Lecture Notes in Computer Science 12201

More information about this series at http://www.springer.com/series/7409

Aaron Marcus · Elizabeth Rosenzweig (Eds.)

Design, User Experience, and Usability

Design for Contemporary Interactive Environments

9th International Conference, DUXU 2020
Held as Part of the 22nd HCI International Conference, HCII 2020
Copenhagen, Denmark, July 19–24, 2020
Proceedings, Part II

 Springer

Editors
Aaron Marcus
Aaron Marcus and Associates
Berkeley, CA, USA

Elizabeth Rosenzweig
World Usability Day and Bentley User
Experience Center
Newton Center, MA, USA

ISSN 0302-9743   ISSN 1611-3349 (electronic)
Lecture Notes in Computer Science
ISBN 978-3-030-49759-0   ISBN 978-3-030-49760-6 (eBook)
https://doi.org/10.1007/978-3-030-49760-6

LNCS Sublibrary: SL3 – Information Systems and Applications, incl. Internet/Web, and HCI

This Springer imprint is published by the registered company Springer Nature Switzerland AG
The registered company address is: Gewerbestrasse 11, 6330 Cham, Switzerland

Foreword

The 22nd International Conference on Human-Computer Interaction, HCI International 2020 (HCII 2020), was planned to be held at the AC Bella Sky Hotel and Bella Center, Copenhagen, Denmark, during July 19–24, 2020. Due to the COVID-19 coronavirus pandemic and the resolution of the Danish government not to allow events larger than 500 people to be hosted until September 1, 2020, HCII 2020 had to be held virtually. It incorporated the 21 thematic areas and affiliated conferences listed on the following page.

A total of 6,326 individuals from academia, research institutes, industry, and governmental agencies from 97 countries submitted contributions, and 1,439 papers and 238 posters were included in the conference proceedings. These contributions address the latest research and development efforts and highlight the human aspects of design and use of computing systems. The contributions thoroughly cover the entire field of human-computer interaction, addressing major advances in knowledge and effective use of computers in a variety of application areas. The volumes constituting the full set of the conference proceedings are listed in the following pages.

The HCI International (HCII) conference also offers the option of "late-breaking work" which applies both for papers and posters and the corresponding volume(s) of the proceedings will be published just after the conference. Full papers will be included in the "HCII 2020 - Late Breaking Papers" volume of the proceedings to be published in the Springer LNCS series, while poster extended abstracts will be included as short papers in the "HCII 2020 - Late Breaking Posters" volume to be published in the Springer CCIS series.

I would like to thank the program board chairs and the members of the program boards of all thematic areas and affiliated conferences for their contribution to the highest scientific quality and the overall success of the HCI International 2020 conference.

This conference would not have been possible without the continuous and unwavering support and advice of the founder, Conference General Chair Emeritus and Conference Scientific Advisor Prof. Gavriel Salvendy. For his outstanding efforts, I would like to express my appreciation to the communications chair and editor of HCI International News, Dr. Abbas Moallem.

July 2020   Constantine Stephanidis

HCI International 2020 Thematic Areas and Affiliated Conferences

Thematic areas:

- HCI 2020: Human-Computer Interaction
- HIMI 2020: Human Interface and the Management of Information

Affiliated conferences:

- EPCE: 17th International Conference on Engineering Psychology and Cognitive Ergonomics
- UAHCI: 14th International Conference on Universal Access in Human-Computer Interaction
- VAMR: 12th International Conference on Virtual, Augmented and Mixed Reality
- CCD: 12th International Conference on Cross-Cultural Design
- SCSM: 12th International Conference on Social Computing and Social Media
- AC: 14th International Conference on Augmented Cognition
- DHM: 11th International Conference on Digital Human Modeling and Applications in Health, Safety, Ergonomics and Risk Management
- DUXU: 9th International Conference on Design, User Experience and Usability
- DAPI: 8th International Conference on Distributed, Ambient and Pervasive Interactions
- HCIBGO: 7th International Conference on HCI in Business, Government and Organizations
- LCT: 7th International Conference on Learning and Collaboration Technologies
- ITAP: 6th International Conference on Human Aspects of IT for the Aged Population
- HCI-CPT: Second International Conference on HCI for Cybersecurity, Privacy and Trust
- HCI-Games: Second International Conference on HCI in Games
- MobiTAS: Second International Conference on HCI in Mobility, Transport and Automotive Systems
- AIS: Second International Conference on Adaptive Instructional Systems
- C&C: 8th International Conference on Culture and Computing
- MOBILE: First International Conference on Design, Operation and Evaluation of Mobile Communications
- AI-HCI: First International Conference on Artificial Intelligence in HCI

Conference Proceedings Volumes Full List

1. LNCS 12181, Human-Computer Interaction: Design and User Experience (Part I), edited by Masaaki Kurosu
2. LNCS 12182, Human-Computer Interaction: Multimodal and Natural Interaction (Part II), edited by Masaaki Kurosu
3. LNCS 12183, Human-Computer Interaction: Human Values and Quality of Life (Part III), edited by Masaaki Kurosu
4. LNCS 12184, Human Interface and the Management of Information: Designing Information (Part I), edited by Sakae Yamamoto and Hirohiko Mori
5. LNCS 12185, Human Interface and the Management of Information: Interacting with Information (Part II), edited by Sakae Yamamoto and Hirohiko Mori
6. LNAI 12186, Engineering Psychology and Cognitive Ergonomics: Mental Workload, Human Physiology, and Human Energy (Part I), edited by Don Harris and Wen-Chin Li
7. LNAI 12187, Engineering Psychology and Cognitive Ergonomics: Cognition and Design (Part II), edited by Don Harris and Wen-Chin Li
8. LNCS 12188, Universal Access in Human-Computer Interaction: Design Approaches and Supporting Technologies (Part I), edited by Margherita Antona and Constantine Stephanidis
9. LNCS 12189, Universal Access in Human-Computer Interaction: Applications and Practice (Part II), edited by Margherita Antona and Constantine Stephanidis
10. LNCS 12190, Virtual, Augmented and Mixed Reality: Design and Interaction (Part I), edited by Jessie Y. C. Chen and Gino Fragomeni
11. LNCS 12191, Virtual, Augmented and Mixed Reality: Industrial and Everyday Life Applications (Part II), edited by Jessie Y. C. Chen and Gino Fragomeni
12. LNCS 12192, Cross-Cultural Design: User Experience of Products, Services, and Intelligent Environments (Part I), edited by P. L. Patrick Rau
13. LNCS 12193, Cross-Cultural Design: Applications in Health, Learning, Communication, and Creativity (Part II), edited by P. L. Patrick Rau
14. LNCS 12194, Social Computing and Social Media: Design, Ethics, User Behavior, and Social Network Analysis (Part I), edited by Gabriele Meiselwitz
15. LNCS 12195, Social Computing and Social Media: Participation, User Experience, Consumer Experience, and Applications of Social Computing (Part II), edited by Gabriele Meiselwitz
16. LNAI 12196, Augmented Cognition: Theoretical and Technological Approaches (Part I), edited by Dylan D. Schmorrow and Cali M. Fidopiastis
17. LNAI 12197, Augmented Cognition: Human Cognition and Behaviour (Part II), edited by Dylan D. Schmorrow and Cali M. Fidopiastis

38. CCIS 1224, HCI International 2020 Posters - Part I, edited by Constantine Stephanidis and Margherita Antona
39. CCIS 1225, HCI International 2020 Posters - Part II, edited by Constantine Stephanidis and Margherita Antona
40. CCIS 1226, HCI International 2020 Posters - Part III, edited by Constantine Stephanidis and Margherita Antona

http://2020.hci.international/proceedings

9th International Conference on Design, User Experience, and Usability (DUXU 2020)

Program Board Chairs: **Aaron Marcus, Aaron Marcus and Associates, USA, and Elizabeth Rosenzweig, World Usability Day and Bentley User Experience Center, USA**

- Sisira Adikari, Australia
- Claire Ancient, UK
- Silvia de los Rios, Spain
- Marc Fabri, UK
- Juliana J. Ferreira, Brazil
- Josh Halstead, USA
- Chris Hass, USA
- Wei Liu, China
- Martin Maguire, UK
- Judith A. Moldenhauer, USA
- Kerem Rızvanoğlu, Turkey
- Francisco Rebelo, Portugal
- Christine Riedmann-Streitz, Germany
- Patricia Search, USA
- Marcelo M. Soares, China
- Carla G. Spinillo, Brazil
- Virgínia Tiradentes Souto, Brazil

The full list with the Program Board Chairs and the members of the Program Boards of all thematic areas and affiliated conferences is available online at:

http://www.hci.international/board-members-2020.php

HCI International 2021

The 23rd International Conference on Human-Computer Interaction, HCI International 2021 (HCII 2021), will be held jointly with the affiliated conferences in Washington DC, USA, at the Washington Hilton Hotel, July 24–29, 2021. It will cover a broad spectrum of themes related to Human-Computer Interaction (HCI), including theoretical issues, methods, tools, processes, and case studies in HCI design, as well as novel interaction techniques, interfaces, and applications. The proceedings will be published by Springer. More information will be available on the conference website: http://2021.hci.international/.

General Chair
Prof. Constantine Stephanidis
University of Crete and ICS-FORTH
Heraklion, Crete, Greece
Email: general_chair@hcii2021.org

http://2021.hci.international/

Contents – Part II

Usability Aspects of Handheld and Mobile Devices

Designing Games and Immersive Experiences

UX Studies in Automotive and Transport

Interactions in Intelligent and IoT Environments

Recommendation Systems and Machine Learning: Mapping the User Experience

Luiz Agner[1]([✉]), Barbara Necyk[2], and Adriano Renzi[3]

[1] Faculdades Integradas Helio Alonso; IBGE, Rio de Janeiro, RJ, Brazil
luizagner@gmail.com
[2] Universidade do Estado do Rio de Janeiro/ESDI; PUC-Rio,
Rio de Janeiro, Brazil
07barbara@gmail.com
[3] Universidade Federal Fluminense/UFF, Niterói, Brazil
adrianorenzi@gmail.com

Abstract. Human-algorithm interaction emerges as the new frontier of studies involving interaction design and interface ergonomics. This paper aims to discuss the effectiveness and communicability of streaming media recommendation systems, based on machine learning, from users' mental model point of view. We examined the content consumption practices on the Netflix platform, identifying some sensitive aspects of the interaction with recommendation algorithms. One-on-one semi-structured interviews were applied to a sample of students from three different universities in Rio de Janeiro, Brazil. We realised that interviewees had not correctly understood how the system works and have not formed an adequate mental model about tracked data and how it is processed to create personalised lists. Another issue concerns data privacy: Users have revealed a suspicion concerning algorithms and what might happen to usage data, not only in the Netflix platform but also in other services that use algorithm-based recommendation. Interviewees' responses suggested that there may be communication failures, and UX designers should strive to make it visible how the system tracks and processes user interaction data.

Keywords: User experience · UX design · Recommendation systems

1 Introduction

This paper aims to study and discuss the effectiveness and communicability of entertainment content recommendation systems, based on machine learning, from users' mental model point of view. An exploratory interview research method was used to map how young college students in Rio de Janeiro, Brazil, interact with machine learning-based systems in entertainment applications such as Netflix.

Nowadays, there is a rush for applying artificial intelligence (AI) among major Internet companies, and interest grows in the same proportion as research investments. Machine learning has emerged as a topic of great importance within the field of artificial intelligence. Bengio [1] cites artificial intelligence application's disruptive examples: industrial production, medicine, transportation, agriculture, personal

© Springer Nature Switzerland AG 2020
A. Marcus and E. Rosenzweig (Eds.): HCII 2020, LNCS 12201, pp. 3–17, 2020.
https://doi.org/10.1007/978-3-030-49760-6_1

assistants, translations, voice recognition, facial recognition, among other areas. Industry often applies AI as recommendation systems that feature personalised entertainment and information content for the user's interaction.

What is possible to know about the experience quality based on these interactions? Are users able to formulate a mental model on how recommendation systems work? Are users satisfied with custom recommendations? What is the mental model built by users regarding machine learning algorithms? Do users understand how machine learning operates and can interact with these algorithms to improve their outputs and better match them to their goals?

In this research, we chose to focus on interaction with the Netflix platform, studying the user experience on its recommendation algorithms. The reason for that choice is that Netflix is the most popular streaming service in the Brazilian market with broad dissemination among young people and is a reference concerning recommendation systems.

2   A Brief Introduction to Recommendation Systems

Nowadays, due to the Internet and information technology, people are facing the problem of enormous information overload and an ever-increasing amount of options to choose from, concerning several aspects of our lives. From choices for videos, music, books, travel itineraries, and restaurants, to health security, courses, or dating partners, the act of deciding is increasingly hard. Frequently, making a choice is a significant, challenging, and complicated task.

For instance, according to Pandey [2], the less popular products are abundant, yet they are not found easily in physical stores and are only available online, constituting what can be called a Long Tail [3]. Even these products may be adequate, but finding them on a website often becomes an arduous task. Therefore certain filters are important.

Machines are much more capable than humans in managing an extensive set of data and in learning from them. Thus, we can observe that computer programs, known as recommendation systems, may have a lot to assist us. They can be supporting the task of quickly establishing data generalisations and helping our decision-making processes, as Gomez-Uribe and Hunt [4] have suggested.

The so-called recommender systems (or recommendation engines) are programs that belong to the category of information filtering systems, and seek to predict which classification a user will give to an item of information, based on calculations and statistical inferences. According to Rocca [5], in a very generic way, recommendation systems can be defined as "algorithms designed to suggest items relevant to the user." Those items can be movies to watch, texts to read, products to buy, or anything else depending on specific industries. According to Pandey [2], they aim to solve two types of problems: prediction (data used to predict the evaluation a user will give to an item he has not interacted with) and ranking (defining a finite list of items to be presented to the system's user).

For Rocca [5], recommendation systems now play an increasingly central role in our lives. From e-commerce (suggesting to buyers articles that might interest them) to digital marketing (suggesting to users the right ad that can generate the highest clickthrough rate), recommendation systems have now become inevitable in online journeys.

These systems are increasingly employed in commercial services that people use on a day to day basis, such as Netflix, YouTube and Spotify playlist generators, Amazon product offerings, or friend recommendations or social media content like Facebook, Linkedin and Twitter. According to Pandey [2], IMDB, Trip Advisor and Google News are other examples of platforms that continually send personalised suggestions and recommendations to their users.

The purposes of recommendation systems, according to Aggarwal *apud* Pandey [2], are:

(i) Relevance - The items to be purchased should interest users;
(ii) Novelty - This makes more sense to recommend items that users do not already know;
(iii) Serendipity - Recommend unexpected or surprising items;
(iv) Diversity - Internal variability in a list of items.

Recommendation systems often use the collaborative filtering approach or content-based filtering, as well as other approaches. Collaborative filtering builds a model based on past user behaviour (purchased or selected items, or ratings given to items), as well as similar decisions made by other users. This model can point out which items the user may be interested in. Content-based filtering approaches use discrete and pre-identified characteristics of each item to recommend new items with similar properties. The most widely used recommendation systems, on the market today, combine one or more approaches into one hybrid system.

2.1 Collaborative Filtering

Collaborative filtering can recommend complex items (e.g. series or movies) without presupposing an understanding of the content. That is because it is based solely on the - often questionable - assumption that people who have agreed in the past will also agree in the future, and people will like items similar to what they have liked in the past.

Rocca [5] points out that collaborative methods for recommendation systems are methods based only on past interactions recorded among users and items to produce new recommendations. These interactions are stored in the so-called "item-user interaction matrix."

The main advantage of collaborative approaches is that they do not require information about users or items and can, therefore, be used in a wide variety of situations or contexts. Also, the more the users interact with the items, the more accurate the recommendations become. That is, for a fixed set of users and items, interactions recorded over time generate new data and make the system increasingly effective, said Rocca [5]. However, we should note that these collaborative filtering approaches often suffer from problems such as cold starting, which we will discuss later.

Furthermore, we should consider that the data collected to model user behaviour can be either explicit or implicit. Explicit forms of data collection include: search terms, asking a user to sort items or creating a wish list. Implicit forms of data collection include: observing browsing times, registering purchased products, viewing product lists, or analysing the social network. According to Pandey [2], implicitly collected data are derived from user interactions with the system and interpreted as indicators of interest or disinterest. With a broad set of tracked user data, it is possible to identify clusters representing user communities with very similar tastes to observe their collective behaviour (Kathayat) [6].

There are two subcategories within collaborative approaches: the so-called memory-based approaches and model-based approaches. The memory-based approaches assume that there is no model and are based only on records of observed interactions between close neighbours (for example, they search for users that are closest to a user of interest and find the most popular items among those neighbours). Model-based collaborative approaches assume that there is an underlying model capable of explaining interactions and attempt to identify it from a matrix of interactions to generate their predictions [5]. According to Pandey [2], these approaches employ machine learning methods.

2.2 Content-Based Filtering

According to Rocca [5], while collaborative methods depend only on item-user interactions, content-based approaches need additional information about users and items. They need a description of each item as well as a profile of user preferences. In this case, keywords are entered to describe the items and a user profile created. If we consider the example of a movie recommendation system, this additional information may be, for example, age, gender, profession or any other personal user data, as well as genre, main actors, duration, country of origin, awards or other features for movies.

The concept of content-based methods is based on building a model that explains the observed interactions among items and users. If the system can get this model, it is easy to make new predictions for a user: just have to check their profile (age, gender, etc.) and, based on that information, select relevant movies to suggest them.

Content-based recommendation systems may also ask users to write a review or some feedback about catalogue items. Based on what the user has liked in the past or is currently looking for, the algorithm finds and presents new similar items. According to Pandey [2], the disadvantage of these methods is their inability to learn from interactions so that there is no improvement over time.

2.3 Hybrid Recommendation Systems

Pandey [2] points out that both collaborative and content-based approaches have strengths and weaknesses. Therefore, most of the recommendation systems we currently use take a hybrid approach, merging collaborative filtering solutions with content-based approach methods, as well as other approaches. Approach hybridisation can be achieved by forecasting each method separately and then combining them, adding features from one approach to another or even unifying them into a single model.

Pandey [2] argues that Netflix is an excellent example of hybrid recommendation systems because its recommendations are based not only on browsing and consumption habits (collaborative approach) but also on similar feature videos (content-based). In order to do so, the company employs several algorithms, as we will see later.

2.4 Success Factors for Recommendation Systems

Nowadays, among the critical success factors of recommendation systems, one must consider points that go beyond the pure mathematical precision of recommendations, since the quality of the experience and user satisfaction involve many other equally relevant aspects. Some of the factors that impact the user experience are highlighted below:

(i) Diversity - Diverse recommendation lists tend to generate greater user satisfaction, so it is essential to recommend items that fit the users well but are not overly similar to each other, which avoids locking them into an "information bubble";

(ii) Privacy - Creating user profiles using collaborative filtering can be problematic from a privacy point of view, and it is crucial to protect sensitive user data. European countries, as well as Brazil, have passed recent laws aimed at protecting their citizens' data;

(iii) Demographics - Demographic aspects and other characteristics of users may become very relevant in the evaluation of recommendation systems. Beel, Langer, Nuenberger and Genzmehr [7] pointed out that maturer users tend to be interested in clicking on system recommendations more often than younger users;

(iv) Persistence - Resubmitting recommendations may be an appropriate strategy, as users tend to ignore items that are first presented to them due to a lack of time;

(v) "Rich gets richer" effect - According to Gomez-Uribe and Hunt [4], these approaches are still unable to deal with the strong bias caused by positive feedback, in which items that users are most involved with are recommended for many other members, leading to even greater involvement. The problem is especially real for collaborative memory-based algorithms (Rocca) [5], and tends to create an "information confinement area";

(vi) Explainability - If users do not understand why a particular item was presented to them, they tend to lose confidence in the recommendation system, so they must be able to build a mental model of the system (Rocca) [5];

(vii) Response Time - Complexity poses a problem: Generating a new recommendation list can be time-consuming for recommendation systems that handle a massive amount of data for millions of users and millions of items.

(viii) Cold Start - This is a recognised condition that negatively impacts novice users' experience in interacting with collaborative approach algorithms since, for these users, there is not enough data to generate accurate recommendations.

(ix) Serendipity - This feature refers to the system's ability to recommend unusual items and surprise the user, not only give him miscellaneous items or novelties, as Pandey [2] noted. Consequently, Serendipity is distinct from simple Diversity.

Due to the listed circumstances, user satisfaction studies are the order of the day. In addition to the standard performance metrics captured in online reviews (A/B testing) and offline reviews, often criticised today, it is also essential to conduct qualitative studies and tests. They must be focused on user experience (UX) evaluation and describe her interaction with recommendation algorithms, such as the studies conducted by Budiu [8] and Harley [9] [10], which we will summarise later.

3   UX and Machine Learning Systems

According to Lovejoy and Holbrook [11], machine learning (ML) is the science of helping computers discover patterns and relationships in data instead of being programmed manually. Today, ML capabilities are becoming increasingly accessible to developers, and there is an impulse to be added to services to enhance the user experience. It's a powerful tool for creating personalised, engaging user experiences and is already directing everything from Netflix recommendations to autonomous cars.

As the authors said, as more user experiences incorporate ML, it is clear that UX designers still have a lot to learn about how to make users feel in control of the technology and not the other way around.

It is known that the most valuable ML systems evolve in connection with users' mental models. When people interact with these systems, they influence and adjust the kind of effects they will see in the future. These adjustments, in turn, will change the way users interact with the system, the models, and so on in a feedback cycle.

However, this can result in "conspiracy theories," in which people create incorrect or incomplete mental models of a system and try to manipulate the results according to imaginary rules. It is necessary to guide users to build accurate mental models that encourage them to give feedback. This fact will be mutually beneficial to them and the model (Lovejoy and Holbrook) [11].

In a study focused on users of ML-based systems, Budiu [8] inferred that people could not make the interfaces do what they want because they form weak mental models. Usability research has observed that these algorithms are not transparent to users. They do not identify which actions are considered by these systems and do not have a clear understanding of their outputs.

To users, lists of suggestions and recommendations often seem random and meaningless. Frequently, these algorithms create categories and group items according to obscure and not mutually exclusive criteria. While these groupings may make sense from a strictly statistical or mathematical point of view, they go against the traditional intuitive way of building an information architecture.

One of the problems pointed out by Budiu [8] is the so-called black-box model. Users necessitate developing a mental model of how the system works, and it needs to be clear about how they can change the outputs. Users perceive the system as a black box with cryptic inputs and outputs out of control.

Not only are people unaware of the universe of possible inputs, but there is a significant delay between input and output, which creates higher confusion. Occasionally, imperfect metrics of relevance cause items of interest to be hidden from the user. This problem also causes the order of items on a list neither understandable nor predictable. Also, Budiu [8] says, items of low relevance are presented to the user (low precision) who will need to ignore them. However, the cost of ignoring a weak recommendation may be high depending on each specific service (in Spotify, this cost is higher than in Netflix, for example).

Repeated recommendations, as well as session-specific thumbnails, descriptions and headings, often increase the cost of interaction. Furthermore, the practice of homepage customisation, according to a session or device, restricts the learning of the layout, reducing usability.

Budiu [8] presents us with some guidelines that should be considered by the machine-learning algorithm based interface developers in order to increase user satisfaction and experience quality. These are some of them:

(i)   Be transparent - Inform people about which actions are considered by the algorithm to help the user build a transparent mental model of interaction.

(ii) Provide easy controls over the output - Give the user the means to reorganize the output in a way that is more relevant or familiar to him.

(iii) Do not repeat content items within several categories - in order to decrease the cost of interaction.

Harley [10] also suggested a list of guidelines to support user experience (UX) in ML-based recommendation systems:

(i)   Transparency concerning data source - The recommendation system should be specific and clear about what user data is tracked and processed to generate personalised lists. This information indicates that the content is unique, individualised to the user. A clear explanation (for example, showing that it was based on the viewing history) helps users decide if recommendations are relevant and add credibility to the system.

(ii) Highlight recommendation lists - The user always prefers suggested content in comparison to generic lists since recommendations are seen as a valuable navigation resource amid information overload. Therefore, recommendations need to be well highlighted and easy to find.

(iii) Recommendations in subcategories - One should avoid showing all recommendations allocated in an extensive "Recommendations" category. It makes more sense for users to search for content in specific subcategories, especially in environments with huge inventories, such as e-commerce or entertainment sites (Harley) [10].

(iv) Allow users to improve recommendations - Loyal and frequent users will want to interact to make recommendations more relevant. Therefore, it is necessary to provide an effective method of entering feedbacks or editing the data used to create the recommendations. An example is the possibility to edit past actions, such as deleting items from browsing history or previous purchases. This task empowers users to instruct the algorithm to forget behaviours irrelevant to their profile. Netflix users view their past activities by visiting the viewing history. In this platform, users are allowed to remove items they consider atypical from their profile.

(v) Recommendations update - According to Harley [10], if users choose to opti-
      mize their recommendations (by performing a rating, adding items to a
      favourites list or updating their profile), they should expect the effect to be
      immediate, especially when the feedback is negative.

4 Netflix and Its Recommendation Algorithms

Netflix's recommendation systems are made up of a collection of different algorithms
and are an essential part of its business model in a growing market such as internet
television. In this business, unlike cable TV or broadcasting, choosing what to watch
and when to watch is the main challenge, as humans are known to be deficient in
dealing with large volumes of information and choices, and are quickly overwhelmed.

For example, according to Gomez-Uribe and Hunt [4], a typical user loses interest
within 60 to 90 s after reviewing around 10 to 20 titles (only 3 in detail) and browsing a
maximum of two screens. The challenge is to make sure that on both of these screens,
each user finds some video they consider appealing and understands why it might be
interesting.

Gomez-Uribe and Hunt [4] say that personalisation, along with a recommendation,
is critical to Netflix's business model and has been able to save $ 1 billion a year by
avoiding subscriber cancellation and high subscriber turnover. Each user experience is
customised in a variety of ways: suggested videos and their rating, video rows and
pages arrangement, and even the poster thumbnails display. For in-depth customisation, Netflix combines several different algorithmic approaches to address each unique
member, stated Netflix Research [12].

For Kathayat [6], traditional TV networks use standard demographic methods such
as age, race, gender, or geography to plot their segmentation. Netflix tracks its members' viewing habits to define, through clustering processes, about 2,000 "taste communities" that play a central role in generating its recommendations. Algorithms create
recommendations based on the assumption that similar visualisation patterns represent
similar tastes.

The recommendation algorithms used in combination by Netflix are as follows:

(i)   Personalised Video Ranker (PVR) - The Netflix interface is usually made with
       40 lines on the homepage (depending on the access device) with up to 75
       videos per line. The videos on each line usually come from a single algorithm,
       the PVR. This feature sorts the entire catalogue of videos (or subsets of genres)
       customised for each user member. This way, the same genre line displayed to
       different users can present completely different videos. PVR can be combined
       with some non-personalised popularity indicators to generate more relevant
       results (Gomez-Uribe and Hunt) [4].
(ii) Top-N Video Ranker - This algorithm aims to find the best-personalised rec-
       ommendations from the entire catalogue for each member and show them in the
       Top Picks line.
(iii) Trending Now - Short-term time trends accurately predict videos that users will
       watch and can be combined with a certain amount of customisation. These

trends are of two types: periodically recurring events (for example, a romantic video showing trend around Valentine's Day; and short-term one-off events such as a decisive soccer game covered by traditional media may increase interest in videos about sports competitions or the World Cup. According to Kathayat [6], Netflix also applies a type of near-real-time (NRT) recommendation because it knows that batch processing, used by most Internet companies, it is not agile enough to handle highly time-sensitive scenarios.

(iv) Video-Video Similarity - Lines classified as Because You Watched (BYW) are a type of item classification, grouping them according to a single video watched by individual user members, and are listed by the similarity algorithm (also called "sims"). The choice of which BYW lines enter the home page, as well as their specific subset of videos, are defined in a customised manner by the BYW algorithm (Gomez-Uribe and Hunt) [4].

(v) Continue Watching - Gomez-Uribe and Hunt [4] explain that this is the agent who places the videos in the Continue Watching line based on estimation to continue viewing or abandoning a not so exciting show. It works with data that measures the time elapsed since viewing, the point of abandonment (beginning, middle or end of the video), as well as which devices were used.

(vi) Evidence - This type of algorithm is responsible for the additional information of each program. They decide whether to show the synopsis, cast, awards, and other metadata, including which of the poster arts, among the various possible layouts, will be presented to represent the video. According to Kathayat [6], for each title, different images can be flagged, using taste communities as a starting point for choosing it. These images can be hundreds of millions and are continually tested among the subscribers base. Creating these designs employs machine learning techniques.

(vii) Page Generation: Row Selection and Ranking - This page generation algorithm employs the output of all previous algorithms to create recommendation pages taking into consideration the relevance to each member. One challenge is handling users' mood fluctuations in each session in addition to the fact that more than one family member may share an account. According to Gomez-Uribe and Hunt [4], this problem is addressed by Netflix with diversification. By producing a diverse selection of rows, the Page Generation algorithm allows the user to skip items suitable for another occasion, or another family member, and identify something relevant to her.

(viii) Search - On Netflix, over 80% of what users see comes from recommendations, said Basilico [13]. The remaining 20% comes from keyword search, an experience that relies on a set of specific algorithms and also involves recommendation issues (Gomez-Uribe and Hunt) [4]. An algorithm can try to find video titles that match a given word search, even if incomplete. Another algorithm will try to predict interest in a concept or genre of a program, and a third algorithm will try to find video title recommendations for a particular concept sought. Sometimes the user may search for specific videos, genres or actors that are not available in the catalogue, so the algorithm will recommend other programs that resemble the searched title.

Summarily, recommendation and personalisation are essential features of Netflix's business model, as it allows each member to see a different cutout of content tailored to her interests. However, Gomez-Uribe and Hunt [4] admit that there still are some issues regarding Netflix's recommendation algorithms. These include the goal of developing global algorithms capable of managing the full complexity of different languages, licenses and specific catalogues. Another challenge is account sharing, where multiple individuals with different tastes can use a single account. The algorithms must be able to provide useful suggestions to anyone in the family viewing at any given time.

According to Basilico [13], recommendation problems have not yet been solved because each user is unique and has a wide variety of interests. What people want to watch is dependent on the context and their mood, and data scientists still do not have devices capable of reading users' minds.

Experience personalisation is the next stage in the evolution of personalisation approaches. At the level of interaction, it is necessary to customize it through a more adaptive user interface, which can present more or less information depending on the user's needs, affirmed Basilico [13].

We also conjecture that there is a certain amount of distrust by users. They worry about which interaction data is tracked, with whom this data is shared, and what criteria are used to generate the recommendations due to the lack of transparency of ML algorithms.

5 Research Method: User Interviews

According to Courage and Baxter [14], one technique often used to study the user experience is the interview. An interview is a guided conversation in which one person seeks information from another. There are a variety of types of interviews, depending on restrictions and needs. A semi-structured interview is a combination of the structured and unstructured types. The interviewer begin with a set of questions to answer but can deviate from them from time to time.

The authors followed the idea that interviews are appropriate if the inquiry is looking to collect information from a small sample of the population. A screening questionnaire was used among students to select participants. Being a paying user and an experienced Netflix member were selection requirements.

We applied one-on-one semi-structured interviews to a small sample of design and communication students from three different universities in Rio de Janeiro, Brazil, with distinct characteristics and backgrounds:

(i)   Universidade Federal Fluminense (UFF) is a federal university with a recently created design course within the engineering school;

(ii) Escola Superior de Desenho Industrial (ESDI) is a state university and the first design university of South America;

(iii) Faculdades Integradas Helio Alonso (Facha) is a private university with a bachelor's program in social communication.

The participators selected for the conversation are undergraduate or graduate university students aged 19 to 34. They have been paying members of Netflix for over five years, managing personal profiles.

They access the internet every day and use applications such as email, news, social networks, instant messages and entertainment, among others. They consume streaming videos using smart TVs, notebooks or cell phones, via Wi-Fi or downloaded content, at home or on the bus while shuttling to college. They are also frequent users of Netflix platform.

We asked students what influences the discovery of new video content. Some of them answered that they notice and like Netflix's recommendations. However, several respondents stated that they prefer recommendations from other sources, such as friends, social networks and specialised channels:

"I receive recommendations from Netflix and like them, but I am also very influenced by direct recommendations from friends. In social networks, many people are commenting on the series and films".

"Netflix recommendations are not usually very effective for me. I get informed on Youtube channels that talk about film production like Screen Junkies, Beyond the Trailer and Dalenogare".

"In addition to Netflix recommendations, I'm influenced by three Youtube channels: Carol Moreira, Mikann and Series Maniac".

"I watch the series that have been most reverberated or that have won awards. They're always on social networks, Twitter or Instagram."

"Close friends influence me directly. Netflix's suggestions are completely random..."

A question about wether users could identify where their custom recommendations are was addressed. In that case, they gave conflicting answers. We concluded that they were not sure where their personalised recommendations are on the home page:

"Sometimes, they put recommendations... But I don't know if I can identify them."

"Only when they put 'Because you watched such a thing.'"

"I think my specific recommendations appear here..." (points to 'Because you added The End of the F**ing World to your list').

"The specific recommendations for me are not highlighted enough because the first ones that appear are 'The Most Watched' or 'The Most Popular.' That is what everyone is having".

The interviewed users showed that they do not have an adequate mental model, when asked how Netflix's algorithms work. Many were unable to define accurately what actions the algorithm considers to create the lists of recommendations. The answers revealed that there is a "black box" feeling:

"Man, I have no idea... The algorithm on Facebook works great. But on Netflix, I have no idea because it's so commercial."

"It's just the search and watched programs."

"I think the likes (formerly stars), I think it sees what I save on my list."

"I think it's from what I see. When it scored. (...) Maybe the trailers I watch. I don't know very well."

"Watch, watch and stay, watch and leave... Staying a long time, opening the video description many times."

"I believe they see in my history the series I watched, and the series I put on my list, and if I give positive feedback, leaving a Like there. In my perception, it collects all this… I believe that the search can also influence."

"What I say on the cell phone influences for sure. It happened several times I talk 'I Love How To Get Away with Murder' and this series was emphasised on my Netflix home."

"I don't know if it gets stuff from outside, from another site…"

Another question we asked was whether users knew how they could interact to improve the quality of their recommendations. From their answers, we realised that several respondents would not know how to do this:

"I don't know how I could do that."

"I don't know, and I don't see any alternative."

"I usually ignore bad recommendations. (…) I spend a lot of time away from Netflix for not receiving a relevant recommendation the moment I finish watching a series."

"If I watched a show and gave negative feedback… I can't think of another way."

"Maybe by giving Dislike even without having watched it. In fact, I never got to do that."
(When giving a Dislike in a video, the interviewee did not realize that the thumbnail had become black and white).

"Dislike is unfair. I may not have liked the Queer Eye series, but from the moment you give a Dislike, the algorithm will stop showing you LGBT content".

After, we asked respondents how they understood the matter of their data protection, and the likelihood of potential threats to privacy, due to the use of navigational data. In these responses, some users manifested distrust and reinforced the idea of the "black box." Some conspiratorial theories appeared, including political implications:

"I am very suspicious of these things. (…) On the cell phone, sometimes you're talking about something, and then a lot of advertising starts to appear."

"I watched 'The Edge of Democracy' [1] *and loved it. But I'm not sure if they're gonna create a list of all the people who were interested in the Netflix left-wing movie… Got it?"*

"All social networks are a way to map people in a very clear way. Not only the film ones but… I think we give too much information! But we have no choice: either we give the information or we don't live in the modern world!"

"My data is all sold! I'm conscious of that, and I've already accepted it. About two or three years ago, people started talking about this, about how Facebook was selling our data while Marc Zuckerberg was investigated. Then, I had a credit card cloned…"

"Everyone feels invaded and surveilled by the algorithms. This is the truth, in everything you access on the internet. Not on Netflix because the algorithm seems a little random to me".

"Through the algorithm they work on the social groups and the niches… I think this is dangerous or wrong because you are limiting free access to information."

"If I search for something I want to buy on the internet, then this product appears in different forms and different prices in ads everywhere. This is the feeling of invasion of privacy that I have…"

"I keep thinking and thinking: man, everything I do these guys from those big companies know. Damn, they're watching me!"

"This is the invasion of privacy. At first, you get scared, but then you see that in a way, it's cool."

"I feel a little uncomfortable: if I spend the whole day searching a shopping site, the recommendations of these products appear on Instagram, Facebook or Youtube for me soon. But in Netflix's case, it brings comfort: more content that I like."

---

[1] Brazilian political documentary nominated for the Oscar 2020.

"I would be sad if Netflix made my data available to another company."
"To tell you the truth, I never stopped to think about it."
"I don't know, one thing I don't like is that my mother finds out what series I'm watching..."

6 Conclusions and Notes for Discussion

During our user interviews, we examined the content consumption practices on the Netflix platform, identifying some aspects of their interaction with recommendation algorithms. We intended to understand more in-depth about the quality of these experiences.

This investigation tried to respond to the following questions: What mental model users created concerning ML-based interfaces? Users were able to form a satisfactory mental model about how recommendation systems work? Are users satisfied with their custom recommendations? Can users interact with the recommendation algorithms in order to improve their outputs and better balance them for their purposes?

As Budiu [8] stated, in order to increase user satisfaction and experience quality, designers should regard the requirement that machine-learning algorithm based interfaces be transparent. Interfaces should inform users about which actions are considered by the algorithm to create recommendations lists. However, concerning the transparency of the information, we realised that interviewees had not correctly understood how the system works and have not formed an adequate mental model about tracked data, as well as did not understand how it is processed to create personalised lists. As Rocca said, explainability is quite important: users must understand why a particular item was presented to them; otherwise, they may lose confidence in the system.

Interviewees' responses suggested that there may be communication failures. Therefore, UX designers should strive to make it obvious how the system tracks and processes user interaction data. It would be advisable to achieve reasonable transparency and help users build appropriate mental models as well as deconstruct the "black box" feeling mentioned by Budiu [8].

Another issue concerns data privacy. Users have revealed a suspicion concerning algorithms and what might happen to usage data, not only in the Netflix platform but also in other services that use algorithm-based recommendation. When asked about the issue of personal data privacy, respondents broadened the spectrum of reporting their experiences to other services as if everything were part of the same system. Fears of political manipulation, restriction of freedom of information, and even credit card hacking have emerged. Additionally, an interviewee reported the concern that the streaming platform would share her data with other online services. These suspicions seem to be manifestations of the "conspiracy theories" pointed out by Lovejoy and Holbrook [11].

Likewise, users did not seem to be completely aware of how they could interfere with the recommendation system and what actions they could take to generate more relevant items lists in line with their goals and mood.

Respondents were unaware of the universe of possible inputs to improve the experience. Responses seem to indicate that UX designers should provide an effective method to encourage Brazilian users to record feedbacks or edit user data in order to create better recommendations. Frequent users do not know how to interact with recommended content to help the algorithm improve its recommendation lists to better suit their profile and personal preferences. Instead of answering the question about improvement, some students criticised the recommendation system.

Human-algorithm interaction emerges as the new frontier of studies involving interaction design and interface ergonomics. This research has addressed the sensitive and emerging recommendation system issues that are often considered too new or unknown by practitioners in the field of ergonomics and user experience design. The sample of interviewed users, although limited, pointed to several aspects that impact the interaction that young Brazilians had with streaming content recommendation algorithms such as Netflix's.

Recommendation problems have not yet been solved since each user is unique and has a wide variety of interests (Basilico) [13]. Therefore, UX designers must keep in mind that they still have a lot to learn and to contribute to the reinforcement of the user's control over technology during the interaction with widely adopted machine learning algorithms.

References

1. Bengio, Y.: Yoshua Bengio on intelligent machines. https://youtu.be/ePUSElR0o9o. Accessed 27 Dec 2019
2. Pandey, P.: The remarkable world of recommender systems. https://towardsdatascience.com/the-remarkable-world-of-recommender-systems-bff4b9cbe6a7. Accessed 28 Jan 2020
3. Anderson, C.: A Cauda Longa: Do mercado de Massa para o Mercado de Nicho. Elsevier, Rio de Janeiro (2006)
4. Gomez-Uribe, C.A., Hunt, N.: The Netflix recommender system: algorithms, business value, and innovation. ACM Trans. Manag. Inf. Syst. 6(4), Article 13 (2015)
5. Rocca, B.: Introduction to recommender systems. https://towardsdatascience.com/introduction-to-recommender-systems-6c66cf15ada. Accessed 19 Dec 2019
6. Kathayat, V.: How Netflix uses AI for content creation and recommendation. https://medium.com/swlh/how-netflix-uses-ai-for-content-creation-and-recommendation-c1919efc0af4. Accessed 15 Jan 2020
7. Beel, J., Langer, S., Nürnberger, A., Genzmehr, M.: The impact of demographics (age and gender) and other user-characteristics on evaluating recommender systems. In: Aalberg, T., Papatheodorou, C., Dobreva, M., Tsakonas, G., Farrugia, Charles J. (eds.) TPDL 2013. LNCS, vol. 8092, pp. 396–400. Springer, Heidelberg (2013). https://doi.org/10.1007/978-3-642-40501-3_45
8. Budiu, R.: Can Users Control and Understand a UI Driven by Machine Learning? Nielsen Norman Group, https://www.nngroup.com/articles/machine-learning-ux/, last accessed 2020/01/02
9. Harley, A.: Individualized Recommendations: Users' Expectations & Assumptions. https://www.nngroup.com/articles/recommendation-expectations/. Accessed 28 Nov 2019
10. Harley, A.: UX Guidelines for Recommended Content. https://www.nngroup.com/articles/recommendation-guidelines/, last accessed 2019/11/29

11. Lovejoy, J., Holbrook, J.: Human-Centered Machine Learning. https://medium.com/google-design/human-centered-machine-learning-a770d10562cd. Accessed 10 Dec 2019
12. Netflix Research: Machine Learning: Learning how to entertain the world. https://research.netflix.com/research-area/machine-learning. Accessed 28 Dec 2019
13. Basilico, J.: Recent trends in personalisation: a Netflix perspective. In: ICML 2019 - Adaptative and Multi-Task Learning Workshop. https://slideslive.com/38917692/recent-trends-in-personalization-a-netflix-perspective. Accessed 10 Jan 2020
14. Courage, C., Baxter, K.: Understanding Your Users: A Practical Guide to User Requirements Methods, Tools, and Techniques. Morgan Kaufmann, San Francisco (2005)

Just a Natural Talk? The Rise of Intelligent Personal Assistants and the (Hidden) Legacy of Ubiquitous Computing

Gabriele Barzilai⬡ and Lucia Rampino$^{(\boxtimes)}$⬡

Politecnico di Milano, Dipartimento di Design, Milan, Italy
{gabriele.barzilai,lucia.rampino}@polimi.it

Abstract. In this paper we trace the connection between the paradigm of *disappearing computers* and the design of today's Intelligent Personal Assistants (IPAs). We show how the concept of natural interaction stems from the emergence of a specific interpretation of the idea of disappearing computers (ubicomp). This interpretation has emerged as a technology centred perspective, losing the link with the complex philosophical principles which inspired the founders of UbiComp. As a result, the dominant understanding of natural interaction reflects this loss of complexity, influencing the way IPAs are currently developed. To better understand the implications of having adopted this paradigm, we carried out a literature review of recent academic studies on the use of IPAs. Using a three-lenses framework helped us identify six major assumptions behind the design of IPAs. The paper ends with a discussion of the emerging design challenges in the field of voice-activated devices and how these relate to the dominant paradigm of natural interaction.

Keywords: Disappearing technologies · Natural interaction · Voice-based interfaces

1 Introduction

Over the last few years, Intelligent Personal Assistants, also referred to as Intelligent Vocal Assistant, Virtual Personal Assistants, Voice-Enabled Assistants, to name a few, have become increasingly popular. Machines that can be spoken to via "natural talk" have a considerable heritage in both fiction (e.g. HAL 9000 from 2001: A Space Odyssey, KITT from the Knight Rider series, JARVIS from Iron Man comics) and research. Only in recent years, however, Voice User Interfaces have matched a similar degree of advancement, to the point of being embedded in a multitude of devices such as smart phones, TVs and cars. In this context, voice interface is on the way to becoming the primary UI in standalone screenless devices (e.g., Amazon Echo and Google Home), which are making popular the idea of *smart home* across millions of households in the US, Europe and Asia [1]. Such devices are described as agents that operate on users' behalf, answering their queries and performing tasks by means of various applications.

© Springer Nature Switzerland AG 2020
A. Marcus and E. Rosenzweig (Eds.): HCII 2020, LNCS 12201, pp. 18–39, 2020.
https://doi.org/10.1007/978-3-030-49760-6_2

Given the role that these systems are acquiring in people's everyday life, it is worth tracing back the process through which voice interaction has come to be so extensively employed today. Our point is that the way Intelligent Personal Assistants (from now on, IPAs) are currently designed and implemented reflects the longstanding principle of technologies "disappearing" into the environment, so dear to the theorists of Ubiquitous Computing. However, IPAs are the result of a particular interpretation of the vision underlying ubicomp, which stresses (and stretches) the concept of natural interaction while applying a technology-driven perspective to the understanding of user experience.

To provide an account of how IPAs have come to embody a specific idea of disappearance in HCI, we follow two stages. First, we present the legacy of two concepts that we believe influence the design of today's IPAs: *disappearing technology* and *natural interaction*. In particular, we highlight the link between the concept of *disappearing technology* and the idea of *touchless interaction*, which inspired the development of voice-based interfaces. Next, we address the current academic discourse on IPAs extensively. To organise such a discourse, we propose a three-lenses framework. The first lens examines the "theory" of IPAs: how they are designed and advertised; what are their potential benefits; and what users expect from them. The second lens scrutinises IPAs in practice, e.g., what happens when users interact with such devices. The third lens covers the emerging issues related to the use of IPAs, from usability problems up to social and ethical concerns. Finally, six assumptions on the design of IPAs are presented and challenged.

2 The Paradigm of "Disappearing Technologies"

2.1 Calm Computing: Where It All Began

The age of IoT we live in shows that the endeavours of computer scientists and engineers to attain *ambient intelligence* have borne fruit. However, well before technology reached maturity, a theoretical condition for a widespread use of computers was the development of the concept of "disappearing technologies", a paradigm that has galvanized a new wave of research on computational technology in the last thirty years: *ubiquitous computing*. Its founding father Mark Weiser, a visionary computer scientist working at Xerox PARC in the late 1980s, was the first to develop the idea of a world where computers seamlessly intertwine with each other, dissolving into the environment. Since then on, UbiComp has grown into an established research field, thriving on the most cited maxim of Weiser: *"The most profound technologies are those that disappear. They weave themselves into the fabric of everyday life until they are indistinguishable from it"* [2].

The Lost Philosophical Bequest. While almost any research published in the field of HCI and UbiComp pays its tribute to the legacy of Weiser's thought, very few researchers seem to account for the deep philosophical background that inspired the vision of ubiquitous and yet unobtrusive computing technologies. Driven by the eagerness to realise the envisioned scenario of computers infused into the environment, researchers have been focusing on technology development, around the principle of *disappearance*. What this view seems to forget, however, is that making computing technology ubiquitous in Weiser's original thought was a technically sophisticated stratagem to gain back the richness of social relationships, jeopardised by the intrusiveness of computers. Therefore, spreading technology everywhere was not conceived as an end. Rather, it was contrived as a technical means to achieve a social – nontechnical – goal.

2.2 Technology First: The Big Misunderstanding of UbiComp

The Philosophy of Ubicomp. When taking a closer look at the historical roots of ubicomp, an extraordinarily rich philosophical background emerges, rendering a picture of the actual motivations that inspired the foundation of this field. About this matter, Takayama's research [3] offers a comprehensive interpretation of how Weiser came to theorise the *disappearance* of computing technologies, emphasising the deep concern Weiser had regarding the future of social relationships in a world pervaded by computers.

Social Relationships First. Ubicomp was envisaged primarily to allow for a socially sustainable spread of advanced computational technology. This perspective was influenced by the thought of three generations of phenomenologists (Martin Heidegger, Hans-Georg Gadamer, and Michael Polanyi) and by that of two influential scientists, the psychologist James Gibson and the economist Herbert Simon, with which Weiser was well acquainted. According to Takayama [3] there has been a lack of proper translation of those philosophical concepts into technical realisation by those who have carried the ubicomp project forward. This failure has occurred despite the development of a rather elaborate discourse on the key principles identified by Weiser in his famous Scientific American article. Perhaps that very article became a source of misunderstanding as most of its dissertation focused on the description of demo-artefacts (proof-of-concepts), squeezing the humanistic issues into one brief paragraph.

Overturning of Priorities. Whatever the actual reason, much of the research that followed that article, which laid the foundation of a rather prolific research community, focused principally on how to achieve technically the major goals set by the founders. Artefacts became the centre of attention in experimental research, considered alone as embodiments of the ubicomp's dream. As a result, the social calling that had driven the original concept of ubiquitous computing took a back seat, leaving the stage to the technological achievements. While Weiser tried to envisage a harmonious, non-dystopian coexistence between computers and human beings (between the natural and the artificial), current ubicomp research looks to user experience and social interaction as a chance for experimenting with new ubicomp systems – rather than developing new systems to achieve the desired quality of sociability.

2.3   The Multifarious World of UbiComp

From Ubicomp to Ubicomps. Despite the discontinuity with its philosophical roots, UbiComp has grown a rather large research community, capitalising on the key concepts embodied by the artefacts that Weiser describes in his article: *context aware*; *mobile*; *networked*. The emphasis on one concept or the other, over time, has given rise to a diverse set of research areas, forming a constellation of different slants on ubiquitous computing. These have come to be characterised by what computers should become (ideally) in the future: *pervasive; unremarkable; transparent; embedded; everyday; calm.* None of them, however, seem to be consistent with the objectives identified by Weiser at the time, as their focus has shifted to the very computers rather than remaining faithful to the search of a new form of sociality that such computing paradigm would enable.

Artefact-Driven Research. Takayama renders a clear picture of this universe, listing the main areas of research active today [3, p. 565]: The internet of things, Context-aware computing; Mobile computing; Pervasive computing; Embodied interaction and Tangible interaction; and Social computing. Interestingly enough, there are no specific conferences on Calm computing and Unremarkable computing, the two perspectives most congruous with Weiser's original conception of ubicomp. This would uphold the argument that the design and development of systems attracts more than the speculative research on the tide of ubiquitous computing, that is, the future of a society where ubiquitous computing becomes reality. In fact, some researchers have argued that ubiquitous computing is already a given and that, therefore, ubicomp would be obsolete as a research topic. Regarding this position, Takayama holds some reservations arguing that what has been attained by the community is the technological advancement (e.g., sensors, network systems, mobility), not necessarily the preferable social interaction in the age of ubiquitous computing [3]. That is to say, the user experience with ubicomp systems still needs to be investigated, especially if one acknowledges that the current solutions fail to foster the kind of social interaction initially hoped.

The Rhetoric Behind IPAs. Whether or not the quest of ubicomp has been already accomplished lies outside the scope of this paper. However, understanding the way ubicomp has turned into a technology-centred field of research does have bearing on our case as it helps better frame the rationale behind the design of today's IPAs. In this respect, we argue that a particular rhetoric around the concept of disappearing computers – pursued in the field of ubicomp over the years – has influenced the design of the interaction modality on which IPAs are based. Indeed, smart systems based on vocal interaction embody a perspective on *disappearing interfaces* that holds a tight relationship with the ubicomp dream of computers blending with the environment.

All things considered, it is worth examining the different interpretations of the concept of *disappearance* and *disappearing interfaces* in HCI.

2.4   Disappearing Interfaces: Definitions and Nuances

Disappearing Computers in HCI. There is little doubt that the concept of *disappearing interfaces* comes from the theoretical legacy of ubicomp. Notably, the terms *calm* and *disappearing* are often used interchangeably (close to that of *computers*) as alternative designations of ubiquitous computing. That said, the exact meaning of the concept is anything but shared in the field of HCI, varying in substance depending on the specific attribution given to the idea of *disappearance*.

In this respect, two ways of interpreting the concept are mostly spread, referring directly to the way systems are implemented and used in the context [4, pp. 11–12].

Two Main Interpretations. According to the first interpretation, disappearance is conceived of as the result of having made systems an invisible presence (e.g., implants and embedded systems). In this case, the systems are integrated in everyday objects or in the body, resulting as imperceptible to users. In the second interpretation, instead, disappearance is regarded as the result of having made systems unnoticeable, that is, out of the limelight. In this other case, the systems are peripheral with respect to human attention (and senses), although still perceptible.

The two interpretations share a metaphorical use of the term *disappearance* as both refer to a seeming invisibility (or non-discernibility) of computers. Yet, their way of understanding the interaction with seemingly invisible computers differs substantially.

Degrees of Disappearance: Implicit and Explicit HCI. The term invisible (or disappearing) acquires a rather figurative sense when used to describe systems that operate at the periphery of users' perception. In this form of interaction, the (seeming) invisibility of the systems is attained by letting them in and out of the users' focus. Indeed, this conception is the closest to Weiser's original idea of ubicomp.

A more literal understanding of the term, on the other hand, refers to systems that are hidden either in the environment or in the users' dressing. In this modality, the systems are made no longer perceivable by the users, except when the interaction occurs. Such a removal from the users' perceptual field entails the shift to an *implicit* form of interaction, that is, a type of HCI in which the system(s) detects the users' behaviours automatically, understanding them as inputs (without an explicit command from the part of the users) [4, p. 12].

Nuances of Interpretation. The complexity emerging from the paradigm of disappearance is made further problematic by a diversity of nuances attributed to the notion of disappearing computers.

Unnoticeable vs Imperceptible. Dey et al., e.g., identify three levels of "invisibility" of UI [5]: *truly invisible* (when made unperceivable to users); *transparent* (when the interface is "forgotten" for it becomes like an extension of the body during the execution of specific actions); *subordinated* (when the functional aspects of the interface take second place in favour of more symbolic and personal aspects such as aesthetics). Although less differentiated, a similar understanding of invisible computers is provided by Streitz, who distinguishes between *physical* and *mental* disappearance [6].

The general idea is to aim for the least cognitively demanding interaction modalities, drawing on everyday people's practical experience. In this respect, an explicit reference is made to gesture-based interaction, which anticipates the much-discussed issue of the removal of interfaces in relation to the concept of natural interaction.

Interfaces as Hurdles. The understanding of interfaces as barriers to be removed has become widely popular in the field of HCI, linking directly to the concept of disappearing computers. Lim describes interfaces as obstacles that prevent users from having free access to the digital content [7]. From this perspective, more "natural" – that is, direct – forms of interaction between users and computers are needed. Such a view on the design of interfaces rejects any aesthetic frills as deviating from the functional goals of the HCI.

The Inevitable Mediators. A more holistic view on the disappearance of computers is offered by van Dam, who envisages a multisensory mix of new generation interfaces (post-WIMP) and interaction styles that combine speech and gesture [8]. He understands interfaces as unavoidable mediators between humans and computers (a "necessary evil"), acknowledging their fundamental role.

Bringing the research forward, Hui and Sherrat coined the definition of DUI (Disappearing User Interfaces) [9]. The researchers refer to those ubiquitous interfaces (e.g., IoT), both tangible and intangible, that are made invisible – namely, unnoticeable – with the aim of allowing users to have a more natural (direct), intuition-based interaction with ubiquitous systems.

A Critical Perspective. According to Ryan [10], vanishing interfaces in the field of wearable-technology lead to a suppression of the cultural and social roots embedded in dressing. Aiming for invisibility (disappearance of interfaces) carries a paradigm of interaction based on efficiency, functionalism, reductionism, essentialism. Ryan's provocative pun on this term (*natural-neutral*) highlights the ideological use of the concept of natural interaction and the related disagreement over its semantic interpretation.

Implications for the Design of IPAs. The terms of the disagreement above mentioned are relevant to the focus of this paper as the way IPAs have been conceived heavily reflects *one* ideal of "natural" interaction. In particular, the ideal based on a usability-centred perspective, which aims at removing interfaces altogether. Indeed, the emergence of this ideal is exemplified by the central role that vocal interaction has gained in the design of IPAs. This also explains why speech as interaction modality is nowadays becoming ubiquitous across different devices.

3 The Advocacy of Natural Interfaces

3.1 Natural Interaction and Disappearing Computers

The use of the term *natural* to describe interfaces and related interaction modalities is strictly tied to the concept of disappearing computers. Indeed, adopting a "natural" form of interaction is often presented as a direct consequence of having made computers disappear. However, this seems to be more a promise than a fact.

The Promise of Natural Interaction. To accomplish ubicomp's dream, the merger between technology and physical objects needs to be complemented by a further form of simplification, that is, a direct (less mediated) form of interaction. This idea is at the base of Lim's concept of disappearing interfaces [7], which has come to be popular in the field of HCI. In this view, touchscreens are considered a step forward towards the disappearance of interfaces as they reduce the level of intermediation between digital content and users, allowing for manipulating the *"digital material"* in a direct way. The epithet natural, in this case, indicates that the type of interaction is more direct (or less mediated) than others, which are based on old interaction modalities (e.g., mouse or pointers). In this context, gesture is understood as a natural form of interaction par excellence, if used in a non-codified, non-communicative fashion.

3.2   The Controversy Over the Concept of Natural Interaction

An Ontological Issue. The main dispute over the definition of natural interfaces revolves around an ontological problem, that is, whether and to what extent interfaces can be regarded as natural. What natural means exactly, however, depends on the interpretative criteria and specific perspectives adopted by the single researchers. Despite the lack of a common definition, the term is generally used to describe ways of interacting with computers that rely on spontaneous behaviour – namely, behaviour that is not based on specific learnings.

Positivistic Critique. Norman's critique on this matter [11] highlights role and limitations of what computer scientists call NUIs (Natural User Interfaces). He holds that natural interfaces – especially gesture-based interfaces, the focus of many studies in HCI – are not inherently natural as they entail one or more specific languages to be learnt (based on standards that are to be necessarily developed). In this regard, Norman specifies that the strength of GUIs – and the reason why they are heavily used still nowadays – is not the graphics itself, but the nature of interaction, which allows users to explore, remember and learn. In one word: visibility. Removing visibility, Norman argues, can have negative consequences.

In line with Norman's critical view, Hansen and Dalsgaard hold that users need to learn how to interact with the so-called natural interfaces in the same way as with any other type of interface [12]. Moreover, they question the very promise behind NUIs: the removal of input devices. Not only are input devices still in play in many examples of NUIs, but also the human body itself can be considered as an input instrument. In this view, "natural interfaces" is an erroneous definition and it should be replaced by that of *"intuitive interfaces"*.

Phenomenological Critique. A different concept of naturalness in HCI is developed by Hara et al., who reject the mechanistic understanding of the human experience behind the prominent definition of natural interaction [13].

Although in line with Norman's critique of NUIs, Hara et al. take a different perspective based on phenomenology (i.e., situated interaction, embodied cognition), which calls into question the idea that the interface itself is the unique *"source of explanation"* for the presence or absence of usability, naturalness, learnability, etc.

Indeed, they contrast what they regard as a *representational* perspective, which implies that natural interfaces would (and should) be based on common (or natural) forms of human expression. This view assumes that human forms of expression come from nature. The main problem with this view, Hara et al. hold, is that the role of the social context seems to be neglected. As an alternative approach, they commit themselves to the concept of *lived body* (Merleau-Ponty) and to the idea that the meaningfulness of individual experience emerges from the social context (Wittgenstein and Garfinkel), being situated in the specific community where the very experience occurs (Wenger's notion of *Communities of Practice*) [13, p. 5].

The "Naturalness" of IPAs Interaction. The way today's IPAs are designed reflects the prominent interpretation of the concept of natural interaction. This is exemplified by the extensive use of vocal interaction, which has long since been considered as natural. As shown so far, however, this concept carries a variety of meanings, in some cases mutually opposed. Consequently, there are multiple perspectives and interpretations, some of which are either under-developed or simply underrated. The implication for personal assistants is that the design of the interaction with them follows the most widespread conception, which "happens" to be usability and technology centred as well as anchored to a positivistic understanding of the human being.

The question to be raised, therefore, is not whether the interaction with IPAs is truly natural. Rather, the question is what implications adopting the paradigm of naturalness entails, with respect to the social relationships taking place in the age of IoT.

4   Intelligent Personal Assistants in Theory and in Practice

The advertising of IPAs promises a *natural way* of interacting with technology. In this regard, however, several issues arise, feeding a debate both in academic research and in mainstream media (e.g. web articles or YouTube videos). According to Murad and Munteanu [14], there is the need to face the specific challenges emerging from new paradigms of interaction, adapting existing heuristics and design guidelines.

As shown in the first part of this paper, having applied a specific understanding of natural interaction to the development of IoT has caused vocal interaction to become central in the design of IPAs. To pursue the understanding of the implications of this choice, we performed a specific literature review on IPAs that we present as the second part of this paper. The review was guided by a pre-defined framework, structured into three lenses. Each lens is described in details hereafter (Fig. 1).

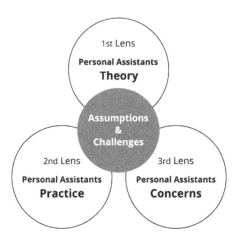

Fig. 1. Three-lenses framework: IPAs in Theory, in Practice, Issues and Concerns.

4.1   First Lens: Personal Assistants in Theory

IPAs are described as embodying the idea of a virtual butler that helps you "get things done" [15]. Already in 2002 Baber depicted intelligent personal assistant as "*an application that uses input such as the user's voice [...] and contextual information to provide assistance by answering questions in natural language, making recommendations and performing actions*" [16].

General Features. Intelligent personal assistants support conversational interaction, most often with no visual output. Placed in the home environment, they are "always-on" and "always listening". From a technical point of view, they combine speech recognition, language understanding, dialogue management, language generation and speech synthesis to respond to user requests. The infrastructure used to operate them has advanced rapidly in recent years, becoming more and more efficient.

In general, IPAs process a wide variety of verbal instructions to run Internet searches, access information and multimedia content, and dictate text messages. In advertising, IPAs are depicted as being particularly suited for helping with cooking, playing music, retrieving news and information, playing games [15]. In the home-context, systems like Amazon Echo and Google Home can also be used as the interface to verbally control a set of compatible appliances (heating, lighting, TV, radio, security devices, etc.).

Most IPAs (Siri, Alexa and Cortana) have female-gendered names and female default voices. Using female-gendered personalities for voice user interfaces is not new: navigation systems (e.g., for cars) are also typically equipped with female-gendered voices.

Commercial Design Assumptions. Branham et al. [17] conducted a qualitative review of the commercial design guidelines published by the five top vendors: Amazon, Google, Microsoft, Apple and Alibaba. From their analysis, a common underlying assumption emerged: the interface of intelligent personal assistants is modelled after human-human conversation metaphor. Thus, IPAs should be designed to reproduce a unique personality while interacting with users. To this aim, designers need to define a *persona*, that is, the personality and profile of the virtual assistant that the user will be interacting with. Moreover, they need to establish the interaction flow, designing the exact answer of the assistant according to the given (or predicted) situation [18].

Analysing reviews of some users Purington et al. [19] conclude that personification of intelligent personal assistants is a marker for the users' satisfaction. This explains why companies try to ensure that users personify their IPAs.

According to the design guidelines reviewed by Branham et al. [17], the conversation should also be personal and efficient. In this view, the design guidelines suggest using contextual data to cooperate with the individual. People appreciate when their IPA remembers the past conversations, especially if there is *"static information and frequent actions"* that will likely often occur.

Users' Expectations. Expectations of users influence their acceptance of novel technologies. The Expectation Confirmation Model (ECM) proposed in 2001 by Bhattacherjee [20] postulates that the acceptance of a system is directly related to the discrepancy between the initial expectations of the users and their actual experience. When betrayed, high expectations cause the users' satisfaction to dwindle [21].

The ability of voice-activated assistants to manage dialogue in a "natural" manner (i.e., fluid, simple, effortless) is at the centre of the message aimed at promoting them. In this respect, one of the most spread – and mismatched – expectations among users is that there would be no need for them to learn how to interact with their IPA. To specify, users expect the conversation with their IPA to unfold "naturally", the same way as it happens in a standard human-human conversation. Moreover, they do not expect applications to behave inconsistently and imperfectly, even if this is often the case when it comes to Artificial Intelligence. According to Kocielnik et al., [21] little research has been carried out so far on methods for setting appropriate users' expectations of AI-powered technologies, (prior to use).

Benefits for Specific Groups of Users. Speech recognition technologies enable hands-free interaction, supporting multi-tasking and allowing users to spare time for other activities. On average, the most popular context of use seems to be the home environment, where activities such as cooking are carried out with the help of IPAs.

Thanks to voice input, writing-impaired users can retrieve information from the Internet. Moreover, new potential users may be involved: very young children (seven-year-old or younger) and illiterate people. According to Lima et al. [1], the rapid spread of voice-controlled systems will impact particularly in countries where large sections of the population is functionally illiterate (e.g. Brazil). These population groups, Lima et al. argue, will take advantage of the possibility to interact with technology through voice. Moreover, people who are physically impaired are assumed to be empowered by voice-interaction. On the other hand, the extensive use of voice-based interaction may exclude people with speech problems. In spite of the benefits for special groups of users, overall, today's IPAs are not yet designed with disable users in mind [17].

4.2   Second Lens: Personal Assistants in Practice

The spread of IPAs raises questions about the kind of user experience to which these assistants give rise: What is the nature of people's interactions and relationships with IPAs? How do families take possession of them, and for which aims? What benefits can the current assistants bring to people's home life? To shed light on these matters, user studies have been conducted in the home environment, often examining specific demographic categories (e.g., older adults, young children, and people with disabilities).

Through our second lens, we scrutinised these studies, paying attention to what happens during the interaction. Our aim was to gain a better understanding of the real user experience with intelligent personal assistants.

There are numerous assistants available on the market. However, Alexa (Echo smart speaker device) is the most popular one, with a market share of about 70% in US households in 2018 [22]. Therefore, most studies focused on Alexa, sometimes comparing it to Siri, the Apple's counterpart.

Categories of Users. As mentioned above, several studies have focused on specific user categories. Hereafter, we summarise some of the results for the following four groups of users: older adults, children, disabled people and low-income users.

Older Adults. Pradhan et al. [23] deployed Amazon Echo Dot Devices in the homes of seven older adults for a three weeks period, with the aim of assessing how individuals experience and ontologically categorise the interactions with IPAs. Their findings indicate that Alexa is categorised as "object like" or "human like" depending on both the responsiveness of the system and whether the users seek social connection.

Children. By means of voice interfaces, even young children, still unable to read and write, can interact with computers. Lovato and Piper [24] enquired into the purposes for which children use IPAs. Their results show that children mainly use these systems to explore and seek information. Exploration can be either aimed at understanding or having fun (playful, humour). Seeking information, on the other hand, is generally for pictures and other facts of their interest.

People with Disabilities. Branham et al. [17] argue that IPAs, optimised to comprehend voices of young adults and middle-aged people, have not been designed for impaired users. In this respect, researchers studying populations with speech impairments found that the current timeout period for IPAs is insufficient. Indeed, people with Alzheimer's disease and intellectual disabilities take longer to utter their command. Likewise, blind users found this time-out frustrating as it restricts their capability of performing complex voice commands. Prior studies showed that blind users aspire to perform complex tasks, with a level of control finer than it is currently possible with commercial voice interfaces.

Specific Languages and Income Groups. Bhalla [25] presents an ongoing study on the use of Voice-User Interfaces by Indian users from low-income and middle-income groups. Since August 2017, search facilities are available in nine vernacular Indian languages. This has prompted the researcher to examine whether people use vernacular language to enter queries on Google.

The initial findings show that people seem to prefer to enter the queries on Google using English rather than vernacular languages. This is probably due to the social stigma associated with the use of vernacular languages, which the participants involved in the study linked to low-income audiences with very little or no literacy.

Personification of IPAs. As IPAs simulate the human voice, users are led to personify them. Personification is the phenomenon of attribution of human-like characteristics to objects or nonhuman agents. There are two main lines of thought regarding the interpretation of this phenomenon; some researchers think that there are psychological reasons ("purposive" explanation) and some other think that the phenomenon arises from a so-called "overlearned politeness" that is substantially mindless [26].

The studies on this matter so far conducted suggest that people who personify their IPAs experience a greater degree of satisfaction [17].

Personification or Overlearned Politeness? In Lopatovska and Williams' [26] study, most of the participants appeared not to personify Alexa and similar IPAs. Therefore, the authors are inclined to believe that people do not tend to personify these devices as argued in other studies. Moreover, their results confute the findings from previous research that suggested a link between personification and satisfaction: all users involved in the study reported high levels of satisfaction, even in absence of person-ification. Finally, the authors argue that the majority of those participants who showed to personify their IPA might have been driven by mindless behaviour, result of an "overlearned social behaviour".

Personification Reflects the Social Context. Pradhan et al. [23] conducted a study to investigate how people personify IPAs, involving seven elderly people living alone. The results show an open-ended ontological categorisation, ranging between the two opposite poles "human-like" and "object-like" based on *"the voice assistant capabilities (e.g., responsiveness), desire for personalization and companionship, sustained use over time, and location and moment of interaction with the voice assistant"* (p. 214:3). The researchers suggest that someone in need of social contact may be likely to personify a piece of technology and at times seek social connection through it. Thus, the ways in which users personify devices would be deeply linked to the social dimension of their lives.

IPAs as Social Agents. Porcheron et al. [15] studied how interacting with Amazon Echo influences everyday social practices of users, involving five households for a month-long qualitative enquiry. During the test, the researchers observed that Echo was "recruited" and adapted to the intricate communication (and actions) at the base of everyday family life. This led the researchers to argue that the use of Echo became part of the "politics of home" ("regulative work" among participants). Porcheron et al. conclude that the use of voice-based assistants such as Echo is constructed through situated actions, thus "embedded" in the social order that the family members produce and elaborate upon.

The Betrayal of Users' Expectations. Recent studies conducted in household settings highlighted how IPAs generate "the illusion of [a] natural conversation" [27]. In this respect, human-like traits attributed to IPAs play a dual and contradictory role. On the one hand, they engage users in the interaction. On the other, they cause users to develop unrealistic expectations.

False Expectations. In the field of human-robot interaction, research found that endowing robots with human-like voices can lead users to overestimate the robots' intelligence, creating false expectations about their performance [28]. The same happens in the interaction with IPAs, where users give their personal assistants credit for capabilities that they do not truly possess. In this regard, Velkovska and Zouinar [27] mention the fact that users often turn to their IPAs vainly, making use of indexical terms (such as "now" or "here"). In fact, these terms, which refer to contextual elements, are not understood by IPAs.

Lee et al. [18] report that besides simple commands, IPAs receive several emotional inputs from users, including rough and aggressive ones. IPAs' inability to understand the context and the user's emotional state is considered to be one of the biggest challenges that AI developers currently face.

Mismatching. As already noted, the mismatch between users' expectations and the reality of an artificial speech-based interaction can undermine the quality of the user experience. Doyle et al. [29] conducted a study addressing how users conceptualise the experience with IPAs such as Siri and Alexa, with respect to the perception of humanness. Their results show that some users found the conversation with both Siri and Alexa inauthentic while some others found them devoid of emotional engagement as well as incapable of showing warmth as humans do.

Speech Recognition Mistakes. The most common technical challenge with voice-based IPAs is speech recognition. In a study performed on a group of 20 Siri's infrequent users, Cowan et al. [30] found that Siri could not properly understand users' accent. Participants in the study mentioned various examples of misunderstanding. Moreover, participants reported the strategies that they adopted to prevent speech recognition mistakes. These included specifying the subject of the request, speaking very slowly and using extremely articulate phrasing.

4.3 Third Lens: Issues and Concerns

According to several authors [e.g. 31, 32, 33] what compromises the overall user experience with IPAs is the difficulty that people have with elaborating a clear mental model of the assistants' behaviour. In addition, the use of this novel technology raises a variety of social and ethical concerns. In this section, we elaborate upon both aspects.

The Lack of a Clear Mental Model. A variety of studies show that the voice-only modality of IPAs – i.e., their "invisible" nature – makes it difficult for users to discover the capabilities and limitations that such devices have [31]. Ghosh et al. [32] stress the difference between visual mapping and the creation of a mental model in usability testing. Indeed, only relying on hearing, with the exclusion of sight, entails a larger cognitive burden for users. When they are not provided with visual menus, users can have trouble understanding the functioning of the system.

Along the same lines, Cowan et al. [30] report that most people perceive IPAs as non-competent due to the fact that they lack a clear mental model of the type of interface on which these devices are based. The user's mental model is largely recognised as being a critical issue in speech interface interaction because it heavily influences people's behaviour during the interaction.

"Since conversational user interface is lacking in visual affordance, one of the major challenges of designing intelligent assistant is figuring out how users discover and learn the way of interaction" [18, p. 176].

Reinforcement of Cultural and Gender Biases. The sound of voice conveys a diversity of cues that humans are accustomed to recognize such as gender, age, and personality of the speaker [28]. Using female voice – with the aim of attributing a "supportive" and "humble" personality to IPAs – raises controversy over gender discrimination and stereotype reinforcement.

According to Søndergaard and Hansen [33], IPAs, mainly designed in the Silicon Valley, epitomise the dominant narrative of *"female servants and secretaries that are part of our collective imaginings"* (p. 878). Moreover, not only does Alexa use words that can be ascribed to women, but also reproduces expressions that can be associated with people (male or female) with a low social status [34].

Nass et al. (cited in [34]) showed that users do transfer gender stereotypes to machines, ascribing precise roles to male-gendered and female-gendered voices. In particular, it was found that female-gendered voices are perceived as helpful and acquiescent, whereas male-gendered voices are felt as domineering. The problem arises from developers' gender stereotypes, which are somewhat transferred to the designed "personality" of IPAs. As a result, people who interact with such a voice will likely reproduce, amplify and strengthen the emerging stereotypes.

Lima et al. [1] conducted a lab experiment aimed at analysing the presence of cultural biases in the interaction with voice-based intelligent assistants. The researchers were interested in verifying whether gender and accent affect the ability of IPAs to process users' speech. In the study, Google Assistant and Siri were tested, involving people of both genders with different accents. Preliminary results suggest that accent and wrong pronunciation due to regional and socioeconomic differences significantly affect the quality of the speech-recognition. The role of gender, instead, remains still unclear (comparison between genders showed a significant difference only when the speech-recognition was performed by Google Assistant).

Development of Controversial Interaction Modalities. Can the interaction that users have with digital objects, intended as social objects, affect the way they interact with other human beings? This social issue is raised by Habler et al. [34], who investigated how gendered voices and specific language affect the perception of personal assistants such as Apple's Siri, Amazon Echo, Microsoft's Cortana and Google Assistant. Results show that the assistants with lower-class language received higher ratings by the participants involved, because they were thought to perform better. The voice's gender, instead, seems to be a factor of less importance.

Lovato and Piper [24] raised the issue of how the asking question behaviour – typical of children – is influenced by the use of technology. If children are beginning to see voice agents as a potential source of answers to their questions, how can these interfaces better support children and their parents? In this respect, Lovato and Piper mention a study by Kahn et al. *"about children seeing robots as both social entities and objects, which could lead them to establish a master-servant relationship with robots that could bring about negative developmental outcome"* [35, p. 338].

Social and Ethical Issues. The rapid spread of IPAs is raising social and ethical concerns as they are designed to be "always-on" and "always-listening".

Mitev et al. [22] report on recent multiple attacks – consisting of unauthorized commands being sent by hackers – against devices that utilise voice-based UIs. To check the level of security of Alexa, they designed and implemented an attack to Echo's smart lock and home security system. Their experiment demonstrates that it is feasible to exploit the interaction model of the specific Skill installed to design a malicious one, which can cause damage to the system (*Skills* are programmatic expansions that provide functionality beyond the basic operations of the IPA).

Ethical concerns arise when technology imitates human-human conversation – the human voice – to such an extent that users are driven to wonder whether they are interacting with a real person or with a machine. Exemplar is the case of Google speech synthesis engine booking an hairdresser's appointment over the phone, without the person at the other end realising she was talking to an artificial system [36].

At a social level, personification of technology can have both a positive and negative impact. Positive aspects include therapeutic benefits for certain user groups. Negative consequences, on the other hand, include a reduced level of human interaction and the risk of manipulation. For instance, users who tend to personify their IPAs might be more likely to reveal personal information [23].

Researchers' Commitment. Aylett et al. [36] regret the lack of commitment by academic designers and HCI professionals to designing and testing alternative speech recognition systems. According to them, this reluctance results in large corporations dictating how speech-recognition technology must be implemented and deployed. The main consequence is that the whole point of Echo remains *"to get you buy stuff from Amazon"* [36, p. 9]. It is the duty of the research community to enlarge the scope of this technology, addressing all the social and ethical issues and supporting vulnerable groups.

5   Assumptions and Challenges

What emerges from the literature review is that IPAs have been conceived and designed based on specific assumptions. The latter can be summarised as follows:

1st assumption: **Human-human conversation mimicry is the best metaphor to be used in IPAs' voice-interaction.**
(Argument based on [17] – see Sect. 4.1, First Lens, *Commercial Design Assumptions*).

2nd assumption: **The interaction between users and IPAs can be standardised, regardless of the context.**
(Argument based on [17] and [18] – see the whole Sect. 4.1, First Lens – as well as on [15] – see Sect. 4.2, Second Lens, *Personification of IPAs*, esp., *IPAs as Social Agents*).

3rd assumption: **Users' expectations regarding the performance of IPAs are a marketing, not a design issue.**
(Argument based on [20] and [21] – see Sect. 4.1, First Lens, *Users' Expectations* – as well as on [27] – see Sect. 4.2, Second Lens, *The Betrayal of Users' Expectations*).

4th assumption: **The same voice – young, female, friendly, and polite – fits all users.**
(Argument based on [18, 27–30] – see Sect. 4.2, Second Lens, *The Betrayal of Users' Expectations* – as well as on [28, 33, 34] – see Sect. 4.3, Third Lens, *Reinforcement of Cultural and Gender Biases*).

5th assumption: **Visual features – both tangible and intangible – are not a priority for the design of IPAs.**
(Argument based on [18, 31, 32] – see Sect. 4.3, Third Lens, *The Lack of a Mental Model* – as well as on [28]).

6th assumption: **IPAs behave in a neutral and innocent way.**
(Argument based on [1, 24, 28, 33–35] – see Sect. 4.3, Third Lens, *Development of Controversial Interaction Modalities* and *Reinforcement of Cultural and Gender Biases*).

These assumptions may be regarded as convenient "shortcuts", used for making voice-activated devices both technologically viable and economically affordable; IPAs can be still considered products in a growing market phase. However, the time has come for manufacturers to focus on the unsolved design issues, challenging the aforementioned assumptions (Fig. 2).

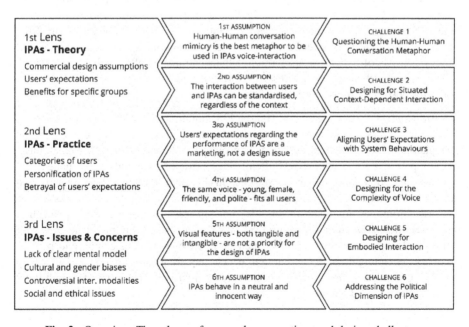

Fig. 2. Overview: Three-lenses framework, assumptions and design challenges.

5.1   Six Design Challenges

1st Challenge: Questioning the Human-Human Conversation Metaphor. Porcheron et al. [15] reject the idea that IPAs are "conversational" in nature and that the interaction with them is a "true" conversation. The fact that the responses from the part of the device do not necessarily follow the input in a coherent way makes such an interaction substantially different from human-human interaction. In this respect, developers should consider whether humanness is the right metaphor to be used for the design of IPAs. Indeed, it is the mismatch between the users' expectations and the system's performance that affects the experience that people have with IPAs [30].

Drawing on prior work about the needs of people with visual impairments, Branham et al. [17] critically assess the taken-for-granted human-human conversation metaphor, arguing that this paradigm restricts usage for a variety of users, including blind people. The researchers solicit a more inclusive models of conversation length, complexity, speed, and other aspects pertaining to the interaction. According to them, not only blind people, but also other groups with disabilities would benefit from IPAs adopting such an inclusive approach.

2nd Challenge: Designing for Situated Context-Dependent Interaction. The interaction between the user and the IPA unfolds in a specific context of use, which implies a specific set of cultural values. This cultural milieu influences the user experience and thus needs to be considered when designing IPAs.

Context-of-Use. According to the analysis performed by Velkovska and Zouinar [27], the inability of AI technology to be context-aware is one of the main usability issues currently faced by developers. To improve the intelligibility of conversational technologies, two strategies are identified. The first strategy consists of supporting users in understanding the answers of the system and the source of the problem – both if the system gives a wrong answer and if the system is unable to respond. The second strategy consists of helping users formulate their commands effectively.

This specific challenge is addressed by Braun and Alt [37] who propose a user model for designing user-aware virtual assistants.

Cultural Context. Søndergaard and Hansen [33] highlight that collective imaginary of IPAs varies across cultures. American collective imaginary, for instance, are built on dystopian narratives of technology (e.g. Frankenstein). Japan, on the other hand, has a more utopian narrative, with robots often being portrayed as friends (e.g., manga). As contemporary IPAs are mostly developed in Western cultures, Søndergaard and Hansen ask themselves how the Japanese culture might influence their design as well as their use. Moreover, linguistic factors play an important role in the user's perception and expectations. As an example, research has shown that people prefer devices with an informal way of speaking and that their preferences regarding gender and personality vary depending on both the region in which they are located and the language they use [28, p. 10]. Therefore, there is no globally optimal voice that resonates with users across contexts and devices.

3rd Challenge: Aligning Users' Expectations with System Behaviours. As emphasised by Gürkök et al. [38], the user experience cannot be evaluated merely considering the performance or usability of IPAs. Indeed, the evaluation is highly influenced by the prior users' expectations as well as by the specific context of use. The findings of the study performed by Kocielnik et al. [21] show that shaping the expectations of users can be an effective way of improving the user acceptance of AI technologies.

The alignment of the users' expectations with the actual systems' behaviour is the focus of a 2019 paper by Azmandian et al. [39]. They found that the users' expectations over smart agents' behaviour are shaped by the users' assumptions. In light of these results, Azmandian et al. acknowledge that designing the behaviour of IPAs is a challenging task: the alignment of the expectations of end users with an agent's actual behaviour is influenced by many factors. One of them is how the agent is introduced to users, i.e., what users retain from the way the agent is presented, which will then contribute to shaping the user's biases. What makes it harder for designers to address the issue is that there may be more than one correct answer to the question of how an agent should behave in a specific situation. Moreover, even if designers create personas to achieve the desired user experience, that very voice-assistant-persona will be perceived differently by different users. This is the concept of the "second-order understanding", well-illustrated by Krippendorff in [40]. Therefore, designers should include the perspectives of the end users when creating a persona, gathering information about what different user groups or individuals would expect from their IPAs [23].

4th Challenge: Designing for the Complexity of Voice. Aylett et al. [36] suggest moving the design focus from mimicry to "vocal performance", which entails conveying complex meaning without relying on the imitation of reality (i.e., human conversation). In other words, voice should be used as actors do when they perform, aiming for representation rather than mimicry. The storytelling at the base of performing is what can make speech technology engaging and immersive, generating a fulfilling experience for users. In this respect, neutral voices should be replaced by more radical vocal styles, taking inspiration from theatre performances.

Cambre and Kulkarni [28] wonder how user would react if IPAs' voice was gender-neutral. In this regard, some researchers have already proposed gender-neutral voices for voice interfaces. A further issue is the controversy over the reproduction of realistic human voices. The concern is that users can be deceived by the system, namely, made believe that they are interacting with a true human. The researchers suggest that using non-human voices (e.g., deliberately robotic) might solve the problem as it would make immediately clear the identity of the system.

According to Kim et al. [41] communication based on a single channel (i.e., voice) restricts expressiveness and richness of information. Therefore, IPAs' designers should explore multimodal interaction modalities. To sustain their point, the authors developed a prototype system adopting thermal interaction to enrich people's experiences with IPAs.

5th Challenge: Designing for Embodied Interaction. To date, designers and researchers have largely focused on the conversational aspects of IPAs. What has been neglected, however, is the form and embodiment of this technology as well as how that makes a difference in the user experience. Cambre and Kulkarni [28] believe that, besides the specific context of use and the characteristics of the voice interface, the user experience is also influenced by the physical features of the devices. According to the them, adopting a human-robot interaction (HRI) perspective would offer a more holistic approach as HRI already merges embodiment and voice in its research.

6th Challenge: Addressing the Political Dimension of IPAs. According to Sønder-gaard and Hansen [33], IPAs are neither innocent nor neutral. Indeed, they are political entities that elicit ethical and philosophical issues. These issues must be addressed by all the parties concerned, included design. For instance, instead of reproducing tradi-tional gender roles, IPAs could be designed to question them and leave them open.

In the same vein, Aylett et al. [36] claim that merely analysing the systems in place – as most HCI researchers have been doing – will not innovate or change speech interaction. Therefore, researchers and designers should take an active role in this process, e.g., developing provocative artefacts that challenge the dominant perspective on the design of IPAs.

6   Discussion

It is worth discussing how and to what extent the identified assumptions are influenced by the dominant paradigms of natural interaction and disappearing computers, addressed in the first part of this paper. In this respect, we want to highlight several points.

First, not all the assumptions underlying the design of IPAs are strictly related to the adoption of the concept of natural interaction. To specify, the third assumption is independent of the discourse about natural interaction. In other words, a market-driven approach may well be adopted even in case a different paradigm of interaction was to be employed in the design of IPAs.

Second, each assumption holds a different degree of relevance with the concept of natural interaction. As an example, a lack of proper understanding of the context-dependence (second assumption) and the embodied nature of interaction (fifth assumption) is a common issue in HCI research, across different types of device and interaction modality. On the other hand, the assumption that mimicry is the optimal choice to design vocal interaction (first assumption) does share some peculiar principles with the paradigm of natural interaction (i.e., natural as authentic and thus better). Finally, although not specifically related to the concept of natural interaction, some controversial aspects regarding the use of speech synthesis (fourth and sixth assump-tion) are the direct consequence of having adopted a voice centred interaction modality. To summarise, the issues that emerge from following these assumptions are of a broad scope, touching upon aspects that go beyond the type of interaction modality adopted. Nevertheless, some specific issues (e.g., criticism of human voice mimicry) derive from having made vocal interaction the main interaction modality of IPAs.

Lastly, although most of the challenges mentioned may be relevant to a large spectrum of devices and interaction paradigms, the related assumptions pertain specifically to IoT devices that rely exclusively on voice as input modality. In other words, the assumptions to be challenged regard the interaction with voice centred – touchless – IoT devices, the design of which embodies the dominant paradigm of natural interaction.

7   Conclusions

By analysing some recent studies on the use of IPAs, a complex set of issues regarding people's experience emerged. We understand that the scope of these issues cannot be limited to the debate around the paradigm of natural interaction and the consequences of its adoption. In fact, the massive spread of computers and the growth of IoT systems produce inevitably a vast range of new types of phenomena, from humanisation of technology to cognitive overload and hypermediated social relationships, just to mention a few. We also think, however, that these phenomena happen in the wake of a framework that led the development of ubiquitous computing to acquire the form it has nowadays. Therefore, understanding the conceptual roots behind the design of today's IPAs is crucial to addressing the main challenges that the use of this new technology entails.

As Søndergaard and Hansen [33] remind us, technological futures stem from and, at the same time, replicate collective imaginaries, which connect technology with social, cultural, and political matters. Such technological futures, therefore, are not predetermined, although not entirely open either. Indeed, it is the designer's task to challenge the dominant narratives in order to propose different and still possible futures.

References

1. Lima, L., Furtado, E., Furtado, V., Almeida, V.: Empirical analysis of bias in voice-based personal assistants. In: Companion Proceedings of the 2019 World Wide Web Conference, WWW 2019 (2019)
2. Weiser, M.: The computer for the 21st century. Sci. Am. **265**(3), 94–104 (1991)
3. Takayama, L.: The motivations of ubiquitous computing: revisiting the ideas behind and beyond the prototypes. Pers. Ubiquit. Comput. **21**(3), 557–569 (2017)
4. Poslad, S.: Ubiquitous Computing. Smart Devices, Environments and Interactions, p. 473 (2009)
5. Dey, A.K., Ljungstrand, P., Schmidt, A.: Distributed and disappearing user interfaces in ubiquitous computing. In: CHI 2001 Extended Abstracts on Human Factors in Computing Systems, CHI EA 2001 (2001)
6. Streitz, N.: From cognitive compatibility to the disappearing computer: experience design for smart environments. In: Proceedings of the 15th European Conference on Cognitive Ergonomics: The Ergonomics of Cool Interaction, ECCE 2008 (2008)
7. Lim, Y.K.: Disappearing interfaces. Interactions **19**(5), 36–39 (2012)
8. van Dam, A.: User interfaces: disappearing, dissolving, and evolving. Commun. ACM **44**(3), 50–52 (2001)

9. Hui, T.K., Sherratt, R.S.: Towards disappearing user interfaces for ubiquitous computing: human enhancement from sixth sense to super senses. J. Ambient Intell. Hum. Comput. **8**(3), 449–465 (2017)

10. Ryan, S.E.: Re-visioning the interface: technological fashion as critical media. In: ACM SIGGRAPH 2009 Art Gallery, SIGGRAPH 2009, vol. 42, no. 4, pp. 307–313 (2009)

11. Norman, D.A.: Natural user interfaces are not natural. Interactions **17**(3), 6–10 (2010)

12. Hansen, L.K., Dalsgaard, P.: Note to self: stop calling interfaces "natural". In: Proceedings of the Fifth Decennial Aarhus Conference on Critical Alternatives, CA 2015 (2015)

13. Hara, K.O., Harper, R., Mentis, H., Sellen, A., Taylor, A.: On the naturalness of touchless: putting the "interaction" back into NUI. ACM Trans. Comput.-Hum. Interact. (TOCHI) **20** (1), 1–27 (2013)

14. Murad, C., Munteanu, C.: I don't know what you're talking about, HALexa": the case for voice user interface guidelines. In: Proceedings of the 1st International Conference on Conversational User Interfaces (2019)

15. Porcheron, M., Fischer, J.E., Reeves, S., Sharples, S.: Voice interfaces in everyday life. In: Proceedings of the Conference on Human Factors in Computing Systems (2018)

16. Baber, C.: "Speech output," in developing interactive speech technology. In: Baber, C., Noyes, J.M. (eds.) Interactive Speech Technology: Human Factors Issues in the Application of Speech Input/Output to Computers, pp. 1–18. Taylor & Francis (2002)

17. Branham, S.M., Roy, A.R.M.: Reading between the guidelines: how commercial voice assistant guidelines hinder accessibility for blind users. In: 21st International ACM SIGACCESS Conference on Computers and Accessibility, ASSETS 2019 (2019)

18. Lee, S.S., Lee, J., Lee, K.P.: Designing intelligent assistant through user participations. In: Proceedings of the 2017 ACM Conference on Designing Interactive Systems, DIS 2017 (2017)

19. Purington, A., Taft, J.G., Sannon, S., Bazarova, N.N., Taylor, S.H.: "Alexa is my new BFF": social roles, user satisfaction, and personification of the Amazon Echo. In: Proceedings of the Conference on Human Factors in Computing Systems, vol. Part F1276, pp. 2853–2859 (2017)

20. Bhattacherjee, A.: Understanding information systems continuance: an expectation-confirmation model. MIS Q. **25**(3), 351–370 (2001)

21. Kocielnik, R., Amershi, S., Bennett, P.N.: Will you accept an imperfect AI? Exploring designs for adjusting end-user expectations of AI systems. In: Proceedings of the Conference on Human Factors in Computing Systems, Glasgow, UK (2019)

22. Mitev, R., Miettinen, M., Sadeghi, A.R.: Alexa lied to me: skill-based man-in-the-middle attacks on virtual assistants. In: Proceedings of the 2019 ACM Asia Conference on Computer and Communications Security, ASIACCS 2019 (2019)

23. Pradhan, A., Findlater, L., Lazar, A.: "Phantom friend" or "just a box with information": personification and ontological categorization of smart speaker-based voice assistants by older adults. In: Proceedings of the ACM on Human-Computer Interaction, vol. 3, no. CSCW, p. Art No. 214 (2019)

24. Lovato, S., Marie Piper, A.: "Siri, is this you?": Understanding young children's interactions with voice input systems. In: Proceedings of IDC 2015: The 14th International Conference on Interaction Design and Children (2015)

25. Bhalla, A.: An exploratory study understanding the appropriated use of voice-based Search and Assistants. In: Proceedings of the 9th Indian Conference on Human Computer Interaction, IndiaHCI 2018 (2018)

26. Lopatovska, I., Williams, H.: Personification of the Amazon Alexa: BFF or a mindless companion? In: Proceedings of the 2018 Conference on Human Information Interaction and Retrieval, CHIIR 2018 (2018)

27. Velkovska, J., Zouinar, M.: The illusion of natural conversation: interacting with smart assistants in home settings. In: CHI 2018 Extended Abstracts (2018)
28. Cambre, J., Kulkarni, C.: One voice fits all? Social implications and research challenges of designing voices for smart devices. In: Proceedings of the ACM on Human-Computer Interaction, vol. 3, no. CSCW, pp. 223:1–223:19 (2019)
29. Doyle, P.R., Edwards, J., Dumbleton, O., Clark, L., Cowan, B.R.: Mapping perceptions of humanness in intelligent personal assistant interaction. In: Proceedings of the 21st International Conference on Human-Computer Interaction with Mobile Devices and Services, MobileHCI 2019 (2019)
30. Cowan, B.R., et al.: "What can i help you with?": Infrequent users' experiences of intelligent personal assistants. In: Proceedings of the 19th International Conference on Human-Computer Interaction with Mobile Devices and Services, MobileHCI 2017 (2017)
31. Furqan, A., Myers, C., Zhu, J.: Learnability through adaptive discovery tools in voice user interfaces. In: Proceedings of the Conference on Human Factors in Computing Systems (2017)
32. Ghosh, D., Foong, P.S., Zhang, S., Zhao, S.: Assessing the utility of the system usability scale for evaluating voice-based user interfaces. In: Proceedings of the Sixth International Symposium of Chinese CHI, ChineseCHI 2018 (2018)
33. Søndergaard, M.L.J., Hansen, L.K.: Intimate futures: staying with the trouble of digital personal assistants through design fiction. In: Proceedings of the 2018 Designing Interactive Systems Conference, DIS 2018 (2018)
34. Habler, F., Schwind, V., Henze, N.: Effects of smart virtual assistants' gender and language. In: ACM International Conference Proceeding Series, pp. 469–473 (2019)
35. Kahn, P.H., Gary, H.E., Shen, S.: Children's social relationships with current and near-future robots. Child. Dev. Perspect. 7(1), 32–37 (2013)
36. Aylett, M.P., Clark, L., Cowan, B.R.: Siri, echo and performance: you have to suffer darling. In: Proceedings of the Conference on Human Factors in Computing Systems (2019)
37. Braun, M., Alt, F.: Affective assistants: a matter of states and traits. In: Proceedings of the Conference on Human Factors in Computing Systems (2019)
38. Gürkök, H., Hakvoort, G., Poel, M., Nijholt, A.: User expectations and experiences of a speech and thought controlled computer game. In: Proceedings of the 8th International Conference on Advances in Computer Entertainment Technology, ACE 2011 (2011)
39. Azmandian, M., Arroyo-Palacios, J., Osman, S.: Guiding the behavior design of virtual assistants. In: Proceedings of the 19th ACM International Conference on Intelligent Virtual Agents, IVA 2019 (2019)
40. Krippendorf, K.: The Semantic Turn. A New Foundation for Design, p. 368. CRC Press, Boca Raton (2005)
41. Kim, S., Row, Y.K., Nam, T.J.: Thermal interaction with a voice-based intelligent agent. In: Proceedings of the Conference on Human Factors in Computing Systems (2018)

Understanding How Visitors Interact with Voice-Based Conversational Systems

Heloisa Candello[1]([✉]), Fabrício Barth[2], Eduardo Carvalho[3], and Ruy Alves Guimarães Cotia[3]

[1] IBM Research, São Paulo, Brazil
hcandello@br.ibm.com
[2] IBM Cloud and Cognitive Software, São Paulo, Brazil
fbarth@br.ibm.com
[3] Museu do Amanhã, Rio de Janeiro, Brazil
{eduardo.carvalho,ruy.guimaraes}@idg.org.br

Abstract. Museums and Art exhibition spaces are adopting Artificial Intelligence (AI) systems to engage and attract visitors in several contexts. The use of AI can boost visitors' attention, promote informal learning through conversations in front of the exhibits, and motivate visitors to act socially. In this paper, we describe a voice-based conversational system Iris+, in which visitors are inquired to answer questions to an agent. It is a proactive agent that invites visitors to reflect and take action to improve future world. First, we will describe how this system works. Second, we will show the outcomes of evaluation studies with visitors in situ and, a survey shows how visitors engaged in social action after interacting with IRIS+ and public demographics. Based on those visitors' studies, we propose a set of challenges to design conversational systems in public spaces and the improvements were incorporated into the redesign of IRIS++.

Keywords: Conversational systems · Artificial intelligence · User studies · Exhibitions · Museum installations

1 Introduction

The use of new technologies in museums encourages the creation of new genres of experience, which need to be developed with excellent design, marketing campaigns and proper functioning, fundamental characteristics for a customer of goods and services, and who will also look for this in experiences (Pine and Gilmore 1999). However, what does it take to make an experience unforgettable? (Boswijk et al. 2006) describe characteristics based on an extensive literature inspired by the concept of flow (Csikszentmihalyi 1991), a mental state that is reached when the individual is involved in an activity, with absolute focus, making it spontaneous and productive.

Another way to make an experience enjoyable is to use the conversational experience that the museum exhibits promote to infer meaning and reflection on certain perspectives or challenges. Traditionally, conversation promotes a space for learning in museums: visitors engage with museum content and develop conversations from

© Springer Nature Switzerland AG 2020
A. Marcus and E. Rosenzweig (Eds.): HCII 2020, LNCS 12201, pp. 40–55, 2020.
https://doi.org/10.1007/978-3-030-49760-6_3

exhibits for learning (Leinhardt 2002, Falk and Dierking 2016). To understand how to introduce and design conversations with chatbots in museums, researchers should know the purposes and intents of the design as well as the purposes and experience of visitors. Content plays a central role in the experience of informal learning by promoting conversations and reflections generated by exhibits. What are the main ways museums can connect with visitors? Several cultural and scientific institutions have adopted technologies to connect beyond labels displayed next to the artworks. These include: chatbots (Boiano 2018), robots (Shiomi 2006), QR codes (Schultz 2013), RFID tags (Hsi 2005), and augmented reality (Wojciechowski 2004). This paper presents a conversational voice-based system and, supporting user studies for understanding how visitors engage with the experience and content by acting in society.

2 Background

2.1 Artificial Intelligence in Museums

The state of the art of museum experiences points to a long list of studies on the use of technology to captivate the visitor (Falco and Vassos 2017). For Wright (2017, p. 109), "technology is inevitable in a museum, so what is the advantage of museums in resisting them?". However, the author emphasizes that experiments should not be developed around technology, which changes so quickly that museums lose time and money invested in hardware that can quickly become out of date. For the author, investments in digital experiences need to be in content - the narratives that museums want to tell about their collections, the place, and their stories. Falco and Vassos 2017 present different technological artifacts that would contribute to the visitor's journey. For example, there are mobile apps, such as audio guides or video guides, interactive with virtual reality (VR) or augmented reality (AR); wearable; sensor technologies. Those might employ voice or movement to trigger specific commands; and natural language processing technologies - NLP. Majd and Safabakhsh (2017) explain that machine learning technologies have improved the experience of users in museums, going beyond its technical function of extracting information of any kind for later analysis of the institution. The same authors explain that machine learning and computer vision have opened up a new way to access information in museums more naturally and with less invasive methods. Vassos (2016) shows in a study the use of machine learning to create dialogues between the visitor and works of art at the Mario Praz Museum, in Rome, Italy. The exhibition also used the Messenger application. The conversational exhibition had the objective of drawing the attention of "digital natives" (Vassos et al. 2016, p. 434). According to our review, there is a small number of conversational applications based on AI technologies in museums, that aim to engage visitors to act in the society.

3   About IRIS+

3.1   The Experience of IRIS+ at Museum of Tomorrow

The Museum of Tomorrow offers a narrative about how we can live and shape our next 50 years on this planet. The museum traces a journey towards possible futures. From the big questions that humanity has always asked, such as: *Where do we come from? Who are we? What are we? Where are we going? How do we want to get there?*. This space also seeks to promote innovation, spread the word about the advances of science, and publish news about the vital signs of the planet. IRIS+ is the first expansion of the central exhibition held at the Museum of Tomorrow since its opening. The launch of the new experience gives new meaning to the museum's call: *Tomorrow is Today and Today is the Place of Action*. The dialogue system (IRIS+) placed at the end of the exhibition trail was developed to questioning visitors who passed through the central exhibition (Cosmos, Earth, Anthropocene, Tomorrows and Us). The IRIS+ inspires the visitor to think about their role in society and truly participate in the search for more awareness, tolerance and a sustainable tomorrow. The initial interaction of the visitor with Iris+ is through a voice dialogue. The conversation system guides this discussion. The dialog begins with a question from IRIS+: *Considering what you saw in the Main exhibition, what are you most concerned about?*. The visitors can answer, and IRIS+ will provide more questions based on the visitor's response. Follow an example of visitor interaction with Iris+:

```
01     IRIS+ (I): The Museum of Tomorrow shows in its main exhibition the opportunities and challenges
of this era of great transformation. Thinking about it, what worries you the most in today's world?
02     The visitor (V): Pollution.
03     (I): Pollution is something of concern. Within this great theme, what else worries you?
04     (V): Contamination of waters.
05     (I): Can you change that scenario? What can you do?
06     (V): Propose not to throwing garbage anywhere.
07     (I): Thank you very much for your participation.
```

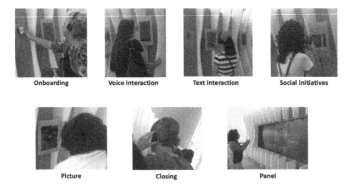

Fig. 1. Visitor experience with IRIS+.

At the end of a conversation, IRIS+ recommends some social initiatives connected to the concerns mentioned by the visitor. IRIS+ has a database of previously registered efforts, and a recommendation component is responsible for identifying up to 3 social initiatives that are consistent with the concerns of the visitor. Subsequently, to seeing recommendations, the visitor can take an optional photo. This photo is projected on a large visualization video wall to highlight the most relevant themes for visitors, and it reveals clusters of people concerned about the same issues. The whole experience lasts 5 to 7 min.

3.2 The Technology Behind IRIS+

The IBM Watson Assistant Service[1] was employed to obtain the IRIS+ response for the text transcription of the visitors' utterances from a set of pre-defined statements created by the museum curators. The recognition of user intents (phrases of visitors) was trained before the start of the exhibition. The curators (Subject Matter Experts - SMEs) from the museum are responsible for the curatorship activities.

To have most of the conversation by voice, the solution uses Speech to Text and Text to Speech components. The solution also uses a recommendation algorithm to recommends social initiatives to visitors. A high-level description of the IRIS+ architecture is presented in Fig. 2.

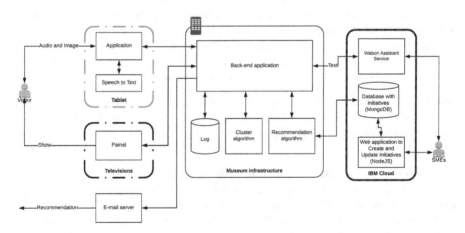

Fig. 2. High-level architecture

The intents, dialogs, and initiatives can be updated by curators over time using an administrative web interface. This allows them to change the solution behavior in real-time.

---

[1] https://cloud.ibm.com/docs/assistant.

4 Understanding Visitor's Perceptions

4.1 Quantitative Survey

Considering that one of the leading objectives of IRIS+ is to inspire people to embrace initiatives related to their concerns for the Planet, we undertook a study six months after the launch of interactive AI, to discover to what degree visitors had actually engaged. The six-month period was established as a means to allow visitors to absorb the experience and reflect on their visit, giving them time to get involved with an initiative. The study took the form of a quantitative survey combined with a set of open-ended questions (Onwuegbuzie and Leech 2005). We conducted the survey with Museum of Tomorrow visitors aged over 15 years old and who had interacted with the IRIS+. Aware of the importance of gathering information on visitors from all over the world, we recruited the participants based on their location precedence to answer the online questionnaire (Evans and Mathur 2005). The survey was answered by 116 participants between July 17, 2018 and August 4, 2018. It was divided into three sets of questions that, together, contained 13 closed-ended questions and 10 open-ended questions. Responses were tabulated and analyzed using *Excel* and *R* software.

Sociodemographic and Cultural Profile of Participants. Regarding the profile of the sample, there was a balance between male (51%) and female (49%) participants. There was a higher number of visitors aged 30 and over (73%) and, 27% of visitors were under 30 years old. There was an expressive participation of visitors from Other States of Brazil beside Rio de Janeiro (53%). Additionally, most of the visitors were within the bracket of up to 2 minimum wages (33%), followed by a group with monthly income ranging from 5 to 10 minimum wages (27%). For most of the participants (81%), it was the first visit to the Museum of Tomorrow.

Results. Follow our results after analyzing the data. It is important to mention that survey was conducted after six months of the visitors interacted with IRIS+, and our aim was also to identify visitors' engagement in the social actions recommended by the exhibit.

Perceptions Regarding the Interaction. Visitors were given the opportunity to assess their experiences through a score ranging from 1 to 5, with the higher score indicating a better evaluation. Most participants (63%) assessed the conversation with IRIS+ positively, allocating the highest possible score, while only 1% scored the experience between 1 and 2. The 4.53 average, along with public opinion, seems to show that the idea of interactive AI was approved. The most frequent comments were related to raising visitors' awareness about contemporary problems; the acknowledgment that we are all responsible when it comes to environmental issues; and reflections on human-machine interaction. This can be observed in participant 25 and participant 28 quotes:

> *"This project with IRIS+ is essential in reminding visitors to the Museum of Tomorrow about their responsibility when it comes to environmental issues" (P25)*

> *"Despite feeling "strange/uncomfortable in interacting with artificial intelligence" it was really fantastic! I'll certainly be back" (P98)*

When questioned on possible reflections as a result of the conversation, visitors were emphatic in identifying the striking aspects of IRIS+, whether through comments like *"My interaction led me to think that the planet I want for the future is not the one I cultivate in my daily routine"* (P14), admitting they should already be doing more for the planet than what they are, or in other comments like *"It provoked me unexpectedly, I had never stopped to think about what humans have done and are doing to our planet. It opened my eyes to the new challenges in my life"* (P1) by visitors who have begun questioning themselves about global issues based on the interaction.

Engagement. We asked visitors whether, six months after the launch of IRIS+ if they had become engaged in a social project or changed their individual behaviors based on the exhibit recommendations. Of all the participants, 37% had become engaged in an initiative related to their concerns about the planet. Assessing the most common topics in this engagement, we noted links with the most frequent concerns recorded through the IRIS+ system (Table 1). This data reveals that visitors seem more likely to act on issues part of their daily routine, like environmental conservation and waste management.

Table 1. 10 most common concerns recorded in the IRIS+ system, 2017–2019

Concern recorded in the IRIS+ system	Related area	Frequency
Environmental Degradation – Overall	Planet	12%
Pollution – Overall	Planet	10%
Global Warming – Climate Change	Planet	6%
Violence - Overall	Society	6%
Environmental Degradation – Deforestation	Planet	5%
Coexistence – Lack of Empathy	Society	4%
New Technologies – Overall	Human	3%
Social Inequality – Overall	Society	3%
Education – Overall	Human	3%
Lack of Resources - Water	Planet	3%

Among engaged visitors, we noted a greater probability to get involved in personal initiatives, that is, those which do not require association to any institution. Selective waste collection, saving water and electricity and cutting down on the use of plastic are examples of individual practices adopted by the participants. Of the 37% that took action, 86% opted for this type of engagement described here by participants 14, 50 and 105.

"A personal initiative, about saving water at home." (P14)

"I'm involved in an initiative to help youths and adolescents find their first job. It's a way I found to apply my expertise to benefit society." (P50)

"It's not an institution. I organized a campaign to recycle waste and cooking oil in the building complex where I live." (P105)

Among the group that became affiliated with an institution (14% of those engaged) there were people involved with NGOs, collaborating and promoting environmental causes; there were teachers providing lessons on environmental conservation and education; and even some related to reducing the use of fossil fuel powered vehicles.

"Campaigns warning about the use of fossil fuel powered vehicles, leveraging the generation of new energies. I encourage people to walk and pedal." (P84)

"I came up with material on EcoEducators (for "AppaiEducar" magazine), through which Environmental Engineering students undertake volunteer work at schools to raise awareness about environmental preservation." (P103)

"I help to promote causes (for Greenpeace)." (P110)

Aimed at understanding the potential for engagement in different groups in the study, cross tables were created between the "engagement" variable and the variables of gender, age bracket, origin, monthly income and the dichotomous question of *"Have you previously visited the Museum of Tomorrow?"*. Table 2 illustrates the main variable leveraging engagement, namely monthly income. To reach this conclusion, a dummy variable (Caudill 1987) was created, wherein we allocated all the individuals that earned up to (and including) 5 minimum wages per month in a group coded as 0; and those individuals who earned over 5 minimum wages per month in a group coded as 1. The first exploratory analysis of the data shows us that, of the visitors earning up to 5 minimum wages per month, 27% were engaged. Those who earned over 5 minimum wages per month presented an engagement rate of 47%. We chose to use Fisher's exact test to assess the null hypothesis that answers were evenly distributed in the contingency table.

The p-value of 0.04928 is an indication that the null hypothesis at a 5% significance level was not rejected, allowing us to infer that there are signs that visitors with a monthly income over 5 minimum wages are more likely to be engaged.

Another interesting result was linked to the age bracket. We parameterized age brackets according to dummy variables whereby individuals aged up to and including 30 years old were coded as 0, while those aged over 30 were coded as 1. The first exploratory analysis showed that 29% of the younger visitors (aged up to 30) had become engaged against 39% of the older visitors (over 30 years old). Although Fisher's test results are inconclusive for this cross reference ($p > 0.1$), we feel it important to look more closely at this data. The IRIS+ system shows that of the users who initiated a session with the AI, 52% are aged up to 30 years old. On the other hand, of those who completed the experience all the way to the end (when the photo appears on the panel), only 32% are aged up to 30 years old.

This data, along with information from the previous paragraph, led us to reflect on the potential engagement among younger visitors. If they make up the majority of visitors to the Museum, and they are also the majority in initiating a session with IRIS+, why are they the minority in the "conversations completed with IRIS+" indicator and why do they present a lower engagement percentage according to the survey data?

Now, we will look at the subject of "no engagement". We asked visitors who had not engaged what their leading motives were. A lack of time appears most common, together with the convenience factor of statements like *"Involvement with other personal issues, but which do not really justify my lack of involvement" (P100)* and *"Not entirely convenient, unfortunately" (P2)*. In other words, these are visitors who are aware of the problems but who, due to other priorities, end up doing nothing. We also discovered that non-engaged visitors living outside the city of Rio de Janeiro were unaware of any initiatives close to home, through statements like *"There's no time! I don't know of any initiatives in my city" (P34)*.

This valuable information can help bolster the responsibility of the Museum of Tomorrow in studying and adding new institutions, organizations and foundations from all over Brazil to the system.

Table 2. Monthly income and engagement (*Source:* IRIS+ Satisfaction and Engagement Survey, 2018.)

Have you engaged in an initiative?	Monthly income Up to 5 MW (0)	Monthly income Over 5 MW (0)
Engagement	15	18
No engagement	41	20
Total	56	38

4.2 Observation Studies in the Wild

The objective of this study was to understand in the wild the user experience with IRIS+ (Schuman 1987). The field study included observations and brief interviews with visitors. The semi-structured interviews were designed to be short and not to disturb or delay visitors. Twelve visitors described their experience to a researcher. The interviews were audio-recorded and consisted of only one question

> *Q1: Please tell us how you would describe your experience with this exhibit for a friend that will not be able to visit it.*

Four employees also contributed to the study sharing their views. The interviews also served as a clarification of the behaviors observed by the researcher during visitor's sessions. We also gathered the text interaction logs of 380 visitors, and audio/video recorded a day of visit interactions with IRIS+.

The Data Analysis. This analysis was a first attempt to understand visitors experience with IRIS+ in situ. We investigated, inspired by other conversation analysis studies (Porcheron 2016), (Moore 2013), Suchman 1987), (Yamazaki 2009) how visitors structure their interaction with Iris+ in a public museum space and which kind of social actions occurred because of this interaction. To investigate the rational social action of visitors, we first explore here onboarding interaction situations that were directly observable and reportable to people present in situ. (Garfinkel 1967). And then, we describe the perceptions of visitors reporting their own experience with IRIS+.

Results. We highlight the main issues identified in the observation studies grounded by the video and audio recordings gathered during this investigation. Analyzing the sequence details of interactions, we identified visitors' reactions to an intelligent voice-based exhibition. We selected a couple of interaction fragments to illustrate attitudes and some strategies visitors used to interact with IRIs+.

Visitors' Interaction Strategies. Iris+ is localized at the end of the main museum trail. Although most of the visitors interact with it after seeing the main spaces of the museum, some go across the corridor and interact first with Iris+. We notice an evident difference from the ones who interacted with the museum spaces before. Those visitors, we call here *experienced visitors*, they knew what to ask and answered the questions with more words and property. The others requested ideas of what to ask from the museum attendants or give up more easily in the middle of the interaction. The *experienced visitors*, in most of the observed cases, knew how to start the interaction using the museum card, it is also used in other museum spaces. (Figure 3 (6)). Due to similar shape displayed on the tablet screen, not experienced visitors more often tap the card on the screen mistakenly. The right place to tap it is on the figure on the wall beside the tablet. This behavior happens even though, there is written information on the screen: "*To start, tap on the logo beside the tablet and wear the pair of headphones.*" We also observed that both types of visitors often laid the card on the logo beside the tablet through the whole experience. They were afraid the exhibit would stop working if they take the card out. What it was a misconception.

Another curious and misconception behavior was to lean forward and to whisper to IRIS+. It was like they were telling a secret to Iris+. Visitors were aware that Headphones had microphones because attendants advised them to hold the microphones to have a better experience, even so, they engaged in this behavior. In Fig. 3 (7), we can see a visitor pointing to the tablet of his partner to advise to talk near the screen. Visitors are familiar with audio guides in museums, but not used to respond back to devices. The museum attendants helped visitors that did not know how to react to IRIS+ advising them that was a voice-based interaction. We observe visitors' behavior before asking for this kind of help. In those situations, they tap the screen for more information, they looked at the next visitor interacting with the installation, or they verbalized the need for assistance to the museum attendant. An excerpt of the data illustrates this:

((participant looks for clues looking at her neighbor interacting, and turns to the museum attendant and ask a question))
    01   P12: Do I have to answer here, right?

Fig. 3. (1) Visitor tap the card to start the experience. (2) IRIS+ Interface shows a question asked by IRIS+. (3) Visitors interacting with IRIS+. (4) Visitors taking pictures of their displayed pictures. (5) Panel showing visualizations with clusters of causes. (6) Visitor using a card to interact with IRIS+. (6) Visitor showing his partner how to interact with the installation. (7) Visitor lean forward to talk to IRIS+. (8) Social interaction between visitors.

Visitors also enjoyed the exhibit accompanied. We observed the cases when visitors were alone; they frequently repeated the experience inviting acquaintances for the second or third time. Second, third-time visitors usually taught the novices they invited and evoked conversations around the IRIS+. (Figure 3 (9)). Additionally, we noticed that several times when visitors were accompanied, only one was wearing the headphones, which caused some misinterpretation from the person who was only seeing the screen. The person who was observing sometimes tap on the screen, resulting in discomfort for the one wearing the headphones, who had to gesticulate signs (waiting, stop hand signs).

The flow of the interaction was also shaped by the multi-modal interaction proposed by the system. Visitors tapped the card and were requested to use the voice-based mode to dialogue with IRIS following the experience. Visitors have an option to take a picture and share their concerns with other visitors that previously interacted with IRIS+. For having this option available for them, they are asked to fill out a form typing their home city, age, and their email. Only people that have more than 18 years old are allowed to take their pictures to display on the Initiative panel. Visitors have the option to skip the form, and we observed that most of them act like that. They were concerned with the use of their data that was not so clear on the interface. Also, some visitors with their parents observed that they could only show up their concerns visually if they filled out the form, so they lied about their age to participate in this step of the interaction. The change of mode from voice to the text input in this stage was also confusing for old visitors that asked the guide for help in this stage, some of them did not have emails, and for this reason, they could not complete the form. After filling out the form, IRIS+ change the mode back to voice-interaction, so users continue tapping on the screen, even though the mode of input was not the same. When visitors saw the initiatives suggested by IRIS+, they also tapped on the screen to know more about each of them, although the square of the initiatives were not touchable. They also took pictures of the screen (Fig. 1), to record the suggested initiatives. It was not clear the initiatives were sent by e-mail if they filled out the form.

Another change in interaction mode also affected the visitors' experience. When the option to take the picture was available, we observed visitors taking off the headphones to tap the screen to take their pictures, and they did not put them back. Therefore, those users did not hear the final statements of IRIS+. They did not know the voice-based interaction was not over yet.

Visitors Perceptions of Talking with Intelligent Systems. Visitors also reported how they felt talking to an artificial intelligence system. IRIS+ invited participants to reflect on museum themes and connect those to their own lives. It surprised participants and created a social situation where sharing those concerns with a machine was not natural. A participant accompanied by his partner commented:

01   Researcher: Please, tell me how your experience with this installation was?

02   P6: I found it very strange when the machine asked me: What is your concern for the future? I was not even thinking about it. (.) when I left the museum exhibition. It is a very personal and very comprehensive question. So, I was like this, with no way to talk (0.2), and I already had to speak in public, too, right? I'm ashamed to speak in public.

More visitors displayed the same behavior, and many More visitors displayed the same reaction, and many verbalized they did not know what to answer to Iris+. In that situation, IRIS+ employed repairs actions (Schegloff 1977) to avoid interaction breakdowns in the dialogue. In line 03 and line 05 of next fragment, Iris+ applies repair mechanisms to bring P8 back to the dialogue subject.

```
01  I: considering what you saw in the main exhibition, what are you
    most worried about?
02  P8: I don' t know. I don' t know. ((smile)).
03  I: Think a little more. Are there any issues related to sustainability
    or coexistence that worry you?
04  P8: It was cool. ((smiles and turns to see others interacting with
    IRIS+))
05  I: It is possible to have several opinions on the same subject.
    But here at the Museum of Tomorrow, we seek answers that value the
    coexistence, with dialogue and respect. Let's go back to the
    question. From what you saw at the Main Exhibit at the Museum of
    Tomorrow, tell me what you care about in today's world?
06  P8: Nothing
```

IRIS+ also captured some environment noises, likewise a sound similar to waves from another exhibit and utterances of visitors talking to each other. In those situations, IRIS+ continued the script and recognized the utterance as not related to the questions asked. Visitors hear a repair question when a not recognized utterance is verbalized for the first time (line 3). And for the second time, IRIS+ processes the ((sound of another exhibit)) and asks a new question (line7).

```
01  I: considering what you saw in the main exhibition, what are you most
    worried about?
02  ((sound of another exhibit))
03  I: I could not understand what you said. I' ll repeat the question.
    Considering what you saw in the main exhibition, what are you most
    worried about the world today?
04  P11: Population growth
05  I: By 2050 the trend is for the world to have 10 billion people. This
    growth must be reconciled with economic, social and environmental
    development. In your opinion, what are the main challenges that this
    population will face
06  ((sound of another exhibit))
07  I: Considering what you are able to do, how can you change it?
08  P11: It' s through recycling
09  I: Thank you very much for your participation!
```

In this case, P11 answered the second question (line 3) and responded to the question in line 7 considering the line 5 information provided by Iris and his previous answer (line 4). In this case, P11 ignored the question at the end of line 5.

Next we show a transcription of a semi-structured interview with three visitors that know each other (P3, P4, P5). P3 grabbed the audio recorder from the researcher (R) and interviewed her companions.

01   R: she ((looking at P3)) did not hear the voice of the Iris, right?
      [If you had to tell her how it felt to talk to a machine.
      P3:[I   feel   (.)   with   her].
      P5:   First   the   daughter,   (.)   then   the   false   nephew.
      ((P3 grabs the audio recorder and points to P4))
02   P3: What did you think of Iris?
03   P4:I found it very strange, actually because I kept the microphone in
      my hand talking to a machine, (.) I felt kind of stupid.
04   P3: she made you afraid?
05   P4: no ((laughs)). In fact she was very nice.
06   P3: so why to be afraid, thinking you are an idiot?
07   P4: because I was talking on my own (0.2) in theory.
08   P3: no you were not alone in your imagination.
09   P4: only in my imagination? ((laughs))
10   P3: what about you?
11   P5: I was a little anxious. Because we did not [Not obviously, right
      ((laughs)) I'm single.
12   P3 [wanted to meet the iris? You wondered what Iris would look like,
      green, blue eyes?]
13   P5: because you really have no idea where it goes, what path of
      discussion we will have [when we are talking to a human being has a
      self-driving discussion, we became subordinate to her initiative, it
      causes certain anxiety, but I did not feel scared.
14   P3: [but it depends on your answer, you lead]
15   P3: just anxious (.) congratulations you are the future.
16   R: Thank you all!

In this fragment, we notice that P4 share her feelings of embarrassment to others by feeling she was talking by herself in a public space (line 03). And P5 demonstrates his anxiety of controlling the interaction (line 11 and 13). We also notice, P3 expectation of why P4 felt stupid (line 4). P4 and P5 also leaned towards the tablet and whispered to the machine, what shows evidence of P4 uncomfortable feelings in public. Likewise, P4 and P6, other visitors we interviewed reported similar feelings.

This analysis shows that integration with visual and verbal elements are essential for onboarding interaction with the intelligent voice-based devices. We also unveiled visitors' social actions in situ while interacting with IRIS+. Highlighting those behaviors may help designers, developers and museum curators to think carefully on how to tailor conversation technologies to visitors and how to take advantage of those social actions to intensify visitors experience in museums and promotes the engagement in social themes outside the institutions. In the next session we present the main lessons learned and challenges to deploy AI voice-based systems in museums.

5 Challenges on Designing Voice-Based Interfaces for Public Spaces

We identified the following challenges for AI voice-based installations in public spaces.

- Diverse modes of interaction in the same exhibition might affect the visitors'experience.
- Social interaction is an essential element in informal learning spaces.
- Share personal information and opinions in public spaces might affect participation.
- Repairing the conversation with visitors is essential.
- Design integrated conversational interactions considering previous knowledge of the museum content acquired by visitors.
- Engaging audiences of different ages in the experience.
- Enroll participants of different location and economic backgrounds displaying information that motivate them to act.

6 Iris++

The second phase of IRIS+ is in development. The new design of IRIS+ is using more colors and an advanced format to catch the dialog (using more voice mode and less text mode input). The contents are now linked with the Sustainable Development Goals (SDGs) from United Nations, and there is a connection between the initiatives of action presented by IRIS+ connected to the themes from the Main Exhibition of the museum.

The IRIS+ project allows knowing concerns based on different profiles of visitors, being able to recognize the significant worries and desires that are influencing the collective awareness about the future. The storytelling of the experience was developed to inspire the visitors for a sustainable and plural tomorrow, connecting to the SDG issues. Besides that, IRIS+ allows its partners to come with strategic narratives that may push people into acting and to be engaged with their communities. In 2020, the project is going to be enhanced in their second stage of development, putting the visitors in discovery about the concerns linking into the areas of the Museum's content, making them more deeply knowledgeable about the themes that they want to connect. The research about the audience of IRIS+ was fundamental because it helped to create new parameters and interactions in the experience to attract the attention of the young audience and address some of the challenges described in the previously. The curatorial team has searched initiatives all over the country related to youngsters and social themes as inequality, gender equality, and women empowerment. The IRIS+ appearance was redesigned, and the model presented in its new version allows the visitor to notice his social connection with other visitors, meaning that more people can engage in similar themes. Because of this, they are willing to change reality.

7 Final Remarks and Further Work

Artificial Intelligence is a data science tool that has positively impacted much of the goods and services we use. Its effectiveness in use in Museums is not yet fully known, but institutions have taken the risk of learning more about this technology. The results should be known later, over time. Far from being thought of as a solution for the development of an unforgettable experience, the application of the use of Artificial Intelligence needs to be understood before being used in the context of museums. It is necessary, above all, to reflect on the content that will cover the technology, more important than presenting it itself - the AI - only as an innovation, as there is a risk of obsolescence of the activity.

In the case of the use of AI in an experiment, another point to be emphasized is the need to identify what enhances the participation and engagement of visitors, checking if the methods adopted and the results meet the expectations created by the developers and the users. We understand that its use in this context requires a good deal of understanding and learning on the part of Museum teams and professionals involved in the implementation of a complex project such as the IRIS+ object and that this is particularly one of the significant challenges in our reality.

This research helped to unveil those issues and redesign the experience being more social and considering the issues that affected the visitors 'experience with the exhibit. The idea is that Artificial Intelligence applied in Museums will, in the future, be a possible way to search for experiential solutions aimed at engagement. It is understood that the use of Artificial Intelligence in the IRIS+ experience to instigate engagement, according to data from the Museum of Tomorrow, efficiently promoted the activation of the visitor to actions related to social or environmental issues. Moreover, the results showed that this experience allowed visitors to the Museum of Tomorrow to experience a dynamic experience with Artificial Intelligence and made accountable their perceptions of having a conversation with an AI.

We hope museum curators, designers and developers use our study as a motivation to use AI in their projects, and be aware of expectations and actions visitors might have while and after interacting with voice-based AI systems.

References

Suchman, L.: Plans and Situated Actions: The Problem of Human-Machine Communication. Cambridge University Press, Cambridge (1987)

Porcheron, M., Joel, E., Sarah, S.: "Do animals have accents?": Talking with Agents in Multiparty Conversation. University of Notthingham, Notthingham (2016)

Moore, R.: Ethnomethodology and Conversation Analysis: Empirical Approach es to the Study of Digital Technology in Action. The SAGE Handbook of Digital Technology Research. Sage (2013)

Yamazaki, K., et al.: Revealing Gauguin: engaging visitors in robot guide's explanation in an art museum. In: Proceedings of the SIGCHI Conference on Human Factors in Computing Systems, pp. 1437–1446. Boston (2009)

Garfinkel, H.: Studies in Ethnomethodology. Prentice-Hall, Upper Saddle River (1967)

Evans, J., Mathur, A.: The value of online surveys. Internet Res. **15**, 195–219 (2005). https://doi. org/10.1108/10662240510590360

Onwuegbuzie, A., Leech, N.: On becoming a pragmatic researcher: the importance of combining quantitative and qualitative research methodologies. Int. J. Soc. Res. Methodol. **8**, 375–387 (2005). https://doi.org/10.1080/13645570500402447

Caudill, S.: Dichotomous choice models and dummy variables. J. Roy. Stat. Soc.: Ser. D **36**(4), 381–383 (1987). https://doi.org/10.2307/2348835

Schegloff, E., Gail, J., Harvey, S.: The Preference for Self-Correction in the Organization of Repair in Conversation, vol. 2, pp. 361–382. Language (1977)

Pine, J., Gilmore, J.: Welcome to the Experience Economy. Harvard Business Publishing, Massachusetts (1998)

Boswijk, A., Thijssen, T., Peelen, P.: A New Perspective on the Experience Economy. The European Centre for the Experience Economy, Blithovenm, The Netherlands (2006)

Falco, F., Vassos, S.: Museum experience design: a modern storytelling methodology. Des. J. **20**, S3975–S3983 (2017)

Majs, M., Safabakhsh, R.: Impact of Machine Learning on Improvement of User Experience in Museums. Artificial Intelligence and Signal Processing, AISP, Teerã (2017)

Vassos, S., Malliaraki, E., Falco, F., Di Maggio, J., Massimetti, M., Nocentini, M.G., Testa, A.: Art-Bots: toward chat-based conversational experiences in museums. In: Nack, F., Gordon, A. S. (eds.) ICIDS 2016. LNCS, vol. 10045, pp. 433–437. Springer, Cham (2016). https://doi. org/10.1007/978-3-319-48279-8_43

Boiano, S., Borda, A., Gaia, G., Rossi, S., Cuomo, P.: Chatbots and New Audience Opportunities for Museums and Heritage Organisations. EVA London 2018 (2018). https://doi.org/10. 14236/ewic/eva2018.33

Wright, L.: New frontiers in the visitor experience. In: Lord, G.D., Lord, B. (eds.) Manual of Digital Museum Planning. Rowman & Littlefield (2017)

Schultz, M.K.: A case study on the appropriateness of using quick response (QR) codes in libraries and museums. Libr. Inf. Sci. Res. **35**(3), 207–215 (2013)

Shiomi, M., Kanda, T., Ishiguro, H., Hagita, N.: Interactive humanoid robots for a science museum. In: Proceedings of the 1st ACM SIGCHI/SIGART Conference on Human-Robot Interaction (2006)

Leinhardt, G., Crowley, K.: Objects of learning, objects of talk: changing minds in museums. Perspectives on object-centered learning in museums (2002)

Hsi, S., Fait, H.: RFID enhances visitors' museum experience at the Exploratorium. Commun. ACM **48**(9), 60–65 (2005)

Wojciechowski, R., Walczak, K., White, M., Cellary, W.: Building virtual and augmented reality museum exhibitions. In: Proceedings of the Ninth International Conference on 3D Web Technology (2004)

Falk, J.H., Dierking, L.D.: The museum experience revisited. Routledge (2016)

What Are People Doing About XAI User Experience? A Survey on AI Explainability Research and Practice

Juliana J. Ferreira[1(✉)] and Mateus S. Monteiro[1,2]

[1] IBM Research, Av. Pasteur 146, Rio de Janeiro 22290-240, Brazil
jjansen@br.ibm.com, msmonteiro@ibm.com
[2] Universidade Federal Fluminense (UFF), Rio de Janeiro 24210-510, Brazil

Abstract. Explainability is a hot topic nowadays for artificial intelligent (AI) systems. The role of machine learning (ML) models on influencing human decisions shed light on the back-box of computing systems. AI based system are more than just ML models. ML models are one element for the AI explainability' design and needs to be combined with other elements so it can have significant meaning for people using AI systems. There are different goals and motivations for AI explainability. Regardless the goal for AI explainability, there are more to AI explanation than just ML models or algorithms. The explainability of an AI systems behavior needs to consider different dimensions: 1) who is the receiver of that explanation, 2) why that explanation is needed, and 3) in which context and other situated information the explanation is presented. Considering those three dimensions, the explanation can be effective by fitting the user needs and expectation in the right moment and format. The design of an AI explanation user experience is central for the pressing need from people and the society to understand how an AI system may impact on human decisions. In this paper, we present a literature review on AI explainability research and practices. We first looked at the computer science (CS) community research to identify the main research themes about AI explainability, or "explainable AI". Then, we focus on Human-Computer Interaction (HCI) research trying to answer three questions about the selected publications: to whom the AI explainability is for (who), which is the purpose of the AI explanation (why), and in which context the AI explanation is presented (what + when).

Keywords: AI explainability · Explainable AI · Artificial Intelligence design · AI for UX

1 Introduction

The usage of Artificial Intelligence (AI) has increased into many contexts and to a more diverse audience [70], such as agriculture, manufacturing, transportation, finance, and healthcare [52]. The role of Machine Learning (ML) models on

© Springer Nature Switzerland AG 2020
A. Marcus and E. Rosenzweig (Eds.): HCII 2020, LNCS 12201, pp. 56–73, 2020.
https://doi.org/10.1007/978-3-030-49760-6_4

influencing human decisions shed light on the black-box of computing systems. In this new disruptive context of AI, explainability plays a vital role, since, in many [70] or all cases [32], the user needs more information than just the output from the model. The model is just one element for the design of an eXplainable AI (XAI) and needs to be combined with other data so it can have significant meaning for users.

The authors Ribera and Agata [70] affirms that explanations cannot be singular since each stakeholder looks for the explanation with their own expectations, background, and needs. Besides, there are different goals and motivations for XAI, such as legal constraints, like the General Data Protection Regulation (GDPR) regulation, for transparency of how an AI system suggests recommending users on some action, for audit purpose when an AI system is part of a regulated process, and its actions need to be traceable and verified, among many others.

In this sense, the explainability of an AI systems behavior needs to consider different dimensions: 1) in which context and other situated information the explanation is presented, 2) who is the receiver of that explanation, and 3) why that explanation is needed. In this sense, the explanation can be adequate by fitting the user needs and expectations in the right moment and format. The design of an AI explanation user experience is central to the pressing need from people and the society to understand how an AI system may impact on human decisions (see [2,55]).

In this paper, we present a survey on AI explainability research and practices. First, we looked at the computer science (CS) community research as a whole to identify the main research themes about AI explainability, or "explainable AI." Then, with this overall view on the AI explainability research, we tried to answer three questions about the selected studies: to whom the AI explainability is for (who), which is the purpose of the AI explanation (why), and in which context the AI explanation is presented (what).

After the mapping of those three dimensions for all selected investigations from the CS community, we focused on the researches executed by the human-computer interaction (HCI) community. By focusing on HCI publications, we aimed to identify how HCI researchers and practitioners have been addressing AI explainability challenges for designing the user experience. We also checked which and how the three dimensions ('who,' 'why,' and 'what') were present on AI explainability HCI research.

Results inside the HCI community highlights some concerns about promoting UX (User eXperience) throughout the authors' discourse, such as adoption, acceptance, engagement, persuasion, among others. Regarding both communities, there is a large number of publications in a few contexts (e.g., health and education) and many others with no context. The result is worrying considering the growth and the recent indispensability of ML components within any kind of application [57] and, as mentioned before, being the explanation an individual experience, posing as a challenge for real-world problems in real-world contexts. [32].

2   Related Efforts on XAI Surveys

While there is an existing recent interest among XAI, as we have seen in Fig. 1, the literature regarding surveys on XAI is not extensive. Nunes and Jannach [64] present a systematic literature review on the topic of explanations for recommender systems. Hohman and colleagues [40] and Garcia [30] advances through the lens of visual analytics.

Ribeira and Lapedriza [70] present an interesting review the state of the art of XAI and highlight the lack of attention regarding who the explanations are targeting. Besides, it also presents a few goals and a discussion regarding WHY would be a need for explainability, and propose the discussion of the WHAT question concerning the explanation definition.

Different from the aforementioned literature reviews, our mapping provides an overview of XAI using as guides the three questions mentioned before: WHY would be a need for explanation, WHAT is the context, and WHO the explanation targets. Furthermore, we review how CS researchers and HCI researchers are approaching these explanation dimensions. Other publications envisioned mapping issues regarding the HCI community and ML (e.g., [96]). The goal of this paper is to provide a conceptual taxonomy regarding the WHY-WHAT-WHO dimensions for XAI. Therefore, bringing attention to opportunities and compromises of each community.

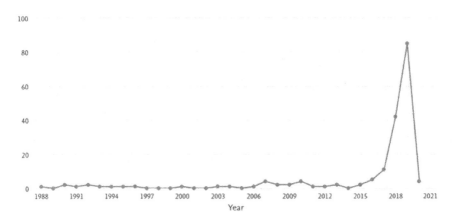

Fig. 1. The 2018 "Boom" - a frame of indexed publications on Scopus regarding XAI.

3   Materials and Methods

The primary goal of our review is related to explanation features in AI systems regarding the final affected people, the motivations or reasons for making the system explainable, and the context within. In this sense, for both inside and outside of the HCI community, we formulate the following questions:

- (RQ1) What is the taxonomy for explainability?
- (RQ2) What are the main contexts within the explanations?
- (RQ3) Who are the main affected by the explanations?
- (RQ4) What are the main reasons or motivations for providing explanations?

In order to answer those questions, we perform a literature survey. Similar to Petersen [69], we found it useful to exclude papers that only mentioned the focus, explainability, in introductory sentences or in the abstract. This approach was needed since it is a central concept and thus frequently used in abstracts without papers addressing it any further.

- Inclusion: Full papers, work in progress papers, and position papers.
- Exclusion: Explanation is not part of the contributions of the paper, the terms are only mentioned in the general introductory sentences of the abstract or no access to the file.

We used two extensive and trusted academic databases: Scopus and Web of Science. In order to find an appropriate Search String, we did an initial Search string refinement (synonyms and acronyms), the Resulting Search String is presented as follows:

Search String
Explanation related keywords ("explanations" or "explainable" or "explaining" or "transparency") AND AI-related keywords ("AI" or "artificial intelligence" or "deep learning" or "ML" or "Machine learning" or "XAI" or "decision-making algorithm" or "model interpretation" or "algorithmic transparency") AND ("design")

After that, an initial screening it was proceeded to apply the exclusion criteria. Then, two researchers did the screening (title, abstract, keywords, and conclusion) individually. Then, a pair session was held to gather the publications that converged and exclude the ones that diverged. The results for outside the HCI community selected **43 papers** out of 250 (Scopus and Web of Science). For the HCI publications, we looked specifically at publications of three major HCI conferences: the ACM conference on Designing Interactive Systems (DIS), the ACM Intelligent User Interfaces (IUI), and the ACM CHI Conference on Human Factors in Computing Systems (CHI). After the same process (of outside HCI community), we were able to select **52 papers** out of 125.

4   Findings and Discussion

In this section, we present the answers we found for our research guiding questions. We did not have the goal to provide definitive answers to those questions, but plausible answers to guide further investigation. For example, a taxonomy of XAI should be an dynamic entity that evolves along with the research on the challenges and technologies related to the subject. But an initial taxonomy is an resourceful reference for future investigation on XAI research.

4.1   What Is the Taxonomy for XAI?

To obtain a better comprehension of XAI regarding the community, we built a taxonomy based on the reviewed papers, as shown in Fig. 2. The primary purpose of this taxonomy is to categorize recurrent ideas by organizing concepts and connections [58]. Therefore, the nodes are detailed in terms of attributes, describing how state of the art in the field addresses each of the characteristics. The first node, (Why) defines the reason for using XAI in Intelligent Systems. The second node, (Who) defines the type of user that the XAI aims. The third node, (What) defines the contexts for using XAI.

4.2   What Are the Main Contexts for Providing the Explanations?

Meta explanation/transparency are publications that are related to an epistemic discussion about a subject (WHAT) within explanation or transparency. Publication categorized as 'no context' are publications with no participation of a domain expert or a study regarding a specific context or discipline. In Fig. 3, we present the main contexts inside and outside HCI communities that we identified on our scope of literature search. Regarding the main contexts inside the HCI community we identified the following:

– Educational [2, 12, 45, 68]
– Health [50, 84, 91, 95]
– Military [38, 79]
– Entertainment [49, 55]
– Environment [82, 83]
– Crowdsourcing [11, 62]
– Real-time strategy games [20]
– Nutrition [23]
– Human resources [10]
– IT services [94]
– Game design [8]
– Fact-checking [100]
– E-commerce [11]
– Design AI [63] selecting AI model [92]
– Arts [21]

Inside the HCI community, there is a significant concern about explaining the explanation (meta) regarding many directions: causality analysis [17], designing transparency and accountability [46, 81], prototyping ML experiences [6], minimalist explanations [74], materializing interpretability [4], dark patterns [13], AI transparency in enterprises [9], paradigms within explanations [24], and anticipation of scenarios [31]. No context publications were characterized by being experts-centered, with the intention to define, analyze or describe, for example, the understandability of data scientists [39], the understanding of annotators [62], the internal model state of robots [71], and the visualizations of models and attributions [16]. The primary contexts outside the HCI community, include these scenarios:

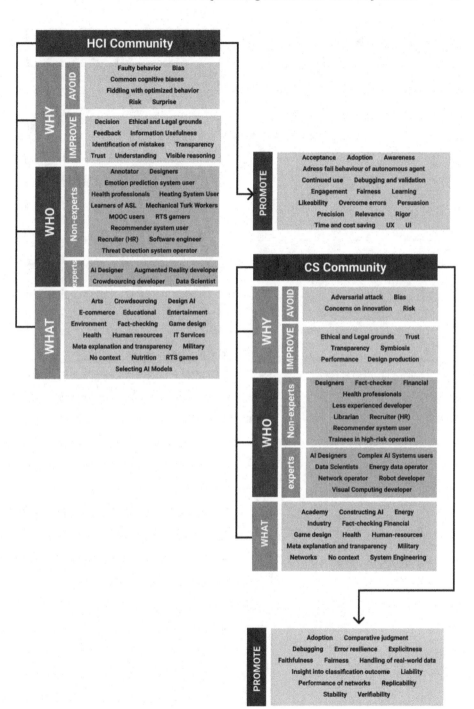

Fig. 2. Taxonomy of XAI among communities.

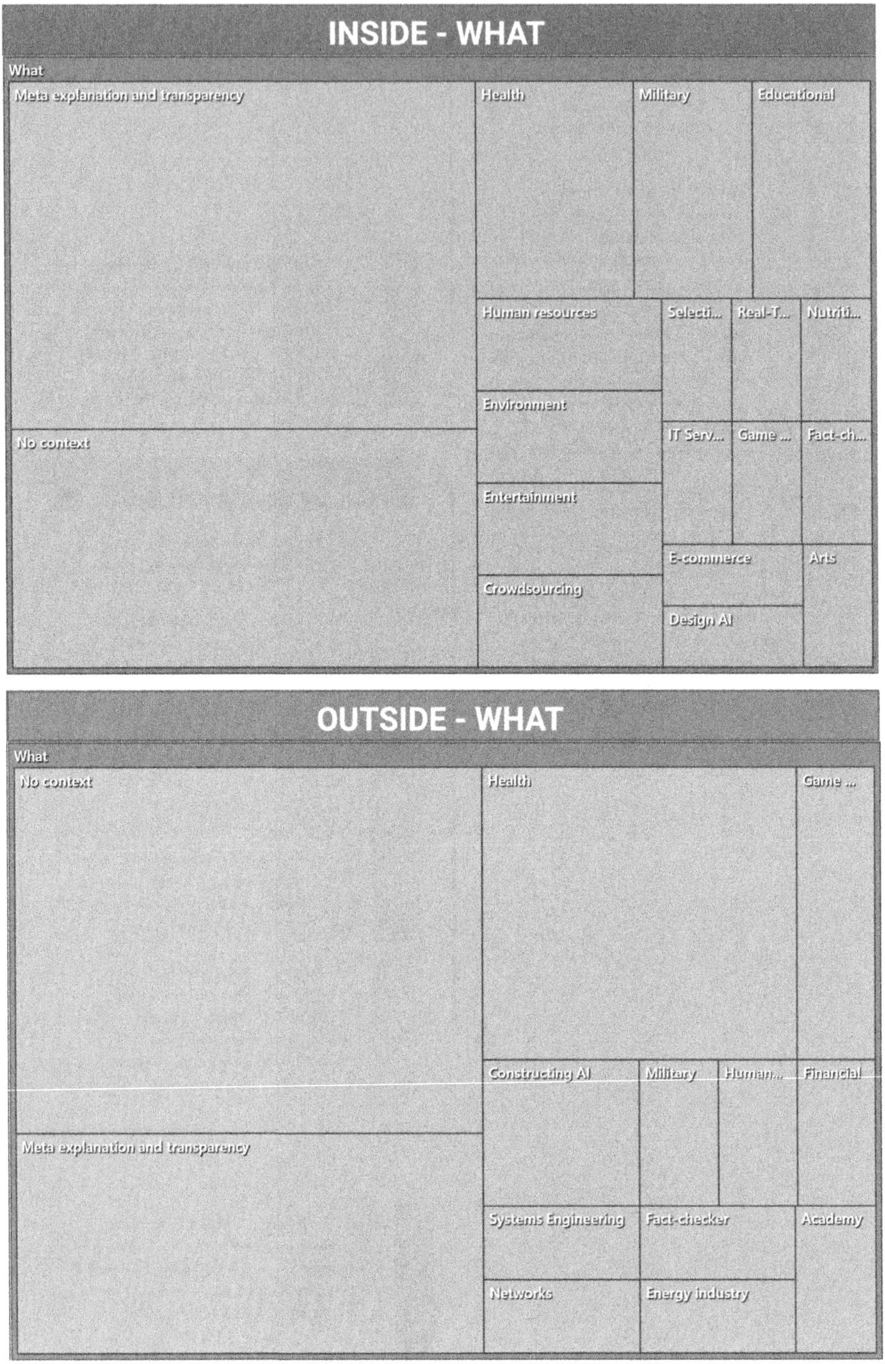

Fig. 3. Main contexts in both inside and outside HCI community

- Health [42,48,54,56,76,88,90]
- Constructing AI [18,25]
- Design [36,101]
- Developing systems [47]
- Energy industry [5]
- Networks [89]
- Risk scenarios, military [14] and financial [99]
- Human resources [28]
- Fact-checker [61]
- Academy [43]

Differently from the inside (HCI community), the CS community presented a large number of publications with no context (see [1,7,15,26,44,73,97]), and is mainly focused on technical experts. The publications that deal with meta-explanation bring to the discussion challenges and directions for [32], new frameworks [93], fuzzy advances [42,76], design criteria for explainability in legal AI [67], and other privacy and data protection related [41].

4.3   Whom Are the Main People Affected by the Explanations?

As seen in our taxonomy, shown in Fig. 2, our research considers two types of people (WHO): 1) Non-ML-experts, which are people not skilled with ML concepts that, in some dimensions, use ML tools to perform tasks on different domains, and 2) ML experts, which are people capable of building, training and testing machine learning models with different datasets from different domains.

Regarding the HCI Community, we found mainly studies related to Non-ML-experts, such as recommender system users in general (see [98]), news (see [46]), music (see [55]), education (see [2]), e-commerce (see [11]), followed by learning scenarios, such students in general [12], or MOOC (Massive Open Online Course) users [45] or Learners of ASL (American Sign Language) [68]; Health workers with medical diagnosis [95], health practitioners [91]; Designers [6,8]; Crowdsourcing user, such as annotators [35,37] and other MTWs (Mechanical Turk Workers) workers [19]; and risk operators [38,79].

Other less focused publications approach gamers [20], software engineers [94], fact-checkers [100] and even heating system user [82]. Only a few publications focus on experts. Two publications focus on visualization for designers of AI [16,84], others on developers of augmented reality [71], crowdsourcing [62], and data scientists [39].

It is worth to mention that some publications did not let clear who are affected by the explanations. The reason can be the context within the publication, such as the ones that focus on agnostic contexts (e.g., [13,51]) or no contexts at all (see [78]), which usually relates the user as an affected, or user-centric, but not tells who is it. Outside the HCI community, this happened with many publications (see [1,7,65,67]). The Non-ML-experts profiles, for example, are less diverse when compared to inside the HCI Community.

However, concerning the publications that defines the user, also focus on recommender system users in general [93] and design recommendation [25]; health

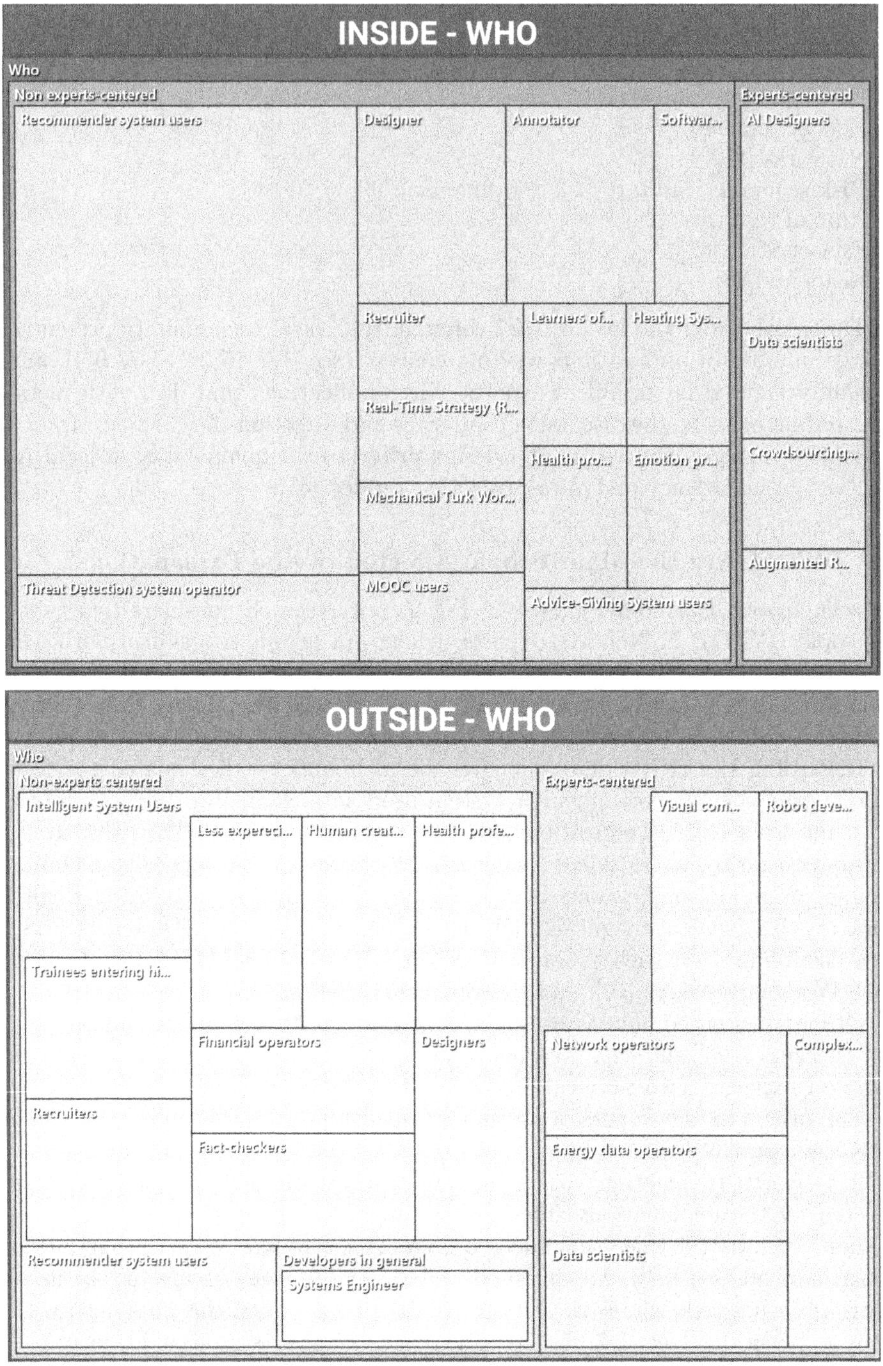

Fig. 4. Main affected people in both inside and outside HCI community

professionals for patient re-admittance and medical application [54], for analysis of medical records through visualization [48,88]; Fact-checkers [61], promoting partnership between human and agents; Human-resource recruiter [28]; risk operators in military training [14] and financial operations [99], developers in general, such as less experienced developer [73], system engineers [47]; human-creativity-related, such as architects [26] and designers [36,101].

On the other hand, in the group of ML experts, the authors presented a more diverse profile, such as complex AI system users [59], data scientists [42], energy data operators [5], network operators [89], autonomous robot developers [85] and also visual computing developers [72]. It is interesting to mention that even those previously mentioned are domain-specific tasks, there is an expert-centered approach to these publications. Different from some efforts in HCI related mainly to decision-making in the domain. Other publications are related to causality analysis [29], fuzzy related [33,97], argument stance recognition [27], and designing AI [18].

4.4 What Are the Main Reasons for Providing Explanations?

As shown in our taxonomy (Fig. 2), our research considers two categories for motivations or reasons (WHY): 1) Improve - focus on using explanations to improve an aspect, a part of the system, among others; and 2) Avoid - consequences, which somehow affects the context, the project, or the system. It is essential to mention that the reasons for using the explanations were extracted from the papers we reviewed and can be more than one if explicitly presented.

Inside HCI, transparency as motivation has a focus on non-experts and not necessarily no-context. For example, recommender systems users in video entertainment [49] and design principles for social recommendation [86], real-stime strategy gamers [20], software engineer [94] in IT services domain, human-resources domain for both job seeker and job mediator [10], and nutrition [23]; on the other hand, for experts, transparency comprehends motivation for designing AI [63], and selecting AI models [92].

Another more substantial amount of publications is motivated by improving trust for non-experts. The health domain appeared at the top for improving trust [50,84,91,95]. Followed by fact-checker [100], designer [6,8], threat detection operator [79], and annotator [35,37]. No publications regarding experts used trust as motivation.

Ethical and legal grounds were focused almost exclusively by agnostic context publications, regarding discussing UI (User Interface) strategies [12], GDPR implications [46], interpretability [4], and paradigms of explanations [24]. Other specific motivation included improving decision [22], identification of mistakes and learning [68], a mental model of the internal state [71], understanding [78], and visible reasoning [38]. Finally, avoid motivation is related to reducing faulty behavior, bias [84], cognitive bias [91], fiddling with optimized behavior [83], risk [77], and surprise [31].

However, outside HCI, transparency motivation is related to publications with no context [7,26,73,80]; transparency also appeared with better model

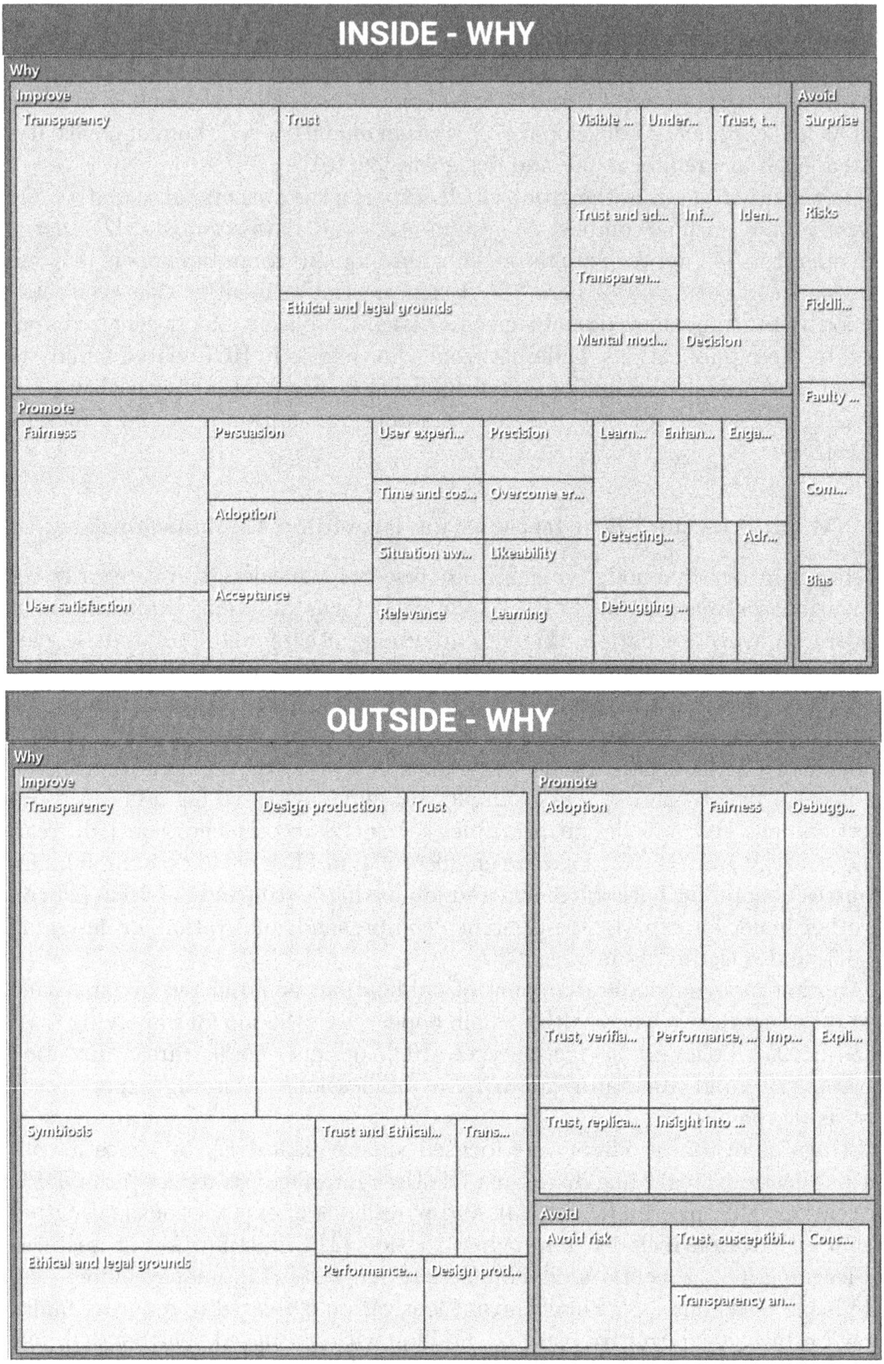

Fig. 5. Main motivations in both inside and outside HCI community

design and faster experimentation [75] in an expert-centered research. Design production motivation is related to both ML experts [1,3,25] and for designers [36,101]. Similarly, ethical and legal grounds also relate to both groups, but with a majority approach to non-experts in context-agnostic contexts, discussing privacy and personal data [41] and design requirements for it [67], and also interpretability in fuzzy systems [53], accompanied by human-resources [28].

Another compelling motivation result is symbiosis, which means improving the relationship between human-machine. This motivation is exclusive to the non-experts group, interested in promoting sympathy actions of agents [44], fact-checking partnership [61], and the discussion about the symbiosis itself [34,60]; last improving motivation was the performance and handling of real-world [72]. Still, outside the HCI community, avoid is a motivation related to non-experts and with a considerable amount of publications with context. Some publications intend to avoid risk, as seen in the military [14] and financial [99] contexts, followed by avoiding bias [65,90], concerns on innovation for the academy, and also adversarial attack [43].

5   Conclusion and Final Remarks

While there is an intention from the HCI community to promote UI aspects (User Interface) and UX of XAI [81], other publications also study the variables that improve UX, such as adoption [9,98], acceptance [22,81], satisfaction [82,83], engagement [66], persuasion [87], continued use; and variables of UI, such as likeability [71], feedback into the system [79], learning [2], learning from mistakes [68], overcome errors [78].

Even though outside the community of HCI, presumably is focused on promoting technology-related attributes, not a single publication has mentioned "user" in the title. A few portions focus on the promotion of user-centric variables, such as adoption [48,54,56,88], which, are all from the health context; fairness [28] from the human-resources context, acceptance [15,32] from meta explainability. Other variables are very related to technology and for experts, such as debugging and error resilience [17,85], verifiability [97], the performance of communication networks [72], among others.

The reality of practical AI applications in sensitive areas reveals the inability of those systems to communicate effectively with their users [32]. Health, for example, demonstrated to be a compelling and focused problem by the researchers. However, there is still a significant number of publications with a pair or single presence on the context, as seen through the mapping with Environment, Human resources, Nutrition, E-commerce, and others. Imputing a problem that Goebel [32, pp.296] has already stated as a challenge for the future - exploratory models for real-world problems. However, XAI is critical across all areas where ML is used [32] and we must properly understand the user in order to promote an adequate explanation [70].

Our research presented an overview of some attributes between CS and HCI communities. While presenting a taxonomy to sum the resulting dimensions, we also present the main characteristics of each dimension of each community. That may serve as a detailed overview of what has been done and provide starting and provocative points for both communities and practitioners. One limitation of our work is the number of bases for the outside HCI mapping. However, this initial step helped us to craft the base for such an objective. Future work includes increasing the bases, still qualitatively, to see if there is a saturation point of the aspects we argued during the paper.

References

1. Apicella, A., Isgro, F., Prevete, R., Tamburrini, G., Vietri, A.: Sparse dictionaries for the explanation of classification systems. In: PIE, p. 009 (2015)
2. Barria-Pineda, J., Brusilovsky, P.: Making educational recommendations transparent through a fine-grained open learner model. In: IUI Workshops (2019)
3. Belle, V.: Logic meets probability: towards explainable AI systems for uncertain worlds. In: IJCAI, pp. 5116–5120 (2017)
4. Benjamin, J.J., Müller-Birn, C.: Materializing interpretability: exploring meaning in algorithmic systems. In: Companion Publication of the 2019 on Designing Interactive Systems Conference 2019 Companion, pp. 123–127. ACM (2019)
5. Bhatia, A., Garg, V., Haves, P., Pudi, V.: Explainable clustering using hyper-rectangles for building energy simulation data. In: IOP Conference Series: Earth and Environmental Science, vol. 238, p. 012068. IOP Publishing (2019)
6. Browne, J.T.: Wizard of OZ prototyping for machine learning experiences. In: Extended Abstracts of the 2019 CHI Conference on Human Factors in Computing Systems, p. LBW2621. ACM (2019)
7. Cabitza, F., Campagner, A., Ciucci, D.: New frontiers in explainable AI: understanding the GI to interpret the GO. In: Holzinger, A., Kieseberg, P., Tjoa, A.M., Weippl, E. (eds.) CD-MAKE 2019. LNCS, vol. 11713, pp. 27–47. Springer, Cham (2019). https://doi.org/10.1007/978-3-030-29726-8_3
8. Cai, C.J., Jongejan, J., Holbrook, J.: The effects of example-based explanations in a machine learning interface. In: Proceedings of the 24th International Conference on Intelligent User Interfaces, pp. 258–262. ACM (2019)
9. Chander, A., Srinivasan, R., Chelian, S., Wang, J., Uchino, K.: Working with beliefs: AI transparency in the enterprise. In: IUI Workshops (2018)
10. Charleer, S., Gutiérrez, F., Verbert, K.: Supporting job mediator and job seeker through an actionable dashboard. In: Proceedings of the 24th International Conference on Intelligent User Interfaces, pp. 121–131 (2019)
11. Chen, L., Wang, F.: Explaining recommendations based on feature sentiments in product reviews. In: Proceedings of the 22nd International Conference on Intelligent User Interfaces, pp. 17–28. ACM (2017)
12. Cheng, H.F., et al.: Explaining decision-making algorithms through UI: strategies to help non-expert stakeholders. In: Proceedings of the 2019 CHI Conference on Human Factors in Computing Systems, p. 559. ACM (2019)
13. Chromik, M., Eiband, M., Völkel, S.T., Buschek, D.: Dark patterns of explainability, transparency, and user control for intelligent systems. In: IUI Workshops (2019)
14. Clewley, N., Dodd, L., Smy, V., Witheridge, A., Louvieris, P.: Eliciting expert knowledge to inform training design. In: Proceedings of the 31st European Conference on Cognitive Ergonomics, pp. 138–143 (2019)

15. Datta, A., Sen, S., Zick, Y.: Algorithmic transparency via quantitative input influence: theory and experiments with learning systems. In: 2016 IEEE Symposium on Security and Privacy (SP), pp. 598–617. IEEE (2016)
16. Di Castro, F., Bertini, E.: Surrogate decision tree visualization interpreting and visualizing black-box classification models with surrogate decision tree. In: CEUR Workshop Proceedings, vol. 2327 (2019)
17. Dimitrova, R., Majumdar, R., Prabhu, V.S.: Causality analysis for concurrent reactive systems. arXiv preprint arXiv:1901.00589 (2019)
18. Ding, L.: Human knowledge in constructing AI systems-neural logic networks approach towards an explainable AI. Procedia Comput. Sci. **126**, 1561–1570 (2018)
19. Dodge, J., Liao, Q.V., Zhang, Y., Bellamy, R.K., Dugan, C.: Explaining models: an empirical study of how explanations impact fairness judgment. In: Proceedings of the 24th International Conference on Intelligent User Interfaces, pp. 275–285. ACM (2019)
20. Dodge, J., Penney, S., Anderson, A., Burnett, M.M.: What should be in an XAI explanation? what IFT reveals. In: IUI Workshops (2018)
21. Dominguez, V., Messina, P., Donoso-Guzmán, I., Parra, D.: The effect of explanations and algorithmic accuracy on visual recommender systems of artistic images. In: Proceedings of the 24th International Conference on Intelligent User Interfaces, pp. 408–416. ACM (2019)
22. Ehsan, U., Tambwekar, P., Chan, L., Harrison, B., Riedl, M.O.: Automated rationale generation: a technique for explainable AI and its effects on human perceptions. In: Proceedings of the 24th International Conference on Intelligent User Interfaces, pp. 263–274. ACM (2019)
23. Eiband, M., Buschek, D., Kremer, A., Hussmann, H.: The impact of placebic explanations on trust in intelligent systems. In: Extended Abstracts of the 2019 CHI Conference on Human Factors in Computing Systems, p. LBW0243. ACM (2019)
24. Eiband, M., Schneider, H., Buschek, D.: Normative vs. pragmatic: two perspectives on the design of explanations in intelligent systems. In: IUI Workshops (2018)
25. Eisenstadt, V., Espinoza-Stapelfeld, C., Mikyas, A., Althoff, K.-D.: Explainable distributed case-based support systems: patterns for enhancement and validation of design recommendations. In: Cox, M.T., Funk, P., Begum, S. (eds.) ICCBR 2018. LNCS (LNAI), vol. 11156, pp. 78–94. Springer, Cham (2018). https://doi.org/10.1007/978-3-030-01081-2_6
26. Eisenstadt, V., Langenhan, C., Althoff, K.-D.: FLEA-CBR – a flexible alternative to the classic 4R cycle of case-based reasoning. In: Bach, K., Marling, C. (eds.) ICCBR 2019. LNCS (LNAI), vol. 11680, pp. 49–63. Springer, Cham (2019). https://doi.org/10.1007/978-3-030-29249-2_4
27. Eljasik-Swoboda, T., Engel, F., Hemmje, M.: Using topic specific features for argument stance recognition
28. Escalante, H.J., et al.: Design of an explainable machine learning challenge for video interviews. In: 2017 International Joint Conference on Neural Networks (IJCNN), pp. 3688–3695. IEEE (2017)
29. Finkbeiner, B., Kleinberg, S.: Proceedings 3rd workshop on formal reasoning about causation, responsibility, and explanations in science and technology. arXiv preprint arXiv:1901.00073 (2019)
30. Garcia, R., Telea, A.C., da Silva, B.C., Tørresen, J., Comba, J.L.D.: A task-and-technique centered survey on visual analytics for deep learning model engineering. Comput. Graph. **77**, 30–49 (2018)

31. Gervasio, M.T., Myers, K.L., Yeh, E., Adkins, B.: Explanation to avert surprise. In: IUI Workshops, vol. 2068 (2018)
32. Goebel, R., et al.: Explainable AI: the new 42? In: Holzinger, A., Kieseberg, P., Tjoa, A.M., Weippl, E. (eds.) CD-MAKE 2018. LNCS, vol. 11015, pp. 295–303. Springer, Cham (2018). https://doi.org/10.1007/978-3-319-99740-7_21
33. Gorzałczany, M.B., Rudziński, F.: Interpretable and accurate medical data classification-a multi-objective genetic-fuzzy optimization approach. Expert Syst. Appl. **71**, 26–39 (2017)
34. Grigsby, S.S.: Artificial intelligence for advanced human-machine symbiosis. In: Schmorrow, D.D., Fidopiastis, C.M. (eds.) AC 2018. LNCS (LNAI), vol. 10915, pp. 255–266. Springer, Cham (2018). https://doi.org/10.1007/978-3-319-91470-1_22
35. Guo, K., Pratt, D., MacDonald III, A., Schrater, P.: Labeling images by interpretation from natural viewing. In: IUI Workshops (2018)
36. Guzdial, M., Reno, J., Chen, J., Smith, G., Riedl, M.: Explainable PCGML via game design patterns. arXiv preprint arXiv:1809.09419 (2018)
37. Hamidi-Haines, M., Qi, Z., Fern, A., Li, F., Tadepalli, P.: Interactive naming for explaining deep neural networks: a formative study. arXiv preprint arXiv:1812.07150 (2018)
38. Hepenstal, S., Kodagoda, N., Zhang, L., Paudyal, P., Wong, B.W.: Algorithmic transparency of conversational agents. In: IUI Workshops (2019)
39. Hohman, F., Head, A., Caruana, R., DeLine, R., Drucker, S.M.: Gamut: a design probe to understand how data scientists understand machine learning models. In: Proceedings of the 2019 CHI Conference on Human Factors in Computing Systems, p. 579. ACM (2019)
40. Hohman, F.M., Kahng, M., Pienta, R., Chau, D.H.: Visual analytics in deep learning: an interrogative survey for the next frontiers. IEEE Trans. Vis. Comput. Graph. **25**(8), 2674–2693 (2018)
41. Ishii, K.: Comparative legal study on privacy and personal data protection for robots equipped with artificial intelligence: looking at functional and technological aspects. AI Soc. **34**, 1–25 (2017)
42. Jain, A., Keller, J., Popescu, M.: Explainable AI for dataset comparison. In: 2019 IEEE International Conference on Fuzzy Systems (FUZZ-IEEE), pp. 1–7. IEEE (2019)
43. Jentzsch, S.F., Höhn, S., Hochgeschwender, N.: Conversational interfaces for explainable AI: a human-centred approach. In: Calvaresi, D., Najjar, A., Schumacher, M., Främling, K. (eds.) EXTRAAMAS 2019. LNCS (LNAI), vol. 11763, pp. 77–92. Springer, Cham (2019). https://doi.org/10.1007/978-3-030-30391-4_5
44. Kampik, T., Nieves, J.C., Lindgren, H.: Explaining sympathetic actions of rational agents. In: Calvaresi, D., Najjar, A., Schumacher, M., Främling, K. (eds.) EXTRAAMAS 2019. LNCS (LNAI), vol. 11763, pp. 59–76. Springer, Cham (2019). https://doi.org/10.1007/978-3-030-30391-4_4
45. Kizilcec, R.F.: How much information?: Effects of transparency on trust in an algorithmic interface. In: Proceedings of the 2016 CHI Conference on Human Factors in Computing Systems, pp. 2390–2395. ACM (2016)
46. Krebs, L.M., et al.: Tell me what you know: GDPR implications on designing transparency and accountability for news recommender systems. In: Extended Abstracts of the 2019 CHI Conference on Human Factors in Computing Systems, p. LBW2610. ACM (2019)

47. Krishnan, J., Coronado, P., Reed, T.: SEVA: a systems engineer's virtual assistant. In: AAAI Spring Symposium: Combining Machine Learning with Knowledge Engineering (2019)
48. Kwon, B.C., et al.: RetainVis: visual analytics with interpretable and interactive recurrent neural networks on electronic medical records. IEEE Trans. Vis. Comput. Graph. **25**(1), 299–309 (2018)
49. Lee, O.J., Jung, J.J.: Explainable movie recommendation systems by using story-based similarity. In: IUI Workshops (2018)
50. Lim, B.Y., Wang, D., Loh, T.P., Ngiam, K.Y.: Interpreting intelligibility under uncertain data imputation. In: IUI Workshops (2018)
51. Lim, B.Y., Yang, Q., Abdul, A.M., Wang, D.: Why these explanations? selecting intelligibility types for explanation goals. In: IUI Workshops (2019)
52. Loi, D., Wolf, C.T., Blomberg, J.L., Arar, R., Brereton, M.: Co-designing AI futures: Integrating AI ethics, social computing, and design. In: A Companion Publication of the 2019 on Designing Interactive Systems Conference 2019 Companion, pp. 381–384. ACM (2019)
53. Magdalena, L.: Semantic interpretability in hierarchical fuzzy systems: creating semantically decouplable hierarchies. Inf. Sci. **496**, 109–123 (2019)
54. Meacham, S., Isaac, G., Nauck, D., Virginas, B.: Towards explainable AI: design and development for explanation of machine learning predictions for a patient readmittance medical application. In: Arai, K., Bhatia, R., Kapoor, S. (eds.) CompCom 2019. AISC, vol. 997, pp. 939–955. Springer, Cham (2019). https://doi.org/10.1007/978-3-030-22871-2_67
55. Millecamp, M., Htun, N.N., Conati, C., Verbert, K.: To explain or not to explain: the effects of personal characteristics when explaining music recommendations. In: IUI, pp. 397–407 (2019)
56. Ming, Y., Qu, H., Bertini, E.: RuleMatrix: visualizing and understanding classifiers with rules. IEEE Trans. Vis. Comput. Graph. **25**(1), 342–352 (2018)
57. Montavon, G., Samek, W., Müller, K.R.: Methods for interpreting and understanding deep neural networks. Digit. Signal Proc. **73**, 1–15 (2018)
58. Montenegro, J.L.Z., da Costa, C.A., Righi, R.D.R.: Survey of conversational agents in health. Expert Syst. Appl. **129**, 56–67 (2019). https://doi.org/10.1016/j.eswa.2019.03.054. http://www.sciencedirect.com/science/article/pii/S0957417419302283
59. Nassar, M., Salah, K., ur Rehman, M.H., Svetinovic, D.: Blockchain for explainable and trustworthy artificial intelligence. Wiley Interdisc. Rev.: Data Min. Knowl. Discovery **10**(1), e1340 (2020)
60. Neerincx, M.A., van der Waa, J., Kaptein, F., van Diggelen, J.: Using perceptual and cognitive explanations for enhanced human-agent team performance. In: Harris, D. (ed.) EPCE 2018. LNCS (LNAI), vol. 10906, pp. 204–214. Springer, Cham (2018). https://doi.org/10.1007/978-3-319-91122-9_18
61. Nguyen, A.T., et al.: Believe it or not: designing a human-AI partnership for mixed-initiative fact-checking. In: The 31st Annual ACM Symposium on User Interface Software and Technology, pp. 189–199. ACM (2018)
62. Nguyen, A.T., Lease, M., Wallace, B.C.: Explainable modeling of annotations in crowdsourcing. In: IUI, pp. 575–579 (2019)
63. Nguyen, A.T., Lease, M., Wallace, B.C.: Mash: software tools for developing interactive and transparent machine learning systems. In: IUI Workshops (2019)
64. Nunes, I., Jannach, D.: A systematic review and taxonomy of explanations in decision support and recommender systems. User Model. User-Adap. Inter. **27**(3–5), 393–444 (2017)

65. Olszewska, J.I.: Designing transparent and autonomous intelligent vision systems. In: Proceedings of the International Conference on Agents and Artificial Intelligence (ICAART), pp. 850–856 (2019)

66. van Oosterhout, A.: Understanding the benefits and drawbacks of shape change in contrast or addition to other modalities. In: Companion Publication of the 2019 on Designing Interactive Systems Conference 2019 Companion, pp. 113–116. ACM (2019)

67. van Otterlo, M., Atzmueller, M.: On requirements and design criteria for explainability in legal AI (2018)

68. Paudyal, P., Lee, J., Kamzin, A., Soudki, M., Banerjee, A., Gupta, S.K.: Learn2sign: explainable AI for sign language learning. In: IUI Workshops (2019)

69. Petersen, K., Feldt, R., Mujtaba, S., Mattsson, M.: Systematic mapping studies in software engineering. In: Ease, vol. 8, pp. 68–77 (2008)

70. Ribera, M., Lapedriza, À.: Can we do better explanations? A proposal of user-centered explainable AI. In: IUI Workshops (2019)

71. Rotsidis, A., Theodorou, A., Wortham, R.H.: Robots that make sense: transparent intelligence through augmented reality. In: IUI Workshops (2019)

72. Santos, T.I., Abel, A.: Using feature visualisation for explaining deep learning models in visual speech. In: 2019 IEEE 4th International Conference on Big Data Analytics (ICBDA), pp. 231–235, March 2019. https://doi.org/10.1109/ICBDA. 2019.8713256

73. Schmidmaier, M., Han, Z., Weber, T., Liu, Y., Hußmann, H.: Real-time personalization in adaptive ides (2019)

74. Schuessler, M., Weiß, P.: Minimalistic explanations: capturing the essence of decisions. arXiv preprint arXiv:1905.02994 (2019)

75. Sellam, T., Lin, K., Huang, I., Yang, M., Vondrick, C., Wu, E.: DeepBase: deep inspection of neural networks. In: Proceedings of the 2019 International Conference on Management of Data, pp. 1117–1134 (2019)

76. Singh, M., Martins, L.M., Joanis, P., Mago, V.K.: Building a cardiovascular disease predictive model using structural equation model & fuzzy cognitive map. In: 2016 IEEE International Conference on Fuzzy Systems (FUZZ-IEEE), pp. 1377–1382. IEEE (2016)

77. Sliwinski, J., Strobel, M., Zick, Y.: An axiomatic approach to linear explanations in data classification. In: IUI Workshops (2018)

78. Smith, A., Nolan, J.: The problem of explanations without user feedback. In: IUI Workshops (2018)

79. Smith-Renner, A., Rua, R., Colony, M.: Towards an explainable threat detection tool. In: IUI Workshops (2019)

80. Sokol, K., Flach, P.A.: Conversational explanations of machine learning predictions through class-contrastive counterfactual statements. In: IJCAI, pp. 5785–5786 (2018)

81. Springer, A., Whittaker, S.: Progressive disclosure: designing for effective transparency. arXiv preprint arXiv:1811.02164 (2018)

82. Stumpf, S.: Horses for courses: making the case for persuasive engagement in smart systems. In: Joint Proceedings of the ACM IUI 2019 Workshops, vol. 2327. CEUR (2019)

83. Stumpf, S., Skrebe, S., Aymer, G., Hobson, J.: Explaining smart heating systems to discourage fiddling with optimized behavior. In: CEUR Workshop Proceedings, vol. 2068 (2018)

84. Sundararajan, M., Xu, J., Taly, A., Sayres, R., Najmi, A.: Exploring principled visualizations for deep network attributions. In: IUI Workshops (2019)

85. Theodorou, A., Wortham, R.H., Bryson, J.J.: Designing and implementing transparency for real time inspection of autonomous robots. Connect. Sci. **29**(3), 230–241 (2017)
86. Tsai, C.H., Brusilovsky, P.: Explaining social recommendations to casual users: design principles and opportunities. In: Proceedings of the 23rd International Conference on Intelligent User Interfaces Companion, p. 59. ACM (2018)
87. Tsai, C.H., Brusilovsky, P.: Designing explanation interfaces for transparency and beyond. In: IUI Workshops (2019)
88. Vellido, A.: The importance of interpretability and visualization in machine learning for applications in medicine and health care. Neural Comput. Appl. 1–15 (2019)
89. Vijay, A., Umadevi, K.: Secured AI guided architecture for D2D systems of massive MIMO deployed in 5G networks. In: 2019 3rd International Conference on Trends in Electronics and Informatics (ICOEI), pp. 468–472. IEEE (2019)
90. Vorm, E.S., Miller, A.D.: Assessing the value of transparency in recommender systems: an end-user perspective (2018)
91. Wang, D., Yang, Q., Abdul, A., Lim, B.Y.: Designing theory-driven user-centric explainable AI. In: Proceedings of the 2019 CHI Conference on Human Factors in Computing Systems, p. 601. ACM (2019)
92. Wang, Q., et al.: ATMSeer: increasing transparency and controllability in automated machine learning. In: Proceedings of the 2019 CHI Conference on Human Factors in Computing Systems, p. 681. ACM (2019)
93. Wang, X., Chen, Y., Yang, J., Wu, L., Wu, Z., Xie, X.: A reinforcement learning framework for explainable recommendation. In: 2018 IEEE International Conference on Data Mining (ICDM), pp. 587–596. IEEE (2018)
94. Wolf, C.T., Blomberg, J.: Explainability in context: lessons from an intelligent system in the it services domain. In: IUI Workshops (2019)
95. Xie, Y., Gao, G., Chen, X.: Outlining the design space of explainable intelligent systems for medical diagnosis. arXiv preprint arXiv:1902.06019 (2019)
96. Yang, Q., Banovic, N., Zimmerman, J.: Mapping machine learning advances from HCI research to reveal starting places for design innovation. In: Proceedings of the 2018 CHI Conference on Human Factors in Computing Systems, p. 130. ACM (2018)
97. Yeganejou, M., Dick, S.: Improved deep fuzzy clustering for accurate and interpretable classifiers. In: 2019 IEEE International Conference on Fuzzy Systems (FUZZ-IEEE), pp. 1–7. IEEE (2019)
98. Zhao, R., Benbasat, I., Cavusoglu, H.: Transparency in advice-giving systems: a framework and a research model for transparency provision. In: IUI Workshops (2019)
99. Zheng, X.l., Zhu, M.Y., Li, Q.B., Chen, C.C., Tan, Y.C.: FinBrain: when finance meets AI 2.0. Front. Inf. Technol. Electron. Eng. **20**(7), 914–924 (2019)
100. Zhou, J., et al.: Effects of influence on user trust in predictive decision making. In: Extended Abstracts of the 2019 CHI Conference on Human Factors in Computing Systems, pp. 1–6 (2019)
101. Zhu, J., Liapis, A., Risi, S., Bidarra, R., Youngblood, G.M.: Explainable AI for designers: a human-centered perspective on mixed-initiative co-creation. In: 2018 IEEE Conference on Computational Intelligence and Games (CIG), pp. 1–8. IEEE (2018)

Design for the Decentralized World: Democratization of Blockchain-Based Software Design

Vladislav Gladyshev[✉] and Qiong Wu

Academy of Arts & Design, Tsinghua University, Beijing, China
fuld18@mails.tsinghua.edu.cn, wla9d@yandex.com,
qiong-wu@tsinghua.edu.cn

Abstract. The decentralized future is now. The blockchain technology and decentralized applications are changing the way we think about digital software products and the value they bring to our lives. Traditional ways of software design and development are not fully applicable, as there is no central authority to control, decide or direct the future of the product. The blockchain-based software is not controlled by anyone, and at the same time, it belongs to everyone, because the value is distributed among all members in the form of a cryptocurrency. Current product design workflows and methods combined with the blockchain technology need a transformation to become even more inclusive, democratic, autonomous, seek user participation and decision-making. The design solution that is accessible, usable and user-centered can be formed only through the optimization of the product around the users, rather than forcing the users to change their behavior to accommodate the product. Research methods like participatory and non-participatory observations, literature and white paper reviews, analyses, interviews with field experts, are all combined with case studies and explorations of decentralized technology, user-centered design, and democratization. All of which is united in the concept of the decentralized autonomous software, or DAS, which is a software that has decision-making mechanisms embedded in an open distributed peer-to-peer network, that requires vote-based human participation to determine the future direction of its lifecycle, development, and design.

Keywords: Decentralization · Democratization · Blockchain-based software · User-centered design · Decentralized autonomous software

1 Introduction

On June 12, 1992, Victor Papanek delivered a lecture at Apple (originally Apple Computer; with less than 10 thousand employees at the time) entitled *Microbes in the Tower* [1] in which he said: "I also believe very strongly in decentralization, largely because I have the conviction ... that nothing big works, ever, in any circumstances." His design and research at that time were focused on environmental issues and tools that can promote greater autonomy for people in developing countries: with the final aim being economical changes and improved quality of life. Victor's theory is an

© Springer Nature Switzerland AG 2020
A. Marcus and E. Rosenzweig (Eds.): HCII 2020, LNCS 12201, pp. 74–86, 2020.
https://doi.org/10.1007/978-3-030-49760-6_5

example of a bottom-up approach, which suggested affordable design solutions based on user needs that can solve the existing problem from an entity level.

Fast forward 28 years and Apple (now having more than 137 thousand employees [2]) became one of the biggest software companies that dominate cyberspace, and people's everyday life; along with Google, Amazon, Facebook, Microsoft, and Netflix. Nevertheless, Victor's beliefs in decentralization are slowly becoming a reality, with his lecture just becoming another irony of history.

After the widespread of the World Wide Web and advancements of globalization, FAANG and BAT together got control of almost all possible user data, thus the network, making users vulnerable [3]. Therefore, people, that from the beginning allowed their personal information sharing with these companies, are now exposed and face many risks that are out of their control. Moreover, the data of users' daily activity will be further used to analyze behavior patterns that will help to generate targeted advertisements, create new paid product features, and other profit-generating schemes for the companies.

In other words, users helped companies to become big and are continuously keeping the growth with each product interaction. The generated data could be used in almost any way the companies want or any bad actor, that gets control of it. Centralization of data makes companies vulnerable to attacks and hacking, thus makes users vulnerable [3].

Above all, the user experience of the product is quite often being designed mainly with business values in mind, not necessarily focusing on the ease of use or the usability; sometimes even using human psychology as an opportunity to gain users, or make users perform actions that they didn't initially intend to. These design practices of user interface or user experience design are called dark patterns [4]. Put differently, it is psychological manipulation of people for the sake of business profit. Centralized data gives power to the companies, that average user is unable to compete with; so, things like dark patterns can easily happen and be neglected. Here are some of the famous examples: LinkedIn's email spamming, Amazon's account deletion [5] or country changing process, Microsoft's aggressive Windows software update, Facebook's data leaking, Apple's automatic two-factor authentication enabling, just to name a few.

The invention of blockchain and Bitcoin (first cryptocurrency and decentralized application) brought many new possibilities for people, businesses, developers, designers, economists and many others. More importantly, blockchain and decentralization are leading the Web 4.0 and the Fourth Industrial Revolution, as it brings fundamental changes and groundbreaking questions to our society, economy, government, physical and moral values, thus changing us and the way we think. As the founder and executive chairman of the World Economic Forum, Klaus Schwab said [6]: "One of the features of this Fourth Industrial Revolution is that it doesn't change what we are doing, but it changes us."

The invention of the blockchain brought many new possibilities to an innovative way of global value decentralization and exchange: which is led by a new technology of distributed information structuring. New industrial changes are supported by new ideas. The same way Henry Ford invented the assembly line technique of mass production and forever changed manufacturing; Satoshi Nakamoto invented the technology of decentralized information and value exchange, and forever changed how we think about money, freedom, and technology. So, it is for us to find the new methods and processes that can support the evolution of blockchain adoption and further innovation.

Decentralization brings challenges to the traditional ways of software product design: there is no central authority to control, decide or direct the future of the product, which adds another dimension and requires process automation as its main factor. The blockchain software is not controlled by anyone and at the same time being controlled by everyone: as the value is distributed among all members of the network. Current product design workflows and methods need a transformation to become open, inclusive, democratic, and autonomous.

2 Research Methods

Methods of research used in this paper are mostly qualitative. Personal participatory and non-participatory observations are combined with software design experience inside and outside the blockchain field: as the basis of the problem definition and understanding of practical blockchain usage. Literature and white paper reviews, analyses of the decentralization trends and tendencies are coupled with the examination of design and development tendencies before and after the existence of decentralized technology. Consultations and interviews with field experts, further brainstorming and feedback sessions helped to test the proposed concept and compare it to the other possible solutions. Multiple case studies and comparisons serve as examples of current state of blockchain technology and decentralized applications, along with the explanations of its possible disadvantages. The final outcome of the discussion is presented in the form of a blockchain-based autonomous software concept that suggests a more democratic way of product creation, usage, and development.

3 Research Background

Each part of the research background block will define a concept and question its possible usage, improvement or advancement in the present and future of the decentralized world. It also discusses the applicability of certain ideas and methods used in current software design processes. Below are the angles from which the problem of blockchain software design could be viewed.

3.1 Blockchain

Blockchain is a technology that was created to serve the first digital cryptocurrency called Bitcoin. At its core, it is an open distributed database, managed by a peer-to-peer network through protocols and cryptography, supported by a consensus algorithm. Block is an encrypted group of new transactions and chain is the network of computer nodes [3].

Satoshi Nakamoto created Bitcoin as an electronic cash system that would allow online payments without a financial institution. Above all, it was aimed to solve the weaknesses of the trust-based model of the value transaction, through a system based on cryptographic proof; that allows the exchange without the need for a trusted third party [7]. In fact, Satoshi's anonymity and non-intervention is another eliminated weakness of trust-based model: nobody knows who he is, thus there is no personal trust involved, everyone can see the code and decide if the system works for them or not.

Will the problem of the third party and trust management remain if the creator of the blockchain network is not anonymous, and participates in further development of the blockchain? How can a blockchain system work in an even more autonomous way, at the same time create consensus between the users and developers?

3.2   Decentralized Applications

Decentralized application (also called dapp) is a software that has been built and runs on top of a blockchain system; often being Ethereum or Bitcoin. Compared to non-decentralized application it usually has different computational mechanisms, file storage methods, monetization, and payments. Dapps represent the second generation of blockchain evolution and advance the technology with more applicable functionalities through smart contracts, at the same time giving an excellent start for Web 3.0 and decentralization of the World Wide Web. These applications could be compared to apps on a smartphone or websites, with the main difference being the decentralized blockchain technology behind its data storage and transfer.

One of the most popular blockchain platforms for decentralized applications is Ethereum, created by Vitalik Buterin and launched in 2015. Its general idea is that blockchain can have general-purpose flexibility and allow developers to build applications upon the core technology; which will give the application trustworthiness through the mechanism it's being built on: the dapps will always run on Ethereum as they were programmed. In other words, they would be decentralized and no single person or entity can control them [8].

Blockchains that allow the development of dapps are becoming ecosystems (similar to Apple iOS/macOS, Microsoft Windows or Linux), that enable design, development, and usage of the software that is based on open, public and decentralized algorithms. These decentralized applications combine the new technology of trust management with already existing methods of application design, and as a result produce public product that would be able to innovate and replace the prior relationships between the internet, software, and money.

Bitcoin has fundamental application in money or value transfer that is not controlled by any financial institution; at the same time, because of that, it has limited functionality. Otherwise speaking, for the first generation of blockchain technology the protocol is in service of the currency, when for blockchains that have the dapp ecosystem built on top, the currency is in the service of the protocol. So, for Ethereum the power of the system is increased (compared to Bitcoin) through the level of its generalized purpose, which at some point also changes the value concept of two blockchain generations on a deeper level. Either way, technical issues, scalability and application of the technology are still the main problems in the mass adoption of decentralized applications.

Dapps add another level of complexity to the blockchain trust and value paradigm, as the decentralized application, blockchain, and currency are all involved at the same time; certain qualities of one are not necessarily being transferred to the other. What could be the optimal relationship between them and how can the transparency of the decision-making be maintained? Can the processes of development and design be autonomous in a way that would originate a better agreement between creators and users of the blockchain and dapps?

3.3   User-Centered Design

User-centered design is a set of design methods, processes, and practices that focus on user needs in order to create a product that would be highly usable and accessible. In other words, designers need to study and research possible future users of the product to create an interaction that would best serve their needs. The term user-centered design was coined by Donald Norman and further popularized in his book called *The Design of Everyday Things*. In it he defines and explains the four main principles of good design: visibility, good conceptual model, good mappings and feedback [9]. All of which require user research, exploration and understanding of user needs, problem definition, design proposal and solution with further iterations. On a product level, the process will consist of these steps: understanding the context of use, specification of user requirements, design solution and iterative evaluation that will loop further product updates [10]. Consequently, a design solution that is accessible, usable and user-centered can be formed only through the optimization of the product around the users, rather than forcing the users to change their behavior to accommodate the product.

Usability and user-centered design approach in business-to-consumer products have got great attention in recent years: more companies saw the rise in numbers of daily active usage and retention, increase in usage duration of apps and websites that have good user experience; which in combination brought greater adoption and higher profits. If before it was gaining industry acceptance, now it is a core part of every design process behind many successful digital products [11].

On the one hand, there are technical problems and issues with scalability. On the other hand, difficulties with user adoption. Concepts of blockchain and decentralized applications are technical and complex, thus require knowledge beyond average in order to build trust and recognize benefits. Also, the field is new, not yet enough explored and popularized, thus like most of the early technologies it is not necessarily user-friendly and doesn't necessarily have the best user experience design. At the same time, there are problems that have the potential to be solved with a user-centered design, like clarification of blockchain and dapp benefits compared to currently available technology, problems with onboarding and accessibility, quality of the user experience and usability, and reevaluation of the platform-based constraints [12].

What are the possible ways for blockchain developers and businesses to incorporate the user-centered approach in the software product design process? Are there any possibilities to introduce user research and inclusion in the updates of the software in a way that would be autonomous and automated?

3.4 Participatory Design

Participatory design (often called co-design) is an approach to design that actively involves all stakeholders and brings customers to the core of the design process to form design-led innovation that would be able to give the full potential of user-centered design approach, and at the end create results that would meet user needs and have high level of usability [13].

At some point, it is a form of idea generation or exploration of the possible solutions that involve the end-user as the test subject, after which, designers would be able to decide if suggested solutions are applicable or what are the outcomes that could be used in future designs. As the user-centered design is for users, participatory design is with the users. This form of design process seeks to enable those who will use the technology to share their thoughts during design creation, without the need to speak the design language or know the technological sides of the problem [14].

Distributed participatory design approach supports the direct participation of users and other stakeholders in system analysis and design work that is often technological or around a certain digital product. This type of design has a very close practical connection with blockchain and decentralized applications and its core beliefs and values, as decentralization is a form of distribution. If blockchain, cryptocurrencies and dapps are being open and used by people that have a direct financial investment in them, the decisions about updates and directions of development should as well include their involvement, participation and decision-making.

What are the possible ways to combine key benefits of decentralized technology like transparency, security, trust management and value transferring with greater user involvement and participation? It could potentially lead to new explorations in the problem of technological understanding, thus mass adoption. Similar to Xerox Alto that had the first GUI that allowed people with non-technological backgrounds to use different functionalities of the personal computer that before were only available through command line in text-only interfaces. What are the possible solutions to automate the participatory design process so it would be more democratized, and people that are invested in it would be able to make decisions of its future evolution?

3.5 Agile Software Design

Agile software design and development is a combination of approaches under which requirements and solutions evolve through the self-organized collaboration of cross-functional teams and their end-users [15]. Many of the principles of agile philosophy are being at the core of a lot of successful products and services. Scrum and Kanban are the main practical solutions for the product creation process, both for test-driven development and behavior-driven development as they bring flexibility and structure to the overall workflow.

Agile principles of software design and development have a close connection with user-centered design and in combination can create software that is understandable, easy to use and bring value to the end-user, at the same time keep everyone in the loop and make participation in decision-making a key solution in the innovation of the product. Here are some agile software principles that form the mindset: the highest priority is to satisfy customer, welcome changing requirements, deliver frequent updates, members of the business and development team work together on many problems, continuous attention to technical excellence and good design, focus on simplicity and ROI of features and functionality, self-organizing principles of team structure, constant reflection and improvement of the design, development and product features [16]. The agility of the methodology creates an enabling factor in frequent implementations of the user research insights and solutions found in the participatory design sessions.

What are the possible ways to combine participatory nature and clarity of the process in the agile philosophy with blockchain-based development and design? How can the workflow be changed to involve more people in the evaluation and assessment of possible product decisions?

4   Case Studies

4.1   Ethereum

Ehtereum was mentioned in this paper before. In summary, it is a next-generation smart contract and decentralized application platform [17]. Vitalik Buterin, the creator of this blockchain, took the core concept from Bitcoin and expanded the technology so it could become more relevant and solve different problems, not just transfer and exchange of cryptocurrencies. As a result, a global open-source platform based on blockchain with focus on dapps was created.

Ethereum improved the technological side of blockchain, compared to Bitcoin, but didn't necessarily make it more costumer or user-friendly. Decentralized applications do create value for some users and solve some problems, but the relationship between the blockchain and dapps is quite subordinative: anyone who would like to use a dapp, first need to understand how Ethereum works, and in order to do that, they need to understand Bitcoin and blockchain. Additionally, concepts and technology behind it all is hard and complex. The onboarding process is difficult especially with many unfamiliar technical words like consensus, chain, nodes, miners, etc. There is definitely some potential for improvement with the change of the mindset and a bit of work from user research and user experience writing.

Bitcoin was a solution to transfer value without any involvement of a third party and reevaluation of trust management; Ethereum on the other hand is mainly a platform for decentralized applications that is built on the same technology. Having the same or similar technology does not necessarily create or transfer the same values, because the solutions are different. Methods of design and development of a peer-to-peer electronic cash system should be different and have additional focus points compared to a platform or an ecosystem for decentralized applications. Ethereum is great compared to Bitcoin in the aspects of functionality and application of the blockchain technology, but compared to any other similar application ecosystem, like Apple iOS/macOS, Microsoft Windows or Linux, it is very poor and does not necessarily solve all the problems an ecosystem should. There are many things missing from a good ecosystem: quality and consistency of the system design and development, synchronization and constant communication between developers and users, high quality user experience and usability, ecosystem based native solutions, clarity of definitions and functionalities, strong user and development base, robust collaboration capabilities, high level of support, just to name a few.

It is said that Ethereum is a foundation of the internet where infrastructure is neutral, not controlled by any company or person [17]. Contrary to the creation of Bitcoin, founder of Ethereum and the team behind it is public, so there is no anonymity involved in the trust management between the developer and the user, which means that the team behind the blockchain or events associated with them can easily influence the consensus, value of the cryptocurrency, or the open nature of the platform. Right now autonomy or neutral aspects are additional to the platform and are not in the core of its processes. Developers of the blockchain have most of the power over the design and implementation of future updates so the final product does not necessarily give a user-centered solution. Even if the project has world class professionals, their decisions are not necessarily driven by user needs and arrangements as a result will not bring good user experience. Community, participation and discussions of the solutions are not necessarily very open, and could be very technical; which leaves the average user in a vague area.

There are different outside occasions that still influence the course and outcome of people's interaction with Ethereum: artificially created rumors about Vitalik's car accident made the ETH market value drop by four billion dollars, a blockchain update led to a break in some smart contacts which created failures in many dapps, decisions about consensus algorithm for Ethereum 2.0 might be a combination of PoW and PoS. All of the above suggests that there is openness in the blockchain as a technology, but not necessarily in the value of the cryptocurrency or in the decisions of the product design and development; as openness leads to constant participation of many entities with a result of a consensus.

There are projects similar to Ethereum that have already solved the problem through implementation of voting mechanisms for the future upgrades: in Cosmos, validators can vote for the direction they think would work best in the next update of the blockchain so the solution that got most of the votes gets implemented. On the other hand, there are projects like Tezos that similarly to Ethereum leave their users behind the decision-making and create frustrations: after the Babylon update the type of a delegation address was changed from KT to tz leading to constant errors in the transaction processes.

Ethereum would move to the next level if it will become more inclusive and transparent about its decisions and build a better communication between developers and users. A voting mechanism on the blockchain is needed to truly make it neutral, open and not controlled by any company or person. Just claiming the values of the technology is not enough, removing one middleman and adding another one that is less visible is not a solution.

Vitalik once mentioned in the VICE interview that, "a community can make money for itself wherever it wants." Only through democratic principles community will define the value, logic, and qualities of the currency. ETH can be used by the community, same way it can use gold, but none of them are truly created by it, as only an agreement of value is made.

4.2   CryptoKitties

CryptoKitties is a popular decentralized application built on the Ethereum network. It uses the technology of the non-refundable token and smart contracts to record, breed, and exchange digital collectibles in a visual form of a cat, that from the code perspective describes the relationship between the phenotype and genotype [18]. Many similar games focus their mechanics and interactions on digital collectibles: Axie Infinity, Etheremon, Gods Unchained, just to name a few.

Some problems of the Ethereum blockchain are also applicable to dapps. Although these applications run on the blockchain, it doesn't necessarily mean that the application itself is decentralized, as they have the single point of failure being the team behind it. The development team makes decisions, fixes bugs and decides on the features of the new version of the dapp. Openness could also be arbitrary or limited as the genetic algorithm that drives the cat reproduction is secret. Either way, users still need to trust the team in order to trust the dapp and the network. Most of the decentralized applications are not censorship-resistant as the team behind it would always be politically centralized. Some even question the application side of the decentralized applications, because they are being frequently used to do ICOs and raise money. In other words, a dapp-specific token is used to raise money without any further obligations from the team to deliver, also the project might not be a registered company or business. In recent years, there were a lot of scam projects that took money from the users and have never delivered anything.

Dapps are very blockchain specific and are highly dependent on the development and updates of the chain and price of the cryptocurrency. Even though Ethereum enables the development of dapps, the process is still hard and each update of the blockchain might potentially bring some disruptions in the dapp ecosystem. People that develop blockchain updates and people that develop decentralized applications are often different, so each might not necessarily know of the possible problems that the other side has. That is why, there is no surprise if a new Ethereum update will shut down many of the dapps, as it happened before, and influence the economy of the applications.

The gaming and entertainment parts of the applications on the blockchain are quite questionable. CryptoKitties didn't go far from concepts of coins or cryptocurrencies, combined with the lack of play elements, dapps leave users with a collection of pure visual-based value collectibles. Crypto-collectibles work the same way as the cryptocurrencies with its main value being the price and the ability to collect, buy or sell; in the end, it just becomes another form of investment. The reason behind it could be that just the original execution of the game was not focused on the entertainment, but on how to find a way to apply the technology; making the game an added value to the blockchain, not a created value of the game itself. Moreover, dapps are expensive to use and require prior studying, which makes the trust a first step of the application validation for the user. Last but not least, there is not much practical usage of the dapps, people don't use them that much, especially if numbers of non-blockchain-based applications are compared side by side. CryptoKitties is a technology looking for an application, not a technology solving a problem or creating engaging ways of entertainment: dapps have a steep learning curve that doesn't lead to entertainment, but at the end creates a beautiful visual investment based on sophisticated technology.

From a broader socioeconomic perspective, dapps like CryptoKitties are trying to explore if a digital good could be rare. With all the possibilities of breeding, combined with the variety of cats on the market, it is almost impossible to understand what is rare without any definition from the game designers. The concept of scarcity in the game is also hard to understand because many of the users are driven by their subjective attraction of the cats' appearance. Besides, digital scarcity is brand new and unfamiliar. Last but not least, only the code of that particular digital good belongs to the user, the visual representation of the cat or the image doesn't. The CryptoKitties company owns all rights to the graphical elements of the cat, making it impossible to legally use the image of the cat elsewhere.

Each user of the game has financial investments in it, as the cats can cost from tens of dollars to thousands of dollars. But the design, development, other related solutions, and updates are carried out by the developers that don't necessarily communicate with the users. Otherwise speaking, the development team can easily implement an additional feature to the overall cat genome and reshape the economy of the dapp, making old cat genome combinations loose value, if they wanted.

At some point, we removed one middleman being a financial institution, added back another middleman in the form of Ethereum and added another middleman being the decentralized application development team. It is not as bad as it sounds and there are some good dapps with teams that do a lot of user research, care to create something good and highly usable, and solve problems, but it is a very small minority.

5 Discussion

Blockchain and decentralized applications are aiming to be open, transparent, solve the problem of trust, value transfer, and bring solutions that would not require a third party. In reality, due to the lack of democratic decision-making, participation of developers and users in the process, user-centered design practices and autonomous voting mechanisms, it only remains a slogan. The blockchain technology itself is open and people can use it instead of a trusted third party, similar to how people use Bitcoin, but the method through which it has been developed and designed remains subjective to a small development community that lacks transparency in their decisions. Each blockchain project, depending on its aim and audience should adjust and incorporate project-specific processes and values. The design of Ethereum should inevitably be different from the design of Bitcoin, as their nature and core functions are different. Ethereum is an ecosystem or a platform with a high level of user and development interactions, because of that it should focus on democratic, participatory decision-making and constant involvement of the community.

Autonomous ideas in processes and structure of decentralized organizations are truly revolutionary and with proper design similar values could be incorporated into the design of blockchain technology and decentralized applications. The greatest value of decentralization is autonomy, and the greatest problem with autonomy is its governance and rules that should at the end create an agreement between entities. The decentralized autonomous organization is an organization created through a set of rules encoded in a transparent computer system that is controlled only by shareholders and not influenced by any government [19]. Its biggest potential is to define decision-makers in an organization and enable a democratic voting mechanism that would lead to further agreement and development of the organization. The blockchain technology behind it can record and keep all the information like names, titles, documents, interactions, numbers, transactions, but most importantly create a consensus mechanism around it, that will allow democratized and fair voting at any step that would require a decision. Even though there was an example of The DAO project (first ever decentralized autonomous organization) that had a vulnerability in the code that led to the stealing of its funds, which subsequently lead to the hard-fork of the Ethereum blockchain [20], the concept and the fact that is was the largest crowdfunding campaign in history gives hopes that more projects like this will happen and maybe lead to a new form of organization design. Decentralized autonomous organizations represent the future of the decentralized economy with collective work, openness, automation, algorithms, votes and revenue sharing.

The proposed solution to the questions previously mentioned in this paper and a possible direction for further advancement of the practices in the blockchain field is a concept of decentralized autonomous software. Similarly, to decentralized autonomous organization it might lead to new ways of software design and development.

Decentralized autonomous software, or DAS, is a software that has decision-making mechanisms embedded in an open distributed peer-to-peer network, that requires vote-based human participation to determine the future direction of its life-cycle, development, and design. It combines key values of blockchain, user-centered design and agile methodology in the form of an autonomous and democratized solution to ensure trust management and transparency of the product design process. Decentralized autonomous software could be created in a form of blockchain or decentralized application with the main value being inclusion and openness of the product decisions.

The incentive of a solution proposal, further design and development could be given in a form of a cryptocurrency mined or locked from the beginning of the project creation. Similar to the current workflow of agile development it will follow the steps of planning, definition, design, development, testing, and deployment, just with an added step of voting that will ensure that the stakeholders (developers, designers, users) are on the same page about the decision of the feature or update, at each step of the process. In other words, voting and democratized decision-making would be the main force in the selection of project features and functionalities. On the other hand, rules for voting could be further defined, it may be possible to vote for addresses that have a certain amount of coins or that remained active during a certain period of time.

In its ideal form, decentralized autonomous software is a combination of democratized practices that help to further develop the values of the decentralized world: blockchain and decentralized applications create the technical background for the software, user-centered approach in the form of participatory design creates direction and evaluation of the software application, agile software methodology creates the process that would connect and systemize all the pieces in a form of a self-driven software evolution.

6 Conclusion

Even though blockchain technology and decentralized applications create a certain openness and trust, it is not enough to fully support the open blockchain-based software design and development, as there are no processes that would help to democratize the decision-making. Decentralized autonomous software is a concept that rethinks the software design and development, potentially leading it to a new way of execution that would truly be autonomous and potentially not only reevaluate the blockchain technology, but also change the way people think about decision-making and participation in the new decentralized economy.

Acknowledgments. Conference registration grant of this research was supported by the National Social Science Foundation as part of the Artificial-Intelligence-Based Interaction Design Method Research project in 2019, with the associated grant number being 19BG127. I would also like to thank and acknowledge the support of Pine Du, Jun Soo Kim, Dmitrii Vasilenko, Alessio Casablanca, and professor Qiong Wu for their precious contributions and constructive feedback.

References

1. YouTube: Design Learning Network, Victor Papanek June 1992 Presentation at Apple Computer - "Microbes in the Tower". https://youtu.be/nMdnjGQQlQU. Accessed 30 Jan 2020
2. Wikipedia: Apple Inc. https://en.wikipedia.org/wiki/Apple_Inc.. Accessed 30 Jan 2020
3. Finch, T.J.: Decentralized: Blockchain and the Future Web: An Introductory Guide. CreateSpace Independent Publishing Platform, Scotts Valley (2018)
4. Gray, C.M., Kou, Y., Battles, B., Hoggatt, J., Toombs, A.L.: The dark (patterns) side of UX design. In: Proceedings of the 2018 CHI Conference on Human Factors in Computing Systems, CHI 2018, pp. 1–14. ACM Press, Montréal (2018). https://doi.org/10.1145/3173574.3174108
5. Dark Patterns: What are dark patterns? https://www.darkpatterns.org. Accessed 30 Jan 2020
6. YouTube: World Economic Forum, What is the Fourth Industrial Revolution? https://youtu.be/kpW9JcWxKq0. Accessed 30 Jan 2020
7. Nakamoto, S.: Bitcoin: a peer-to-peer electronic cash system. Bitcoin Project (2008). https://bitcoin.org/bitcoin.pdf. Accessed 30 Jan 2020
8. Ethereum.org: What is Ethereum? https://ethereum.org/what-is-ethereum. Accessed 30 Jan 2020
9. Norman, D.A.: The Design of Everyday Things: Revised and Expanded Edition, Revised edn. Basic Books, New York (2013)
10. The Interaction Design Foundation: What is User Centered Design? https://www.interaction-design.org/literature/topics/user-centered-design. Accessed 30 Jan 2020
11. Mao, J.Y., Vredenburg, K., Smith, P.W., Carey, T.: The state of user-centered design practice. Commun. ACM **48**, 105–109 (2005). https://doi.org/10.1145/1047671.1047677
12. Glomann, L., Schmid, M., Kitajewa, N.: Improving the blockchain user experience - an approach to address blockchain mass adoption issues from a human-centred perspective. In: Ahram, T. (ed.) AHFE 2019. AISC, vol. 965, pp. 608–616. Springer, Cham (2020). https://doi.org/10.1007/978-3-030-20454-9_60

13. Wikipedia: Participatory design. https://en.wikipedia.org/wiki/Participatory_design. Accessed 30 Jan 2020
14. Simonsen, J., Robertson, T.: Routledge International Handbook of Participatory Design, 1st edn. Routledge, London (2013)
15. Collier, K.: Agile Analytics: A Value-Driven Approach to Business Intelligence and Data Warehousing (Agile Software Development Series), 1st edn. Addison-Wesley Professional, Upper Saddle River (2011)
16. Stellman, A., Greene, J.: Learning Agile: Understanding Scrum, XP, Lean, and Kanban, 1st edn. O'Reilly Media, Sebastopol (2013)
17. GitHub: Ethereum White Paper, A Next-Generation Smart Contract and Decentralized Application Platform. https://github.com/ethereum/wiki/wiki/white-paper. Accessed 30 Jan 2020
18. CryptoKitties: Technical Details, White Pa-purr. https://www.cryptokitties.co/technical-details. Accessed 30 Jan 2020
19. Wikipedia: Decentralized autonomous organization. https://en.wikipedia.org/wiki/Decentralized_autonomous_organization. Accessed 30 Jan 2020
20. Wikipedia: The DAO (organization). https://en.wikipedia.org/wiki/The_DAO_(organization). Accessed 30 Jan 2020

Babe: An Experience Sharing Design for Enhancing Fatherhood During Pregnancy

Jingyu Lin📵 and Danni Chang$^{(\boxtimes)}$

Shanghai Jiao Tong University, Shanghai, People's Republic of China
dchang1@sjtu.edu.cn

Abstract. The distribution of family responsibilities between men and women is still unfair in modern families. The design theme of this work particularly focuses on the issue that father-to-be often lacks the awareness of fatherhood. For this purpose, several design research methods such as literature research and questionnaire were applied to explore the relationship between female and male during pregnancy. According to the research and analysis results, the user needs can be identified: males' consciousness of being a father should be enhanced and father-to-be should be encouraged to be more proactive in caring for the fetus and wife. Therefore, a pair of wearable devices for couples is designed, which enables the male to feel the fetal heartbeats and movements in real time. Through this way, father-to-be can also share part of females' experience during pregnancy. At last, a prior usability test was performed in a laboratory environment. Both the usability of the wearable devices and the supportive application were tested. In conclusion, Babe provides a new way of interaction and creates an artificial connection between father and fetal. Sharing experience through devices can be a creative way of alleviating gender conflicts.

Keywords: Father involvement · Experience sharing · Pregnancy · Creative product design

1 Introduction

Under the traditional culture of East Asia, women have always been "The Second Sex". Under the control of Confucianists, the moral rule that women should defer to the authority of men is unquestionable [15]. Therefore, women in China had failed to gain the respect and the status they deserve in their family life for thousands of years.

After the establishment of the People's Republic of China, the core status of family is greatly impacted by the new form of government [3]. According to Yan, new laws and regulations on sex and marriage penetrated in family and lifestyle through the women's liberation movement [20]. More and more women in the new era have independent personality, their own career and life goals. Female started to play an indispensable role not only in the family but also in the labor market.

The great change in gender concept gave rise to new conflicts. Although the opinion on women today is no longer the same as that in the feudal era, it is still far away from the true gender equality. In modern families, most of the women keep obtaining new knowledge in the process of raising children and trying to fulfill the

© Springer Nature Switzerland AG 2020
A. Marcus and E. Rosenzweig (Eds.): HCII 2020, LNCS 12201, pp. 87–98, 2020.
https://doi.org/10.1007/978-3-030-49760-6_6

duties of the mother. However, it appears that a number of men gradually lose their roles in the family and leave the burden of housework and cultivating children to their wives. Some studies in Canada and Australia examine the time that two genders spend on caretaking preschool children [5, 13]. Although subjects are all from dual-earner families, fathers only spend two-thirds as much time as mothers do.

Moreover, the inequality is especially obvious during pregnancy. There is a nature connection between a mother-to-be and her fetal, which leads to stronger ties and the sense of responsibility [2]. But it is quite difficult for men to recognize their father's identity before the child is born. A study in Singapore shows that only 35.2% of the first-time fathers are considered highly involved during pregnancy [19].

This paper focuses on addressing the issue of gender inequality during pregnancy from the design perspective. The period of pregnancy, as a turning point of family role, plays a key role in cultivating healthy parenting attitude and family relationship. In this regard, researches have shown that the involvement of father-to-be is closely related with postpartum depression and females' parenting anxiety [14]. Therefore, increasing father involvement during pregnancy is especially significant for improving maternal and infant health outcomes [7].

It is shown that men are becoming more and more aware of their own deficiency and have a growing will to support their wives during pregnancy [1, 18]. Therefore, creating more communication and interaction opportunities for both sexes appears a promising design direction, and the problem of uneven distribution of childbearing responsibilities during pregnancy deserves deeper investigation.

For this end, a creative design solution, named Babe, was proposed, and the following contributions are expected:

Firstly, a creative interactive way is built for sharing experience. The unique experience of female can be imitated and regenerated by Babe, which gives male a whole new experience. Thusly, an opportunity can be provided for father-to-be to feel the fetal heartbeats and movements.

Secondly, this paper offers evidence that gender conflicts can be alleviated through design approach. By sharing experience with wearable devices, new parents will show more empathy in each other. It can indicate the potential of HCI methods in solving gender issues over a larger range.

2 Related Works

In order to confirm the feasibility and creativity of the idea, competitive analysis on related works has been carried out. A small number of researchers have noticed the meaningfulness of regenerating pregnant experience on the male. *Mommy Tummy* is a pregnancy experience system, which can be worn by the male and is designed to be a jacket in appearance [10]. *Mommy Tummy* can simulate the growth of fetal in weight and size, but it can only be experienced in a lab. *Fibo* is a wearable jewelry designed for men [4]. It is able to receive real-time data based on digital devices like *BloomLife* and imitate fetal movements by pearls on the wrist. Movement patterns of kick, push and hiccups can be simulated by presses, hits and prodding against skin on the body of father-to-be.

Some services and campaigns also exist for the sake of letting father-to-be experience the feeling of pregnancy. A project called "3 Pregnant Dads" was run in the UK [16]. Three fathers in their mid-40 s took the challenge to wear sets of fully-blown pregnancy suits for a month. Another popular way of sharing experience is through TENS machine. Some well-known people such as Piers Morgan experienced the feeling of labour pains through a simulation machine on telecasts [12]. Similar campaigns are also held in China [8]. Some hospitals provide lessons for couples on Mother's Day, in which father-to-be has to wear artificial bellies and complete pre-natal yoga courses. Through such devices, men could have a better understanding of their wives' pain and hardship.

However, obvious shortages still lie in these products and services:

Firstly, some of the products do not effectively simulate the pregnant experience that women have. Wearable devices should be placed on the abdomen to simulate the experience to the greatest extent.

Secondly, most of the products and services cannot be used in daily life, which means couples can only share experience in a certain period of time. When the father-to-be go back from working, he will lose the connection with the fetal.

Therefore, the following part is intended to improve the two shortages above-mentioned and especially address the following question: Can a design solution of wearable device enable male to experience fetal heartbeats and movements when they are working through as vivid experience as possible? Specifically, the goal can be further separated into two main points: the detection of fetal movements and heartbeats and the simulation of such signals against skin. To realize these goals, the technologies available in existing products are researched.

2.1 Products Measuring Fetal Heartbeat and Movement

The platform JD.COM (an e-commerce platform famous for selling electronic products in China) was chosen for collecting information of related products on sale.

All products that can measure fetal heartbeats and movements are arranged according to sales volume and different brands and functions. The technique principle, function, usage and registration time of each product is recorded and the information is then summarized and compared (see Fig. 1).

Generally, the product *Mengdong* is especially small in size and light in weight owing to the passive mode tech of detection. Considering that many women keep working at 7 months of pregnancy, the wearable product should be as small as possible. The size of Mengdong is about 60 mm*60 mm*5 mm and the weight is around 15 g, so it is quite suitable to wear at work. Considering the tech modes, active mode tech of detection is not appropriate in this case because of its complicated use flow. Passive detecting tech, on the other hand, is based on stethoscope principle so there is no extra radiation when measuring the fetal heartbeats.

When analyzing the products according to the timeline, it clearly shows that the combination of software and hardware equipment has gradually become the mainstream of the market. Supplementary application is usually designed to provide detailed data and records for users. And sometimes related services such as exercising suggestions and medical advices are provided.

Tech of Detection

▪▪ Active mode (Doppler baby's heart instrument)
▪▪ Passive mode (Principle of stethoscope)

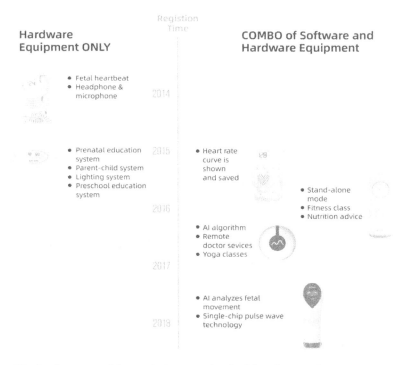

Fig. 1. Summary of the products measuring fetal heartbeats and movements

2.2   Products Prodding Against Skin

In order to simulate the experience of fetal movements and fetal heartbeats through a wearable device on abdomen, two choices are available: mechanical vibration and low-frequency electrical pulse stimulation. The stimulus intensity should be limited in a certain range, so that the device will not bring trouble to the father-to-be in working. In this respect, the wearable products with the function of massage can provide similar functions, and are especially studied as technique references.

Considering the size and weight of the product, we find the products based on TENS quite suitable. Transcutaneous electrical nerve stimulation, TENS in short, is a treatment method that delivers pulsed electrical currents across the intact surface of the skin so as to achieve the purpose of relieving pain [3]. The technique is inexpensive, noninvasive and self-administered. According to meta-analysis by Johnson, TENS techniques can be divided into conventional TENS and acupuncture-like TENS. The former one uses low intensity and high frequency currents, while the latter one uses high intensity and low frequency currents, which will provide stronger stimulation on the skin. The device used to simulate the fetal heartbeats and movements can refer to the conventional TENS technique. And the frequency, wave width, and intensity range of currents must be strictly controlled. Users should feel comfortable when placing the de-vice on abdomen and there should be no muscle contraction reaction.

Referring to the related products on sale, the massage instruments based on TENS can be divided into two part, the host and the patch. The host is responsible for outputting suitable low-frequency electrical currents. The patches have electrodes that fit the locations of the lesion and can deliver electrical stimuli to the skin. The normal size of the host part is about 50 mm*50 mm*15 mm, and the size of the patches depends on different locations they are going to fit.

To sum up, TENS is an ideal solution to prod against skin. When regenerating the feeling of fetal movements, a suitable number of pressure sensors and electrodes positions can be set, and the intensity of pressure can be converted into corresponding levels of currents frequency and intensity. When regenerating the feeling of fetal heartbeats, the wearable device can control the frequency of the output electrical stimulation to keep it the same as the real fetal heart rate.

3 Design and Implementation

3.1 Design Concept

According to the research above, the user needs can be identified: enhance males' consciousness of being a father and encourage them to be more proactive in caring for the fetus and wife. Studies have shown that if parents take care of their baby personally, their parental awareness will rise significantly [6]. Creating connections between father-to-be and fetus might be useful to encourage male to pay more attention to fetus.

The main purpose of this design is to lead male to spend more time on caring for fetus and their wives. A wearable device for father-to-be, which enables male to feel the fetal heartbeats and movements in real time, may fulfill this purpose. But which part of a day is appropriate for a working father-to-be to have some connections and interactions with their fetus? And how could they interact with fetus naturally? As the connection and interaction between mother-to-be and fetal are instinctive, women's behaviors and habits could be good answers to these questions.

Structured interviews are carried out on women who have given birth to a baby recently. The four subjects range from 25 to 35 in age and are now living in Shanghai, China. They all gave birth to a baby within a year when the interview was conducted. The questions are about how they and their husbands arrange a day in their six month's pregnancy, when they interact with their fetus and how they react to fetal movements.

After the interviews were performed, we summarize the behavior patterns of male and female in an experience board (see Fig. 2). From the board we can see clearly where opportunities lie for men to pay attention to fetus and communicate more with their wives.

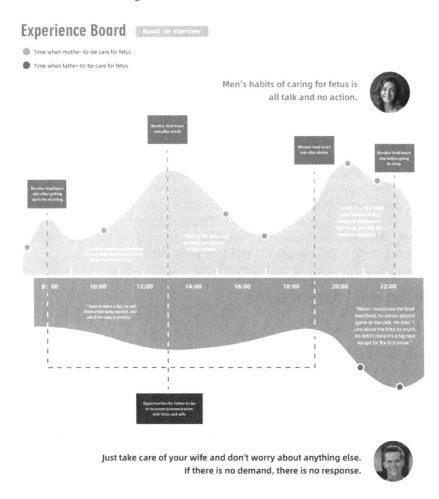

Fig. 2. Experience board of a working day of the couples in six month's pregnancy

Generally, Mother-to-be interact with fetus 10 times a day on average and monitor fetus heartbeats 4-8 times varying from person to person. By contrast, father-to-be only think of fetus after work and no more than twice a day. As females usually monitor fetal heartbeat during morning, evening and short break after meals, these time periods can be the opportunity for reminding working males to pay attention to fetus without influencing their work. The habits are easier to maintain with a regular and feasible time plan.

The interviewees agreed that feeling fetal heartbeats and movements can stimulate their sense of responsibility. So the real-time experience sharing may have the same effect on males, improving their sense of participation and strengthening the connection between them and fetus.

When it comes to the way of interacting with fetus, all female mentioned petting and touching as the most frequent way. We take it as reference of the design of the interaction way between father-to-be and their wearable device to add verisimilitude. The whole system design and interaction will be interpreted in details in the next part.

3.2   System Design

The main functions of the design concept include: detecting and collecting the fetal heartbeats and movements data, data transmission with the mobile phone terminal as well as simulating the fetal heartbeats and movements experience. Based on deliberate data collection and technology research (as discussed in Sects. 2.1 and 2.2), it can be proved that this design concept is technologically feasible and creative.

The appearance and scenario for mother-to-be and father-to-be are shown below (see Fig. 3 and Fig. 4).

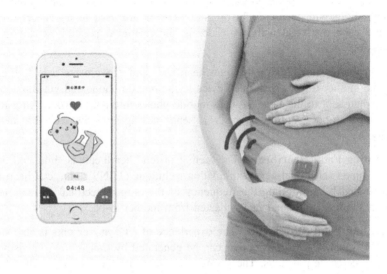

Fig. 3. Babe: scenario for mother-to-be

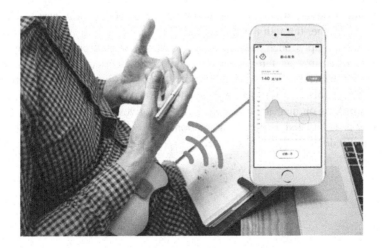

Fig. 4. Babe: scenario for father-to-be

The main functions of *Babe* are performed as follows:

Fetal Heartbeats Detection. Whenever mother-to-be wants to monitor the fetus's status, she can paste *Babe* on the abdomen and start detecting by pressing the open button on the side of the host part. If the device is working, a breathing light will display according to the rate of the detected heart rate. Fetal heartbeats data can be collected from mother-to-be through the passive stethoscope fetal heart rate measurement technology.

Fetal Movements Detection. When mother-to-be intends to monitor the fetal movements, she can paste *Babe* on the abdomen and double press the open button and an indicator light will be on. Eight pressure sensors are used to tag the positions and measure each one's intensity, considering the restricted position sensitivity of the human abdomen.

Data Transmission. All of the fetal heartbeats and movements data is transmitted from the mother-to-be's wearable device to the mobile phone end via Bluetooth. And data is then sent to the father-to-be's mobile phone through network. After receiving data, father-to-be's mobile phone will send messages to his wearable device via Bluetooth.

Generating Fetal Heartbeats. The feeling of fetal heartbeats is simulated using the transcutaneous electrical nerve stimulation technique (TENS). The fetal heart rate can be generated by controlling the frequency of the output electrical currents to be the same as the real-time heart rate collected from mother-to-be.

Generating Fetal Movements. The experience of fetal movements is also simulated using TENS. The fetal movements can be generated by transmitting intensity data to different electrode positions. The stronger the intensity, the higher the intensity of the currents and the lower the frequency. There is a strictly controlled mapping relationship between the pressure intensity level (the mother-to-be's device) and the feature of the currents (the father-to-be's device).

Feedback and Conversation. During the process of detecting, both parents can send message to each other through the application. If father-to-be is busy with his work, he can answer it by simply touch *Babe*, just like mother-to-be comfort the fetus by petting it. And in the meantime, an auto message will be sent to the mother-to-be's application, for example "I am feeling my baby now! Sorry that I am busy with my work now". After a monitor process is finished, a detailed report of the status of the fetus will be sent to both parents on their applications. The report gives advice on whether the fetus is healthy or needs related medical examination. And both parents can share the report with the family doctor for further advice.

4 Usability Test

4.1 Method: Lab Experiment

We enrolled 4 participants (2 males, 2 females) from Shanghai as participants for a user experiment. The average age of the couples was 30.0 years old and had given birth to a baby within 2 years (SD 2.12). The participants were asked to go to the lab in the morning (about 10 a.m.) and were instructed to fill in a questionnaire in different rooms. The questionnaire investigates how much they were aware of their identity as a mother/father during the sixth month of pregnancy. In the meantime, they were informed that the test was to investigate whether experience sharing can affect the awareness of parent identity.

After that, the participants were kept separated and we explained how Babe works. Different experiments were designed for male and female. On one hand, for male participants, they were asked to imagine that their wives were at their sixth month of pregnancy and paste Babe on their abdomen. The fetal heart rate and movement were given by a researcher in another room. The male subjects were asked to fill in the questionnaire again after experiencing the functions of Babe. On the other hand, for female participants, they were asked to paste a device with TENS on their abdomen and evaluate how much it was similar to the feeling of fetal movements.

The last step is to ask the participants' opinion on the color, modelling, weight, wearing experience and other suggestions on Babe.

4.2 Method: Heuristic Evaluation

Since the prototype is mainly operated by mother-to-be, we enrolled only five female participants to complete the usability test. According to the rule proposed by Nielsen, 85% of the product usability problems can be found under the condition of involving five participants. So five is an economical number for testing [17]. The average age of the participants was 22.2 years old (SD 0.97). The test method is heuristic evaluation as this test was carried out for finding problems and iteration [11]. The participants were asked to finish three tasks which could cover the main functions. The completion time, rate and subject evaluation of each participant are all recorded.

5 Results

5.1 Usability of the Wearable Devices

The usability of the Wearable Device can be divided into three parts: how much can it inspire the awareness of being a father, how much is it similar to the real fetal movements and how much the participants like the appearance and using experience do.

Firstly, how much can it inspire the awareness of being a father? Male subjects rated their awareness of being a father on average 4.5/10 before using Babe, from 1 "totally have no awareness" to 10 "be fully aware of being a father". After using Babe, the average score rose to 6.5/10 (both male subjects' rated higher). Com-pared to the average score of the awareness of being a mother (8.0/10), males' awareness was still lower despite the fact that it had risen after experience sharing. This result could be partly affected by the faked experiment condition and the limited experience time.

Secondly, how much is it similar to the real fetal movements? Female subjects rated the similarity on average 3.5/5 after experiencing Babe. One participant gave comments like "I think it is quite like the experience of my baby kicking the belly".

The last aspect is how much the participants like the appearance and using experience. All the four participants showed preference in color and weight, both on average 4.75/5, from 1 "totally dislike" to 5 "like very much". Babe got a lower score in modelling and wearing experience, both on average 3.50/5. The male participants stated that they would appreciate sports style more than the gentle design style. And for wearing experience they worried that when sitting down or standing up Babe might loose and drop from the abdomen. The most mentioned problem is that the patch feels very cold when it contacts with the skin, which could cause discomfort.

5.2 Usability of the Supportive Application

Except for a participant failed in task two because of misunderstanding the task, all the participants successfully finished the three tasks within the reference time. Hence, the efficiency and effectiveness of Babe can be proved. And the participants on average rated 1.4/5 in difficulty and 4.4/5 in favorability. Only one participant gave suggestion that "Some instructions can be shown when detecting the fetal movements and heartbeats, or I will be a little confused about what to do as it takes such long time".

6   Limitations and Future Work

We observed effective interactions between father and fetus through the wearable device Babe, yet the number of participants (n = 4) is limited. The main reason is that subjects who have experienced birth-giving recently is quite difficult to recruit. However, it is necessary to carry out experiments and usability tests in a proper sample size, which will make the results more valid and collect more valuable suggestions on Babe. Therefore, a larger-scale user experiment will be conducted.

Due to the fact that the completeness of the prototype is limited by our ability of applying technology, it is impossible to conduct experiments in a real-life environment. The effect of wearing Babe for long time still need to be investigated, and it might be different from the short-time experience tested in this paper. Therefore, our next step is to enhance the technical design and organize longer experiment session.

Moreover, some people, mainly males, may doubt whether it is convenient for them to wear the device for a whole day, especially when they are working. The specific way of using Babe can also be further studied.

The novelty of the research lies in the creative interaction way between father and fetus and the new idea of alleviating gender conflicts through experience sharing. Babe provides the possibility for males to experience fetal heartbeats and movements on their own body. Through the new way of interaction, an artificial connection between father and fetus was achieved. Males can feel the fetus and comfort the fetus just like what females do. As a result, the father-to-be's habits of childcare can be naturally culti-vated, and the mother-to-be's pressure of parenting can be shared. What's more, we tried to solve gender issues from the design perspective. We believe that if the two genders can understand each other better and feel what the other feel, there will be more tolerance and care instead of suspicion and indifference.

References

1. Alio, A.P., Lewis, C.A., Scarborough, K., Harris, K., Fiscella, K.: A community perspective on the role of fathers during pregnancy: a qualitative study. BMC Pregnancy Childbirth **13**(1), 60 (2013). https://doi.org/10.1186/1471-2393-13-60
2. Bird, C.E., Rieker, P.P.: Gender matters: an integrated model for understanding men's and women's health. Soc. Sci. Med. **48**(6), 745–755 (1999)
3. Bøe, C.A.: Women and Family in contemporary urban China; contested female individualisation, Master's thesis. The University of Bergen (2013)
4. Carpenter, V.J., Overholt, D.: Designing for meaningfulness: a case study of a pregnancy wearable for men. In: Proceedings of the 2017 ACM Conference Companion Publication on Designing Interactive Systems, pp. 95–100. ACM (2017)
5. Craig, L.: Does father care mean fathers share? A comparison of how mothers and fathers in intact families spend time with children. Gender Soc. **20**(2), 259–281 (2006)
6. Erlandsson, K., Christensson, K., Fagerberg, I.: Fathers' lived experiences of getting to know their baby while acting as primary caregivers immediately following birth. J. Perinat. Educ. **17**(2), 28 (2008)
7. Giurgescu, C., Templin, T.: Father involvement and psychological well-being of pregnant women. MCN. Am. J. Matern. Child Nurs. **40**(6), 381 (2015)
8. How painful is childbirth? Men experience birth and everyone screams "unbearable". http://news.sina.com.cn/o/2017-05-12/doc-ifyfekhi7442437.shtml. Accessed 16 Jan 2020
9. Johnson, M.I.: Transcutaneous electrical nerve stimulation (TENS). e LS (2001)
10. Kosaka, T., Misumi, H., Iwamoto, T., Songer, R., Akita, J.: "Mommy tummy" a pregnancy experience system simulating fetal movement. In: ACM SIGGRAPH 2011 Emerging Technologies, p. 1 (2011)
11. Nielsen, J., Molich, R.: Heuristic evaluation of user interfaces. In: Proceedings of the SIGCHI Conference on Human factors in Computing Systems, pp. 249–256 (1990)
12. Piers Morgan experiences labour pain through a simulator and is left SCREAMING and begging for the 'torture' to stop on GMB, 8 May 2019. https://www.dailymail.co.uk/femail/article-7004973/Piers-Morgan-left-agony-experienced-pain-labour-simulator-GMB.html. Accessed 16 Jan 2020
13. Silver, C.: Being there: The time dual-earner couples spend with their children. Can. Soc. Trends **57**(11–008), 26–30 (2000)
14. Stapleton, L.R.T., Schetter, C.D., Westling, E., Rini, C., Glynn, L.M., Hobel, C.J., Sandman, C.A.: Perceived partner support in pregnancy predicts lower maternal and infant distress. J. Fam. Psychol. **26**(3), 453 (2012)
15. Stockman, N.: Understanding Chinese Society. Wiley, Hoboken (2013)
16. Three Pregnant Dads. The Book of Everyone, 12 May 2006. http://3pregnantdads.com/. Accessed 16 Jan 2020
17. Why You Only Need to Test with 5 Users, 18 March 2000. https://www.nngroup.com/articles/why-you-only-need-to-test-with-5-users/. Accessed 22 Jan 2020

18. Widarsson, M., Engström, G., Tydén, T., Lundberg, P., Hammar, L.M.: 'Paddling upstream': fathers' involvement during pregnancy as described by expectant fathers and mothers. J. Clin. Nurs. **24**(7–8), 1059–1068 (2015)
19. Xue, W.L., He, H.G., Chua, Y.J., Wang, W., Shorey, S.: Factors influencing first time fathers' involvement in their wives' pregnancy and childbirth: a correlational study. Midwifery **62**, 20–28 (2018)
20. Yan, Y.: The Chinese path to individualization. Br. J. Sociol. **61**(3), 489–512 (2010)

Designing Human-Centered Interactions for Smart Environments Based on Heterogeneous, Interrelated Systems: A User Research Method for the "Age of Services" (URSERVe)

Alexandra Matz[1][✉] and Clarissa Götz[2]

[1] S/4HANA Industries User Experience, SAP SE,
Walldorf, Germany
alexandra.matz@sap.com
[2] Digital Supply Chain User Experience, SAP SE, Walldorf, Germany
clarissa.goetz@sap.com

Abstract. Heterogeneous, interrelated systems leveraging the Internet of Things (IoT) in smart environments such as a smart factory or smart city, pose many challenges for software design and development. Capturing and addressing the human needs is one of them and designing the interactions within smart applications is another. There are several reasons for this, for example diverse personas for both human as well as digital actors, a large variety of usage scenarios, a vast number of data exchange protocols, as well as data privacy and ethical concerns.

On top of this, the service-based architecture of smart environments has widened the gap between software development teams and their end users. Services are highly modular, decoupled units of application logic, developed for specific task units and as such they are one or even several hierarchy layers removed from the business logic of main applications, and, in consequence, from the applications' users. Therefore, in our experience, service development groups often refrain from identifying their users and doing any kind of user research at all. The reasoning being that, because their services will only be used by applications or other services, and not directly by human or non-human users, these users cannot be identified at all or are of no importance. This paper proposes a bidirectional, complementary method to approach user research for smart environments, such as smart cities. It describes how service development teams can reach beyond the applications which consume their service to the users of these consuming apps and how, at the same time, the smart city projects can reap the benefits of the technological expertise that resides in the service development groups. Ultimately, the method helps to create a shared knowledge base which arguably fosters innovation within an organization responsible for the design, development and operation of smart environments.

Keywords: Human-centered design · Knowledge management · Microservices · User centered design · User experience · User research · Services · Smart cities · Smart environments · Smart factory

© Springer Nature Switzerland AG 2020
A. Marcus and E. Rosenzweig (Eds.): HCII 2020, LNCS 12201, pp. 99–116, 2020.
https://doi.org/10.1007/978-3-030-49760-6_7

1 Introduction

The continuous advancement of Information Technology (IT) has caused devices to become smaller and faster at an ever-increasing rate. In the Internet of Things (IoT), both humans and things enjoy instant access to innovative digital products and services. These enable them, via the Cloud, to connect with each other and retrieve, use and store data at any time and from anywhere. Gone are the days when people had to observe office opening hours in order to speak with or obtain information from authorities or organizations. Today, such information can be exchanged 24 h a day and without human-to-human interaction via Websites and other cloud-supported platforms. Real-time updates of public transport schedules help commuters catch the nearest bus to their destination or enjoy a leisurely cup of coffee instead of waiting for their delayed train on a cold station platform. Air quality sensors installed at busy thoroughfares report measurements to citizen apps, which alert their users to take protective measures before leaving home or take an alternative route. Specialized devices built into production machines, construction equipment or sustainability monitoring facilities detect the smallest deviations from normal operations and enable corrective or preventive measures.

These are only a few examples to illustrate how smart environments, specifically smart cities and smart factories, are made possible by the availability and interoperability of a vast numbers of sensors, audio or video recording and processing devices, and other digital equipment. They are operated either by people ("human-to-machine interaction") or by autonomous, intelligent systems ("machine-to-machine interaction") [10]. The basis of these interactions are applications which consume and combine any number of software "services" as well as the underlying technological architecture, all of which are connected and enabled by IoT technology. Cook and Das [5] define smart environments as "a small world where all kinds of smart devices are continuously working to make inhabitants' lives more comfortable". Pourzolfaghar and Helfert [22] add that through utilization of the technology which connects and links data in the Internet, individualized, user friendly applications can be provided to these inhabitants. In a smart city, "inhabitants" represent all kind of actors, such as citizens, commuters, visitors etc. They are either direct/active (e.g. someone using a city's weather app) or indirect/passive (e.g. a late-night stroller whose walk through the park is lit up by smart streetlights) users of applications fused into the smart city's technological landscape. In a smart factory, the "inhabitants" are users working and interacting with production machines or being assisted in their tasks by robotic and autonomous, intelligent systems [17]. These systems, again, are linked through IoT technology in order to increase the efficiency, sustainability and safety of the production process [27].

1.1 Effects of a Growing User Base in Smart Environments

A key priority of human computer interaction (HCI) and user experience (UX) is understanding human users' needs and, by applying human-centered design methodologies, helping to solve the users' challenges in their use of technology or when navigating the numerous services on offer in a smart city or smart factory. For the purpose of this paper and the methodology described therein, both the human inhabitants of the real world and the intelligent things, devices, systems and applications (as the humans' digital counterparts) are considered users of, or actors in, a smart environment.

Capturing and analyzing the needs of the diverse actors with research methods and catering for them when designing and developing appropriate software solutions poses a number of challenges. These actors are involved in large variety of usage scenarios, with a vast number of data exchange protocols, and numerous distributed computing platforms available to store and interpret smart data [15]. Moreover, these actors no longer exist and act within known and established geographic, social or demographic boundaries - in smart environments they may start to figure in new, unheard-of contexts that are hard to predict or research. Therefore it is no surprise that the personas (as user research artefacts) for both human and digital actors tend to be undefined and blurry [19]. Data privacy and ethical concerns also must be considered when designing and developing for smart environments. Examples are the non-exclusion of individuals from smart offerings, caused, for example, by unaffordable technology [26], biased decisions of systems or administrators, or the right of citizens to own their data processed in smart cities.

1.2   Effects of a Deconstructed Software Architecture in Smart Environments

For a long time in software development, the ratio between user and application or backend functionality seemed to be relatively manageable. It could be described, for example, as one-user-to-one-application (1:1) or maybe one-to-many (1:n) or many-to-one (n:1), only rarely was it many-to-many (n:n). With the rise of the IoT technology and its distributed, decomposed service architecture, developing a software product today often means providing functionality by selecting and combining any number of suitable services or micro services ("Age of (Micro-)Services" [20]). The resulting effect is that the ratio today is not only between user and application but between user and potentially many services called by different applications. Now, the ratio tends to be many-to-many (n:n), where the n on either side of the colon potentially represents a very high number of unknown elements, for example human and non-human actors, applications, (business) services or microservices. Trying to get a handle on all the possible actor – app – service – microservice interaction possibilities and mapping them out is difficult.

Considering that it has already been a challenge for software developers to keep up with their users' needs and requirements in the past, this is becoming an even more daunting task in smart environments. Not only because today's software development lifecycle for cloud products is high-paced, and products often are developed in an agile setup and shipped through continuous delivery, but also because the number of potential actors and usage scenarios seems too huge to handle. This can lead to developers claiming that, since their service or microservice is not exposed to the user directly, any knowledge about the user or usage context is of no relevance or consequence to them or their product. Oftentimes the sheer complexity and difficulty of mapping out the potential users causes development teams, especially those who develop (micro)services, to throw in the towel, often to the detriment of a user-friendly and adequate product.

1.3   The Proposed Approach for Smart Environments

The approach described in this paper aims to overcome this deadlock by disentangling the n:n relationship described above to a certain degree, and helping service development teams to better understand which actors they are developing for. In a pragmatic view of the world, an actor's (in this case, a person or an IoT device) goal is to make informed decisions (e.g. to walk the dog by a different route because of bad air quality) while the goal of the developers of software solutions, all the way down to individual (micro)services is to enable this decision making process, using the big data, machine leaning and cloud capabilities and tools available to them.

The method we propose for this purpose is illustrated in Fig. 1 and can be described as a double-sided funnel which ensures a high coverage of actor needs by (a) funneling these needs, for example, the results from user research, into the design process of an application, business service or (micro)service (left funnel: outside-in), and by (b) identifying the services, applications, and consumers of (micro)services based on the knowledge of the development team (right funnel: inside-out). The information collected via the two funnels is fed into a defined space for knowledge sharing. Working collaboratively and iteratively with the information in the shared knowledge space, the involved project teams can make informed decisions about the (micro)services to be developed, taking into consideration all their possible users and actors. In the proposed method, the "shared knowledge space" is not a physical space. Rather it is the concept and the provision of all that is required for people to collaborate and may comprise room, technology, infrastructure, material, time, mental space, permission, in

Fig. 1. The double-sided funnel to collect outside-in and inside-out information for knowledge sharing

short: everything that fosters knowledge sharing among experts. This may differ depending on individual project circumstances.

This guided approach to proactively get experts to share their information from both outside-in and inside-out, became necessary because of, and was developed in response to, the effects described in Sects. 1.1 and 1.2.

By and large, the knowledge generated from the "outside-in" and the "inside-out", as described in Fig. 1, is owned by different persons or stakeholders in a software development project. Knowledge about the users and usage scenarios typically rests with user researchers or other UX roles, whereas the knowledge owners of technology trends and the different technologies incl. their capabilities and limitations are the software developers/architects. Business process and market related knowledge is owned by product management. This knowledge is not necessarily shared between these stakeholders by default, if at all.

The benefits and user research methods for the outside-in approach have been extensively discussed for example in [1, 7, 13, 14, 24], and therefore will not be covered in this paper. The description of the proposed method focuses on how service development teams can reach beyond the applications which consume their service to the actors that use their services either directly or indirectly via these applications. In this method, which is described in detail in Sect. 3, the guided sharing of expert knowledge is a key enabler.

2 The "Smart City" Project – A Real Business Case and Testbed for the URSERVe Method

The method presented in this paper was developed during the assignment of the authors as User Experience Researchers to the IoT topic and a smart city project within a major enterprise software company between 2015 to 2017. After the initial concept of the smart city project was implemented by international city authorities (e.g. Buenos Aires [2]), the method was extended and refined alongside follow-on projects in 2018 and 2019.

2.1 Focus on Smart Lighting

The smart city project focused specifically on smart lighting scenarios and belonged to one of several coordinated work streams for smart cities that the company has been running over a longer period of time. Smart lighting can be seen as a fundamental component for smart cities [21]. Smart lighting [28] refers to intelligent, technology-enabled ways of managing and optimizing the energy consumption of a city's lighting systems, as well as the efficiency and speed of their maintenance. It further refers to extending an existing or future lighting infrastructure and outdoor luminaires by equipping them with smart technologies such as wireless hotspots and repeaters, sensors (air quality, precipitation etc.), motion detector equipment or even electric mobility charging points. This enables the connected, centralized management of lighting operations, for example, smart guiding of human and motor traffic, emergency routing through variable intensity of light, and the transmission of sensor data to a backend system where data is analyzed, and appropriate actions can be triggered.

Some scenarios of the smart lighting project that were implemented in global cities included: the optimization of the lighting network and management with a focus on cost reduction and citizen participation (e.g. through predictive maintenance and citizen-enabled reporting of defects), improved security and emergency responses (e.g. through monitoring of weather conditions, or motion behavior analysis and change stimulation [15]) and advanced sustainability management (e.g. through adaptive traffic or parking navigation, based on environmental measures or the frequency and quantity of cars).

2.2   The Left Side of the Funnel: Input from Market and User Research

The project was conducted under the umbrella of a "Co-Innovation Lab (SAP COIL)". A co-innovation setup enables customer or company-internal projects to join up and collaborate with external experts from partnering organizations. The goal is to identify and embrace new technology opportunities and foster innovation in a legally safe environment with regard to intellectual property, and the provision of appropriate technical infrastructure [4].

The core smart city project team was convinced that by including the potential users and actors in a smart lighting context, and inviting them to provide opinions, insights, challenges or needs ("observable, tacit and latent" [6]) about their experience in a city environment, it could build user-accepted smart solutions and more solid, future-proof technical or administrative services. Therefore, in the early project phase, intensive market and user research activities were conducted in a close cooperation of product managers, user researchers, development architects as well as technical/solution experts for lighting or wireless technology and sensor equipment, from both internal departments and partnering companies.

The goal was to identify relevant scenarios through opportunity assessment, involvement of users, workshops for idea generation and early prototyping. To obtain input from the future active or passive users of a smart lighting solution, extensive participatory user research activities were performed, such as contextual interviews, observations, surveys (online and in-person), the definition and validation of personas and storyboards, as well as co-creation and validation of prototypes. Figure 2 below illustrates the manifold participating human and non-human actors (the latter being represented by the respective human technical experts): Citizens and visitors to the city (commuters, shoppers, sports fans, tourists etc.), city planning officials, urban light designers or light management personnel, service planning and maintenance staff, city administrators for sustainability and finance.

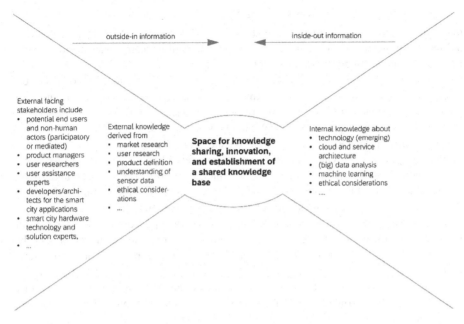

External facing
stakeholders include
* potential end users
  and non-human
  actors (participatory
  or mediated)
* product managers
* user researchers
* user assistance
  experts
* developers/archi-
  tects for the smart
  city applications
* smart city hardware
  technology and
  solution experts,
* ...

External knowledge
derived from
* market research
* user research
* product definition
* understanding of
  sensor data
* ethical consider-
  ations
* ...

**Space for knowledge
sharing, innovation,
and establishment of
a shared knowledge
base**

Internal knowledge about
* technology (emerging)
* cloud and service
  architecture
* (big) data analysis
* machine learning
* ethical considerations
* ....

outside-in information

inside-out information

Fig. 2. The outside-in stakeholders

The data collected in these activities was extensive and multi-faceted. In addition to filling the human-centered, outside-in funnel of the USERVe method for the smart lighting project, the information generated benefitted further smart city projects later on. One of these was a "smart waste management" solution which was implemented by the City of Heidelberg, Germany [12].

2.3 Right Side of the Funnel: Input from Internal Technical Experts

Up till now, software solutions were rather monolithic [16], usually combining all relevant functional and technical capabilities, such as user interface (UI), application logic and database management under one architecture model. Such applications range from small, consumer focused apps with a limited set of functions and use cases to large scale business solutions, such as production planning or service maintenance systems. Business applications may span several business processes and scenarios within the given domain, each of which covering various use cases in which humans interact with application interfaces.

Technically speaking, monolithic applications can also have their architecture layers and functions decomposed into modules, to enable reuse within the application system and for better scalability, e.g. when equipped with application programming interfaces (APIs) that can be accessed from within a system or outside of it. In this situation, the design and development of small, related applications typically can be handled by few teams or team members, and the chances of close collaboration and knowledge exchange theoretically are relatively high.

Large-scale applications or business solutions, however, usually are developed by many development teams in different disciplines (UI design, UI development, technology or application specific development etc.) as well as teams catering for centralized tools and technology such as database management. The multi-team setup of large-scale development projects requires tight and well managed collaboration between the different roles and between the teams. Sharing the knowledge required to jointly build an adequate application is no small feat, and in our experience the potential knowledge gap is particularly wide between user centered information on the one side and the technological expertise on the other. Still, even such a large-scale project setup has the advantage that all project stakeholders usually are aware of the involved applications, the user interfaces with their respective users and the underlying business processes. Identifying the users of such systems and gaining empathy for them through user research activities and artifacts such as personas (prototypical users) is still manageable. Personas represent the key users of an application, and in the case of monolithic applications, typically the following user-to-application ratios can be observed: many-to-one (n:1), i.e. different key users access parts of one monolithic application (e.g. the planning function and the scheduling function), one-to-many (1:n), i.e. one user accesses several (sub-) applications and the underlying architecture through one user interface. Non-human actors also feature in monolithic applications. Like human actors, they can be identified and integrated more readily as their functions and data requirements are easier to define in the application scope. This scope may be large, but nevertheless it is still bounded.

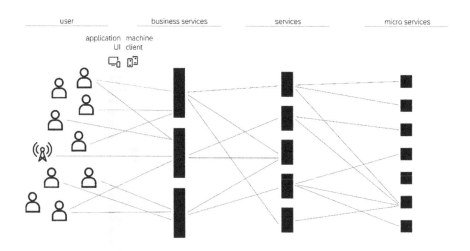

Fig. 3. user:application ratio with service hierarchy (simplified)

In contrast to this, in smart environments which, like most cloud based applications, are based on a service architecture, the functional decomposition into sets of services [16] is a standard paradigm, offering partitions of very small (microservices) to small (services) sized functionality which communicate through interface calls. Supported by new techniques of modularization and virtualization through packaging software in containers [20], this allows for scalable, reusable and reliable architecture landscapes. In the SAP Cloud Platform architecture, on which the smart city project was based, (micro)services are meshed up with services providing business specific application content (so called Business Services [9]). And these Business Services, in turn, can be consumed by yet a larger system or application, approximating the functional scope of a monolithic application as described above. Such a hierarchy of services is illustrated in Fig. 3.

From the perspective of a (micro)service, this architecture allows for potentially unlimited numbers and types of human and non-human users on the left side of the user:application ratio. Likewise, there are endless possible combinations and permutations of the (micro)services on the right side of the user:application ratio. The ratio to reckon with here typically is n:n.

The development teams of (micro)services and the respective internal experts (see Fig. 4) have a difficult task understanding the larger usage contexts and the various actors of their services when these are consumed in a multi-layer architecture. This is especially true if they are developing "in limbo", that is, disconnected from the application layer, which was the case in the smart city project. In the prototyping phase of the project, and after the extensive market and user research activities, the project team had validated use cases and other documented requirements regarding the services underlying the planned smart city solution. However, until they were contacted by the smart city project team, the responsible service development teams had created their (micro)services primarily under functional aspects alone. They had not thought of tracking or finding out which business services and applications, and ultimately which actors were consuming their services.

To ensure that the smart city solution provides the most innovative and appropriate services to their actors meant involving the service teams with their technical and subject matter experience, so that stakeholders from both ends of the spectrum (i.e. the funnels, see Fig. 4) could share and integrate their knowledge - the human-centered and the technical (see also Pourzolfaghar and Helfert [22] or Ryan and O'Connor [23]). The former makes for application pull, whereas the latter provides the technology push [15]. Referencing Dell'Era and Landoni's classification of smart city case studies [6], our approach enabled the project to move towards an open, user-involving mode and thus embrace both a "value capturing" (innovating with existing technology) and a "value creating" strategy (innovating with possibilities of new technology).

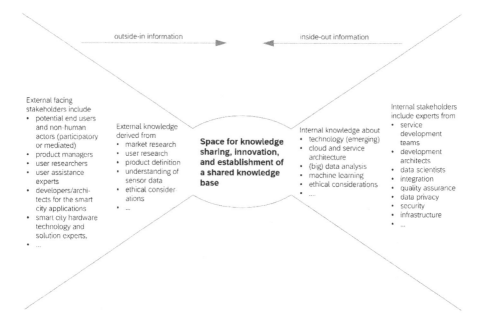

Fig. 4. The stakeholders in the outside-in and inside-out processes of the funnels

3   The URSERVe Method

Our method draws on findings from research on knowledge management, in particular the position that expert knowledge as held by individuals is primarily tacit [18] and that not all team members of a software project necessarily know everything it takes to develop their product [23]. Bringing tacit expert knowledge out into the open and sharing it among the team, for example, face-to-face in a workshop setting, is of utmost importance to the success of a software product.

3.1   Goals of the Method

Faced with the challenges described above, and in an attempt to address them and mitigate their effects, we defined a set of methodological goals for the smart city project. These goals were later generalized and adapted in the URSERVe method to be used by other smart environment projects. They are:

– Determine the teams and stakeholders that need to collaborate
  Identifying all relevant teams or stakeholders and completing the overall team set-up can be complicated, especially in a decomposed service architecture. It is an iterative, step-by-step process, potentially spanning several project phases. In the smart city project, the project team was already large, collaborating closely with and bringing in a diverse set of experts: users, product management, UX experts, development architects, user assistance, sales experts, from both the business software company and from partnering companies. Once all the user and actor

requirements were available and the necessary services identified, the representatives from the service development teams needed to be included.

- Share and manage the diverse expert knowledge (human-centered, business, market, technical) of the project team and the affected service development teams
  This goal focuses on detecting, compiling and bringing out in the open the various stakeholders' expert knowledge about the requirements, challenges and expectations from the actors on the one side and the current and future possibilities and limitations of technology, all the way down to the (micro)services on the other. The shared information is the basis for innovative and appropriate design of smart city solutions.
- Develop a shared stakeholder language
  When sharing knowledge, learning must have taken place beforehand or it happens at the moment of sharing. Jointly arriving at a common understanding or "project language" that is shared by all actors and stakeholders in a smart environment project helps to discuss and share knowledge. "A language is an ecosystem functional to information exchange. It is alive, dynamic and flexible, evolving according to the needs of its community of speakers" [8].
  The members of a software development project team already have quite different backgrounds and roles (information or data scientist, business experts, UI designers, to name a few), each talking in their particular lingo and using their own terminology. Looking at the potential actors in a smart environment there is even more diversity, starting from someone walking in a park in the dark, to professionals responsible for designing elements of a smart city, such as architects and urban planners. Each of them speaks a different "expert language". The language and the way people convey their knowledge needs a joint and moderated space where listening, translating between "expert languages", and learning enable the effective sharing of knowledge. This aspect becomes even more relevant in smart environments, where knowledge is not only created by human actors but also by IoT devices, sensors, the analysis of Big Data or social network sentiments. This learning contributes to the overall knowledge of a project or organization and ultimately to its economic success [11].
- Create an environment that fosters human-centered innovation opportunities (a shared knowledge space)
  Innovation can happen on different levels, for example the technological, societal or economic. To avoid the possible loss of innovation opportunities due to missing knowledge sharing, one explicit goal is to create a knowledge sharing space to invite synergies of knowledge, help create ideas beyond given organizational affiliations or hierarchies and functional boundaries, and take advantage of established innovation methods such as Design Thinking workshops. Human actors were explicitly included both indirectly, by capturing and funneling their needs and challenges into the shared knowledge space through user research and directly, for example by their participation in workshops, to draw on their creativity as the future users of smart city offerings.
- Document results and build up a knowledge repository other projects can profit from

After having created a knowledge space to elicit and share the tacit knowledge that resided with individual experts [25], the need to capture and document this knowledge and disseminate it to other stakeholders and projects was formulated as another goal. This documentation could be in the form of personas, best practice guides and other information artifacts, to be reused and added to with own findings by subsequent projects. This increases the organization's knowledge base and helps to avoid duplicate efforts.

– Meta goal: Document the URSERVe method
  The final goal was to track the evolvement of the method as it is being used in additional projects, and to continually improve and document it as a guided process and best practice for user researchers and other project stakeholders.

3.2   Steps of the URSERVe Method

In order to reach these goals, the following high-level steps are recommended to set up and execute a smart environment project. These steps differ depending on which team initiates the method: the project team focusing on the smart environment application (left side of the funnel), or the team(s) requested to provide the underlying (micro)-services for a smart application (right side of the funnel).

Steps of the method when the process is initiated from the left side of the funnel

1. After in-depth market and user research activities are completed and the research data is consolidated and analyzed, the project team defines and documents the relevant usage scenarios, activity flows and use cases. Most importantly: It sets up an information architecture to understand and sketch out the complete solution with its holistic interaction flows before starting to design any high-fidelity UI prototypes.

2. In parallel with the UI design prototyping and validation phase, the smart environment project team starts with technical prototyping and determines the functionality required to satisfy the user's needs and challenges, as identified in step 1. Cascading down the hierarchy, all required types and levels of services are analyzed and documented.

3. At least one representative of each service development team in this cascade is briefed about the consolidated market and human-centered research results. In return, the service development teams share detailed knowledge about their service (s), for example the scope and limitations of a service, and in which contexts it is already being used. If certain functional requirements are not yet offered by the services, a software development cycle is initiated to develop the service. Alternatively, the functionality may be recruited from other (micro)services, whose responsible development teams would then be ramped up to the same level of knowledge as indicated above.

4. With the enlarged project team thus set up, the stakeholders jointly continue to design the smart solution, drawing on their shared knowledge and contributing their respective expertise. Suitable techniques to employ in this phase are, for example,

ideation, prototyping and end user validation methods from Design Thinking, preferably in face-to-face settings.

Steps of the method when the process is initiated from the right side of the funnel
This process applies when a service development team starts a cooperation with a higher-level consuming service or application which may or may not have performed (user) research activities as outlined above. It also applies to situations in which service development teams create services from scratch.

1. The service development team identifies all future or existing consuming applications (consumers) of their service. This can be achieved by contacting the other service or application teams or by tracking the usage/call history of their service, if existing and in use. Depending on the degree of nesting, the service team might first need to identify superior services in the service hierarchy, thus working their way up to the consumers.
2. The service development team identifies the consumers' end users by getting in touch with the product management or user experience representative responsible for the application, to understand the end users' needs and challenges. This information may already be documented, e.g. in a knowledge management system.
3. The service development team pairs up with the applications' project teams to understand the exact usage contexts (business processes, activity flows, use cases) in which the users of the consuming apps will be exposed to the functionality covered by their service. From this point on, the teams collaborate with each other, sharing their respective knowledge.
4. If no human-centered information is available yet, the service development team performs or initiates user research activities (as outlined in step 1 for the left sided funnel initiation) with the users and actors of the different consuming applications and analyzes the findings across the various applications and users and actors. If there are many different consumers with different users and actors, the data can be heterogenous. Extracting findings then can be a challenge; still, this can also offer an opportunity for consistency, a functional extension of the service or further decomposition, as required.
5. The service development team adapts the service's interface and logic to enable the consuming applications to furnish all relevant aspects based on the research learnings. If the service itself bequeaths UI elements to consuming applications, they should be designed in a way so that they cover the human needs and challenges and adapt to the consuming application and its end users.
6. Finally, the service development team validates and tests their service with their consumers' users and actors. In order to ensure user acceptance as well as functional quality, this should be in the form of usability studies with various consuming application teams as well as functional integration tests. These tests must be scripted such that the development team's services are executed (or mimicked in a prototype set-up).

4 Findings

The incremental and iterative development of the URSERVe method alongside a smart city case project revealed several findings.

By applying the method, product teams which develop (micro)services were able to identify and better understand which applications consume their service, which, in turn, led to increased collaboration and alignment between the service and consuming application's teams. The extensive user research activities performed in the context of the smart city application project in which the method was applied and developed, proved to be of benefit to both the service and the application development teams. As such it represented a strong collaborative value, and resulted in iterative, cross team and stakeholder workshops and discussions, which generated innovative ideas and solutions.

The method not only engenders a higher degree of collaboration between teams, it also provides a defined space for joint idea generation and innovation, by deliberately connecting the findings from outside-in research (such as personas, usage scenarios and user requirements) with the inside knowledge residing within the team (such as opportunities provided by existing and emerging technologies). In the context of the smart city project, this type of knowledge sharing by the various stakeholders resulted in qualitative improvements in both discussions and results: We noticed a change towards a more human-centered mindset and service design because it became tangible for the service teams who they are developing their services for. This became evident, amongst others, in the project teams' discussions where the fictive names of the personas were frequently used to describe the user's perspective, or by the fact that posters of the personas were hung up in the project spaces of the different teams.

Projects that have employed the method showed that both approaches (outside-in and inside-out) complement each other and enrich the design and development process. They helped to identify the relevant personas, define the usage contexts and develop use cases. Further, the teams realized that a holistic design approach is helpful and necessary and that users must not be confronted with the underlying complexity related to a service architecture. At the same time, the method enabled the teams to adapt and extend their services' interface and logic, which helped the consuming applications to further drive modularization and re-use by leveraging the services' capabilities. This made the services more valuable and viable as they became more exposed within the development organization.

Moreover, the market and user research results had a bearing on several follow-up projects. The intensive collaboration and co-innovation activities of all stakeholders in the smart city project created knowledge that outlasted the project's duration. This knowledge included findings and artefacts from market and user research (such as process and scenario documentation, personas and use cases, as well as best practices templates created for solution definition), learnings from UI and technical prototyping, solution implementation. Because this knowledge was documented it could be shared with and used by subsequent smart city projects and noticeably reduced the risk of duplication of work (e.g. developing the same service functionality twice).

According to Yin et al. (quoted in Pourzolfaghar and Helfert) "knowledge, experience and technology of all disciplines and stakeholders" need to be regarded in smart environments in particular [22]. Semertzaki [25] adds that, especially in knowledge or information driven industries, knowledge needs to be distributed and passed on for an organization to remain innovative and competitive. Given the fact that knowledge generated and owned by the different roles and stakeholders in a company frequently is tacit knowledge held in people's minds and usually remains unshared [18] the method can help companies to express, translate, combine, capture, collect and consolidate the knowledge right down to their (micro)services, and map out the users and actors as well as the usage contexts of these services. Ultimately, the goal for a company employing this method could be to create a knowledge base or knowledge management system in which to share and disseminate this knowledge within the organization, as proposed by (Pourzolfaghar and Helfert [22]).

5   Limitations and Further Research Opportunities

To date, the method was successfully employed in smart city projects of a global IT company. To evaluate and quantify the applicability and scalability of the method, projects in companies of various sizes will need to be observed when using the method and the results evaluated, both qualitatively and quantitatively. Further research opportunities will therefore benefit from the method evolving over time with more projects and teams adopting it.

While cultural and regional differences in user base and project teams do matter, our method has not considered these in detail yet. A smart city is the perfect set up for going beyond standard solutions to more local ones, tailormade for citizens right down to the level of city quarters or even individual streets. This is because the data from the very sensors and devices that make the IoT foundation [3] of the smart city can be used to further enrich, and provide focus to, the left side, outside-in information funnel in future smart city projects. In the context of our method, this source and type of information has not been extensively researched.

The topics of ethics (especially in the context of digital actors and artificial intelligence), data privacy and data security are very important in smart environments and were taken into account in the user research process. They were included in the research results but as these are major, standalone topics, covering these here would go beyond the scope of this paper.

We learned that the method could not be executed to the full scale with all projects. Realistically, it was not possible to get the message across to all teams of how knowledge sharing and gaining can benefit human-centered and innovative software design. We also had to accept that deadlines can beat knowledge gain even against the wishes of the project teams.

In our projects we noticed that local or team-specific knowledge bases that store user research results, market and innovation documents on a shared network or in collaborative team applications are insufficient. We see the need for further research on how to scale up the concept of a shared knowledge space and the documentation of the learnings from individual projects to the complete organization, thus strengthening the organization's learning and innovation capabilities. All three elements, "knowledge acquisition, knowledge creation and knowledge dissemination" [25] are required to achieve this.

Finally, we aim to research into how to further bolster the participatory, creative, and innovative capabilities in a project and encourage stakeholders to go beyond the known, the feasible, or the imaginable. Especially in the scattered persona landscape of smart cities we felt that we might have missed a potential user, an interesting new feature extension or innovation possibility.

6 Summary

The methodology outlined in this paper lends itself to being used in smart environments that are enabled by a highly decomposed architecture of hierarchically nested services. The method focuses on the sharing of expert knowledge, that is, knowledge generated outside-in by the market and user facing members of a software development organization, and the knowledge that exists inside-out and is based on the expertise of the development and technology groups which, amongst others, create the underlying (micro)services. By applying the method, capturing and documenting the findings and the shared knowledge, and by disseminating this to other stakeholders, project teams can contribute to the company-wide knowledge base, thus helping to establish and promote a learning organization. There is room for enhancement of this method. Further application of the method in different settings will help to improve it and answer some of the open questions.

References

1. Beyer, H., Holtzblatt, K.: Contextual Design. Defining Customer-Centered Systems. Morgan Kaufmann, San Francisco (1998)
2. Casini, M.: Green technology for smart cities. In: IOP Conference Series: Earth and Environmental Science, vol. 83, no. 1, p. 12014 (2017). https://doi.org/10.1088/1755-1315/83/1/012014
3. Cauteruccio, F., Cinelli, L., Fortino, G., et al.: Using sentiment analysis and automated reasoning to boost smart lighting systems. In: Montella, R., Ciaramella, A., Fortino, G., et al. (eds.) Internet and distributed computing systems. Lecture Notes in Computer Science, vol. 11874, pp. 69–78. Springer, Cham (2019). https://doi.org/10.1007/978-3-030-34914-1_7
4. Condea, C., Cruickshank, D., Hagedorn, P.: What co-innovation can mean for digital business transformation: sharing and managing risk to achieve IT Business innovation. In: Oswald, G., Kleinemeier, M. (eds.) Shaping the Digital Enterprise, pp. 287–307. Springer, Cham (2017). https://doi.org/10.1007/978-3-319-40967-2_14
5. Cook, D., Das, S.K.: Smart Environments: Technology, Protocols, and Applications. Wiley, Hoboken (2004)
6. Dell'Era, C., Landoni, P.: Living lab: a methodology between user-centred design and participatory design. Creat. Innov. Manag. 23(2), 137–154 (2014). https://doi.org/10.1111/caim.12061

7. Gianni, F., Divitini, M.: Designing IoT applications for smart cities: extending the tiles ideation toolkit. Interact. Des. Archit. J. - IxD&A, **35**, 100–116 (2017)
8. Gobbi, A., Spina, S.: Smart cities and languages: the language network. IxD&A – Interact. Des. Architect. **16**, 37–46 (2013)
9. Hofstaetter, U.: SAP cloud platform – more than just PaaS (2018). https://blogs.sap.com/2018/10/12/sap-cloud-platform-more-than-just-paas/. Accessed 13 Feb 2020
10. Hui, T.K.L., Sherratt, R.S., Sánchez, D.D.: Major requirements for building smart homes in smart cities based on internet of things technologies. Fut. Gener. Comput. Syst. **76**, 358–369 (2017). https://doi.org/10.1016/j.future.2016.10.026
11. Jennex, M.E.: Big data, the internet of things, and the revised knowledge pyramid. SIGMIS Database **48**(4), 69–79 (2017). https://doi.org/10.1145/3158421.3158427
12. Kleinemeier, M.: How governments use AI to create better experiences for citizens (2019). https://www.forbes.com/sites/sap/2019/11/07/how-governments-use-ai-to-create-better-experiences-for-citizens/. Accessed 02 Feb 2020
13. Kujala, S.: User involvement: a review of the benefits and challenges. Behav. Inf. Technol. **22**(1), 1–16 (2003). https://doi.org/10.1080/01449290301782
14. Kuniavsky, M.: Observing the User Experience. A Practitioner's Guide to User Research. Morgan Kaufmann Series in Interactive Technologies. Morgan Kaufmann Publishers, San Francisco (2003)
15. Latre, S., Leroux, P., Coenen, T., et al.: City of things: an integrated and multi-technology testbed for IoT smart city experiments. In: Conference IISC (ed.) Improving the Citizens Quality of Life. IEEE Second International Smart Cities Conference (ISC2 2016), 12–15 September 2016, Trento, Italy, Proceedings, pp. 1–8. IEEE, Piscataway (2016)
16. Li, S., Zhang, H., Jiaa, Z., et al.: A dataflow-driven approach to identifying microservices from monolithic applications. J. Syst. Softw. **157** (2019). https://doi.org/10.1016/j.jss.2019.07.008
17. Lom, M., Pribyl, O., Svitek, M.: Industry 4.0 as a part of smart cities. In: 2016 Smart Cities Symposium Prague, pp. 1–6 (2016)
18. Wright, J.D. (ed.): International Encyclopedia of the Social & Behavioral Sciences, 2nd edn, pp. 4–8. Elsevier, Amsterdam
19. Mylonas, P., Siolas, G., Caridakis, G., et al.: Modeling context and fuzzy personas modeling context and fuzzy personas towards an intelligent future internet smart home paradigm. In: Botía, J.A., Charitos, D. (eds.) Workshop Proceedings of the 9th International Conference on Intelligent Environments, pp. 732–743. IOS Press, Amsterdam (2013)
20. Panda, A., Sagiv, M., Shenker, S.: Verification in the age of microservices. In: Association for Computing Machinery-Digital Library (ed.) Proceedings of the 16th Workshop on Hot Topics in Operating Systems, pp. 30–36. ACM, New York (2017)
21. Petritoli, E., Leccese, F., Pizzuti, S., et al.: Smart lighting as basic building block of smart city: an energy performance comparative case study. Measurement **136**, 466–477 (2019). https://doi.org/10.1016/j.measurement.2018.12.095
22. Pourzolfaghar, Z., Helfert, M.: Investigating HCI challenges for designing smart environments. In: Nah, F.F.-H.F.-H., Tan, C.-H. (eds.) HCIBGO 2016. LNCS, vol. 9752, pp. 79–90. Springer, Cham (2016). https://doi.org/10.1007/978-3-319-39399-5_8
23. Ryan, S., O'Connor, R.V.: Acquiring and sharing tacit knowledge in software development teams: an empirical study. Inf. Softw. Technol. **55**(9), 1614–1624 (2013). https://doi.org/10.1016/j.infsof.2013.02.013
24. Sauro, J., Lewis, J.R.: Quantifying the user experience Practical Statistics for User Research, 2nd edn. Morgan Kaufmann, Amsterdam (2016)
25. Semertzaki, E.: Knowledge management. In: Semertzaki, E. (ed.) Special Libraries as Knowledge Management Centres, pp. 57–119. Chandos, Oxford (2011)

26. Stephanidis, C., Salvendy, G., Antona, M., et al.: Seven HCI grand challenges. Int. J. Hum.-Comput. Interact. **35**(14), 1229–1269 (2019). https://doi.org/10.1080/10447318.2019.1619259
27. Strozzi, F., Colicchia, C., Creazza, A., et al.: Literature review on the 'Smart Factory' concept using bibliometric tools. Int. J. Prod. Res. **55**(22), 6572–6591 (2017). https://doi.org/10.1080/00207543.2017.1326643
28. de Loo, J.: Smart lighting: integration intelligenter beleuchtungssysteme in smart cities. In: Etezadzadeh, C. (ed.) Smart City – Made in Germany, pp. 757–767. Springer, Wiesbaden (2020). https://doi.org/10.1007/978-3-658-27232-6_77

Improving the Usability of Voice User Interfaces: A New Set of Ergonomic Criteria

Caroline Nowacki[1]([✉]), Anna Gordeeva[1], and Anne-Hélène Lizé[2]

[1] frog Design, Paris, France
{caroline.nowacki,anna.gordeeva}@frogdesign.com
[2] frog Design, Lyon, France
anne-helene.lize@frogdesign.com

Abstract. Technological progress has made possible to create voice user interfaces that feel more natural, as smart speakers notably show. As those develop, issues of usability have also been spotted that underline the fact that the way we are used to designing interfaces do not apply directly to voice interactions. Since heuristic and ergonomic criteria are the first way designers can improve their interfaces, we propose a new set of criteria for VUIs, based for the first time on an extensive review of academic and professional guidelines, and plugged into existing general heuristics. These criteria underline the need for VUIs to make up for the lack of visual cues, to take into account the social nature of conversations, as well as the need to own the fact that talking objects will be interpreted as full characters with a personality, and therefore need to be designed as such.

Keywords: Ergonomic criteria · Heuristic evaluation · Voice user interface · Conversational agent · Usability

1 Introduction

In 2018, 66.4 million adults in the U.S. owned a smart speaker, showing an impressive increase of 40% owners in just one year [1]. According to comScore, 50% of requests will be made orally in 2020, making voice a serious contender to touchscreens and keyboards. The voice user interfaces (VUIs) of smart speakers have made enormous progress compared to automatic phone systems. Instead of series of choices symbolized by numbers, smart speakers promise a "conversational interface" in which the interaction feels natural. However, even when the technology makes requests better understood and frees the user from answering according to a decision tree, the user experience with smart speakers has unveiled many problems. These spans from reinforcement of gender stereotypes through the feminine voice of the assistant [2] to negative influence on children's politeness [3]. Indeed, as we create VUIs, we're forced to think about new design norms that adapt to the way we use voice rather than the way we have used screens.

In parallel, a multitude of blog posts give advice about how to design better VUIs, underlining the differences of this medium compared to screens. Academically published, famous heuristics also warn that new technologies might require a revision of

© Springer Nature Switzerland AG 2020
A. Marcus and E. Rosenzweig (Eds.): HCII 2020, LNCS 12201, pp. 117–133, 2020.
https://doi.org/10.1007/978-3-030-49760-6_8

these heuristics. However, today's guidelines represent an expert's opinion and do not systematically build upon on the current literature.

This article aims to propose an improved set of existing guidelines, the ergonomic criteria of Scapin and Bastien (1997) [4], based on a systematic review of 26 existing guidelines for VUIs. We show that 4 original sub-criteria are not useful anymore, 6 take on significantly different meaning and need adapting, while we propose to add 7 new sub-criteria specific to VUIs.

2   Prior Work

2.1   Assessing the Usability of an Interface

Usability is key in human-computer interactions and defined by the International Organization for Standardization (ISO) as "the extent to which the product can be used by specified users to achieve specified goals with effectiveness, efficiency, and satisfaction in a specified context of use" [5].

Testing the usability of an interface takes three main forms: user tests, expert-based evaluations, and model-based evaluations [5]. Although ultimately user-tests are the most telling and reliable, expert-based evaluations are the cheapest and least time-consuming. They allow for a fast screening of the interface at several phases of its conception [5]. Indeed, expert-based evaluations can happen at the design phase, or to audit an interface already developed and improve it before user tests.

Most commonly, expert evaluations are based on one own's opinion. However, the use of a heuristics has been shown to greatly improve expert-based evaluations [6]. A heuristic is a set of guidelines that can support the evaluator in his/her task and improve his/her ability to spot flaws in the interface. An evaluation using heuristics or ergonomic criteria is analytical and predictive: It compares the characteristics of an interface to principles or desirable ergonomic dimensions to support a diagnosis on its likely use [4].

Heuristic and guideline evaluations are widely used thanks to their intuitiveness and ease of implementation [7]. Although this evaluation is often done intuitively by one or two designers, Nielsen and Molic (1990) [6] showed that 5 evaluators screening the interface for defaults individually and then collectively enabled to identify twice as much flaws, as compared to a single evaluator. Although heuristic evaluation alone is rarely enough to reach the highest level of usability of an interface, its wide use and ability to improve the result of an expert evaluation justify that we search to improve existing heuristics and adapt them to new types of interfaces. We now turn to a review of the specificities and challenges of VUIs.

2.2   The Challenges of Voice-User Interfaces and Conversational Interfaces

The most widely known and used academically published heuristic were developed in the 1990s, primarily for interfaces that involved a screen. However, interfaces today are evolving toward "natural" interfaces, meaning they are based on natural modes of communication such as conversations.

However, the term "natural" and "conversational" have been questioned [8]. Indeed, talking to a machine and not a human being is not natural, and users adapt their ways of talking to access the service they desire. One of the most telling difference lies in the fact that human conversations consists in turn-taking arrangements that are contextual and negotiated in real time by participants. On the contrary, VUIs rely on voice commands with a built-in fixed turn-taking: The user asks a question or make a request, to which the VUI answers, and so on [9].

Observations of users' interactions with VUIs show that talking to objects leads users both to change their attitudes to accommodate an object and to give human traits and interpretations to some of the VUI's features. For example, users take turns in talking, simplify their commands and decrease background noise when uttering a command to maximize the chances of success. On the contrary, when the VUI takes too much time to answer, the silence is interpreted as a sign of trouble and leads to describe the system as a human "not liking something" [10]. Because VUIs use a medium so far exclusive to people, some interactions are interpreted using human traits and often elicit emotional responses such as distrust in users when the interaction is unexpected [11].

These observations indicate that as technology evolves to increase the accuracy of both understanding and uttering human speech, the use of such interface is still creating a new kind of interaction, with expectations from the user and possible ways for designers of VUIs to improve their ease of use.

In parallel though, we should note that VUIs do not pose only usability [12], or performance problems [13, 14] but have led to underline many ethical challenges as well. If some of those are linked to the recording, storage and use of data from users, others question the very rules of social relationships, such as politeness or authority of parents over children. Here, we'll touch incidentally on some of these ethical questions, but our criteria are not meant as a guide to tackle ethical challenges.

2.3   The Limits of Generic Heuristics to Assess the Usability of VUI

The most well-known heuristics were created in the 1990's without specifying the type of interface they were intended to. Nielsen tested its heuristic both on visual and voice interfaces, but the voice interface assessed was a phone answering system that followed a predetermined tree much like a computer at that time.

As new interfaces and media developed, heuristics dedicated to those also developed, with the basis that generic heuristics might miss domain-specific concerns. Such heuristics exist for video games, virtual worlds, and mobile phones among others [15]. Inostroza et al. (2012) [16] showed that a specific heuristic designed for touch-screen mobile devices helped evaluators find more errors than the use of Nielsen's generic 10 principles. Scapin and Bastien (1997) also warned that their ergonomic criteria might not be valid to assess an interface based on new technology.

This motivates us to question the applicability of widely used generic heuristics (Nielsen, 1994) and ergonomic criteria (Bastien and Scapin, 1993 [17]; Scapin and Bastien, 1997) to voice user interfaces. Our research question is: **How can we improve**

these existing criteria to help design more usable VUIs, based on the research and experience that exists today for this media?

Today, one can find a variety of advice about how to design vocal interfaces, particularly for vocal assistant applications. However, each of these guidelines are based on one company's or researcher's singular experience, without any formal comparison with other guidelines. We therefore propose an adaptation of generic guidelines to VUIs based on the existing academic and professional research on this topic, and preliminary empirical tests.

3   Methodology

The present article systematically reviews and compares existing design guidelines for VUIs between each other, and to the heuristics of Nielsen (1994) and ergonomic criteria of Scapin and Bastien (1997). The end result is a new set of design guidelines adapted to VUIs based on a wide range of experiences and research, and preliminary tested by designers at frog design.

3.1   Choice of Nielsen and Bastien and Scapin as Reference Heuristics

We chose these two sets of criteria because of their wide recognition by academics and professionals. Nielsen enjoys a global recognition and is credited with inspiring the tradition of creating heuristics to guide the design and assess the usability of interfaces through his 1990 article co-authored with Molic. This paper has been cited 3,915 times according to google scholar and his 1995 publication of 10 usability heuristics has been cited 726 times (google scholar).

The ergonomic criteria of Bastien and Scapin are the most widely known and used in France, where they were first published as a technical report by the INRIA in 1993 before being published in an academic journal in 1997. The English version of these criteria have been cited 601 times for their 1993 publication, and 451 for the version in 1997. We kept these two sets as reference because of their different level of abstraction, with the ultimate goal of not producing a new set of guidelines from scratch, but to improve the guidelines that would seem best fitted to help experts assess the usability of VUIs.

3.2   Systematic Review of Existing Guidelines for VUI

Rusu et al. (2011) [18] have proposed a methodology to establish better heuristics. It involves 6 steps: (1) an exploration of the literature to find heuristics linked to an area; (2) A description stage to formalize the main concepts associated with the research; (3) a correlation stage to identify the characteristics the new heuristic should have; (4) an explicative stage describing the guidelines; (5) A validation stage testing the heuristic; (6) A refinement stage improving the guidelines based on the feedback from the validation stage. In this paper, we have followed the first 4 steps completely, and have started step 5 and 6, testing and refining the guidelines, but with a number of tests too low to yield robust results.

3.3   Establishing the New Set of Guidelines

First, the authors looked for academic papers available online with the keywords "voice-user interface", "vocal assistants", "conversational agents", and "heuristics", "design guidelines", "ergonomic criteria" using google scholar. Among the references returned, we selected as relevant 2 books [19, 20] and 7 academic papers [12, 21–26].

We also searched the web with the same keywords and included in our review 17 sets of guidelines from websites specialized in design, user interface, voice-user interface and user experience (Muzli; Interaction Design Foundation; Magenta; CX partners; Nielsen Norman Group; Career Foundry; Telepathy; Voicebots; Octane AI; Medium; Smashing Magazine; Voice Principles; Magenta; Google AI Blog). Finally, we added 9 sets of guidelines published by large tech and design companies (Apple, Google (x2), Amazon, Microsoft, IBM, Fjord, Voysis, Accenture-Fjord).

The second author read all 35 references and compared them to the reference guidelines of Nielsen and Bastien and Scapin. She recorded in a table which new guidelines from the literature corresponded to existing one, either exactly or with adjustment, and adding below guidelines with no correspondence. Each of the 35 references was then read by at least one additional designer from frog design. We then organized a working session with the 6 designers involved to review and confirm the correspondence between new and reference guidelines and agree on a final list of guidelines. During this session, we also proposed and compared modifications to Nielsen's guidelines, versus Bastien and Scapin's, and agreed that the modifications to Bastien and Scapin's allowed to show more details related to VUI and would potentially be more helpful.

3.4   Preliminary Tests

For the validation stage, we created 2 possible dialogues with vocal assistants and recorded them. One dialogue presented the case of a vocal assistant helping a mother and her son to cook a chocolate cake, while the other portrayed a vocal assistant helping a customer to buy a watch. We purposefully incorporated 37 «errors» in total: sentences, attitudes and tones of voices in the vocal assistant that corresponded to problems identified in the literature.

We asked 8 designers with experience auditing inferfaces in our studio to find errors in the scenarios we provided. 5 of them had a booklet with our guidelines, while 3 did not have them. Each group were comparable in terms of variety of experience levels (1 to 10 years) and familiarity with Bastien and Scapin.

We found that on average, testers with the guidelines identified 59% of the errors we had included, against 39% for testers without the guidelines. The minimum share of errors found was 41% with guidelines, and 24% without guidelines. The maximum share of errors found was 78% with guidelines, and 62% without guidelines. The average in this experiment are very encouraging as they show that twice as many errors were found with our guidelines. This experimentation is still in progress and the very small size of our sample and the unbalance between the number of testers in each group require to stay prudent when using these results.

4   Comparison with Nielsen (1994) and Scapin and Bastien (1997)

Looking at Nielsen, we found that all of the principles hold for voice interface except for Aesthetic and Minimalist Design, which we suggest should be replaced by a section on the personality induced by choices of language, behavior and identity. All the other principles also need slight changes or warning in their description to address specific challenges of vocal interfaces, such as the need to adapt to different situations of use as the same product can be used at home, outside, alone or with other people present, hence opening the field also to *qualitative* evaluations.

We also found that though each source did not have more 20 principles, they all proposed guidelines that were more detailed and specific to the voice medium than Nielsen's principles, and that it would be difficult to show those by modifying Nielsen's principles. We found that less information was lost when we tried to modify the ergonomic criteria of Bastien and Scapin (1993, 1997). Figure 1 shows our proposed

1. Guidance
   1.1. Prompting
   ~~1.2. Grouping and distinguishing items~~
       ~~1.2.1.Grouping and distinguishing items by location~~
       ~~1.2.2.Grouping and distinguishing items by format~~
   1.3. *Immediate feedback*
   ~~1.4. Legibility~~
2. Workload
   2.1. Brevity
       2.1.1.Conciseness
       2.1.2.Minimal actions
   2.2. *Information density*
3. Explicit control
   3.1. *Explicit user actions*
   3.2. *User control (incl. Ethics & Privacy)*
   3.3. Pro-active user confirmation
4. Adaptability
   4.1. Flexibility
   4.2. Users' experience level
   4.3. Multi-user
5. Error management
   5.1. Error protection
   5.2. Quality of error messages
   5.3. Error correction
6. *Consistency*
7. ~~Significance of codes~~
8. *Compatiblity*
   8.1. **Short & Long-term memory**
   8.2. **Environment**
9. **Personality**
   9.1. **Identity**
   9.2. **Behavior**
   9.3. **Language (natural conversation)**

Fig. 1. List of criteria from Scapin and Bastien (1997) with the changes we suggest making (in italic the guidelines that change slightly, in bold the new guidelines, and in strike-through the ones that are not applicable for VUI).

set of guidelines as a modified version of Bastien and Scapin's list. Unchanged guidelines are in black, slight modifications are in italic and blue, new criteria are bolded and green, and criteria that we suggest erasing are crossed out.

5   Results: New Guidelines for Voice Interfaces

Below, we explain each criterion. We give context compared to Scapin and Bastien's ergonomic criteria, then a principle and illustrate it with an example. When needed, we add a rationale to explain further the guideline. Although reference guidelines were not illustrated, the feedback from our colleagues and testers was that an illustrated example greatly helped them understand and use the guidelines.

5.1   Guidance

Guidance refers to the "means available to advise, orient, inform, instruct, and guide the users throughout their interaction". They help the user know what the system can do and learn how to use it. Because VUIs support interactions with a system with limited capabilities, this principle remains very important. It is even more important when users rely solely on voice and cannot have visual signs to help them know what is possible in general and right away. However, among the original guidelines, grouping/distinction of items and legibility were very focused on visual cues and change drastically for voice interactions. Prompting and immediate feedback stay very important and we keep them but transform their phrasing into guidelines adapted to VUIs below.

Prompting. Users should always know the status of the conversation, if the system is listening or processing the request. Visual and verbal cues, nonverbal sounds and conversational markers help to communicate the status. Users should also know how they can interact with the system and what the system can and cannot do.

Rationale: This is particularly complex because users usually rely on visual cues as much as vocal ones in conversations to know if the person is listening, thinking, about to talk or if there is any other problem. In conversations based solely on voice, there is often a physical object such as a telephone that indicates when the conversation starts or stop. These need to be indicated with voice or sound when there is no visual cue. Some linguistic markers can be used to help orient the users, such as "first, then, finally", and the end of the utterance can be marked by a question to the user to confirm the end of the conversation or give the opportunity to continue it.

Immediate Feedback. Feedback allows users to feel understood or to take corrective actions. It reassures them in social and conventional ways and makes up for the lack of visual cues.

Rationale: The quality and the rapidity of the feedback increase the confidence and satisfaction of users. This is important because silence in conversations are easily interpreted as trouble and decrease the quality of the interaction. For VUIs, the sentences and tone used create a type of relationship with the system and an emotion in the user. If they seem robotic, they risk alienating the user, whereas a personal feedback, with some varieties and contextuality are an opportunity to increase satisfaction (Fig. 2).

Fig. 2. From left to right, examples for Prompting and Immediate Feedback (All illustrations were created by Anne-Hélène Lizé and Julie Charrier)

5.2   Workload

The criterion workload is exactly the same as in the original guidelines. It aims at reducing the perceptual and cognitive workload for the user and increase the dialogue efficiency. We focus their description to the voice medium.

Brevity. Brevity concerns individual commands needed to perform an end goal and the responses from the system. They include both conciseness and minimal actions.

Conciseness. Respond concisely without extra words to avoid increasing the time users must spend listening. When listing the options, avoid listing all of them at once, it's better to indicate how much information there is, then list 3 ($\pm$1) items, and ask what the user would like to do next.

Rationale: Listening is longer than reading and oral sentences are usually shorter and more direct than written ones. Shorter responses will optimize the time of the user and allow to better direct the information toward what the user wants to know or do.

Minimal Actions. Limit the number of steps a user has to go through to achieve a goal and make it as short and intuitive as possible.

Rationale: Often one user command requires the system to engage in several steps. These need not be explicit since they do not matter to the user. Forcing the user through

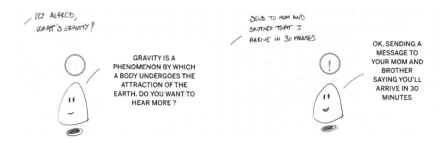

Fig. 3. From left to right, examples for conciseness and minimal actions.

them would annoy him/her. In the illustration, one command for the user requires several actions for the system: opening the messaging app, choosing two recipients, writing the core of the message and sending it. The system should not force the user to break into those steps, but only asks for the confirmation of the overall action (Fig. 3).

Information Density. This part describes the whole set of information presented to the user rather than one command. One should manage peaks of user attention and focus the user attention on what is important. One of the strategies is using the "End Focus Principle". It suggests placing new important information at the end of the sentence. Others include pauses, emphasis, and diversity in questions and answers to catch the attention.

Rationale: The brain does not process visual and oral information the same way and remembering long lists is troublesome for many people. In conversations we use pauses, emphasis, and break up the information into several questions and answers to avoid asking users to remember. While we remember better the first thing we read, we remember better the last thing we heard. The positioning of information is therefore reversed between visual and voice interfaces (Fig. 4).

Fig. 4. Example for information density

5.3 Explicit Control

Same as in the original guidelines, explicit control "concerns both the system processing of explicit user actions, and the control users have on the processing of their actions by the system." This criterion helps reducing errors and ambiguities but is also key to increase user acceptance and trust in the system. Two criteria that are strongly underlined for VUIs but were already present in Bastien and Scapin's guidelines.

We keep the original division in "explicit user action" and "user control" and add the new sub-criteria "pro-active user confirmation".

Explicit User Action. "The computer must process only those actions requested by the users and only when requested to do so". In addition, the VUI should require explicit confirmation before accomplishing an action that can have a negative impact on the user. Giving full disclosure on the impact and double-checking is crucial.

Rationale: Spontaneity from the system can be felt as scary or intrusive, as examples of bugs such as the spontaneous laugh of Alexa have shown. Users are also dreary of suggestions based on personal data they did not explicitly agreed to share.

User Control. User should be allowed to interrupt the system or initiate another command at any moment without having to wait for the VUI to finish its sentence or task. "Emergency exit" command to leave the unwanted state, undo and redo should be available and intuitive. (e.g. saying "stop" should immediately interrupt the action and confirm that the action has been interrupted).

Rationale: Buttons and visual commands can be more reassuring than voice in terms of control. The lack of visual indicators should be made up by the ease and speed in stopping and correcting actions to increase user trust (Fig. 5).

Fig. 5. From left to right, examples for explicit user action and User control

Pro-active User Confirmation. If users don't express their full intention in their request, anticipate what they might want to ask or do, and propose it in the answer.

Rationale: the lack of visual menu and options and the difficulty to deal with lists orally mean that users will explore what can be done by the system with commands that may have several possible answers. Proposing an option instead of engaging in a long list of questions to determine what the user exactly wants will increase the fluidity of the interaction and create some good surprises. However, one should be careful to keep these suggestions to responses to commands and balance it with the criterion "explicit user action" in which spontaneous actions and commands can be scary for the user (Fig. 6).

Fig. 6. Example for pro-active user confirmation.

5.4   Adaptability

Adaptability keeps its original meaning of the "capacity to behave contextually and according to the users' needs and preferences". We add a new sub-criterion to the existing two, "multi-users" about dealing with groups of users.

Flexibility. Adapt the experience to users' particular needs, capability or style. For VUIs, this include the ability to understand accents, speaking styles, but also the change in voice when the person has a stuffed nose or is sick.

Rationale: Adapting to personal traits such as accents is also particularly important as failure to do so can result in the discrimination of categories of the population.

Users' Experience Level. Offer shortcuts for expert users and help for beginners. Give the user the possibility to choose their own shortcuts. Ideally, the VUI could learn them from past interactions with users & create personal shortcuts.

Rationale: An experienced user will like to gain in speed and fluidity while beginners will appreciate being accompanied. For VUIs, the idea of personalization of the interface goes hand in hand with the personal character of talking with a system and its personification (Fig. 7).

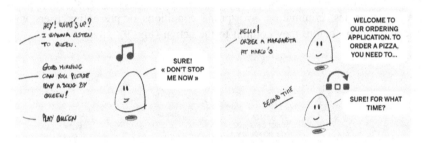

Fig. 7. From left to right, examples for flexibility and users' experience level.

Multi-user. The VUI should be able to recognize the "owner" user from other people that might speak to the system (ex. children) and provide information adapted to the user. VUIs need to be designed to take into account the potential interactions of several users with the system at the same time, or by different users over time. This often means that some users will have more rights and others to give orders to or get information from the system.

Rationale: Conversations often involve more than two people. Additional people can listen in, interject, and try to redirect the conversation. Porcheron et al. (2018) show that in a family context, the VUI not recognizing that parents' commands have a higher priority to children's created confusion and trouble. In that case, this might mean letting the user decides if some users should have more rights than other. This can also mean withholding some information for at-risk users such as children. However, Frejus et al. also show that social use of VUIs mean that the entire family tries to help in finding the right command, in which case a child might have the answer and not taking his or her input into account might not be appropriate. Therefore, different rules regarding different users should be considered depending on the context of use (Fig. 8).

Fig. 8. Example for multi-user.

5.5   Error Management

This refers to "the means available to prevent or reduce errors and to recover from them when they occur".

Error Protection. Systems should prevent errors from occurring by developing error prevention strategies, eliminating error-prone conditions or presenting users with a confirmation option before they commit to the action (Fig. 9).

Fig. 9. From left to right, examples for Error protection and quality of error message.

Quality of Error Message (Propose Action). Avoid error messages that only say that the system did not understand the user correctly. The message "I didn't understand you" leaves the user confused about what went wrong and does not give him/her a chance to correct the command, thus creating a feeling of frustration. Instead, add the information or question that would help users explicit their request and prevent the error from happening again.

Error Correction. Accept corrections, even in the middle of a command. In case of non-recognition of a command, give users another chance by prompting again. When possible, propose the closest command to what was not understood, and ask for confirmation, as shown in the vignette (Fig. 10).

Fig. 10. Example for error correction.

5.6   Consistency

Internal Consistency. The same type of commands should lead to the same type of answers. The tone of voice and speaking style should be consistent. Actual sentences used can vary, through the use of synonyms notably, to increase the natural character of the conversation.

Rationale: Users need some consistency to learn how to use the system and feel confident that a request will give them what they want. In addition, the same way a visual interface has a style, a VUI has a personality that appears in the tone and speaking style. Changing it brutally will break the flow of the conversation, while using a unified tone of voice can help create familiarity. However, some variations in wording are recommended, notably because people use synonyms and vary the wording of answers naturally to break the monotony and direct the attention to what is most important.

External Consistency. Respect existing external norms and conventions. Users are already surrounded by systems that make some sounds to mean error, turn on, turn off, finish etc. These conventions need to be respected to avoid confusion. If breaking them, a clear intention must support this choice (Fig. 11).

Fig. 11. Example for external consistency.

5.7   Compatibility

Although the initial criterion includes the idea of a match between the system and the user's memory, and the system and the environment, the VUI guidelines we reviewed referenced those more explicitly, which is why we included them as sub-criteria.

Short & Long-Term System Memory. The VUI should act according to the context and track the history of information given if users allow it. In conversations, one does not expect to repeat oneself, which means some answers must be memorized at least in the short term. Memorizing long-term preferences can also make commands more fluid for the user, as shown in the vignette.

Environment. The voice medium directly insert itself in an environment characterized by a noise level, and a context with potentially other people that can listen in or participate. The VUI should be designed based on all potential contexts of use, and ideally provide different options and behaviors to adapt to different environments. The sound level can be automatically adjusted based on sensors for noise levels the same way screen lighting now automatically adapts. In addition, the information given about a user's preference or information can be sensitive and should not be given without certainty that it will not put the user in a difficult position (Fig. 12).

Fig. 12. From left to right, examples short & long-term memory of the system, and environment.

5.8   Personality

We underlined in the introduction that speech is a medium associated with characters, real or fictitious. As such, a VUI will be interpreted as a character, no matter how neutral its design is. We therefore created this criterion of personality and propose the following sub-criteria to incentivize designers to fully take responsibility for and control the impression given to the user by choices made in writing the dialogues of a VUI.

Identity. Thinking of a personality for the VUI is important to engage the user and avoid the feeling of frustration that comes from "talking to a machine". The persona of the VUI can be built using the following essential elements: a name, age, gender (or gender-neutral), voice pitch, pace, accent, level of speech (familiar, professional, ...) (Fig. 13).

Fig. 13. Example for identity.

Behavior. To gain trust and empathy with users, develop the following elements: intonations, deciding how serious or playful the VUI will be, degree of politeness, use of humor (and which type), deciding on the emotions or lack thereof shown in different situations (notably when the user expresses emotions, or makes fun of the system).

Match the personality & behavior to the context of use, the brand image, the capacity of the VUI (dumb bots can build empathy to make up for their limitations), and the users' expectations.

Language (Natural Conversation). The commands and responses should be as natural as a regular conversation with a human. The construction of the sentence should be the same as in everyday life. VUI should be trained to understand basic rules of conversation and grammar (Fig. 14).

Fig. 14. From left to right, examples for behavior and language (natural conversation).

6 Concluding Discussion

This paper has proposed a set of usability criteria tailored to VUIs, as a modified version of Bastien and Scapin's ergonomic criteria (1993) that incorporate the advice from 26 design guidelines for VUIs from both academic and professional sources.

The result is a list of 8 criteria and 18 sub-criteria, of which one of the original criteria was erased and one new criterion was added, 2 sub-criteria were erased, and 7 sub-criteria were added. The fact that the majority of the criteria could be kept and adapted is for us a proof that building upon this existing heuristic instead of creating a completely new one was worth it.

The added and modified criteria relate particularly to the fact that VUIs touch to a social context, conversations, with established but also moving and flexible rules. This work shows that one of the main challenges designers of VUIs will face consists in the interpretation of the interface as a fictitious character, as one can find in movies or books. However, it is accessed through a new medium, and with apparently more flexibility. This means new expectations and standards will emerge as more VUIs are created, but that in the meantime, users might feel uneasy as to what this new medium is and how to use it.

A second challenge consists in the social use of a VUI, and the difficulty for VUIs to negotiate the turn taking in conversations the way people do and take into account the relationships of authority that might exist in a group.

A third challenge lies in the fact that voice and image are more easily read and understood together than voice alone. People interpret many conversations based on what they see in addition to what they hear. Voice alone as an interface is limited by potential misunderstandings, by the longer time it takes to talk rather than read and press buttons, and by the fact that the environment (noise level, large number of people, public settings) will affect the quality of the VUI. This means that before following the guidelines presented here, the first question should always be: why is a VUI a better option than another interface? Will it be able to perform the function of the system by itself or does it need to be complemented? The case for using a VUI needs to be made as users will quickly lose interest if it shows too many limitations or not enough added value for the context of use.

Finally, the present work has limits. First, VUIs are still only emerging and we might still miss some issues and solutions that yet need to be discovered as we create more VUIs. Second, the progress in technology also risk changing what is possible to do with the VUI, notably, the time it takes to process a request, potentially changing again what we propose here. Third, we have not had the opportunity to test these guidelines in an experimental setting with experts to measure their quality. A logical next step will be to test the quality of these guidelines by asking experts to find problems in VUIs, with our guidelines for one group, and without for the other.

References

1. Voicebot.ai. https://voicebot.ai/2019/03/07/u-s-smart-speaker-ownership-rises-40-in-2018-to-66-4-million-and-amazon-echo-maintains-market-share-lead-says-new-report-from-voicebot/. Accessed 29 Jan 2020
2. New York Times article. https://www.nytimes.com/2019/05/22/world/siri-alexa-ai-gender-bias.html. Accessed 29 Jan 2020
3. Forbes article. https://www.forbes.com/sites/cognitiveworld/2019/02/28/should-my-child-be-polite-to-alexa-navigating-the-complex-world-of-human-ai-interaction/#7a7caa781b9f. Accessed 29 Jan 2020
4. Scapin, D., Bastien, C.: Ergonomic criteria for evaluating the ergonomic quality of interactive systems. Behav. Inf. Technol. **16**(4/5), 220±223 (1997)
5. Scholtz J.: Evaluation methods for human-system performance of intelligent systems. In: Proceedings of the 2002 Performance Metrics for Intelligent Systems (PerMIS) (2002)

6. Nielsen, J., Molich, R.: Heuristic evaluation of user interfaces. In: Proceedings ACM CHI 1990 Conference, Seattle, WA, pp. 249–256 (1990)
7. Nielsen, J.: Enhancing the explanatory power of usability heuristics. In: Proceedings ACM CHI 1994 Conference, Boston, MA, 24–28 April, pp. 152–158 (1994)
8. O'Hara, K., Harper, R., Mentis, H., Sellen, A., Taylor, A.: On the naturalness of touchless: putting the "Interaction" back into NUI. ACM Trans. Comput. Hum. Interact. **20**(1), 1–25 (2013)
9. Pelikan, H.R., Broth, M.: Why that Nao?: how humans adapt to a conventional humanoid robot in taking turns-at-talk. In: CHI 2016: Proceedings of the 2016 CHI Conference on Human Factors in Computing Systems, pp. 4921–4932 (2016)
10. Porcheron, M., Fischer, J.E., Reeves, S., Sharples, S.: Voice interfaces in everyday life. In: CHI 2018, Montréal, Canada (2018)
11. Mennicken, S., Zihler, O., Juldaschewa, F., Molnar, V., Aggeler, D., Huang, E.M.: «It's like living with a friendly stranger»: perception of personality traits in a smart home. In: UBICOMP 2016 (2016)
12. Smith, D., Liberman, H.: Helping users understand and recover from interpretation failures in natural language interfaces. In: CHI 2012, 5–10 May 2012, Austin, Texas, USA (2012)
13. Luger, E., Sellen, A.: Like having a really bad PA: the gulf between user expectation and experience of conversational agents. In: CHI 2016, San Jose, CA, USA (2016)
14. Sauvage, O.: «Comment les français utilisent les enceintes intelligentes» Livre Blanc publié par Wexperience.fr. (2019)
15. Quinones, D., Rusu, C.: How to develop usability heuristics: a systematic literature review. Comput. Stand. Interfaces **53**, 89–122 (2017)
16. Inostroza, R., Rusu, C., Roncagliolo, S., Jiménez, C., Rusu, V.: Usability heuristics for touchscreen-based mobile devices. In: Ninth International Conference on Information Technology – New Generations (2012)
17. Bastien, C., Scapin, D.L.: Ergonomic criteria for the evaluation of human-computer interfaces. RT-0156, INRIA, p. 79 (1993)
18. Rusu, C., Roncagliolo, S., Rusu, V., Collazos, C.: A methodology to establish usability heuristics. In: ACHI 2011: The Fourth International Conference on Advances in Computer-Human Interactions (2011)
19. Pearl, C.: Designing Voice User Interfaces. O'Reilly, Sebastopol (2016)
20. Bouzid, A., Ma, W.: Don't Make Me Tap! A Common Sense Approach to Voice Usability. CreateSpace Independent Publishing Platform (2013)
21. Lahoual, D., Fréjus, M.: Conception d'interactions éthiques et durables entre l'humain et les systèmes d'intelligence artificielle. Le cas de l'expérience vécue des usagers de l'IA vocale. Revue d'intelligence artificielle **32**(4) (2018)
22. Meyer, J., Miller, C., Hancock, P., de Visser, E.J., Dorneich, M.: Politeness in machine-human and human-human interaction. In: Proceedings of the Human Factors and Ergonomics Society Annual Meeting, vol. 60, no. 1, pp. 279–283 (2016)
23. Dubinsky, Y., Catarci, T., Kimani, S.: A user-based method for speech interface development. In: Stephanidis, C. (ed.) UAHCI 2007. LNCS, vol. 4554, pp. 355–364. Springer, Heidelberg (2007). https://doi.org/10.1007/978-3-540-73279-2_39
24. Hua, Z., Ng, W.L.: Speech recognition interface design for in-vehicle. In: Automotive. UI 2010 Proceedings of the 2nd International Conference on Automotive User Interfaces and Interactive Vehicular Applications, pp. 29–33 (2010)
25. Minker, W., Néel, F.: Développement des technologies vocales. Le travail humain **65**(3), 261–287 (2002)
26. de Villiers, J.: The interface of language and theory of mind. Lingua. Int. Rev. Gen. Linguist. **117**(11), 1858–1878 (2007)

Dive2Views: A Mobile Camera Application that Dives into Another Device's Camera View

Takashi Ohta[1]([⊠])[iD] and Kansei Fujikawa[2]

[1] Tokyo University of Technology, Tokyo, Japan
`takashi@stf.teu.ac.jp`
[2] Graduate School of Tokyo University of Technology, Tokyo, Japan

Abstract. As one of the attempts to propose an interaction design of using multiple devices in collaboration, we devise an application that allows users to use another camera's image through their smartphones by simply directing their smartphone's camera toward the other camera. By using this application, taking photos from any vantage point becomes possible, while remaining at the same location. We implement a prototype application and confirm that it is possible to switch to images of multiple cameras. Moreover, it is also possible to capture a scene from any direction from the viewpoint of other cameras as we introduce 360-degree cameras as target devices to connect. We expect this interaction would provide an impression of diving into the other camera's view. The objective of this research is to design such a new experience, but not to realize the function of connecting dynamically with other cameras. We would like to design an interaction that makes a user feel it natural for using the function. Experiment results with a prototype convinced us of the validity of the interaction design.

Keywords: UX design · Multi-device interaction · Mobile device

1 Introduction

Ever since digital cameras have been integrated into smartphones, people take photos frequently because they always have their phones with them and also because of their desire to post them on social networking sites. Taking pictures using digital cameras is very easy and convenient. However, there are cases in which one cannot be at a vantage point for a variety of reasons. For example, often there are cases in which the zoom function is not sufficient to capture the desired object large enough in screen or the line-of-sight to the object is blocked (Fig. 1). Naturally, it would be more convenient and favorable if one can move to a vantage point.

Bearing this in mind, we consider that an ideal solution would be borrowing the view from another device, which is at a more convenient angle and location. Technically, it is not difficult to implement such a function as it only requires

© Springer Nature Switzerland AG 2020
A. Marcus and E. Rosenzweig (Eds.): HCII 2020, LNCS 12201, pp. 134–145, 2020.
https://doi.org/10.1007/978-3-030-49760-6_9

Fig. 1. Situations in which it is difficult to be at a vantage point

pairing two devices and transmitting the captured video from one device to the other. Furthermore, the capability of switching between multiple devices will lead to better usability. Such functions would typically provide an interface that displays the thumbnails of images of available cameras and lets the user to choose the desired one. However, we do not want this overhead of browsing images because it interrupts the user from the action of taking photos. We prefer to offer a function that maintains continuity for the ease of taking photos. We consider it ideal if users can use another camera's view simply by directing their cameras toward it. In such interactions, users can keep holding their smartphone for choosing the desired view. However, we have not designed the interaction for the sake of usability or convenience. Instead, we attempt to offer a fascinating user experience similar to diving into another camera's view merely by capturing the other camera with one's own camera. We aim to offer this new experience.

We have previously performed a preliminary study [1] and implemented a prototype application that works with multiple smartphones and tablet PCs. With that prototype, users could not control the borrowed view based on the direction of the device in their hand because the target device was fixed or held by someone else. We noticed that such a restriction contradicts the user's intuition and frustrates him/her. We therefore considered improving the interaction by employing 360-degree cameras as target devices. This change achieves controllability by providing an image for the desired direction, which is extracted as a part of the entire spherical image.

This work aims to achieve better user experience while taking photos. This is an attempt in a series of studies conducted by us to design innovative usages and interactions when using multiple mobile devices in collaboration. For realizing this goal, we attempt to design interactions that users find intuitive and natural when using the corresponding functions. We believe that the Internet of Things cannot be a part of people's daily life without offering such interactions.

2   Concept and Interaction Design

We implement Dive2Views as a camera application for smartphones. It dynamically accesses 360-degree cameras and receives their video stream, which is displayed on the smartphone. With this application, people can take ideal photos by choosing a camera at the best vantage position among several devices.

For realizing this function, we design an interface such that there will be no interruption in switching from one's own camera to one of the other devices. Especially, considering there would be multiple cameras to choose from, we do not require an additional action every time the camera is switched, such as opening the configuration panel and choosing the desired one. Moreover, we do not aim to realize the function itself. Our objective is to create a new experience for using multiple devices in collaboration. For fulfilling these objectives, we design an interface so that one can access another device's camera merely by directing one's device toward it (Fig. 2).

Fig. 2. Dive2Views concept: accessing another camera's view by directing one's camera toward it

The basic interaction with the application is as follows. When the application starts, it shows captured images on the screen like a standard camera application; the user can take photos by tapping on the screen. When the user directs his/her smartphone to one of the 360-degree cameras placed in the surrounding area, the application automatically begins to receive a video stream and the screen gradually changes to show the images captured by the corresponding camera (Fig. 3). Again, the user can take photos by tapping on the screen. Therefore, the operation for taking photos is consistent and continuous regardless of the application status.

We provide two ways to terminate the network connection with a 360-degree camera. First, the connection is terminated when the smartphone deviates from the direction of the camera (Left, Fig. 4). Second, the connection is terminated by shaking the smartphone (Right, Fig. 4). After the connection is terminated, the application returns to displaying the view of the smartphone's camera. Thus, two different operation modes that are slightly different in terms of viewing the surrounding are offered. In the first one, users will feel like they are accessing another camera's view temporarily. They can change the view only by altering the smartphone's direction. The connection will cease easily if the user tilts the device too far from the direction of the 360-degree camera. In contrast, the second mode will provide an experience in which the user will feel as if he/she is moving to and standing at a different position because all directions can be viewed until the connection is broken forcibly by shaking the smartphone.

Fig. 3. Core interaction idea of Dive2Views

Fig. 4. Two different methods to terminate network connection

We believe Dive2Views would be useful in situations such as a sports stadium, which is generally too large for the audience to take clear pictures of the scenes on the field. If multiple 360-degree cameras are installed around the field at certain intervals, the audience would be able to take photos from their seat by directing their smartphones toward the most appropriately placed camera. Similarly, this would also be useful for an event like a parade at a theme park. A crowd of people may block one's view to the parade; it would not be easy to be at a vantage point for taking photos. A camera facing a sightseeing spot can also be useful for taking selfies for Instagram. Moreover, there would be various places where cameras can be placed to capture unusual scenes, a balloon would be a such candidate.

3   Related Research

Many attempts have been made in this field so far. Various mechanisms have been introduced to establish a connection between multiple devices. Some approaches use an extra sensor to detect physical contact between devices [2,3], which is used as a trigger for establishing a network connection between the devices. Google's "Tone" utilizes the detection of a tone as a trigger [4]. These works focus on creating a temporary co-working environment and file-sharing system; therefore, only a signal for deciding which devices to pair is sufficient for these applications. Some studies aimed to create a large display using multiple devices; therefore, they required information on each device?s relative position. Hinckley's work used a trail drawn by a stylus pen across the screens of multiple devices [5]. Another primary approach was to use an external camera for detecting device placements [6,7]. The common objective of these studies was to realize the function of each research theme. The interfaces were provided for setting up the environment to use the content.

We have also been researching on utilizing dynamic relationships between multiple devices. In one research, we proposed the use of a pinching gesture on two annexed touch screens to make the applications on the devices work in collaboration [8,9]. This interaction offered users an experience of handling digital content like physical objects. In another research, a physical object bridges between the contents running on different devices [10]. Our objective in these works was to create a novel experience rather than realizing the new functionality. Therefore, the interaction is not an auxiliary, but the design of it is the primary objective of these research works.

4   Implementation

4.1   System Overview

We implemented Dive2Views as an iOS application. The cameras used were Android-based 360-degree cameras (Ricoh Theta V). The system's overview is illustrated in Fig. 5. Because the application identifies the cameras based on their direction, the cameras' geometrical positions were required to be known. We used GPS for locating the smartphones and cameras, assuming the application would be used outdoors. We employed a smartphone as a GPS device and paired it with each camera because the camera did not have the sensor. The location data of multiple cameras was gathered at a location server, from which the application could retrieve information. The location server stored the coordinates of each camera's position along with the device ID number. Location data was updated whenever the cameras moved. Therefore, the application retrieved data repeatedly during its use. Each aspect of the process is explained in detail in the next subsections.

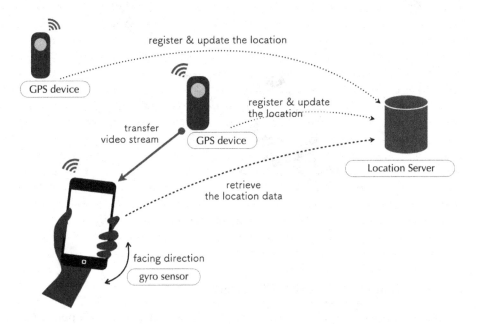

Fig. 5. Overview of the Dive2Views system structure

4.2 Camera Detection

Among the multiple cameras, the application detects one in the direction in which the user is pointing his/her smartphone. Therefore, the application needs to know the direction in which the smartphone is facing and the relative direction to each camera. The direction in which the smartphone is facing θ is obtained by a built-in gyro sensor. The relative direction to a cameras ϕ is calculated by the devices' geometric positions, as shown in Fig. 6. When the user moves the smartphone's direction, the application updates θ and compares it to the direction of every camera. When θ is within a certain threshold from ϕ, the application determines that it detects one of the cameras. For the first attempt, we set this threshold as 5° regardless of the distance between the smartphone and the camera. After detecting a camera, the application requests the camera to start streaming the captured video. Because the location of the cameras is obtained automatically by using GPS, the pre-configuration step of registering their positions is not necessary. This aspect is different from the former work [1], which requires the registration of the location of the target devices manually.

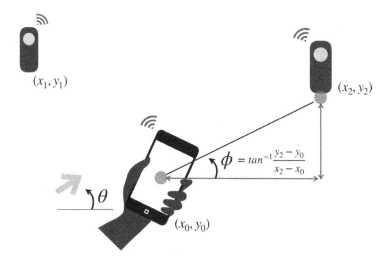

Fig. 6. Camera detection

4.3   Termination of Network Connection

When the smartphone moves away from a camera's direction, the application detects the event and terminates the network connection between devices. The user can change the smartphone's direction within a small range because moving too far results in termination of the connection with the camera. The threshold for the angle for disconnection is set to be larger than that for discovering a camera to allow some flexibility to tilt the smartphone. This method of disconnection is consistent with the concept of accessing a camera's view only by pointing one's smartphone. However, this restricts the freedom of movement for viewing in a desired direction. Therefore, another method for disconnection is proposed to avoid this issue. In this method, the user can terminate the connection by shaking the smartphone. This interaction allows the user to look around freely once the connection is established. Such operability would offer the user an impression of standing at the connected camera's position. However, the ease of switching between multiple cameras just by moving a smartphone around would be lost. Therefore, both these methods have been made available and users can select one based on their preference.

4.4   Image Extraction

The video sent from the camera is a 360-degree view. Therefore, an appropriate part from the entire video needs to be extracted based on the direction of the smartphone. This idea is illustrated in Fig. 7. For this, we use a spherical model provided by iOS's SceneKit; the 360-degree image is mapped to it as a texture. The appropriate scene is displayed on the screen automatically by mapping the direction in real time to the camera's view in the SceneKit model. Because this approach extracts a fragment from the entire 360-degree image, the resolution of the extracted image is low. Using a stepping motor to rotate the camera would be another approach to achieve viewing flexibility. We did not employ this approach because it restricts the access to the camera to only one person at one time. Instead, the 360-degree image is sent to the device and the application on the device extracts the required fragment; this allows multiple users to access a camera at the same time.

Fig. 7. Viewing a fragment from the entire 360-degree image

4.5   Visual Effect

A visual effect is required to let the user to know that the application is detecting a 360-degree camera. When the smartphone?s pointing direction is close to a camera, the screen starts to fade out. As the user keeps holding the smartphone in that direction, the image on the screen then switches to the image received from the detected camera (Fig. 8). Such visual effect is essential for providing a better user experience. Without such effect, users would find it difficult to determine whether a camera is detected. At the same time, this effect contributes to creating an impression of diving into another camera's view. A similar visual effect is also provided when the application stops using the camera.

Fig. 8. Visual effect of diving into another camera's view

5   Experiments and Discussion

We developed a prototype Dive2Views application on iOS with an Android-based 360-degree camera (Ricoh Theta V). We performed several experiments to examine the basic functionality.

First, we checked whether camera detection works as expected. We created a scenario by placing a 360-degree camera outdoors; a person stood beside it as the target object (Fig. 9). Another person with a smartphone with the Dive2Views prototype stood approximately 10 m away from the camera; this person started to capture the scene from a slightly deviated angle and rotated the smartphone gradually toward the target. The screen transition of the smartphone is shown in Fig. 10. It can be seen that the display gradually fades as the angle of the smartphone coincides with the direction of the camera. The image of the target person then appears larger on the screen as the application starts to receive video stream from the directed camera.

Although the fundamental function seems to work, further improvement is needed. Currently, camera direction detection is not sufficiently accurate. We suspect that there are several reasons for this. First, the currently equipped GPS is not sufficiently accurate. The calculated direction error between two devices becomes more substantial if the several meters differences are at both ends. In addition, the built-in gyro sensor does not detect the direction accurately. The error seems to accumulate while the smartphone is moved around continuously. Further, the threshold of the angle to detect a camera is fixed to a specific value regardless of the distance between the camera and user's smartphone. With this

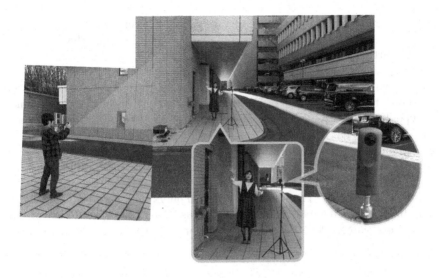

Fig. 9. Experimental setup

Fig. 10. Transition of the screen when a camera is detected

fixed threshold, the range of the angle for detecting a camera varies according to the distance. This value should be smaller as the distance reduces. Another aspect is the image quality. The image appearing on screen is an extracted part of the entire 360-degree image; the image displayed on the screen is an expanded version of the extracted part and so the resolution is low. We intend to use a newer version of the camera that provides a higher resolution to attempt to resolve the issue.

For the second experiment, we examined whether switching of video input between multiple cameras works by directing the smartphone at each of them. We positioned two devices in different directions. We directed a smartphone to one of the cameras first and then pointed it to the other, and then moved it back to the first one. We could observe the changes of the images appearing on the screen. We have not yet examined a case with more than three cameras.

Sometimes, the application failed to change the view after repeatedly switching between cameras several times. Thus, reliability is another issue that should be examined further in the future.

Finally, we tested two interactions for the different ways of terminating the connection with a camera. In our previous prototype, the image on the screen did not respond to the movement of the user's smartphone. In our newly designed prototype, however, the user can browse the camera's view by tilting the smartphone (Fig. 11, Left). Though not much viewing flexibility is provided, this succeeds in removing the unnaturalness that a user would feel with the first prototype. We were also able to confirm that the user can view in all directions when the application uses the second method for disconnecting from the detected camera (Fig. 11, Right). The former interaction offers ease in switching from one camera to another when multiple cameras are used. The latter would be suitable for use of one camera located at a vantage point, which cannot be approached easily.

Fig. 11. Different operability modes for terminating a network connection

6 Conclusion

We designed an interface that allows users to access another device's camera function easily through a simple interaction. We have thus far developed the application and examined its operability to evaluate the interaction concept. For this prototype, we could confirm that the interaction will offer operability as designed. From several experiments, we verified that the new application design improves upon the previous work. However, even our primary objective is to design an interaction that can provide a novel experience in taking photos, the function should work on the premise to appreciate the interaction's uniqueness. Considering this, there is still scope for improvement to make the application more complete.

References

1. Ohta, T.: SIGHT DIVE: directing for viewing through other device's camera. In: 5th IIEEJ International Workshop on Image Electronics and Visual Computing, IEVC2017 2017, Da Nang (2017)
2. Hinckley, K.: Synchronous gestures for multiple persons and computers. In: Proceedings of the 16th Annual ACM Symposium on User Interface Software and Technology, UIST 2003, pp. 149–158. ACM, New York (2003)
3. Merrill, D., Kalanthi, J., Maes, P.: Siftables: towards sensor network user Interfaces. In: Proceedings of the 1st International Conference on Tangible and Embedded interaction, TEI 2007, pp. 75–78. ACM, New York (2007)
4. Tone: an experimental Chrome extension for instant sharing over audio. https://research.googleblog.com/2015/05/tone-experimental-chrome-extension-for.html. Accessed 24 Jan 2020
5. Hinckley, K., Ramos, G., Guimbretiere, F., Baudisch, P., Smith, M.: Stitching: pen gestures that span multiple displays. In: Proceedings of the Working Conference on Advanced Visual Interfaces, AVI 2004, pp. 23–31. ACM, New York (2004)
6. Rädle, R., Jetter, H.C., Marquardt, N., Reiterer, H., Rogers, Y.: HuddleLamp: spatially-aware mobile displays for ad-hoc around-the-table collaboration. In: Proceedings of the Ninth ACM International Conference on Interactive Tabletops and Surfaces, ITS 2014, pp. 45–54. ACM, New York (2014)
7. MIT media lab, viral communications, Project Junkyard Jumbotron. https://www.media.mit.edu/projects/junkyard-jumbotron/overview/. Accessed 24 Jan 2020
8. Ohta, T., Tanaka, J.: Using pinching gesture to relate applications running on discrete touch-screen devices. Int. J. Creative Interfaces Comput. Graph. 4(1), 1–20 (2013)
9. Ohta, T., Tanaka, J.: MovieTile: interactively adjustable free shape multi-display of mobile devices. In: SIGGRAPH ASIA 2015, Kobe (2015)
10. Ohta, T.: Using physical objects to connect multiple mobile applications. In: 16th International Conference of Asia Digital Art and Design (ADADA 2018), Tainan, November 2018

A Method for Increasing User Engagement with Voice Assistant System

Daehee Park$^{(\boxtimes)}$, Heesung Park, and Scott Song

Samsung Electronics, 56, Seongchon-gil, Seocho-gu, Seoul, Republic of Korea
daehee0.park@samsung.com

Abstract. Voice interaction is becoming one of the major methods of human interaction with computers. Several mobile service providers have introduced various types of voice assistant systems such as Bixby from Samsung, Siri from Apple, and Google Assistant from Google that provide information including the schedule for a day, the weather, or methods to control the device to perform a task such as playing music. Although the voice assistant system provides various types of functions, generally, the users do not understand what functions the system can support. We conducted a control task analysis based on expert interviews and found that the main bottleneck of using a voice assistant system is that the user cannot know all the commands. Thus, we believe that presenting recommendable commands is an effective way to increase user engagement. Through buzz data analysis, we discovered what functions could be used and determined the relevant usage context. Subsequently, we performed context modelling and designed the user interface (UI) of a voice assistant system and conducted a case study. Through this case study, we proved that presenting commands on a UI induced more user engagement and usability.

Keywords: Voice interaction · Voice assistant system · Human-computer interaction · User engagement

1 Introduction

1.1 The Trends of Voice Interaction

Recently, voice interaction has become one of the major methods for people to interact with computers. According to Fortune Business Insights, the global speech and voice assistant system market size was valued at USD 6.9 billion in 2018, and it is anticipated to reach USD 28.3 billion by 2026. It indicates that the compound annual growth rate for the forecast period will be 19.8% [1]. Several mobile service providers have introduced various types of voice assistant systems like Bixby from Samsung, Siri from Apple, and Google Assistant from Google that provide information including the schedule for a day, the weather, or methods to control the device such as playing music. Google announced in 2014 that among teens 13-18, 55% use voice assistant systems every day, and 56% of adults said that using these systems makes them "feel tech-savvy" [2]. Business Insider presented the shares of the market in voice assistants: Apple Siri possesses 45.6%, Google Assistant possesses 28.7%, Amazon Alexa possesses 13.2%, Samsung Bixby possesses 6.2%, and Microsoft Cortana possesses 4.9%

© Springer Nature Switzerland AG 2020
A. Marcus and E. Rosenzweig (Eds.): HCII 2020, LNCS 12201, pp. 146–157, 2020.
https://doi.org/10.1007/978-3-030-49760-6_10

[3]. Kiseleva et al. (2016) indicated that smart voice assistants are increasingly becoming a part of the daily lives of users, in particular, on mobile devices [4]. They introduce a significant change in how information is accessed, not only by introducing voice control and touch gestures, but also by enabling dialogues where the context is preserved. Significant change in information access, not only by introducing voice control and touch gestures but also by enabling dialogues where the context is preserved.

However, voice systems cannot recognise many types of natural languages; currently, they only provide limited functions based on recognised user voice inputs. Generally, the users do not know all of the functions the voice assistant system can support. Additionally, the users give commands with short words or phrases to these systems as they do not know what the system will accept. The user will try to use the voice assistant system several times but will easily give up when they cannot fulfil their purpose. If the voice assistant system understands all commands naturally from the users and all functions of the mobile phone can be supported through voice, the system does not need a screen to present possible commands. However, current systems only provide limited functions to the users; thus, the voice assistant systems equipped on the mobile phones try to support the users by providing recommend voice commands on the screen.

The contents of the first screen of a system can present instructions on how to use it. Thus, we can consider that the first screen of the voice assistant system is regarded as a first step to use the voice assistant system, and it determines the user's engagement. Some voice assistant systems only provide a message such as "What can I help you with?" Whereas, some voice assistant systems present a home screen consisting of recommended commands.

To guide the users on how to use a voice assistant system, only presenting a few possible commands is not sufficient. We hypothesised that recommending commands based on context would induce higher user engagement for voice interaction. To design a context-based voice assistant system, we need to find out the purpose of using a voice assistant system, examine a variety of usage scenarios, and determine usage bottlenecks.

However, we could not collect data, which include an individual user's voice assistant system usage due to limited resources and privacy issues. Thus, we analysed buzz data regarding two current voice assistant systems, Google Assistant and Apple Siri, collected during a specific period (90 days prior from 9 December 2019). In addition, we conducted cognitive work analysis based on the result of buzz analysis, to analyse the tasks of the users using these voice assistant systems in detail. Then, determined a data index for context-awareness through analysis of the purpose of using voice assistant systems, usage scenarios, and usage bottlenecks. The home screen had to present example context-based options that were consistent with the purpose required by the users to increase user engagement. After developing the data index for context-awareness, we developed a prototype that applied the context-aware voice assistant. Next, we measured the user engagement of each voice recognition system through a modified user engagement scale (UES) [5]. We validated the effectiveness of the context-aware voice assistant system by measuring the UES.

Although there is some research regarding user satisfaction while using voice assistants, there is still a research gap because there is little research regarding user engagement using voice assistants. In addition, designing a context-aware voice assistant has not yet been researched. Thus, we propose three main objectives of this paper. The first objective is to provide a comprehension of user behaviours based on the buzz analysis, i.e., how the users use the voice assistant system. Then, we provide context modelling for easy use of the voice assistant system. Finally, we validate the effectiveness of the context-aware assistant system by measuring the UES.

2   Related Works

According to Burbach et al. (2019), voice assistant systems have been one of the major changes in user interaction and user experience related to computers recently [6]. They already support many tasks such as asking for information, turning off the lights, and playing music, and are still learning with every interaction made with the users.

The study completed by Burbach et al. (2019) presented acceptance of relevant factors of virtual voice-assistants. They insisted that although individual users frequently use voice assistant systems in their everyday lives, their use is currently still limited. Currently, voice assistant systems are mainly used to call people, ask for directions, or search the Internet for information. One of the reasons for such limited use is that automated speech recognition can cause users to be dissatisfied if errors occur. Another reason is interactions between users and voice assistant systems are more complex than web searches. For example, the voice assistant systems must be able to comprehend the user's intention and context so that they can choose the proper action or provide a proper answer. Burbach et al. (2019) conducted a choice-based-conjoint analysis to find out factors, which influence acceptance of voice assistant systems. The method aimed to study consumer choices or preferences for complex products. Their study presented that "privacy" was the most important factor in the acceptance of voice assistant systems rather than "natural language processing-performance" and "price." It means that the participants did not want the assistant always to be online; it would be expected that they would rather reject this option.

In this study, we believe that the first screen design of the voice assistant systems influences the user engagement. One of the first screens of the voice assistant system should consist of recommendable commands, and we believe that if it can become one of the factors for acceptance of voice assistant system, then it may influence the level of engagement.

3   An Analysis of Using Voice Assistant Systems

3.1   Buzz Data Analysis

We hypothesised one of the important bottlenecks of using voice assistant system is that the user does not know the supported functions and command words because the voice assistant system can neither recognise all natural languages nor provide all functions of the mobile phone via voice. This indicates that learnability is one of the improvement points in the voice assistant system. We tried to analyse the usability issues of voice assistant systems. Rather than collecting user data or performing a user survey, we used big data to find UX insights in the voice assistant system as well as to discover users' natural opinions regarding the voice assistant systems. Various kinds of data are currently collected to find out new trends in the market. According to Lavalle et al. (2011), recent studies of predictive analytics are not limited to specific areas, such as marketing or customer management, due to the growth of various analytical data [7]. Data analysis performed online has expanded to financial management and budgeting, operations and production, and customer service.

Samsung Electronics has a big data system called BDP; it has collected a variety of buzz data from social network systems such as Twitter, Facebook, Instagram, news, and other forums. Through the BDP, we can collect English written buzz data about Google Assistant and Apple Siri from the 9th of December 2019 to 90 days prior. The system can categorise whether buzz data is positive, neutral, or negative. Table 1 indicates that negative posts comprised 17% of buzz data regarding Google Assistant. Table 2 indicates that negative posts comprised 38% of buzz data regarding Apple Siri. We hypothesised that presenting only "What can I help you with?" is not sufficient to guide users; thus, there were more negative posts about using Apple Siri. We will discuss the context of using voice assistant systems through work domain analysis (WDA) and the voice assistant system users' decision-making style through Decision Ladder based on some expert interviews in Sect. 3.3.

Table 1. Buzz data analysis for Google Assistant (last 90 days from 9th/Dec/2019).

	Number of buzz
Total	54790
Positive posts	8088 (15%)
Neutral posts	37387 (68%)
Negative posts	9315 (17%)

Table 2. Buzz data analysis for Apple Siri (last 90 days from 9th/Dec/2019).

	Number of buzz
Total	100000
Positive posts	23383 (23%)
Neutral posts	38346 (38%)
Negative posts	38271 (38%)

3.2 Work Domain Analysis Based on Buzz Data

We analysed buzz data specifically pertaining to Google Assistant and Apple Siri to determine various contexts of using voice assistant systems. The result of WDA indicates that the users normally use these voice assistant systems for several different events as detailed in Fig. 1. In addition, their environment can influence events.

According to the buzz data, the users use the voice assistant systems to control light, air conditioners, or even set an alarm at night. The users regularly send e-mails, set a schedule, and receive weather information and news through their voice assistant systems. While driving, users use it for calling, playing music, finding information about songs, controlling functions of the vehicle, and setting a destination on their navigation system. Through the WDA, we can assume that time and location information can be an important factor to recognise the context of using the voice assistant system. Additionally, GPS data can also be regarded as a significant factor because it can recognise where the user is driving.

Fig. 1. Work domain analysis of the contexts of using voice assistant systems.

3.3   Control Task Analysis Based on Expert Interview

We recruited four experts in voice assistant systems, and then we conducted in-depth interviews to analyse how users control their voice assistant system. Based on the results of these in-depth interviews, most experts indicated that many potential voice assistant systems users could not overcome the first stage of system use; the user thinks about how to say the command and cannot get any further. In the early days, when voice recognition came on the market, the main issue of voice assistant systems was the recognition rate. Although the recognition rate has improved, the main bottleneck of using the voice assistant system is still that the users do not know what functions the system can support because the voice assistant systems only present one sentence; "What can I help you with?" (Fig. 2).

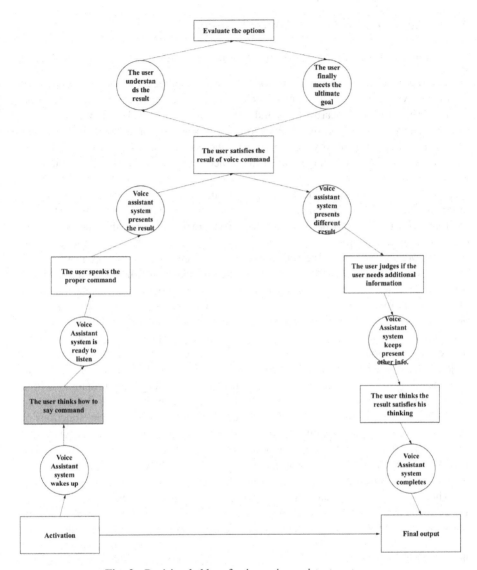

Fig. 2. Decision ladder of using voice assistant systems.

Thus, the experts argued that only presenting one sentence is not a sufficient guideline for users because they could not know the functions of voice assistant systems without being given more information. They try to use their voice assistant several times, and unsuccessful trials cannot lead to continuous usage.

4   A Suggestion of Context-Based Design

4.1   Context Modelling for the Voice Assistant System

Dey and Abowd (1999) insisted that context must be regarded as an important factor for interactive applications [8]. In the field of mobile computing, some information such as user's location, nearby users and their devices, time of day, and user activity can be manipulated to improve latency time or boost the communication signal by using bandwidth from nearby devices (Chen and Kotz, 2000) [9]. In this study, we suggest user context modelling of using the voice assistant system based on the buzz analysis.

The buzz data analysis identifies that the users use the voice assistant system differently according to the time of day. In general, at home, the users want to start the morning with useful information; thus, they want to listen to weather, news and get daily briefing information from the voice assistant system. On the other hand, at night, the users prepare to sleep. The relevant commands analysed include controlling IoT devices, setting the alarm, and setting a schedule on a calendar. During the daytime, the user uses a voice assistant system for application behaviours that operate via touch interaction. For example, they may send e-mail, share photos, send text messages, etc. When the user is walking or driving a car, the user's context changed. When the user is walking, opening the map application and voice memo applications generally are used to avoid uncomfortable touch interaction while walking. While driving a car, the user's vision should focus on scanning the driving environment, and the user's hands should hold the steering wheel; the user feels uncomfortable when they need to interact with a touch device due to driver distraction. The buzz data analysis described that calling, setting a destination, and playing music are regarded as the higher priority functions of the voice assistant system while driving. Furthermore, the voice assistant system can recognise the user context through the sound input. If the system determines that music is playing, it can provide song information. Alternatively, if the system determines that the user is in a meeting, it can suggest recording voices.

The quantity of buzz data has arranged the order of commands in each context. Based the context modelling from the buzz data, we designed a user interface (UI) for the first screen of the voice assistant system. The UI presents several recommendable commands, which are consistent with the user's context and are easily accessible. In the next section, we will evaluate how the suggested UI influences the user engagement of the voice assistant system (Fig. 3).

Cat-egory	Home			Outside		If input da-ta available
	Morn-ing	Day-time	Night	Walk-ing	Driving	Sound
Rec-om-mended func-tions	Weath er info	Send e-mail	IOT control	Open map	Call	Find a song
	News	Share photos	Alarm on/off	Voice Memo	Set a destination	Voice Memo
	Daily Briefing	Send text mes-sages	Set a schedule on a cal-endar		Play a music	
		Set a schedule on a cal-endar	Call		Find a song	
		Call	Send text mes-sages		Control functions of vehicle	
			Send e-mail		Voice memo	
			Share photos			

Fig. 3. Context modelling based on the buzz data analysis

5   Is Presenting Recommendable Commands Better?

To design a more effective voice assistant system, we conducted expert interviews to determine the bottleneck of using a voice assistant system. Previously, we discussed expert interviews; the result indicated that the users do not properly use their voice assistant systems because they do not know the functions of the system. Thus, we designed the UI of the proposed voice assistant system consisting of recommendable commands. For suggesting recommendable commands, we developed context modelling based on the buzz data analysis. We believe that a voice assistant system, which involves recommendable commands can create more user engagement than current voice assistant systems, which only involve a guide sentence. Thus, through the experiment, we tried to compare two different UI screens in the level of engagement; the first one presents recommendable screen, the second one only presents "What can I help you with?" (Fig. 4)

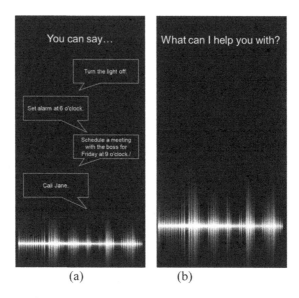

Fig. 4. First screen of each type of voice assistant system: (a) Recommending commands; (b) Presenting a guide sentence

5.1   Method

We measured user engagement regarding the two different types of voice assistant systems. According to O'Brien (2016a), user engagement is regarded as a quality of user experience characterised by the depth of user's cognitive, temporal, affective, and behavioural investment when interacting with a specific system [10]. In addition, user engagement is more than user satisfaction because the ability to engage and sustain engagement can result in outcomes that are more positive. To measure user

FA-S.1	I lost myself in this experience.
FA-S.2	The time I spent using this voice assistant system just slipped away.
FA-S.3	I was absorbed in this experience.
PU-S.1	I felt frustrated while using this voice assistant system .
PU-S.2	I found this Voice Assistant System confusing to use.
PU-S.3	Using this Voice Assistant System was taxing.
AE-S.1	This Voice Assistant System was attractive.
AE-S.2	This Voice Assistant System was aesthetically appealing.
AE-S.3	This Voice Assistant System appealed to my senses.
RW-S.1	Using Voice Assistant System was worthwhile.
RW-S.2	My experience was rewarding.
RW-S.3	I felt interested in this experience.

Fig. 5. Questions of UES from O'Brien's study (2018)

engagement, the UES, specifically UES-SF provided by O'Brien et al. (2018) was used in this experiment. Questions of UES consist of several dimensions, focused attention (FA), perceived usability (PU), aesthetic appeal (AE), and rewarding (RW) (Fig. 5) [5].

5.2 Experimental Design and Participants

The within-subject design was used to measure two kinds of voice assistant systems. The order of the voice assistant systems presented was random. The independent variable was each UI screen of the voice assistant system. The dependent variable was the score of UES. A total of 24 participants were recruited, ranging in age from 26 to 46 years (mean age of 34.4 years). They were instructed about the experiment first; then they answered the UES questions about each voice assistant system.

5.3 Results

Figure 6 presents the average UES score of each voice assistant system. The total UES score of the "Presenting recommendable commands" voice assistant system was 46.09, out of a maximum score of 60. The total UES score of the "Presenting guide sentence" voice assistant system was 26.09. Through statistical analysis, there was a significant difference between the two systems ($p < 0.05$). In the aspect of dimension, the average UES score of the "Presenting recommendable commands" was significantly higher than "Presenting guide sentence." It describes that "Presenting recommendable commands" voice assistant system induces more user attention, usability, aesthetic appeal, and rewarding than the voice assistant system which only presents a guide sentence.

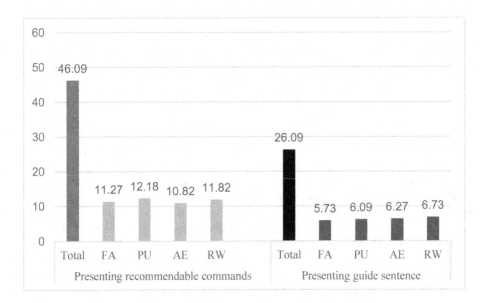

Fig. 6. Bar graph of user engagement score for each voice assistant system

6 Discussion, Limitations, and Future Work

The result indicated that most participants chose the version of the voice assistant system, which can present recommended commands. It means that the voice assistant system presenting recommended commands led to more user engagement than the voice assistant system that only includes a guide sentence. In the aspect of dimensions, the recommended commands UI had the greatest effect on usability. The score of perceived usability was relatively higher than in other dimensions. However, the score of perceived usability in other systems was not higher than other dimensions. Presenting recommended commands led to a higher level of usability, and it induced more user engagement. Therefore, the result described that presenting commands helped the users to learn how to use the voice assistant system, and it led to higher user engagement.

Several studies are needed for further research. First, in this study, we developed context modelling based on the buzz data as we could not collect personal data. The buzz data consists of user's preference functions. The context modelling was developed based on events and functions that were generally more useful for many users rather than individual data analysis. Defining individual context and recommending function is the first challenge. The voice assistant system cannot listen the user's voice every time due to privacy issues. Burbach et al. (2019) suggested that "privacy" is the most important factor in using a voice assistant system. It means that voice assistant system users do not want the system to continue to listen to their voices. Thus, the system only can check voice data when it is activated through the user's intention such as pushing the activation button or saying an activation command. At that time, the problem is that the system cannot analyse a novice user's context. In addition, if the period of using the system is short, the data must be sufficiently cumulated. We believe that if the user tries to use the voice assistant system for the first time, our context modelling based on the buzz data might be effective. However, for experienced users, the voice assistant system should sufficiently possess enough individual data to present recommended commands based on user context. The second challenge is presenting hidden functions to the users. The voice assistant system cannot present all functions on the first screen. Only two or three functions can be presented to avoid the complexity of the UI. This limitation requires further study in the future.

7 Conclusion

In recent years, voice assistant systems have changed user interaction and experience with computers. Several mobile service providers have introduced various types of voice assistant systems like Bixby from Samsung, Siri from Apple, and Google Assistant from Google that provide information such as the schedule for a day, the weather, or methods to control the device such as playing music. Although the voice assistant systems provide various kinds of functions, generally, the users do not know what functions the voice assistant system can support. Rather than collecting user data or performing a user survey, we used big data to find UX insights in the voice assistant system as well as to discover users' natural opinions regarding voice assistant systems.

Through the Samsung Big Data Portal system, we collected English buzz data about Google Assistant and Apple Siri. The system categorised whether the data is positive, neutral, or negative. The proportion of negative opinion of Apple Siri is higher than that of Google Assistant. We hypothesised presenting only "What can I help you with?" is not a sufficient guide for users. We discussed the contexts of using voice assistant systems through WDA and the voice assistant system users' decision-making style through a control task analysis based on some expert interviews. The results of the control task analysis described that the main bottleneck of using the voice assistant system is the user cannot know all of the useful commands. Thus, we believed that presenting recommended commands is an effective way to increase user engagement. Through the buzz data analysis, we could discover what functions can be used and the usage contexts. Hence, we performed context modelling, designed the UI of a prototype voice assistant system, and conducted a case study. Through the case study, we proved that presenting commands on the UI induced more user engagement and usability. However, a method of finding out user context based on individual data and presenting hidden functions will be the subject of future work.

References

1. Fortune Business Insights. https://www.fortunebusinessinsights.com/industry-reports/speech-and-voice-recognition-market-101382. Accessed 09 Jan 2020
2. Google Inc. https://www.prnewswire.com/news-releases/teens-use-voice-search-most-even-in-bathroom-googles-mobile-voice-study-finds-279106351.html. Accessed 09 Jan 2020
3. Business Insider. https://www.businessinsider.com/siri-google-assistant-voice-market-share-charts-2018-6. Accessed 09 Jan 2020
4. Kiseleva, J., et al.: Understanding user satisfaction with intelligent assistants. In: Proceedings of the 2016 ACM on Conference on Human Information Interaction and Retrieval, pp. 121–130. ACM (2016)
5. O'Brien, H.L., Cairns, P., Hall, M.: A practical approach to measuring user engagement with the refined user engagement scale (UES) and new UES short form. Int. J. Hum Comput Stud. **112**, 28–39 (2018)
6. Burbach, L., Halbach, P., Plettenberg, N., Nakayama, J., Ziefle, M., Valdez, A.C.: "Hey, Siri", "Ok, Google", "Alexa". Acceptance-relevant factors of virtual voice-assistants. In: 2019 IEEE International Professional Communication Conference. IEEE (2019)
7. LaValle, S., Lesser, E., Shockley, R., Hopkins, M.S., Kruschwitz, N.: Big data, analytics and the path from insights to value. MIT Sloan Manag. Rev. **52**(2), 21–32 (2011)
8. Dey, A.K.: Understanding and using context. Pers. Ubiquit. Comput. **5**(1), 4–7 (2001). https://doi.org/10.1007/s007790170019
9. Chen, G., Kotz, D.: A survey of context-aware mobile computing research. Dartmouth Computer Science Technical report TR2000-381 (2000)
10. O'Brien, H.: Theoretical perspectives on user engagement. In: O'Brien, H., Cairns, P. (eds.) Why Engagement Matters, pp. 1–26. Springer, Cham (2016). https://doi.org/10.1007/978-3-319-27446-1_1

Holistic Assessment of Situated Cooking Interactions: Preliminary Results of an Observational Study

Stephanie Van Hove[(✉)], Anissa All, Peter Conradie,
and Lieven De Marez

imec-mict-Ghent University, Ghent, Belgium
Stephanie.Vanhove@Ugent.be

Abstract. This study presents the preliminary results of in situ observations of 2 cooking moments among 16 households. The aim of the study was to map the domestic cooking ecosystem from a user's perspective and define which components of that environment influence the user's cooking experience. Preliminary results show that contextual components and in particular, situations, shape cooking experiences in the domestic kitchen. Four opposite situational contexts, i.e., cooking for oneself or cooking for guests, cooking on a weekday or cooking during the weekend, cooking routine dishes or cooking dishes for the first time, and cooking alone or cooking together were distinguished. Situational context will influence temporal context, social context, physical context perceptions and information and task context of the cooking activity. These will in turn influence interactions with objects (i.e., ingredients, kitchen utensils), kitchen technology and their interfaces, content and other people present during the cooking activity. This study suggests that future kitchen technologies can match or enhance current practices only if designers and user researchers understand and define their situational context. This study goes beyond the state of the art, as this is the first study that aims to provide a holistic analysis of the current state of domestic cooking experiences using in-situ observations in order to inform design of future technologies. Implications for design are discussed.

Keywords: Kitchen · Cooking · Home · Family · Situational context · Situated action · Contextual inquiry · Retrospective think-aloud

1 Introduction

Studying the home is a difficult endeavor, let alone kitchen practices, as meaning is created through informal agreements, tacit knowledge and embodied interactions [36]. The majority of people's actions within the home occur in an unstructured manner and are not just part of routines [11]. Notwithstanding, smart home research either focuses automating routines or improving performance [10].

Other design strategies should be taken into account when designing experiences for the home, and in particular for todays kitchens. Experiences cannot be boiled down to human-system interactions, but stretch from interactions with other people, content, dumb and smart objects to a multitude of situational contexts [51]. Therefore, it is

© Springer Nature Switzerland AG 2020
A. Marcus and E. Rosenzweig (Eds.): HCII 2020, LNCS 12201, pp. 158–174, 2020.
https://doi.org/10.1007/978-3-030-49760-6_11

important that technology design is informed by understanding the needs of people, activities they perform in the kitchen, and the situations taking place in household kitchens [38]. Further, design choices should enhance (and not distract) traditional living, and match (instead of conflicting with) the original interactions [8]. Joint HCI and cooking literature typically limit their focus to one type of interaction of the cooking experience, solely focusing on either content interactions, object interactions or social interactions. In an IoT context, however, interactions with technology have become multidimensional and multimodal and woven into everyday interactions [52]. Hence, the authors of this paper strongly support a holistic approach applied in successful user experience design [40], taking into account all interactions that might impact or result from the envisioned human-system interactions. Therefore, the empirical contribution of this study lies in the holistic assessment of the kitchen ecosystem from a user-centered approach. Moreover, this study also provides a practical contribution for designers and engineers by means of design requirements.

2   Related Work

2.1   Experience Design

Experience design is in essence about problem setting and problem solving, which strives to design the right functionality and the right concept [7, 12]. All product components, such as its functionalities, content, interactions, interface and tangible objects should be aligned with the foreseen experience. Therefore, Hassenzahl suggests to first 'consider experience before products' [22:76]. Moreover, it is argued that researchers should relate empirical insights in the context-of-use with theories and models [4, 22].

Domestic cooking experiences are complex experiences consisting of a multitude of interactions, such as interactions with food, with kitchen appliances, with recipes, with other household members, with devices and tasks unrelated to cooking, etc. By considering the holistic context-of-use and all these interactions, designers are able to make more informed decisions regarding future kitchen products and services.

In the next section, we will give a short overview of the main components studied in HCI research regarding domestic cooking experiences.

2.2   HCI in the Domestic Cooking Experience

Efficiency Versus Experiential Quality
Since the advent of smart homes, HCI has also moved into the kitchen. Ethnography studies suggest that kitchens are not only goal-oriented places [5], but rather places where common everyday experiences take place [36]. However, the innovations that have entered modern kitchens or that are presented at HCI conferences merely focus on automating habits and assisting household cooks. For example, KitchenSense, translates clusters of routines into personalized information on tasks (e.g., safety alarm on cooking temperature, cooking technique instructions) [26], and the visual prompting system of Ikeda et al. [24] assists elderly in multi-step tasks in the kitchen.

The strong focus on efficiency over experiential quality has led to a wide arsenal of kitchen appliances, such as microwaves, deep fryers and food processors, which resulted in faster, but not necessarily better food [2]. Grimes and Harper [17] also found in their review of food research in HCI that technologies are informed by a corrective approach and are thus designed to fix problems that individuals are thought to have with food. Therefore, Bell, Blythe and Sengers see potential for HCI research to resolve the borders of design spaces by criticizing the assumptions that underlie the design of everyday objects [2]. In their research they defamiliarized the home through the use of ethnography of English and Asian homes, and a cultural history of American kitchen technology and translated it into twelve design recommendations. None of the 12 design statements values efficiency, whereas two statements are related to hedonic experiences (i.e., creating new experiences and supporting serious play), and four shed light on the needs and motivations of the user. The remaining six statements take the broader socio-cultural and situational context into account. Hence, recent efforts in HCI research encourage 'celebratory technologies', that complement existing positive interactions or with food instead of focusing on problematic interactions that technology might 'solve' [17]. One such technology is the Living Cookbook [47], by means of which people can share live cooking experiences with others or teaching how to cook.

In order to avoid that celebratory technology ideas turns an already positive experience into a negative experience, however, the authors emphasize the importance of understanding the behavior being addressed [17].

Social Interaction in the Domestic Cooking Environment
Kitchens are inhabited by different household members, each with different motivations for being there. One could see the kitchen as the ultimate play zone, whereas others perceive it as a place to rest, to connect with others or to improve their cooking skills. The social context of living together with others impacts cooking experiences and the meaning people attach to it. Multiple studies found that living together with other people structures cooking practices, because sharing homemade meals serves as a symbol of their family life [53, 54]. In contrast, people living alone, such as widows, consider cooking rather as a chore and are less willing to invest time and effort to cooking [44].

In a qualitative study that explored hedonic eating experiences of 16 people, was found that social interactions positively contribute to hedonic eating [33]. In particular the presence of others and the eating activity serve as a venue to other social activities (e.g., talking about food, sharing thoughts, preparing meal together).

A video observation study on the gestural interactions during family cooking acknowledged the importance of social context for gestural interactions [36]. Whether people preferred verbal or gestural interactions, depends on the social characteristics of the situation, such as age, ethnicity, type of relationship, and food related knowledge and skills. However, it is this presence of multiple people packed in one space that inhibits the successful recognition of gestures and different people by gestural sensors [38]. With regard to the cooking stage, it is argued that cooking food is a more individual activity than food preparing, with the latest holding the opportunity to be a 'powerful bonding mechanism', as intimate social interactions take place while preparing ingredients [32:282, 35]. Not only the cooking stage, but far more the physical context of kitchens facilitates socializing among significant others [32] and should be considered as an integral part of the cooking experience [21]. The physical activity of preparing food in combination with intimate conversations are even considered 'kitchen therapy' [32:282].

Interaction Modalities Kitchens are multisensory spaces that cater to the experience of processing and combining ingredients during which odors and flavors emerge. However, systems that are present in today's kitchens do not respond to these type of experiences. Interfaces of ovens, scales, hobs, and even novel innovations that are presented at HCI conferences are primarily graphical user interfaces with touch interaction modalities [13, 20, 27 e.g., 42]. Tangible technologies mostly facilitate pragmatic experiences, and to a lesser extent social and hedonic experiences [30, 36, see: 49]. Based on their ethnographic study on family cooking, Nansen, Davis, Vetere et al. [36] see potential for tangible technologies to support special cooking occasions and for (non-verbal) system-mediated communication. Furthermore, they suggest that especially younger cooks will benefit from grip-sensitive sensors and adults rather from speech input. This was also found in a preliminary evaluation study of an interactive recipe system [35]. Its tangible tags that visualize the available ingredients facilitate social interaction and decision-making.

An observational pilot study towards the development of the MimiCook system, in which recipes are embodied in the kitchen counter, discovered that people misread the amount of ingredients or overlook a step when reading step-by-step instructions of a recipe [42]. This is a common difficulty with graphical user interfaces, and hence also traditional paper recipes, due to a decoupling of the perception and action space [43]. Tangible interfaces that unify input and output can overcome this difficulty [43]. Once the technology was tested, researchers discovered that the display time of instructions is critical, as well as the interpretation of instructions such as "mix well" [42]. Moreover, the study showed that people were confused what measuring tools or utensils to use [42].

The Broader Situational Context of Cooking

Situational context has shown to impact user requirements regarding design and features of kitchen technology [14]. To our knowledge only one study evaluated the potential of interaction modalities of a cooking assistant prototype for different situations, such as cooking new versus known dishes, busy cooking (i.e., while multitasking) and mobile cooking (i.e., cooking outside of anybody's home) [50]. This study found that how features are perceived, largely depend on context and age. Social context raise as an important not a priori defined context as one to impact preferences of interaction modalities. In situations where other people are present during the cooking process, for example, speech input is considered socially inappropriate [50]. The cooking assistant prototype could also automatically adapt to the context of use, such as postponing audio messages until a conversation break, which was highly appreciated by the participants [50]. However, turning an ubiquitous system into blind and deaf mode was not yet implemented, although much sought after [50].

2.3   Towards Situated Cooking Action Observations

While several studies have been conducted regarding user experience of domestic cooking technologies, these are limited to either the investigation of one specific component of the cooking environment and/or the evaluation of a specific technology. A study mapping the domestic cooking ecosystem can provide an interesting step back in order to define both problems and current positive aspects of the domestic cooking experience. This can provide a meaningful framework for the conceptual design stages of kitchen technology and thus design by understanding the activity [36]. While several studies have conducted research aiming to understand the domestic cooking activity, these were either a) a small discussed step in a technology evaluation oriented paper [42] b) not conducted in a domestic environment [42] and/or c) aimed towards a subcomponent of the whole cooking experience [38]. The present manuscript goes beyond the state of the art by investigating the domestic cooking experience in a holistic manner.

Moreover, this manuscript goes beyond the state of the art through its methodology. Previous research aiming to get insight in the domestic cooking experience, either asked participants to gather visual data of themselves that was later used during in-depth interviews [55], conducted (video-) observation of the cooking activity at home with a researcher present [55] and/or created an artificial domestic cooking experience outside the homes of the participants while being observed by a researcher [42, 50]. This results in representations and versions of events, produced by the researcher and/or the participant [55]. More specifically, these are either reconstructions and/or projections of actions. According to Suchman, however, actual *in situ* action needs to be distinguished from projected actions (i.e., a priori rational plans) and reconstructions of courses of actions (i.e., post-hoc interpretation of actions) [45]. Actions depend upon the action's circumstances and comprises of ad hoc responses to contingencies of particular situations and the actions of others [45]. This means that the investigation of domestic-cooking experiences should occur in its authentic environment, not only referring to the physical environment, but also to the presence of other household members during this activity and other relevant events or interactions that influence actions of the household cooks. A study of situated action of the domestic cooking experience is not only important to gain an ecologically more valid view on this experience, but is also important in order to gain insight in which situations influence actions and how these influence action. This is important in HCI design as machines do not have the same resources as humans to interpret situations of actions. Successful interaction between people is however, the result of mutual understanding of situation and through the detection, repair and exploitation of possible differences in understanding [45]. Successful interaction between 'smart' technology and humans should thus also thrive for the same, as a machine's insensitivity to situations have previously resulted in negative user experiences [45, 50].

By using video cameras in the home context, without the presence of a researcher and without actively asking participants to shoot content, we aim towards a more ecologically valid view of the domestic cooking experience, its actions and its situations of actions. The present manuscript discusses preliminary results.

3   Methodology

The aim of this study was to gain a better understanding of cooking experiences in today's Western kitchens. For this purpose, in-depth interviews have been conducted with 16 people facilitated by retrospective think-aloud protocol (RTA). Prior to the interview, the interviewees participated in in-situ video-observations that have been conducted in their kitchens during two cooking moments. The observations (only video, no audio) took place on a weekday and a weekend day. The observations lasted approximately 1–3 h per cooking moment. The research design has been approved by the faculty's ethical committee.

3.1   Video Observations

One week before the in-depth interview, two Nest cameras were installed in the kitchen of the participant. One camera (cooking camera) was installed nearby the cooking hob that captures all interactions with the hob, hood, and pots. The other camera (context camera) captures the broader physical context of the kitchen, focusing on the back of the cook and the most frequently used passages (see Fig. 1). During the camera setup, participants were asked when they would be cooking during the next week and weekend. Accordingly, only data is collected during these agreed-upon cooking moments using the calendar functionality of Nest. A Nest camera can be remotely switched on and off, and family members are notified of its power state through a green led on the camera. Before data collection starts, all adult family members are provided with a consent that informs them about the purpose of the study and the data that is going to be collected. This informed consent requests their voluntary participation in the observational study and a follow-up interview with the focal participant afterwards. In case the participating family has one or more children younger than 16 y/o, parents also have to give their consent to videotape the children.

Fig. 1.   Video observation set-up

The video observations served as probing material of the Retrospective Think-Aloud Protocol. During the qualitative data analyses of the interviews, the videos recordings also served as additional contextual information.

3.2   Retrospective Think-Aloud Protocol

In the retrospective think aloud (RTA) protocol participants verbalized their thoughts while watching the video recordings of their cooking. In contrast to concurrent think-aloud (where participants think out loud while working on a task) this method yields more explanatory insights, as no cognitive effort is imposed on participants while undertaking the cooking task [19]. Playback speed was altered to four times the original speed, resulting in playback durations from 40" to 1h40" for the recordings of the combined cooking moments. Video recordings were paused if needed. Moreover, if particular interactions or contextual characteristics were not coined by the end of the RTA, a semi-structured topic guide was followed covering questions, such as 'Is there a division of roles between you and your partner in the kitchen?', 'What would you like to change in your kitchen?', 'What makes you insecure while cooking?', 'What is the meaning of your kitchen?', 'How would you describe yourself as a cook?

3.3   Data Analysis

The in-depth interviews are transcribed and coded in NVivo 12. Data coding proceeded following the analytical process of Grounded Theory [16], which consists of multiple waves of open, axial and selective coding. Preliminary results in the open coding stage revealed interactions with ingredients, kitchen utensils, kitchen technology, kitchen technology interfaces, other people, non-related kitchen technology and content. Additionally, time-related variables, space-related variables and dish type resulted from open coding. By means of axial coding, these open codes were subdivided into the following categories: social context, information and task context, physical context, temporal context and situational context. In the selective coding phase, the authors decided to select the situational context as core category, as it serves as a lens for people to motivate and perceive people's cooking experiences. In the results section different situational contexts are delineated and how these impact the perceived interactions with objects, cooking appliances, content and other people in the household, across the different cooking stages.

3.4   Participants

Participants were recruited from a profiling survey that has been conducted as part of the same research project. While a full description of this profiling is beyond the scope of this paper, in brief, it was based on a k-means clustering of survey questions relating cooking motivation and behavior. It resulted in three profiles of increasing levels of motivation to cook and action cooking behavior (i.e.: 1) persons least motivated to cook, 2) those struggling to find a balance between cooking and other pressing activities and, 3) those with a motivated and creative cooking profile). These three cooking profiles were also present among the 16 participating cooks in this study. Ten participants are female, and the average age is 33.69 years (SD = 7.74) with the youngest 27 and the oldest participant 52 y/o. Six participants live together with their partner, another six with their partner and children, and three people live alone. The least motivated cooking profile with the lowest cooking frequency is represented by three people, the family cook that struggles with a healthy work-life balance is represented by six participants and another seven people fit the most motivated and creative cooking profile. The names of participants, family members and identity-sensitive video data are anonymized.

4 Results

4.1 Physical Context

Half of the observed households have a semi-open plan kitchen (i.e., the kitchen is separated from the living room through a kitchen island or low wall). Two open-plan kitchens (i.e., kitchen and living room are perceived as one room) and three closed-plan kitchens (i.e., the kitchen is located in a closed room separated from the living room) set also the scene for the observations. Participants who are delighted about the kitchen's physicality, most of all they praised the kitchen's atmosphere, i.e., soundscape and lighting. Whereas some prefer the radio to be on, the other prefers its silence. Also, its lighting seems to be crucial for the positive evaluation of a kitchen. Further, cooks positively perceived their kitchen's ergonomics, openness, and size. In their kitchens everything was within easy reach and open-plan kitchens served as a venue to more social contact. With regard to kitchen size, they are satisfied about the large surface or in case of a small kitchen, it forces them to be creative with the available resources. A man who rents a small house with a closed-plan kitchen describes this tradeoff between lack of space and creativity:

> Look, right now, over there is not enough space. That kettle was on the floor. I will put it back on the hob. It is really a matter of a lack of space, but I like to cook in a small kitchen. It challenges me to be creative though it is frustrating. It structures my cooking and forces me to create less chaos.

(P12, man, 31 y/o)

More often, on the other hand, household cooks are bothered with the physical characteristics of their kitchen, with atmosphere (i.e., gloomy lighting, environmental noise, and size (i.e., lack of space) as the most disturbing elements. A kitchen that always turns out to be messy, that forces the cook to do the dishes in between cooking, or that offers the cook limited space to prepare ingredients are often-mentioned small kitchen annoyances.

Objects

Kitchen utensils, pots, pans and ingredients are the main objects where household cooks interact with in the domestic cooking environment related to cooking. Smartphones are a non-cooking related object that is present among almost all participants and often used during 'dead' moments. Pots that need to be stirred and require attention, such as saucepans, are put on the front of the hob. High pots with contents requiring less attention are put in the back.

When cooking alone, cooks get a positive experience from efficiency-oriented practices, such as optimizing utensil use in order to limit dishes. Related to this, negative experiences are created when size of pots and pans needed for preparing a dish are underestimated, and one has to change pans resulting in more dishes.

Kitchen Appliances

Main kitchen technology that participants interact with are the oven, the hood, the hob and the fridge. The hood is turned on if the stove is turned on or when the pots are getting warm, because of its integrated lights. The hood is not always turned on and two main reasons can be distinguished for this: either it is unintentional (i.e., forgotten) or intentional, as the hood makes too much noise. When turned on, either the middle or highest hood level is used: The lowest hood level is almost never used, as *'it is so quit, it can't possibly extract fumes'* Only a minority leaves the cooking hood on after cooking, which is related to the quality of the hood (i.e., too noisy).

The hob is –besides actual cooking- also used as a source of warmth, keeping food warm while eating. The residual heat is also often used for cleaning burnt remains. Mixing soup is also an activity that occurs on the hob.

Remarkably, cooks who were used to physical button as interface with the kitchen technology prefer this over their current touch interfaces. They are perceived as more easy, fast and reliable. Also, implicit interactions such as in the induction system, are sometimes considered frustrating. For instance, when the stove is turned off as a result of over boiling water.

One participant stated that she loved to cook with the oven, because *'you don't have to keep an eye on the oven all the time and you don't have to stay in the kitchen'.*

4.2   Social Context

A difference between active and passive household members can be made. More specifically, active household members refer to household members involved in the cooking process. Passive household members refer to members present in the physical context around the cooking experience, not involved in the cooking process, influencing the domestic cooking experience.

Only three participants prepared a meal alone during both cooking moments and only two were supported by their partner during both sessions. However, cooking alone does not mean that no one was nearby; they were accompanied by their partner, children, both, cohousing friends or a household help. Hence, it is noteworthy that people who cook alone often talk with others who are present in the kitchen or in the semi-attached living room. The observations show that couples tend to cook together more often (all but one participant cooked at least once together) and families with children tend to divide chores between both parents with one being occupied with dinner preparation and the other mostly occupied with the children. Only three couples cooked together or with their children, the remaining eight family cooks prepared a meal alone during one or both cooking moments.

All but one participant mentioned the social context as determining for their cooking experience in either a good or bad way. Especially in terms of arousal, such as talking, intimate affection, and the pleasant feeling of having someone around. One participant also mentioned the increase in efficiency as and advantage of cooking together.

> It's not like we need each other to cook. We don't wait till the other is home to start preparing dinner. It is more fun, I mean, being together in the kitchen is the first thing that happens if we turn back from work. That is our main reason, to have a little chat. (P07, man, 27 y/o)

Contrary, the social presence of others or even cooking together leads to a plethora of frustrations and conflicting processes among 8 participants. Especially the presence of children, which negatively impacts the feeling of control, leads to unforeseen conditions, and makes it difficult to divide attention between cooking and children. When cooking together with others, people mentioned conflicting priorities (slow vs fast, precise vs loose, ...) or processes (more dishes, getting in each other's way, no multitasking, already in use utensils or cooking zones ...). Moreover, cooking together appears more chaotic and inevitably it results in waiting for one another. One woman (52 y/o) also mentioned that cooking with other people than her partner makes her insecure about her cooking skills. Another woman with two children of 1 and 3 years old explains why she strives to do the dishes together with her partner in the weekends:

> Mostly my daughter grabs on to my leg and then I can't do much anymore. Now (referring to the video observation) both kids are in the storage room opening and closing the door over and over again, but I give them a hand slap and tell them to stop it.

(P05, woman, 33 y/o)

Another woman describes why she prefers to cook alone instead of together with her partner:

> I have the feeling that when I cook alone on weekdays, it occurs more efficiently if no one disturbs me: I immediately clean everything. But, if we cook together, the dishes start to pile up and everything gets everywhere. During those moments I think 'that doesn't belong over there'. Maybe I think I am more efficient if I do it all by myself?

(P02, woman, 27 y/o)

4.3   Information and Task Context

Seven participants cooked one or both cooking moments with a recipe. While not all cooks cook with a recipe, those who do, follow it closely. Insecurities raise as a result of non-detailed description of quantities, and not knowing how something should look like and when something is done.

In this study, cooks explained that they prepared new recipes more often for guests than for their family. When cooking for guests, they prepare more elaborate meals, which provides more pressure, but is also worth it according to three people. Only one observed cooking moment was for guests (single woman, cooking for a friend) and all other participants cooked both observed moments for their family.or in case of singles for. Remarkably, participants evaluated the preparation of a family meal based on other parameters than a meal for guests. When describing the cooking process for guests it is both evaluated in terms of its result and the overall experience, whereas family meal cooking is described in terms of its result, i.e., goal-oriented cooking. A single woman who cooked dinner for a friend explains why her attitude during the think-aloud was rather negative:

It seems like I don't like cooking, but it's just because I'm under time pressure. You are cooking for someone else. So, it has to be good, because you want her to like it. The day before it didn't really matter, because I had to eat it myself.

(P01, woman, 27 y/o)

Almost everyone (n = 15, f = 22) prepared a routine dish at least once, whereas eight cooks prepared a new dish with a recipe (f = 7, n = 6) or improvised a meal from scratch (n = 2, without recipe support). People oftentimes explained their choice for familiar dishes in terms of the needs and restrictions of family members, or depending on the week of the day (weekdays vs weekend). These household cooks prepare a dish that everyone likes, which are mostly simple and fast dishes. Furthermore, the narrow preferences of children and food intolerance negatively impact meal variation. The most prepared meal during the observations is a typical Flemish meal, consisting of sausages, apple compote and mashed potatoes (WAP).

We prepared WAP, but we used frozen mashed potatoes, since there were no potatoes left. On Sunday evenings it is mostly a quite simple meal, which is not an exception over here.

(P07, man, 27 y/o)

4.4   Temporal Context

All participants cooked once on a weekday and once during the weekend as prescribed in the research design. The majority prepared a familiar dish on weekdays (n = 13), whereas a more equitable distribution of dish type can be noticed during the weekend (familiar dishes, n = 9 - new dishes, n = 6). This is indicative for the close relationship between temporal and task context. If participants considered the temporal context of their cooking experience, it is mostly described in terms of time pressure and routines. Time pressure results especially from the cooking event as part of a chain of events, such as after grocery shopping and before sports activities, but can also result from the cooking experience itself. One woman who works fulltime and has two children describes her personal experience with cooking on weekdays.

P03: There is a big difference between cooking on weekdays and in the weekend. I don't feel at ease when I don't have enough time to cook. It's like going for a run to relax, but you have to be back within half an hour!
Interviewer: Why is it similar?
P03: Then I don't cook, or I opt for something very easy
Interviewer: When do you not feel at ease to cook?
P03: If I arrive late home or if we have to go somewhere.

(woman, 32 y/o)

Another single participant who cooks for a friend feels agitated while cooking, due to unforeseen circumstances. She has to switch pots and the cooking process proceeds faster than expected.

I used a small pan to fry the onion, but then I realized I need a bigger one to add the other ingredients. I switched pans, while I thought 'now I have more dishes'. Now I add the olive oil, which warmed up quickly and I get even more agitated.

(woman, 27 y/o)

5 Conclusion and Discussion

Based on the preliminary analysis of the in-depth interviews, we can deduct the following situations:

- cooking for a guest (external household) or cooking for family/cooking or for yourself (internal household)
- cooking routine dishes or cooking new dishes
- cooking on weekdays or cooking on weekend days
- cooking alone or cooking together

These situations impact requirements regarding development and design of kitchen technology and applications. Situational context impacts temporal context, information and task context and how the physical context is perceived. Temporal context, information and task context and physical context in turn impact the interaction with objects, content, kitchen technology and other household members present in the direct domestic cooking environment. When aiming to develop IoT technology for the kitchen, a system should be able to detect these situations and adjust its behavior depending on these situations.

When cooking during weekdays, for instance, temporal context takes the upper hand: people are often under time pressure because of other activities before or after the cooking activity. This results in people resorting to routine dishes and thus cooking without a recipe (information and task context). During weekdays, children are present during these cooking moments, possibly distracting the cook (social context). Main frustrations are thus related to not being able to finish the meal in time or that separate subcomponents of the dish are not finished in time and being distracted while cooking. A smart kitchen system that can support households in reducing time pressure during weekdays, both during preparation including grocery shopping and cooking phases would be of added value. Even more if it allows the cook to being distracted, without having to sacrifice time or dish quality. This system should, however, allow for input of the cook -and not rely on recipes of the system- as during these time pressured moments one falls back on own recipes.

When cooking during weekend days there is less time pressure and more opportunity for hedonic cooking. More specifically, trying out new dishes and learning new cooking techniques (task context). A smart kitchen system should thus also be able to inspire cooks before (e.g. system-suggested recipes that require more time/skill so the cook can learn new dishes) and during the cooking process (e.g. trying out a new slicing technique when cooking in the weekend).

Cooking alone is often considered more efficient than cooking together. This is mainly caused by differences in speed of separate cooking processes, different ways of following a recipe (e.g. one wants to follow the recipe rigorously while the other likes to follow it more freely, changing several components/information and task context) or lack of space (physical context), all resulting in frustration. However, people like to cook together as it is a 'social moment', a moment to talk about how the day went, to show some affection, etc. Here, we thus see a clash between temporal context elements (efficiency) and social context elements (social interaction with family members). Cooking together for most of the time, means that different participants of the household participate in different steps of the cooking process, such as preparing (cutting vegetables) and actual cooking. In these interactions, it is also noticeable that there is always one 'chef' in this cooking process and one 'sous-chef'. A smart kitchen technology that supports this cooking together process in terms of several stages of the cooking process and several roles, might reduce frustrations during the 'together cooking' situation and make it as efficient as cooking alone. It might also offer the opportunity for the less experiences cooks in the household to learn from the household 'chefs'. When cooking alone and for oneself, efficiency regarding time (temporal context) and object-use (i.e., reducing dishes) are more important.

When cooking a dish for the first time, the information and information context and temporal context variables are most important. More uncertainties exist and more interaction with content will be required (information context) A technology focusing on not only user-content interaction (user following recipe) but also for system-user interaction, in the form of feedback content to address these uncertainties might be an interesting opportunity. Cooking a dish for the first time also influences temporal context, as one typically chooses for a moment when more time is available to experiment. If there is a clash with temporal context, a negative experience will be generated. When cooking routine dishes, there are little frictions in the cooking experience. However, the choice of routine dishes is often out of comfort considerations. More specifically, a sense of control regarding time (i.e., one knows approximately how long it takes to make the dish and outcome and outcome (i.e., one knows family members will like it). Kitchen technology enhancing the experience, providing small alterations or suggestions for similar dishes regarding time of preparation and taste might be an interesting opportunity.

While this manuscript only discusses preliminary results of an *in situ* video-observational study combined with in-depth interview research using retrospective think-aloud, we can state that situational context is an important starting point when developing new technologies for the domestic cooking environment. It will influence temporal context, social context, physical context and information and task context. These will in turn influence requirements regarding kitchen technologies and applications. However, other objects present in the direct context-of-use, other users (passive or active) and other content, will also influence the user experience of cook with a kitchen technology. This study has contributed to the state-of-the-art, as – to our knowledge- no studies have systematically analyzed domestic cooking experiences using a situated action approach. One study had previously defined relevant situations to take into account when evaluating technology features [50]. This was, however, not based on previous analysis of possible situational contexts. In this study, the contexts were created and impact of the context on feature preferences were examined. In line with their assumptions, we have defined the 'cooking a routine dish versus cooking a new dish' and the 'cooking together versus cooking alone' situation.

6 Further Research and Limitations

These results need to be further validated, as for instance, in only one occasion did the 'cooking for an external household guest' situation occur. Moreover, relationships between the different broader (non-tangible) contexts and elements within the direct context-of-use (i.e., objects, kitchen appliances, content and other household members), need to be further investigated.

Another important aspect that has not been taken into account is the impact of user characteristics. Previous research has however shown that quality of experience of technologies is the result of an interaction between contextual variables and user characteristics [14]. In a previous step in this research project, three types of household cooks have been defined based on socio-demographic, attitudes towards cooking and cooking behavior (see Sect. 3.4). In a further analysis, we will differentiate results based on these user profiles.

Acknowledgements. This research was conducted in the context of the imec.icon project IOT chef that focuses on the design of a connected cooking system that enhances the cooking and eating experience.

References

1. Angkananon, K., Wald, M., Gilbert, L.: Towards a technology enhanced interaction framework. GSTF J. Comput. (JoC) **3**(2), 25–31 (2013). https://doi.org/10.5176/2251-3043
2. Bell, G., Blythe, M., Sengers, P.: Making by making strange. ACM Trans. Comput.-Hum. Interact. **12**(2), 149–173 (2005). https://doi.org/10.1145/1067860.1067862
3. Blasco, R., Marco, Á., Casas, R., Cirujano, D., Picking, R.: A smart kitchen for ambient assisted living. Sensors (Switzerland) **14**(1), 1629–1653 (2014). https://doi.org/10.3390/s140101629
4. Blythe, M., Wright, P., McCarthy, J., Bertelsen, O.W.: CHI '06 extended abstracts on Human factors in computing systems - CHI '06. *CHI '06 extended abstracts*: 1691–1694 (2006). http://portal.acm.org/citation.cfm?doid=1125451.1125764%5Cnpapers2://publication/doi/10.1145/1125451.1125764
5. Bonanni, L., Jackie Lee, C.-H., Selker, T.: CounterIntelligence: Augmented Reality Kitchen. Association for Computing Machinery (ACM) (2004)
6. Bradbury, J.S., Shell, J.S., Knowles, C.B.: Hands on Cooking, p. 996 (2003). https://doi.org/10.1145/766098.766113
7. Buxton, B.: Sketching User Experiences - Getting the Design Right and the Right Design. Elsevier (2007)
8. Chi, P.P., Chen, J., Liu, S., Chu, H.: Designing smart living objects – enhancing vs. distracting traditional human–object interaction. In: Jacko, J.A. (ed.) HCI 2007. LNCS, vol. 4551, pp. 788–797. Springer, Heidelberg (2007). https://doi.org/10.1007/978-3-540-73107-8_87
9. Chi, P.-Y.P., Chen, J.-H., Chu, H.-H., Lo, J.-L.: Enabling calorie-aware cooking in a smart kitchen. In: Oinas-Kukkonen, H., Hasle, P., Harjumaa, M., Segerståhl, K., Øhrstrøm, P. (eds.) PERSUASIVE 2008. LNCS, vol. 5033, pp. 116–127. Springer, Heidelberg (2008). https://doi.org/10.1007/978-3-540-68504-3_11

10. Crabtree, A., Rodden, T.: Domestic routines and design for the home. Comput. Support. Coop. Work **13**, 191–220 (2004)
11. Davidoff, S., Zimmerman, J., Dey, A.K.: How routine learners can support family coordination. In: Conference on Human Factors in Computing Systems – Proceedings, pp. 2461–2470 (2010). https://doi.org/10.1145/1753326.1753699
12. Desmet, P.M.A., Schifferstein, H.N.J.: From Floating Wheelchairs to Mobile Car Parks: A Collection of 35 Experience-driven Design Projects. Eleven International Publishing, Utrecht (2011)
13. Doman, K., Kuai, C.Y., Takahashi, T., Ide, I., Murase, H.: Video cooking: towards the synthesis of multimedia cooking recipes. In: Lee, K.-T., Tsai, W.-H., Liao, H.-Y.M., Chen, T., Hsieh, J.-W., Tseng, C.-C. (eds.) MMM 2011. LNCS, vol. 6524, pp. 135–145. Springer, Heidelberg (2011). https://doi.org/10.1007/978-3-642-17829-0_13
14. Geerts, D., et al.: Linking an integrated framework with appropriate methods for measuring QoE. In: 2010 2nd International Workshop on Quality of Multimedia Experience, QoMEX 2010 – Proceedings, pp. 158–163 (2010). https://doi.org/10.1109/QOMEX.2010.5516292
15. Gherardi, S.: Situated knowledge and situated action: what do practice-based studies promise? In: The SAGE Handbook of New Approaches in Management and Organization, pp. 516–525 (2008). https://doi.org/10.4135/9781849200394.n89
16. Glaser, B.G., Strauss, A.L.: The Discovery of Grounded Theory: Strategies for Qualitative Research. Aldine Transaction, New Brunswick (1967). https://doi.org/10.2307/2575405
17. Grimes, A., Harper, R.: Celebratory technology, p. 467 (2008). https://doi.org/10.1145/1357054.1357130
18. Gummerus, J., Pihlström, M.: Context and mobile services value-in-use. J. Retailing Consumer Serv. **18**(6), 521–533 (2011). https://doi.org/10.1016/j.jretconser.2011.07.002
19. Van Den Haak, M.J., De Jong, M.D.T., Schellens, P.J.: Retrospective vs. concurrent think-aloud protocols: testing the usability of an online library catalogue. Behav. Inf. Technol. **22**(5), 339–351 (2003). https://doi.org/10.1080/0044929031000
20. Hamada, R., Okabe, J., Ide, I., Satoh, S.I., Sakai, S., Tanaka, H.: Cooking navi: assistant for daily cooking in kitchen. In: MM 2005, 6–12 November 2005, Singapore, pp. 371–374 (2005). https://doi.org/10.1145/1101149.1101228
21. Hammer, F., Egger-Lampl, S., Möller, S.: Quality-of-user-experience: a position paper. Qual. User Experience **3**, 9 (2018)
22. Hassenzahl, M.: Experience Design: Technology for All the Right Reasons. Morgan & Claypool Publishers (2010). https://doi.org/10.2200/S00261ED1V01Y201003HCI008
23. Hooper, C.J., et al.: The french kitchen, p. 193 (2012). https://doi.org/10.1145/2370216.2370246
24. Ikeda, S., Asghar, Z., Hyry, J., Pulli, P., Pitkanen, A., Kato, H.: Remote assistance using visual prompts for demented elderly in cooking, 1–5 October 2012. https://doi.org/10.1145/2093698.2093744
25. ISO 13407. 1999. Human-centered design processes for interactive systems
26. Lee, C.H.J., Bonanni, L., Espinosa, J.H., Lieberman, H., Selker, T.: Augmenting kitchen appliances with a shared context using knowledge about daily events. In: IUI '06 Proceedings of the 11th international conference on Intelligent user interfaces, 29 January-1 February 2006, Sydney, Australia, pp. 348–350 (2006). https://doi.org/10.1145/1111449.1111533
27. Ju, W., Hurwitz, R., Judd, T., Lee, B.: CounterActive. CHI '01 extended abstracts on Human factors in computing systems - CHI '01, p. 269 (2001). https://doi.org/10.1145/634067.634227
28. Jumisko-pyykkö, S., Vainio, T.: Framing the context of use for mobile HCI. Int. J. Mob. Hum. Comput. Interact. (2010). https://doi.org/10.4018/jmhci.2010100101

29. Kirman, B., Linehan, C., Lawson, S., Foster, D., Doughty, M.: There's a Monster in my Kitchen Using Aversive Feedback to Motivate Behaviour Change (2010)
30. Kranz, M., et al.: Context-aware kitchen utilities, p. 213 (2007). https://doi.org/10.1145/1226969.1227013
31. Latour, B.: Science in Action. Harvard University Press, Cambridge (1987). https://oca.korea.ac.kr/link.n2s?url=http://search.ebscohost.com/login.aspx?direct=true&db=cat00139a&AN=korb.000045573719&lang=ko&site=eds-live&scope=site
32. Locher, J.L., Yoels, W.C., Maurer, D., van Ells, J.: Comfort foods: an exploratory journey into the social and emotional significance of food. Food Foodways 13(4), 273–297 (2005). https://doi.org/10.1080/07409710500334509
33. Macht, M., Meininger, J., Roth, J.: The pleasures of eating: a qualitative analysis. J. Happiness Stud. 6(2), 137–160 (2005). https://doi.org/10.1007/s10902-005-0287-x
34. Mennicken, S., Karrer, T., Russell, P., Borchers, J.: First-person cooking: a dual-perspective interactive kitchen counter. In: Proceedings of the 28th of the International Conference Extended Abstracts on Human Factors in Computing Systems, pp. 3403–3408 (2010)
35. Mou, T.Y., Jeng, T.S., Ho, C.H.: Sociable kitchen: interactive recipe system in kitchen island. Int. J. Smart Home 3(2), 27–38 (2009)
36. Nansen, B., Davis, H., Vetere, F., Skov, M., Paay, J., Kjeldskov, J.: Kitchen kinesics: situating gestural interaction within the social contexts of family cooking. In: Proceedings of the 26th Australian Computer-Human Interaction Conference, OzCHI 2014, pp. 149–158 (2014). https://doi.org/10.1145/2686612.2686635
37. Paay, J.: Indexing to Situated Interactions. Information Systems, February 2006
38. Paay, J., Kjeldskov, J., Skov, M.B.: Connecting in the kitchen: an empirical study of physical interactions while cooking together at home. In: CSCW 2015, pp. 276–287 (2015). https://doi.org/10.1145/2675133.2675194
39. Palay, J., Newman, M.: SuChef: an in-kitchen display to assist with "everyday" cooking. In: Proceedings of the 27th International Conference Extended Abstracts on Human Factors in Computing Systems - CHI EA 2009, pp. 3973–3978 (2009). https://doi.org/10.1145/1520340.1520603
40. Partala, T., Saari, T.: Understanding the most influential user experiences in successful and unsuccessful technology adoptions. Comput. Hum. Behav. 53, 381–395 (2015). https://doi.org/10.1016/j.chb.2015.07.012
41. Roto, V.: Web browsing on mobile phones - characteristics of user experience web browsing on mobile phones - characteristics of user experience. Doctoral Dissertation (2006). https://doi.org/10.1007/s10681-006-9218-0
42. Sato, A., Watanabe, K., Rekimoto, J.: MimiCook: a cooking assistant system with situated guidance. In: Proceedings of the 8th International Conference on Tangible, Embedded and Embodied Interaction, pp. 121–124 (2013). https://doi.org/10.1145/2540930.2540952
43. Sharlin, E., Watson, B., Kitamura, Y., Kishino, F., Itoh, Y.: On tangible user interfaces, humans and spatiality. Pers. Ubiquitous Comput. 8(5), 338–346 (2004). https://doi.org/10.1007/s00779-004-0296-5
44. Sidenvall, B., Nydahl, M., Fjellström, C.: The meal as a gift - the meaning of cooking among retired women. J. Appl. Gerontol. 19(4), 405–423 (2000). https://doi.org/10.1177/073346480001900403
45. Suchman, L.A.: Plans and Situated Actions: The Problem of Human-Machine Communication. Cambridge University Press, Cambridge (1987)
46. Suchman, L.A.: Human-Machine Reconfigurations: Plans and Situated Actions. Cambridge University Press, Cambridge (2007)

47. Terrenghi, L., Hilliges, O., Butz, A.: Kitchen stories: sharing recipes with the Living Cookbook. Pers. Ubiquitous Comput. **11**(5), 409–414 (2007). https://doi.org/10.1007/s00779-006-0079-2

48. Tran, Q.T., Calcaterra, G., Mynatt, E.D.: Cook's collage. In: Sloane, A. (ed.) Home-Oriented Informatics and Telematics. IIFIP, vol. 178, pp. 15–32. Springer, Boston. https://doi.org/10.1007/11402985_2

49. Uriu, D., Namai, M., Tokuhisa, S., Kashiwagi, R., Inami, M., Okude, N.: Experience "panavi,": challenge to master professional culinary arts. In: CHI '12 Extended Abstracts on Human Factors in Computing Systems, pp. 1445–1446 (2012). https://doi.org/10.1145/2212776.2212478

50. Vildjiounaite, E., et al.: Designing socially acceptable multimodal interaction in cooking assistants. In: Proceedings of the 15th International Conference on Intelligent User Interfaces - IUI 2011, p. 415 (2011). https://doi.org/10.1145/1943403.1943479

51. Van Hove, S., et al.: Human-Computer Interaction to Human-Computer-Context Interaction: Towards a Conceptual Framework for Conducting User Studies for Shifting Interfaces. In: Marcus, A., Wang, W. (eds.) DUXU 2018. LNCS, vol. 10918, pp. 277–293. Springer, Cham (2018). https://doi.org/10.1007/978-3-319-91797-9_20

52. Poppe, R., Rienks, R., Van Dijk, B.: Evaluating the future of HCI: challenges for the evaluation of upcoming applications. In: Proceedings of the International Workshop on Artificial Intelligence, Artifical Intelligence for Human Computing Conference IJCAI, vol. 7, pp. 89–96 (2007)

53. Kemmer, D., Anderson, A.S., Marshall, D.W.: Living together and eating together: changes in food choice and eating habits during the transition from single to married/cohabiting. Sociol. Rev. **46**(1), 48–72 (1998)

54. Kjærnes, U. (ed.): Eating patterns: a day in the lives of Nordic peoples. National Institute for consumer research (2001)

55. Wills, W.J., Dickinson, A.M., Meah, A., Short, F.: Reflections on the use of visual methods in a qualitative study of domestic kitchen practices. Sociology **50**(3), 470–485 (2016)

Flatpack ML: How to Support Designers in Creating a New Generation of Customizable Machine Learning Applications

Marcus Winter[⊠] and Phil Jackson

School of Computing, Engineering and Mathematics,
University of Brighton, Brighton, UK
{marcus.winter,prjll}@brighton.ac.uk

Abstract. This paper examines how designers can be supported in creating a new generation of interactive machine learning (ML) applications that run locally on consumer-level hardware and can be trained and customized by end-users for their specific context and use case. It delineates the proposed applications against research into Interactive Machine Learning and Machine Teaching, examines the challenges designers face in these contexts and their relevance for designing the proposed new applications, and reports on the findings of a survey exploring designers' interest in ML, their understanding of ML capabilities and concepts, and their preferences for learning about ML. Based on findings from the literature and the survey, the paper identifies three overlapping research challenges in supporting designers to ideate, design and prototype the proposed ML applications.

Keywords: Machine Learning · Customization · User experience · Design

1 Introduction

Many current applications of Machine Learning (ML) run on cloud infrastructure and are driven by business needs, based on large data sets about users' demographics, preferences and behaviors. Our interaction with this kind of ML is usually implicit, indirect and mostly unaware: based on data that is accumulated in the background, often in a different physical, digital or temporal context than the one in which it is used to predict our needs and preferences. When these systems produce wrong or unexpected results, users often discover that they have limited options to find out how decisions are made or what information the system holds on them, and that it might be difficult or even impossible for them to correct misleading information, leading to well documented user experience problems related to transparency, control and trust.

By contrast, explicit interaction with ML that runs locally and is driven primarily by user needs to address problems in their specific context is comparatively rare and currently mostly limited to research prototypes addressing the needs of domain experts in specific contexts (e.g. [3, 4, 7, 17, 18, 24, 31]), mainly due to the complexities of designing and training ML models and their requirements for substantial computing power. Recent developments, however, are eroding these barriers, with specialized

© Springer Nature Switzerland AG 2020
A. Marcus and E. Rosenzweig (Eds.): HCII 2020, LNCS 12201, pp. 175–193, 2020.
https://doi.org/10.1007/978-3-030-49760-6_12

hardware emerging to run ML models locally in a performant and energy-efficient manner [8, 20, 23, 38], a host of open repositories offering free, high-quality, pre-trained ML models for a range of problems [33–35, 42] and several ML frameworks allowing these models to be used on consumer-level hardware [37, 40, 41, 43]. While the ready availability of pre-trained models and high-level development tools shifts the focus from ML research to ML applications research, the ability to run models on edge devices such as browsers, mobile phones and single-board computers broadens deployment options and enables ML applications to take advantage of device sensors and user interaction. Combined with transfer learning approaches, which drastically reduce training times and the amount of required training data by retaining pre-trained models' previous learning derived from large general data sets [48], this enables a new generation of interactive ML applications that run locally on consumer hardware and can be trained and customized by end-users for their specific context and use case. Reflecting that fact that these applications typically rely on off-the-shelf pre-trained base models for specific problem classes and require a setup process by end-users to train and customize them in the target environment, we use the term *Flatpack ML* in reference to a popular distribution format for mass furniture that is assembled by customers at home.

This paper examines what designers need to know to ideate, design and prototype this new generation of ML applications and how they can be supported in making them relevant, usable and meaningful for users. Its main contributions are to (i) situate and delineate the proposed new generation of local, end-user customizable ML applications, (ii) provide a snapshot of designers' current understanding of ML concepts and capabilities, and (iii) identify a number of challenges that can inform the research agenda for this emerging class of ML application.

2 Related Work

Situated broadly in the field of Human-Centered Machine Learning (HCML) [19], the work relates to various research efforts in the literature adopting a more user-centered perspective on ML. Regarding the user experience of ML applications and services, it draws on literature discussing the transparency, explainability and debuggability of ML systems [1, 16, 27]; regarding users' direct interaction with ML, the work draws on literature on Interactive Machine Learning (IML); and regarding the shift in focus from optimizing the accuracy of learning algorithms towards improving the efficacy of the people who "teach" algorithms how to behave [46], the research draws on literature on Machine Teaching (MT). Finally, the work draws on a range of previous efforts exploring end-users' understanding of ML concepts [16, 46] and the role of designers in creating ML applications [45, 47].

2.1 Interactive Machine Learning and Machine Teaching

The literature offers various definitions of Interactive Machine Learning (IML) in an effort to distinguish it from traditional ML. In [15], IML is defined as "an interaction paradigm in which a user or user group iteratively builds and refines a mathematical model to describe a concept" (p.4), without specifying the type of user providing the input or the context in which the machine learning happens. In [2] IML is characterized by "rapid, focused, and incremental interaction cycles", which "facilitate end-user involvement in the machine-learning process" (p.108). As this involves a tight coupling between user and system, it "necessitates an increased focus on studying how users can effectively influence the machine-learning system and how the learning system can appropriately influence the users" (p.108). The clear focus on end-users in this definition leads the authors to call for more research into the interaction between end-user and ML system, and how the process gradually advances learning and understanding by both end-user and ML system - an aspect highly relevant to ML systems that can be trained and customized by end-users as it indicates the need to account for this development in the interface and interaction design. A third definition [36] proposes that IML "focuses on methods that empower domain experts to control and direct machine learning tools from within the deployed environment, whereas traditional machine learning does this in the development environment" (p.12). Here the focus shifts from development environment to the target environment in which the ML system is used. An important implication is that IML application design needs to support users to control and direct the IML process in-situ, shifting the focus to the support system enabling users to train and optimize ML applications.

Further emphasizing this shift in context and perspective are definitions of the field of Machine Teaching (MT). For instance, [39] see ML and MT as related but distinct research fields, where "Machine Learning research aims at making the learner better by improving ML algorithms", while "Machine teaching research aims at making the teacher more productive at building machine learning models" (p.3). An almost identical interpretation is offered in [46], which states that ML focuses on improving the accuracy of learners (i.e. learning algorithms), while MT focuses on improving the efficacy of teachers (i.e. people who interact with data and "teach" algorithms how to behave). Overall, [46] asserts that MT refers to a human-centered perspective to the process of ML, while [39] point out that MT research has "more in common with programming and human-computer interaction than with machine learning" (p.3).

Considering these definitions of IML and MT, we can delineate the problem space for Flatpack ML application design as being concerned with:

- end-users training and customizing ML applications for their specific context
- pre-trained base models and transfer learning techniques rather than custom models
- consumer-level hardware rather than high-performance professional equipment
- personal use environments rather than work environments or lab environments

Given that designers have well-developed methods to research and design for end-users and their use-contexts, this paper focuses in particular on designers' understanding of ML capabilities and concepts necessary to design the user experience and interaction of end-users training and customizing ML applications for their specific context.

2.2   Challenges for Designers Working with Machine Learning

According to [46] there are three categories of people who build ML systems, including experts, intermediate users and amateurs. As these categories have different perspectives and operate at different levels of ML expertise, they face different sets of challenges. While ML experts are of limited interest in the context of this paper, both intermediate users and amateurs need to be considered: designers who ideate and prototype customizable ML applications arguably fall into the intermediate user category, while end-users who train and customize ML applications for their specific context can be assigned to the amateur category. Both of these perspectives are relevant when designing customizable ML applications. With regard to the former, the authors [46] identified many challenges including (c1) understanding the limits of what an ML system can learn, (c2) exploring alternative formulations of an ML problem and (c3) evaluating the performance of ML models in the context of its specific application. Regarding the latter, identified challenges include (c4) translating real-world problems into achievable learning tasks, (c5) improving the design of a ML model rather than trying to improve performance by adding more training data, and (c6) assessing model performance and accounting for bias and overfitting. There is a considerable overlap in the identified challenges for intermediate users and amateurs, with (c1, c2, c4) all relating to understanding ML capabilities and being able to map them to practical uses and (c3, c6) relating to the ability to assess how well a trained model does in a specific environment.

Focusing in particular on problems faced by UX designers, [47] identifies six distinct challenges in three case studies involving attempts to integrate UX and ML aspects in system development. They include that (c7) UX is often an afterthought rather than being thought of throughout the project, (c8) UX designs are constrained by available data, (c9) designers struggle to proactively work with data scientists, (c10) designers have limited access to competent data scientists, (c11) ML is difficult to prototype and does not integrate well with designers' *fail early fail often* approach, and (c12) designers struggle to understand ML's capabilities in the context of UX. Reflecting the context in which these challenges were identified, several relate to development methodology (c11) and communication in mixed project teams (c7, c9, c10) while others are more fundamental in nature: (c8) highlights a mismatch between ML as a design material that cannot be easily prototyped and design methodology that relies on quick iterations and successive improvement, while (c12) relates to understanding ML capabilities and applying them to problems in a specific context.

Based on a survey of 51 UX practitioners, most of whom had previous experience in collaborating with ML experts, [13] found that designers (c13) have fundamental difficulties in grasping ML as a design material due to the differences in human and machine perspectives (c14) lack suitable prototyping tools to experience ML in realistic situations, and (c15) often have misconceptions about ML capabilities and limitations. All of these are variations of previously identified challenges, with (c13, c15) relating to conceptual knowledge about ML and its possible applications, and (c14) relating to difficulties in prototyping ML in tandem with evolving design iterations.

Interestingly, [15] discuss not only problems that users face when interacting with IML systems but also problems that IML systems face when interacting with users.

Among the former, they list (c16) the open-ended character of training and the related problem of assessing model accuracy and knowing when to stop, (c17) the co-adaptive character of interaction with an evolving model where both user and model influence each other's behavior and (c18) that users associate computers with precision and struggle to interpret prediction uncertainty. Among the latter, they list that (c19) users can be imprecise and inconsistent, and that (c20) there is a degree of uncertainty when relating user input to user intent. As this aspect can be exacerbated by non-experts' lack of understanding of ML concepts and terminology (see c1, c3, c5, c6, c14, c16, c18), it suggests a need for a shared language for ML interaction not derived from the ML expert community but developed together with users from an HCML perspective.

Other challenges mentioned in IML literature cited in [2] include that (c21) users, unlike machines, easily get tired of repetitive tasks in IML workflows, (c22) users are biased towards giving more positive than negative feedback, (c23) users prefer to give guidance to ML systems rather than feedback on past decisions and (c24) users naturally provide a wide variety of input types to an ML system. Just like (c19, c20) above, all of these challenges can be seen as problems that an IML system faces when interacting with users, reinforcing the view that designers need to balance the needs of both users and ML systems to support effective interaction.

Table 1. Challenge categories and their relevance to Flatpack ML application designers.

Challenge category	Relevance to Flatpack ML
Conceptual knowledge of ML: capabilities and limitations of ML and how they can be mapped to problems in a specific context (c1, c2, c4, c12, c13, c15)	Relevant in particular during the ideation stage for new consumer-level applications for ML
Technical knowledge of ML: modifying the design of a model or tuning its hyper-parameters to improve performance (c5)	Contingently relevant as designers typically use off-the-shelf pre-trained base models and do not engage in model design or optimization
Operational knowledge of ML: evaluating model performance for a specific context and determining when to stop training (c3, c6, c16)	Relevant as it informs designers' decisions on how to guide users through the training and customization process
Development culture: ensuring that UX aspects are considered throughout and communicating with data scientists and ML experts (c7, c9, c10)	Contingently relevant as projects are typically design-led, but might still require ML experts to engineer transfer learning mechanisms and custom models
Design methodology: prototyping ML aspects of an application in tandem with evolving design iterations (c8, c11, c14)	Contingently relevant as the issue essentially becomes a design problem when training and customization is left to users
Interaction design: supporting effective interaction between ML systems and user while accounting for the evolving nature of that interaction and for human biases and preferences (c17, c18, c19, c20, c21, c22, c23, c24)	Relevant given the challenges of guiding users through the initial training process, supporting them in selecting suitable training data and assessing model performance

There are many overlaps between the challenges discussed in the literature, with several distinct challenge categories emerging. However, not all of the challenges discussed in the literature are equally relevant to Flatpack ML application design. The mapping in Table 1 shows conceptual and operational knowledge of ML and interaction design challenges in ML applications all being highly relevant as designers take the lead in ideating ML applications and design interactions and interfaces supporting end-users in training and customizing these applications, while challenges relating to technical knowledge of ML, development culture and design methodology are less relevant in design-led projects using off-the-shelf pre-trained base models.

2.3   Making Machine Learning More Accessible to Designers

Making ML more accessible to designers is not a new idea but has been subject to discussion in both popular and academic literature for some time. There are numerous online publications and books around the topic (e.g. [10, 11, 14, 22, 28, 29]) and an evolving body of academic research exploring the problem from various angles (e.g. [13, 15, 30, 45–47]). According to [45] efforts fall broadly into two categories: one taking a didactic approach based on the assumption that a better conceptual and technical understanding of ML helps designers to make better use of it, and the other taking an experiential approach based on the assumption that sensitizing designers to ML capabilities and design possibilities through hands-on engagement is more fruitful. In addition to this dichotomy of approaches, there is also a dichotomy of uses of ML: those discussing ML as a creative tool for designers that opens up new possibilities and disrupts traditional design processes, and those discussing ML as a design material that can improve, augment or allow for completely new applications and services. The work discussed in this paper focuses primarily on ML as a design material, reflecting the key idea behind Flatpack ML as a design-driven effort to develop customizable products that use ML to address user needs in a specific context.

Both the idea of sensitizing designers to the capabilities of ML through hands-on engagement [45] and the call for "research on new tools and techniques that make it easier for designers to ideate, sketch and prototype what new forms ML might take, and new contexts in which ML might be appropriate" [13, p.279] support the case for experiential learning rather than more didactic methods. Recent research exemplifying this experiential approach is described in [30], which discusses ObjectResponder as a tool for designers to quickly prototype ML applications and test them in their context of use. The tool takes the form of a smartphone application using an online computer vision service with live camera images. It provides designers with a simple interface to associate recognized objects with spoken responses using text-to-speech technology. An evaluation of the tool with design professionals found that looking at specific use contexts from a ML perspective helped designers to think more broadly about ideas, and that immediately testing them in the target environment provided valuable learning opportunities about the capabilities and limitations of ML.

2.4   Conclusions

The literature helps to distinguish the proposed Flatpack ML applications from related efforts such as IML and MT through its focus on training and customization by end-users, transfer learning techniques, consumer-level hardware and personal use environments. It also helps to inform research exploring how designers can be supported in ideating, designing and prototyping these applications. Flatpack ML application design poses a particular set of challenges with respect to communicating ML concepts to end-users and guiding them through the training and customization process. Tackling these challenges will require both conceptual and operational understanding of ML as well as suitable prototyping tools and techniques. Given that established design practice typically involves the iterative development of design artefacts, experiential approaches helping designers to develop their knowledge skills through active experimentation with ML seem a promising way forward.

3   Survey: Designers' Understanding of ML

In order to complement and further qualify findings from the literature, we carried out a survey exploring designers' knowledge, understanding and interest in ML. Besides informing our work to make ML more accessible to designers, the survey also aimed to establish a baseline of current understanding and use of ML among designers, against which the outcomes of future interventions can be measured.

3.1   Instrument

The survey used an online questionnaire structured into seven sections:

1. An introduction to the research, simple definition of ML, contact details of the investigators and a question for participants to confirm their consent to take part.
2. Questions relating to participants' previous experience of designing ML applications, awareness of ML in everyday applications and ideas for novel ML applications.
3. Questions exploring participants' understanding of ML capabilities, focusing in particular on capabilities relevant to Flatpack ML due to their generality, availability of pre-trained models and suitability to run on edge devices.
4. Questions asking participants to self-rate their understanding of various conceptual and operational aspects of ML related to training, performance, uncertainty and bias.
5. Questions exploring how useful designers would find various approaches to support them in designing and prototyping ML applications.
6. Demographic questions relating to participants' age, gender, job or course title and self-rated design and programming skills.
7. A final open question asking for any other thoughts on the topic.

The questionnaire design involved a member of staff with a design background to ensure that questions made sense from a design perspective and used appropriate language for the target group, resulting in several iterations refining the introduction as well as the wording and sequence of questions. It then was piloted and discussed post-hoc with two designers (not included in the sample), resulting in further changes to wordings and the removal of six non-essential questions. The final version of the questionnaire takes 10–15 min to complete.

3.2 Methodology

Participants were recruited through calls posted on popular discussion groups for various disciplines, emailed to professional networks and personal contacts of the investigators, and distributed to design students via lecturers at the University of Brighton. The questionnaire was open for a duration of three weeks and during that time was completed by 102 participants.

Answers to closed questions were analyzed quantitatively while answers to open questions were analyzed in an emergent coding process described in [32], involving first a data reduction step, where responses were coded to identify emerging themes, and then a data visualization step, where the coded data was structured into key themes for interpretation. In order to mitigate investigator bias when interpreting responses and identifying themes, both data reduction and data visualization were carried out independently by two researchers before being discussed and synthesized in a collaborative interpretation session.

Given that the survey aims to broadly inform future research across design disciplines, no attempt was made at this stage to differentiate answers between design domain or participant demographics. For the same reason, interrelations between responses to different answers were not examined at this stage, although they might be interesting to explore in future work.

3.3 Ethical Considerations

Ethical considerations concerning the involvement of professionals and students in the survey are based on Anderson's guidelines for using volunteers in research projects [6]. Participants were not pressurized to participate in the survey and were informed about the context and purpose of the research. The introduction to the survey clarified that the data collection and analysis is anonymous; collected data is used only in the context of the research and not made available to third parties; and that participants can withdraw at any time without giving a reason.

With regard to student participants, calls to take part in the survey were issued by lecturers in an inclusive, non-discriminatory way, emphasizing that participation is voluntary and not connected to the curriculum or any assessment.

In order to reduce pressure on participants while filling in the survey questionnaire, all questions were optional, allowing respondents to skip questions they had no answers to or did not want to answer, without abandoning the questionnaire altogether. The survey was scrutinized and cleared by the University of Brighton's ethics approval process prior to commencement.

3.4 Sample

The survey includes 102 participants with various backgrounds, demographics, skill levels and previous experience in designing ML applications. The age distribution in the sample (Fig. 1a) is indicative of calls for participation being directed at both design students and design professionals, with the 18–25 year group being the largest segment at 34% and other segments gradually decreasing with age. However, all age groups, including over 65 years, are represented in the survey. There is a substantial gender gap (Fig. 1b) with 33% of respondents identifying as female and 64% identifying as male, while 1% identified as non-binary and 3% preferred not to answer the question. This is very similar to UK labor marked statistics for design professions including traditional designers, web designers and designers in engineering, which combined have a gender split of 32% female to 68% male [44]. Only 12% of respondents report to ever having designed an application that uses ML (Fig. 1c). Answers to open questions suggest that this includes applications using ML behind the scenes rather than designing user interaction with ML components as envisaged in the customizable ML applications proposed in this paper. Most respondents rate their design skills considerably higher than their programming skills (Fig. 1d), with 21% having no programming skills at all and a further 38% having only minimal programming skills, while at the other end only 3% rate their programming skills as expert level.

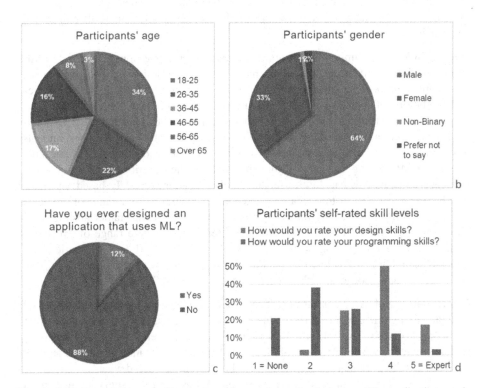

Fig. 1. Participants' (a) age, (b) gender, (c) experience in designing ML applications and (d) self-rated skill levels in design and programming.

Answers to an open question asking for participants' job or course title suggest that respondents were from a wide range of design disciplines, with the largest segments in user experience design, product design, digital media design, graphic design and building design. Answers also include more specialized disciplines such as typeface design or motion design as well as general descriptors such as studio director or creative director. The sample also includes five participants who describe themselves as artists and/or academics teaching in design disciplines.

3.5   Findings

Awareness of ML. In order to assess designers' awareness of ML in their everyday lives, the survey began with an open question asking participants to name some common applications that use ML. The fact that 72% of respondents provided at least one, often multiple, examples of common applications and services using ML suggests a high level of awareness among designers. By far the largest proportion of applications mentioned were large online services such as Google, Amazon, Facebook or Netflix, typically cited by name but in some cases referred to as "search", "social media" or "shopping recommendations", closely followed by personal assistants such as Siri, Alexa, Google Assistant used on smart speakers and mobile phones. Other answers referenced specific ML capabilities such as face recognition or object classification, or, in some cases, application areas such as predictive keyboards, financial trading and weather forecasting.

Interest in ML. Assuming that designers' actual (rather than espoused) interest in ML would manifest itself in creative engagement with it as a design material, and to see how realistic proposed applications might be as a measure of how well the capabilities and limitations of that design material are understood, the next question asked participants whether they had ever thought about possible applications that use ML, and if so, to explain in a few words what they would do. The fact that 44% of respondents answered this question with more or less concrete application ideas suggests substantial interest in ML among designers. More than half of the described application ideas reference concrete ML capabilities related to classification, typically based on image data but in some cases custom data sets, and content generation for a range of problems of varying complexity. Many other application ideas were either rather abstract (e.g. "Medical diagnostics", P53) or very complex, requiring a whole range of ML capabilities, wider AI technologies and sensors, if possible at all (e.g. "Electric Rollerblades: Braking and accelerating, reading shifts of rider's weight and moments [sic], proximity of one boot to the other when both are powered." P26).

Understanding of ML Capabilities. The next set of questions asked participants how well they thought ML would perform on a range of problems, using a generic scale of 1 (Poor) to 5 (Good). The ML problems in these questions were chosen with regard to their relevance to the development of Flatpack ML applications indicated by generality, availability of pre-trained models and suitability to run on edge devices.

The overall trend in answers across capabilities (Fig. 2) suggests that most respondents assume ML to perform rather well at the specified problems, even though many are reluctant to give it the highest rating. However, there is also a substantial tail of medium to poor ratings reflecting more critical assessments of these ML capabilities. While there are marked differences in ratings for some capabilities, with generic object recognition, body pose estimation and image style transfer attracting higher ratings, while age recognition from faces, image generation and written style transfer attracting lower ratings, average ratings for all capabilities range between 3.24 and 4.03 (SD = 0.23) indicating that respondents overall assume better than par performance for these capabilities. One aspect particularly relevant in the context of Flatpack ML is that most respondents seem to assume that ML performs better at generic object recognition (e.g. cat, bottle, car) than at specific object or gesture recognition (e.g. your cat, thumbs up), which is typically not the case as the latter requires less generalization and can be achieved through transfer learning with comparatively small training data sets.

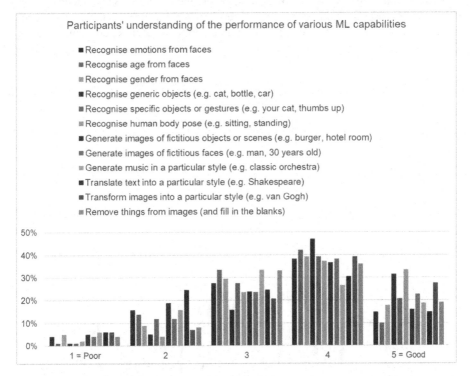

Fig. 2. Participants' understanding of the performance of various ML capabilities.

This section also included open questions asking what other ML capabilities or applications participants had heard of or would find useful, with responses describing a surprisingly wide range of ML capabilities and applications. With regard to capabilities or applications participants had heard of (50% response rate), some applications were mentioned more often that others (e.g. self-driving cars and personal assistants) and some application areas were more prominent than others (e.g. privacy and security-related applications). However, answers also included a large number of niche applications such as "Deep Fakes" (P30, P44) or "Reviewing images of crops to find disease resistant plants" (P73). With regard to capabilities of applications participants would find useful (43% response rate), many respondents suggested applications that either already exist (e.g. "Trying glasses online and see how they fit", P11) or are actively researched (e.g. "recognising tumours or cancer from images", P29). Some suggested applications were genuinely novel, such as the idea of ML for automated usability testing of interface designs (P19) or image search based on purpose rather than content (P73). Many respondents suggested general application areas such as health or sustainability rather than specific applications and only few suggested ML capabilities not included in the provided examples, all of which either already exist (e.g. "Voice recognition" P14) or are actively researched (e.g. "precise gaze detection", P18).

Understanding of ML Aspects. When asked about their awareness and understanding of various ML aspects, a large majority of respondents answered that they had never heard of, heard of but knew nothing or only knew little about these concepts (Fig. 3).

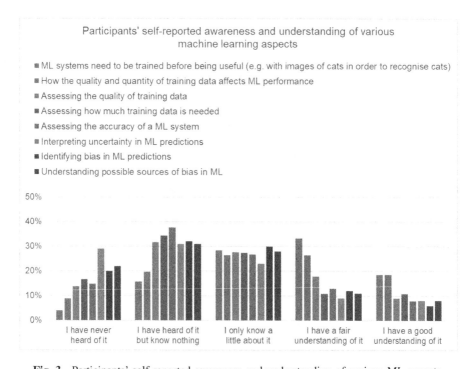

Fig. 3. Participants' self-reported awareness and understanding of various ML aspects.

In particular this included critical aspects such as assessing the quality of training data, assessing how much training data is needed and assessing the accuracy of an ML system, as well as interpreting uncertainty and identifying bias in ML predictions and understanding possible sources of bias. Notable exceptions were more fundamental aspects such as that an ML system needs to be trained before being useful and how the quality and quantity of training data affect its performance, which almost half of respondents reported to have a fair or good understanding of. A rather surprising result is that 29% of respondents answered that they had never heard of the need to interpret uncertainty in ML predictions. The formulation of the question does not allow for inferences about whether respondents were not aware of ML systems producing confidence scores rather than definite predictions, or whether they just never heard of the need to interpret these confidence scores. However, given that a further 31% answered that they had heard of it but knew nothing about it, this is certainly a key aspect to address in any support measures as uncertainty is particularly relevant in customizable ML applications where designers might need to support end-users in setting threshold values for predictions depending on the specific use case and context. For similar reasons, it will be important to improve designers' knowledge about assessing the accuracy of an ML system, which 15% answered they had never heard of and 38% had heard of but knew nothing about, as they must find ways to meaningfully communicate this information to users.

Usefulness of Support Measures. When asked to rate the usefulness of various ways to support them in designing ML applications, respondents indicated that all suggested measures would be quite useful of very useful (Fig. 4). However, there is a clear preference for working examples to see and try out different ML capabilities, and for practical workshops where they build ML prototypes with guidance from an expert. Articles and tutorials, too, are seen as useful to some extent while code snippets for re-use in prototyping were rated least favorably. While the ratings for code snippets are higher for the sub-sample of participants who rated their programming skills 4 or 5 on a scale of 1 (None) to 5 (Expert), they are still lower than the ratings for working examples and practical workshops in the whole sample, underlining the importance of experiential learning methods for designers.

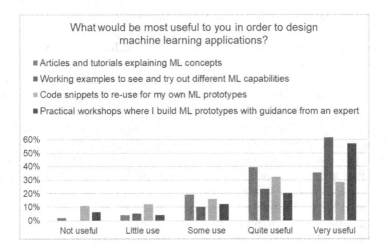

Fig. 4. Perceived usefulness of various support measures.

When asked what else could help participants to design ML applications (34% response rate), respondents expressed a strong interest in interactive, multimedia and experiential ways of learning about ML with several mentions of "step-by-step guides", "video tutorials", "workshops" and "conferences". There were also calls for more formal and comprehensive training, in particular with regard to coding and ML-related technologies, and a distinct interest in learning about ethical aspects of ML, including bias and potential misuse, and how to address these issues.

Ethical aspects were also touched on in answers to a final open question asking for any other thoughts on ML in a design context (31% response rate). Several answers had a note of apprehensiveness (e.g. "its our future so don't mess it up", P53; "Don't take our jobs away!!!", P92), however, many respondents acknowledged that ML opens up new opportunities, both as a design material to improve the capabilities of their products and as a tool to support and speed up the design process, with some emphasizing this aspect with adjectives such as "exciting" (P2, P23, P39), "interesting" (P38, P60) and "liberating" (P37). Several respondents pointed out the general importance of ML for design professionals and expressed a need to learn more about it, with one participant stating that "it seems a bit behind the times that these tools are not more mainstream in design education" (P23).

3.6 Discussion

The findings both underline the need for this research and inform its various aspects with regard to how designers can be supported in creating ML applications that can be trained and customized by end-users.

Participants' answers suggest that designers have good awareness of ML in their everyday lives, with most participants being able to name several applications making use of the technology, and a strong interest to learn more about it. The latter is supported not only by the fact that many participants had already thought about potential ML applications, but also by statements emphasizing its importance for design professionals and calling for training and support in this area.

There is much variation in how participants rated the performance of various ML capabilities, however, above par mean ratings for all capabilities suggest that a majority of designers is rather optimistic about ML capabilities. Detailed responses indicate a misconception about ML performance in recognizing generic versus specific objects, which is of particular relevance for customizable applications using transfer learning to contextualize ML models, however, overall the results suggest that most designers have a fair understanding of what problems are more or less difficult for ML to solve. While this only applies to the particular set of ML capabilities included in the survey, it nonetheless puts into perspective claims in the literature about designers often having misconceptions about ML capabilities [13] or difficulties understanding the limits of what ML can learn [46], indicating that these difficulties might apply less to well-defined generic ML problems designers might have heard of or read about, such as object recognition or face interpretation.

Participants' self-assessed understanding of various ML aspects suggest that most designers would benefit from learning about basic concepts related to training, assessing the performance and interpreting the outputs of ML systems. While some aspects are better understood than others, there is a significant proportion of respondents who indicated that they had never heard of these aspects and a large majority who knows little or nothing about them. This includes aspects particularly relevant to Flatpack ML, as designers need to be able to encode and operationalize them in their designs in a manner that is easy to learn and understand by end-users.

How designers can be supported to learn about and use ML as a design material is a key question in this paper, and the survey findings provide clear indications towards suitable learning approaches and materials. Participants' responses show a strong preference for experiential ways of learning about ML. Experiential learning theory [26] tells us that hands-on experimentation and reflection on the concrete experience lead to deep understanding and facilitate the transfer of learned concepts to new situations and contexts, which is particularly important when designers are asked to ideate and design novel ML applications. It also resonates with design theory, where Material Driven Design [25] provides a conceptual framework for design explorations inspired by the qualities of a design material rather than necessarily starting with a problem, while emphasizing that engagement with the design material "should also elicit meaningful user experiences in and beyond its utilitarian assessment" (p.35).

Finally, the survey findings document strong interest in ML among designers and desire to learn about it, evidenced by respondents' explicit calls for training and support. They underline the need to explore this topic further and develop suitable learning materials and programmes to support designers' engagement with ML.

3.7 Limitations

The survey involved 102 design professionals and students covering all age groups and broadly reflecting the gender distribution among UK design professionals, however, it cannot be claimed to be based on a representative sample due to the employed convenience sampling and, perhaps more importantly, the broad range of design domains and lack of a clear definition of what constitutes design or the act of designing.

Closely related to this diversity, no attempt was made to distinguish between different design domains, skill levels or demographic segments in the data analysis, although this might yield valuable insights in the future. As such, the findings can only provide a broad understanding of designers' interest, understanding and support needs, and help to inform future more targeted research efforts into making ML accessible to specific demographic groups and design domains.

4 Research Challenges

Based on findings from the literature and survey, a number of overlapping research challenges emerge in the effort to support designers in ideating, designing and prototyping Flatpack ML applications.

1. Designers need conceptual knowledge about ML, in particular with regard to its capabilities, limitations and data requirements, in order to ideate realistic applications that address end-users' needs and fit a particular context. Designers also need

operational knowledge of ML, in particular with regard to the quality and quantity of training data, the assessment of ML performance and the identification of bias in trained systems. The literature suggests that designers struggle with these aspects [13, 15, 46] and survey results confirm this for the most part: while many designers seem to have a fair understanding of which classes of problems are more or less difficult for ML to tackle, they assign themselves low ratings when it comes to their understanding of operational aspects of ML. Considering that survey results show a clear preference for experiential learning methods among designers, a key research challenge in this context is to develop suitable environments and tools that enable designers to learn about ML through hands-on engagement and experimentation.

2. Experiential learning theory tells us that active reflection on concrete experience is a key mechanism to conceptualize learning, leading to deep understanding and helping learners to transfer their knowledge to new contexts [26]. A related research challenge is therefore how to encourage and support designers' reflection when engaging with these environments and tools, and how to help them relate concrete aspects of their experience to abstract ML concepts and operational knowledge. Key in this context is to recognize learning opportunities in the engagement with ML and to address wider problems relating to transparency and explainability [1, 16, 27].

3. Helping designers to encode their conceptual and operational knowledge of ML in their designs to create a good user experience for end-users training and customizing Flatpack ML systems for their specific context is another important research challenge. While the literature identifies interaction design with ML as a challenge in general [2, 15], this aspect is of particular relevance when user interaction with ML extends to training systems and assessing their performance. Key in this context is a suitable terminology and/or visual language that can describe ML aspects in ways that make sense to end-users, and design patterns and conventions for ML training and customization that increase the recognition and learnability of these features. The latter in particular can draw on recent efforts in developing design guidelines for Human-AI interaction [5, 9, 12, 15, 21].

Other more specific challenges include finding effective ways to communicate uncertainty in ML predictions, supporting end-users in identifying acceptable context-specific thresholds for that uncertainty, and helping end-users to be aware of and avoid bias when training Flatpack ML applications.

5   Summary and Conclusions

Picking up on the opportunities of running ML models locally on consumer-level hardware, this paper proposes a new generation of ML applications that can be trained and customized by end-users for their specific context and use case. In reference to flat pack furniture that requires a setup process at home before it can be used, we used the term *Flatpack ML* for this type of application. While sharing many aspects with research into IML and MT, Flatpack ML design has its own problem space as it focuses on end-users training and customizing a generic application for a specific context;

pre-trained base models and transfer learning techniques rather than custom models; consumer-level hardware rather than high-performance professional equipment; and personal use environments rather work- or lab environments.

The literature discusses a variety of challenges designers face when working with ML, not all of which are equally relevant in Flatpack ML design (Table 1). As this type of application uses readily available pre-trained base models, it does not require deep technical ML knowledge, is less reliant on ML experts and typically design led, mitigating many of the challenges in more traditional ML-driven projects, where UX design is often an afterthought [47]. At the same time, challenges around operational ML knowledge and interaction design become more pertinent as designers need to guide end-users through the initial training and customization process for these applications.

In order to gauge designers' interest and understanding of ML, and to find out how they can be supported in designing and prototyping ML applications, we carried out a survey of 102 design professionals and students. The results indicate a strong interest in ML among designers and a readiness to learn about it. While many designers seem to have a fair understanding of which problems are more or less difficult for ML to solve, the findings largely support claims in the literature that designers often have little understanding of basic ML concepts. There was a clear preference among participants for experiential approaches to learning. Working examples to see and experiment with ML capabilities and practical workshops to build ML applications with guidance from an expert were the most popular options, with many other suggestions involving hands-on engagement with ML.

Based on the survey results and findings from the literature, the paper identified three overlapping research challenges in supporting designers to ideate, design and prototype the proposed new generation of ML applications. They include (i) developing suitable environments and tools to support designers' exploration and hands-on engagement with ML, (ii) facilitating designers' reflection when engaging with these environments and tools to support their experiential learning, and (iii) helping designers to encode their conceptual and operational knowledge of ML in their designs to improve the end-user experience of training and customizing applications. Addressing these challenges will require substantial and multi-faceted research, to which we plan to contribute in future work.

Acknowledgements. We would like to thank the participants of our survey for volunteering their time and sharing their valuable thoughts.

References

1. Abdul, A., Vermeulen, J., Wang, D., Lim, B.Y., Kankanhalli, M.: Trends and trajectories for explainable, accountable and intelligible systems: an HCI research agenda. In: Proceedings of 2018 CHI Conference on Human Factors in Computing Systems, paper 582. ACM (2018)
2. Amershi, S., Cakmak, M., Knox, W.B., Kulesza, T.: Power to the people: the role of humans in interactive machine learning. AI Mag. **35**(4), 105–120 (2014)

3. Amershi, S., Fogarty, J., Kapoor, A., Tan, D.: Examining multiple potential models in end-user interactive concept learning. In: Proceedings of 2010 CHI Conference on Human Factors in Computing Systems, pp. 1357–1360. ACM (2010)

4. Amershi, S., Fogarty, J., Kapoor, A., Tan, D.: Overview based example selection in end user interactive concept learning. In: Proceedings of 22nd Annual ACM Symposium on User Interface Software and Technology, pp. 247–256. ACM (2009)

5. Amershi, S., et al.: Guidelines for human-AI interaction. In: Proceedings of 2019 CHI Conference on Human Factors in Computing Systems, Paper 3. ACM (2019)

6. Anderson, G.: Fundamentals of Educational Research. Falmer Press (1990)

7. Andriluka, M., Uijlings, J.R., Ferrari, V.: Fluid annotation: a human-machine collaboration interface for full image annotation. In: Proceedings of 2018 ACM Multimedia Conference on Multimedia Conference, pp. 1957–1966. ACM (2018)

8. Apple A13 Bionic Chip. https://www.macworld.com/article/3442716/inside-apples-a13-bionic-system-on-chip.html. Accessed 29 Jan 2020

9. Argarwal, A., Regalado, M.: Lingua Franca: A Design Language for Human-Centered AI (2020). https://linguafranca.standardnotation.ai/. Accessed 31 Jan 2020

10. Christina, C.: The Designer's Guide to Machine Learning. Digitalist (2017). https://digitalist.global/talks/the-designers-guide-to-machine-learning/. Accessed 17 Jan 2020

11. Clark, J.: Why Machine Learning and AI Matter for Design Teams. Big Medium (2019). https://bigmedium.com/ideas/why-machine-learning-and-ai-matter-for-design-team.html. Accessed 17 Jan 2020

12. Corbett, E., Saul, N., Pirrung, M.: Interactive machine learning heuristics. In: Proceedings of Machine Learning from User Interaction for Visualization and Analytics Workshop at IEEE VIS 2018. IEEE (2018)

13. Dove, G., Halskov, K., Forlizzi, J., Zimmerman, J.: UX design innovation: challenges for working with machine learning as a design material. In: Proceedings of 2017 CHI Conference on Human Factors in Computing Systems, pp. 278–288. ACM (2017)

14. Drozdov, S.: An intro to Machine Learning for designers (2018). https://uxdesign.cc/an-intro-to-machine-learning-for-designers-5c74ba100257. Accessed 17 Jan 2020

15. Dudley, J.J., Kristensson, P.O.: A review of user interface design for interactive machine learning. ACM Trans. Interact. Intell. Syst. 1, Article 1 (2018)

16. Eiband, M., Völkel, S.T., Buschek, D., Cook, S., Hussmann, H.: When people and algorithms meet: user-reported problems in intelligent everyday applications. In: Proceedings of 24th International Conference on Intelligent User Interfaces, pp. 96–106. ACM (2019)

17. Fails, J.A., Olsen Jr., D.R.: Interactive machine learning. In: Proceedings of 8th International Conference on Intelligent User Interfaces, pp. 39–45. ACM (2003)

18. Fogarty, J., Tan, D., Kapoor, A., Winder, S.: CueFlik: interactive concept learning in image search. In: Proceedings of 2008 CHI Conference on Human Factors in Computing Systems, pp. 29–38. ACM (2008)

19. Gillies, M., et al.: Human-centred machine learning. In: Proceedings of 2016 CHI Conference Extended Abstracts on Human Factors in Computing Systems, pp. 3558–3565. ACM (2016)

20. Google Edge TPU. https://cloud.google.com/edge-tpu/. Accessed 29 Jan 2020

21. Google: People + AI. Designing human-centered AI products. https://pair.withgoogle.com/. Accessed 29 Jan 2020

22. Hebron, P.: Machine Learning for Designers. O'Reilly Media, Sebastopol (2016)

23. Huawei Kirin 980. https://consumer.huawei.com/en/campaign/kirin980/. Accessed 29 Jan 2020

24. Jo, Y., Park, J.: SC-FEGAN: Face Editing Generative Adversarial Network with User's Sketch and Color. arXiv preprint arXiv:1902.06838 (2019)

25. Karana, E., Barati, B., Rognoli, V., Zeeuw van der Laan, A.: Material driven design (MDD): a method to design for material experiences. Int. J. Des. **9**(2), 35–54. (2015)
26. Kolb, D.A.: Experiential Learning: Experience as the Source of Learning and Development. Prentice-Hall, Upper Saddle River (1984)
27. Kulesza, T., Burnett, M., Wong, W.K., Stumpf, S.: Principles of explanatory debugging to personalize interactive machine learning. In: Proceedings of 20th International Conference on Intelligent User Interfaces, pp. 126–137. ACM (2015)
28. Liikkanen, L.: Applications Of Machine Learning For Designers. Smashing Magazine (2017). https://www.smashingmagazine.com/2017/04/applications-machine-learning-designers/. Accessed 17 Jan 2020
29. Lovejoy, J.: The UX of AI. Google Design, (2018). https://design.google/library/ux-ai/. Accessed 17 Jan 2020
30. Malsattar, N., Kihara, T., Giaccardi, E.: Designing and prototyping from the perspective of AI in the wild. In: Proceedings of 2019 Designing Interactive Systems, pp. 1083–1088. ACM (2019)
31. Manshaei, R., et al.: Tangible tensors: an interactive system for grasping trends in biological systems modeling. In: Proceedings of 2019 Conference on Creativity and Cognition, pp. 41–52. ACM (2019)
32. Miles, M.B., Huberman, A.M.: Qualitative Data Analysis. Sage (1984)
33. Modelzoo. https://modelzoo.co. Accessed 30 Oct 2019
34. ONNX Model Zoo. https://github.com/onnx/models. Accessed 30 Oct 2019
35. Open Model Zoo. https://github.com/opencv/open_model_zoo. Accessed 30 Oct 2019
36. Porter, R., Theiler, J., Hush, D.: Interactive machine learning in data exploitation. Comput. Sci. Eng. **15**(5), 12–20 (2013)
37. PyTorch Mobile. https://pytorch.org/mobile/home/. Accessed 30 Oct 2019
38. Samsung Neural Processing Unit. https://www.samsung.com/global/galaxy/what-is/npu/. Accessed 17 Jan 2020
39. Simard, P.Y., et al.: Machine Teaching: A new paradigm for building machine learning systems. arXiv preprint arXiv:1707.06742 (2017)
40. TensorFlow Lite. https://www.tensorflow.org/lite. Accessed 30 Oct 2019
41. TensorFlow.js. https://www.tensorflow.org/js. Accessed 30 Oct 2019
42. TF Hub, TensorFlow Hub. https://tfhub.dev. Accessed 30 Oct 2019
43. TorchJS. https://github.com/torch-js/torch-js. Accessed 30 Oct 2019
44. UK Office for National Statistics. Annual Population Survey - Employment by occupation by sex. October 2019 - September 2019. https://www.nomisweb.co.uk/datasets/aps168/reports/employment-by-occupation?compare=K02000001. Accessed 25 Jan 2020
45. Yang, Q., Scuito, A., Zimmerman, J., Forlizzi, J., Steinfeld, A.: Investigating how experienced UX designers effectively work with machine learning. In: Proceedings of 2018 Designing Interactive Systems, pp. 585–596. ACM (2018)
46. Yang, Q., Suh, J., Chen, N.C., Ramos, G.: Grounding interactive machine learning tool design in how non-experts actually build models. In: Proceedings of 2018 Designing Interactive Systems, pp. 573–584. ACM (2018)
47. Yang, Q.: Machine learning as a UX design material: how can we imagine beyond automation, recommenders, and reminders? In: AAAI Spring Symposium Series (2018). https://www.aaai.org/ocs/index.php/SSS/SSS18/paper/viewFile/17471/15475. Accessed 30 Oct 2019
48. Yosinski, J., Clune, J., Bengio, Y., Lipson, H.: How transferable are features in deep neural networks? In: Advances in Neural Information Processing Systems. NIPS, vol. 27, pp. 3320–3328 (2014)

Speak to Me: Interacting with a Spoken Language Interface

Xiaojun Yuan[(✉)] and Ning Sa

University at Albany, State University of New York, Albany, NY, USA
{xyuan,nsa}@albany.edu

Abstract. This study addresses the importance of encouraging effective interaction of users with information systems. We examined the interaction between users and a spoken language interface through a user-centered Wizard of Oz experiment, in which the user behavior of a spoken language search interface which allows only spoken query and touch behavior, was compared with a generic keyboard baseline interface. Forty-eight participants joined the experiment, with each searching on 12 different topics of three types. Results showed that using the spoken interface resulted in significantly less interaction measured by the number of iterations, number of viewed webpages, and number of clicks/touches, than using the baseline interface. In terms of query length, participants using the spoken interface issued significantly longer queries than those using the baseline interface. Results also indicated that participants spent significantly more time in completing tasks, dwelling on each document, and making decisions on each document using the spoken language interface than using the baseline interface. Design criteria and implications for spoken language systems were discussed.

Keywords: Scanning · Searching · Adaptive information retrieval · Interactive information retrieval · Personalization · Spoken language interface

1 Introduction

As users are increasingly relying heavily on their daily use of information systems or applications on mobile devices, it has become ever more challenging to provide easy and effective access to a various user.

Jansen, Spink and Saracevic [1] point out that information system users have a tendency to initiate their information search with very short queries. This leads to the mismatch between how users address information systems, and what information systems need to respond effectively. Another contributing factor is the need of typical "best match" retrieval algorithms to have long queries in order to do effective matching of information needs to documents.

There are several reasons for user of information systems to begin their searches with brief queries. For example, users may not be able to precisely specify what information they need to resolve their information problems (cf. [2]); users may have difficulty in finding terms that can describe their information problems, and matching such terms to describe the documents in the database of the information system;

© Springer Nature Switzerland AG 2020
A. Marcus and E. Rosenzweig (Eds.): HCII 2020, LNCS 12201, pp. 194–211, 2020.
https://doi.org/10.1007/978-3-030-49760-6_13

interfaces for typical information retrieval systems were designed in a way that long queries were discouraged.

Different methods and techniques have been proposed to address these issues. For example, researchers have (1) developed interface techniques to encourage users to input longer queries (e.g. [3, 4]); (2) tried to automatically enhance the initial query, either through "pseudo-relevance feedback", or through query expansion based on thesauri or similar tools (cf. [5]). In addition, systems have offered to users, based on their initial queries, either terms which could be used to enhance their initial queries (e.g. [6]), or to directly offer query suggestions based on queries submitted by other users, as in the query suggestion devices provided by current Web search engines. However, none of these approaches could address the issues of uncertainty of the information problem, or interaction mode. There is an urgent need in the field to involve users in developing and understanding their information problems, finding better ways to express their information "needs", and greatly improving both retrieval effectiveness and user satisfaction with the interaction.

To enable the users to effectively interact with the information systems, we propose to move from keyboard-based interaction to spoken language and gestural interaction of the users with the information system. Our proposal is further supported by the increasingly widely used mobile devices. Spoken language input is one obvious way to address this limitation, as Apple's Siri and Google's spoken language search interface demonstrate.

The project contributes to improve the design and development of intelligent spoken language information systems.

In this study, we were interested in the following research questions (RQs).

RQ1: How does the mode of query input affect user information search behavior?
RQ2: Will allowing users to talk to the system to some extent improve their experience of interacting with information systems?

In this paper, we focus on comparing the user behavior of the spoken language interface with that of the baseline interface. [7] and [8] have reported respectively how users perceived the spoken language interface and which factors affected user perception, and how task type has an impact on the query behavior.

2 Previous Work

There have been arguments against taking the spoken language and gesture approach to query input and interaction. For example, doubts about whether such interaction will actually result in more effective results; if users would like to engage in such interaction; and, most importantly, if there is robust speech understanding technology to support such interaction. However, research has shown that the longer queries and more extensive response to search results that would be afforded by this mode of interaction does improve retrieval effectiveness (e.g. [4, 9]). Also, users are willing to fully describe their information problems when being encouraged to do so [4, 10]. Speech recognition technology is already in place in a mobile environment [11] and some of the work reported near human level performance [12]. Nowadays, Apple's

Siri, Amazon's Echo and Google's Now can respond to commands that require search. In the near future, the more effective and accurate spoken language interaction with information systems will be widely accepted and used.

This study was motivated by Taylor's study on question negotiation between user and librarian in special libraries [13], and the research on eliciting verbal descriptions of users' information problems in Anomalous State of Knowledge (ASK)-based information systems (e.g. [9, 14]). In the types of interactions that he studied, Taylor found that librarians engaged in conversations for the purpose of eliciting different aspects of the users' information problems, and that the users were indeed able to address these different aspects in the interaction process. According to Belkin and his colleagues [9, 14], when appropriately prompted, users were able to offer search intermediaries extended verbal descriptions of their information problems. Subsequently, Saracevic, Spink and Wu [15] analyzed user and intermediary interaction with information systems and found that there was substantial direct commentary by both user and intermediary on results retrieved with respect to a query put to the system. In a recent study, Trippas et al. [16] investigated how a pair of users, one as seeker and the other as intermediary, interacted in an audio-only search setting. The authors reported increased complexity and interactivity in the search process.

Crestani and Du [17] have shown that asking for expression of information problems in verbal terms results in significantly longer queries than those expressed through a keyboard interface. Crestani and his colleagues have examined spoken language queries and their effectiveness in various contexts [17–20]). They have investigated the effectiveness of spoken queries, as well as their length, but in simulated rather than real interaction. [19] also proposed a system design for verbal interaction in information systems. [21] considered technical issues of spoken language input compared to text input of the same query, and found no significant differences. Zue, et al.'s [22] work is relatively more complete in terms of spoken language query understanding, but it has only been applied in limited domains. More recently, [23] reported that due to the recognition errors, voice queries did not generate better search results, though the spoken queries were longer and more complex than the text queries.

In the studies based on mobile search data, Schalkwyk et al. [24] reported that voice queries were shorter than text queries while Guy [25] found that voice queries were significantly longer than text queries. According to Guy [25], voice queries were closer to natural language which were longer and used richer language such as 'take me to' and 'please'. [24] found that compared with written queries spoken queries were more likely about local service, and less likely about sensitive subjects or interaction intensive tasks. [26] reported that users tended to speak a query when they could get quick answers without having to get further detailed information. A survey [27] about Google voice search indicated that 55% of the teens between 13 and 18 used voice search on mobile phones every day. Direction-related search was one of the most frequently performed voice search. It was also reported that voice search was often issued when the users were doing activities including cooking or watching TV.

In a content analysis of the interview data of a user experiment [7], results have shown that users' familiarity with the system, ease-of-use of the system, speed of the system, as well as trust, comfort level, fun factor, and novelty were all factors that affected users' perception of a spoken system. Survey studies [27, 28] also showed that one of the top reasons why the users preferred voice search was 'for fun.' In [8], it was reported that spoken queries involved more stop words and more indicative words than written queries since they are similar to natural language used in our everyday conversation. This is consistent with the findings of [29] in which most participants preferred the human dialogue or using full sentences in interacting with information systems.

3 Method

3.1 Wizard of Oz

The Wizard of Oz method has been applied to test natural language dialogue systems (e.g. [30]) and multimodal systems (e.g. [31, 32]) and has been proved powerful and useful in supporting the design process and evaluating user interfaces and information systems [33]. In such studies, a human being (the Wizard) plays the role of the system itself in performing some aspect of a complex system. That being said, the wizard, who is unknown to the subject, simulates that aspect of the system. The main reason for doing Wizard of Oz studies is that, in general, the particular aspect of the system is one which is not yet actually possible or feasible to implement, but which is understood to be implementable in the near future. For the purpose of accurately examining the efficacy of spoken language input, and satisfying all the constraints of our research, including accurate interpretation of input, we chose to use the Wizard of Oz method. Some of the research most directly relevant to this study includes [34] and [35].

The experimental environment was a usability laboratory with two separate rooms. In one room, the participants performed their tasks, while in the other one, an experimenter (the Wizard) had a monitor that was tied to the participants' monitor. The Wizard observed the participants, listened to the participants' spoken input and observed their gestures, interpreting what was said and pointed to, and then sent that interpretation to the participants' interface device.

3.2 Tasks and Topics

In the experiment, each participant performed twelve different search tasks. These tasks were presented in the form of scenarios that attempt to involve the participants in the context of the search, as proposed by [33], so that some degree of ecological validity could be given to the experiment. The 12 tasks belonged to three categories in terms of the analysis by Kim [36]; i.e., factual task, interpretive task and exploratory task. According to Kim, factual tasks are close-ended and collect facts by asking questions. Interpretive tasks and exploratory tasks are open-ended and include evaluation, inference, and comparison. The difference is that interpretive tasks are more focused and goal oriented than exploratory tasks.

Below, we give an example topic for each task type. Table 1 shows the topics of all the tasks.

Table 1. Tasks and topics

Task	No.	Topic
Factual Task (FT)	1	The largest cruise ship in 2006
	2	NASA imaging program
	3	Hypermarket in Spain
	4	The name of an actress and a movie
Interpretive Task (IT)	1	Differences between Organic food, genetically modified food, and raw food
	2	Eating disorders in high school
	3	Charter school, public school, and private school
	4	Growing fruits
Exploratory Task (ET)	1	Lead paint poison
	2	Reasons for vegetarians and vegans
	3	Beer brewing at home
	4	Feline intelligence, temperament, and behaviors

Task type 1 (Factual task)

Topic: Professor Doe, your astronomy professor spoke of a NASA (National Aeronautics and Space Administration) imaging "program" which includes four large, powerful space-based telescopes. You recall that each of these satellites performs specialized imaging along the electromagnetic spectrum. For example, one satellite uses infrared imaging. You can't recall the name of the actual program.

Task: Find the name of the NASA program which includes four large, powerful space-based telescopes. One of the telescopes uses infrared. Find the name of this telescope. Save the document(s) where you have found the information required.

Task type 2 (Interpretive task)

Topic: You have heard your niece, who is a freshman in high school, talk about friends who are struggling with eating disorders. You are concerned and want to learn more about eating disorders experienced by children at her age.

Task: Identify at least three types of eating disorders experienced by children at the age of your niece, and their characteristics, risk, and treatment. You want to have a better understanding of what your niece is dealing with. Save the document(s) where you have found the information required.

Task type 3 (Exploratory task)

Topic: You have recently moved to Boston and you are interested in buying a home. You have heard that most homes built before 1978 have some lead paint, but that their paint status is often reported as "unknown." You are concerned because you have two small children and know that lead paint is extremely toxic.

Task: You want to have a better understanding about lead poisoning from lead paint in housing before you buy a home. You want to see if there are resources available to help you become better informed. The Web seems like a good place to locate this information. Save the document(s) where you have found the information required.

3.3 Experimental Design

The experiment was designed to be a within-subject experiment, where the participants performed searches using both systems, one after the other. For each system, participants first searched a training topic, then worked on six different topics. These six topics belong to three task categories, as described above. The first test topic was of the same task type as the training topic, the second topic was of another task type, and so on. The order of the task types and topics was rotated across participants and the experiment was replicated by exchanging the order of the two systems. This design led to 48 participants.

3.4 System Design and Implementation

Both the Baseline and Experimental systems used the same interface and the same underlying information retrieval system constructed using the Apache Lucene information retrieval toolkit.[1] Functions provided by the Lucene core were used to build the index, analyze the queries, and perform the searches.

Baseline System. A standard keyboard and mouse were used by the participants to conduct searches. The participants were instructed to type a natural language statement of their information problems in a search query box. Belkin, et al. [10] reported that this interface structure could lead to significantly longer queries than the usual single query line, and to significantly more satisfactory searches. The search results were organized as a list of retrieved documents, each with a title, and a brief description. The participants could view the full text of an article by clicking on the title, and could save the relevant articles to a window in the interface by clicking on a "save" button. (See Fig. 1, the screenshot of a training topic).

Experimental System. The interface for the experimental system (also see Fig. 1) was identical to the baseline system. The only difference was that there was no keyboard or mouse. Instead, there was a touch-screen monitor on which the participants could point out full documents, or parts of documents they would like to select.

Participants were instructed that the system they used was an experimental speech recognition system for information retrieval. They were told that they would interact with the system by describing their information problem (using the same instruction as in the baseline system) and by touching the screen and thereby selecting or highlighting the relevant items. Participants were asked to speak slowly and clearly. The experimenter in the control room typed the spoken query into the query box on that system. The query appeared on the participants' monitor after the participants finished uttering the query. In order to modify a query, the participants needed to speak the complete query to the system. The participants initiated the search by saying "search" when they were satisfied that their query had been correctly interpreted by the system. The underlying retrieval system searched on the query and returned a list of results to the interface. All other activities were performed by the participants using the touch screen (e.g. scrolling, viewing, saving, exit).

---

[1] http://lucene.apache.org/.

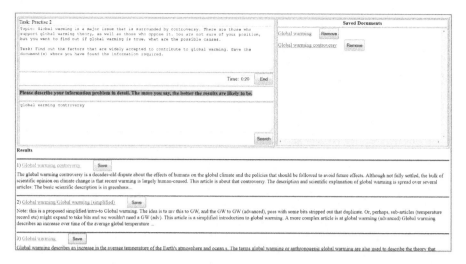

Fig. 1. System interface screenshot

3.5   Participants

Forty-eight graduate students from University at Albany participated in the experiment. There were more undergraduate students than graduate students (37 vs. 11). Demographic characteristics of the participants are shown in Fig. 2. Computer and information searching experience were determined in an entry questionnaire, using a 7-point scale, with 1 = low, and 7 = high. Those data are displayed in Table 2.

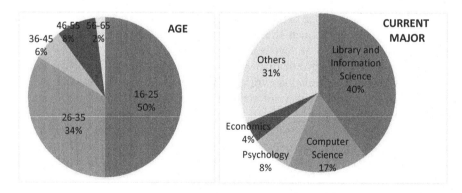

Fig. 2. Demographic characteristics of the participants

Participants conducted searches very frequently, and their Internet searching experience was high. Their touch interface use was at a medium level. However, their use of vocal search and their use of commercial spoken language software were very low.

Table 2. Computer and searching experience of the participants (7-point low to high scale)

Type of computer/search experience	Mean (s.d.)
Computer daily use	7.00 (0.00)
Expertise of computer	5.50 (0.99)
Searching experience of library catalogs	5.23 (1.13)
Searching experience of commercial system	3.58 (1.93)
Searching experience of WWW	6.73 (0.64)
Touch screen interface use	5.13 (1.78)
Voice search use with search engines	2.42 (1.70)
Commercial spoken language software use	1.85 (1.13)
Frequency of Search	6.40 (1.47)
Success in finding information	6.17 (0.72)
Expertise of searching	5.48 (0.71)
Number of years of searching experience (open question)	10.21 (3.31)

3.6 Dataset

We selected an English subset of "The Wikipedia XML Corpus For Research" [37] as the document collection. The collection 659,388 XML documents from Wikipedia and encoded in UTF-8. The documents of the Wikipedia XML collections are structured as a hierarchy of categories defined by the authors.

3.7 Data Collection

The computer logs and the logging software, "Techsmith Morae 3.1"[2] were used to collect log data, including the interaction between the user and the system. Morae was also used to record the users' speech during the search, and in the exit interview. An entry questionnaire elicited demographic and search experience information; a pre-task questionnaire gathered information about participants' knowledge of the topic; a post-task questionnaire collected participants' opinions about the last search; a post-system questionnaire elicited perceptions about the specific system; and, an exit interview compared users' search experience and opinions of the two systems.

3.8 Procedure

In our human computer interaction lab, participants first filled out an informed consent form. This consent form included detailed instructions about the experiment. An entry questionnaire was then given to the participants. Next, participants went through a general tutorial of the interface and how to use the two systems. After that, they practiced on a training topic to get familiar with the first system they would use. Following the training topic, participants conducted six search topics on the same

---

[2] http://www.techsmith.com/morae.html.

system. For each topic, they completed a pre-task questionnaire, performed the search and saved the answers in the given place in the system. Participants had up to 10 min on each topic. When participants felt that a satisfactory answer was saved, or they ran out of time, they answered a brief post-task questionnaire. Upon completing the six topics, participants finished an end-of-system questionnaire. The same procedure was applied for the second system. At the end, an exit interview was conducted. After completing the experiment, each participant was paid $30 for compensation.

4 Results

4.1 Effect of System Type on User Behavior

To answer the research questions, we first tested if system type had a significant impact on user behavior. Particularly, we were interested in discovering if allowing users to speak, point and touch would make a difference in their search behavior in comparison to their using a typed-input system. User behavior was measured by three types of time, including time of task completion, dwell time, decision time, and five interaction measures (the user characteristics of user interaction with the system and of user effort) including the number of iterations (e.g. the number of queries in each search), the total number of saved documents, the total number of viewed documents, the mean query length and the total number of clicks or touches.

According to [38], dwell time was defined as the time duration between when the user starts reading a document and when the user leaves the document. Each dwell time is thus the total of all of the times that a user dwells on the document. Decision time was defined as the first dwell time. Table 3 displays the behavior results. Significance tests were through t-test.

Table 3. Behavior measures (* significant at < .05 level, ** significant at < .01 level)

Variables	Systems		
Behavior measure	Baseline	Experimental	t, sig
Time of task completion	322.96 (159.46)	359.32** (174.65)	$t(574) = 2.61, p = 0.009$
Total Dwell Time	23.95 (27.57)	30.46** (35.24)	$t(2936) = 5.62, p < 0.00$
Decision Time	19.13 (21.04)	24.63** (27.91)	$t(2936) = 6.09, p < 0.00$
Number of iterations	6.66** (4.52)	5.05 (3.03)	$t(574) = 5.04, p < 0.00$
Number of final saved documents	3.16 (2.13)	2.87 (1.98)	$t(574) = 1.68, p = 0.09$
Number of viewed documents	6.07** (3.87)	4.89 (3.02)	$t(574) = 4.08, p < 0.00$
Number of clicks	45.75** (30.51)	36.07 (21.01)	$t(574) = 4.44, p < 0.00$
Query length	3.38 (2.12)	3.60** (2.17)	$t(3371) = 2.88, p = 0.004$

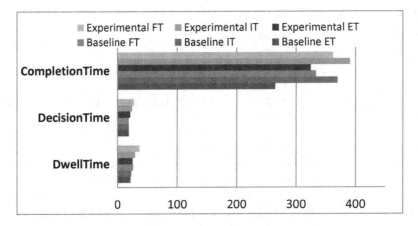

Fig. 3. Average time by system and task type (in seconds)

Participants spent significantly more time in the experimental system than those in the baseline keyboard system. Also, query length is significantly longer in the experimental system than in the baseline system. However, the number of iterations per search is significantly lower in the experimental system and the viewed documents and the number of clicks was significantly lower in that system. There were no significant differences in the other variables.

4.2 Effect of Task Type on User Behavior

There were three task types in the study. We investigated how users behaved in different systems when they worked on different tasks in terms of time, and interaction. There was a significant impact of task type on participants' time of task completion, $F = 13.19$, $p < 0.01$ Fig. 3 displays the results of this comparison of the task/system effect.

Further analysis (Table 4) shows that participants using the experimental system spent significantly more task completion time than using the baseline system, in the exploratory tasks. Participants using the experimental system spent significantly more dwell time and decision time in both factual tasks and interpretive tasks than in the baseline system.

Table 4. Average time comparison (* significant at < .05 level, ** significant at < .01 level)

Variables		System		
Behavior measure		Baseline	Experimental	t, sig
Time of task completion	FT	333.82 (178.18)	362.46 (184.10)	t(190) = 1.10, p = 0.27
	IT	369.88 (138.74)	390.82 (165.32)	t(190) = 0.95, p = 0.34
	ET	265.16 (141.79)	324.68** (169.42)	t(190) = 2.64, p = 0.009
Decision time	FT	18.96 (15.99)	27.73** (29.55)	t(895) = 5.71, p < 0.00
	IT	19.20 (24.42)	24.77** (29.31)	t(1159) = 3.53, p < 0.00
	ET	19.21 (21.04)	21.69 (24.15)	t(878) = 1.63, p = 0.104
Dwell time	FT	26.18 (25.66)	37.1** (40.97)	t(895) = 4.90, p < 0.00
	IT	23.38 (31.20)	29.77** (34.58)	t(1159) = 3.30, p = 0.001
	ET	22.20 (23.91)	25.39 (29.17)	t(878) = 1.78, p = 0.075

As can be seen from Table 5 and Fig. 4, participants viewed significantly fewer documents in the experimental system in both the factual tasks and the interpretive tasks than in the baseline system. This result correlates to the findings shown in Table 4, that when completing factual and interpretive tasks, participants spent more time in viewing the relevant documents so they viewed fewer documents in spoken interface than the textual interface.

Table 5. Comparison of interaction behavior (* significant at < .05 level, ** significant at < .01 level)

Variables		System		
Behavior measure		Baseline	Experimental	t, sig
Number of iterations	FT	6.80** (4.31)	4.70 (2.83)	t(190) = 4.00, p < 0.01
	IT	7.78** (4.84)	5.55 (3.03)	t(190) = 3.83, p < 0.01
	ET	5.41 (4.09)	4.90 (3.19)	t(190) = 0.96, p = 0.34
Number of documents viewed	FT	5.75** (3.22)	4.14 (2.26)	t(190) = 4.03, p < 0.01
	IT	7.10** (3.91)	5.59 (2.74)	t(190) = 3.10, p = 0.002
	ET	5.35 (4.23)	4.94 (3.72)	t(190) = 0.73, p = 0.47
Number of documents saved	FT	2.09 (1.16)	1.98 (1.18)	t(190) = 0.68, p = 0.5
	IT	3.93 (1.83)	3.58 (1.59)	t(190) = 1.39, p = 0.17
	ET	3.45 (2.69)	3.04 (2.56)	t(190) = 1.07, p = 0.29
Number of mouse clicks/touches	FT	49.40** (32.02)	36.52 (23.05)	t(190) = 3.2, p = 0.002
	IT	51.28** (29.04)	39.01 (19.56)	t(190) = 3.43, p = 0.001
	ET	36.58 (28.52)	32.69 (19.97)	t(190) = 1.10, p = 0.27
Query length	FT	4.05 (2.60)	4.16 (2.46)	t(1102) = 0.70, p = 0.48
	IT	3.08 (1.78)	3.44** (2.18)	t(1278) = 3.26, p < .01
	ET	2.97 (1.63)	3.23** (1.71)	t(987) = 2.42, p < .05

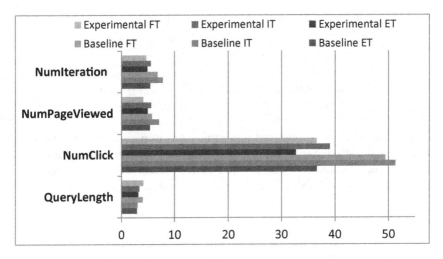

Fig. 4. Interaction measures by system and task type

With regards to the number of iterations, results show that participants initiated significantly fewer iterations in the experimental system than in the baseline system for both factual tasks and interpretive tasks.

In analyzing the total number of clicks or touches, results showed that participants made significantly fewer clicks or touches in the experimental system than in the baseline system for both factual tasks and interpretive tasks.

Participants input significantly longer queries in the experimental system than in the baseline system for both interpretive tasks and exploratory tasks.

4.3 Effect of System Type on Search Effectiveness

Search effectiveness was measured in terms of answer correctness for the factual tasks, and aspectual recall for both the interpretive and exploratory tasks. Answer correctness was measured in a 4-point scale (0: no answer; 1: wrong answer; 2: partially correct answer, and 3: right answer). Participants using the experimental system found fewer correct answers than using the baseline system, but the difference was not significant. Aspectual recall was measured for interpretive and exploratory tasks. Based on the method provided by [10], one assessor read all the documents saved by the participants and determined the aspects discussed in each document. The aspectual recall was calculated by the number of aspects saved by each participant divided by the total number of aspects identified by all participants [10]. Table 6 shows the results.

Table 6. Task and system types on search effectiveness

Task	Baseline	Experimental	Chi square test/t test
FT	2.58 (0.79)	2.51(0.85)	$X^2(3) = 0.832$, p = 0.842
IT	0.715 (0.055)	0.696 (0.081)	t(46) = −0.960, p = 0.342
ET	0.402* (0.076)	0.361 (0.053)	t(46) = −2.198, p = 0.033

From Table 6, it can be observed that participants using the experimental system identified significantly fewer aspects using experimental system in exploratory tasks. No other significant differences were found. Figure 5 presented the search effectiveness of each individual interpretive task and exploratory task.

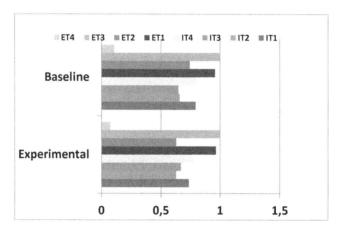

Fig. 5. Search effectiveness on each interpretive task and exploratory task

4.4   User Perception of the Systems

In the post system questionnaire, user perception of the systems was measured in terms of ease of learning to use the system, ease of use of the system, understanding of the system, and usefulness of the system (all on 7-point scales, 1 = low; 7 = high).

Results of wilcoxon signed rank test show that participants found the baseline system (Mean = 6.00, SD = 1.11) was significantly easier to learn to use than the experimental system (Mean = 5.43, SD = 1.18), W = 831.5, p = 0.015. There was no significant difference between the rest of the variables. In [7], participants' comments recorded in the interviews were analyzed to understand more about both their opinions and their behaviors. Participants felt that the baseline system was easier to learn to use because "I am a little more biased towards typing, I am practicing that for a longer period. Searching is a lot easier with the typing." "we are used to this kind of search. it is almost as same as we used the web browse Google, Yahoo…" However, they also commented that "it is just so much fun to talk to the computer, have it do all the work" and "But, eventually, that (touch) is the future."

5 Discussion

This study compared user interaction behavior in using a spoken language interface with a keyboard interface. Forty-eight participants participated in the experiment, with each searching on 12 different topics of three task types.

There were significant differences in favor of the spoken language interface on interaction measures. The number of iterations, the number of viewed documents and the number of clicks or touches were significantly lower. This is a good indication that speaking and pointing are appropriate techniques in reducing interaction between users and information systems, thus in turn improving interaction experience of users in the long run. Regarding query length, our results agree with the findings of [17] and [25] that asking for expression of search need in verbal terms results in significantly longer queries than those expressed through a keyboard interface. Since it is known that longer queries perform better in best match systems, the result is of some general interest.

Participants spent significantly more time in completing tasks, dwelling on each document, and making decisions on each document using the spoken language interface than when using the typed input interface. To better understand why longer task completion time led to fewer iteration, we then further looked into the effect of system and task types on the interaction measures, behavior measures, and search effectiveness and found significant impact. In both factual and interpretive tasks, there were no significant differences in task completion time, the number of saved documents, and search effectiveness. But the use of the experimental interface led to significantly longer decision time and dwell time, fewer iteration, fewer viewed documents, and fewer clicks or touches in these two types of tasks. We conclude that when performing factual tasks and interpretive tasks in the spoken interface, the users spent longer time on fewer documents, issued fewer queries but finished the tasks as fast as in the baseline interface and achieved similar search effectiveness. Liu and Belkin [38] showed that total dwell time is positively related to the usefulness of documents. It could be interesting to see if our findings on dwell time and decision time correlate with document usefulness. It is likely that the findings in this direction would logically explain our results.

When performing exploratory tasks in the spoken interface, the users read and saved fewer documents, spent more time on reading each document and making decision, issued fewer queries than in baseline system though the differences were not significant. However, the task completion time was significantly longer and the search effectiveness was significantly lower than in the baseline system. Since exploratory tasks require users to use various querying and browsing strategies to "describe an information-seeking problem context that is open-ended, persistent, and multi-faceted" [39], the users might need more time to perform the tasks. The experimental settings asked the user to finish the task in 10 min so the users might feel more pressure when working with an unfamiliar system.

[23] reported that compared with text queries, the longer and more complex voice queries yielded worse retrieval results. We further analyzed the search effectiveness by task type. In factual tasks and interpretive tasks, the two interfaces were not significantly different in search effectiveness. However, in exploratory tasks, participants

identified significantly fewer aspects using the spoken language interface than the typed interface. In a study comparing system effectiveness by taking into account the CPU time of query processing, Buttcher et al. [40] found that systems using more CPU time performed better in terms of the system effectiveness. Our results did not confirm this finding. It seems that participants liked to spend more time reading documents, and making decision in completing tasks in the spoken interface than in the textual interface. We believe it may be interesting to further explore if a slow search is expected by the users in a spoken language system.

In an analysis of the query characteristics, [8] found that participants used significantly more stop words in the spoken language input interface than in the textual input interface for both interpretive and exploratory tasks. They employed significantly more intention-indicative words (e.g., how, what, why) in the spoken language input interface than that in the textual input interface for factual tasks. In searching for exploratory tasks, users need both querying and browsing strategies to "foster learning and investigation" in order to find something from a domain where they have general interest but not specific knowledge [41]. [42] categorized questions into factual and procedural, and found differences in the types of documents relevant to these two different types. This suggests, combined with our results, that taking account of such "intention-revealing" words could be a useful strategy in future information systems, as opposed to the current practice of discarding them. As pointed out in [7], interview comments indicate the need of a hybrid system that allows users to alternate between a spoken language and textual input interface, depending upon users' particular need. For example, some users desired a hybrid system because speaking or typing might be a better option in different situations: a spoken language system seemed more appealing to use when users were alone, while textual input was more feasible to use when they were around other people.

6   Conclusions

We did an experiment to test user behavior difference of a spoken language interface in comparison with a baseline keyboard interface. We found interesting results on the interaction measures in favor of the experimental, spoken language input system.

In the future, we plan to conduct more user experiments to see if our findings can be generalized in a mobile environment and if task stage and task difficulty play a role in this new method of interaction.

This user experiment has its limitations. The limited types of tasks, the number of topics, and the sample pool limit the generalization of the findings. Despite the limitations, the results of this series of research will contribute to the field with the evaluation of a new method of interaction with information systems, as compared to a normal keyboard-based interaction, and design criteria for a spoken language and gesture input interface to information retrieval systems.

Acknowledgments. We thank the Institute of Museum and Library Services (IMLS) grant #RE-04-10-0053-10.

References

1. Jansen, B.J., Spink, A., Saracevic, T.: Real life, real users, and real needs: a study and analysis of user queries on the web. Inf. Process. Manag. **36**, 207–227 (2000)
2. Belkin, N.J.: Anomalous states of knowledge as a basis for information retrieval. Can. J. Inf. Sci. **5**, 133–143 (1980)
3. Karlgren, J., Franzén, K.: Verbosity and interface design (1997). http://www.ling.su.se/staff/franzen/irinterface.html
4. Kelly, D., Dollu, V.J., Fu, X.: The loquacious user: a document-independent source of terms for query expansion. In: Proceedings of the 28th Annual ACM International Conference on Research and Development in Information Retrieval (SIGIR 2005), Salvador, Brazil, pp. 457–464 (2005)
5. Efthimiadis, E.N.: Query expansion. In: Williams, M.E. (ed.) Annual Review of Information Systems and Technology, vol. 31, pp. 121–187 (1996)
6. Belkin, C.C., Kelly, D., Lin, S.-J., Park, S.Y., Perez-Carballo, J., Sikora, C.: Iterative exploration, design and evaluation of support for query reformulation in interactive information retrieval. Inf. Process. Manag. **37**(3), 403–434 (2001)
7. Begany, G.M., Sa, N., Yuan, X.: Factors affecting user perception of a spoken language vs. textual search interface: a content analysis. Interacting with Computers, **28**(2), 170–180 (2015). https://doi.org/10.1093/iwc/iwv029
8. Yuan, X., Sa, N.: User query behaviour in different task types in a spoken language vs. textual interface: A wizard of Oz experiment. In: The Information Behaviour Conference (ISIC), Zadar, Croatia (2016)
9. Belkin, N.J., Kwasnik, B.H.: Using structural representations of anomalous states of knowledge for choosing document retrieval strategies. In: SIGIR 1986: Proceedings of the 1986 ACM SIGIR International Conference on Research and Development in Information Retrieval, Pisa, Italy, pp. 11–22. ACM (1986)
10. Belkin, N.J., et al.: Query length in interactive information retrieval. In: SIGIR 2003. Proceedings of the 26th Annual International ACM SIGIR Conference on Research and Development in Information Retrieval, pp. 205–212. ACM, New York (2003)
11. Stone, B.: Google Adds Live Updates to Results. New York Times, December 8 Issue (2009). http://www.nytimes.com/2009/12/08/technology/companies/08google.html
12. Xiong, W., et al.: Toward human parity in conversational speech recognition. In: 2017. IEEE/ACM Trans. Audio Speech Lang. Process. **25**(12), 2410–2423 (2017). https://doi.org/10.1109/TASLP.2017.2756440
13. Taylor, R.S.: Question negotiation and information seeking in libraries. Coll. Res. Libr. **29**, 178–194 (1968)
14. Belkin, N.J., Oddy, R.N., Brooks, H.M.: ASK for information retrieval. Part I: background and theory; part II: results of a design study. J. Documentation **38**(2&3), 61–71; 145–164 (1982)
15. Saracevic, T., Spink, A., Wu, M.-M.: Users and intermediaries in information retrieval: what are they talking about? In: Jameson, A., Paris, C., Tasso, C. (eds.) User Modeling. ICMS, vol. 383, pp. 43–54. Springer, Vienna (1997). https://doi.org/10.1007/978-3-7091-2670-7_6
16. Trippas, J.R., Spina, D., Cavedon, L., Joho, H., Sanderson, M.: Informing the design of spoken conversational search: perspective paper. In: Proceedings of the 2018 Conference on Human Information Interaction & Retrieval, pp. 32–41. https://doi.org/10.1145/3176349.3176387
17. Crestani, F., Du, H.: Written versus spoken queries: a qualitative and quantitative comparative analysis. J. Am. Soc. Inf. Sci. Technol. **57**(7), 881–890 (2006)

18. Du, H., Crestani, F.: Spoken versus written queries for mobile information access. In: Crestani, F., Dunlop, M., Mizzaro, S. (eds.) MUIA 2003. LNCS, vol. 2954, pp. 67–78. Springer, Heidelberg (2004). https://doi.org/10.1007/978-3-540-24641-1_6

19. Du, H., Crestani, F.: Retrieval effectiveness of written and spoken queries: an experimental evaluation. In: Christiansen, H., Hacid, M.-S., Andreasen, T., Larsen, H.L. (eds.) FQAS 2004. LNCS (LNAI), vol. 3055, pp. 376–389. Springer, Heidelberg (2004). https://doi.org/10.1007/978-3-540-25957-2_30

20. Du, H., Crestani, F.: Spoken versus written queries for mobile information access: an experiment on Mandarin Chinese. In: Su, K.-Y., Tsujii, J., Lee, J.-H., Kwong, O.Y. (eds.) IJCNLP 2004. LNCS (LNAI), vol. 3248, pp. 745–754. Springer, Heidelberg (2005). https://doi.org/10.1007/978-3-540-30211-7_79

21. Fujii, A., Itou, K., Ishikawa, T.: Speech-driven text retrieval: using target IR collections for statistical language model adaptation in speech recognition. In: Coden, Anni R., Brown, E. W., Srinivasan, S. (eds.) IRTSA 2001. LNCS, vol. 2273, pp. 94–104. Springer, Heidelberg (2002). https://doi.org/10.1007/3-540-45637-6_9

22. Zue, V., et al.: JUPITER: a telephone-based conversational interface for weather information. IEEE Trans. Speech Audio Process. **8**(1) (2000)

23. Arguello, J., Avula, S., Diaz, F.: Using query performance predictors to reduce spoken queries. In: Jose, J.M., et al. (eds.) ECIR 2017. LNCS, vol. 10193, pp. 27–39. Springer, Cham (2017). https://doi.org/10.1007/978-3-319-56608-5_3

24. Schalkwyk, J., et al.: "Your word is my command": Google search by voice: a case study. In: Neustein, A. (ed.) Advances in Speech Recognition, pp. 61–90. Springer, Heidelberg (2010). https://doi.org/10.1007/978-1-4419-5951-5_4

25. Guy, I.: Searching by talking: analysis of voice queries on mobile web search. In: Proceedings of the 39th International ACM SIGIR Conference on Research and Development in Information Retrieval, pp. 35–44 (2016). https://doi.org/10.1145/2911451.2911525

26. Kamvar, M., Beeferman, D.: Say what? Why users choose to speak their web queries? In: Interspeech (2010)

27. Google. Teens Use Voice Search Most, Even in Bathroom, Google's Mobile Voice Study Finds (2014). http://www.prnewswire.com/news-releases/teens-use-voice-search-most-even-in-bathroom-googles-mobile-voice-study-finds-279106351.html. Accessed 23 Oct 2015

28. Sa, N., Yuan, X.: Improving voice interaction through examining user voice search behavior: an empirical study. Presented at the Chinese CHI 2017 (2017)

29. Berg, M.M.: Survey on spoken dialogue systems: user expectations regarding style and usability. In XIV International Ph.D. Workshop, Wisla, Poland, October 2012 (2012)

30. Johnsen, M., Svendsen, T., Amble, T., Holter, T., Harborg, E.: TABOR – a Norwegian spoken dialogue system for bus travel information. In: Proceedings of 6th International Conference of Spoken Language Processing (ICSLP 2000), Beijing, China (2000)

31. Gustafson, J., et al.: AdApt-a multimodal conversational dialogue system in an apartment domain. In: Proceedings of 6th International Conference of Spoken Language Processing (ICSLP 2000), Beijing, China (2000)

32. Salber, D., Coutaz, J.: Applying the Wizard of Oz technique to the study of multimodal systems. In: Bass, Leonard J., Gornostaev, J., Unger, C. (eds.) EWHCI 1993. LNCS, vol. 753, pp. 219–230. Springer, Heidelberg (1993). https://doi.org/10.1007/3-540-57433-6_51

33. Bernsen, N.O., Dybkjær, H., Dybkjær, L.: Designing Interactive Speech Systems, pp. 127–160. Springer, London (1999). https://doi.org/10.1007/978-1-4471-0897-9

34. Akers, D.: Wizard of Oz for participatory design: inventing a gestural interface for 3D selection of neural pathway estimates. In: CHI'06 Extended Abstracts on Human Factors in Computing Systems (Montréal, Québec, Canada, 22—27 April 2006), pp. 454–459. ACM Press, New York (2006)

35. Klein, A., Schwank, I., Généreux, M., Trost, H.: Evaluating multimodal input modes in a Wizard-of-Oz study for the domain of web search. In: Blandford, A., Vanderdonckt, J., Gray, P. (eds.) People and Computer XV - Interaction without Frontiers: Joint Proceedings of HCI 2001 and IHM 2001, pp. 475–483. Springer, Heidelberg (2001). https://doi.org/10.1007/978-1-4471-0353-0_29

36. Kim, J.-Y.: Task as a Predictable Indicator for Information Seeking Behavior on the Web. Unpublished Ph.D. dissertation, Rutgers University, New Brunswick (2006)

37. Denoyer, L., Gallinari, P.: The Wikipedia XML corpus. In: Fuhr, N., Lalmas, M., Trotman, A. (eds.) INEX 2006. LNCS, vol. 4518, pp. 12–19. Springer, Heidelberg (2007). https://doi.org/10.1007/978-3-540-73888-6_2

38. Liu, J., Belkin, N.J.: Personalizing information retrieval for multi-session tasks: the roles of task stage and task type. In: Proceedings of the 33rd Annual International ACM SIGIR Conference on Research & Development on Information Retrieval (SIGIR 2010). Geneva, Switzerland, 19–23 July 2010

39. White, R.W., Muresan, G., Marchionini, G.: Evaluating exploratory search systems: introduction to a special topic issue. Inf. Process. Manag. **44**(2), 433–436 (2007)

40. Buttcher, S., Clarke, C.L., Soboroff, I.: The TREC 2006 terabyte track. In: TREC, vol. 6, p. 39 (2006)

41. White, R.W., Kules, B., Drucker, S., Schraefel, M.C.: Supporting exploratory search. Spec. Sect. Commun. ACM **49**(4), 36–39 (2006)

42. Murdock, V., Kelly, D., Croft, W.B., Belkin, N.J., Yuan, X.-J.: Identifying and improving retrieval for procedural questions. Inf. Process. Manag. **43**(1), 181–203 (2007)

BlueJourney for AI – A Study Beyond Design Thinking to Develop Artificial Intelligence Solutions

Raquel Zarattini Chebabi[(✉)] and Henrique von Atzingen Amaral[(✉)]

IBM Research, São Paulo, Brazil
{rchebabi,hvon}@br.ibm.com

Abstract. BlueJourney is a program from ThinkLab Brazil, the innovation laboratory of IBM Research. BlueJourney was designed to connect customers, IBM researchers and other technical areas by using Design Thinking techniques. We have a specific space of immersion and co-creation and a team of professionals specialized in software development, business, engagement, design, ecosystem, education, marketing and content production. BlueJourney was created on 2018 to attend our clients' transformation needs. We study their challenges, and with clients' specialists, researchers and technical areas from IBM, we explore deeply their problems and opportunities to innovate. Therefore, we create viable solutions that truly meet people's needs and expectations. In 2019, some clients brought the challenge to develop projects by using Artificial Intelligence (AI). Sometimes because they knew exactly how AI could help their business and sometimes just because it's a buzz word, it's a movement that they don't want to stay out. In all the cases, we run the BlueJourney program to find out viable solutions with AI. But as AI is already a theme of solution with technology, we had problems to seek a perfect way to do it. Design Thinking is a method to study problems and opportunities and to create solutions. So, it's an assumption not starting with a predetermined technology. For these cases, when we need to discuss how to apply AI as a solution for some problems, we already have the technology determined. Also, for most of AI solution we need to have the data available to build the solution, that is not always the true in client reality. For these reasons, we decided to create a way to work with Design Thinking methodology when we have the premise to work with AI. In this paper, we will present a study about Design Thinking for AI. We will show how we simulated a challenge and developed the steps this method suggested, and all the conclusion about this process. We will also propose an approach about Design Thinking and AI based in the study.

Keywords: User centered design · Artificial Intelligence · Design Thinking · Innovation

1 Introduction

ThinkLab has been working since 2015 with Design Thinking techniques to connect customers, IBM researchers and other technical areas. We have a team with professionals specialized in software development, business, engagement, design, ecosystem,

A. Marcus and E. Rosenzweig (Eds.): HCII 2020, LNCS 12201, pp. 212–221, 2020.
https://doi.org/10.1007/978-3-030-49760-6_14

education, marketing and content production. Also, we have a space for co-creation where it's possible to join specialists from clients and IBM to explore the challenges to innovate client's process or products.

BlueJourney is a program created in 2018 to attend the transformation needs of our clients by leading them to a deep study about their challenges.

Since the launch and success of IBM's Artificial Intelligence products branded as Watson, several clients started to imagine future solutions that could solve business challenges at their corporations. Although the big investment of IBM and other technologies players to teach the market about what is real and what is unreal on AI, there are still lots of misconceptions about what is possible to achieve using this technology.

In 2019, we saw lots of our BlueJourney engagement drive AI solutions ideas, but as we mentioned, some of the ideas are based on misconceptions of what is possible leading to a not practical neither feasible solution. We discovered that a new approach was necessary. We needed a new framework that would guide the sessions away from doubts, and drive the solutions to be based on well stablished AI technical solutions.

In order to design the model to work with AI, we tested some tools and based on feedbacks, we studied possibilities with data specialists. In this paper, we will explain BlueJourney, the test and new approach.

2   Method and Materials

In this section, we will describe references for BlueJourney, the program developed at ThinkLab in 2018 to work with our clients in their digital transformation journey. And we will describe a technique to map data to be possible to create solutions based on Artificial Intelligence.

2.1   BlueJourney Program

BlueJourney uses Design Thinking tools to explore problems and opportunities and to develop viable solutions and to innovate. Based on Design Thinking methodology from IDEO.org [1], we defined the steps by using the concept of Inspiration, Ideation and Implementation. The Inspiration step is to understand the problems from our clients with them, and to define the challenges they have and want to explore; the Ideation is to create possible solutions for the challenges. In the Implementation step, we have real projects to select, implement and test. The most important for us is the fact of Design Thinking being a human-centered design method that brings the importance of people needs and the concept of co-creation.

Another reference is the IBM Design Thinking Framework [2]. This framework has three steps: observe, reflect and make; and defines principles like:

- Focus on the user outcomes (to achieve the users goals);
- Restless reinvention (treating everything as a prototype);
- Diverse empowered teams (to be fast and efficient).

The Fig. 1 is the Loop. The idea is to understand deeply the problems and challenges from people how knows about that; to create solutions based on this knowledge

Observe >   Reflect >   Make >

Immerse yourself in the   Come together and look   Give concrete form to
real world.   within.   abstract ideas.

Fig. 1. IBM design thinking loop.

and to make solutions, keeping in mind that as fast we test and observe and reflect again, as fast you have the best solution.

Based on IDEO [1] and IBM [2] references, BlueJourney [3] has a model with well-defined steps to facilitate to create, develop and test ideas to identify the best solution. The steps are Investigation, Ideation, Prototype, and Pitches and Selection. Usually, the process lasts 2 or 3 weeks, but for each project, we customize all detail, even the time. The most important is the engagement of specialists, the immersion and collaboration and to put focus on people's needs.

In the Investigation step, we explore the client's company, their needs, why they are thinking to innovate. Through meetings, interviews and ethnographic method, we organize the information and find out the real challenges of the client. It's very important also to bring to this conversation people who work with the outstanding challenges to know their problems and difficult in more detail. At this moment, everyone involved in the client company is aware that the process must be participatory, that the more the experts are engaged and dedicate time to the project, the greater are the possibilities of transforming their processes and systems. This steps usually takes two week and the output is a well-defined challenge.

In the Ideation step, we bring who understand most from the challenge chosen in the Investigation, for a day of co-creation in the ThinkLab space. We bring also the specialists from IBM to participate. Depending on the challenge we plan the activities selecting tools like Personas, Empathy Map, Scenario Map, Hopes and Fears, Map of Stakeholders, Ideation etc. Usually, it takes one entire day and it's on our lab to have the real immersion. The output is a list of prioritized solution ideas to develop in the next step.

In the Prototyping step, the prioritized ideas are developed in more details by teams formed by client and IBM specialists. Ideas are transformed into projects and they develop prototypes. Sometimes it's necessary to access more information, areas and specialists to go deep in details and understand the viability of proposal projects. This stage takes one or two entire days.

In the Pitches and Selection step, the participants present their prototypes in pitches format (quick presentation technique), usually in 5 (five) min, for client executives who will evaluate them. This evaluation will consider mainly, the technical and business viability, so that the winning solution (or more than one) is really a project that will be implemented in the company. It takes some h in the end of Prototype day.

Always, we adapt the techniques and schedule to attend the client's needs and the scope of their challenges. In all cases, the output is selected solutions to be developed to solve the problems that emerged from the co-creation, and to innovate the company.

2.2 Artificial Intelligence Data

As we started to work with Artificial Intelligence solutions [4], it was necessary to map the data our clients have, or they need to have, to implement the solutions created for their challenges. So, we decided to add to BlueJourney a new element, a tool to describe the data related to the challenge. This information is important to understand the viability of solutions from the Ideation step. In this cases, after the Ideation, we added a brainstorming to map all the data the client' specialists think that are related to the solutions created.

Figure 2 represents the data mapping from AI Essentials Framework [5]. The objective is to write every public, private and user data that would be useful in this context. Public data is the data available to anyone. Maybe it's open in articles, journals, magazines. Some examples are weather data, traffic data, schedule of flights. Private data is available just for a company or a specific area; so, it's necessary to respect compliance rules to access. An example of Private Data is customer satisfaction. User data is personal, like data contact (phone number, email, address) or documents data.

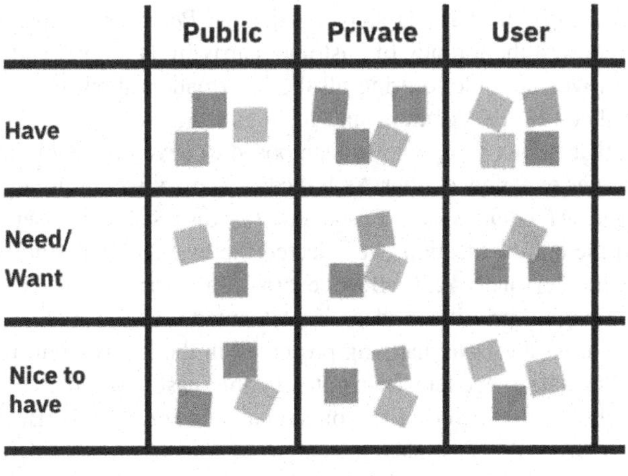

	Public	Private	User
Have			
Need/ Want			
Nice to have			

Fig. 2. Data mapping.

The column Have is for data the client already has, it's something that is available right now. Need/Want is data that we don't have but it's necessary to implement the solutions created on Ideation step. Nice to Have, is the data that is not available and it's not necessary, but would help to improve the ideas.

This table is just a first brainstorming to think about the projects we plan to execute, based on Ideation step. Looking at all data mapped, it's still necessary to discuss what is the minimum and maximum to have in this table, and it's possible to think about the viability of the projects.

With this method and tools, BlueJourney has steps to create an opportunity to rethink processes and products, to innovate business and to improve experience for people. But, is it enough to work with a specific technology like AI? In the next session, we will describe the problems we had to work with BlueJourney to Artificial Intelligence with the techniques we described until now, and the conclusions about that.

3   A Case to Test the Model

In order to test the possibilities to work with Design Thinking tools for AI projects, we created a case to test the model. In this session, we will describe this exercise and the difficulties and problems the participants described.

3.1   The Test and Results

In October 2019, we started to test some tools with ThinkLab team. They are experts in Design Thinking and specially in BlueJourney. We created a case to simulate a real challenge. In this case, the objective was to improve the customer experience for a hotel.

Like in BlueJourney with clients, we started the Investigation step to define the challenge. We discussed the possibilities to work with customer experience and the limits for this challenge. In the next step, we defined Personas, Empathy Map, As-Is Scenario Map to design the journey of customers arriving at a hotel and staying there. With this tools, it was possible to bring all the information about the actual scenario, the problems, difficulties, expectations and feelings from each Persona.

Considering that in this case, we were supposed to develop a solution by using AI to improve customer experience, after As-Is Scenario map, we discussed what kind of problems mapped, AI could solve. Based on this discussion, we set minds to the Ideation step. In the end of Ideation, we selected the best and viable ideas to have the best experience for Personas. A To-Be Scenario Map was designed to describe the perfect journey, imaging prioritized ideas implemented.

After that, we used the Data mapping presented in the last session. It was possible to simulate all the data the client (the hotel in this case) would have and need to implement the solutions defined on Ideation step and designed in To-Be Scenario Map to have the best journey for Personas.

The last activity was Hills, a tool that allows the participants to focus on define exactly what is important to deliver to people with the solutions and the impact we expected to achieve. With Hills, we defined who would receive the solution, what would be the solution and what is the factor that determines that it would bring innovation and impact to people. So, we defined exactly what kind of solution we want to deliver and how it would bring impact.

After this workshop, all the participants listed the good points, the problems and difficulties on this simulation, as we were testing the model.

The conclusion was that is possible to work with Design Thinking tools to define projects based on AI, even though AI is a predetermined kind of solution. The importance of the deeply study about the people needs and the co-creation that Design Thinking promotes has to be considering also in this case. The problems the participants listed about this test are:

1. About data:

The participants we usually bring to a BlueJourney have the knowledge about the business and people, but not about data. It's necessary to include specialists with data knowledge. And data scientists are indispensable.

Even so, it's possible the participants don't know or forget data during the mapping. So the Data mapping is a tool to be complemented somehow.

2. About Ideation for AI:

Traditional BlueJourney has an Ideation step with no limits of ideas. Participants can create ideas about processes or products, with or not including technology, without thinking about viability in this phase. They can even create ideas so different that is not easy or possible to implement. It's an important moment of creative process for everyone.

When we have to start an Ideation about AI, what kind of limits we have? How the participants know what is possible or not in this brainstorming? The discussion about the AI possibilities we had on the test was not sufficient to identify this scope and to guide the participants to go to Ideation step.

3. About desire and viability:

Usually the Ideation has a time to prioritize the ideas based on importance (impact for people) and viability (about resources to implement). In this case, the data is the most important factor to determine if a solution is viable to implement or not. It's not just about if we have the data or need to have, as we consider in the Data mapping, but it involves another aspect like data security and law aspects. Maybe, we choose in the BlueJourney, some ideas that we cannot develop because it's difficult to consider all the specificities at this moment.

Based on the test, study and feedbacks, we started to recreate the model in order to have a better method to work with BlueJourney for AI. We will present a proposal in the next session.

4   BlueJourney for AI Proposal

The model we're proposing will maintain the first step of BlueJourney, the Investigation. Also, the Prototype, and Pitches and Selection. All the difference is in the Ideation, where we have to consider the AI as a prerequisite to create solutions. Figure 3 illustrate the steps of BlueJourney, now with a different aspects for Ideation.

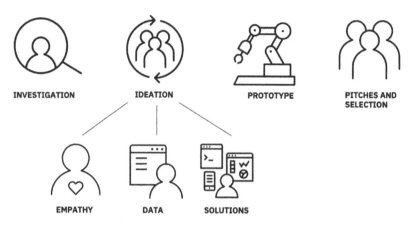

Fig. 3. BlueJourney for AI steps.

4.1   The Ideation Considering AI

As we start the Ideation based on Investigation step, in this moment we have the challenge defined. So, it's time to start the Empathy phase, by using Personas, Empathy Map, As-Is Scenario Map to design the journey of customers. These tools allow us to study the customer's needs, expectations and problems.

After that, we include a table to explain the possibilities to use AI. The objective is to present use-cases as examples to clarify how AI can be part of solutions and impact the specific industry. If we don't present an example, the participants will have difficult to create solutions to use AI, so they will create ideas based on their previous knowledge and it usually doesn't include AI.

This table has a title (the business) that specifies the business or industry we're talking about. It's necessary to present the table with examples to represent the necessity and reality for the audience. The table (Fig. 4) has three dimensions: the areas from this specific industry [A], the AI technologies [B], the use-cases [C].

Business	Impact area [A]
AI Technology [B]	Use-case [C]

Fig. 4. Use-cases about AI projects.

In the Fig. 5, we explain an example for the tridimensional table, relating some applications of AI in Finance business. Each row is an internal unit of a financial sector company (Impact areas) and each line is an AI task (AI technology). In the center, we describe example of application that we could develop inside the bank (Use-cases).

Financial Sector Company	Marketing	Credit	Retail	Investments
Predictive Modeling	Target customers	Credit offering, credit score	New products that customer is willing to buy, insurance for instance Chance of a customer be a default client	Predict better investments by understanding customer profiles
Computer Vision	Simplify customers journeys through mobile apps	Fast input of documents to approve credit scoring	Signature conference, address checking, face recognition, document evaluation	Creation of investment knowledge base of available investment funds
Natural Language	Talk with customers	Assistance to offering credit	Assistance to sell products	Assistance to help invest
Data Mining	New segments, new markets	Money laundry, fraud, default	Product recommendation, customer behavior, merge of sme (small medium entrepreneur) and personal account	Analysis of fund's performance to drive new investments

Fig. 5. An example of AI table with use-cases for finance business

The importance of this tool is to show to participants the possibilities to apply the technology as solutions for problems. The problems were explored in the Investigation step and in the Empathy (Ideation step). So, participants understand use-cases as examples and choose what kind of solution they are willing to create. In the end, they have some of use-cases selected to inspire to create solutions.

After this study, next step is to describe the data by using Data Mapping (Fig. 2). Based on the kind of use-cases the participants are focus on, it's possible to relate all the data they have, need or want, and it's nice to have. This exercise is a brainstorming, so it's not closed just to attend the ideas of use-cases, but it's important to give some space to put all data the audience remember. In the end of this step, they have data mapped.

Next step is the brainstorming to create solutions. The ideas from an original Ideation are very open, related to all kind of problems mapped on the Empathy step. In this Design Thinking, considering AI, it's important to focus on the study of use-cases to create solutions by using AI technology. The AI table (Fig. 5) and Data mapping (Fig. 2) will direct to viable solutions. Also, it's important to have a space to describe ideas about everything that it's not AI, like processes improvement, new products and so one.

After the brainstorming, the participants can divide the ideas in tree spaces: solutions with AI that are viable (it's possible to implement and the data is available), solutions with AI that are not viable now (they don't have data available yet, but maybe in the future) and other kind of solutions. Solutions are related to business impact, so it's the importance to start the process studying problems, opportunities, necessities from company and costumers. It's why Design Thinking has a lot of value, because in the end, we have solutions that reflects people's and business' needs.

Another important aspect is the data security. Each data considered to be part of solutions has to be in according to LGPD (General Data Protection Regulation) for Brazil in our case [6].

In the end of this process, the participants have a deep knowledge about problems and opportunities, and ideas to implement to achieve the innovation, considering AI technology. They also have another kind of ideas that natural emerge to improve processes and products. All the ideas were prioritized. Next step is the design of each solution. And it's possible to include a data project, planning to have data for future solutions.

5   Conclusion

Design Thinking is a framework to create innovation by studying deeply problems and opportunities. It is an approach that allow participants to work with all kind of problems and solutions, depending on the information that naturally emerges on the sessions. So, it's a premise to not define previously a technology as solution.

At the same time, nowadays, we have the necessity to create projects based on AI, and Design Thinking has tools to think the company's and people needs. To attend this demand, we created a model to work with Design Thinking tools to create empathy, to study client's problems, to understand people expectations and to create viable solutions by using AI technology. We included a data table to allow the visibility of all data involved in the possible projects, now and in the future. And we included also, a use-cases table to share examples to clarify how to work with this technology for each industry. Moreover, we decided to create spaces to maintain the premise to work with brainstorming, so it's possible to suggest ideas beyond AI, to improve processes, services and products.

Acknowledgment. We appreciated the contribution from ThinkLab team that tested our model. Their important feedbacks improved this study and our development process. Thank you, Rodrigo Bandarra dos Santos, Paula Fernanda Pereira and João Cícero Ferreira. And a special thanks to Ana Paula Appel, whose contribution about AI made a lot of difference for this study.

References

1. IDEO Homepage. https://www.ideo.org/approach. Accessed 09 Jan 2020
2. IBM Homepage. https://www.ibm.com/design/thinking/page/framework/. Accessed 09 Jan 2020
3. Chebabi, R.Z., von Atzingen Amaral, H.: A solution development model for industry based on design thinking. In: Marcus, A., Wang, W. (eds.) HCII 2019. LNCS, vol. 11586, pp. 253–262. Springer, Cham (2019). https://doi.org/10.1007/978-3-030-23535-2_19
4. Russell, S.J., Norvig, P.: Artificial Intelligence: A Modern Approach. Pearson Education Limited (2016)
5. IBM Homepage. https://www.ibm.com/design/thinking/page/toolkit. Accessed 09 Jan 2020
6. LGPD Homepage. https://www.lgpdbrasil.com.br/lgpd-english-version. Accessed 05 Feb 2020

Interaction Design of Smart Fitness Reminder in Car Based on Internet of Vehicle

Yan-cong Zhu[1], Wei Liu[1(✉)], and Yu-zu Shen[2]

[1] Beijing Normal University, Beijing 100875, China
{Yancong.zhu,Wei.liu}@bnu.edu.cn
[2] Lenovo Research, Beijing 100085, China
shenzy6@lenovo.com

Abstract. With the development of Internet of Vehicle (IoT), people have paid more attention on physical exercise depending on cars. In this study, we focus on the smart fitness based on IoT, taking the office workers as the target users and commuting as the main scene, exploring an in-vehicle health reminder service to promote them persist in effective exercise. We introduce the definition of car networking and smart fitness and analyze target users' pain points and psychological motives by questionnaire and interview. By transforming the user's pain points and needs, we designed an interactive high-fidelity interface, which is simulated by the SCANeR Studio platform. This study can promote users to adhere to effective exercise and improve the health.

Keywords: Internet of Vehicles (IOV) · Smart fitness · Reminder service · Interactive interface · SCANeR · Health

1 Introduction

After the popularity of the Internet, the Internet of Things (IoT) is also developing at a rapid speed [1]. The Internet of Vehicle (IoV), as the most typical one in the application of the Internet of Things, has attracted increasing attention from various automobile manufacturers [2]. The emergence and development of connected car technologies have made possible, such as intelligent traffic management, intelligent information services, and vehicle intelligent control [3]. The Internet of Vehicles combines advanced information technology and network technology to connect vehicles, infrastructure, and pedestrians into an organic whole. Each part of the whole can realize information interconnection and information sharing and provide various convenient services to each other [4]. Through the three-network interconnection, the Internet of Vehicles can obtain information from the cloud in real time, provide customized services for drivers and passengers, and improve the driver's experience during driving [5].

More research on smart fitness focuses on management systems, applying Internet technology and SAAS (Software-as-a-Service) software, integrating information management, intelligent operation, data interconnection and sharing, and lightweight operation, and expanding the scope of services and improving the user's fitness experience. However, due to the contradiction between fitness needs and lack of time,

© Springer Nature Switzerland AG 2020
A. Marcus and E. Rosenzweig (Eds.): HCII 2020, LNCS 12201, pp. 222–237, 2020.
https://doi.org/10.1007/978-3-030-49760-6_15

no fixed fitness plan and fitness place, are becoming an urgent problem in smart fitness in urban commuters.

At present, there are many researches on connected car and smart fitness. However, few researchers have combined the two to study how to provide users with more convenient health monitoring and fitness reminder services in the context of car networks. This article takes urban office workers as the target users, commuting to and from work as the main scenario, researching their fitness-related needs and pain points in this scenario, and using this as a breakthrough, combining car networking technology to design a new smart fitness reminder service.

Based on the main characteristics of Chinese city office workers, this article explores the pain points and needs of users in the commuting situation and combines the Internet of Vehicles with smart fitness to improve the health care of target users. After the design, this article simulates to verify whether the design has good usability.

2 Related Work

Telematics services are undergoing rapid development. At present, technologies such as vehicle location sharing, traffic situation perception, intelligent navigation system and intelligent parking management system, license plate number recognition, intelligent traffic signal control, automatic search for parking spaces and automatic parking have been implemented. Due to the introduction of the Internet of Vehicles, the internal information of automobiles has changed more and more complex, and new interaction methods have gradually appeared [10]. Tesla has mass-produced and commercialized self-driving technology under road conditions in the United States, and can implement automatic car following, automatic lane changing, automatic parking, and emergency braking on urban roads. As early as 2015, Mercedes-Benz also released a self-driving concept car, which can not only identify road markings, but also human-vehicle interaction, can automatically identify pedestrians who want to cross the road, and use lights to shoot zebra crossing images [11, 12]. A patent from Google, using GPS and other on-board sensors, can identify the undulations and potholes on the road and upload them to the cloud database in real time. In this way, when the vehicle is navigating, it is possible to choose a route with good road conditions to avoid accidents such as bumps and bumps [13]. Augmented Reality (AR) technology is also being applied to cars. For example, Toyota combines AR technology with the front windshield, which can display basic driving information such as vehicle speed, rotating speed, navigation, etc. The combination can also use the on-board camera to step in real-time around the vehicle, identify lane markings and obstacles, and locate the front windshield, to display on the windshield to remind drivers to pay attention to road conditions and improve driving safety [14]. Alibaba Group has released the Zebra Wisdom Connected System, which integrates vehicle control, path planning, and social behavior. With this system, data flow and calculation are realized, so that users can better feel the fun of driving when driving. Many universities and laboratories are also conducting research on the Internet of Vehicles, such as the human-computer interaction laboratory established by the Innovation and Entrepreneurship Education Center of Beijing Normal University, the vehicle interconnection simulation platform established by Beijing University of Aeronautics and Astronautics, and the vehicle-road integration test established by Tongji University. Platform [15] and so on. The research investment of institutions of higher learning has provided solid theory and broad prospects for the rapid development of the Internet of Vehicles. However, at present, there is still a certain distance to achieve information sharing and communication between vehicles, vehicles and people, vehicles and transportation facilities. This is undoubtedly the most critical link in vehicle network technology [16].

The rapid development of Internet of Vehicles has further promoted the driving experience, making the research method of driving experience more comprehensive and systematic. For example, based on artificial intelligence technology, researchers use more user experience maps [17], and do research on improving the usability of language and user interface in cars [18]. Zhu et al. used a statistical method to design a traffic condition prediction model. This model uses a single channel and a single frequency spectrum to analyze historical information, thereby iteratively estimating real-time traffic conditions on the road. Other studies will consider family travel scenarios to ease travel fatigue and improve the driving experience [19]. After the technology matures, experience will become one of the core issues in the research of the Internet of Vehicles.

In terms of fitness, a mature industry has been formed. Eime [24] (2013) and others analyzed the relationship between 11 dimensions, such as metabolic health, energy balance, and mental health, and physical fitness by studying the health levels and living habits of people in different countries and regions. The results show that regular physical activity can Promote people's physical health. Compared to traditional sports, people now rely more on the Internet for related activities. For example, in the United States, more than 20% of mobile phone users will install sports apps to urge themselves to achieve fitness goals [20]. Liu Meijin and Huang Daidai analyzed how the Internet will manage sports health, how to effectively monitor physical fitness, and h how to learn fitness knowledge online to promote the people's familiarity and love of sports. Wallis and others have found through research that people tend to exercise and exercise with friends of equivalent physical strength, so that they are more likely to set an example for others and strive to reach the same level as their peers [24].

This research will combine the research and design methods of applied psychology and user experience, through literature research, to understand the development status of connected car and smart fitness, and related theoretical knowledge. Through questionnaires and interviews, target user characteristics, scenarios, pain points, needs, etc. were further explored, and the results of questionnaires and interviews were summarized and analyzed to obtain design opportunities. According to design opportunities, this study draws interactive high-fidelity prototypes and simulates them through a virtual driving platform to perform usability tests to ensure a good user experience in the design.

3   User Research

This user research is divided into two parts. First, through survey data analysis, we investigate the current working and living status of the target population and their commuting situation; then explore the two dimensions of commuting scenes and motivational factors of training through user interviews. The conclusions obtained through user research provide a basis for subsequent design transformation.

3.1   Questionnaire Survey and Analysis

This questionnaire is mainly distributed through online questionnaire platforms and disseminated through social channels such as WeChat and QQ. The target group is urban drivers and passengers. A total of 605 questionnaires were collected, and a total of 463 valid questionnaires were received based on the restrictive factors such as the city of work, the nature of work, and fitness. The main questions of the questionnaire involve five dimensions: geographic information, job information, demographic information, commute status, health status, and exercise status. Then use Excel and SPSS to perform cross-analysis and correlation analysis on the 463 valid data recovered. As shown in Fig. 1.

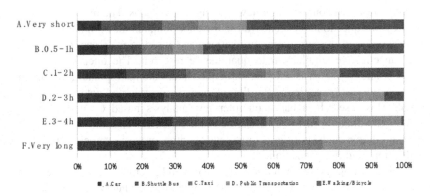

Fig. 1. Cross analysis of commute status and commute stress.

Through the questionnaire survey, we obtained the following points: (1) The daily life and work status of the research subjects is not optimistic. 71.3% of the subjects are in the working status of "low-headed people" every day. 67.0% feedback state after returning home was "I lie down and don't want to move after work." Most of the subjects were in a sub-health state, sitting in a sedentary state during the day, and lacking exercise after returning home. (2) Most of the participants who chose to commute by bicycle or walk to work concentrated in the interval of commuting time less than 1 h. At the same time, when commuting time was longer than 3 h, no one chose to commute by bicycle or walking. Two ways of commuting to work by company shuttle. More than 65.9% of the participants commuted for more than 2 h, this part of the time was not fully utilized; the health status of the participants was positively related to the exercise frequency; nearly 50% of the participants did not take the time to exercise because of "Too tired to move off work" and "Trying nothing but giving up." (3) A correlation analysis was conducted between the exercise frequency and the health status of the participants, and the results showed that there was a significant negative correlation between the exercise frequency and the probability of having obesity ($r = -0.195$, $p < 0.01$), suffering from lumbar muscle strain ($r = -0.148$, $p < 0.01$). There was a significant positive correlation between exercise frequency and the probability of no illness ($r = 0.424$, $p < 0.01$). In other words, exercise can help your body (as shown in Table 1).

Table 1. Correlation analysis of exercise frequency and health status (N = 463).

	Obesity	Hypertension	Diabetes	Cervical spondylosis	Lumbar muscle strain	No
Frequency of exercise per week	$-.195^{**}$	.041	$-.076$	$-.034$	$-.148**$	.424**
	.000	.378	.103	.468	.001	.000
	463	463	463	463	463	463

3.2 Qualitative Research

Quantitative research contains interview, coding and analysis. The interviews are based on the previous questionnaires, excavating the pain points in the commuting process of going to work, and the behaviors, motivations and motivation factors of fitness exercises as an effective supplement to quantitative research. The interviews were conducted on a one-to-one basis with the participants, and the main points and opinions of the participants were recorded. After the interviews, the recorded data were coded and analyzed. This research is based on interview analysis based on grounded theory. Interview recordings need to be transcribed and coded for analysis with NVivo software. The coding analysis uses a three-level coding process, namely labeling, conceptualization, and genericization.

A total of 5 subjects were interviewed, 2 males and 3 females, aged between 25 and 35, all of whom were working in Beijing. The content of the interview was mainly two dimensions. One focused on the commuting situation, about behavior of the participant during the commute, and which behaviors were intended to occur during the commute. The other focused on being healthy, including the current physical condition, frequency and type of physical activity, and reasons for promoting adherence or non-physical activity.

In the coding, the transcription texts of different subjects were numbered '01, 02, 03', etc.; male subjects were marked as 'M', female subjects were marked as 'F'; driving to work was marked as 'C', public transportation is marked as 'S'; 'a' was commuting process experience dimension, 'b' was the dimension of keeping healthy needs. For example, if the first woman was driving to work, her label was FC01, and each label of the interview content was FC01a1, FC01b1, FC01a2, etc. Through the integration of secondary and tertiary coding, the five central themes are: the need for professional fitness guidance, the need for adequate rest and relaxation, the need for supervision and motivation, the need for precise and controllable commute time, and the efficient use of fragmented time. Table 2 shows the final encoding results.

Table 2. Correlation analysis of exercise frequency and health status (N = 463).

Generic	Concept	Generic frequency	Concept frequency	Involved labels
Professional fitness instruction	More professional gym	12	2	FC03b22, FS05b24
	Gym appointment trouble		3	FC03b19, FC03b20, FC03b18
	Fitness need guidance		2	FC03b12, FC03b13
	Do simple exercises after getting home		3	FC03b17, FC03b11, FS05b5
	Improve sitting posture and relieve fatigue		2	FS05b13, MS04b5
Rest and relax	Tired and just want to rest	54	11	FC02b10, FC03b4
	Busy work and have no time to exercise		11	FC02b6, FC02b9
	Relax during work		3	FC03b9, MS01b6, FS05b26
	Need to work overtime at night		10	FC03b1, FC03b2
	Sub-health		15	MS04b1, FS05b8
	Exercise for weight loss		4	FS05b7, FS05b16
Supervision and motivation	Unwilling to exercise	16	4	MS04b16, MS04b18
	More like do exercise with companion		8	FC03b21, FS05b41
	Exercise must be effective to persist		4	FS05b38, FS05b37
Precise and controllable commute time	Time to work needs to be fixed	26	4	MS04a3, FC02a3
	Controlled subway travel time		5	FS05a4, MS04a4
	Easy to drive and not hurry		7	FC02a2, FC03a1
	Long taxi ride		3	FC02a7, FC02b2, MS04a6
			7	

(continued)

Table 2. (*continued*)

Generic	Concept	Generic frequency	Concept frequency	Involved labels
	Severe peak congestion			FS05a6, MS04a18
Applying fragmentation time efficiently	Subway commuting is crowded	23	5	MS01a1, FS05a3......
	Hate driving jams		6	FS05a14, FC03a2
	Commute time is working		2	FC03a7, MS01a6
	Looking at mobile phone on commute		5	MS01a5, MS01a3
	Short commute time		5	FC02a5, MS01a4

3.3   Persuasive Design Based on Motivation Theory

We further classified and integrated the conclusions, converted them into user needs and pain points, and combed the opportunity points. As shown in Table 3.

Table 3. Function point analysis

Problem	Cause analysis	Chance point
Long commutes and inefficient use	1. Home is far from the company 2. Poor commuting environment (many people, traffic jams, no seats, etc.)	1. Plan your trip reasonably, shift to and from work 2. Make the most of traffic jams to do other things
Inability to exercise effectively after returning home	1. Weak will and insufficient exercise stimulation 2. Tired of working during the day	1. Increase interaction 2. Intrinsic motivation to stimulate exercise
Difficult to keep exercising	1. No timely feedback on exercise effects 2. Lack of supervision and incentives	1. Show off the sports results in time 2. Give rewards for achieving goals 3. Increase the supervision and encouragement mechanism among friends

As shown in the Table 3 above, the last two questions are about how to urge users to adhere to effective exercise. From the perspective of the problem, on the one hand, because the user is inherently inert and has a low level of motivation to exercise after going home, he does not want to go out to exercise; on the other hand, because of the specific nature of the exercise, it is impossible to get an immediate effect after an exercise. Instead, they are exhausted, which leads to a lack of timely positive incentives to keep the practice of exercise. There are two ways to solve this problem: increasing the level of internal motivation and giving external stimuli to make this behavior sustainable. We use persuasive design theory and motivation theory in psychology to explain the relationship between motivation level, stimulus and behavior occurrence, to solve this problem.

Motivation theory explains the nature and mechanism of internal psychological motivation behind external behavior and is a systematic and theoretical explanation of motivation in the field of psychology. Achievement goal theory is a kind of motivation theory. The main point is that the reason why people constantly strive to reach a set goal is to get a sense of accomplishment when they achieve the goal. In addition, cognitive evaluation theory is also a kind of motivation theory, which mainly explains the relationship between external stimuli, internal stimuli, and motivation levels. If someone did something out of interest and was unexpectedly rewarded, over time, the individual would think that the behavior was to get the reward and forget that it was originally because of their own interest. Once the reward stops, the individual will not do this again.

In our research, we found that participants "needed timely feedback on their results," and they thought "as long as I let me know that my exercise today is fruitful, I can continue to exercise." The feedback mentioned here is giving users a sense of accomplishment. The theory has two main concepts, goal setting and goal orientation. The goal setting is to determine what the goal is to achieve; the goal orientation refers to the individual's participation in this goal task, that is, his purpose. Therefore, setting a specific goal with a suitable difficulty will help users to more actively generate behaviors that point to this goal and finally complete the goal. If users want to use the product for a long time, they should be motivated to stimulate their intrinsic motivation, that is, to do something in their own interest. The level of external stimulus should be appropriate, otherwise the user will rely too much on external stimulus, which ultimately affects the continuation of behavior. In addition, the persuasive design proposed by BJ Fogg (2003) at Stanford University is to reflect the theory of behavior motivation in product design, so that users can be attracted to the product without knowing it and can continue to trigger the behavior of using the product. He believes that change in behavior includes three dimensions: motivation, ability and stimulus. To trigger an action, individuals need to have sufficient internal motivation, behavioral execution capabilities, and certain external stimuli. Brainstorm based on this theory, and finally determine the product information architecture as shown in Fig. 2.

In the early stage of users' use of products, external motivation is dominant, and users should be given timely feedback and incentives to encourage users to keep exercising. For old users, the ways to improve user stickiness should be the ways from external motives transformed into internal motives so that users can't help exercising.

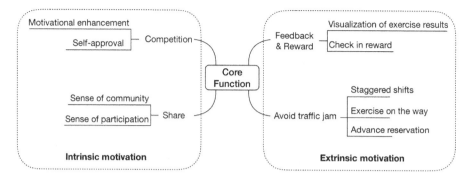

Fig. 2. Information architecture.

4 Interaction Design

Finally, we designed the car-side APP, which mainly implements commuting route planning, time scheduling, and exercise reservation functions; at the same time, the car-side data can be synchronized to personal mobile phones through the Internet, and users can implement data recording, exercise results display, and sharing and communication functions on the mobile phone. After drawing a high-fidelity page using Sketch, the car end is imported into the iPad to simulate the central control screen and combined with the SCANeR Studio simulation driving platform for simulation.

4.1 Prototype Design

The scene focuses on the commute scene. The current problem in this scenario is mainly serious traffic jams in the morning and evening. Part of the time is wasted during traffic jams, and users cannot reasonably plan this time. Therefore, the main function of this design is to reasonably plan the route and arrange the time, travel on peaks, and take the opportunity to exercise appropriately.

Combined with the information architecture diagram, we first draw a low-fidelity page flow as shown in Fig. 3. Among them, the main pages are the home page (PK information page), today's overview page, historical data page, and sports results page. The above pages and navigation pages can jump to each other. The home page is the PK information presentation page. Based on the theory that comparing users with each other is also an effective way to stimulate exercise motivation, users open the APP and the default is a PK page to let users always know their exercise situation with their opponents. The opponents are automatically matched by the system, and the physical data of the two are like the daily target exercise amount. Today's overview page presents the user's current exercise data. The historical data page presents the user's

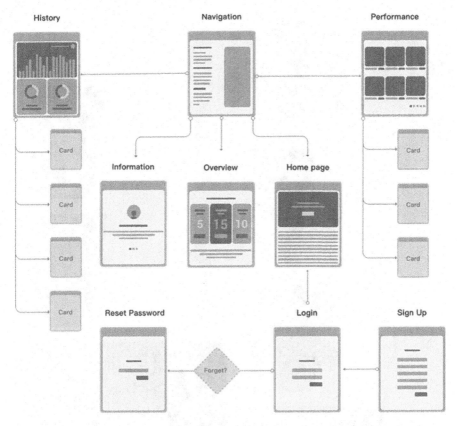

Fig. 3. Low-fidelity page flow.

daily exercise volume and daily PK wins and losses in the past 6 months. Each tab can be clicked to view detailed exercise volume data and compare the curve with the opponent's data. The exercise results page is set to automatically jump when the user opens the app for the first time after the exercise, mainly showing the amount of exercise.

Combined with the conclusions of the user research in the previous chapter, the amount of exercise is represented by the amount of food consumed, which is more intuitive and impactful. Exercise data can be shared by other devices worn by users while exercising.

After traversing the page flow to determine that there are no logical issues and cover all the functional points, you can draw a high-fidelity page. The resulting high-fidelity page is shown in Fig. 4.

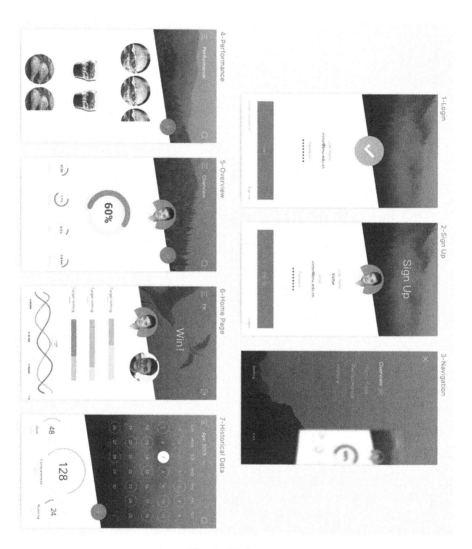

Fig. 4. Hi-fi page.

The interface function of the vehicle is relatively simple, as shown in Fig. 5. In addition to basic route navigation functions, it can also obtain real-time traffic conditions information and perform intelligent analysis to predict the duration and elimination time of congestion conditions. Furthermore, it recommends the nearby places where users can exercise and relax for a short period of time, and then continue driving on the road after the peak time is over. After the calculation, the time saved or wasted will be displayed for users to choose.

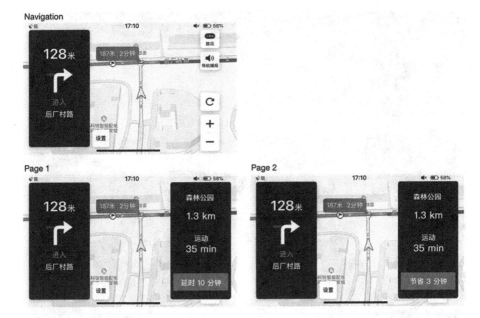

Fig. 5. Car page.

The navigation page is consistent with the existing content and contains distance information, road information, and traffic information. When the system detects that the current route is heavily congested and finds that there is a place suitable for relaxing sports along the way, the background will analyze and predict how long the congestion will be reduced, and then get a time suitable for sports. Of course, the premise is that it will not take more time to go to the destination after the exercise than the default route, and even if the congestion is reduced, you may arrive at the destination early. After the calculation is completed, it will automatically jump to the sports route recommendation page. Compared with the navigation page, an additional label will be displayed on the right side of the page to display the name of the sports venue, distance, recommended exercise time, and time consumption compared with the default recording Differences and other data.

4.2 Simulation

This study is under the premise of self-driving commute scenarios, and user tests should also be conducted under driving scenarios. Although real road driving is closer to the real environment, for safety and repeatability of experiments, the best solution is to simulate driving through a virtual driving platform. Studies have proven that the use of simulation methods in measuring visual attention information and driving subtask performance still has ideal validity and reliability.

The simulation uses the driving simulator of the Human-Computer Interaction Lab of Beijing Normal University. This system includes software system and hardware system. The hardware includes a cockpit, a computer, a projector, a display screen, and

Fig. 6. Human-computer interaction laboratory hardware composition.

sound, as shown in Fig. 6. The software mainly uses the SCANeR Studio simulation driving platform developed by OKTAL, France. This simulation driving software platform has been used by many automobile companies, including Renault Motors, with high reliability.

The simulation principle is to connect the cockpit with a computer, read the driving data in the cockpit in real time through the software, and then control the 3D animation to make corresponding changes after computing by the computer, and finally project it on the screen through a projector. Among them, the 3D animation scene needs to be built inside the software. Because the driver's cabin has only traditional physical buttons and no screen, the imported high-fidelity interface is imported into the iPad and placed in the middle of the front row to simulate the central control screen, which is convenient for users to operate while driving. As shown in Fig. 7.

Fig. 7. Simulated cockpit interior.

5   Discussion

This research work is centered on office workers in urban areas. In a strict sense, the research results have limitations. Interested researchers in the later period can supplement the research results of office workers in other first-tier cities, and it is more meaningful to synthesize the research results of this paper.

Although this article simulates the usability test through simulation, and the result feedback is good, there are still some problems. For example, user feedback hopes that the driving route can be customized and supports sports recording and other functions. These issues should have been analyzed and then prototyped. However, due to time, the prototype cannot be upgraded iteratively. But this does not affect the conclusion that users are generally satisfied with the current design prototype.

In the later stages of the study, the design prototype used traditional touch interaction, and the visual cue was simulated with a central control screen (using iPad). It did not use currently popular methods such as voice control, gesture control, and head up display (HUD). This is because the focus of this research is not on exploring new ways of interaction and presentation. At the same time, other researchers are also required to focus on HUD's in-vehicle interaction, and subsequent research results can be merged.

6 Conclusion

The design proposed in this study, on the one hand, intelligently predicts road conditions in the future through traffic big data analysis, so that people working in different areas can travel off peaks or use the time of traffic jams to perform simple exercises along the way. On the one hand, you can save your time, and you can relax your body properly. At the same time, you can reduce the time jammed on the road and reduce the waste of resources. On the other hand, by presenting exercise results to users in a timely manner, the motivation level of exercise is improved based on external incentives. In addition, by comparing with other people, you can make yourself feel crisis and promote timely and effective exercise.

In future research, the vehicle-mounted end can combine gesture recognition and voice recognition technology to replace the traditional touch interaction with a more secure and efficient interaction method. The multi-screen integration on cars, that is, the central control screen, dashboard, HUD, multi-function steering wheel, etc., has become a trend. From this bold prediction, in the short time to come, there will be more ways to present information in the car. For different roles in the car, the information is presented in zones. The driver only needs to pay attention to the information related to driving safety, and the passengers can browse the content of their interest without interfering with each other. As for the mobile terminal, it is possible to combine biometric technology and other sensors to more accurately obtain the user's own health status and exercise volume. By comparing the body data before and after exercise, the relevant results can be displayed more intuitively and in detail for the user.

Acknowledgments. We thank HMI lab in Beijing Normal University, who provide the context of our simulation. Moreover, thank all the participants for their contribution.

References

1. Giusto, D., Iera, A., Morabito, G., Atzori, L. (eds.): The Internet of Things: 20th Tyrrhenian Workshop on Digital Communications. Springer, New York (2010). https://doi.org/10.1007/978-1-4419-1674-7
2. Wang, J., Li, S., Zeng, J.: Analysis of development model of internet of vehicles. Comput. Technol. Dev. 21(12), 235–238 (2011)
3. Shi, X., Huang, A., Zhang, T.: Research and development of sensing technologies in internet of cars. J. Hubei Autom. Ind. Inst. 25(3), 39–44 (2011)
4. Goel, A., Gruhn, V.: Solving a dynamic real-life vehicle routing problem. In: Haasis, H.D., Kopfer, H., Schönberger, J. (eds.) Operations Research Proceedings. ORP, vol. 2005, pp. 367–372. Springer, Heidelberg (2006). https://doi.org/10.1007/3-540-32539-5_58
5. Atzori, L., Iera, A., Morabito, G.: The Internet of Things: a survey. Comput. Netw. 54(15), 2787–2805 (2010)
6. Liu, Z., Kuang, X., Zhao, F.: Development status, bottlenecks and countermeasures of China's automobile networking industry. Sci. Technol. Manag. Res. 36(4), 121–127 (2016)
7. Zheng: Wirel. Internet Technol. (13), 67–68 (2016)
8. Tong: Research on development model of Beijing community sport based on the Internet of Things fitness (2014)

9. Xing, D.: Contemp. Sports Technol. **7**(32), 251–252 (2017)
10. Schmidt, A., Spiessl, W., Kern, D.: Driving automotive user interface research. IEEE Pervasive Comput. **1**, 85–88 (2010)
11. Lee, E.K., Gerla, M., Pau, G., Lee, U., Lim, J.H.: Internet of vehicles: from intelligent grid to autonomous cars and vehicular fogs. Int. J. Distributed Sens. Netw. **12**(9) (2016). https://doi.org/10.1177/1550147716665500
12. Sun, L., Chang, R.: Research status and prospect of driving style. Hum. Ergon. **19**(4), 92–95 (2013)
13. Tbatou, S., Ramrami, A., Tabii, Y.: Security of communications in connected cars modeling and safety assessment. In: Proceedings of the 2nd International Conference on Big Data, Cloud and Applications, p. 56. ACM, March 2017
14. Kaiwartya, O., et al.: Internet of vehicles: motivation, layered architecture, network model, challenges, and future aspects. IEEE Access **4**, 5356–5373 (2016)
15. Sun, J.: An integrated simulation platform for connected vehicle system experiments. Res. Explor. Lab. **33**(2), 75–78 (2014)
16. Liu, He, Li: J. Hubei Univ. Econ. (Hum. Soc. Sci.) **12**(3), 81–82 (2015)
17. Martins, M.M., Santos, C.P., Frizera-Neto, A., Ceres, R.: Assistive mobility devices focusing on smart walkers: classification and review. Robot. Auton. Syst. **60**(4), 548–562 (2012)
18. Kim, D.H., Lee, H.: Effects of user experience on user resistance to change to the voice user interface of an in vehicle infotainment system: implications for platform and standards competition. Int. J. Inf. Manag. **36**(4), 653–667 (2016)
19. Cycil, C., Perry, M., Laurier, E.: Designing for frustration and disputes in the family car. Int. J. Mob. Hum. Comput. Interact. (IJMHCI) **6**(2), 46–60 (2014)
20. Duggan, M., Brenner, J.: The Demographics of Social Media Users, 2012, vol. 14. Pew Research Center's Internet & American Life Project, Washington, DC (2013)
21. Liu, H.: Method of physical education informationization requirement analysis. Jo. Beijing Sport Univ. (4), 80–84 (2016)
22. Kumar, S., Dolev, E., Pecht, M.: Parameter selection for health monitoring of electronic products. Microelectron. Reliab. **50**(2), 161–168 (2010)
23. Mozaffarian, D., et al.: Executive summary: heart disease and stroke statistics—2015 update: a report from the American Heart Association. Circulation **131**(4), 434–441 (2015)
24. Wallis, C.J., Ravi, B., Coburn, N., Nam, R.K., Detsky, A.S., Satkunasivam, R.: Comparison of postoperative outcomes among patients treated by male and female surgeons: a population based matched cohort study. Bmj **359** (2017). https://doi.org/10.1136/bmj.j4366
25. Wang, J., Li, S., Zeng, J.: Research on develop model of Internet of Things. Technol. Dev. Comput. **12**(10), 34–37 (2011)

Usability Aspects of Handheld and Mobile Devices

Does the Kindle Conform to Chinese Users' Usage Habits? A Usability Assessment of the Kindle Paperwhite

Yuxi He, Fang Lin, Jinyao Song, Tao Su, Marcelo M. Soares[(✉)],
Zhixin Gui, and Jiayu Zeng

School of Design, Hunan University, Hunan, People's Republic of China
shijiuxx@foxmail.com, 1634817102@qq.com,
pinzilian@163.com, 2542817167@qq.com,
soaresmm@gmail.com, 649651069@qq.com,
jiayuzeng@163.com

Abstract. It is predicted that electronic book readers will become the mainstream of ways of reading in the future, and this sign has been seen in China recently. According to statistics from Taobao Tmall (Fig. 1), China's biggest online-shopping website, the amount of people purchasing Kindle Paperwhite4 is more than 5000 per month. In this research, we performed a detailed usability assessment on the Kindle Paperwhite to see whether it conforms to the usage habits of Chinese users. Then we compared the Kindle Paperwhite with another e-book reader designed at home, to explore the differences in interaction design and design style. Finally, we summarized the weakness of Kindle Paperwhite and made our suggestions. This research hopes to give some new insights into e-book readers design for the Chinese market.

Keywords: Kindle · Usability assessment · Interaction design · Chinese users

1 Introduction

With the development of technology, using electronic book readers to read has been trending upwards, especially in China. While there is a variety of devices to choose from, people naturally turn to the giant in this field, which is Amazon and its classic product Kindle. Since Kindle has been launched in the Chinese market in 2013, it obtains constant attention among Chinese netizens [1]. According to the statistics analyzing Taobao's quantity of sales, we made a sales comparison between three kinds of kindle (Fig. 1), more than 5000 Kindle Paperwhites are sold within a month in Kindle's flagship store. While the demand for e-book readers continues to increase, it is undeniable that the user experience of Asians was not given priority to when designing Kindle in the first place. A more user-friendly product, which is oriented towards the prosperous Chinese market, is in need imperatively.

Previous researches have mainly focused on the general usability and user experience of Kindle product. For instance, John V. Richardson Jr and Khalid Mahmood [2] present a comprehensive evaluation of user satisfaction and usability concerns related

A. Marcus and E. Rosenzweig (Eds.): HCII 2020, LNCS 12201, pp. 241–248, 2020.
https://doi.org/10.1007/978-3-030-49760-6_16

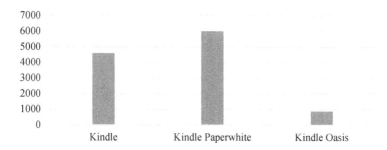

Fig. 1. Three kinds of kindles' monthly sales according to statistics from Taobao Tmall

to five e-readers, including the Amazon Kindle. And Jakob Nielsen also did Kindle Fire Usability Findings in 2011 [3].

But what motivated us are some more specific questions: Is Kindle suited for Chinese users? Does it conform to the Chinese's habitual ways of interaction and their mental models? In our research, we tried to narrow down to find the most severe and detailed problems that Chinese users might encounter when using Kindle. To supplement our findings, we made a comparison with iReader, a domestic e-book reader which is popular in China as well. With our result, we aim to provide some new insight into the design of e-book readers for the Chinese.

2   Research Subject

Since there is a series of Kindle products, we decided to take Kindle Paperwhite (Fig. 2) as the research example for two reasons. First, this type of Kindle is rather full-featured, with both essential functions and more advanced ones like built-in reading

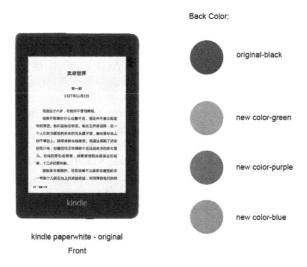

Fig. 2. Kindle Paperwhite (source: https://www.amazon.cn/)

lights, which gives it the edge over Kindle 499. Second, Kindle Paperwhite ranks above other kinds of Kindle in sales according to Taobao (Fig. 1), which implies that it is more wide-spread currently compared to Kindle Oasis and Kindle 658, thus the conclusion we draw would be more universally applicable.

3 Research Method and Process

Our research contains both quantitative and qualitative methods to explore the usability of Kindle Paperwhite. The experiment can be divided into four steps. In the first step, task analysis and property checklist were used to draw a rough idea of the product, and we did these two methods by ourselves. In the second step, we handed out a questionnaire and interviewed with typical Kindle Paperwhite users. We also conducted think-aloud protocols and co-discovery with volunteers in the third step. And at last, we compared Kindle to iReader based on the problems we had found.

To see the instinctive reaction of using Kindle Paperwhite, the volunteers we selected in the third step were mostly novices and had not used Kindle products before, without particular restrictions in other variables such as age and gender. The participants in other method were not particularly defined.

3.1 A Rough Assessment Using Task Analysis and Property Checklist

At the beginning of the research, we did a property checklist using principles of usable design [4]. The outcome of the property checklist was only for locating the problems, so we would not discuss it further. We conducted this method with the simple purpose of making hypotheses in advance of the next two steps.

A qualitative task analysis (Fig. 3) was another method acting as a provision. We set up a task: read *the three-body* and adjust the font size before reading, and then listed every step required to complete the task to see whether the process was simple and straightforward enough. Because the task we set was not too complicated, there were no critical problems shown in the result of the analysis. We also observed our volunteers based on the task analysis process while they performed other tasks in the third step. The result of which will be discussed later.

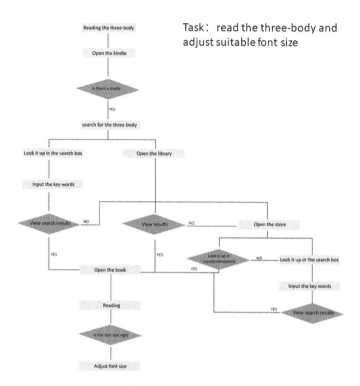

Task：read the three-body and adjust suitable font size

Fig. 3. The task analysis

3.2   Questionnaires and Interviews with Typical Kindle Users

In the second step, we used the questionnaire, to get a general idea that users held about Kindle Paperwhite. We handed out questionnaires in several Kindle interest forums for two days and received from 31 participants. Unfortunately, we had to discard the quantitative data from 14 users since what they were not our target users, so our statistics were based on the remaining 17 users.

In the survey, the physical properties and design style of Kindle Paperwhite were mainly questioned. For example, the participants were asked to rate in a 5-point Semantic Differential scale (Fig. 4) about their general feelings of Kindle Paperwhite. The adjectives used were collected from the reviews and comments about it on the Internet. The result shows that most participants viewed Kindle Paperwhite as a classic, succinct product. The questionnaire also included more detailed questions such as question (9): Do you think the size of Kindle Paperwhite is comfortable for you to use? And question (11): Do you think it convenient to press the button? The questionnaire is given in the Appendix A.

After analyzing the results of the questionnaires, we invited five typical Kindle Paperwhite users to participate in an in-depth interview, in which their opinions were discussed at length. Besides the necessary information such as the frequency of usage, they were required to talk about their personal experience on several given topics. Then they were asked to answer some unstructured questions. The specific usability

(13) What's your overall feeling about Kindle?

	1	2	3	4	5		Average point
Fashion	0	11.76%	35.29%	29.41%	23.53%	Retro	3.65
Soft	17.65%	11.76%	29.41%	23.53%	17.65%	Hale	3.12
Classic	47.06%	17.65%	35.29%	0	0	Fancy	1.88
Cheap	5.88%	0	47.06%	17.65%	11.76%	Expensive	3.41
Light	11.76%	11.76%	47.06%	17.65%	11.76%	Heavy	3.06
Technological	17.65%	17.65%	17.65%	23.53%	23.53%	Leisure	3.18
Concise	29.41%	35.29%	29.41%	5.88%	0	Complex	2.12

Fig. 4. The 5-point semantic differential scale

problems were known through these questions. In short, the major problem is that there are lots of hidden operations that users do not know. Since these operations were not shown in the beginner's guide, most users discovered them by accident.

3.3 Think-Aloud Protocols and Co-discovery

At the third stage of our experiment, we conducted a think-aloud test. The participants were asked to complete the task which we had set up in the task analysis and speak about what were they doing and thinking simultaneously. The whole process was filmed by a moderator with the consent of the participants. We collected several usability problems in this research and ranked them by times.

In subsequent, three groups of participants were invited to do a co-discovery test based on the same task as before. Each group is composed of two people, and at least one of them is a novice. When working together to accomplish the task, they were encouraged to help each other and verbalize their thoughts. After analyzing the video recordings, we found that the same problems appeared in this research, which was also related to the interaction of Kindle Paperwhite.

3.4 A Comparison Between Kindle Paperwhite and iReader

At the last step, we compared Kindle Paperwhite with iReader (Fig. 5), a China-produced e-book reader, in the usability problems found previously. The type of iReader we choose was iReader A6, which was launched in 2019.

We compared these two devices in three aspects. The first aspect was the weight and size. iReader is thinner and lighter than Kindle Paperwhite, and a curvier back with the texture of metal makes it comfortable to hold. However, it is worth mentioning that during our research, there was little people complain about Kindle Paperwhite's weight. One participant even reported that the shape and weight of it gave him a sense of the paper book. The second aspect was the design of the button. The button of Kindle Paperwhite was on the bottom of the device, while iReader A6 on the top. And

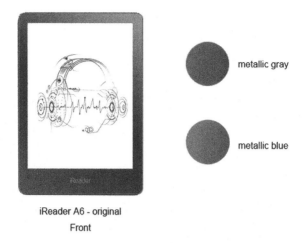

iReader A6 - original
Front

Fig. 5. iReader A6 (source: https://ireader.tmall.com/)

the latter one is more suited for Chinese users' habits. The last aspect being compared was the reading experience. Although Kindle Paperwhite's interface is not as clear as iReader A6, it is still superior when it comes to the overall reading experience.

4   Analysis and Results

4.1   Results of Interviews

When providing a series of operations and asking the participants which ones they were not accustomed to, 3 of 5 said that they had trouble finding the way to adjust the font size and line spacing at first. One participant said that when she habitually tapped the center of the screen to wake up the menu, it turned to the next page. This is because most reading APPs use the interaction of tap on the center to wake up the menu, while on Kindle users have to tap the upper part of the screen to achieve that goal. There were also 3 participants did not know the way to take screenshots on Kindle Paperwhite (press two opposite corners on the screen simultaneously), and one reported that it was unnecessary to have all these tricks in an electronic reading device.

When required to rate in a 5-point Semantic Differential scale (the same as in the questionnaire), their common feelings for Kindle Paperwhite were classic, succinct, and lightweight.

4.2   Results of Think-Aloud Protocols

There are three significant problems shown in the research. First was that the screen flickers a lot, which bothers some of the participants. Secondly, participants had difficulty finding the way to wake up the TAB bar (the menu): they slide downwards or tap on the wrong places. Thirdly, when asked to adjust the font size, one participant, after failing a lot of times, eventually succeeded by habitually using two figures to zoom in. However, this operation was neither included in the beginners' guide nor the standard step set by us.

4.3   Results of Co-discovery

The most severe usability problem was found in the group of two novices. The overall task went smoothly, but when asked to adjust the font size, they tried a solid two minutes and still failed. They reported after the task that they had no clues how to call out the command. And for other groups, one group of a novice and a common user and another of a novice and an expert, there is no obvious problems, since the novices were guided by the non-novices.

5   Conclusion

Although Amazon Kindle is nowadays one of the most common electronic reading platforms, it still can be improved when it comes to the usage of Chinese users. The conclusions of this research and our suggestions are drawn as follows:

Firstly, too many ways to achieve a simple task may confuse users. Tricks or hidden operations may sound intriguing, but if there were too many of them, it could bewilder users. From what we have researched, Chinese users prefer surprises with clues. So, the simplest way may be completing the beginners' guide to include all the operations. A less clumsy way is adding hints which imply available actions, in order to release users' workload. It is also suitable for other fundamental operations such as adjusting the font size.

Secondly, as an electronic e-book reader with rather specialized functions, it is better to simplify the procedures of other operations. It is shown in our research that Chinese users concern about the experience of reading the most when choosing an e-book reader. Thus, making other operations smooth and straightforward is of great importance, by which we can ensure that users can enjoy the reading part to the utmost.

Thirdly, it is evident that the basic interaction of Kindle Paperwhite does not ideally suit for Chinese users. If changing the patterns of interaction is beyond consideration, remind users of the interactions from time to time may be a choice worth considering.

Lastly, Chinese users prefer laconic interface and interaction. The priority of the information given on Kindle Paperwhite's interface could be thought again thoroughly. It is advised to give a larger space for the reading part where the users can browse through his/her library.

6   Discussion and Limitation

The specific usability problems are investigated and evaluated in this research. However, due to the limited time, limited access to new techniques, and some other factors, there are still limitations in the following two aspects:

Limitation 1. When interviewed with unstructured questions, it is difficult for interviewees to recall the problems they have met when using the Kindle Paperwhite. Their first answers are quite ambiguous, so researchers have to lead them to help recollect their experience. It might influence the rigor of the research.

Limitation 2. It is widely acknowledged that a large number of samples is needed to support a precise result. However, we fail to recruit enough participants, especially for questionnaires. Since we intend to focus on Chinese users, it would be more accurate if we had had adequate samples.

This research mainly discusses the usability problems that Chinese users may encounter or already encountered when using the Kindle Paperwhite. There is still a lot of space for research and experiment. Our research can be used as an inspiration for further studies, not only for Chinese users but also for users worldwide. Meanwhile, the project will also be improved in our next phase of research.

Appendix A. Questionnaire

(1) What is your gender?
(2) What is your age?
(3) Have you ever used Kindle products?
(4) Have you ever used other e-book readers?
(5) Why did you choose this rather than Kindle?
(6) Which parts are more important to you if you want to buy an e-book reader?
(7) What times do you use Kindle Paperwhite in one week?
(8) Do you think the size of Kindle Paperwhite is comfortable for you to use?
(9) Do you think the weight of Kindle Paperwhite is comfortable for you to use?
(10) Did you buy the protect cover for your Kindle?
(11) Do you think it convenient to press the button?
(12) For the following operations, which operations you do not know?
(13) What are your overall feelings about Kindle?

References

1. Lei, Y.: Amazon's day one in China: the role of Amazon's Kindle in China. Pub. Res. Q. **29**, 365–370 (2013). https://doi.org/10.1007/s12109-013-9334-3
2. Richardson, J.V., Mahmood, K.: eBook readers: user satisfaction and usability issues. Libr. Hi Tech **30**(1), 170–185 (2012)
3. Nielsen, J.: Kindle Fire Usability Findings. Alertbox (2011)
4. Jordan, P.W.: An Introduction to Usability, pp. 25–37. CRC Press, Boca Raton (1998)

Study on Size Coding Identification of Manual Rotary Knob

Huimin Hu[1], Junmin Du[2(⊠)], Hui Lu[3], and Haoshu Gu[2]

[1] SAMR Key Laboratory of Human Factor and Ergonomics,
China National Institute of Standardization, Beijing, China
[2] School of Transportation Science and Engineering, Beihang University,
Beijing, China
dujm@buaa.edu.cn
[3] Beijing WellinTech Inc., Beijing, China

Abstract. Size coding is a common coding method of assigning different size to a manipulation device during design process. It is widely used in industrial product design and human-machine interface design that need to quickly identify or distinguish alignment devices. In this study, the effects of size coding of manual rotary knob on identification rate and identification time were studied experimentally. The identification correct rate and identification time for paired manual rotary knobs with different diameters were obtained. The results showed that when using the size coding to identify the manual cylindrical rotary knob devices, the knobs with a diameter difference in 4 mm could be distinguished correctly by 100% of female and more than 96% of male. The knobs with a diameter difference in 6 mm could be distinguished correctly by all of the participants. The increase of the knob diameter reduced the number of people who could distinguish the difference in size of 2 mm. The identification time increased with the increasing of the knob diameter. The larger the difference between the two knobs diameter paired, the higher the identification correct rate and the faster the identification time. Female's identification time was significantly faster than male. The results are helpful to understand human's identification limit of the dimension, as well as the gender difference at dimension identification ability. The data could provide reference for product ergonomic design related with dimensional coding of manual rotary knobs.

Keywords: Size coding · Dimension identification · Manual rotary knob · Human-machine interface

1 Introduction

Coding is a method of assigning different types of information (such as size, shape, color, etc.) to a manipulation device during design process, so as to achieve more reliably identification. When there are multiple manipulators in the work system simultaneously, for the purpose of allowing operator to identify the manipulators quickly, accurately and prevent misoperation, the manipulators should be coded (GB/T 14775-93, 1993). The coding method is widely used in the layout design of the control device. In the design of the control device layout, in order to make it easy for the

A. Marcus and E. Rosenzweig (Eds.): HCII 2020, LNCS 12201, pp. 249–256, 2020.
https://doi.org/10.1007/978-3-030-49760-6_17

operator to observe, detect, recognize and follow the information flow, make timely selection and action suitable for the current situation, the control device should be laid out in an appropriate manner, and coding is one of the methods. Control devices with the same function use the same code. Different function controls use different code or feature to ensure the controls have significant difference in appearance. As a method of grouping, segmentation, highlighting and identification, coding can coordinate the presentation of information, identify and interpret the information in the system state and process, explain the functional structure of the system, and describe the relationship between components and groups. It can promote the convenience of human-machine interaction and reduce the cognitive load in human-machine interaction (BS EN 894-4, 2010). Coding is an effective method when an operator or a device is required to be identified or be distinguished quickly from a similar set of controls.

According to manipulator's respective functions, each manipulator is encoded with different feature or code. The recommended encoding style includes shape coding, position coding, size coding, color coding, operation method coding, character encoding (GB/T 14775-93). Size coding is a commonly used coding method that is coded in different sizes. It is suitable for highlighting specific components in a group, and connecting the same functional components from a large distance. When the size coding method is used, sufficient space between the controls should be left, so as to allow the operator to identify the component by touch. Dimensional codes for distinguish purpose should not exceed three dimensions. Further, coding design should also consider the type of task, user classification, performance requirements (e.g., accuracy, speed, quality, quantity, duration, frequency of use), installation space, cultural customs, habits and so on. Coding can be used in combination. For example, size-encoded knobs can be second-coded with shapes. This is helpful for optimizing the selection, combination and interpretation of components in more complex interactions, ensuring the identification and interpretation of the different functional components with similar appearance.

The key index for size coding is size. When products are designed in size coding method, the size difference should be measured as a percentage. For instance, for a circular (column) steering device (such as a knob) with a diameter of 13 mm to 100 mm, the diameters of two sizes should differ by at least 20% (in terms of larger control device diameter calculation) (GBJ/Z 131-2002, GB/T 14775-93). In order to ensure the identification correct rate of the size difference, this percentage selection is much larger than human's identification limit. In order to understand human ability on identifying the smaller size of the code, this study carried out the identification test of the manual knob, which has the outer diameter between 10 mm and 30 mm. This diameter range is commonly used for the knob controllers on small industrial equipment, household equipment and vehicle cab devices. The experiment obtained the identification correct rate and identification time of the paired size coded knobs, as well as the gender difference in the identification of the size codes. The results are helpful to understand human's identification limit of the dimension, as well as the gender difference at dimension identification ability. The data could provide reference for product ergonomic design related with dimensional coding of manual rotary knobs.

2   Experimental Materials and Methods

2.1   Experimental Materials

The experimental materials included cylindrical knobs (two sets), knob base, cardboard, timing system, table and seats. The operation objects were two sets of customized cylindrical knobs. The knobs were placed on a base to analog rotary switches. The outer diameter of the knobs was from 10 mm to 30 mm with the step of 2 mm (see Fig. 1).

Fig. 1. One set of cylindrical knobs by size

2.2   Participants

A total of 54 participants, aged 18–55 years, attended the experiment. Half of them were male and half were female. All of the participants were in good health, no joint disease, and right-handed. Participants were recruited by responding to the posting notices on the Internet and in the community. Participants were volunteered to participate the experiment. The experiment objective, content and procedure were explained to the participants before the experiment to obtain their consent.

2.3   Experimental Scene

Experimental scene is shown in Fig. 2. The participants were asked to operate the paired knobs one by one and distinguished whether the dimensions of the paired knobs were same. The knobs were placed behind a cardboard with no visual feedback to participants during the operation and identification period. A pair of knobs (example) is shown in Fig. 3. The test monitor recorded the outer diameters of the paired knobs and the identification time when the participant could identify the difference.

Fig. 2. Experimental scene

Fig. 3. A pair of knobs (example)

2.4   Experimental Steps

The steps of the experiment implementation were as follows:

1. The test monitor introduced the experimental objective, content and procedure to the participant and the participant signed the informed consent form.
2. Participant filled in the personal basic information form. The test monitor measured the upper limb size of the participant.
3. The participant sat down and adjusted the height of the seat until the he (she) felt comfortable.
4. Carried out the 30 mm outer diameter knob comparison test firstly.
    a. Two cylindrical knobs, with one of them was 30 mm outer diameter, were put into the base behind the cardboard plate.
    b. The participant pressed down the timing button with the left hand, operated the paired knobs with the right hand to identify whether or not they had the same outer diameter. The participant pressed down the timing button again when he (she) completed the identification. Then the participant spoke out his (her) identification result: the same, different, or could not be distinguished. Based on the identification result, the paired knobs were changed by the test monitor. Repeat these steps until the participant distinguished the paired knobs size correctly. This meant the minimum size different from 30 mm was found. The data was recorded by the test monitor.

c. The identification time recorded by the timing system was monitored by the test monitor in real time. Only the identification time of the size that can be distinguished correctly was saved into the data file.
5. Carried out the 28 mm, 26 mm, up to 10 mm outer diameter knob comparison test in sequence.

3   Experimental Results

3.1   Identification Rate

The number of female and male participants who could correctly identify each pair of knob sizes are showed in Table 1 and Table 2. It can be seen that as the diameter of the knob increased, the number of people who correctly identify the difference in size of 2 mm showed a downward trend. Among them, the number of female who could correctly identify the difference of 2 mm was reduced from 27 (all female participants) to 24, and males from 27 (all male participants) to 22. All female participants were able to identify a 4 mm knob size difference, while 3 of male participants were not able to identify 4 mm size difference. All male participants could identify 6 mm size difference.

Divide the number of people who could correctly identified by the total number of female or male participants to get the identification rate. It can be obtained that for the cylindrical knobs used in this experiment, more than 89% of females and more than 81% of males could identify a difference of 2 mm in diameter, 100% of females and 96% of males could identify a difference of 4 mm in diameter, 100% of males could identify a difference of 6 mm in diameter.

Table 1. Number of female participants who could correctly identify each pair of knob sizes

Participant number/person /mm Knob size/mm	28	26	24	22	20	18	16	14	12	10
30	24	3								
28		24	3							
26			24	3						
24				25	2					
22					25	2				
20						24	3			
18							27			
16								25	2	
14									26	1
12										27

Table 2. Number of male participants who could correctly identify each pair of knob sizes

Participant number/person Knob size/mm	28	26	24	22	20	18	16	14	12	10
30	22	4	1							
28		24	3							
26			23	3	1					
24				23	4					
22					26	1				
20						26	1			
18							24	2	1	
16								25	2	
14									26	1
12										27

3.2   Identification Time

The identification time of the paired knob size difference by female and male participants are shown in Table 3 and Table 4. It can be seen that as the diameter of the knob increased, the participants' (both females and males) identification time for the difference in size of 2 mm was on the rise. Among them, those who could correctly identify the difference in size of 2 mm, the identification time of females increased from 5.07 s up to 7.21 s, and the identification time of males increased from 5.74 s up to 7.56 s.

For the participants with a minimum distinguish size difference of 4 mm or 6 mm, their identification time was significantly shorter. It can be concluded that the larger the difference in outer diameter between the pair of knobs, the higher the identification accuracy rate and the shorter the identification time.

The gender difference in identification time of 2 mm diameter difference of the knobs is shown in Fig. 4. It can be seen that female's identification time was significantly faster than male in each size of paired knobs with 2 mm diameter difference ($p < 0.001$).

Table 3. Identification time of female participants on size differences

Knob size/mm	28	26	24	22	20	18	16	14	12	10
30	7.21	4.74								
28		6.53	4.58							
26			7.38	1.3						
24				5.69	6.96					
22					5.73	2.95				
20						5.61	3.84			
18							5.61			
16								5.39	5.54	
14									5.5	7.16
12										5.07

Table 4. Identification time of male participants on size differences

Knob size/mm	28	26	24	22	20	18	16	14	12	10
30	7.56	6.98	3.17							
28		7.99	4.97							
26			7.98	5.28	2.36					
24				6.36	5.27					
22					7.2	2.02				
20						6.51	3.31			
18							7.08	2.29	2.59	
16								6.62	3.92	
14									5.93	3.22
12										5.74

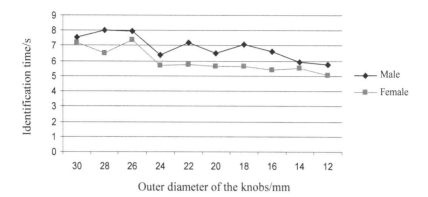

Fig. 4. The gender difference in identification time of 2 mm diameter difference of the knobs

4   Conclusions

According to the experimental results, the following conclusions are obtained for the use of size to code the manual cylindrical rotary knob devices with outer diameter between 10 mm and 30 mm:

1. As the diameter of the knob increases, fewer people can correctly identify the 2 mm size difference.
2. 100% of females and more than 96% of males can correctly identify knobs with a diameter difference of 4 mm, and everyone can correctly identify knobs with a diameter difference of 6 mm.
3. As the diameter of the knob increases, the identification time for the difference in size of 2 mm increases.
4. The larger the difference in the outer diameter of the knob, the higher the accuracy of identification and the shorter the identification time.
5. Female's identification time of diameter difference is significantly faster than male.

Acknowledgement. This research was supported by National Natural Science Foundation of China (project number 71601007) and President Foundation of China National Institute of Standardization (project number 522018Y-5984).

References

GB/T 14775-93: General ergonomic requirements for manipulators. State Technical Supervision Bureau of China (1993)

BS EN 894-4: 2010 Safety of machinery - ergonomics requirements for design of displays and control actuators - Part 4: Location and arrangement of displays and control actuators (2010)

GBJ/Z 131-2002: Human Engineering Design Handbook for Military Equipment and Facilities. General Equipment Department of the People's Liberation Army of China (2002)

Effects of the Chinese Character Size, Page Spacing and Scrolling Frequency on Reading Time of Smartphones

Shih-Miao Huang[(⊠)]

National Formosa University, Yunlin 632, Taiwan
smhuang@nfu.edu.tw

Abstract. Previous studies found text in small Chinese Characters had better readability than larger ones, and concluded that the behaviors of scrolling text might degrade readability because of length increases of text in large character size. However, they did not manipulate sliding behaviors in the study. Therefore, the purpose of this study is to explore relations among sliding frequency, reading time, Traditional Chinese character size and page spacing. Results showed that both character sizes and screen sizes affect sliding frequencies. Texts written in 14 pt. characters had more sliding frequencies than 10 pt and 12 pt both which did not significant differ; and the sliding frequencies were the most when using the 0.5H page spacing size, followed by 0.25H and 0H. Besides, the correlation analysis showed no significant correlation between them. It indicated that the sliding frequency might be not a covariate when exploring effects of character size and page spacing on reading time. Finally, the effect of character size and page spacing on reading time was tested. Results showed no significant effects of character size on reading time. The reason might be that the legibility of texts written in these character sizes was high enough because participants could adjust their viewing distances to see them clearly. Besides, the reading time is significantly shorter when using the 0.25H than 0H, while the reading time does not differ significantly between 0.5H and 0H, and between 0.5H and 0.25H. It implied that the display area which is too large or small is harmful for text reading.

Keywords: Character size · Page spacing · Sliding frequency · Reading time

1 Introduction

Due to the convenience of smartphones, users use them at any time, place or occasion. The penetration rate of smartphone users is growing rapidly. According to eMarketer estimate, 73.4% of Taiwan's population uses smartphones [1]. Smartphones are no longer cutting-edge communication gadgets but are now necessities in peoples' lives. The Global Views Survey Research Center [2] reported that 46.4% of the Taiwan population had reading experiences on e-books and that 27.1% of them used a smartphone to read an e-Book. The population reading either e-news or e-books on smartphones should continuously increase due to increasing penetration of smartphones in Taiwan. Moreover, Taiwanese are accustomed to reading articles written in

© Springer Nature Switzerland AG 2020
A. Marcus and E. Rosenzweig (Eds.): HCII 2020, LNCS 12201, pp. 257–269, 2020.
https://doi.org/10.1007/978-3-030-49760-6_18

traditional Chinese characters. Hence, it is necessary to explore effects of traditional-Chinese characters on readability on smartphones for Taiwanese.

Reading is a complex "cognitive process" of decoding symbols in order to construct or derive meaning [3], involving top-down processing and bottom-up processing. While the top-down processing explains why reader expectation or knowledge background and text context influence reading comprehension and efficiency, the bottom-up processing addresses the importance of character legibility for reading performance. Previous studies concluded that large alphanumeric characters had high legibility, which would facilitate text readability in alphanumeric systems [4–8].

Table 1. The literatures related to studies of Chinese character sizes

Author (s)	Size	Viewing distance	Size(visual arc)	Characters in text	Performance measure	Display type
Chan and Lee [12]	14pt > 10pt	450 mm	38'arc > 27'arc	289(270–308)	1. reading time 2. reading comprehension 3. subjective preference reading comfort reading ease reading fatigue overall preference	15-inch color CRT
Huang et al. [13]	2.2 mm, 2.6 mm, 3.0 mm	350 mm	21.61'arc 23.57'arc 25.54'arc	1500–2000	1. reading speed 2. searching time 3. subjective evaluation ease of read tiredness preference	mobile phone
Chan and Ng [14]	14pt > 12-pt	400 mm	Ming style 0.51'arc > 0.71' Hei style 0.71' > 0.51'arc Kai style 0.71' > 0.51'arc	483–600	1. proofreading time 2. accuracy (n.s.) 3. subjective evaluation comfort proofreading Ease fatigue	17-inch LCD monitor
Cai et al. (2001)	Not specified	Not specified	Above 20–39'		identification legibility threshold	15-inch CRT
Yen et al. [18]	24 pixels > 32 pixels	Not specified	41' > 60'	18–21 pages 1866–2358	1. eye-movement indicators total reading time per passage, number of fixations, first fixation duration, gaze duration, saccade length regression rate, 2. comprehension score 3. preference rating	19-inch CRT
Huang [20]	10 > 12 > 14 pt	Adjustable			reading speed	5.5" mobile phone
Huang [25]	10 > 12 > 14 pt	Adjustable			reading speed	5.5" mobile phone

Note: ">" denotes superiority in performance.

As Table 1 shown, for traditional-Chinese characters, large Chinese characters had high legibility [9, 10] and that the high legibility of the large Chinese characters significantly influenced readability [11–15]. For example, Chan and Lee [12] suggested that the 14 pt (point) Chinese character (38' arc) was superior to the 10 pt one (27' arc) in terms of performance on total reading time, reading comprehension, and subjective preference in a 15-inch color CRT. They also found that subjects reported less fatigue, more reading ease, and more comfort when reading text with larger font sizes. Moreover, Huang et al. [13] found that the reading speed of a large Chinese font (ex. 26' arc) was significantly faster than a small font (ex. 14' arc) when the viewing distance of thee was fixed. In addition, Chan and Ng [14] found that 14-point characters were rated significantly superior to 12-point characters in a 17-inch LCD monitor.

Nevertheless, the conclusions reached in previous studies which claimed better readability for larger characters were based on the assumptions that the viewing distance to the screen was confined to a fixed distance and that the experiment must be performed under well-controlled conditions to comply with the ergonomic principles of desktop displays (ex. OSHA 3092). However, everyday smartphone reading behavior bears little resemblance to such experimental conditions. By bending his elbow, the smartphone user can hold the phone and adjust his viewing distance at will, which puts the screen much closer than the suggested ergonomic VDT design for comfortable reading [16]. Besides, to see the text clearly, users can adjust their viewing distance to attain an optimal visual angle subtended to the retina: short (near) for small character sizes; and long (far) for large character sizes. Consequently, both large and small characters may be legible enough for readers. Hence, small font size might not significantly perform worse on smartphones because the visual angles of various character sizes formed on the retina may be similar with adjustment to the viewing distance. In such situations, the effects of character size would have been not significant on readability. The findings of Darroch et al. [17] supported this assertion for alphanumeric text. They arranged a proof-reading experiment, which did not set up a rigid viewing distance, and asked subjects to hold a PDA handheld device and to read the messages written in English from a comfortable position. Provided that the English text messages were all legible, they found no significant difference in text-reading performance.

However, Yen et al. [18] found that the large characters do not show significantly higher readability than the small ones when both the character sizes are legible enough. They found that text in 24-pixel characters (41') was read faster than text in 32-pixel characters (60'arc) when both sizes are larger than the minimal recommended character size (33' arc) [19]. Besides, Huang and Li [20] also found that the smaller character size was better than the larger one for reading tasks as subjects could adjust their viewing distance in their will.

1.1   Scrolling Effect

It is possible that the scrolling behavior affect the results. Due to the size limit of displays, the text on the small screen may overflow onto multiple screens, prompting users to scroll the screen in order to read the text. Previous studies suggested that scrolling might negatively affect alphanumeric reading performance [21, 22], including reduction of reading comprehension on full-size displays [23], and memory overload when reading on small screens [24].

Text written with a large font may cost more space and lengthen the text on the screen, and readers may increase the frequency of scrolling to read through the lengthened text. For example, the length of text participants read is ranged from 18-22 pages in the study of Yen et al. [18]. The participants had to scroll to read through the text. The large characters lengthen the text and resulting in increasing scrolling frequencies. Consequently, text written with large characters may degrade reading performance owing to increased scrolling behavior, and text with a small font may facilitate better reading performance when the characters are legible enough on smartphones.

Therefore, this study suspects that scrolling frequencies is a covariate which affects character size effect, resulting in that the readability of text in small characters on smartphones is superior to that in larger ones. To verify the argument, the study tries to explore the effect of both character size and scrolling behavior on reading performance.

2   Methods

The study suspects the Scrolling Frequency is a covariate of Character size, influencing reading performance. Hence, the study will perform an Analysis of Covariance design with two main effects and one covariate when it is found that the correlation between Sliding frequency and Reading time is high. Two main effects are Character size and Page spacing; the covariate is the Sliding frequency.

The Character size includes three levels, 10 pt, 12 pt and 14 pt. Large character size occupies more space, consequently, the text lines of 10 pt, 12 pt and 14 pt are 20, 24 and 28 lines in the screen, respectively. Page spacing refers to the margin from the top title of the page to the beginning of the text. Sometimes, an illustration would be put in the page spacing. Page spacing is frequently applied to the typography of the first page of texts, or of a children's book. The page spacing includes three levels, no spacing, one-fourth spacing and one-half spacing as shown in Fig. 1. No spacing (0H) refers to the white space between the text title and main text equal to the line spacing. One-fourth (0.25H) or one-half spacing (0.5H) refers to a one-fourth or a one-half length of the screen, respectively.

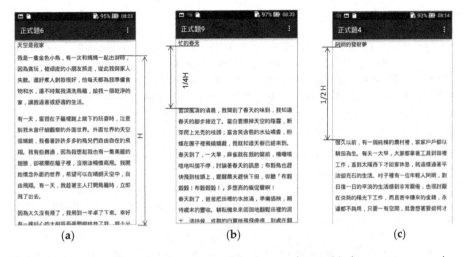

Fig. 1. Three types of page spacing were used in the experiment. (a) shows no page spacing (0H); (b) one-fourth page spacing (1/4H); and (c) half page spacing (1/2H). It also shows parts of three essays in this study.

The purpose of page spacing is to increase scrolling behaviors by increasing the size of page spacing. The larger page spacing size is, the smaller the display area is, and the more display pages occupied by a text, resulting in more sliding frequencies. Table 2 shows the number of pages for typographical combinations of Character sizes and Page spacing.

Table 2. The number of pages for typographical combinations of Character sizes and Page spacing size

Pages	10pt	12pt	14pt
0 H page spacing	2 (1.5) pages	3 (2.25) pages	3 (2.25) pages
1/4H page spacing	2 (2.0) pages	3 (3.0) pages	4 (4.0) pages
1/2H page spacing	3 (2.5) pages	4 (3.75) pages	5 (5.0) pages

However, it is necessary to check the correlation between Reading time and Sliding frequency before performing Analysis of Covariance. Hence, the correlation analysis is performed firstly. The sliding frequency would be a covariate if the correlation coefficient between Reading time and sliding frequency is high.

2.1 Subjects

Eighteen undergraduate students from different Colleges in Taiwan participated in the experiment. The mean age was 21.72 years. (SD = 1.58 years). These participants had taken the Chinese language portion of the General Scholastic Ability Test, which has scores ranging from 0 to 15, and all had scores over 14, indicating high Chinese reading competence. Each was paid about $12 USD for their participation in the experiment. All subjects reported normal ocular health with no clinically significant anomalies of accommodation. Before participating in the test, all subjects consented to perform the trials by signing the agreements outlined by the committee on Governance Framework for Human Research Ethics of National Cheng Kung University in Taiwan.

2.2   Materials

A 5.5-inch smartphone (ZenFone 2 Laser model ZE550KL) with a display resolution of 267 ppi was used to display a reading comprehension test. The screen size is 6.85 cm × 12.18 cm. Its physical size is 148.2 cm × 72.8 cm × 10.34 mm. The smartphone was programmed with Android 5.0 (Lollipop) to control the experimental procedures and collect data.

There are nine essays chosen from reading comprehension tests used in an elementary school in Taiwan. The number of characters in each was close to 501 characters. They were slightly modified to get an identical length. Finally, each essay, including punctuation marks, has 501 characters in length. Each essay includes ten typos classified into three types. First, homophone typos refer to the wrong Chinese characters pronounced identically to the correct ones in the text, but with different meanings and shapes from the correct ones. Second, lookalike typos refer to the wrong characters that are very similar in physical appearance to the correct characters in the text but have different meanings and shapes from the correct ones. Last, spelling typos refer to the location swap of characters of a word composed of the two characters, resulting in different meanings from the correct word in the text. Therefore, participants must read and comprehend the text to find those typos.

The difficulties of comprehension for the nine essays were tested by four participants. The text font was a 12-point Bia style of traditional Chinese characters. The reading time of finding typo are recorded for each essay. The outcomes shows no significant difference on reading times between the essays ($F(8, 24) = 0.299$, $p = 0.959$) in Table 3.

Table 3. An ANOVA table for testing difficulties of comprehension for nine essays in the experiment

Source		Sum of Squares	df	Mean Square	F_0	Sig.
Intercept	Hypothesis	716562.250	1	716562.25	41.695	0.008
	Error	51557.639	3	17185.88		
paper	Hypothesis	703.500	8	87.94	0.299	0.959
	Error	7065.611	24	294.40		
sub	Hypothesis	51557.639	3	17185.88	58.376	0000
	Error	7065.611	24	294.40		

2.3   Tasks and Procedure

Participants performed a typo-finding task by reading essays, after consenting to the experiment. At the start of the trial, a preparing page showed a "To start time counting" button (written in Chinese). Participants were reminded to take a breath and be ready to go before tapping on the button. After they tapped it, the screen showed an essay with one of the design combinations, and the programmed smartphone recorded the start time. Participants discovered and tapped on the typos as soon as possible. The tapped typo was turned red and replaced by a figure indicating the order of the typo in the essay. After participants found the ten typos, the experiment program recorded the ending time of the reading task and calculated the reading time by subtracting the starting time from the ending time.

The typo-finding test was performed until participants completed the nine reading tasks. Each participant had a five-minute break after finishing every two tasks. It took about one and half hours for each participant to complete the tasks. Familiarization was based on three training trials with an additional essay with different typographic variables.

2.4   Performance Measures and Data Analysis

Reading time, as a performance measure, was calculated for each part of the test by subtracting the starting time from the ending time. The less the reading time, the better the design combinations performed. Analysis of Variance was employed to analyze the data. All calculations were made using SPSS.

3   Results and Discussion

3.1   Sliding Frequencies on Character Size and Page Spacing

The text written in large characters or displayed on small screen, which may increase the physical length of the text, needs more pages to display the texts. Users have to increase scrolling frequencies because of the increase of pages presenting text. Hence, it seems that both large characters and small display area may affect sliding frequencies. To verify the argument, it is necessary to test both effects of character size and page spacing on sliding frequency. Results of ANOVA in Table 4 shows that there are significant main effect of both Character size ($F (2, 136) = 8.10$, $p < 0.001$) and Page spacing ($F (2, 136) = 38.38$, $p < 0.001$) on Sliding frequencies, whereas the interaction effect of Character size × Page spacing was not significant ($F (4, 136) = 0.26$, $p = 0.904$).

Table 4. Analysis of variance for sliding frequencies

Source of variation	Sum of squares	df	Mean square	F_0	P-value
Corrected model	5616.747[a]	25	224.670	8.63	.000
Intercept	14018.821	1	14018.821	538.36	.000
subject	3169.290	17	186.429	7.16	.000
Character size	421.568	2	210.784	8.10	.000
Page spacing	1998.901	2	999.451	38.38	.000
Character size * Page spacing	26.988	4	6.747	0.26	.904
Error	3541.432	136	26.040		
Corrected total	9158.179	161			

Note: R Squared = .613 (Adjusted R Squared = .542)

Table 5. Means and standard deviations of sliding frequencies for each level of independent variables

	Level	N	Mean	Standard Deviation	Duncan Groups
Character Size	10 pt.	54	7.52	139.17	A
	12 pt.	54	8.96	131.02	A
	14 pt.	54	11.43	130.59	B
Page Spacing	0H	54	5.59	4.970	A
	0.25H	54	8.30	6.439	B
	0.5H	54	14.02	8.302	C

Note: Different letters in Duncan group indicate significant differences at 0.05 levels.

Table 5 shows the means and standard deviations of sliding frequencies for each level of the independent variables. Multiple comparisons using Duncan's method shows that the sliding frequencies are larger when using the 14 pt character (11.43) than 12 pt (8.96) and 10 pt (7.52); and the sliding frequencies of both 12 pt (8.96) and 10 pt (7.52) are not significantly different. Besides, multiple comparisons show that the sliding frequencies are the most when using the 0.5H (14.02); followed by 0.25H (8.30) and 0H (5.59). The outcomes confirm that both larger characters in text and larger page spacing sizes, resulting in small display area affect sliding frequencies significantly. The outcomes may indicate that extended text physical length would increase sliding frequencies.

3.2 Sliding Impact on Reading Time

As mentioned above, both character size and page spacing size would affect sliding frequencies. The main question arises. Is the text reading time affected by the typo-graphic factors (i.e., character size and page spacing size in this study) or by sliding frequencies resulting from lengthened pages caused by large character size and page spacing size when using a smartphone? The study needs to explore whether the sliding frequency is a covariate influencing reading time. Therefore, the Pearson's Correlation Analysis is performed to test the correlation between Reading time and Sliding frequencies. Results of analysis shows no significant correlations and a low correlation coefficient between Reading time and Sliding frequencies (r = 0.106, p = 0.178, d. f. = 160). It indicated that Sliding frequency could only explain 1.12% (= r^2) variances of reading time, and the correlation between sliding frequency and reading time is little.

The outcome excludes the influences of sliding behaviors on reading time, which does not support the argument of the previous studies [21–24]. Several reasons might explain the contradictions.

Firstly, the reason why the sliding frequencies were not significant correlated with reading time may be that the sliding frequencies confounded with character sizes which actually affected reading time. Previous study found text written with large characters might degrade more reading performance than small ones [16]. In the meantime, large characters also increased scrolling frequencies. When the text is long enough, the sliding frequencies of reading large characters increase significantly larger than those of small characters. Therefore, in the study of Yen et al. [18], the effect of sliding frequencies is large enough to significantly demonstrate the subtle differences of reading time because asking participants to read the long enough text with the lengths ranged from 18–22 pages. However, in this study, the amount of pages of the combinations was ranged from 2 to 4 pages. Consequently, the differences of sliding frequencies between different typographical combinations are not large enough to significantly demonstrate the subtle differences of reading time. Hence, it is suspected that the sliding effect did not affect reading time, but character sizes.

Second, sliding behaviors might negatively affect reading comprehension of the text, but not the typo-finding test. Previous studies demonstrating negative sliding effects on reading used reading comprehension score [23] and memory overload [24] as performance measures, while the present study uses the time spending on finding typos. To answer the assigned questions on the comprehension tests, participants have to look back to find the answers on the text frequently. Due to scrolling the text, the locations of words or sentences they tried to find on the text are changed all the time. Consequently, the participants have difficulties to find the key words or sentences to answer the questions, resulting in degrading reading performance. Conversely, the present study asks subjects to find ten typos in the text. Participants need not to look back to find the answers. In this situation, sliding frequencies may be only related to text length, but not to reading time; even, may reducing reading time for the nine typographic combinations. However, the study did not investigate the effects of reading tasks on sliding effects to confirm the argument. Hence, the effect of reading tasks on sliding frequency will be explored in a future study.

3.3   Reading Time on Character Size

After excluding the sliding effect on reading time, this study will test the effects of Character size and Page spacing on reading time. Results of ANOVA in Table 6 shows no significant effect of Character size (F (2, 136) = .40 p = 0. 672), and no interaction effect of Character size × Page spacing (F (4, 136) = 0. 49, p = 0. 740).

Table 6. Analysis of variance for reading time

Source	Sum of squares	df	Mean Square	F_0	Sig.
Corrected model	466891.557	25	18675.662	2.52	.000
Intercept	3546163.25	1	3546163.248	477.72	.000
Subject	395692.08	17	23276.005	3.14	.000
Character size	5919.45	2	2959.723	.40	.672
Page spacing	50625.79	2	25312.896	3.41	.036
Character size * Page spacing	14654.24	4	3663.560	.49	.740
Error	1009537.15	136	7423.067		
Corrected total	1476428.71	161			

Note: R Squared = .316 (Adjusted R Squared = .191)

Table 7 shows the means and standard deviations of reading time for each level of the independent variables. Multiple comparisons using Duncan's method shows that the reading time does not significantly differ among 10 pt (151.9106 s), 12 pt (152.5352 s) and 14 pt (139.4113 s). The reason might be that the legibility of texts written in 10 pt, 12 pt and 14 pt are not significantly different because participants could adjust their viewing distances.

Table 7. Means and standard deviations of reading time for each level of independent variables

	Level	N	Mean (sec)	Standard Deviation	Duncan Groups	
Character Size	10 pt.	54	151.9106	83.36711	A	
	12 pt.	54	152.5352	129.00470	A	
	14 pt.	54	139.4113	64.44509	A	
Page Spacing	0H	54	171.5422	134.88140	A	
	0.25H	54	128.9883	51.34517		B
	0.5H	54	143.3265	77.92705	A	B

Note: Different letters in Duncan group indicate significant differences at 0.05 levels.

Most previous studies related to Chinese typography on digital screens fixed viewing distances in the experimental trials. However, users can adjust their viewing distance arbitrarily in the real context of using smartphones. In order to simulate the real context in this experiment, this study does not set a fixed viewing distance, and subjects were encouraged to adjust their viewing distance at any time. Obviously, the evidence in this study does not support previous studies. As explained above, experimentation incorporating normal smartphone usage leads to conclusions different from those of previous studies.

The results of this study are very encouraging. In this study, the sliding effect is not obvious because of short text lengths. In the situation of short texts, the findings suggest that small Traditional Chinese characters are not inferior to large ones for reading tasks when the sliding effect is not significantly. However, the study did not investigate the effects of text length on sliding and reading time to support the argument. Hence, the effect of text length will be explored in a future study.

3.4   Reading Time on Page Spacing

Results of ANOVA in Table 6 shows that there were significant main effect of Page spacing (F (2, 136) = 3.410, p = 0.036) on reading time. In Table 7, multiple comparisons using Duncan's method shows that the reading time is significantly shorter when using the 0.25H (128.99 s) than 0H (171.54 s), while the reading time does not differ significantly between 0.5H (143.33 s) and 0H (171.54 s), and between 0.5H (143.33 s) and 0.25H (128.99 s).

The result agrees with the findings of Huang, Li and Tung, [25] (2018). It indicated that too large page spacing is not conducive to reading performances. Oversized page spacing would decrease a display area dramatically, which would limit the number of characters presented in one screen and increase screen pages. Consequently, participants must slide the text frequently, resulting in degraded readability. Therefore, the result showed that the reading performance of moderate page spacing (i.e., 0.25H page spacing) was significantly better than that of the larger page spacing (i.e., 0.5H page spacing).

However, the result also showed the reading performance of the smallest page spacing size (i.e., 0H page spacing) was not significantly better than the moderate page spacing (i.e., 1/3H page spacing). It is possible that too small a page spacing (0H) causes overcrowded typography, not providing readers with visual relief and relaxation in reading tedious text. Accordingly, the smallest page spacing increases loadings of the reading task, degrading reading performances. On the contrary, at the same time, the smallest page spacing size (i.e., 0H) does decrease participants' scrolling frequencies, promoting reading performances. This advantage dilutes its disadvantage. Therefore, the outcomes did not show the difference in reading time between 0H page spacing and 0.25H page spacing.

In conclusion, the reading performance of the 0.25H page spacing is significantly better than that of the 0.5H page spacing and not less than that of the 0H page spacing. Hence, it seems that 0.25H page spacing is suitable for page spacing on smartphones.

The participants in this study did not have design experience. Many people without a design background considered white space wasted space and believed it should house more information or other visual elements to avoid waste [26]. Therefore, the findings agreed with the design laypeople's opinions that the white space would degrade subjective preference [26]. Conversely, design practitioners believed white space would not waste the screen space but improve visual communication and reading comprehension. They promoted the use of white space for elegance and ensuring a high-quality user experience. It seems to be an individual difference between design practitioners and laypersons in page spacing evaluation. Future studies should explore the differences between designers and laypeople.

4 Conclusions

Many tests are performed to verify that the character sizes, but not sliding behaviors, would degrade the reading performance. Firstly, the effects of Character size and Page spacing on sliding frequency are tested. The results show that the effects are significant. Restated, both character sizes and page spacing sizes may affect sliding frequencies. However, the sliding effect is not significant on reading time in this study because of the text lengths for all typographical combinations in this study are not large enough to detect the subtle differences of reading time on different typographical combinations.

Besides, the study suggests that small Traditional Chinese characters are not inferior to large ones for reading tasks when the sliding effect does not significantly affect reading time. In order to simulate the real context in this experiment, this study does not set a fixed viewing distance, and subjects were encouraged to adjust their viewing distance at any time. Consequently, the participants in this study can see the text clearly written in different character sizes. In addition, the sliding effect on reading time is not obvious because of short text lengths in this study. Therefore, the character size effect is not significant in this study.

Last, for Page spacing, the outcomes showed that too large (i.e., 0.5H in this study) or too small (i.e., 0H in this study) page spacing size were not conducive to reading speeds. The results show that 0.25H page spacing provided less reading time.

Acknowledgments. The authors would like to thank the Ministry of Science and Technology, Taiwan for financially supporting this research under Contract No. MOST-106-2221-E-150-034.

References

1. eMarketer: Mobile Taiwan: A Look at a Highly Mobile Market. Country has the highest Smartphone Penetration in the World. https://www.emarketer.com/Article/Mobile-Taiwan-Look-Highly-Mobile-Market/1014877. Accessed 22 July 2017
2. Global Views Survey Research Center. http://www.gvsrc.com/dispPageBox/GVSRCCP.aspx?ddsPageID=OTHERS&&dbid=3098763327. Accessed 22 July 2017
3. Rayner, K., Pollatsek, A.: The Psychology of Reading. Prentice Hall, Upper Saddle River (1989)
4. Bernard, M., Chaparro, B., Mills, M., Halcomb, C.: Comparing the effects of text size and format on the readability of computer-displayed Times New Roman and Arial text. Int. J. Hum.-Comput. Stud. **59**(6), 823–835 (2003)
5. Dyson, M.C., Kipping, G.J.: The effects of line length and method of movement on patterns of reading from screens. Vis. Lang. **32**, 150–181 (1998)
6. Garcia, M.L., Caldera, C.I.: The effect of color and typeface on the readability of on-line text. Comput. Ind. Eng. **31**, 519–524 (1996)
7. Kolers, P.A., Duchnicky, R.L., Feguson, D.C.: Eye movement measurement of readability of CRT displays. Hum. Factors **23**(5), 517–527 (1981)
8. Paterson, D.G., Tinker, M.A.: The effect of typography upon the perceptual span in reading. Am. J. Psychol. **60**(3), 388–396 (1947)
9. Dobres, J., Chahine, N., Reimer, B.: Effects of ambient illumination, contrast polarity, and letter size on text legibility under glance-like reading. Appl. Ergon. **60**, 68–73 (2017)

10. Dobres, J., Wolfe, B., Chahine, N., Reimer, B.: The effects of visual crowding, text size, and positional uncertainty on text legibility at a glance. Appl. Ergon. **70**, 240–246 (2018)
11. Chi, C.-F., Cai, D., You, M.: Applying image descriptors to the assessment of legibility in Chinese characters. Ergonomics **46**(8), 825–841 (2003)
12. Chan, A., Lee, P.: Effect of display factors on Chinese reading times, comprehension scores and preferences. Behav. Inform. Technol. **24**, 81–91 (2005)
13. Huang, D., Rau, P.P., Liu, Y.: Effects of font size, display resolution and task type on reading Chinese fonts from mobile devices. Int. J. Ind. Ergon. **39**, 81–89 (2009)
14. Chan, A.H.S., Ng, A.W.Y.: Effects of display factors on chinese proofreading performance and preferences. Ergonomics **55**(11), 1316–1330 (2012)
15. Liu, N., Yu, R., Zhang, Y.: Effects of font size, stroke width, and character complexity on the legibility of Chinese characters. Hum. Factors Ergon. Manuf. Serv. Ind. **26**(3), 381–392 (2016)
16. Huang, S.-M.: Effects of font size and font style of Traditional Chinese characters on readability on smartphones. Int. J. Ind. Ergon. **69**, 66–72 (2019)
17. Darroch, I., Goodman, J., Brewster, S., Gray, P.: The effect of age and font size on reading text on handheld computers. In: Costabile, M.F., Paternò, F. (eds.) Human-Computer Interaction - INTERACT 2005. LNCS, vol. 3585, pp. 253–266. Springer, Heidelberg (2005). https://doi.org/10.1007/11555261_23
18. Yen, N., Tsai, J., Chen, P., Lin, H., Chen, A.: Effects of typographic variables on eye-movement measures in reading Chinese from a screen. Behav. Inf. Technol. **30**(6), 797–808 (2011)
19. Wu, H.C.: Electronic paper display preferred viewing distance and character size for different age groups. Ergonomics **54**(9), 806–814 (2011)
20. Huang, S.-M., Li, W.-J.: Format effects of traditional Chinese character size and font style on reading performance when using smartphones. In: Proceedings of the 2017 IEEE International Conference on Applied System Innovation (IEEE-ICASI 2017), pp. 13–17. Sapporo, Japan (2017)
21. Morrison, D.L., Duncan, K.D.: The effect of scrolling, hierarchically paged displays and ability on fault diagnosis performance. Ergonomics **31**(6), 889–904 (1988)
22. Piolat, A., Roussey, J.Y., Thunin, O.: Effects of screen presentation on text reading and revising. Int. J. Hum.-Comput. Stud. **47**, 565–589 (1997)
23. Sanchez, C.A., Wiley, J.: To scroll or not to scroll: scrolling, working memory capacity and comprehending complex text. Hum. Factors **51**(5), 730–738 (2009)
24. Sanchez, C.A., Goolsbee, J.Z.: Character size and reading to remember from small displays. Comput. Educ. **55**, 1056–1062 (2010)
25. Huang, S.-M., Li, W.-J., Tung, S.-C.: An effect of white space on traditional Chinese text-reading on smartphone. Appl. Syst. Innov. **1**(3), 24 (2018)
26. Golombisky, K., Hagen, R.: White Space Is not Your Enemy: A Beginner's Guide to Communicating Visually through Graphic, Web & Multimedia Design, 2nd edn. Boston, MA, USA (2010)

Mobile Usability: Review, Classifications and Future Directions

Zhao Huang[1,2(⊠)]

[1] Key Laboratory of Modern Teaching Technology, Ministry of Education,
Xi'an 710119, People's Republic of China
zhaohuang@snnu.edu.cn
[2] School of Computer Science, Shaanxi Normal University, Xi'an 710119,
People's Republic of China

Abstract. Advanced mobile technologies have enabled the thousands of applications to be developed that can be used by people on their move. The ability to easily use and be satisfied with mobile apps is important to users. However, the usability requirements of mobile apps differ due to their specific genres, design purposes, business goals and strategies. Therefore, this study conducts a systematic review of extant literature related to mobile app design, and thereby classifies usability pertaining to usability requirements and user experience in a variety of categories of mobile apps. We believe that it would be useful for researchers and practitioners to better understand mobile app usability.

Keywords: Mobile apps · Mobile usability · Mobile categories

1 Introduction

The rapid evolution of mobile technologies and wireless communication services has stimulated the development of the mobile market. To date, the worldwide sales of mobile devices reach more than 1.7 billion units [1], and in some countries, people have more than one mobile phone [2]. Except the basic functions of mobile phone, such as sending text messages and making phone calls, a diversity of information and services become available and accessible through mobile applications (mobile apps) today [3], covering a wider range of areas, including education, shopping, health care, travel, business, sports, entertainment, lifestyle, news and etc. These mobile apps provide the apps for almost any situation of our life [4], which in turn encourage greater user engagement [5]. The ability to easily use and be satisfied with mobile apps is important to users [6]. In this vein, the usability should be addressed in the course of mobile app development. Otherwise, design goals to mobile apps may not be achieved, which in turn could lead to difficulties of use [7], frustrated users [8] and lost revenue [9]. Therefore, usability design is vital in mobile app development.

Many studies related to mobile app usability can be found in the literature. Some studies explore the methodology for the evaluation of usability of mobile apps (e.g. [7]), some focus on developing usability heuristics for native smartphone mobile apps (e.g. [6]) and others tend to explain the rationale for the usability model of mobile applications (e.g. [10]). Although the prior research provides useful insights into

© Springer Nature Switzerland AG 2020
A. Marcus and E. Rosenzweig (Eds.): HCII 2020, LNCS 12201, pp. 270–276, 2020.
https://doi.org/10.1007/978-3-030-49760-6_19

mobile app usability, it can be arguable that mobile app usability needs to consider the physical constraints of mobile devices, such as small screen, mobile connectivity and context of use. In particular, mobile apps are categorized into a varieties of group based on their key functionalities, which requires different usability. Thus, the usability requirements of mobile apps differ due to their specific genres, design purposes, business goals and strategies.

To this end, the goal of this study is to have a systematic review of extant literature related to mobile app design across various research domains, including Human-Computer Interaction, Computer Science, Economic, Social Science and Marketing Science, and thereby classify usability pertaining to usability requirements and user experience in a variety of categories of mobile apps. By doing so, it would be helpful for researchers and practitioners to better understand mobile app usability and develop more usable mobile apps to meet users' requirements.

The paper is organized as follows. Section 2 presents background notions and related work; Sect. 3 contains a detailed explanation of the review approach; Sect. 4 discusses the results of the usability review, and Sect. 5 draws conclusions and future work.

2   Related Studies

Mobile apps refer to software systems operating on mobile devices, evolving making ubiquitous information access at anytime and anywhere [11]. A variety of mobile apps requires that they be classified into categories [12]. Generally, mobile apps can be categorized, based on the key functionalities, into education apps, shopping apps, health care apps, travel apps, business apps, sports apps, entertainment apps, lifestyle apps, news apps and weather apps. Such categories can be seen, for instance, on major app stores like as Google Play and Apple's App Store.

The term of usability can be defined as the capability of a software product to be understood, learned, operated, and attractive to the users [13]. Usability is normally explained by multiple attributes. For example, Ahmad et al. [14] interpreted mobile app usability by looking at usability attributes, including content, error handing, input method, equitable use, cognitive load and design. Karjaluoto et al. [15] explained mobile app usability by focusing on ease of use, usefulness and functionality.

The physical constraints of mobile devices and wireless technologies raise a number of challenges for mobile app design and development [16]. These challenges include small screen size [7], limited connectivity [11], limited processing capacity [15], different display resolutions [17], limited storage space [18], context of use [19], limited input capabilities [14], and multimodality [11]. Therefore, it is important to understand the usability requirements of mobile apps due to their unique features of mobile devices.

3   Research Approach

To conduct the study, a systematic search process is employed to review existing literature and to determine the needs for developing mobile application usability heuristics. We focus on relevant papers published between 2008 and 2018, which includes the usability evaluation of mobile applications and devices. The performance of the search process consists of six steps (please see Fig. 1).

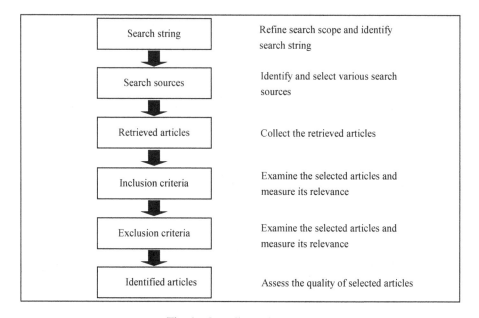

Search string	Refine search scope and identify search string
Search sources	Identify and select various search sources
Retrieved articles	Collect the retrieved articles
Inclusion criteria	Examine the selected articles and measure its relevance
Exclusion criteria	Examine the selected articles and measure its relevance
Identified articles	Assess the quality of selected articles

Fig. 1.   Overall search process

The first step is search string, which searches for the publications from the identified sources. The key search scopes cover mobile devices, mobile applications and usability. A variety of search strings are combined and used, such as mobile or mobile phone(s) or mobile device(s), and mobile application(s) or mobile app(s) or app(s), and usability or usability design or usability evaluation. The second step is to decide search sources, including IEEE digital library, ACM digital library, Science Direct, Springer and Google scholar. This is followed by collecting all of the publications. After that, inclusion criteria are developed to assess the selected articles. For example, the paper is focused on mobile devices, including smart phones or tablets. Furthermore, the exclusion criteria are used to exclude papers from the results that were not related to our study. For instance, the article is not written in English. Finally, the most relevant publications are evaluated for their quality and identified.

4   Results and Discussion

Usability is composed of multiple facets, which is considered as usability attributes. The study identifies a set of usability attributes from literature, include simplicity of systems, ease of use, system support, functions integration, system consistency, learnability, visibility of system status, match system and the real world, aesthetics design, facilitate easier input, screen readability, flexibility and personalization, privacy and social conventions, error management, effectiveness, efficiency, satisfaction, memorability, cognitive load, navigation and control, content provision and usefulness.

Moreover, usability of mobile apps is an active research area as it faces a number of challenges due to unique limitations of mobile devices, including small screen, limited connectivity, limited processing capacity, low display resolutions, low level of storage space, context of use, limited input capabilities, and multimodal mobile apps. These physical limitations and constraints, which are also distinguishing aspects for mobile apps lead to various requirements of usability attributes. Thus, it needs to be carefully considered in mobile app design. Additionally, it is necessary to constrain and distinguish mobile app development from general information system or software development. Table 1 shows the results of the usability attribute relevance with various mobile app design limitations.

Overall, almost all the identified usability attributes are necessarily relevant with the constraints of mobile devices in terms of screen size, display resolutions, context of use, input capabilities and multimodal mobile apps. However, for limited connectivity, limited processing capacity and storage space, less identified usability attributes are required. These findings suggest that mobile devices themselves may play a much more influential role in mobile app usability design compared with desktop computers do in desktop applications. When designing and developing usability for mobile apps, usability and the physical constraints of mobile devices must be considered as whole, minimizing the effect of contextual factors on perceived usability.

Moreover, with respect to each identified usability attribute, significant differences to a variety of mobile design limitations are also found. As showed in Table 8, for example, simplicity of systems is addressed in screen size, display resolutions context of use, input capabilities and multimodal mobile apps. This result is also reflected in the usability attributes of consistency, visibility of system status and aesthetics design. A possible reason might be that these usability attributes are in the areas of design look, which closely support users' visual cognition and understanding when they interacting with mobile apps. However, for the physical constraints of connectivity, processing capacity and storage space, the usability attribute of functions integration is particularly required. These results imply that mobile app usability design needs to match with the characteristics of the physical constraints of mobile devices. This echoes the view of Kumar and Mohite [20] who suggest that design elements should meet the needs of the unique features of mobile devices, which can increase mobile app quality and strengthen user playfulness.

Table 1. Usability attributes with mobile physical limitations

Usability attribute	Mobile physical limitations							
	1	2	3	4	5	6	7	8
U1. Simplicity of systems	√	-	-	√	-	√	√	√
U2: Ease of use	√	-	-	-	-	√	√	√
U3: System support	√	-	-	√	-	√	√	√
U4: Functions integration	√	√	√	-	√	√	√	√
U5: Consistency	√	-	-	√	-	√	√	√
U6: Learnability	√	-	-	-	-	√	√	√
U7: Visibility of system status	√	-	-	√	-	√	√	√
U8: Match system and the real world	√	√	√	×	√	√	√	√
U9: Aesthetics design	√	-	-	√	-	√	√	√
U10: Easier input	√	-	√	-	√	√	√	√
U11: Screen readability	√	-	-	√	-	√	-	-
U12: Flexibility and personalization	√	√	-	√	-	√	√	√
U13: Privacy and social conventions	-	-	-	-	-	√	√	√
U14: Error management	√	-	-	√	√	√	√	√
U15: Effectiveness	√	√	√	√	√	√	√	√
U16: Efficiency	√	√	√	√	√	√	√	√
U17: Satisfaction	√	√	√	√	√	√	√	√
U18: Memorability	√	-	-	-	-	√	√	√
U19: Cognitive load	√	-	-	√	-	√	√	√
U20: Navigation and control	√	-	-	√	-	√	√	√
U21: Content provision	√	-	-	√	√	√	√	√
U22: Usefulness	√	√	√	√	√	√	√	√

Note: 1 = Small screen; 2=Limited connectivity;3=Limited processing capacity; 4=Low display resolutions; 5=Storage space; 6=Context of use; 7=Limited input capabilities; 8=Multimodal mobile applications; √means related; -means not related.

5 Conclusion

Evidence from previous studies indicates that mobile apps usability is a new phenomenon that needs to be better understood. To date, little systematic help has been offered to focus on mobile apps usability or in designing usable mobile apps. This study conducted a systematic literature review for building up a body of knowledge, describing the concept of mobile apps, explaining the usability of mobile apps and its design. Our results present the state-of-the-art in terms of mobile app studies, and provide a deep insight into mobile app usability design by looking at the nature of the usability through two major steps. First, to better understand the concept of usability, this study identifies a number of important usability attributes of mobile app design from the literature. Second, we depict the conceptualization of the identified usability with the physical constraints of mobile devices. We believe that the identified features can help designers to focus on specific elements of the mobile apps to further improve its usability.

Acknowledgments. This study was supported by research grants funded by the "National Natural Science Foundation of China" (Grant No. 61771297), and "the Fundamental Research Funds for the Central Universities" (GK201803062, GK201802013).

References

1. Evanthia, F., Maria, R., Spiros, S.: A usability study of iPhone built-in applications. Behav. Inf. Technol. **34**, 799–808 (2015)
2. Anand, A., FossoWamba, S.: Business value of RFID-enabled healthcare transformation projects. Bus. Process Manag. J. **19**(1), 111–145 (2013)
3. GSMA. Mobile economy (2018). https://www.gsma.com/mobileeconomy. Accessed 20 Sept 2019
4. Xu, R., Frey, R.M., Fleisch, E., Ilic, A.: Understanding the impact of personality traits on mobile app adoption e Insights from a large-scale field study. Comput. Hum. Behav. **62**, 244–256 (2016)
5. Hoehle, H., Aljafari, R., Venkatesh, V.: Leveraging Microsoft's mobile usability guidelines: conceptualizing and developing scales for mobile application usability. Int. J. Hum.-Comput. Stud. **89**, 35–53 (2016)
6. Joyce, G., Lilley, M.: Towards the development of usability heuristics for native smartphone mobile applications. In: Marcus, A. (ed.) DUXU 2014. LNCS, vol. 8517, pp. 465–474. Springer, Cham (2014). https://doi.org/10.1007/978-3-319-07668-3_45
7. Billi, M., et al.: A unified methodology for the evaluation of accessibility and usability of mobile applications. Univ. Access Inf. Soc. **9**, 337–356 (2010)
8. Vélez, O., Okyere, P.B., Kanter, A.S., Bakken, S.: A usability study of a mobile health application for rural Ghanaian midwives. J. Midwifery Women's Health **59**(2), 184–191 (2014)
9. Coursaris, C.K., Kim, D.J.: A meta-analytical review of empirical mobile usability studies. J. Usability Stud. **6**(3), 117–171 (2011)
10. Harrison, R., Flood, D., Duce, D.: Usability of mobile applications: literature review and rationale for a new usability model. J. Interact. Sci. **2013**(1), 1 (2013)
11. Zhang, D., Adipat, B.: Challenges, methodologies, and issues in the usability testing of mobile applications. Int. Hum. Comput. Interact. **18**, 293–308 (2005)
12. Al-Subaihin, A.A., et al.: Clustering mobile apps based on mined textual features. In: Proceedings of the 10th ACM/IEEE International Symposium on Empirical Software Engineering and Measurement, Spain, pp. 1–10 (2016)
13. Fernandez, A., Insfran, E., Abrahão, S.: Usability evaluation methods for the web: a systematic mapping study. Inf. Softw. Technol. **53**, 789–817 (2011)
14. Ahmad, N., Rextin, A., Kulsoom, U.E.: Perspectives on usability guidelines for smartphone applications: an empirical investigation and systematic literature review. Inf. Softw. Technol. **94**, 130–149 (2018)
15. Karjaluoto, H., Shaikh, A.A., Saarijärvi, H., Saraniemi, S.: How perceived value drives the use of mobile financial services apps. Int. J. Inf. Manag. (2018). https://doi.org/10.1016/j.ijinfomgt.2018.08.014
16. Ji, Y.G., Park, J.H., Lee, C., Yun, M.H.: A usability checklist for the usability evaluation of mobile phone user interface. Int. J. Hum.-Comput. Interact. **20**, 207–231 (2006)
17. Díaz-García, J., Brunet, P., Navazo, I., Vázquez, P.: Progressive ray casting for volumetric models on mobile devices. Comput. Graph. **73**, 1–16 (2018)

18. Falloon, G.: Young students using iPads: app design and content influences on their learning pathways. Comput. Educ. **68**, 505–521 (2013)
19. Joyce, G., Lilley, M., Barker, T., Jefferies, A.: Mobile application usability heuristics: decoupling context-of-use. In: Marcus, A., Wang, W. (eds.) DUXU 2017. LNCS, vol. 10288, pp. 410–423. Springer, Cham (2017). https://doi.org/10.1007/978-3-319-58634-2_30
20. Kumar, B.A., Mohite, P.: Usability of mobile learning applications: a systematic literature review. J. Comput. Educ. **5**, 1–17 (2018)

Preliminary Exploration of Interface Design for Senior Citizens: A Study of Smartphone Camera Usage for People Above 50

Jiabei Jiang$^{(\boxtimes)}$, Weiwei Zhang, and Jihong Jeung

Tsinghua University, Beijing, China
jjb19@mails.tsinghua.edu.cn

Abstract. With the popularity of smart devices and the accelerating trend of population aging, more and more people aged above 50 begin to use smartphones. The applications they use mainly range from social communication to entertainment. Few studies have been conducted on the usability of evolution of smartphone for them [1], especially investigation about smartphone camera usage. According to the pre-research about smartphone application usage among the age over 50 years old people, smartphone photography has become very important in their daily lives. Meanwhile, there also exists a lot of problems differ from young people. This study targeted these people to research on their experience using smartphone camera application. It presents two studies on user interface: first, online survey for general information of operation; second, user interview for target people's behavior. The results show that: 1) The user experience study of smartphone camera among the people aged above 50 is very meaningful; 2) Icon combined with text is easier to recognize and operate in the camera interface menu; 3) A simple and safe-operation interface is expected; 4) Gender and education level influence the recognition of icons and needs of functions; 5) Feedback and tips are needed on the interface; 6) Electronic album editor can help to record memory more comprehensive and arrange photos. This research is expected to provide a reference for researchers, designers and mobile phone service providers to think about future designs of smartphone camera interface for the people aged above 50 and explores how to enhance their user experience of taking pictures with smartphones.

Keywords: People aged above 50 · Smartphone · Camera · User experience · User interface

1 Introduction

The smartphone is a valuable technological device for the elderly, aged 50 years and above, as it enables them to communicate with their family, friends and society [2]. Nowadays, China is highly informative. The national network ubiquity rate reached 54.3% by 2016, which was 1% higher than the global average. The proportion of netizens using smartphones had increased from 95.1% to 96.3% by the end of 2016 and now this proportion is still increasing [3]. According to some researches, at present nearly 100 million people aged over 50 in China are using smartphones. They have

© Springer Nature Switzerland AG 2020
A. Marcus and E. Rosenzweig (Eds.): HCII 2020, LNCS 12201, pp. 277–293, 2020.
https://doi.org/10.1007/978-3-030-49760-6_20

become the user group with the largest increase for several times [4]. The ability of using smartphones has become one of the key factors to integrate to society [5–7]. According to several reports, age over-50s people mainly use smartphone for communication and entertainment [8] in general. Before this study, there is a pre-research about the smartphone applications usage among them. It interviewed 35 people. The result shows the top two applications they used is WeChat and phone call. These two apps are related to social communications. Therefore, they are the most popular apps in China [9]. News, smartphone photography and video, which can be categorized as entertainment applications, are next three apps in the ranking list. Nowadays, people over 50 years old are getting used to take photos by smartphone camera. And over 14% of interviewees claimed they took photos almost every day. It indicates that smartphone photography has play a very essential role in their daily life. As such, the user experience of smartphone camera interface needs to be highly valued. There is much prior work that have been investigated, such as smart home and community care for the age over 50 people [10–12], applications specially designed for them [13–16] and their perception and use of smartphone interface [17–20]. Currently available smartphone user interface does not appear to be optimized for age over-50s people [21–23] ,and not much work has yet looked into the use of smartphone camera. This study exploded more details of the usage of smartphone camera by questionnaire and user interview.

2 Method

There are two main purposes of this study (see Fig. 1): 1) Understand problems of smartphone camera operation of target people; 2) Find guidelines of camera application design. The study consists of two parts. First part is an online questionnaire survey, which includes the current situation of target people using smartphone camera app and their perspectives about it. According the statistic analyze by SPSS26, there are two main results can be summarized: the effect of different factors (age, gender and education level) on camera operation and camera interface recognition. As the study 1 was conducted online survey, most of detail operation behavers and specific problems could not be able to dig on, researchers designed the second part, study 2. Combining with the data from study 1, the second part, user interviews is designed to look into user operation and their thoughts. Researchers use self-designed questionnaire in it to conduct one-on-one interviews. At the same time, interviewees are required to use every function and researchers take their behavioral habit down in photographs and videos. The final conclusion was integrated by study 1 and study 2. The following list summarizes related noun explanation for clarity (see Table 1). In the following pages we will discuss them in the form of abbreviated terms. In additional the interface of smartphone camera reference from iPhone and Huawei as these tow brands are the top2 used in our research result.

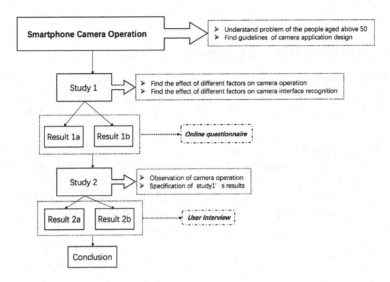

Fig. 1. Structure diagram

Table 1. Noun explanation.

Inconvenient points	
P1	Unable to distinguish picture mode and video mode
P2	Text is too small
P3	Unable to understand icons
P4	Blurred photo
P5	Do not understand the selfie icon
P6	Keys are too close to each other and it's easy to press the wrong key
P7	Unable to understand a lot of functions
P8	Too many functions
P9	Can not find photos just taken
Education level	
L1	Under middle school
L2	High school
L3	Bachelor degree or above
Function needs	
F1	Edit pictures and videos without downloading third-party software
F2	Have tutorials about the camera application
F3	Can make electronic album
F4	Interface more clear and easier to operate
F5	Easier management of electronic albums
F6	No need to add more functions

3 Result

3.1 Result of Study 1: Online Questionnaire Research

The online questionnaire survey interviewed a total of 495 people, which included 227 men and 268 women. Among them, the proportion of people aged 40–50 was 40.2%, 50–60 was 30.1%, 60–70 was 24.85%, 70–80 was 3.23% and people above 80 was 1.62%.

Status of Smartphone Camera Use
As shown in Fig. 2, the most commonly used functions for people above 50 and below are photo-shooting, video-shooting and selfie. Thereinto, 80.74% of the people aged over-50s shoot photos, slightly higher than those under 50 years old. And 15.08% of the people under 50 shoot videos, higher than those above 50. When it comes to taking selfies and recognizing selfie icons, the number of people aged above 50 is bigger than the youngers.

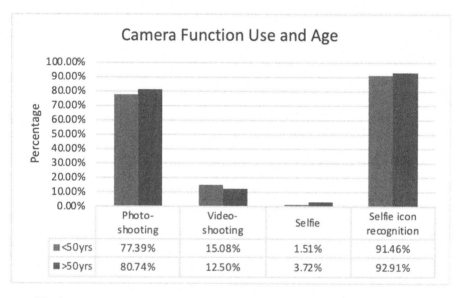

Fig. 2. The status of different age on the function use of smartphone camera app.

Effects of Gender, Age and Education Level on the Inconvenient Factors of Using Smartphone Camera Application
As shown in Fig. 3, the number of people who chose P7 is the most, reaching 44.44%. The second is P8 with 38.18%, and the third is P3 with 33.13%. And according to statistical analysis, the inconvenience of using camera app is different by interviewees' gender, age and education background.

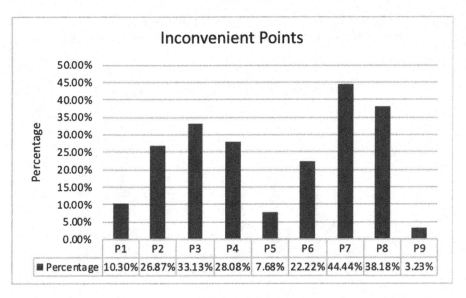

Fig. 3. Inconvenient factors for different crowds to use smartphone camera app.

Gender. There is clear difference between men and women in the choice of P1 (p = 0.011 < 0.05), P2(p = 0.015 < 0.05) and P3(p = 0.039 < 0.05). And more men choose P2 and P3 (see Fig. 4).

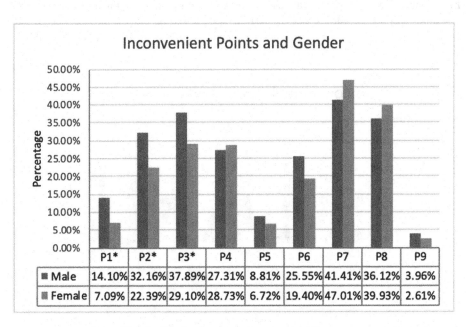

Fig. 4. Gender impact on inconvenient factors.

Age. We can know from Fig. 5 that age has a big influence on P6($p = 0.00 < 0.01$). 31.16% of people under 50 choose P6 while only 16.22% elders choose it.

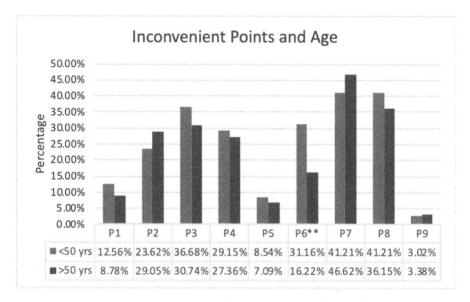

Fig. 5. Age impact on inconvenient factors

Education. Figure 6 shows that education background has a significant impact on the selection of P1($p = 0.012 < 0.05$), P4($p = 0.009 < 0.05$), P8($p = 0.013 < 0.05$) and P9($p = 0.003 < 0.05$). And people with lower education level is more likely to agree

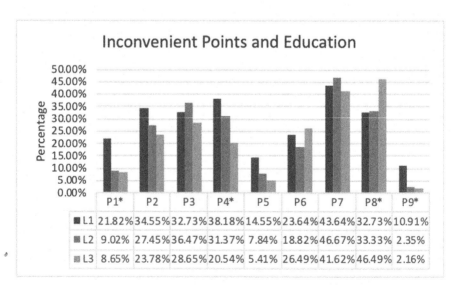

Fig. 6. Education background's impact on inconvenient factors of using camera app.

with P1(21.82%), P4(38.18%) and P9(10.91%) while people with higher education level tend to choose P8(46.49%).

Different Functional Improvements' Impact on the Use of Smartphone Camera Application

We can see from Fig. 7 that 54.75% of them choose F1. It seems that gender, age and education level have little influence on this selection. And people of different ages have significant difference in the choice of F3($p = 0.00 < 0.01$) and F6($p = 0.018 < 0.05$) (as shown in Fig. 8). 54.27% people under 50 years old agree with F3, higher than those over-50s. Among the people who agreed with F6, the number of people aged above 50 who choose this question exceeded half of the number of people under 50, reaching 12.5%.

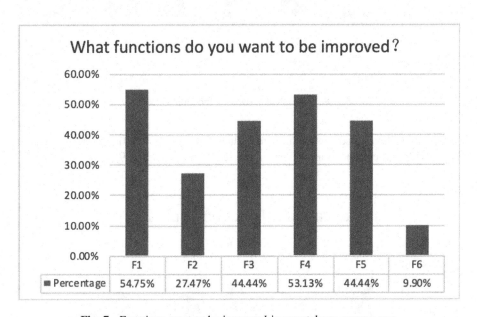

Fig. 7. Functions want to be improved in smartphone camera app.

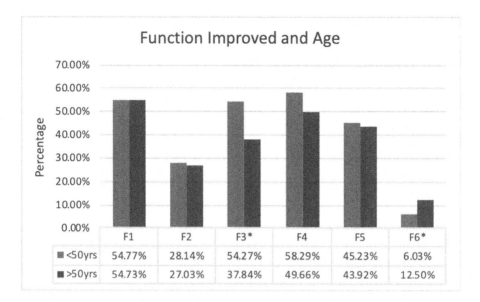

Fig. 8. The effect of age on functional needs.

Education level also has significant influence on F3(p = 0.015 < 0.05). 52.43% people with higher education background agree with it (see Fig. 9).

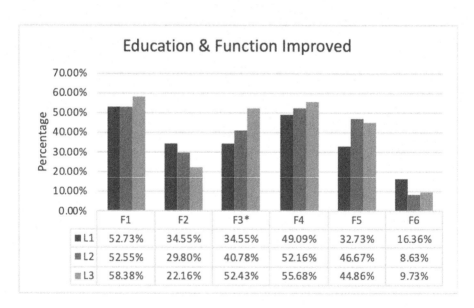

Fig. 9. The effect of education level on functional needs.

3.2 Result of Study 2: User Interview

After the first part, data collection, researchers conducted in-depth interviews with 20 people above 50 years old around the following four questions:

1) Researchers observed whether the interviewees really know how to use the functions in the smartphone camera application and recorded the problems during the usage.
2) Researchers asked interviewees whether they were on their own when they first use some functions and whether they could recognize the icons.
3) Since there were many people agreed with F3 (see Fig. 8), researchers dived deeper into the issue of electronic photo albums.
4) More than half of the people over-50s agreed with F4 (see Fig. 8), so researchers asked interviewees what were the four features they want to keep in smartphone camera application.

The result of interviews and observations are presented below:

1) Usage of different functions and problem exists
Panorama: Most interviewees use it when they come across beautiful scenery. And some interviewees use it at family gatherings because they think this function can record larger scenes. It has text labels and is displayed on the main interface of the camera, so it's easy to find. The main problem is that users find it unclear that whether to start shooting from left or right.
Camera Timer: Most people know the function but haven't used it, because interviewees did not know where this function is, let alone what the icon looked like. One interviewee thought this might be used for selfies.
Time-lapse: Most interviewees have seen the function but haven't use it because they didn't know when to use it.
Selfie: When interviewees couldn't find someone else to take photos for them or when they were with their family members, they used selfie function. Most people thought that the selfie button was easy to recognize, because the reverse arrow icon made it easier for them to understand the meaning of the lens reverse. However, during the operation, due to the limited stretch of the arm, the face often looks big, which makes the photo look unsightly.
Flash: All the interviewees knew about the function but more than 90% of them couldn't recognize the icon and didn't know how to turn it on and off. In most cases, the flash automatically turned on when there was insufficient light, so most of the interviewees thought that the flash was used to shoot night scenes. There were still a few interviewees who used flash to take portraits.
Focus Frame: Most interviewees found the function by accident. Sometimes the focus frame would appear on the screen automatically. Other times, when the user touched the screen, they found that the function appeared automatically. And the screen automatically became brighter and clearer. But they did not know why and how to make the focus frame appear again. There were still a small number of interviewees did not know this function at all until researchers mentioned it (as shown in Fig. 10).

Fig. 10. Focus frame.

2) Simplification of interface

As shown in Table 2, for the people aged over 50, the three traditional functions: photography, video, and photo album are still most important. Photo beautification and selfie are tied for fourth. The camera function is the most important, so the interviewees put forward higher requirements for it, such as whether the camera can switch between distant and near scenes so that they can shoot different targets.

Table 2. Choice for reserved functions.

	Photo	Video	Selfie	Album	Filter	Panorama	Flash
Pct.	90%	45%	25%	35%	25%	15%	15%

4   Discussion

Through statistical analysis, we found that gender, age, and education background had no significant effect on the use of camera functions. However, Fig. 2 shows that the number of people above 50 years old who use smart phones to take pictures is still higher than people under 50 years old. And it is interesting that the number of people over-50s who use phone for selfie is bigger than those who under 50 years old. We can see from that the need for smartphone photography for people aged above 50 can not be ignored. In the previous research, we proposed 9 influencing factors and 5 demand points for the use of smartphone camera applications. Next, we will discuss these factors and demand points.

4.1 Security of Smartphone Use

The cautiousness of the people aged over-50s makes them unable to experience the functions in the smart phone camera application further. Although smartphones are now very popular among them, the use of such technology products still makes them anxious [16] and they sometimes refuse to use these products. In our research, we also found that people over-50s like to use fixed functions. Although they know about some functions, they are unwilling to try. Except that they are not frequently-use in daily life, it is mainly because of fear. They fear that after pressing a certain function key, the mobile phone will be damaged or the switch can not return to the interface where it was just now. They will reduce their error rate by reducing the use of unfamiliar functions and ensure that what they do won't cause a problem [24]. And that's why there is a very significant difference in age on P6 (see Fig. 5). In addition, we learn from Fig. 7 in Study 1 and interviews in Study 2 that many people over-50s are reluctant to download third-party software and prefer to use the phone's own functions to prevent down-loading viruses or operating errors. It can be seen that people aged over-50s are very cautious when using mobile phones, which has also become one of the obstacles for them to learn new skills.

4.2 Smartphone Camera Interface Design

Gender Has an Impact on Icon Identification
As shown in Fig. 4, gender has a significant impact on the P1, P2 and P3. On all three issues, the proportion of male is higher than females. Among them, 82.2% of the men who chose P2 graduated from high school. It shows that it's not low education level that makes them weak at recognizing icons. Men may have weaker cognitive ability in graphics than women. The ability to identify icons may be affected by gender and education level [25]. The researchers Passig and Levin have a same point of view [26].

The Combination of Text and Icons Helps to Understand the Functions
Gender, age and education background have no significant effect on the choose of P7. However, many functions in present smartphone camera applications are not under-stood or used by young people, let alone the people over 50 old years. In Study 2, we conducted detailed user interviews and observations of some functions and found that the functions with text annotations on the main interface menu are still used more because they are clear at a glance. Brazilian researcher Ávila also mentioned that icons combine texts will be easier to understand on her research [27]. For example, people aged over 50 use panorama function more than the other main functions (photography, video, selfie). Panorama is usually displayed in the form of text or text combined with icon on the interface of smartphones, it is easy to find. However, when observing the operation of the interviewees, researchers found that there are some people who are not clear about the specific operation method when using it, because there is only a simple

arrow to indicate but no text. Besides, more than 90% of users are aware of the function of the flash but most of them do not know the icon of the flash, because most of the flash function dose not have the text label. They learn the existence of this function by the automatically opening of flash. The survey also showed that the number of people who agreed with P3 ranked third (see Fig. 3). Nearly half of the people do not understand the icons, which causes some people to fail to use many functions. This possibility was recognized by most of the interviewees in Study 2. Therefore, the recognition of icons will also affect the use of functions.

Simple and Easy-to-Use Interface

As shown in Fig. 7, more than half of the population agrees with F4 and 58.29% of them are over 50 years old (see Fig. 8). This is related to the decline in vision [28] and visual acuity and the perception of color in people aged over 50 [29]. Due to this physiological degradation, some icon size settings and color choices may frustrate some users. That's why it needs to design a simple interface for them [23]. Of course, usability is also very important [13]. Figure 8 shows that age has significant effect on F6. The number of people over-50s who choose this question has exceeded half of the number of people under the age of 50 choosing this question, up to 12.5%. It can be seen that many target people think that there are too many functions in smart phone camera application, and there is no need to increase any more. At the same time, in Study 2 researchers also found that although people over-50s seem to know a lot of smartphone camera functions, they only use a few commonly used functions. Some users hope that the camera can have the functions of distant (wide-angle or panoramic) and close-up (macro) shooting. They also hope it can be more conspicuous and faster to find, which may be related to their habit of shooting landscape photos. What's more, they hope that the album can be browsed quickly. The existence of other functions not only causes them to press the wrong button, but also makes them think that they are consuming smartphone memory. Combining the results of Study 2, researchers found only photos, videos, selfies and photo albums are necessary. As for the switching of the near and far views in the camera function, further research is still needed. Therefore, reducing some functions to ensure the basic needs of people aged above 50 can not only reduce the complexity of the interface, simplify the operation process of them when using the camera to take pictures, but also increase their sense of security.

Interface Feedback

On the camera application interface of many smartphones on the market, although some functions such as camera and photography are marked with text, after the text is clicked, no prompt will appear to tell the user whether the camera mode has been switched. So, this will make some users unclear about camera button and video button. The signs before and after the camera button and video button switch are not obvious so many users are not clear about the difference between them. This problem has also been recognized by many people in Study 2 and they hope to get some feedback after choosing different functions. With the aging of the body, people over 50 years old have severe hearing loss [24]. Researchers propose that the elderly prefer haptic feedback [24], so perhaps vibration might be a good way of feedback [13, 30].

Tips on the User Interface

Tips for photography skills are very important for the people aged over 50. The survey finds that although there are some techniques on the smartphones to help take photos clearly, target people group is easily to take blurred photos because of the aging of their bodies. At the same time, according to Fig. 9, it showed that the lower the education level, the more people choose option F2. So, there might be a certain relationship with the ability to learn and understand. In the interview, researchers continued to make some inquiries around this issue. It is found that some of the people with high education level like to figure out where the problem is and how to solve it and they often have higher requirements for their photos. Conversely, people with low education level simply take a picture and leave it alone. The quality of the photo is not good. This also causes their photo albums to be occupied by a lot of "junk" photos, making the phone run slower. In addition, more people with lower education background choose P1 and P9 (see Fig. 6). This shows that education level also affects the user's ability to observe the interface. And among this group of people, 41.94% people age over-50s want to have tutorials to guide them.

Figure 7 shows that the number of people who choose F1 has the highest proportion of 54.75%. However, the fact is that many smart phone cameras now come with the ability to beautify photos. The function of beautifying pictures can be divided into two parts. One is set at the time of shooting and the other is to edit the photos in the album after shooting. However, there is no clear text description and tutorial guidance on these operations on the interface.

In Study 2, researchers also learned that some people think that the flash is used to shoot night scenes, which may be related to the camera flash's automatic opening at night. Some users know that tapping the screen can brighten the screen although this is only learned when they accidentally make mistakes or they are under the guidance of family and friends. The camera itself does not have related function tips and instructions.

Although timed and time-lapse photography also have text prompts, most users don't know what situation they can be used for and how to use them. There are also a small number of users who believe that timed photography may be available when taking selfies.

Interviewees said that it is not always possible to ask people around them and they are too shy to ask their children all the time. So, it would be much more convenient if the camera could have tips or instructions. And it will increase their frequency of utilization and add fun to their lives.

4.3   Electronic Photo Album

The function of electronic photo album is very attractive to the people over 50 years old. As shown in Fig. 7, a total of nearly half of the people choose F3. In the interview researchers found that making electronic photo albums is very popular among the target people. Since the electronic photo album can be easily spread on WeChat and the circle of friends, many people know this application. Some people think that electronic photo albums can help them to record their feelings at the time, make travel notes or diaries to help them recall this time in the future and also facilitate them to share these feelings and experiences with their relatives and friends conveniently. Although many people are worried that some errors may occur when downloading the operating software or editing, these people who have tried find that the software in existence for editing electronic albums are very easy to use. And the interface of these software is worth consulting. Besides, they also found that there is such software in the WeChat Mini Program, so there is no need to download it anymore. It reduces their alertness. What is more interesting is that some interviewees think that electronic albums can help them to categorize and organize photos.

5 Conclusion

This study presented the investigation of inconvenient points and functions needed on the smartphone camera application among the people aged above 50. There are 6 results as follows:

1. Research on the user experience of smartphone camera applications in people aged above 50 is very meaningful.
2. The text size and icon design need to be suitable with the using habits of people over 50 years old. The combination of text and icons helps them to understand the functions of the camera easier and improve their user experience.
3. People over 50 years old don't have many requirements for the functions in the smartphone camera application. What they need is to take photos, record videos and view albums. What they want is the simplicity, easy and safe-operation of the interface. And they hope to add the function of quickly switching between near and far shooting.
4. Gender does not have much impact on functional requirements, but there are some differences in icon cognition, which probably will be taken into consideration in future designs. And as for education, people with higher education background have simpler requirements for functions.
5. Feedback and tips on the interface will be very helpful for age above 50 people.
6. Electronic photo album helps people over-50s to record their lives in different way and organize photos.

The study hopes to provide a reference for researchers, designers and mobile phone manufacturers. It also expects to offer a better user experience and improve a social life and leisure time through smartphone photography among the people aged above 50 in the future.

6 Limitation and Further Research

The questionnaire survey is mainly conducted online. People over 50 years old who can conduct the questionnaire operation on the Internet should be more familiar with mobile phone usage. So, it may affect our results. In addition, this study is only our preliminary survey on the use of mobile phone camera interfaces of people aged over 50. Based on the results, the questionnaires will be continued to improve for obtaining more objective data to improve user experience and provide real basis for better interface. In addition, due to the improvement of medical standards, there are more and more long-lived elderly people in China. In the later research, the study will subdivide the middle-aged and elderly age groups. What's more, the Chinese one-child policy makes many elderly people living alone or living in nursing homes [31]. As a result, if they have the ability to use a smartphone will become important to these elderly people and their families in the future [32]. The research on camera applications is just a beginning, the future study hopes gradually to improve user experience of the elderly and their quality of life in old age.

Acknowledgement. This work is supported by No. 20197010002, Tsinghua University Research Funding. I would like to thank the Future Lab at Tsinghua University for giving me the opportunity to conduct this research. I would like to thank professor Jihong Jeung, Weiwei Zhang, Dr. Mengyin Jiang, Yuankun Li, Yuhao Huang for their help and support.

References

1. Mohadisdudis, H.M., Ali, N.M.: A study of smartphone usage and barriers among the elderly. In: 3rd International Conference on User Science and Engineering (i-USEr). LNCS, pp. 109–114. IEEE (2014)
2. Salman, H.M., Ahmad, W.F.W., Sulaiman, S.: Usability evaluation of the smartphone user interface in supporting elderly users from experts' perspective. IEEE Access **6**, 22578–22591 (2018)
3. Jhony Choon Yeong, N.G., Sixuan, C., Qingmei, T.: A research on the informatization impact on elderly life: based on the usage and feeling of smartphone users. J. Nanjing Univ. Aeronaut. Astronaut. **21**(2), 58–64 (2019)
4. Jian Guo, W., Zhifeng, H.: Prospect of China's Film & TV in "Internet Plus" Era, 1st edn. Communication University of China Press, Beijing (2017)
5. Klimova, B., Maresova, P.: Elderly people and their attitude towards mobile phones and their applications—a review study. In: Park, J., Jin, H., Jeong, Y.-S., Khan, M. (eds.) Advanced Multimedia and Ubiquitous Engineering. LNEE, vol. 393, pp. 31–36. Springer, Singapore (2016). https://doi.org/10.1007/978-981-10-1536-6_5
6. KuoppamaKi, S.M., Taipale, S., Wilska, T.A.: The use of mobile technology for online shopping and entertainment among older adults in Finland. Telematics Inform. **34**(4), 110–117 (2017)
7. Halmdienst, N., Radhuber, M., Winter-Ebmer, R.: Attitudes of elderly Austrians towards new technologies: communication and entertainment versus health and support use. Eur. J. Ageing **16**, 513–523 (2019). https://doi.org/10.1007/s10433-019-00508-y
8. Biao, L., Zeyu, S., Yi, C., Ziman, Y.: A study of smartphone application usage among the elderly user. Sci. Technol. Innov. **24**, 78–79 (2019)
9. Jiaxing, L., Xiwei, W., Shimeng, L., Liu, Z.: Research on the influencing factors of WeChat use behavior among the elderly group from the perspective of information ecology. Libr. Inf. Serv. **15**, 25–33 (2017)
10. Suryadevara, N.K., Mukhopadhyay, S.C., Wang, R., Rayudu, R.K.: Forecasting the behavior of an elderly using wireless sensors data in a smart home. Eng. Appl. Artif. Intell. **26**(10), 2641–2652 (2013)

11. Ransing, R.S., Rajput, M.: Smart home for elderly care, based on Wireless Sensor Network. In: International Conference on Nascent Technologies in the Engineering Field. LNCS. IEEE (2015)
12. Hussain, A., et al.: Health and emergency-care platform for the elderly and disabled people in the Smart City. J. Syst. Softw. **110**, 253–263 (2015)
13. Plaza, I., Martín, L., Martin, S., Medrano, C.: Mobile applications in an aging society: status and trends. J. Syst. Softw. **84**(11), 1977–1988 (2011)
14. Abdulrazak, B., Malik, Y., Arab, F., Reid, S.: PhonAge: adapted smartphone for aging population. In: Biswas, J., Kobayashi, H., Wong, L., Abdulrazak, B., Mokhtari, M. (eds.) ICOST 2013. LNCS, vol. 7910, pp. 27–35. Springer, Heidelberg (2013). https://doi.org/10. 1007/978-3-642-39470-6_4
15. Harada, S., Sato, D., Takagi, H., Asakawa, C.: Characteristics of elderly user behavior on mobile multi-touch devices. In: Kotzé, P., Marsden, G., Lindgaard, G., Wesson, J., Winckler, M. (eds.) INTERACT 2013. LNCS, vol. 8120, pp. 323–341. Springer, Heidelberg (2013). https://doi.org/10.1007/978-3-642-40498-6_25
16. Nikou, S.: Mobile technology and forgotten consumers: the young-elderly. Int. J. Consum. Stud. **39**(4), 294–304 (2015)
17. Caprani, N., O'Connor, N.E., Gurri, C.: Touch screens for the older user. In: Auat Cheein, F. (ed.) Assistive Technologies. InTech (2012)
18. Czaja, S.J., Charness, N., Fisk, A.D., Hertzog, C., Nair, S.N., Rogers, W.A., et al.: Factors predicting the use of technology: findings from the center for research and education on aging and technology enhancement (CREATE). Psychol. Aging **21**(2), 333–352 (2006)
19. Pattison, M., Stedmon, A.: Inclusive design and human factors: designing mobile phones for older users. PsychNology J. **4**(3), 267–284 (2006)
20. Morris, A., Goodman, J., Brading, H.: Internet use and non-use: views of older users. Univ. Access Inf. Soc. **6**(1), 43–57 (2007). https://doi.org/10.1007/s10209-006-0057-5
21. Balata, J., Mikovec, Z., Slavicek, T.: KoalaPhone: touchscreen mobile phone UI for active seniors. J. Multimodal User Interfaces **9**, 263–273 (2015). https://doi.org/10.1007/s12193-015-0188-1
22. Khan, K., et al.: Influence of design elements in mobile applications on user experience of elderly people. Procedia Comput. Sci. **113**, 352–359 (2017)
23. Al-Razgan, M., Al-Khalifa, H.S.: SAHL: a touchscreen mobile launcher for Arab elderly. J. Mob. Multimed. **13**(1–2), 75–99 (2017)
24. Williams, D., Alam, M.A.U., Ahamed, S.I., Chu, W.: Considerations in designing human-computer interfaces for elderly people. In: 13th International Conference on Quality Software (QSIC). LNCS, pp. 372–377. IEEE (2013)
25. Chung, S., Chau, C., Hsu, X., Lee, J.J.: The effects of gender culture on mobile phone icon recognition. In: Jacko, J.A. (ed.) HCI 2007. LNCS, vol. 4551, pp. 252–259. Springer, Heidelberg (2007). https://doi.org/10.1007/978-3-540-73107-8_28
26. Passig, D., Levin, H.: Gender interest differences with multimedia learning interfaces. Comput. Hum. Behav. **25**(2), 173–183 (1999)
27. Ávila, I.M.A., Gudwin, R.R.: Icons as helpers in the interaction of illiterate users with computers. In: Proceedings of the IADIS International Conference on Interfaces and Human-Computer Interaction, MCCSIS, Portugal, Algarve, pp. 69–77 (2009)
28. Nunes, F.M.C., Silva, P.A., Abrantes, F.: Human-computer interaction and the older adult: an example using user research and personas. In: Proceedings of the 3rd International Conference on Pervasive Technologies Related to Assistive Environments, PETRA 2010, Samos, Greece, pp. 1–8 (2010)

29. Phiriyapokanon, T.: Is a big button interface enough for elderly users? Toward user interface guidelines for elderly users. Masters thesis, Computer Engineering, Mälardalen University, Västerås, Sweden (2011)
30. Yusof, M., et al.: Design for elderly friendly: mobile phone application and design that suitable for elderly. Int. J. Comput. Appl. **95**(3), 28–31 (2014)
31. Runlong, H.: The family condition of empty-nest household in China. Popul. Econ. **2**, 57–62 (2005)
32. Chou, W.H., Lai, Y.T., Liu, K.H.: User requirements of social media for the elderly: a case study in Taiwan. Behav. Inf. Technol. **32**(7–9), 920–937 (2013)

Evaluating One-Handed Usability of Phablets: A Comparative Study into Turkey's Leading Food and Grocery Delivery Applications

Emre Kızılkaya[✉] and Kerem Rızvanoğlu

Galatasaray University, Ciragan Cad. No: 36 Ortakoy, 34357 Istanbul, Turkey
emre.kizilkaya@ogr.gsu.edu.tr, krizvanoglu@gsu.edu.tr

Abstract. The ongoing and enduring adoption of mobile devices with ever-enlarging screens continues to bring new challenges in application development to improve usability. This study aims at providing insights on efficiency, effectiveness and user satisfaction of four leading food and grocery delivery applications in Turkey, when they are used with a single hand on a phablet. We designed a usability test with qualitative and quantitative aspects based on a multi-method approach with a sample of 9 male and 9 female university students from Istanbul. The participants were observed during the execution of 21 tasks on food delivery applications Yemeksepeti and GetirYemek, as well as their inter-linked online groceries, Banabi and Getir. Additional data was collected by the thinking-aloud protocol, video recording, a post-test interview, a System Usability Scale (SUS) survey and anthropometric measuring. By averaging together a standardized version of completion rates, task-times, task-level satisfaction and errors, we also generated Single Usability Metric (SUM) scores for each application. Results were discussed in the dimensions of ergonomics, findability, discoverability and use of conventions. Although all applications scored higher than 78% in 18 of the 21 tasks in Single Usability Metric (SUM) with a confidence level of 90% and 52 error opportunities, their SUS scores were between 54%–74%. Together with this finding, the fact that 9 tasks received lower than 50% in user satisfaction on SUM was used to assert that there was still room to improve one-handed usability of mobile applications.

Keywords: User experience (UX) · Usability · Touchscreen · Phablet · Mobile · Application · One-handed designs · Ergonomics · Thumb movement

1 Introduction

1.1 Statement of the Problem

The ever-enlarging touchscreens of smartphones keep changing the ways in which users interact with their mobile devices. Still, many developers opt to release mobile applications in a one-size-fits-all manner, potentially allowing less effective and less efficient usability on larger screens.

A phablet was described as "the hybrid of both a cellular phone and tablet with a screen size measured diagonally between 5.3–6.9 in." [1]. The market share of the

© Springer Nature Switzerland AG 2020
A. Marcus and E. Rosenzweig (Eds.): HCII 2020, LNCS 12201, pp. 294–312, 2020.
https://doi.org/10.1007/978-3-030-49760-6_21

smartphones with over 5.5 in. display size was predicted to grow to 47% and 52% by 2020 and 2022 respectively [2].

Karlson and Bederson [3] argue that "devices that accommodate single-handed interaction can offer a significant benefit to users by freeing a hand for the host of physical and attentional demands common to mobile activities. But there is little evidence that current devices are designed with this goal in mind." It was observed that many conventional mobile application designs cause friction on phablet-size devices, particularly if they are used with one hand as most users prefer [4] and many others are frequently forced to do in certain situations in their daily lives, such as while they are standing in public transport holding a hanging strap or a grab handle.

Studies into the effectiveness, efficiency and satisfaction of the one-handed use of mobile applications date back to the pre-smartphone era, including one into the map navigation tasks on PDAs [5] and another one into Scalable User Interface (ScUI) techniques for PDAs and cell phones [6]. More recent research investigated ergonomics aspect of the issue in detail, including factors like the rear of the smartphone, index finger reach zone and hand length [7]. As the adoption of smartphone with larger screens continue, many other fields of research into phablets, particularly their one-handed use, remain largely unexplored.

1.2   Purpose of the Study

In Turkey, an emergent market with vibrant demographics and a mobile internet penetration rate of 53% [8], several studies into mobile application usage have been made in various areas [9–11]. One of them investigated left vs. right-handed user experience on Yemeksepeti [12], a popular online food delivery service, on mid-size touchscreen mobile phones. Our study aims to provide insights into the specific case of one-handed mobile application usage on phablets by focusing on four applications produced by two of Turkey's on-demand delivery giants.

Glovo, an on-demand delivery startup headquartered in Spain, pulled out of Turkey in January 2020 [13], cementing the dominant position of locally-originated competitors Yemeksepeti and Getir in the national market. Yemeksepeti, a Turkish startup that was bought by Berlin-based Delivery Hero in 2015, announced that it had 14 million users in 2019 with 81% of them on mobile on its core product, its namesake food delivery service linking restaurants with customers [14]. Yemeksepeti introduced Banabi, an on-demand grocery delivery service, to challenge the market leader of this business line, the Istanbul-based start-up Getir, in 2019. Getir responded by introducing GetirYemek to challenge Yemeksepeti in food delivery business [15]. As the incumbent market leaders and their emergent challengers in the largely-duopolistic markets in Turkey's on-demand restaurant food and grocery delivery sectors, the two companies' interconnected mobile applications – Yemeksepeti and Banabi on the one side, Getir and GetirYemek on the other – present a uniquely comparative environment to conduct the study.

In this context, the study's main purpose is to determine usability problems within the user interface of the four mobile applications, as they are interacted by various groups of representative users under controlled test conditions. Although the study is focused on one-handed use on phablets, it was also hoped that it could provide fresh insights into general usability of these popular mobile applications among Turkish users.

2   Research Methodology

A multi-method research design was preferred to measure one-handed usability scores both qualitatively and quantitatively. In this regard, the research questions were: How efficiently and effectively do the users perform key task on the mobile applications with one hand? How much satisfied are they and what can be proposed to solve the usability challenges that they encountered?

Data was collected by using various techniques in order to answer these questions, including a background questionnaire, task observation, post-test surveys, anthropometric measurement and a debriefing interview. In the first stage, a pre-test questionnaire on users' demographics and prior device usage was completed. It was followed by the discrete target stage, which involved the performing of determined key tasks on a phablet with a single hand. The participants' hand measurements were taken in the last stage, which was concluded by a final interview and a retrospective probing of the session's video record. The total session time was approximately 50 min.

The test for the observation of key tasks was also designed to establish a Single Usability Metric (SUM) [16] for each of the four mobile applications regarding their effectiveness, efficiency and satisfaction in one-handed use. To generate a SUM score, performance metrics such as errors rates, completion rates, task-times and task-level satisfaction were measured. Before the structured debriefing, the System Usability Scale (SUS) [17] was used as part of the post-test survey to enrich the qualitative range of the data, particularly to map application-level satisfaction and user perceptions.

3   User Study

3.1   Sample

18 university students (9 females and 9 males) aged between 20 and 26 (median = 22) from 9 universities in Istanbul voluntarily participated in this experiment. The participants, who were all right-handed, had an experience in the use of phablets from 1 year to 8 years (median = 4). 11 of them reported that they currently use various brands of Android phones, while the remaining 7 named iPhone models. One user for each of the four applications reported that he/she uses it every day, representing "heavy users," while the rest (n = 14) said that they use any one of them for less than twice a week, representing "casual users" or beginners.

Half of the participants reported familiarity with both operating systems as they had switched between Android devices and iPhones in the past. Their daily usage of a mobile phone, which they reported by corroborating with daily usage data collected by their own device, ranged between 180 to 600 min (median = 315). All participants gave informed consent before the start of the experiment, including for the video recording, and reported any physical or health problems involving their hands or fingers.

3.2 Test Device and Medium

An iPhone 7 Plus, which has a 5.5-inch screen with 1920×1080 pixels of resolution and weighing 188 grams, was used for the usability test. Yemeksepeti, Banabi, Getir and GetirYemek applications were installed and kept in unaltered, non-customized form in their default settings, except the entry of a delivery address to enable their functionality. Automatic spell checking and correction features of the phablet were also disabled to provide a level field for all users in the usage of the Turkish keyboard. All participants used the device throughout the session with one hand, holding it at a favorable height from the floor and the table in front of them, which was put there as a precaution against possible slips and falls.

3.3 Procedure

Usability tests were conducted in typical lab environments at Galatasaray and Bahçeşehir universities, as well as the Media Academy operated by the Journalists' Union of Turkey, with the test phablet, supporting software and hardware. While the facilitator, who was seated in the lab, monitored the participant's interaction with the mobile application, an assistant helped him in taking notes, logging data and making an audiovisual recording of the session, which was held in privately with each participant.

The pre-test questionnaire included 14 questions. It covered not only demographics, but also various aspects of the participants' experience on a phablet as a (potential) user of the four applications in question. The survey provided the researchers with data on how a participant engages with a phablet on a daily basis, e.g. which way they usually hold a phablet and whether they use any accessories to let them grip the large screen easier.

In the second stage, the participants were asked to execute a total of 21 tasks while using the four applications with highly comparable designs developed by the two competing companies. In order to avoid order bias, half of the participants started with Yemeksepeti and its sister application Banabi, while the other half did it with Getir and its sister application GetirYemek. Initially, 12 tasks were specified for Yemeksepeti/Banabi and 12 mirroring ones for Getir/GetirYemek. Although the four applications largely overlap in their interface design and functions, one task for switching between Yemeksepeti and Banabi was ultimately removed, as the former application has a distinct opening screen that directly asks the user which application he/she wants to use, rendering such a possible task irrelevant.

As a result, a total of 21 tasks were selected in a way to provide data in both the ergonomics-aspect of the study and other usability dimensions, including effectiveness, efficiency and satisfaction relating to information architecture. Two primary constructs were determined as focal points of study for each task, although findability and ergonomics were common denominators in all of them. Completion rates, task-times, satisfaction and errors for each task were recorded during the second stage. Maximum 5 min of time were given for each task and the participant was then asked to move to the next one even if it was not successfully completed. A think-aloud protocol was used at this stage of the test, which lasted an average of 30 min. A total of 52 error opportunities were determined for all tasks (Table 1).

Table 1. The 21 tasks for four applications can be summarized in five groups.

Group	Task group summary	Main dimensions of study
1	Find and add a product in the basket with search	Findability & discoverability
2	Find and add a product in the basket by browsing	Findability & discoverability
3	Find certain information/touch certain buttons	Ergonomics & conventions
4	Check the basket	Findability & conventions
5	Switch to the sister application	Findability & conventions

The third and the final stage included a standard SUS form for each of the four applications, as well as a six-question post-test questionnaire asking about the tasks that the participants' perceived as the hardest and the easiest, as well as their suggestions of change for better usability. Following the debriefing interview, the test was concluded by measuring the participants' hand breadth at metacarpal, hand length and hand circumference, as it was conventionally applied in research that relates to anthropometry [16].

4   Results

4.1   SUM vs. SUS

See Figs. 1, 2, 3, 4 and 5.

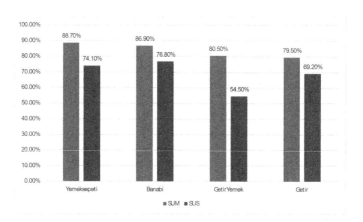

Fig. 1. Although the SUM tests indicated that Yemeksepeti and Banabi performed better than their competition in GetirYemek and Getir, respectively, it should be noted that the differences fell within the margin of error (90% CI). Still, Yemeksepeti and Banabi received significantly higher SUS scores as well, compared to their competition. The substantial difference between GetirYemek's SUM and SUS scores is addressed in the discussion section.

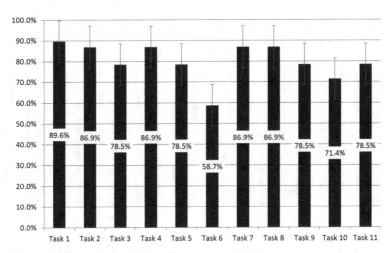

Fig. 2. SUM values for the one-handed tasks for Getir and GetirYemek applications with error bars.

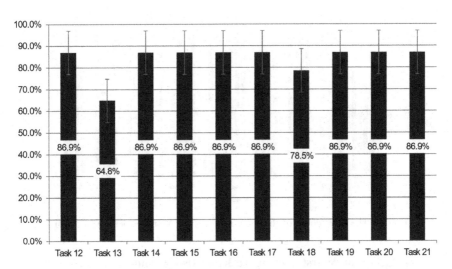

Fig. 3. SUM values for the one-handed tasks for Yemeksepeti and Banabi applications with error bars.

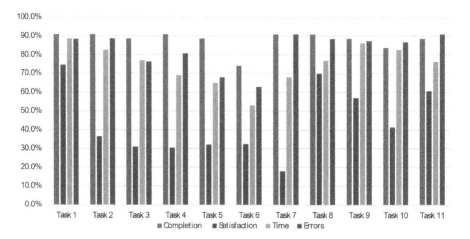

Fig. 4. The breakdown of four measures for Getir and GetirYemek, which are the main components of SUM. Higher percentages for the errors column denote better usability scores.

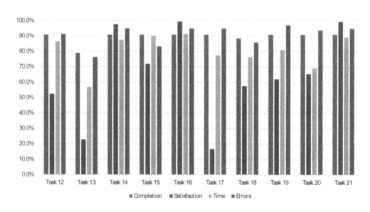

Fig. 5. The breakdown of the four measures for YemekSepeti and Banabi.

4.2   Satisfaction on Worst Scoring Tasks by User Groups

See Fig. 6.

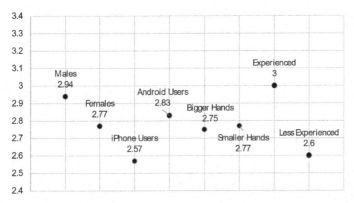

Fig. 6. Task 7 (GetirYemek) and Task 17 (YemekSepeti), during which participants were asked to touch the icons on the top left of both applications' home screen, were the greatest negative contributors of their respective SUM due to the lowest points of satisfaction, although all participants completed them rapidly. The figure shows the average satisfaction rates of various groups of participants on a 5-point Likert scale for these two tasks focused on ergonomics. "Experienced" participants were defined as those above the median of 4.2 years of phablet usage (n = 9), while the participants with "bigger hands" were categorized as those above the median of 4.2 cm in average hand measures on three dimensions (n = 9).

4.3 Errors and Task-Time on Worst Scoring Tasks by User Groups

See Figs. 7, 8, 9 and 10.

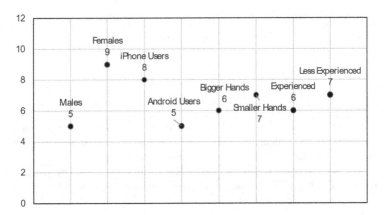

Fig. 7. Task 6 (GetirYemek), during which participants were asked to find and touch the application's Help section, was the greatest negative contributor of GetirYemek's SUM due to higher number of errors, longer task-times and a lower rate of completion (%77.8). The figure shows the total number of errors committed by various groups of participants on this task, which was focused on findability and discoverability. As the figures are total number of errors, not the average, it is important to note again that our sample included 7 iPhone users and 11 Android users. Other groups shown in the figure, though, were formed with equal number of users on two sides.

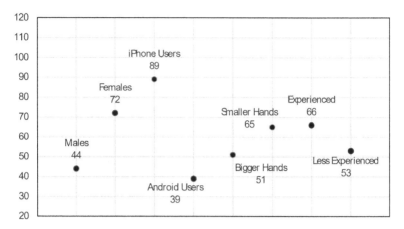

Fig. 8. Average task-time during Task 6 (GetirYemek) by various groups in the test.

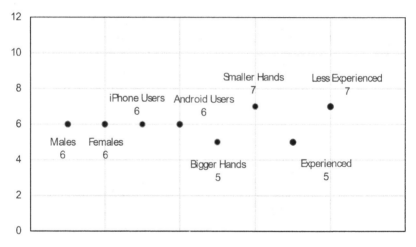

Fig. 9. Task 13 (Yemeksepeti), during which participants were asked to find and add a product to the basket by browsing –without using the search box, was the greatest negative contributor of the application's SUM due to higher number of errors, longer task-times and a lower rate of completion (%83.4). The figure shows the total number of errors committed by various groups of participants on this task, which was focused on findability and discoverability.

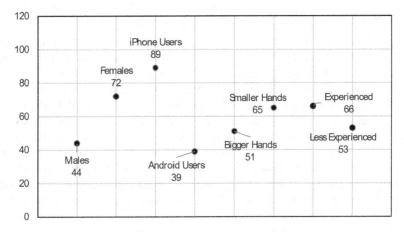

Fig. 10. Average task-time during Task 13 (Yemeksepeti) by various groups in the test.

5 Discussion

The task-specific results are discussed in the comparative context of the four applications' designs, which are not wholly dissimilar, within the framework of ergonomics, findability, discoverability and use of conventions (Fig. 11).

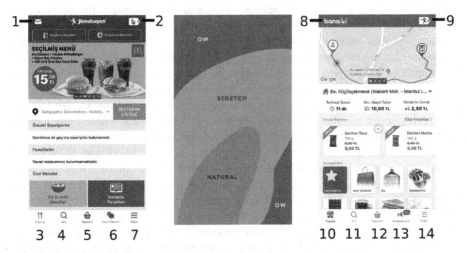

Fig. 11. Home screens of restaurant food delivery application Yemeksepeti (L) and its sister Banabi, a grocery delivery application (R). The interaction areas surrounding the main feed - numbered by the authors- will be explained in the discussion. At the center, the "Thumb Zone" for 5.5-inch screens as of iPhone 7 is seen, according to Hurff [18], whose illustration was based on Hoober's research [4].

5.1   Ergonomics

A few tasks that were included to test the ergonomics in one-handed phablet application use included those that required the user to touch the areas numbered 1, 2 and 7 above, which all fell on uncomfortable-to reach thumb zones cited in earlier research. As the fact that the greatest negative contributors of GetirYemek's and Yemeksepeti's SUM scores were Task 7 and Task 17 showed, the top left (numbered 1) of the screen indeed brought about a significant usability challenge in the one-handed use of a phablet. All participants were able to complete these tasks in a relatively short amount of time, but their significantly lower rates of satisfaction due to their over-stretching of hands and fingers brought down the SUM scores. In the post-test interview, five participants (User 1, 4, 7, 9, 15) directly mentioned these tasks as the most challenging ones in the test. "I have to bend the phone in my hand to touch there," User 7 said, while User 15 admitted that she "could have dropped the phone as 'strong finger muscles' are needed to reach there" while using the phablet with one hand.

Most users (n = 10) also voiced discomfort during various tasks while reaching other areas of the screen. Following 1, the most problematic of the numbered areas according to SUM scores and user feedback were, respectively, 7/14 (bottom right), 2/9 (top right), 3/10 (top left) and 6/13. Yemeksepeti and Banabi use a hamburger menu on 7/14, labelled "Other", while they reserve 2/9 for switching between two applications, and 6/13 for "Live Change" with a dialogue icon. In the Getir/GetirYemek ecosystem, 7/14 is a section for announcements with a gift box icon, 2/9 is for the basket and 6/13 is the profile menu with the icon of a person. For all four applications, 3/10 functions as a shortcut back to the home screen/main feed. Considering these functionalities, the observed ergonomics challenges seemed particularly problematic for one-handed usability of all four applications on 3/10, because this area was more frequently used.

Although most other challenging areas on Yemeksepeti/Banabi are of secondary importance for the user function-wide, Getir/GetirYemek pushes a key function to an ergonomically challenging part of the phablet screen; the top right for the basket button. Task 4 and 11 instructed the users to find and touch the basket on these two applications. Only User 2 totally failed to complete this task, but many other participants experienced significant difficulty. "I don't look at a place where I can't reach easily," User 7 explained after finally finding and touching the basket.

Another significant ergonomics challenge that affected SUM and SUS scores negatively according to the user interviews was the "back" functionality that was observed during most of the tasks (n = 13). All four applications enable the user to go back to the previous screen by either touching the Home buttons on the bottom right or the Back icon on the top left of the screen, which are both not the easiest areas to reach on a phablet. Some users ranked Getir/Getiryemek lower in this regard, pointing that even the Back button on the top left is not available in these two applications in the first phase of a product search. Target size was also mentioned as a problem in this regard as

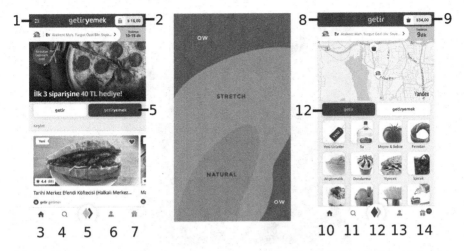

Fig. 12. Home screens of restaurant food delivery application GetirYemek (L) and its sister Getir, a grocery delivery application (R) with Hurff's "Thumb Zone" in the middle.

User 15 observed that "their Back button is too small for my thumb." And this button only appears when a restaurant is selected and not on the search screen, which can be put forward as another usability problem that led to the lower scores for these two applications compared to their competition.

A feature that diverges the two application ecosystems (Yemeksepeti/Banabi vs. GetirYemek/Getir) also has a link to ergonomics of the back function. On Yemeksepeti, a "Joker" card was given to present a flash discount opportunity to the user by occasionally popping up full screen, especially after searching a product. "I always check for the Joker first, as they generally gift me a big discount especially after 2 p.m. everyday," User 14 observed. However, although some users like him welcome this intrusive feature, the only way to close this pop-up is to touch the Back button on the top left of the screen, which brings about another ergonomics challenge in the user journey. Apart from its benefits in other areas, this challenge on the use of Joker feature negatively contributed to lower usability scores in both SUM and SUS for Yemeksepeti, as our post-test interviews confirmed.

Issues related with affordance, which may solve some ergonomics problems in application usage, were also observed as a negative factor. None of the participants were aware of Yemeksepeti's feature of swiping left for the "back" function or iOS/Android feature that pulls down the screen for easier access to the top or the ability to squeeze the virtual keyboard toward the side of the phablet. Furthermore, all participants said that they do not use any accessories, like "rings," for hold and grip of the phablet to ease one-handed use (Figs. 13 and 14).

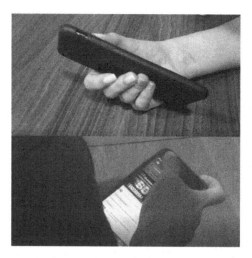

Fig. 13. Two ways to touch the top left of the screen during one-hand phablet usage: While performing the action on Getir, User 15 said she had to support her hand with the desk "otherwise the phone will fall" (top). User 01 moved the device in his hand with a quick jab to reach the letter icon on Yemeksepeti (below the first photo).

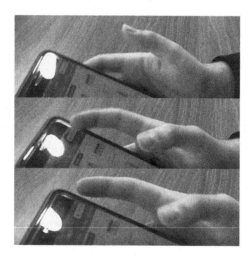

Fig. 14. A peculiar way to touch the top right corner with one-hand on a phablet. User 10 is seen in this screenshot while touching the basket icon of Getir with his index finger. He was the only participant who used an index finger during the test. All the others always used their thumbs.

5.2   Findability

The tasks that were focused on the findability dimension included those that the user was asked to find a certain product through search or browsing, and also to find certain information or functionalities within the applications, like the About section or the Live

Help service. Most users (n = 10) pointed to Getir/GetirYemek as the most challenging ecosystem in finding a product or function, particularly the basket. Four of these users specifically mentioned the difficulty they experienced while trying to find a product on these two applications without using the search box. Users complained that Getir-Yemek lacks some features of Yemeksepeti that ease navigation, like more prominent categories and filters. "I have to do too many scrolls to find a medium-size pizza because the sliding categories appears too late. It is especially bad when you use a heavier device as phablet for a long time with one hand," User 14 said while thinking aloud during the test. "I could never have found the exact food that I looked for by browsing. So, I had to go for another one that was a close match," User 3 elaborated.

Although it ranked higher than browsing, the search function on GetirYemek, too, received several negative comments from the users. As typing a virtual keyboard on a phablet with one hand is even harder than scrolling a relatively long time, this negative feedback on an efficient search functionality can be regarded as significant. "I'm trying to find a pizza with kavurma meat. But when I type it, GetirYemek brings me restaurants that sell pide, not kavurma pizza. It's awful because I had to type that long phrase on the search box with one hand," User 18 explained.

Shortcomings in search functionality, like failing to bring a listed product or restaurant in the results feed, were frequently cited by users during testing GetirYemek. Yemeksepeti and Banabi, on the other hand, were cited for problems of findability by two users who complained that the two applications' navigational features, such as categories, did not work as efficiently as their search boxes. Still, it should be noted that -regardless of the application- users voiced their discomfort in the use of the virtual keyboard, particularly while typing the letters on the left. As most users in Turkey have QWERTY keyboards, whose letters were distributed on the keyboard for faster typing with two hands in English words, they face a constant challenge especially with many frequently-used letters like A and E in Turkish while on typing on phablet screen with one hand. "I have to flex my hand muscles to reach to the left of the keyboard," User 4 said while searching a product on Yemeksepeti.

The participants voiced their expectations that the search boxes should do more to satisfy the users particularly in the one-handed usage of a phablet. For instance, while trying to find the button to switch from Getir to GetirYemek, User 13 initially tried to type "Getir" in the search box of the latter application. "Oh, it didn't work," he then said in disappointment, before continuing his search and finding the switch button in the end. Similarly, two users typed "About" to Yemeksepeti's search box after initially finding to locate this section by browsing. They also failed as all four applications provide only product and vendor based results, not those based on in-app information or functions.

5.3   Discoverability

Beside the Joker feature of Yemeksepeti that was discussed earlier, the four applications provide the users with opportunities of discoverability in their journeys. Sliders for recommended products/menus are used by all of them. The most frequently-used and widely-adopted of these features on Yemeksepeti was the curated food lists, like "Fit and Light Menus." When asked to find a certain product on Yemeksepeti without using the search box, User 6 said: "I don't know where to go now. Perhaps I can browse the Campus Discounts [a curated section with offers for students]. I would pick a high-rate restaurant there or find a place I know. Then I would check their menus and try to find that food there."

Another divergent element between Yemeksepeti and GetirYemek is their particular approach in content organization that also impacts their discoverability perspective. Even though User 10 said that "the best thing to do here is to present both product photos and textual information," the applications chose between one of the two approaches, considering the limited space on the screen and the additional burden of scrolling with a single hand. While Yemeksepeti uses substantially more text both on its home feed and results lists, GetirYemek prefers more images similar to the dashboard-style results and galleries in both ecosystems' grocery applications (Banabi and Getir). "It's so good that GetirYemek has so many photos. Sometimes I don't see them on Yemeksepeti," User 7 said. Similarly, User 6 stressed the benefits of "ease thanks to photos that do not require reading of anything" and admitted that she thought of buying a hamburger instead, as she discovered it thanks to the photo-based recommendation while browsing to find a pizza. Only one user (User 15) outspokenly said that she prefers text-based interfaces because she "reads books everyday and got more used to text than photos."

However, the application-level SUM and SUS scores do not support the participants' task-level verbal feedbacks in this area. Although they were vocally welcoming the GetirYemek's more image-oriented user experience, Yemeksepeti's text-oriented style received better overall scores. This divergence can be observed even in the design of the tab bar. Only Yemeksepeti and Banabi's tabs include textual labels below each icon, which received appraisal from 12 participants. The textual labelling of tabs may not be a key feature for the users who are familiar with the general heuristics in iconography, but it is helpful for beginners as the test showed. "I know that the icon of dialogue bubbles may indicate but Yemeksepeti's decision to also write 'Live Help' below that icon can really help users like my mom," User 15 said.

While users generally complained of "too many options," they hailed navigational elements such as horizontally sliding category tabs of GetirYemek/Getir.

5.4   Use of Conventions

The Yemeksepeti/Banabi duo sticks to a more conventional approach to content organization and heuristics compared to its competition. While performing Task 4 (check the basket on Getir/GetirYemek), User 12 linked the ergonomics challenge with an example in this regard. She explained: "The basket on Getir and GetirYemek appears on the top right of the screen only after I add something to the basket. Usually it should have been on the tabs section below, like Yemeksepeti has. And its icon is also not the conventional basket, but a figure that looks like a lock. Why lock? So irrelevant."

The same functionality is presented as two buttons with texts that prominently read "Getir" and "GetirYemek" side by side in the center of the home screen as well as a rhombus icon in the middle of the tab bar. Both options let the user switch between the two applications. 6 users said that they were used to find the basket in the middle of the tab bar, as in Yemeksepeti and Banabi, and GetirYemek/Getir's choices confused them.

This confusion stemmed not only from the location of the basket and the switch buttons, but also GetirYemek/Getir's unconventional selection of icons. Beside the problem with the basket icon (on top right) voiced by participants like User 12, several heuristics-related usability problems were observed on the tab, which is traditionally used for the most important features of any application. Alongside the rhombuses, which are "totally unknown" for a first time user like User 9, the Getir/GetirYemek's tab icons numbered as 6/13 and 7/14 as seen on Fig. 12 were criticized by most users (n = 10) for failing to address their actual functionality. "They put a gift box figure for a menu that contains a section called "Announcements" and they put a human figure on for a menu that contains sections like "Help". It's wrong", User 18 said. 6 of the participants stressed that an "appealing" icon like a gift box in a relatively harder location to reach in one-handed use (bottom right) is particularly problematic.

The switch buttons between Yemeksepeti and Banabi are located on the top right and consist of the logo of each application in an interchanging way (shown with the numbers 2 and 9 in the figure above). "They are easy to find," User 15 said, "but hard to touch and press. I can't see where I am touching." The difficulty of access is obviously linked to the location, but post-test interviews showed that the uttered ease at finding them is more linked to Banabi's success in brand awareness than broader heuristics of its digital product. While Getir and Getiryemek's text-based logos bring them an advantage in this regard, it can be argued that Banabi compensates it through marketing campaigns and a clever iconography, as can be seen in the comments of the users in post-test interviews:

User 8: Banabi's logo had sticked to my memory after seeing so many pink motorcycles driven by their couriers all over Istanbul.

User 14: I had never used Banabi, but I know its logo, so I found the switch function.

User 16: I haven't seen the Banabi logo before. I don't know it, at least consciously.
But the image on the logo seemed like the gesture of a customer who tries to call the waiter with one hand raised, as if she is calling him "I want a..." [In Turkish, the word "Banabi" or lexically "Bana bir..." means "I want a..."]

Some other choices in the design of the interface of the applications were also linked to the brands' image in the mind of many users. User 4 defended that Getir "hides its Help section inside an obscure menu because it does not have that much confidence in its customer support." User 18, on the other hand, said the fact that Yemeksepeti/Banabi featured its Live Help on its home screen, making it even more prominent by supporting the icon with a text label below it, "is indicative of the company's confidence in itself and its services." It should also be noted that these user statements were made not after a structured interview question specific to this subject, but during think-aloud amid the execution of all tasks.

We also observed that the participants who had used one application even once, carried the prior knowledge to its sister application. For instance, those who had used Getir, but not GetirYemek in the past, said that it was easier for them to find the unconventional location of the basket.

The applications broke away from conventional design in two more areas that task-level scores and observations concluded as challenging for usability with one-hand. GetirYemek and Getir have a white bar near the top of the home screen to enter the delivery address but 9 users confused it with a search box, which is a key feature especially in single-handed use. Yemeksepeti's preference in the use of an "envelope" icon on the top-left also led to lower satisfaction rates, more errors and longer task-times. Before checking the content presented after touching this icon, User 4 and User 15 both predicted that it may enable communication between Yemeksepeti and the user like the Live Help function. "It's hard to reach there anyway and when I managed to do it, I saw that there are useless notifications like 'You have earned a badge' or 'You have won a 5% discount', User 4 explained. According to User 11, this disappointment is due to Yemeksepeti's rarely made choice of ditching the conventions in heuristics. "Normally, a bell icon is used for such notifications. I don't know why Yemeksepeti chose an envelope, which makes me think of messaging," he said. Yemeksepeti's use of a hamburger menu for the icon on its home page's top left corner was also found bizarre by a few users (n = 3). "That three lines [hamburger] are usually used for menus like profile, etc. But Yemeksepeti uses it as a link to another kind of content. I've never seen such a usage before," User 18 explained.

On the other hand, we did not spot any meaningful correlation between any in-group feature of a user and his/her scores and perceptions of usability in any of the tasks or applications that were tested. Further study with a larger sample is needed to make a more enlightening assessment in this area.

6   Conclusion

The ongoing and enduring adoption of phablets continues to bring new challenges in mobile application development to improve usability on ever-enlarging screens. We believe that our study provided insights into the strengths and weaknesses of four leading delivery applications in Turkey in the context of user experience, particularly when they are used with a single hand. 14 of the 18 participants said that they can prefer to use all four applications to make an order with one hand, despite the usability problems that are reflected both in the task observation and in the SUM/SUS scores. Despite their successes on many areas, there is some room to improve the one-handed usability of these applications.

According to Gould et al. [19], three principles can be recommended to improve a system's usability: 1. Focus on users and their tasks. 2. Observe, measure, and analyze their performance with the system. 3. Design iteratively. Considering the qualitative and quantitative findings in this research, the following recommendations to improve the usability of the four applications, as well as other applications that may sport identical or highly similar features, were made:

- Providing easy-to-reach targets on the screen: All corners of the screen, and particularly the top left corner, should be used cautiously and solely for infrequently used functions. Frequently used functions like browsing back or returning to home screen should be placed on easier locations closer to the center and right. 10 users recommended to move key elements out of the top of the screen, two suggesting to create a vertical tab bar on the right. Alternatively, users should be onboarded in a more efficient way to teach them gestures for such features, including swipes. Left-handed users should also be given an option to adjust the interface as per their preference.
- Search: Users expect to see a more efficient in-app search engine and easily accessed search function, particularly when they find it harder to type with one hand. Through search, they should be able to access to all content and services of the mobile application, and not only the products. A more balanced approach in text or photo-oriented interfaces can be helpful.
- Browsing: Horizontally sliding category tabs can be complemented with accordion menus to summarize the content on the first screen, in order the avoid the feeling of being overwhelmed by too much information. Such an approach may also solve the widely voiced usability problem of long scrolling.
- Standards and conventions: Although an industry's dominant actor can also be a trendsetter in certain areas, an over-assertive approach in this regard may backfire in usability. Considering the additional burden of one-handed use on phablets, mobile applications should stick to the common sense in heuristics and take the conventional way, if it is not necessary to act otherwise.

This study was limited to four Turkish mobile applications, sampling university students in Istanbul. Further research can compare our results with the two-handed usage of the same applications, focus on new types of applications, or widen the sample toward other groups as seniors or left-handed people.

References

1. Fraulini, N.W., Dewar, A.R., Claypoole, V.L.: Individual differences and phablet purchase intent: a preliminary study. In: Proceedings of the Human Factors and Ergonomics Society Annual Meeting, vol. 59, no. 1, pp. 897–901. SAGE Publications, Los Angeles (2015)
2. Oh, W.: Smartphone sales forecast by type: phablets and superphones: 2003 to 2022. https://www.strategyanalytics.com/access-services/devices/mobile-phones/smartphone/smartphones/market-data/report-detail/smartphone-sales-forecast-by-type-phablets-and-superphones-2003-to-2022-UPDATED#.WXf7IHxPqUk. Accessed 27 Jan 2020
3. Karlson, A.K., Bederson, B.B., Contreras-Vidal, J.: Understanding single-handed mobile device interaction. In: Handbook of Research on User Interface Design and Evaluation for Mobile Technology, vol 1, pp. 86–101 (2006)
4. Hoober, S.: How do users really hold mobile devices? https://www.uxmatters.com/mt/archives/2013/02/how-do-users-really-hold-mobile-devices.php. Accessed 27 Jan 2020
5. Dong, L., Watters, C., Duffy, J.: Comparing two one-handed access methods on a PDA. In: Proceedings of the 7th International Conference on Human Computer Interaction with Mobile Devices & Services (2005)

6. Karlson, A.K., Bederson, B.B., SanGiovanni, J.: AppLens and launchTile: two designs for one-handed thumb use on small devices. In: Proceedings of the SIGCHI Conference on Human Factors in Computing Systems (2005)
7. Lee, S., Kyung, G., Lee, J., Moon, S.K., Park, K.J.: Grasp and index finger reach zone during one-handed smartphone rear interaction: effects of task type, phone width and hand length. Ergonomics **59**(11), 1462–1472 (2016)
8. Digital 2019 Q4 global digital statshot, we are social. https://wearesocial.com/blog/2019/10/the-global-state-of-digital-in-october-2019. Accessed 27 Jan 2020
9. Namli, C.: Mobil uygulama kullanılabilirliğinin değerlendirilmesi. Master's thesis, Istanbul Technical University (2010)
10. Kaya, Y., Çetin, M.K., Yildirim, S.O.: Lokasyon Tabanlı Mobil Kampus Uygulaması ve Kullanılabilirlik Değerlendirmesi. In: Ulusal Yazılım Mühendisliği Sempozyumu UYMS (2014)
11. Demir, H., Arslan, E.T.: Mobil sağlık uygulamalarının hastanelerde kullanılabilirliği, hastane yöneticileri üzerine bir araştırma. KMÜ Sosyal ve Ekonomik Araştırmalar Dergisi **19**(33), 71–83 (2017)
12. Aşçı, S., Rızvanoğlu, K.: Left vs. right-handed UX: a comparative user study on a mobile application with left and right-handed users. In: Marcus, A. (ed.) DUXU 2014. LNCS, vol. 8518, pp. 173–183. Springer, Cham (2014). https://doi.org/10.1007/978-3-319-07626-3_16
13. Lomas, N.: Glovo exits the Middle East and drops two LatAm markets in latest food delivery crunch. TechCrunch. https://techcrunch.com/2020/01/21/glovo-exits-the-middle-east-and-drops-two-latam-markets-in-latest-food-delivery-crunch/. Accessed 27 Jan 2020
14. Ulukan, G.: 2019'da 3,2 milyon üye kazanan Yemeksepeti'nin toplam kullanıcı sayısı 14 milyona ulaştı. Webrazzi. https://webrazzi.com/2019/12/30/yemeksepeti-kullanici-sayisi/. Accessed 27 Jan 2020
15. Ulukan, G.: Getir ve Banabi rekabetinde taraflardan gelen açıklamalar, gelecek tahminlerini şekillendiriyor. https://webrazzi.com/2019/12/24/getir-ve-banabi-rekabetinde-taraflardan-gelen-aciklamalar-gelecek-tahminlerini-sekillendiriyor/. Accessed 27 Jan 2020
16. Sauro, J., Kindlund, E.: A method to standardize usability metrics into a single score. In: CHI Conference, pp. 401–410 (2005)
17. Brooke, J.: SUS-a quick and dirty usability scale. Usability Eval. Ind. **189**(194), 4–7 (1996)
18. Hurff, S.: How to design for thumbs in the era of huge screens. https://www.scotthurff.com/posts/how-to-design-for-thumbs-in-the-era-of-huge-screens/. Accessed 27 Jan 2020
19. Gould, J.D., Boies, S.J., Levy, S., Richards, J.T., Schoonard, J.: The 1984 Olympic message system: a test of behavioral principles of system design. In: Preece, J., Keller, L. (eds.) Human-Computer Interaction (Readings), pp. 260–283. Prentice Hall International Ltd., Hemel Hempstead (1990)

A Study of Middle-Aged User's Acceptance in Mandarin Chinese Font Display on Smart Phones

Shih-Chieh Liao[1,2]([⊠]), Chih-Cheng Sun[2], Shu-Hsuan Feng[2], and Chi-Hin Choy[2]

[1] Department of Industrial Design, National Cheng-Kung University, Tainan 70101, Taiwan (R.O.C.)
alfietw@stust.edu.tw
[2] Southern Taiwan University of Science and Technology, Tainan 71005, Taiwan (R.O.C.)

Abstract. Population aging has been a severe problem in recent years, there is over 14% of the elderly citizens in Taiwan [1], in addition, the rising number of smart devices use, the middle-aged to elderly smartphone user base has grown significantly and taken a considerable portion of the user demographic, occupying 53.3% of the total smartphone user population [2]. Although the screen sizes on modern smartphones have become larger over the years, making the average size of phones screen over 5 inches, many users still find them suffering from discomfort in reading text on the screen, especially reading Mandarin Chinese due to its calligraphy, plus the increasing number of people suffer from eye diseases such as myopia and presbyopia, making it a significant problem for future user interface designer to solve.

Our study is trying to find out the optimal font size and design in the Mandarin Chinese user interface for middle-aged and elderly users, this research may be helpful for future designers to design an interface catering to those who found the standard user interface hard to read.

Keywords: Font · Chinese · User interface · Smartphones

1 Introduction

Population aging has been a serious problem in Taiwan, with over 14% of the elderly citizens (Over 65 years old), the country has already surpassed the average of 8% of the world. With the increasing number of smart devices used and the popularity of mobile internet service, the middle-aged to elderly citizens are beginning to adopt the usage of smart devices, making this demographic of smartphone user base grow significantly and take a considerable portion of the whole user demographic, occupying 53.3% of the total smartphone user population.

With the advance of technology and the change in user habits, the average screen size of the smartphones have become larger over the years, making the average screen size over 5 inches now, but instead of displaying larger font and icons, most smartphones choose to show more delicate and small fonts and icons for the aesthetics. This

© Springer Nature Switzerland AG 2020
A. Marcus and E. Rosenzweig (Eds.): HCII 2020, LNCS 12201, pp. 313–321, 2020.
https://doi.org/10.1007/978-3-030-49760-6_22

design choice makes a large number of middle-aged and elderly users, especially those who are suffering from myopia and presbyopia, difficult to read the words display on-screen efficiently and effortlessly. With the penetration rate of the smartphone in the elderly demographic over 68%, this may cause a serious problem in user experience.

To compensate for this issue, some phone companies provide a new breed of phones specially made for middle-aged to elderly users named Phones for Seniors. These unusual phones feature old-school design, large screen, and large physical buttons, forgoing touch screen, smart operating system, and more complex function-alities to ease those users who are less familiar with technology into having a phone. Due to their simplified functions compared to standard smartphones, they limit the ways users can connect with others, and the name "Phones for Senior" may even be beneath the user's dignity.

Our study aims to find out the optimal font size and design direction in Traditional Chinese within middle-aged and elderly Mandarin Chinese users, sorting out the design guidelines for user interface designers to create an interface catering to those who found the standard user interface difficulty to read efficiently and yet still maintain the whole aesthetics of the interface itself.

2 Backgrounds

2.1 Population Aging

Due to increasing life expenses and change in social expectation, fertility rate in Taiwan has declined drastically in recent years. On the other hand, advanced medical technology and national health insurance system extended average life expectancy rapidly, Taiwan has an accelerated rate of aging more than twice of European countries and the United States, equal to Japan, making it one of the fastest-aging societies in the

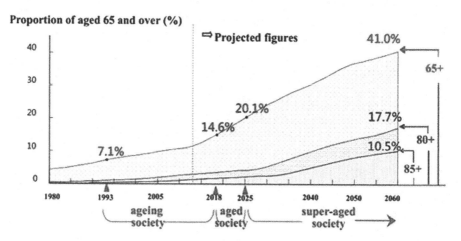

Fig. 1. Proportion of aged 65 and over (%) in Taiwan. Source: Population projections for Republic of China (Taiwan): 2014–2060.

world [3]. According to World Health Organization, with the currently over 14% of elderly citizens in Taiwan, it is regarded as an "aged society", and it is estimated that by 2025 it will become a "super-aged society", which means that 20% of the population are above the age of 65 (Fig. 1).

2.2 Increasing Smartphone Usage

According to a study performed by Institute of Information Industry of Taiwan, over 80% of the citizens use their smartphones for over 2 h a day, 51.5% use 2 to 5 h and 28.1% have an average daily smartphone use time of 5 h and up [4]. Entertainment related usage has increased drastically compared to 2014, more people are using their smartphone to watch videos, listen to music, play games and browse social media, it has been an inseparable part of citizens daily life.

Users in different age group enjoys different activities on their smartphones, users aged between 25 to 44 mostly use their smartphones on social media and messenger programs, users aged 45 and up spent most of their time on the phone browsing news and take photos.

2.3 Smartphone Related Eye Disease

Ophthalmologists also address that excessive smartphone use may harm users in three different ways. First is viewing the screen in short distance for a long time, which may cause presbyopia. Second is damage from bright light, which is the most serious danger, exposing under bright monitor may cause cataract and macular degeneration, damaging users' eye permanently. Damage from blue light is the most significant one due to the short wave length and high power in blue light. The last one is dry eye disease, researches have found that use of smartphones is a risk factor in pediatric dry eye disease. A study performed by Moon (2016) noted that smartphone use in children was strongly associated with pediatric dry eye disease [5].

Presbyopia is not caused by the use of smartphones, but it seriously affect the user's experience with it. Presbyopia a normal part of aging and people over age of 35 are prone to suffer from this disease and has affected over 25% of the global population [6]. This eye disease associate with aging of the eye that hinders ability to focus clearly on close objects, which may cause difficulty when using a smartphone.

2.4 Screen Sizes and Readability

Many users nowadays utilize multiple devices at once to increase their productivity, except from smartphones, personal computer is the most commonly used device with the usage rate of 62.1%, others are 55% of laptop computers, 44.8% of tablet computers and 26.7% of wearable devices [4]. These devices all have varied screen sizes even in the same category, and their user interface design and font sizes can vary vastly as well. Viewing on smartphones, personal computers and tablet computers all have their individual preferred viewing distance, according to study conducted by Yuliya Bababekova (2011), the average viewing distance for text messages and internet viewing on smartphones was 36.2 cm and 32.2 cm respectively. Otherwise preferred viewing distance for personal computer is between 50 and 100 cm, and for tablet computer is between 33 and 40 cm, which may require different user interface design and optimized font sizes (Fig. 2).

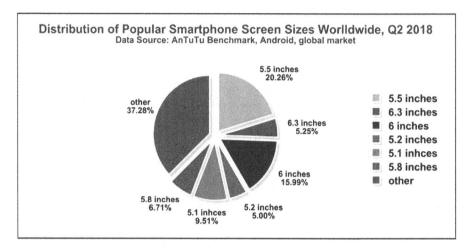

Fig. 2. Distribution of popular smartphone screen sizes worldwide. Source: AnTuTu benchmark

2.5   Phones for Seniors

Smartphones feature more functions and are more complex than traditional feature phones, which may hinder the usability for users unfamiliar with technology. As the demand increased, some companies start producing feature phones with larger physical buttons and screen, also running older operating system with large fonts and simplified user interfaces. Because of the simplified and out-dated operating system, most phones for seniors don't have the ability of downloading applications or browsing internet pages, in addition to the name of these kind of phones, may make the elderly users feel they are beneath their dignity (Fig. 3).

Fig. 3. Phones for senior feature large size font and buttons for accessibility. Source: iNO

2.6   Difference Between Mandarin Chinese and English

Mandarin Chinese and English are two very different languages, especially in their style of writing. English features 26 different characters, by arranging these characters, a word is form. Otherwise Mandarin Chinese features vastly different characters, some are fairly simple with a few strokes, other requires more than twenty strokes, making the average strokes to form a word 13. Also, while English words feature different numbers of characters, making some word short and other longer, Mandarin Chinese characters are mostly square shaped, displaying these two language on screen under the same user interface structure requires a lot of adjustment from the designers and developers (Fig. 4).

Fig. 4. Mandarin Chinese and English features vastly different characters. Source: LTL Mandarin School

3   Materials and Method

3.1   Experiment Method

In order to find out the optimal font size and design in the user interface for middle-aged and elderly users, the study combines two different research methods and is separated into two phases. In the first phase, we utilize a specially made program to find out the preferred way of displaying user interface for different aged users. This program shows the users three identical user interfaces in the same time with different font sizes, users need to pick their preferred one, and the program will display the next set of user interfaces according to their choice. After the first phase ends, there are focused group meetings held in order to discover more about the users choices and their experience about the font size difference in the user interface.

3.2   Participants

In the experiment, the participants will be separated into three different age groups. Adolescence with 18 to 40 years old, middle-aged with 41 to 65 years old and elderly with 65 years old an up. Gender is not restricted. Every participant must have over three years of experience with a smartphone for the accuracy of the outcome. The reason for separate participants in these three specific groups is that presbyopia is usually found on people aged 40 and up, and those users have occupied over 53% of the smartphone user base.

In our experiment, we have a total of 17 participants finished the procedure. There are 7 adolescence participants, 4 male and 3 female; 8 middle-aged participants, 6 male and 2 female; and 2 elderly participants, both are male (Table 1).

Table 1. Age and gender distribution of the participants

Age group/gender	Adolescence	Middle-age	Elderly
Male	4	6	2
Female	3	2	0
Total	7	8	2

3.3 System Structure

The program used in this experiment is made with Unity Engine and is designed to find out the user's preferred font size. To achieve this goal and provide a broader view of user experience, the program contains 4 different scenarios for users to participate in. The 4 scenarios are based on commonly seen on-screen contents including home screen, settings menu, social media and entertainment application. All the demonstrate user interfaces are based on iOS system user interface. In any of the 4 different scenarios, there are two different parameters including font size and bold font, users are asked to choose their preferred way of displaying fonts. To insure the accuracy of the experiment, the experiment is conducted on a 13 in. screen, 3 of the demonstrate user interfaces will be displayed at once, each will be 5.5 in. large, which is the average size of smartphones screen, and the users are asked to maintain the average distance to screen of 36 cm. The font size will start with 28pt on the left, 32pt in the middle, and 36pt on the right. Also, the experiment is conducted in both English and Mandarin Chinese.

3.4 Materials

The demonstrated user interfaces are designed under Apple's iOS Human Interface Guidelines, and the typography of choice are San Francisco for English, Heite TC for Mandarin Chinese, both are designed by Apple and are the default font for iOS devices. There are 4 demonstrated user interfaces ranging from home screen, settings menu, social media pages to entertainment application, reminiscent of common smartphone usage (Fig. 5).

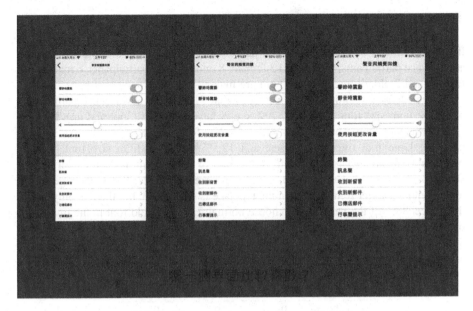

Fig. 5. A screenshot of experiment program

3.5   Procedures

The study is separated into two phases. The first phase is the experiment itself, participants are asked to interact with the test program in a controlled environment. The experiment is held at a lab set with monitoring gear such as camera and microphone to record the participants' action. After a simple introduction, the participants begin the first phase and start with Mandarin Chinese. The program will display 3 identical demonstrated user interface with different font size, small (28pt) on the left, medium (32pt) in between and large (36pt) on the right. Participants have to choose their preferred one in order to proceed. After the participant choose the first one, the next set of user interfaces will appear. The second set of user interfaces is the same to the first one, but the font sizes will be adjusted according to participants' previous choice and the difference between 3 user interfaces will be smaller. This procedure will be repeated 3 times with normal font and also 3 times with bold fonts. After that, participants will be moving to the next scenario. When all 4 scenarios are completed, participants are asked to complete the same experiment with English user interface to find out whether there is a difference between the language and text clarity in user interface.

After the first phase, we will have an interview with the participant to have a further understanding of their preferences in font size and typeface. The interview will be held in a controlled environment to prevent any other interferences. The interview will be focusing on two major subjects, how participants made their decision in the previous test, and how participants interact with their smartphones daily.

4 Results

In our experiment, we have a total of 17 participants finished the procedure. There are 7 adolescence participants, 4 male and 3 female; 8 middle-aged participants, 6 male and 2 female; and 2 elderly participants, both are male.

In the Mandarin Chinese part, we found that 71% of the adolescence participants prefer medium size font (29–35pt), 29% prefer large size font (36pt and up). Middle-aged participants however, mostly prefer large size font, with 87.5% of the participants choosing large font over other sizes, and 12.5% prefer medium size font. Elderly participants all prefer large size font. In this part of experiment, no participant choose small size font (smaller than 28pt) as their preferred font size. Participants generally tend to choose larger font size when the typeface is set to bold, but there is only minor difference. 88% of the participants choose normal font over bold font in the final stage of this experiment (Table 2).

Table 2. Experiment result of Mandarin Chinese part

Age group	Adolescence	Middle-age	Elderly
Small size	0	0	0
Medium size	5	1	0
Large size	2	7	2
Prefer bold	0	1	1
Prefer normal	7	7	1

Otherwise in the English part, 58% of the adolescence participants prefer medium size font (29–35pt), 28% prefer small size font (smaller than 28pt), 14% prefer large size (36pt and up). The result in middle-aged group is similar to the result of the Mandarin Chinese part, 75% prefer large size font, 25% prefer medium size font, no middle-aged participant prefer small size font. Elderly participants all prefer large size font. Participants have a better acceptance of bold fonts compare to Mandarin Chinese, but most participants still prefer normal fonts (Table 3).

Table 3. Experiment result of English part

Age group	Adolescence	Middle-age	Elderly
Small size	2	0	0
Medium size	4	2	0
Large size	1	6	2
Prefer bold	0	2	2
Prefer normal	7	6	0

After the experiment, we had interviews with all the participants to further understand their preference and why they choose those specific font size and typeface.

In the interview, 5 of the middle-aged participants addressed that due to they having both myopia and presbyopia, they need to take off their glasses or put the phone further away in order to have a clear view to the text on screen, larger font and larger screen may help them identify the text easier, thus while medium size font is still usable, they prefer larger size font. On the other hand, 3 adolescence users address that they prefer medium size or small size font only because of aesthetics reason. The 2 Elderly participants address that even with large fonts, sentences with too much word may still hinder their ability to read quickly. Most of the participants prefer normal fonts over bold fonts, an middle-aged participant address that bold fonts are bulkier, the space between the strokes in word is narrower, thus making it more difficult to see the character clearly, this problem is more prevalent in Mandarin Chinese due to it's more complex characters.

5   Conclusion

In our experiment, we found that medium size font which is between 29 and 35pt is mostly suitable for majority of general users while middle-aged users prefer larger size font. Users with eye diseases, especially presbyopia, tend to prefer larger size font because of the limited length between their device and eyes. Bold fonts should be used sparingly and preferably on larger texts due to their thicker strokes, which may hinder their clarity. We also found that the length of a sentence may also cause difference in reading efficiency, users are less likely to read the whole sentence if it is too long and tend to guess with a few keywords instead. Texts in smaller fonts may make the screen seem more clutter and difficult to read, which could lead to users skipping important messages in sentences, causing problem in the user experience.

This study still have a number of limitations and space of improvements. First of all, the sampling size is still too small to represent the majority of the different age groups of users. Secondly, there is only indirect connection between eye diseases and the trend of middle-aged users preferring larger fonts. Finally, users enjoys many different activities on their smartphones, in the limited scope of this study, the selected scenarios may not represent all the users' behaviors.

References

1. Ministry of interior statistics report, 2018 week 15. Ministry of Interior (2018)
2. Study of digital chance in civilian with cellphones. National Development Council (2018)
3. Lin, Y.-Y.: Aging in Taiwan: building a society for active aging and aging in place. Ph.D., Chin-Shan Huang (2015)
4. Activity research on 4G mobile lifestyle. Institute for Information Industry (2017)
5. Moon, J.H., Kim, K.W., Moon, N.J.: Smartphone use is a risk factor for pediatric dry eye disease according to region and age: a case control study. BMC Ophthalmol. 16 (2016). Article number: 188. https://doi.org/10.1186/s12886-016-0364-4
6. Reflected errors. National Eyes Institute (2019)

A Usability Study of a Brother Printer and Improvement with Ergonomic Recommendations

Linlang Shen[(✉)], Ziren Zhou, Xinran Su, Jing Wang,
and Marcelo M. Soares

School of Design, Hunan University, Changsha, People's Republic of China
763675601@qq.com, stevenzzr@hotmail.com,
396073998@qq.com, 237713424@qq.com, soaresmm@gmail.com

Abstract. The product usability is closely related to how users feel and experience when using a particular product to achieve some goals or functions. This study selects the Brother DCP 1618W All-in-One Printer as a research objective to test its usability and current problems which serve as reference for the coming improvements. Several methods, including Likert scale, checklist, think aloud protocols and task analysis, were adopted to conduct the test. With appropriate methodology, researchers measured the size of the machine, viewing angle of the display and other related data to find out the factors which influence the product usability. After analyzing these research results, designers redesigned the printer model with new structure and display according to ergonomics and brand gene. The advantages and disadvantages of methods applied on the study are concluded to improve the current researches.

Keywords: Ergonomics · Usability · Printer · Checklist · Questionnaire · Internet of things

1 Introduction

The printer is an instrument that can quickly and inexpensively printer and copy documents and images onto paper. It was developed in the 1960s and gradually replaced carbon paper copying technology, mimeograph and other copiers in the following 20 years. Its widespread use is one of the reasons why paperless offices that were pioneered in the early days of the digital revolution are still not possible.

Printers are widely used in business, education and government agencies. Many people have estimated that as more and more people use digital technology to transfer documents, the importance of printers as well as the use of paper for document transfer will reduce. However, there is no doubt that it is more acceptable to share files in the form of paper than in the digital form.

Under this circumstance, the usability of the printer is of great significance which can improve not only the efficiency but also the user experience. This study selects the Brother DCP 1618W All-in-One Printer (Fig. 1) as a research objective to test its usability and current problems which serve as reference for the coming improvements.

© Springer Nature Switzerland AG 2020
A. Marcus and E. Rosenzweig (Eds.): HCII 2020, LNCS 12201, pp. 322–334, 2020.
https://doi.org/10.1007/978-3-030-49760-6_23

Fig. 1. Brother DCP 1618W All-in-One Printer [1]

2 Current Problems

Despite of the fact that the printer has been developed for over 100 years, it still has many annoying problems and unfriend experience remained to be solved. For instance, when we command our printer to print a file, sometimes we have don't know whether the paper supply is low or not. If there are other printing tasks queuing before us, it won't tell whether another printer nearby is free or not.

According to general principles for interaction design by Jakob Nielsen, the system should always keep users informed about what is going on, through appropriate feedback within reasonable time [2]. While In many application scenarios, if the user realizes that he has to modify the documents after pushing the Start button and, he must to click the Cancel button as quickly as possible to avoid wasting too much paper and ink. Unfortunately, the computer has already sent more pages to the printer's buffer which makes the printer continue printing. But meanwhile, the application may tell the user that that task had been cancelled. In terms of the feedback, it is not direct and explicit enough to avoid confusion which caused a lot of maloperations and waste when coping material.

Error messages should be expressed in plain language (no codes), precisely indicate the problem, and constructively suggest a solution. If a taskbar icon on the display indicates a problem with a printer, clicking that icon should provide a mechanism to troubleshoot and rectify the problem. When it turns to this printer, users can do nothing if they are reminded that there is something wrong. Even though it is better if the system can be used and problems can be solved without documentation, it may be necessary to provide help and documentation. Any related information should be easy to search, listing concrete steps to be carried out.

Under some circumstances, users need to do a large number of operations which include many steps on the monitor. The application may become slow and unresponsive when performing a lot of data processing. So, it can't be more annoying for users to staring at the small black and white screen for a long time. It is critical and crucial to redesign the monitor on the printer and user interface if the current one is not satisfactory enough [3].

3   Field Study

3.1   Survey of the Field Study

In order to find out the usability of the current small and medium size printer, researchers conducted a survey in the form of a questionnaire, from April 21st, 2019 to June 2th, 2019. It was received 142 effective answers.

Questionnaire. From the total of 142 persons who take parte in the survey, 67 were male and 75 were female. When asked about how often people print by themselves, 10% of them answered that they usually print by themselves and 20% of them sometimes printed, while the rest of them rarely did that. Among the interviewees who had related experience, most of them printed in the printing shop or at school which accounts for 35.2% and 25.3% respectively. The rest people did that at home or in the office. Most users' printers do not have color screens and can see how many printing tasks in progress when printing. If the paper supply is not sufficient, over 80% users replied that they could receive a clear reminder.

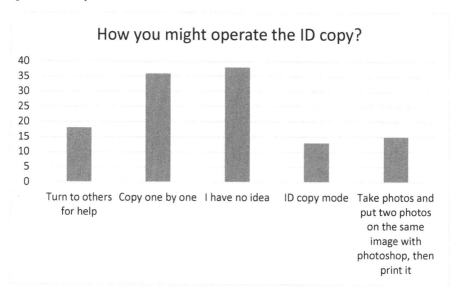

In terms of the ID copy, most users don't know the most efficient way which may waste a lot of time and resources.

According to the result of the questionnaire, most participants don't use often use printer by themselves. They tend to go to print shops, using public printers to print documents or copy paper for the sake of convenience and cost. Few participants chose to buy printers via official websites because of unfriendly price and poor user experience. In comparison to product design, people care more about the function and price, followed by post-sales service. In the consumer-grade market, many of printers are equipped with black and white screens and some of others don't have screens. Though most users can check how many printing tasks are in progress when using the printer, there is still no clear reminder of insufficient paper supply. Fortunately, a large number of participants reported that they could stop printing tasks in time after canceling the task which is a huge progress. Participants usually try to repair printers by themselves or turn to friends for help. When it comes to the features that users lay emphasis on, the traditional functions, which are printing, copying and scanning, matter most. Despite of the fact that more and more printers have the ID copy function, few users know it and most of them prefer to copy one by one which is a little time-consuming and inconvenient.

Likert Scale. The Likert scale is the most commonly used one of the scores plus total scales. These items of the same construct are scored by summation, and individual or individual items are meaningless. It was improved by the American social psychologist Likert in 1932 on the basis of the original total scale. The scale consists of a set of statements, each of which has five answers: "very agree", "agree", "not necessarily", "disagree", and "very disagree", respectively, as 5, 4, 3, 2, 1, the total score of each respondent's attitude is the sum of his scores on the answers to each question, this total score can indicate his attitude or his different status on this scale [4] (Fig. 2).

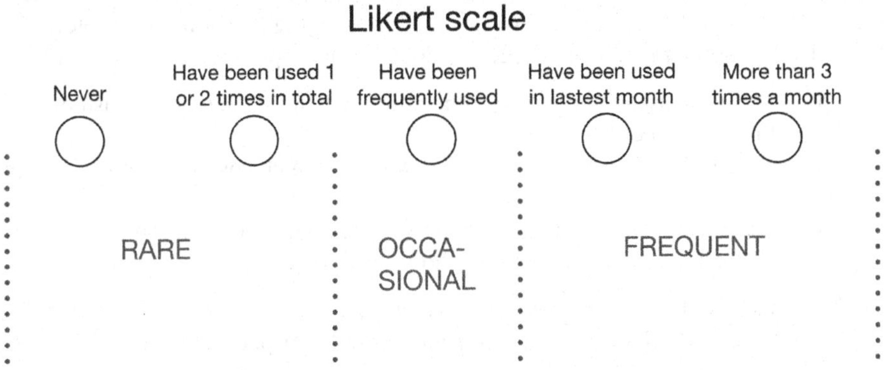

Likert scale

Fig. 2. Frequency definition

In this research, 5 different levels are offered to classify the frequency of using printers by themselves. If they used printers more than 3 times a month or had used them in the latest month, they will be defined as frequent users. It they have never or have used 1 or 2 times in total, they are rare users. The rest of them will be regarded as occasional users.

As a result, participant knew how to classify themselves in the most proper and scientific way instead of choosing subjectively.

Think Aloud Protocols. This method involves a participant speaking about what they are doing and thinking when using an interface. Participants may be asked to perform specific tasks with an interface, or they may simply be given the opportunity for free exploration. During the think aloud session the investigator will usually prompt the participant, in order to encourage him or her to make helpful verbalizations. These prompts may be of, for example, what are you thinking now? Why did you press that button, etc. [5].

Participants were asked what did they search for when operating specific steps and how did they fell when using the printer.

In this way, investigators got a clear view of the users' experience that they might fell a little experience when facing this machine at the first time and it took some time to be familiar with it.

3.2   Field Study on Usability

Two of the most significant functions of the printer is printing and copying which should be laid great emphasis on. The usability of these two functions contributes to user experience as well as user satisfaction. Besides, with the development of Wi-Fi and Bluetooth wireless protocols, electronic devices can frequently connect to and disconnect from each other. Internet of things and smart home connects everything smartly and makes everything into a unity, so the usability of Wi-Fi connection also plays an important role in improving the user experience.

Six users were invited to use the printer to finish some basic tasks which are printing, ID copy and Wi-Fi setting. One of them used printers frequently, two of them used printers at least once, and the other three users seldom used printers before the test. Our researchers used a camera (Canon 760D) to took pictures and record videos.

Step1: Users were asked to print a document which helps them to get accustomed to this machine and relieve their stress.

As a result, all of them were able to finish this task which cost them about 20 s on average.

Step2: Researchers assigned users to copy two sides of an ID card on one page of paper which can be called ID copy in short version.

The standard steps to finish the task are as follows:

Here are feedbacks to every step (user input) on the display screen (Fig. 3):

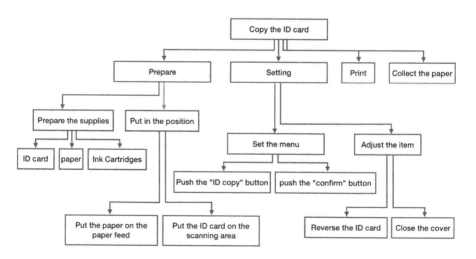

Fig. 3. Task and scenarios

1. Press the ID copy button——**"ID copy"**
2. Press OK button——**"put your ID card inside"**
3. Put the ID card on the scanning area and close the cover
4. Press the Start button——**"Turn the ID card over"**
5. Turn the ID card over, move its location and close the cover
6. Press the Start button——**"Copying"** (Fig. 4)

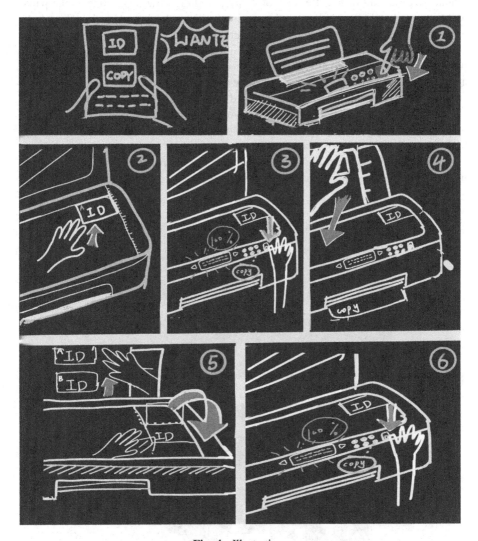

Fig. 4. Illustrations

If users operate as these steps and put the ID card on the proper scanning area, they will succeed in coping both sides of the ID card and making them be arranged vertically. In order to stimulate the real situation and test the usability of the printer without tutor, all users were not taught how to do it before the test so that they had to read the guidance on the body of the machine and rely on their instinct as well as previous experience.

Unfortunately, although most users learned the skill by trial and error and finished the task eventually, they made plenty of mistakes during the process. For instance, someone failed to scan the ID card before printing and got a blank paper from the outlet. For a lack of obvious feedback, they didn't know whether the printer had scanned the ID card or not. Besides, other users didn't know which side of the paper will be printed and failed to located the precise position when scanning the ID card. As a result, they let both sides of the ID card overlapped which wasted a piece of paper. In addition, one user who pressed the Start button in the first step, letting the printer perform the copy task directly, failed in the very beginning. The most common situation was that the majority of users did some unnecessary operations, they copied one side and printed it immediately, then copied another side to print it. Actually, they weren't aware of how the ID copy function works, or in other word, this function is not intelligible enough for novices to have command of it which seriously affects its usability.

Last but not least, the confirming and going back commands play an important role in the interaction system of the printer, while users were confused from time to time

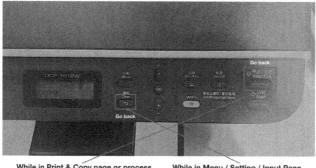

While in Print & Copy page or process   While in Menu / Setting / Input Page

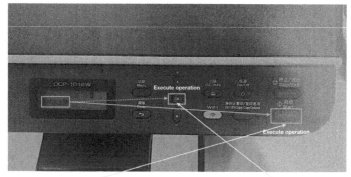

While in Print & Copy page or process   While in Menu / Setting / Input Page

Fig. 5. Images of the go back and execute operation in different pages

due to the poor console setting. For instance, users need to push stop/exit button to go back in print & copy page or process. While they are supposed to push clear button to go back in menu, setting and input page. Situations are similar when it comes to executing operations. Users have to push start button to execute orders in print & copy page or process. While they are supposed to push ok button to let printer work in menu, setting and input page (Fig. 5).

For the third step of the experiment, users were asked to connect the printer with Internet via Wi-Fi, making it possible to control the printer remotely with mobile phone. There is no denying that it's quite hard and tough to finish the Wi-Fi setting, because users had to use the direction key to choose numbers and alphabets which is extremely time-consuming. In the end, only one user succeeded in finishing the task and it took him over 10 min. If the experience of Wi-Fi setting couldn't be improved, the usability of the printer would remain poor.

For the fourth step of the experiment, researchers invited every user to talk about what they had thought and felt when operating the printer. Some users reported that there should have been evident feedback to remind them that the printer is working in case of potential danger. Others thought they couldn't finish tasks without hints from researchers.

For the last step of the experiment, users received a checklist to fulfill.

Q1. Could you finish these tasks finally?
Q2. Do you think it takes a lot of time to finish these tasks?
Q3. Are you satisfied with the product design of the printer?
Q4. Are you satisfied with operating feel of the printer?
Q5. Do you think there are too many interaction steps when operating the printer?
Q6. Do you think the feedback towards your operation is appropriate?
Q7. Do you think the user interface is comprehensible?
Q8. Do you hope that the printer will be able to remember your operation prefer-ence and customize the homepage for you?

The results are as follows.

	user1	user2	user3	user4	user5	user6
Q1	yes	yes	yes	no	yes	yes
Q2	yes	no	yes	yes	yes	no
Q3	yes	yes	no	yes	yes	yes
Q4	yes	yes	no	yes	yes	yes
Q5	yes	no	no	no	no	no
Q6	yes	yes	yes	no	no	yes
Q7	no	yes	no	no	yes	no
Q8	yes	yes	yes	no	yes	yes

Q1. Could you finish these tasks finally?
Five respondents answered positively and only one negatively.
Q2. Do you think it takes a lot of time to finish these tasks?
Four respondents answered positively and two negatively.

Q3. Are you satisfied with the product design of the printer?
Five respondents answered positively and only one negatively.
Q4. Are you satisfied with operating feel of the printer?
Five respondents answered positively and only one negatively.
Q5. Do you think there are too many interaction steps when operating the printer?
Five respondents answered negatively and only one positively.
Q6. Do you think the feedback towards your operation is appropriate?
Four respondents answered positively and two negatively.
Q7. Do you think the user interface is comprehensible?
Four respondents answered negatively and two positively.
Q8. Do you hope that the printer will be able to remember your operation?
Five respondents answered positively and only one negatively.

Comments. Though most users were novices, they were able to finish tasks finally. Some could finish tasks independently, others had to rely on our basic guidance to type. In terms of product design and operating feel, over 80% ($n = 6$) of users were content with them. Although most users could tolerate the interaction steps, some of them though the feedback was not timely enough. What's more, more than 60% users felt it hard and tough to understand the user interface due to the poor translation. An overwhelming number of users were open to the preference threshold which saves interaction steps. In conclusion, this printer is not so perfect that everyone will enjoy the user experience when operating it.

Actually, almost all users failed to copy the ID card perfectly in terms of layout. Some users who thought they were able to finish the task independently didn't make it on their own. It's common that users tend to overestimate their ability and achievement due to cognitive bias, so video recording is quite indispensable while testing users.

Meanwhile, it's obvious that some users were nervous when being tested. They were embarrassed and anxious when they had difficulty in finishing tasks. Therefore, it's of great significance for researchers to implement proper methods to relieve users' tension.

According to their feedbacks, the most representative problem is that participants couldn't finish the ID copy task in the right step for a lack of necessary instructions and clear feedback of the screen.

4 Ergonomics Problems

While it comes to the ergonomics of the printer, our researchers found three indispensable defects which will do harm to users in the long run.

1. Visualization
   When the user was operating the printer, she had to bend down the neck to watch the console since the visual angle of the display screen is limited. After keeping this posture for a long time, she would suffer cervical spondylosis. When the user was pressing the button, she had to press it hard due to the mechanical structure and

shape of the button. Besides, the fonts on the monitor are small and dim which makes it hard for users to watch them clearly. After watching for a long time, users's vision could be harmed. After pressing buttons regularly, users would suffer sore fingers (Fig. 6).

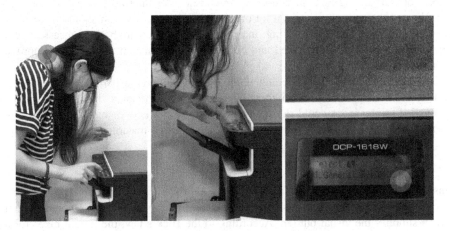

Fig. 6. Images of the postures and the monitor

Researchers measured the size and weight of the printer for product evaluation. The printer which weighs about 7.2 kg is too heavy to move normally. Users may feel confused that which part of the printer can be opened. Some of the mechanical structures are not flexible. The length of the groove of the cover 8 cm and the height and width of that is 0.5 cm and 1 cm respectively. According to the feedback of participants, it is not quite comfortable for their thumbs [1] (Fig. 7).

Fig. 7. Images of the product evaluation

5   Design Concept

According to our interview and questionnaire, users hope that the printer will be able to remember their preference so that they don't need to set again after doing it once. Preference thresholds offer us guidance in user interface design by demonstrating that asking users for successively detailed decisions about a procedure is unnecessary. After choosing to print, users don't need to tell printers how many copies they want or whether the image is landscape or photography. There is an assumption about these things that the first-time users set all of them and then the printer will remember them for all subsequent operations. If users want to alter these settings, they can request the printer options dialog box. In addition, the current user interface is so complex and complicated that it took novices a lot of time to finish tasks which should have been easy like ID copy and Wi-Fi setting. Interactive steps which are both unnecessary and time- consuming will be replaced and convenient shortcut will be added to improve user experience.

Imagine what will be happening if all the objects having pertinent status information on users' desktop or in their application could display their status in this manner. If printer icons could show how close the printer is to completing a print job, users will be less anxious when waiting for their printing materials.

5.1 Final Design

Based on the findings described above, several improvements will be made to increase the usability of this printer. Firstly, there will be fewer buttons on the control panel which simplify the visual burden. According to the Hick's law, the time it takes for a person to make a decision as a result of the possible choices he or she has: increasing the number of choices will increase the decision time logarithmically. Unnecessary buttons are abandoned in the new design and the former layout will be improved which makes it more convenient for users to operate [6]. In order to increase user experience, the original black and white display is replaced by a brand new color LCD display so that it will be easier and more explicit for users to operate the printer. With this display, users can see more information and functions at the same time (Figs. 8 and 9).

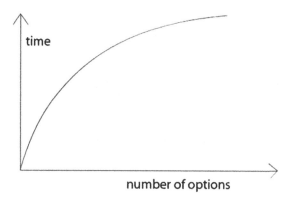

Fig. 8. The link between time and number of options

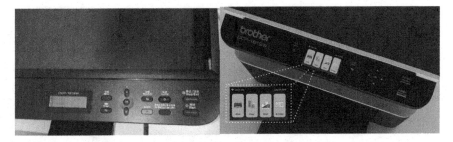

Fig. 9. Contrast between two versions on the screen (the second one is the improved version)

Secondly, the control panel will be tilted by fifteen degrees, preventing users from bending down their necks to watch the display screen. The black and white screen will be replaced by a color and clearer one which increases the viewing angle (Figs. 10 and 11).

Fig. 10. Contrast between two versions on the angle (the left one is the improved version)

Besides, Guidance about how to put the paper and copying materials will be added to help novices in case of wasting paper. And top scanner slotting will be more ergonomic.

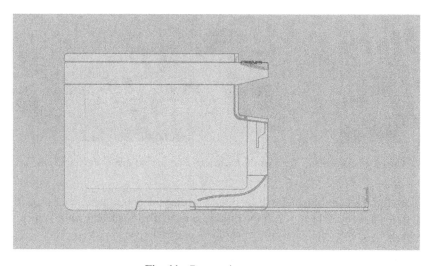

Fig. 11. Perspective structure

References

1. Brother Corporate Data. https://www.brother-usa.com. Accessed 4 Oct 2012
2. Nielsen, J.: Heuristic evaluation (1994)
3. Cooper, A.: About Face 4: The Essentials of Interaction Design. Publishing House of Electronics Industry Inc., Beijing (2015)
4. Likert, R.: A technique for the measurement of attitudes. Arch. Psychol. **140**, 1–55 (1932)
5. Lewis, C. H.: Using the "Thinking Aloud" method in cognitive interface design. Technical report. IBM. RC-9265 (1982)
6. Davis, J.A.: Providing Critical Incident Stress Debriefing (CISD) to Individuals & Communities in Situational Crisis. The American Academy of Experts in Traumatic Stress, Inc. (1998)

Usability Assessment of the Camera GR II

Zhanyan Luo, Tao Ruoyu, Yiling Zeng, Rui Zhang[(✉)],
and Marcelo M. Soares

School of Design, Hunan University, Changsha 410000,
Hunan, People's Republic of China
1620593826@qq.com, 965437377@qq.com,
1601928334@qq.com, zhangruiself@hnu.edu.cn,
soaresmm@gmail.com

Abstract. With the economic development and people's living standards improved, the number of people having the economic strength to buy a digital camera is increasing, and digital camera requirements, such as manual adjustments, picture transfer will also be improved. Therefore, usability level as a vital important reference index is widely concerned by users. Our research is carried out with a camera called GR II, and we measured the main and specific functions of it through a series of tasks [1, 2]. Since it is a product for sale, we define our research as a summative usability assessment [3]. Using several analysis methodologies, we achieved our aim to find the most confusing part and problems of its function. Then, we try to give some recommendations and new insights according to the usability assessment results. Three types of participants were enrolled in our experiment, including novice, normal and expert [4, 5], which guarantee our experiment is credible.

Keywords: Usability · Function · Camera · Measurement · Problems

1 Introduction

Due to the development of technology, the functions of cameras have become more and more diverse as the operation of products has become more and more complicated, which also attributes to the lack of availability of most camera products. With the usability research methods, it is convenient to find some problems in the digital camera interaction design, and then the designer can gradually solve these problems, which can bring a better operating experience to the users.

This study aims to investigate whether the functions of GR II cater to all the users and whether this digital camera exists any usability issues. GR II is not only high-quality enough to take good pictures, but also is convenient and portable, which means it is easy to carry with travelers. But this digital camera occupies a much less market amount than Canon and Nikon, in China. So, we plan to carry out usability experiment investigation, related theoretical research and technical analysis on it, and try to find some aspects imperatively to improve.

© Springer Nature Switzerland AG 2020
A. Marcus and E. Rosenzweig (Eds.): HCII 2020, LNCS 12201, pp. 335–345, 2020.
https://doi.org/10.1007/978-3-030-49760-6_24

2 Experiment Method

The study is based on the user experience measurement and usability metrics [6]. According to the international organization for standardization [7, 8], it is mentioned that the usability of something should be measured in three dimensions: effectiveness, efficiency and satisfaction.

According to ISO 9241. Ergonomics of human-system interaction [9]—(ISO International Organization for Standardization).

The definition of effectiveness refers to whether the user task is completed or not, and whether the task is completed is valid. Efficiency is defined as the speed at which a user's task is completed. Satisfaction is defined as the satisfaction of the user's process of completing related tasks.

We try to measure the main functions of the camera and identify whether the goal is combined well with the function, if not, we will put forward the improvement proposal with the reference to the participants' data.

2.1 Materials

In the experiment, the common type of GR II available on the market was selected, as shown in Fig. 1. Since the images saved in the camera can be displayed on/imported to a communication device by directly connecting both the devices via Wi-Fi and using the dedicated application "Image Sync", a cellphone was needed in this process.

We used video camera to record the behavior of the participants and wrote down what they spoke during the tasks.

Fig. 1. GR II

2.2 Participants

Eight participants were enrolled from Hunan University and Hunan Normal University, after they signed the Informed Consent Form, we used the user information form to distinguish them into three groups: novice, normal and expert. We used task book to guide them to finish the tasks. After that, they were asked to fill the questionnaires immediately. We used these self-reporting questionnaires to collect subjective & qualitative data.

2.3   Questionnaire Design

In the course of the experiment, the participants need to complete three kinds of questionnaires: the user information table questionnaire, the post-mission satisfaction questionnaire, and the product icon recognition questionnaire [10].

User Information Table. The purpose of the questionnaire is to understand the basic situation of the participants, the background of the camera and the experience of using the camera to ensure a balanced group. Through the understanding of the basic information, we divided the participants into three groups, namely novices, ordinary users, and expert groups;

Post-mission Satisfaction Questionnaire. The post-mission questionnaire was based primarily on the SUS System Usability Questionnaire [11], which was used to collect feedback from participants after completing each task, including scoring camera interfaces, icons, and subjective impressions of GR II used in the experiment;

Product Icon Cognitive Questionnaire. The product icon cognition is mainly used to collect the participant's cognition of the camera interface, icons, and button identification, and is conducted by means of interviews and questionnaires [12].

2.4   Task Analysis

Referring to different categories, we defined camera operation into three steps, including 1) getting ready, 2) adjusting parameters and shooting, 3) downloading into the cellphone. Understanding the user's tasks at both a high and a detailed level [13, 14], we decomposed them into the detailed subtasks defining them and developed a hierarchical breakdown, as shown in Fig. 2.

2.5   Think Aloud

Think aloud method was used to let the user speak while thinking about what he wants [14]. During the operation, the user can say "I think the following should be done like this...". In this way, we can grasp which part of the user's attention, what he thinks, and what kind of operation is taken. This is a very effective evaluation method that can figure out why it leads to bad results.

The focus of think aloud observation:

- Has the user completed the task independently? If the task cannot be completed independently, the product has a validity problem.
- Did the user perform an invalid operation or be at a loss during the process of achieving the goal? If there is, the product has efficiency issues.
- Does the user have feelings of dissatisfaction? If there is, there is a problem with the satisfaction of the product.

Then, we quantitatively and statistically evaluated the effectiveness, efficiency and satisfaction of Think aloud, study the cognitive process of users, explore the cognitive factors and variables that affect GR II, and analyze the different stages of the user's use process according to the analysis results. Cognitive features, thus incorporating the

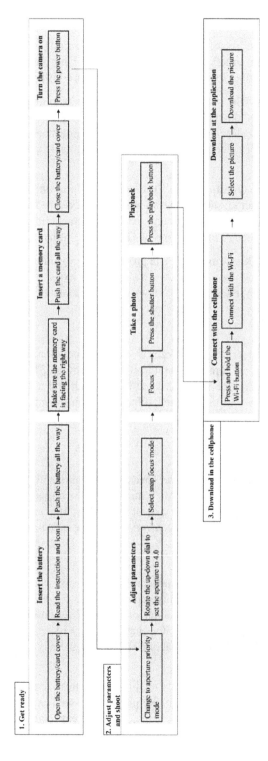

Fig. 2. Flowchart of the ordinary activity of the task of "Using GR II"

user's cognitive characteristics into the user-use process model based on problem-solving theory, to form a more complete model.

Sometimes, there is a problem in the user test, but for some reason we are not convenient to interrupt the user to ask questions in depth, or the user would miss some information by thinking aloud. At this point, after the test is completed, the tester will ask questions about the problems that occurred during the test.

3   Analysis

Behavioral and subjective data were collected to measure the usability of each task. Average and variance were used to compare whether there is significant difference between different tasks; and Chi-square test method were employed to whether performances vary significantly among normal, expert and novice group [15].

3.1   Qualitative Data

Qualitative data includes user's feelings and words. They all are objective comments and reveal the basic problems.

This part is the "Think aloud", we gathered the words and ranked them to get the highest frequent problems, as shown in Table 1. We can find that there exist some problems of the battery cover, mode dial, and some parts of the camera do not conform to users' habits according to the result.

Table 1. The most frequent problems

Think aloud	Problems
Task 1	The battery cover is so hard to close
	It is difficult to find the open button
Task 2	I just subconsciously rotate it without pressing lock release button
	Incredibly it is not a touch screen
	The "Playback" button is not easy to find
Task 3	It is difficult to find the button
	Why is "effect" with "Wi-Fi" button?

3.2   Quantitative Data

Quantitative data includes finish time and accurate rate under each task for three groups, as well as the self-report questionnaires.

Usability Characteristics. We collected and analyzed the mistakes during the three tasks, and calculated the data to describe the effectiveness (As shown in Table 2). We recorded the time consumed during tasks and calculated the the reciprocal to describe the efficiency (As shown in Table 3). We also analyzed the result of post-mission satisfaction questionnaire to arrive at the conclusion of satisfaction (Table 4).

The record of the task time frequency is used to compare the efficiency of the task, after calculating the reciprocal of the time. From the histogram (Fig. 3) above, we can conclude that task 2 is the most time-consuming, which indicates there remain the most issues during task 2 and we will pay much attention to this part in the analysis of the camera interface design (Fig. 4).

Table 2. Experiment result of the effectiveness of the 3 tasks

	U 01	U 02	U 03	U 04	U 05	U 06	U 07	U 08	Average	Variance
Task 1	87.5%	87.5%	75%	87.5%	62.5%	87.5%	62.5%	87.5%	79.68%	131.14
Task 2	81.8%	90.9%	73.33%	81.8%	18.18%	90.9%	72.7%	90.9%	75.06%	583.92
Task 3	88.89%	88.89%	88.89%	77.8%	33.33%	100%	100%	100%	84.73%	491

Table 3. Experiment result of the efficiency of the 3 tasks

	U 01	U 02	U 03	U 04	U 05	U 06	U 07	U 08	Average	Variance
Task 1	80	22	37	60	123	12	632	42	126	43043.71
Task 2	237	135	272	242	740	64	335	123	268.5	44179
Task 3	129	301	310	150	138	56	103	153	167.5	8227

Table 4. Experiment result of the satisfaction of the 3 tasks

	U 01	U 02	U 03	U 04	U 05	U 06	U 07	U 08	Average	Variance
Task 1	2.33	3	1.3	2	0.67	2.67	−1	3	1.75	1.9
Task 2	2.2	0.4	−0.4	1.8	−0.8	2	1.2	0	0.8	1.34
Task 3	4	−1.5	−0.25	1.5	−0.75	2	1.5	2.25	1.09	3.27

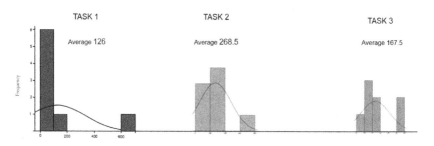

Fig. 3. Histogram for comparison of task time frequency

The three tasks' availabilities vary a little, but the variance of task 2 is much higher, which means task 2 may lead to cognitive errors of new users. And task 2 takes a lot of time to learn. The situations of novice, normal and professional in task 3 vary least of all. So we come to a conclusion that the usability of task 2 is the lowest [13].

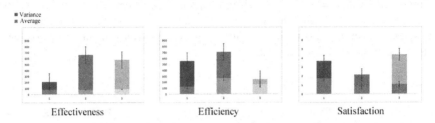

■ Variance
■ Average

Effectiveness   Efficiency   Satisfaction

Fig. 4. Chart for comparison of average and variance

Performance Measurement. We analyzed the task of each participant in 5 dimensions: task success, finish time, errors, efficiency and learnability [10]. And then we got the average mark of each step to compare with each other, with a chart (Fig. 5) ranking the figure, finally found the most severe task or step. We selected one of the participant's measurement results as an example (as shown in Table 5).

Table 5. Measurement of each step's performance (User 01)

U 01		insert the battery		insert a memory card		turn the camera on		ajust parameters		take a photo		playback		connect with the cellphone		download at the application
Task success	3	no problem	3	no problem	2	small problem	2	small problem	3	no problem	2	small problem	3	no problem	3	no problem
time-on-time	3	quickly	3	quickly	3	quickly	2	medium	3	quickly	3	quickly	3	quickly	3	quickly
errors	3	no error	3	no error	2	Can't find the power button, the flash is turned on	1	Directly rotate the kentable Entered the image view	3	no error	2	Long press thumbnail	3	no error	3	no error
efficiency	3	high	3	high	2	medium	2	medium	3	high	3	high	3	high	3	high
learnability	3	very easy	3	very easy	3	very easy	2	very easy	3	very easy	3	very easy	3	very easy	3	very easy
average	3		3		2.4		1.8		3		2.6		3		3	

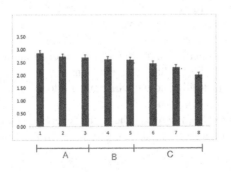

8=ajust parameters
7=playback
6=take a photo
5=turn the camera on
4=download at the application
3=insert a memory card
2=insert the battery
1=connect with the cellphone

*The lower the score is, the worse the usability is

Fig. 5. Chart for average data of performance measurement

- Observed = Observations refer to the number of participants who successfully completed the task for each group of participants.
- expected = Average number of successful completions in each group of participants chi-test = (observed value, expected value)

The table above (Fig. 6) shows the three results of Chi-square Test are lower than "Significance level P = 0.05", so our observation experiment result is close to the theoretical inference. Through inspection, it is necessary to know that the improvement of the problems in task 2 is urging. It will be easy for novices to learn, if the company try to achieve the expected efficiency.

Effectiveness			Efficiency			Satisfaction		
group	observed	expected	group	observed	expected	group	observed	expected
noive	1	1.6	noive	0	1	noive	1	1.3
intermediate	2	1.6	intermediate	1	1	intermediate	2	1.3
experts	2	1.6	experts	2	1	experts	1	1.3
total	5	5	total	3	3		4	4
	chitest	0.04625		chitest	0.002625		chitest	0.0358

Fig. 6. Result of the Chi-square Test

4 Findings

4.1 Preliminary Ideas

Quantitative data reveals that task 2 (Adjusting parameters and shooting) remains the most usability problems, and then we pay attention to the subjective data of task 2 to get to know how do the functions not fit with the user objectives.

Through the videos we recorded during the tasks, we can get to know the position and design of some icons confused the participants, and most of novices get stuck. They tend to make mistakes at that step.

We also use intensive interview to get more details, and experts expressed their experience of using it and gave some opinion of the design.

4.2 Problems and Improvements

Five users think they can close the battery/card cover directly so we will change this structure into a new one that when the users close the cover, they needn't slide the release lever to lock it.

Playback is an important function in camera design, but when a user holds the camera, this button is hidden, so we would like to change its location.

The menu and ok button's function's misleading so we will change it to ok button and then add a new menu button in the top right corner.

And we will change normal screen to touch screen. There are several ways to interact: click; slide switch; double click to enlarge; double fingers to zoom in or out and so on.

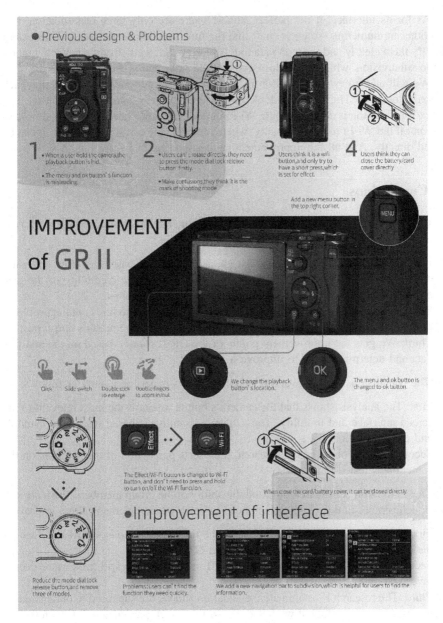

Fig. 7. Improvement of GR II

For the mode dial, there are two problems: 1. Users can't rotate directly, they need to press the mode dial lock release button firstly; 2. The mode dial makes confusions, because users think it is the mark of shooting mode.

For the Wi-Fi button, users may think it is a Wi-Fi button, but only try to have a short press, which is set for effect.

As for its interface, it not perfect, either. There are only three classification, and functions are numerous, so users can't find the function they need quickly. Users can't classify them clearly and the icon meaning is blurred. So, we will add a new navigation bar to subdivision, which can help users find the information which they need.

We will add a new menu button in the top right corner and change the playback button's location. The menu and ok button are changed into the ok button. The Effect/Wi-Fi button is changed to the Wi-Fi button, and don't need to press and hold to turn on/off the Wi-Fi function. Finally, when you close the card/battery cover, it can be closed directly. And all the improvement suggestions are shown in Fig. 7.

5   Conclusions

This paper explores the usability of digital camera interaction design, and the work is as follows:

- First: The paper designs a task list of usability tests based on user operation characteristics. It ensures the usability test method and the credibility of the task chain, and conducts targeted usability tests and questionnaires;
- Second: The paper analyzes the data from the usability test to finds out the problems in the digital camera interaction design and summarizes the reasons and types;
- Third: We gets the improvement points of the GR II camera based on the analysis data and determines how to improve it.

The conclusions and innovations obtained in this paper are mainly as follows:

- First: The analysis shows that the camera's button layout is the most relevant to the screen interface and usability. The camera's usability is based on simple symbols and daily operation.
- Second: In the course of the research, the user's perception of the symbols on the camera was tested innovatively.

Due to the limited research time and the ability of the group members, there are still many deficiencies in this paper, which need to be slowly supplemented and improved.

- First: Ricoh is a good brand. Because of the limited conditions, GRIII has been on the market for a long time when we tested GR II;
- Second: The problem of usability of GR II in this paper is still need more deeper investigation.
- Third: The research is a summative evaluation and we are supposed to obtain a large representative sample, but we failed to recruit enough participants for the test. The result would be more accurate if we had had adequate samples.

Although the research method of this paper is not a new theoretical method system, it is based on the research results of predecessors, and draws on the successful experience of predecessors and strengthens the research in depth. We hope that the research of this paper can be used for subsequent related design. It can provide new design ideas and technical means for the staff. The study of usability needs to be taken seriously, and we hope that through our own efforts, we can make a contribution to usability research.

With the development of technology, cameras will gradually add new features and new usability issues. This requires our team members to continue to pay attention to new developments in such issues, making research more and more perfect and satisfying more users' needs.

References

1. Tricot, A.: Utility, usability and acceptability: an ergonomic approach to the evaluation of external representations for learning (2007)
2. Madan, A., Kumar, S.: Usability evaluation methods: a literature review. Int. J. Eng. Sci. Technology **4**, 590–599 (2012)
3. Kirakowski, J.: Summative Usability Testing (2005). https://doi.org/10.1016/b978-012095811-5/50018-3
4. Jordan, P.W.: Measures of usability. In: An Introduction to Usability, pp. 18–23. Taylor & Francis, London (1998)
5. Booth, P.: An introduction to Human-Computer Interaction. Lawrence Erlbaur Associates Publishers, Hillsdale (1989)
6. Tullis, T., Albert, W.: Measuring the User Experience: Collecting, Analyzing, and Presenting Usability Metrics, 2nd edn. Elsevier, Amsterdam (2008)
7. Hom, J.: The Usability Methods Toolbox Handbook (1996)
8. Leventhal, L., Barnes, J.: Model of User Interface including Usability Engineering (2008)
9. ISO 9241-11:2018(en). Ergonomics of human-system interaction—Part 11: Usability: Definitions and concepts
10. Kirakowski, J.: A List of Frequently Asked Questions, 3rd edn. (2000)
11. Bangor, A., Kortum, P.T., Miller, J.T.: The system usability scale (SUS): an empirical evaluation. Int. J. Hum.-Comput. Interact. **24**, 574–594 (2008). https://doi.org/10.1080/10447310802205776
12. Chin, J., Diehl, V., Norman, K.: Development of an instrument measuring user satisfaction of the human-computer interface. In: SIGCHI Conference on Human Factors in Computing Systems, pp. 213–218 (1998)
13. Nielsen, J.: Usability Engineering. Morgan Kaufmann, Burlington (1993)
14. Jordan, P.W.: An Introduction to Usability. Taylor & Francis, London (1998)
15. Al-Buainain, H.A.: Human Computer Interaction Study on Fujifilm Instax Mini 8 Camera Using Evaluation Techniques. IEEE Reg 8, Saudi Comp Soc, Saudi Arabia Sect. BN 978-1-7281-0108-8 (2019)

Ergonomics Considerations of Usability Test of UAV Handheld Control Unit

Xu Wu[1(✉)], Guoqiang Sun[1], Shuang Liu[2], Lin Ding[1],
Chongchong Miao[1], and Kai An[1]

[1] AVIC China Aero Polytechnology Establishment, Beijing 100028, China
405809790@qq.com, sunguoqiang1213@foxmail.com,
dinglin_1982@163.com, miaochong301@163.com,
sd_ankai@163.com
[2] Beihang University, Beijing 100191, China
liushuangbh@163.com

Abstract. Consumer UAV (Unmanned Aerial Vehicle) has changed our daily life in many ways of aerial entertainment and photography. User experience and usability design were considered as priority factors which determined consumer's purchase selection. Therefore, manufactures of consumer UAV focused on human factors and ergonomics considerations that help to guide UAV deign finalization and verification. Specifically, UAV handheld control unit should be drawn more attention to achieve efficient interaction and user satisfaction. This research firstly reviewed on technical literatures and standard specifications to distinguish key factors of ergonomics design requirements of UAV handheld control unit. And Delphi method was adopted to establish an index system of ergonomics evaluation of UAV handheld control unit involved with control-display interface, warning, and special usage. Finally, usability test method was developed to realize user experience evaluation and expert technical measurement of UAV handheld control unit. Both ergonomics considerations and usability test methods were designed to provide guidance support for relevant consumer UAV designers and testers.

Keywords: UAV handheld control unit · Usability test · Ergonomics evaluation · Index system

1 Introduction

Nowadays, with prosper of consumer UAV industry, its marketing scale has blown out with updating product and expert solutions. The battlefield of consumer UAV market was concentrated on the competition of user experience rather than production technology. For instance, the traditional product test of UAV mainly focused on flight performance and requirement-function realization. However, user experience and usability design became more popular as key points to achieve consumer satisfaction.

As primary interface between user and UAV, the handheld control unit played a significant role of providing effective and efficient interaction, which was ensured to perform remote-control task and realize multi-function task including aerial

A. Marcus and E. Rosenzweig (Eds.): HCII 2020, LNCS 12201, pp. 346–356, 2020.
https://doi.org/10.1007/978-3-030-49760-6_25

photography. The common control device was widely applied in both industry and daily life, therefore, the ergonomics design had direct and significant influence on task performance, user experience even health care and personnel safety. To improve human machine interaction, the control device was required to design in accordance with user physical and psychological characteristics as well as behavior custom.

As shown in Fig. 1, a typical UAV handheld control unit contained various hardware of controls and displays [1]. The controls should be designed including with button, finger wheel, joystick, and switch while the displays were included with display screen and indicating light [2].

Fig. 1. Example of UAV handheld control unit

1.1 Research Reviews

The recent study of ergonomics issues on UAV handheld control unit was hardly found, however, the designers tended to rely on scheme evolution and their experience due to the lack of specifications or standards. In contrast of ergonomics or usability test, realization of functional capabilities drew more attention during test and evaluation phase.

Ergonomics research of controller mainly focused on type selection and design requirement or criteria using physical measurement, subjective evaluation as well as visual simulation. Yao recruited 70 professional truck drivers to carry out ergonomics evaluation for control device of truck cockpit based on subjective feelings and driving experience [3]. Liu developed manipulation classification of control device and analyzed characteristics parameter of ergonomics design for selection [4]. In addition, recent study of ergonomics test and evaluation research concentrated on household electric applications including air conditioner manual [7], household appliances interface [6], TV screen and control unit [5–7].

1.2   Current Standards

With prosper development of UAV industry, relevant standard organization realized the importance of UAV standard and became expert standardize team to promote systematic work. Such as ISO/TC20/SC16, JARUSJ, SAE AS-4 were most active worldwide standard organization. And SAC/TC435/SC1 in China was just established and became the first sub-committee of UAV system in 2018. However, ergonomics requirement of UAV handheld control unit was merely found in the current standards, which still focused on design requirement and overall layout of control device of typical product, especially in automobile or working machine.

For instance, ISO 9241-400 provided ergonomics guidelines of principles and requirements for physical input devices which contained keyboard, mouse, joystick, trackball, touchscreen, and other devices. Generic ergonomic principles were specified and valid for the design and use of input devices [8]. ISO 9241-410 provided ergonomics design criteria for physical input devices which should be coincided with product characteristics under target user task situation [9]. ISO 9241-411 provided ergonomics evaluation methods for the design of physical input devices mentioned in ISO 9241-400 and specified evaluation methods of design attribute and determined criteria based on task situation [10]. Besides, HF-STD-001B specified technical requirements (diameter, length, manipulation power) for thumb tip and fingertip-operated displacement joysticks [11].

In China, there were certain published standards involved with ergonomics design and evaluation of the controls such as GB/T 14775-1997 "General ergonomics requirements for controller" and GB/T 32261.2-2015 "Usability of consumer products and products for public use-part 2: summative test method" [12, 13]. In consideration of specific household electric product, newly-released standards provided technical requirement and ergonomics evaluation for refrigerator (GB/T 36608.1-2018) and air conditioner (GB/T 36608.2-2018) [14, 15].

To sum up, foreign researches of ergonomics consideration of consumer product have realized further achievement and concentrated on problem-solving of daily life issues, which was conformed to the idea of human-centered design. Yet domestic researches in such field were required more promotion and innovation, therefore, study on ergonomics design and evaluation of UAV handheld control unit could be imperative.

2 Ergonomics Considerations of Design Requirements

2.1 Overall Design

The shape and size of UAV handheld control unit should be considered in overall design whereas its geometric size was designed to fit the primary requirement of use and convenience of handheld posture. The shape of contact area with hands should be designed as sphere, cylinder, or ring while that with fingers should have ripples suitable for touch. In addition, the aesthetics of appearance and comfort of operation should also be taken into account.

Moreover, the overweight of UAV handheld control unit should be noticed to avoid the unavailability of special users with uniform distribution of mass and balanced mass center. And the layout of overall design of controls and displays should be considered and coincided with requirements of function allocation, priority grouping, operation order and frequency. Besides, healthy material and comfort color as well as pleasant texture should also be involved with overall design.

2.2 Controls

Selection of the controls should be designed in accordance with actual operation needs which determined the choice of button, finger wheel, joystick, and switch. Therefore, layout of the controls became the next consideration that the spacing and grouping design should be satisfied the requirements of convenience and operability. However, the consistency requirement of control coding was obvious to follow yet this principle was difficult to achieve perfect designed due to the ignorable details with trifles and the counter-balance with other considerations such as usage pattern and update alternatives. Besides, the control coding of color, size, and shape should be also considered.

2.3 Displays

The ergonomics requirement of display screen should be followed with relevant standards or specifications which recommended appropriate design parameters of screen luminance, resolution, and contrast ratio. And the display interface should be well-designed to support friendly and easy user experience. In addition, display information should be shown including flight status, parameters, residual electricity and other auxiliary information that satisfied user's visual acquisition of UAV's current status.

2.4 Interactions

Interaction with UAV through handheld control unit should be designed to ensure usability that realized effective and efficient interaction in multiple interaction modals including hand-control, finger-control, touch screen control or even speech recognition control in order to achieve satisfied user experience. The specific requirements of interaction were contained simplicity requirement, consistency requirement, compatibility requirement, movement relationship requirement, and diversity requirement.

2.5 Warnings

The ergonomics considerations of warnings design contained visual and auditory requirements which should be provided with instant and salient cuing warned if any fault or failure happened. The visual requirement of warnings was mainly involved with blink, salient color or luminance while warning sound loudness and frequency should be taken into account of auditory requirement.

Nonetheless, limitations of night light or poor ambient illuminance should be considered to meet the minimum requirement of visibility. Besides, the workload and fatigue of handheld posture should be improved especially for long-term usage.

3 Ergonomics Evaluation Index System

3.1 Establishment

Based on ergonomics factors analysis of UAV handheld control unit, a primary index system of ergonomics evaluation was put forward in three-layer structure of thirty-two bottom indices.

The top layer of index system was coincided with Chapter 2 that was involved with I_1 overall design, I_2 controls, I_3 displays, I_4 interactions and I_5 special usage (including warnings and alarms).

The middle layer indices were extracted and specified from the upper layer:

1. $I_{1.1}$ appearance, $I_{1.2}$ weight, and $I_{1.3}$ material were belonged to overall design.
2. $I_{2.1}$ selection, $I_{2.2}$ layout, and $I_{2.3}$ coding were belonged to controls.
3. $I_{3.1}$ screen, $I_{3.2}$ information, and $I_{3.3}$ content were belonged to displays.
4. $I_{4.1}$ modal and $I_{4.2}$ usability were belonged to interactions.
5. $I_{5.1}$ warning, $I_{5.2}$ environment adpatation, and $I_{5.3}$ long-term use were belonged to special usage.

And thirty-two bottom indices were dissolved from the middle layer as shown in Fig. 2.

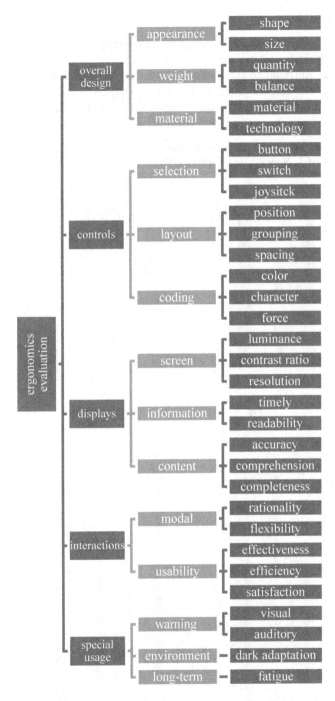

Fig. 2. Three-layer structure of ergonomics evaluation index system

3.2 Optimization

Delphi method was used to select single index and optimize the proposed index system. Six participants including ergonomics experts and UAV designers were recruited in Delphi's survey and required to complete a questionnaire to determine the significance of each index. According to the classic data process of Delphi method, the Mean, Mode and P33 were calculated as statistics results of index system and significant value threshold was set up as 3.0 which suggested an inappropriate index with significance below it.

Top Layer. As shown in Fig. 3, the results of the top layer indicated suggestion of a retained index of I_5 Special Usage (P33 < 3).

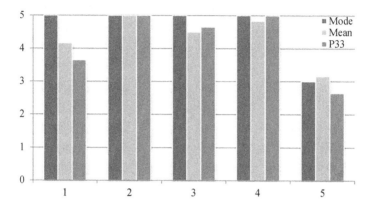

Fig. 3. Delphi results of the top layer

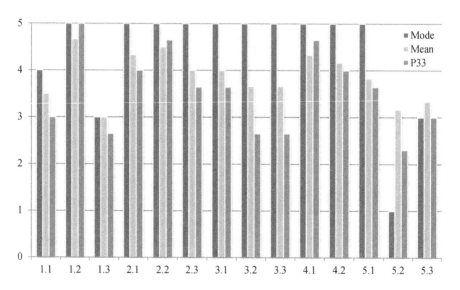

Fig. 4. Delphi results of the middle layer

Middle Layer. As shown in Fig. 4, the results of the middle layer indicated suggestion of retained indices of $I_{1.3}$ Material, $I_{3.2}$ Information, and $I_{3.3}$ Content (P33 < 3) and an abandoned index of $I_{5.2}$ Environment (Mode & P33 < 3).

In addition, certain participants advised to add human error protection into the middle layer followed by I_2 controls and interface design into I_3 displays. And also, transmission delay should be taken into consideration.

Bottom Layer. As shown in Fig. 5, the results of the bottom layer indicated suggestion of retained indices of $I_{1.3.1}$ Material, $I_{2.3.4}$ Color Coding, $I_{2.3.5}$ Character Coding, $I_{3.2.1}$ Timely, $I_{3.3.3}$ Completeness, $I_{4.1.2}$ Flexibility, and $I_{5.2.1}$ Dark Adpatation (P33 < 3).

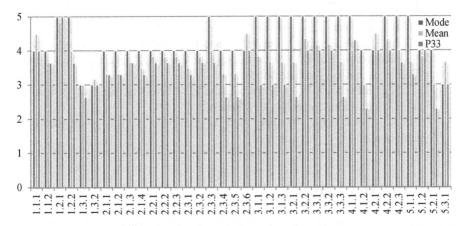

Fig. 5. Delphi results of the bottom layer

In addition, foreign languages should be considered in I3.3 information and battery endurance as well as operation and storage environment should be added into I5.3 long-term usage.

3.3 Verification

Focus team method was used to examine the results of Delphi's questionnaire and verify the determination of index system. Five experts were recruited as focus team which contained two ergonomics experts and three UAV designers. After the demonstration of Delphi's results, the focus team was required to discuss revision of the former index system and recommendation of the final one. To sum up, their conclusion came to an agreement that certain indices should be deleted such as $I_{2.3}$ coding and $I_{5.2}$ environment, while others should be adjusted that layout requirement ($I_{2.2}$) should be moved under I_1 overall design and the middle layer under I_2 controls should be updated into rationality, convenience, and human error protection.

Therefore, the ergonomics evaluation index system of UAV handheld control unit remained three-layer structure with forty-four bottom indices:

- Five indices of the top layer were involved with I_1 Overall Design, I_2 Controls, I_3 Displays, I_4 Interactions, and I_5 Special Usage.
- Fifteen indices of the middle layer were contained with (1) $I_{1.1}$ appearance, $I_{1.2}$ weight, $I_{1.3}$ layout, and $I_{1.4}$ delay, (2) $I_{2.1}$ rationality, $I_{2.2}$ convenience, and $I_{2.3}$ human error protection, (3) $I_{3.1}$ screen, $I_{3.2}$ interface, $I_{3.3}$ information, and $I_{3.4}$ content, (4) $I_{4.1}$ modal and $I_{4.2}$ usability, (5) $I_{5.1}$ warning, and $I_{5.2}$ long-term use.
- Forty-four indices of the bottom layer were contained with:
  - (1.1) $I_{1.1.1}$ shape and $I_{1.1.2}$ size, (1.2) I_{121} quantity and $I_{1.2.2}$ balance, (1.3) $I_{1.3.1}$ position, $I_{1.3.2}$ grouping, $I_{1.3.3}$ spacing, and $I_{1.3.4}$ socket, (1.4) $I_{1.4.1}$ data-link delay and $I_{1.4.2}$ transmission fluency,
  - (2.1) $I_{2.1.1}$ input controls, $I_{2.1.2}$ touch control, and $I_{2.1.3}$ gesture control, (2.2) $I_{2.2.1}$ force, $I_{2.2.2}$ feedback, and $I_{2.2.3}$ custom, (2.3) $I_{2.3.1}$ operation error, $I_{2.3.2}$ false touch, and $I_{2.3.3}$ fool proof,
  - (3.1) $I_{3.1.1}$ luminance, $I_{3.1.2}$ contrast ratio, $I_{3.1.3}$ color rending, and $I_{3.1.4}$ clarity, (3.2) $I_{3.2.1}$ friendliness, $I_{3.2.2}$ aesthetics, and $I_{3.2.3}$ learnability, (3.3) $I_{3.3.1}$ timely, $I_{3.3.2}$ readability, and $I_{3.3.3}$ foreign language, (3.4) $I_{3.4.1}$ accuracy, $I_{3.4.2}$ comprehension, and $I_{3.4.3}$ completeness,
  - (4.1) $I_{4.1.1}$ rationality, $I_{4.1.2}$ flexibility, and $I_{4.1.3}$ diversity, (4.2) $I_{4.21}$ effectiveness, $I_{4.2.2}$ efficiency, and I_{423} satisfaction,
  - (5.1) $I_{5.1.1}$ visual, $I_{5.1.2}$ auditory, and $I_{5.1.3}$ tactile, (5.2) $I_{5.2.1}$ fatigue, $I_{5.2.2}$ endurance, and $I_{5.2.3}$ environment.

4 Usability Test Method

According to the ergonomics factors and index system, the usability test methods to evaluate UAV handheld control unit were developed and involved with both quantitative requirement of technical measurement and subjective assessment of user experience.

4.1 Technical Measurement

Technical measurement of usability test method was used to adopt professional measuring instrument to evaluate the appearance, weight and transmission delay of UAV handheld control unit. The specific requirement of technical measurement contained:

- Appearance evaluation was required to measure geometrics characteristics of overall design parameters which were involved with length, breadth, and thickness. In addition, the size and spacing of the typical controls were also included in appearance evaluation.
- Weight evaluation was required to measure quantitative characteristics of overall weight, center of gravity, and weight distribution.
- Force evaluation was required to measure operation power of button-pressing, switch-turning, and screen/pad-touching.
- Transmission delay evaluation was required to measure delay time, packet loss, and spread spectrum ratio. To be noticed, transmission delay was not strictly considered

as ergonomics evaluation index, however, it surely affected accuracy and efficiency of UAV remote-control which might lead to bad user experience due to graphic disfluency or operation latency. Therefore, it was recommended to include in technical measurement and an acceptable threshold was suggested as "<200 ms" of transmission delay that could be merely perceived during ordinary usage.

4.2 User Experience

User experience of usability test method was used to adopt traditional subjective questionnaire to evaluate preference perception during scenario-based use-case test. The test scenario of user experience was designed as typical usage of UAV which contained with initialization and preparation, basic operation of handheld control unit, and ordinary operation of flight and videography. As shown in Fig. 6, the specific task of use-case was designed in accordance with UAV manual. The whole test procedure of user experience should be included with participant recruitment, training and practice, scenario-based test, and questionnaire research.

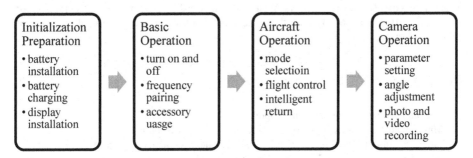

Fig. 6. Use-case of user experience

- Participant recruitment was designed to focus on requirements of participant selection, sample size, and informed consent constraint. Besides, both ergonomics scholars and UAV designers should be invited as technical experts and recruited in this test. And sample size was suggested as twelve participants at least which should be included with four experts and eight UAV users.
- Training and practice were designed to help the participants master the basic UAV operations and become qualified users. It was recommended that the training and practice phase might be skipped when the participants were of rich experience of UAV usage, however, the formal test should not start until they were all familiar with test product and normal operation.
- Scenario-based test was designed as formal test of user experience with specific use-case shown in Fig. 6. During the case of initialization and preparation, the participants were required to initiate UAV system by installation of control unit and battery charging. And the cases of basic and ordinary operations required the participants to experience function and performance of UAV which should be evaluated in the next questionnaire research.

• Questionnaire was used to measure user experience of UAV in five-star grading evaluation using weighted quantization calculation. According to the index system mentioned in 3.3, the questionnaire was designed as satisfaction rating of both static and interactive evaluation. The former one concentrated on physics characteristics evaluation of appearance and layout design, while the latter one contained usability and user experience of UAV interactions of control and display interface.

5 Conclusion

In conclusion, this research firstly analyzed five main considerations of ergonomics design of UAV handheld control unit which were concerned with overall design, controls, displays, interactions, and warnings. And a three-layer index system of forty-four bottom indices was established and verified for ergonomics evaluation using Delphi questionnaire method. Moreover, usability test method was developed in consideration of technical measurement and user experience of UAV handheld control unit.

Acknowledgement. This research was financially supported by National Key R&D Program of China (No. 2017YFF0206604). And the co-authors would like to thank the kindly support of relevant experts and participants.

References

1. DJI Support. http://www.dji.com/support
2. Mavic Mini User Manual, V1.0 2019/11. http://www.dji.com/mavic-mini
3. Liu, S.: Ergonomics design features and selection research of control device. Master Dissertation of Zhengzhou University (2016)
4. Yao, Y.: Study on ergonomics evaluation for control device of truck cockpit. Master Dissertation of Zhengzhou University (2017)
5. Na, L., Jun, T.: Ergonomics evaluation of intelligent TV screen and control unit. China Appl. (1), 72–74 (2017)
6. Shao, G., Luo, H., Zhao, C., et al.: Application of ergonomics evaluation for household appliance's interface. In: Proceedings of 2015 China Appliance technology Conference, pp. 1058–1065 (2015)
7. Chao, C., Zhao, C., Hu, H.: Evaluation research on ergonomics of air conditioners manuals. China Stand. (5), 102–105 (2014)
8. ISO 9241-400: Principles and requirements for physical input devices (2007)
9. ISO 9241-410: Design criteria for physical input devices (2008)
10. ISO 9241-411: Evaluation methods for the design of physical input devices (2012)
11. FAA: Human Factors Design Standard-001B (2016)
12. GB/T 14775: General ergonomics requirements for controller (1997)
13. GB/T 32261.2: Usability of consumer products and products for public use-part 2: summative test method (2015)
14. GB/T 36608.1: Ergonomics technical requirements and evaluation for household appliances-part 1: refrigerators (2018)
15. GB/T 36608.2: Ergonomics technical requirements and evaluation for household appliances-part 2: air-conditioners (2018)

Exploring Food Literacy Through the Use of Mobile Apps in the Era of Human-Food Interaction: Kliktag Case

Kübra Sultan Yüzüncüyıl, Kerem Rızvanoğlu, and Özgürol Öztürk^(✉)

Galatasaray University, Ciragan Cad. No: 36 Ortakoy, 34357 Istanbul, Turkey
kubrayuzuncuyil@gmail.com,
{krizvanoglu,ozozturk}@gsu.edu.tr

Abstract. Everyone eats. It is a fundamental act to human existence. On the other hand, in today's society, achieving healthy food products is challenging. Proliferation of industrialized agriculture has created public health concerns due to rise of obesity and diet-related disease around the world. People who are aware of the effects of food choices on human body, have been trying to become food literate. In other words, they have been trying pursuing to obtain necessary knowledge to select, prepare and consume healthy food. Yet, information pollution and lack of education engenders gastro-anxiety which is a term to describe the suspicion about foodways. In this context, an application called Kliktag introduces itself as "A Healthy Food Advisory." The application seems to alleviate the gastro-anxiety of its users. Due to this impression, this study aims to analyze the competency of this application to empower the level of food literacy among users. It also aims to investigate the user experience of Kliktag through an analysis framework based on parameters such as Onboarding, Search Experience (Findability), Visual Hierarchy, Visibility, Data Visualization, User Collaboration and Editorial Tone. It was also analyzed how user behaviors were changed related to evolving food literacy. To achieve this aim, a multi-method user research based on two separate phases was conducted. The study firstly focused on the momentary first-time user experience through a usability test while the second phase was based on a 10 day-diary study that aims to understand the evolving cumulative user experience on the mobile app. According to the findings, users could tolerate the detrimental effects of user experience issues and maintain a particular level of food literacy in short term.

Keywords: Human food interaction · Food literacy · User experience (UX)

1 Introduction

With the rapid industrialization in food production, decisions people make about food consumption become more complex. In today's cities people can't track where and how their food comes from, who produce it [1]. Although they may benefit from cheaper food, quality and health implications have been under suspicion. Recent studies show that people's dieting habits have been primarily based on low-nutrient high energy food. The lack of knowing what foods are made of, how food labelling

© Springer Nature Switzerland AG 2020
A. Marcus and E. Rosenzweig (Eds.): HCII 2020, LNCS 12201, pp. 357–375, 2020.
https://doi.org/10.1007/978-3-030-49760-6_26

information is read and understood, lead people to gain nutrition promotion and education. The suspicion about foodways has been growing since new media tools might be considered as sources for information acquisition. Yet, new media channels, specifically the ones based on user generated content may let misinformation spread far wide. In this manner, people might get confused and have anxiety in choosing and consuming food properly. In other words, gaining a significant level of food literacy and proficiency in food related skills have been a complex issue [2]. User studies should be conducted to understand the competency of digital platforms in supporting food literacy and behavioral change among users. This study aims to contribute to this context through a multi-method qualitative research based on usability testing and diary study. To address this gap, this study aimed to evaluate "Kliktag" mobile application, which defined itself as the "Healthy Food Advisory". The remainder of this paper presents the literature review, methodology, results and discussion and the conclusion.

2   Literature Review

2.1   Food Literacy

Food literacy is a term that is coined to express the combination of the knowledge, skills, behaviors, selection, management, preparation and consumption about food that meets nutritional and health recommendations [3]. It is defined "as the capacity of an individual to obtain, interpret, and understand basic food and nutrition information and services as well as the competence to use that information and services in ways that are health enhancing [4]. It also identifies the need for both knowledge and capacity in order to make the best use of food [5]. Vidgen and Gallegos presents a conceptual model for the relationship between nutrition and food literacy [6] (Fig. 1).

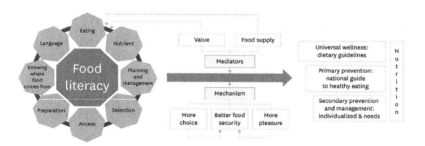

Fig. 1. Food Literacy Chart developed by Vidgen and Gallegos [6]

Due to this model food literacy is consisted of eight basic steps that are eating, nutrient, planning and management, selection, access, preparation, knowing where food comes from, language. According to Nowatschin et al. [7], many individuals in urbanized society are lacking in terms of food related knowledge and skills. They emphasize that food insecurity in cities make difficult to reach clean and sustainable food which is also transparent about its production chains and principles of the producer. French sociologist Claude Fischler [8], coined the term gastro-anomie to imply this issue. He said that food production and processing techniques went further beyond the view of an ordinary consumer. Many of food items are consisted of unknown features and ingredients that cause loss of consumer's confidence. Kanık [9], said that this term needs to be developed as food technology has been improving. Also, the rate of ever-increasing social media use makes reaching exact information related with food difficult. Hence, Kanık proposed the term of gastro-anomie to express the current situation caused by the modern food manufacture system in daily life. By calling the term gastro-anxiety, she attempted to show that gastro-anomie has evolved into a social attitude called gastro anxiety. She indicted that people observed negative effects of industrialized food system on their health and became more self-aware of farmland loss. Occurrence of undesirable consequences of mechanical food production lead individuals to plan an emergency act to organize their food related behavior. Food related social networks like food communities, cooperation, solidarities can be seen as a result of this pursuit. The studies in the field of Human Computer Interaction have been also responding the food related concerns in the society. The phases from how food is grown, cooked, presented, eaten and disposed have been associated with the use of digital technology. The next section presents how food practices and human computer interaction discipline have converged.

2.2   Human Food Interaction Studies

Food practices such as producing, procuring, preparing, eating and digesting of food take time at certain intervals in daily life. As French gastronome Brillat-Savarin [10], indicated we are what we eat. This essential facet of life also is the biggest industry in the World [11]. The rapid evolution of digital technologies has been penetrating into food practices. In the area of Human Computer Interaction (HCI), this penetration is studied and defined by the term of Human Food Interaction (HFI) [12]. This interdisciplinary field is emerged by the studies that illustrates how HFI builds on recent trends within HCI across all phases of the human food cycle [13]. HFI studies offer a glimpse of a possible food future that digital technology is an inseparable part.

Discussions in HFI might be conducted in a range from how food is grown, cooked to how is eaten and disposed. In the beginnings, researchers in the field of HFI were interested in new emerging technologies like food printing [14], virtual reality [15], robotics [16] and changing interfaces. However, following studies focus on how food related applications are used. West et al. [17], focused on health behavior theories in diet applications. They aimed to evaluate the extent to which diet apps' content was guided by health behavior theory in their design and user interface. Furthermore, Eikey and Reddy [18], conducted a qualitative study on how women with eating disorders use weight loss applications and how those applications are designed. Moreover, Taimouri et al. [19], researched usability of online food ordering websites in Iran. The design parameters of these websites have been classified and reviewed in a detail in terms of effectiveness, efficiency, and satisfaction to sort restaurants.

Recently, discussions related with food literacy has been aroused in human food interaction studies. Bomfim and Wallace [20], stated that researches in the field of HCI have generally focused on healthy eating through weight loss and calorie control mobile applications. Before the growing rate of gastro anxiety, the motivation of healthy eating behavior has been of interest to HCI. Due to this fact, development and evaluation of a number of nutrition mobile apps were done. According to Hingle and Patrick [21], food literacy might be associated with mobile health (mHealth). It is an emerging field which means the use of mobile and mobile devices to improve health outcomes. Healthy food choices can be empowered by advances in technology which lead the ease of disseminating knowledge, increasing awareness, and emphasizing the importance of proper eating [22]. McCabe et al. [23], stated that mobile device technology was an example of a potential purveyor of information related to healthy eating. Despite the promise of m-health, studies that focus on their usability remained limited.

Bomfim and Wallace indicated that, the interest of the HCI community is heading towards to a more broadly term, namely food literacy which contains planning, management, selection, preparation and consumption of nutrition. It is also associated with confidence, autonomy and empowerment of the self in relation with healthy food choice. As Hingle and Patrick stated that many applications have been developed via traditional research methods without benefiting from the methodologies of human computer interaction and user centered design.

3 Methodology

In Human-Computer Interaction, research methods have been derived primarily from cognitive sciences. Hence, lab-based observations, quantitative experiments have been adopted to gain empirical insight about the user experience. Yet with ethnographic return of social sciences in 70s, the methods of HCI were also diversified. This study aims to understand the momentary and cumulative user experience of a mobile application, namely Kliktag, and its impact on behaviors related to food literacy, through a multi-method approach based on two phases. The study firstly focuses on the momentary first-time user experience through a usability test based on think aloud protocol. The second phase is based on a 10 day-diary study that aims to understand the evolving cumulative user experience on the mobile app and its impact on the behaviors related with food literacy. The research questions of this study are as follows:

1. How has the informative content of Kliktag been presented in the context of user experience?
2. How does Kliktag change user behavior with respect to food literacy?
3. How does Kliktag help users obtain food literacy skills?

According to Kiefer et al. [24], woman have a higher awareness and better knowledge of nutrition than men. They also seek nutrition counselling more frequently than men do. Also, Su et al. [25], asserted that the men were less likely to use nutrition labels than women. Due to the fact that this study has a variety of factors to analyze, the sample is limited by women to deepen the findings. The sample was composed of ten women between the age of 29 to 35, who had at least bachelor degree. All the participants were skeptic about industrial food system and they tried to construct a healthy diet for themselves. To enrich the sample and observe valid results, participants were chosen from different diet types. Five of them have following omnivorous diets which include animal and plant-based food. Five of them were vegetarians and two of five vegetarians had been trying to consume gluten-free products.

The first usability testing phase with the Kliktag mobile application, was based on three stages: Pre-test, test, post-test. In the pre-test stage, a background questionnaire was utilized to collect demographic data. Afterwards in the test stage, task observation started with the execution of previously selected tasks. Tasks were given in random order in order to prevent the order bias. Participants were asked to think aloud as they were performing the tasks. They were asked to say whatever they are thinking, doing, feeling and looking at each moment of task execution. The behaviors of each participant were recorded by camera. Finally, as part of the post-test stage, a debriefing interview was conducted to understand the experience in detail.

After the execution of the first phase, which was based on the first-time user experience, was completed, field work started. Behaviors are meaningful in their natural context over time [26]. In this context, in order to investigate the cumulative user experience in the Kliktag and its impact on behaviors related with food-literacy in the long-term, diary study was preferred. Diary study is a data collection method that asks users to record actions and thoughts in their own environment in terms of related practice in a diary over a time period. In this study, participants were asked to share their experiences both in the form of text and voice messages through Whatsapp to the researcher. For ten days, participants were asked to complete pre-defined tasks each day. Every three days, researcher conducted semi-depth interviews with each participant through the telephone. After ten days practice, in order to make an overall evaluation, a final semi-depth interview was conducted.

3.1 Kliktag: "Enjoy and Stay Healthy"

"Are you confused? Are you worried? Let us take care of it." The introductory sentence of Kliktag seems to alleviate the gastro anxiety. This application was designed by CMOS technology and software company in Turkey to create awareness about packaged food consumption in society. Kliktag analyzes the ingredients of the packaged foods and indicates whether they are suitable for customer's health and lifestyle. To do this, customers need to scan the barcode by using Kliktag before consuming it. After that, Kliktag monitors and scores the ingredients in packaged foods with nearly 400 additives and 63 allergen components. Its' health score is a systematically assigned "processing" score according to the NOVA criteria considered by the United Nations as a valid instrument. The score, which is also color-coded, changes between 1 (green) and 5 (red) from good to bad. Products with a score above 3 contain over-processed substances. Customers might generate a profile according to their diets (vegan, vegetarian, gluten, halal). They might choose the allergen components and additive materials (starch-based sugars, palm oil etc.), which they don't want to consume, as filters. Kliktag shows the products' features in terms of customers personal preferences. There are three main sections in the home page which are Health, Nutrition and Alternative. The Health section includes health analysis which contains processed level of food, the explanation of risk factor of sugar, saturated fat and additive, the explanation of e-code's and additional informative statements of the related products. In the Nutrition section, food analysis in terms of calorie and daily intake are placed. The alternative section might be used by only Premium users. Premium feature offers customers to present alternative healthier products that they can eat by showing an ordered score (Fig. 2).

Fig. 2. Kliktag interface (Color figure online)

3.2   Analysis Framework

The overall research model of the study is based on two analysis frameworks. First framework relies on the concept of food literacy whereas the second complementary framework relies on user experience parameters. The majority of food literacy definitions put importance on acquisition of critical and functional knowledge about food. By keeping the eight food literacy steps in mind, critical knowledge can be associated with the steps called knowing where food comes from, understanding language, nutrition value. Functional knowledge may contain the steps of eating, planning, management, selection, access and preparation (Table 1).

Table 1. Food literacy

	Critical knowledge	Functional knowledge
Kliktag	Understanding language, nutritional value	Eating, planning, management, selection
	Knowing where food comes from	Access, preparation

By appealing these steps, Kliktag may help to alleviate gastro anxiety. By referring to the steps mentioned above, this article evaluates how the informative content presented in the Kliktag affects user behavior related with food literacy.

Moreover, a complementary analysis framework was also used in understanding the user experience in Kligtag. This framework, included the following parameters:

Onboarding, Search Experience (Findability), Consistency and Standards, Visual Hierarchy, Visibility, Data Visualization, User Collaboration, Editorial Tone, Providing complementary information to support decision making, Uncurated over-abundant use of ads, Unmoderated social media share. Moreover, the study also analyzes Kliktag's effect on changing user behavior related with food literacy.

4   Results and Discussion

This section provides findings due to the two analysis frameworks provided above. Firstly, an in-depth analysis of the user experience is presented. Afterwords, in the final sub-section, by referring to the analysis framework on food literacy, the paper presents findings on how user behaviors were changed due to the evolving food literacy supported by the given application.

4.1   Onboarding

A well engaged onboarding user experience indicates the value of the product. According to the first-time user experience findings, lack of onboarding is a prominent issue. Kliktag doesn't include an onboarding step that informs users about the content of the app. It doesn't support users to know where they are and what they can do next. In the main page of Kliktag there is a line called "last seen product". First-time users (n = 10) spent approximately five minutes to figure it out. This line makes them think why they see it, who sees the product first and the last, why is this product chosen, is it the most preferred item or is it the healthiest one. When they push the "(!)" button on left corner which supposes to explain the purpose and usage of that line they only see the warning "you see the last scanned item." This button creates a strong disappointment and make the user confused (Fig. 3).

Fig. 3.   Presentation of last seen product

In addition to this, Kliktag doesn't explain why it needs to get camera and location permission from users. Due to lack of onboarding, those permissions trigger anxiety on users. All first-time users would like to learn why their data was collected and how it is used. They also would like to know if they have the right to withdraw their consent at any time.

As soon as the users accessed the main page, permission for camera and location were requested. First-time users did not give the permission to camera as they didn't yet use the barcode scanning. They found location permission irrational and intrusive. During the practice, Kliktag insisted on permissions for both camera and location. All users stated that this persistence made them feel insecure. It can be said that privacy management of Kliktag was not properly designed to meet customer expectation. It doesn't build and strengthen trust among users.

On the other hand, during the ten days practice, as time passed by, all users get used to it and gave Kliktag those permissions. It is seen that users get confused along the Kliktag journey because of onboarding lack. Kliktag needs to design an onboarding experience to drive users' satisfaction.

4.2　Search Experience (Findability)

In Kliktag case, First-time users (n = 7) would like to search a product in the database to reach the related information. However, performance related limitations in the search experience such as the lack of a placeholder text to support pre-search and lack of auto-completion/auto-correction, caused frustration and even abandonment of the app. The participants were confused in how to write in to the search bar. P4 hesitated if she should have written the brand or the name of the product.

P5 was also confused if she could write the name of a fruit other than a packaged product. Search box didn't provide alternative suggestions when the user misspelled a term. When P4 couldn't find the "Pringles" through the use of search box, she closed the application, opened Google Chrome and enter the word of "Pringles" to check its spelling. After that she opened the application, past the home page and clicked searching box and entered the spelling again. She could not find it and finally thought may be Pringles is not in the database. On the other hand, when she clicked the category called "snacks - cips" she found the various type of Pringles (Fig. 4).

Fig. 4. Search box

It was observed that the shortcomings of the search engine caused significant cognitive load in terms of search experience: "Should I always find the appropriate category first and then write the brand name? Or the product? This is just so complicated. On the other hand, categories are limited" (P4). According to Agricultural

Research Service of U.S there are fourteen food categories in a human diet such as Milk and Dairy, Grains, Beverages Non Alcoholic, Protein Foods, Snacks and Sweets, Alcoholic Beverages, Water, Fats and Oils, Mixed Dishes, Fruit, Condiment and Sauces, Sugars, Vegetables, Infant Formula & Baby Food, Others (protein powders and etc.) Hence, Kliktag categorization was not appropriate due to valid scientific standards. After ten days of practice, all users indicated that they felt as if the products they were looking for were somewhere in the database but they couldn't find it. This situation generated a dissatisfaction and even trust issues in users (Fig. 5).

Fig. 5. Results of categoric search

After ten days of practice P5 also said that the current data base lacked of vegan or vegetarian products. On the other hand, although the level of findability was low, users did not abandon Kliktag and keep their motivation to find the related food products. All

Fig. 6. User's loading data of unknown products

of them indicated the knowledge they obtain from Kliktag was worth making effort for searching the products (Fig. 6).

The other problem about the search page was that when user entered the name of a food product, brands that produced it were not sorted due to the score parameter. If the user wanted to sort the products in an arranged order due to their scores, they needed to purchase the Premium account. This feature was not persuasive enough to convince the users to buy the Premium. The participants chose to scroll down the page and take a quick glance all the products. However, it was evident that this experience was frustrating. For example, in her first-time use, P5 indicated that when she looked for pekmez in the database, products were listed randomly (Fig. 7).

Fig. 7. Random product list

"I wished I could see them in an order. It doesn't seem neat. Should I browse all the list?" Yet, in her fourth day she said she got used to scrolling down and find the product she was looking for. Although browsing option is confusing, she got used to operate it because of its benefits.

Additionally, users can't display alcoholic beverages on Kliktag database. It says that in accordance with the law no 6487, they can't inform users about the product that involves alcohol. P8 said that she felt disappointed and can't legitimate this warning.

Third problem about the search experience was that the search algorithm didn't classify the products due to their nutrition value. NOVA scores for food processing doesn't consider the ingredient value. In other words, this classification assigns food products based on how much processing they have been through. The ingredients that are engaged in both organic and conventional agriculture can't be separated. The fact that their nutrition values are different from each other can't reflect on NOVA processing scores. This issue was not realized in first-time user experience but through a ten days practice all of the uses were aware of this complexity (Fig. 8).

Fig. 8. Same score with different nutrition values.

Kliktag needs to inform users about the content, what NOVA considers and what does not. Otherwise, reinforcing the trust in users might be hard.

Furthermore, back button creates a huge friction in first-time user experience. When users (n = 10) search an item in the search box and tried go back to enter another item, they clicked the back button. Yet when they do it, instead of leading users to the main search box, the application is closed. Users need to open Kliktag and enter the name of the item again to find the product. Users have to use "restart searching" button which is not visible for them at all. After the ten days of practice it was seen that the users tolerated the use of the back button and started using the button to restart searching.

4.3 Visual Hierarchy

Visual hierarchy is valuable as it provides better context for the user and generalizes key regions of the product. In the home page of Kliktag there is a space between the last seen product box and the advertisements. All first-time users wondered the function of the space. When they realized it only separates the elements on the homepage, they found it too large to be effective. Inefficient use of the white space doesn't match up with users' expectation (Fig. 9).

It can be said that this space is not helping to set vertical rhythm or linespacing of the page. It distracts the overall completeness. It needs to reexamined to catch the intended visual hierarchy and connect elements properly.

Fig. 9. Unproductive space at home page

4.4 Visibility

Visibility is an important element for construction an interaction and user centered design. It focuses on how a user interacts with specific elements of the product. In other words, the level of visibility plays an important role constructing good and bad practice.

First of all, users might register and log in to Kliktag system or they can continue to use it as a guest. But guests have limited interaction as they can't scan the barcode or choose preferences. In this context, five of first-time users chose to continue with Facebook, others (n = 5) were faced with problem in registration. Since the "new user" button can't be realized because of its placement, users found themselves entering the username and password of their e-mail account. When they realized the failure, they erased the entered information and searched the icon for new users. However, they had difficulty in finding the small grey button just under the right side of the password button. The placement of the buttons doesn't indicate what possible actions the buttons offer to users. Because of the size, the color and its placement, visibility is decreased. Contrast colors needs to be used to emphasize the button of new user.

4.5 Data Visualization

Visual elements that Kliktag use have the same purpose as well. In the first-time experience, information display through the visualization of colors and score numbers created a confusion among users. NOVA give colors to food products in terms of being processed from green to red, by giving ranking scores from 1 to 5. Four first-time users linked the green color with the highest number 5. They thought the score of 5 is the healthiest and needs to be green. On the other hand, six of them lived a momentary confusion in understanding the logic of ranking. In the end of first day practice, the mentioned four users adopted the information display of Kliktag. It is learnable, yet it causes a friction which may lead to frustration and abandonment for users from different backgrounds (Fig. 10).

Fig. 10. Users' confusion about colors and score (Color figure online)

On the other hand, after users understand the meaning of scores and colors, they are satisfied with visual consistency. Other than the NOVA groups processing score, the ranking colors of green yellow orange red dark red is also used to classify food additives. All of the users indicated that they all thought every food additive is harmful to human body. Learning food additives that have green colors does not directly cause a disease in the body alleviated users' gastro anxiety to a degree. It can be said that visual consistency that Kliktag has helped users to engage. Moreover, onboarding which supports the learning of the meaning of the colors can enhance the experience.

4.6   User Collaboration

Kliktag is an application which invites users to be active for updating the improvement of the platform. It allows users to upload the images that are not in the database. Users mostly appreciate the feature of uploading after the act of scanning. Once new images are uploaded, they are analyzed by Kliktag and put in their database. Also, since the barcode numbers and ingredients are constantly changing, Kliktag invite users to check if the nutrition values are current. They may report the difference and support Kliktag to stay updated. By doing this, Kliktag positioned users as a self-control mechanism for the application. Moreover, the speed of barcode scanning satisfies the users. On the other hand, the opening time of Kliktag might bothers users. Especially while shopping it takes time to launch it. In first three days, users even indicated that they waited in front of the shop for the Kliktag to open before buying a food product. However, as time passed by, the users learned how to cope with this issue.

On the other hand, users are limited only by the image upload right after the scanning. It is not possible to manually upload an image in the system. User collaboration is promising. Yet collaboration with limited interaction demotivates the users for further engagement. Although the users are willing to find strategies to overcome these limitations, they should be provided with more features to support collaboration.

4.7   Editorial Tone

The tone of the editor shapes how users interact and communicate with the application. It contains the language, words, expressions, phrases and intonations. The way of Kliktag presents the content needs to be revised. The language of Kliktag needs to be balanced in the context of formality. According to findings, the tone of voice was located between formal and informal tone. It is seen that Kliktag tried to create a simple language instead of technical terms. It tries to provide easy explanations and create an empathy with the user. P6 said that "the everyday language of Kliktag sounds good, I think. I felt sincerity. Because we learn very serious things about the things we eat and drink, and the informal language made me relax." This attitude was common among other users. Yet, P8 said that in the "About us" section, the language Kliktag use is full of spelling errors. She indicated that "it doesn't seem professional at all. The content deserves a professional language. I mean expressions don't have to be formal but spelling errors irritate me." Hence, it can be said that the language of Kliktag needs to be revised to catch the right balance between an informal and formal tone.

4.8   Providing Complementary Information

Kliktag provides additional complementary information for the users to support decision making. For example, it alerts users who search Kinoa in the database: For example, Yayla Agro Food brand was in the list of adulteration list of Ministry of Agriculture and Forest in 2016 due to the quantity of yellow food dye in bulgur. Kliktag also made a warning about BEŞLER brand, since it was on the list of adulteration due to the contents of its sausage (Fig. 11).

Other than this, Kliktag also motivates users in using home-made food instead of packaged food. For instance, Kliktag recommends users to make their own home-made crema by referring to the low scores of the ingredients found in the popular crema brands in the market.

Furthermore, while adding informative pop-ups, Kliktag needs to review the use of navigation buttons in carousels that present information. All first-time users have difficulty in understanding the function of these dots and couldn't navigate to the other slides of these carousels. Navigation between the slides in these carousels needs to be enabled through the use of "arrow" signs.

Fig. 11. Information about adulteration list

4.9 Uncurated over Abundant Use of Ads

The abundance of advertisements in the app caused frustration and even the abandonment of the app. All users indicated that showing too much advertisement ruin the visual flow. Kliktag offers the Premium version for those who wouldn't want to see ads. Although this seems to be the core business model of the Kliktag, it was observed that the users were frustrated with this offer.

Moreover, some of the advertisement presented in the app even ruins the core principles and the consistency of the context. Kliktag displays the advertisement of the chicken steak of Şenpiliç brand. However, the food displayed on the content is not listed in the app. Other products of Şenpiliç have the highest score of 5 or 4 in Kliktag's database, which means they are extremely processed. Displaying such an ad engenders a significant level of distrust and frustration. Hence, it can be said that Kliktag needs to minimize the amounts of ads in page transition and reviewed the contexts to reinforce whole integrity (Fig. 12).

4.10 Unmoderated Social Media Share

Kliktag gives users an opportunity to make comments and share the reviewed products on other social media channels. Unfortunately, all of the first-time users could not realize this feature. On the other hand, in the long-term ethnographic study, they discovered that they can read and make comments.

Presentation of unmoderated user-generated content caused the users feel unsecure. P4 indicated that the comment section is so passive and monotone. To create participatory culture and empower the interaction, Kliktag needs to reorganize the comment section to be more attractive for action. On the other hand, the opportunity of sharing the product on other social media channels satisfy the need of the users. P6 said that "I

Fig. 12. Inconsistency in advertisements

would like to share the information I learned from my friends. It is more effective to send direct Kliktag links to them. They may directly open it and see the information on the app of Kliktag. It seems that the sharing option can help users to be engaged.

4.11 "Shopping with Kliktag": Change of User Behaviors Related to Evolving Food Literacy

Kliktag includes features that enables users to gain critical and functional food literacy. By helping users to learn how to read packaging language and the nutrition value, it facilitates the functional knowledge to be obtained. First of all, Kliktag made health analysis by showing health compromising ingredients. It analyzes the food products in terms of food additives such as flavorants, invert sugar, starch-based sugar and palm oil. It explains why they are harmful to human body by using visuals as well. After that, it represents e-code analysis of the product. It makes explanation of the codes and colors them in terms of health risk. This feature helps users to alleviate their gastro anxiety and become aware of the contents. For example, in the second day of practice, P1 said that "I believed that industrial foods have food additives and it is very harmful for human body. I felt guilty when I had to eat it. But now I learned that they don't have any food additives. I'm set at ease. I wish I had used Kliktag before.

In her sixth day, P6 also said that "I am vegetarian and often use pea protein. Kliktag showed me that it is an ultra-processed product. I am searching for different brands with lower scores."

Kliktag also help users obtain functional food literacy knowledge to empower their planning management and selection process. In her fourth day P5 said that "I am a snack lover especially I constantly buy chips. I've already known that all the products I consume is very harmful. Kliktag explains why it is harmful." On the second day, P2 indicated that she changed the bread brand that she got used to eat after using the Kliktag. Furthermore, all users changed water brands that they consumed. Kliktag published a list that ranks the score of water brands. Based on that list, users changed their preferences. It was the most observed behavioral change.

It was seen that the users end up with increasing level of gastro anxiety even in the first-time use of Kliktag. During approximately three days, it continued to rise. For example, on her third day, P2 said that "I was a happier person before I met with this application. It always shows the negative sides of food." P3 said that "I had already known that the food system did not consider human health but valued the money. Our bodies became units through which the system can maximize its profit. It is hopeless." However as time passed and the users became more familiar with Kliktag, choosing healthier products and creating alternative solutions became easier to them. P4 said that "At the beginning, it feels like I will be obsessive compulsive about food. But then I realized that there are some basic criteria to eat healthier.

Vegetarian and vegans also indicated that they feel much more secure about the selection of food products since Kliktag made a deep analysis in terms of animal derived ingredients. Kliktag analyzes the food products in terms of being halal. At first view users thought that (n = 10) this analysis was made for users with Islamic sensibilities. However, Kliktag explains whether the product might not be halal since it may contain pork or some kind of insects. This explanation goes beyond halal certification and become a guide for vegans. Warnings about halal food lead vegans not to consume food products that carry the risk of having animal derived ingredients. As it is seen, Kliktag leads a behavior change for all users in the context of food literacy. All in all, it can be said that from the first-time use till approximately third day, the level of gastro-anxiety has been increased. But once the application has established trust, presence and familiarity with users, the level of gastro-anxiety has been decreased. Users started to use Kliktag to make healthier judgements through a rational process.

During the long-term use of the app for ten days, Kliktag persuaded all the users to achieve the desired behavior. Users took actions to enhance food literacy in accordance with Kliktag. Although there are user experience related issues that minimized the efficiency and effectiveness, there is a conversion. In the interview at the end of the diary study, all users indicated that they wouldn't uninstall Kliktag. They self-reported the desire to continue.

As mentioned in the previous section, Kliktag needs to reformulate some design elements to optimize its effect. On the other hand, none of the users preferred to buy the Premium account. Kliktag can't persuade users to switch to Premium although the price is low: 3.99 TL per month. P5 said that "I felt like there is a coercion. I am subjected to non-stop advertising if I don't buy Premium account. It is not a friendly attitude at all." Kliktag needs to change this perceived aggressive attitude to increase the level of persuasiveness.

5 Conclusion

In today's world, people are seeking for healthy and secure food while harmful effects of industrial food production on human body become a controversial topic. Since non confirmed information about food and eating are circulated through various media channels, developing food literacy skills is getting harder. The problem of information aggregation lead gastro anxiety. However, there is not any study to focus on how it is experienced in daily life. Through a user experience perspective-based framework, this study analyzes Kliktag, which aims to lead users towards healthy foodways. It also evaluates the effect of Kliktag on user behavior in terms of food literacy.

Findings stated the notion that the process of finding information in search box is too complicated. It takes a significant time to search and find the product. It creates a cognitive load since user navigation is not supported by an onboarding process. Due to low findability of products, there's a risk that people will simply abandon it in long term. Furthermore, Kliktag invites users to be active and contribute to Kliktag. Yet, limited interaction, the uncurated over-abundant use of ads and the unmoderated social media share constitute obstacles against the desired experience. On the other hand, users were observed to tolerate the difficulties caused by user experience issues during the long-term diary study. Moreover, despite these issues, they were able to obtain food literacy skills in terms of reading the language of labels, understanding nutrition values, selection and managing the proper food. In first three days, it was seen that the level of gastro anxiety has risen. Yet, the more users become familiar with the application, the more gastro anxiety has been alleviated. It was observed that there is a concrete behavioral change among users since they adopted related food literacy skills. By improving the provided user experience by minimizing the friction in completing relevant tasks, better changes in user behavior towards a healthier life can be achieved.

References

1. Truman, E., Lane, D., Elliott, C.: Defining food literacy: a scoping review. Appetite **116**, 365–371 (2017)
2. Caraher, M., Lang, T.: Can't cook, won't cook: a review of cooking skills and their relevance on health promotion. Int. J. Health Promot. Educ. **37**, 89–100 (1999)
3. Cullen, T., Hatch, J., Martin, W., Higgins, J.W., Sheppard, R.: Food literacy: definition and framework for action. Can. J. Diet. Pract. Res. **76**(3), 140–145 (2015)
4. Kolasa, K.M., Peery, A., Harris, N.G., Shovelin, K.: Food literacy partners program: a strategy to increase community food literacy. Top. Clin. Nutr. **16**(4), 1–10 (2001)
5. Minehan, M.: Green, Healthy and Eat Meat?: A mixed-methods investigation into how meat is used and viewed by meat-eaters in Australia. Doctoral Dissertation (2013). http://www.canberra.edu.au/researchrepository/itms/38b96b3f-97ae-49b5-80bf-eb3eba3ceb95/1/
6. Vidgen, H.A., Gallegos, D.: Defining food literacy and its components. Appetite **76**, 50–59 (2014)
7. Nowatschin, E.: Educational food landscapes: developing design guidelines for school gardens, Master's Thesis. University of Guelph Atrium (2014). https://dspace.lib.uoguelph.ca/xmlui/handle/10214/8057
8. Fischler, C.: Food, self and identity. Inf. (Int. Soc. Sci. Counc.) **27**(2), 275–292 (1988)
9. Kanık, İ.: Gastro-Endişe ve Yeni Toplumsal Hareketler (Gastro-Anxiety and New Social Movements). J. Tour. Gastronomy Stud. **5**, 599–620 (2017)
10. Savarin, B.: You are what you eat. Physiol. Gout **32**, 243–245 (1826)
11. Murray, E.: Origin and Growth of the Thai Food Industry & Thailand - The Kitchen of the World. CAB Calling, CAB-RBI Pune (2007)

12. Comber, R., Choi, J., Hoonhout, J., O'Hara, K.: Designing for human–food interaction: an introduction to the special issue on 'food and interaction design'. Int. J. Hum. Comput. Stud. **72**, 181–184 (2014)
13. Khot, R.A., Mueller, F.: Human-food interaction. Found. Trends® Hum. Comput. Interact. **12**(4), 238–415 (2019)
14. Sun, J., Peng, Z., Zhou, W., Fuh, J.Y.H., Hong, G.S., Chiu, A.: A review on 3D printing for customized food fabrication. Proc. Manuf. **1**, 308–319 (2015)
15. Arnold, P., Khot, R.A., Mueller, F.F.: "You Better Eat to Survive": exploring cooperative eating in virtual reality games. In: Proceedings of the Twelfth International Conference on Tangible, Embedded, and Embodied Interaction (2008)
16. Mehta, Y., Khot, R.A., Patibanda, R., Mueller, F.: Arm-a-dine: towards understanding the design of playful embodied eating experiences. In: Publication of the Annual Symposium on Computer-Human Interaction in Play. ACM (2018)
17. West, J., Hall, P., Arredondo, V., Berrett, B., Guerra, B., Farrell, J.: Health behavior theories in diet apps. J. Consum. Health Internet **17**, 10–24 (2013)
18. Eikey E.V., Reddy M.C.: "It's Definitely Been A Journey": A Qualitative Study on How Women with Eating Disorders Use Weight Loss Apps. Self tracking Mental Health, Denver, USA (2017)
19. Taimouri, A., Emamisaleh, K., Mohammadi, D.: Assesing the usability of online food ordering websites using a new fuzzy Kano method: implications for improvement. Int. J. Bus. Manag. **14**(10), 87–100 (2019)
20. Bonfirm, M.C.C., Wallace, J.R.: Pirate Bri's Grocery Adventure: Teaching Food Literacy through Shopping, Montreal Canada (2018)
21. Hingle, M., Patrick, H.: There are thousands of apps for that: navigating mobile technology for nutrition education and behavior. J. Nutr. Educ. Behav. **48**(3), 213–218 (2015)
22. Riebe D., Greene, G.W. Ruggiero, L., Stillwell, K.M., Nigg, C.R.: Evaluation of a healthy lifestyle approach to weight management. Prevent. Med. **36**(1), 45–54 (2013)
23. McCabe, J., Doerflinger, A., Fox, R.: Student and faculty perceptions of e-feedback. Teach. Pschol. **38**(3), 173–179 (2011)
24. Kiefer, I., Rathmanner, T., Kunze, M.: Eating and dieting differences in men and women. J. Men's Health Gend. **2**, 194–201 (2005)
25. Su, D., Zhou, J., Jackson, H.L., Soliman, G.A., Huang, T.T., Yaroch, A.L.: A sex specific analysis of nutrition label use and health, Douglas County, Nebraska, 2013. Prevent. Chronic Dis. **12**, E158 (2015)
26. Austin, Z., Sutton, J.: Qualitative research: getting started. Can. J. Hosp. Pharm. **67**(6), 436–440 (2014)

A Usability Testing Comparing Two Mobile Phone Gimbals

Keke Zhong[✉], Junfei Liu, Zhixin Gui, Chang Meng,
and Marcelo M. Soares

School of Design, Hunan University, Changsha 410000, Hunan,
People's Republic of China
zhongkeke98@gmail.com, 384814300@qq.com,
649651069@qq.com, 945561012@qq.com, soaresmm@gmail.com

Abstract. In this study, we compared two Mobile Phone Gimbals from DJI and MOZA to investigate usability issues and access which product has better usability and provide iterative recommendations for Mobile Phone Gimbal. The study was conducted from May to June 2019 based on the principle of effectiveness, efficiency and satisfaction in ISO 9241-11 [1]. Then the usability test was carried out in three parts: task design, test exclusion and data statistic. 6 subjects were asked to complete five tasks with two gimbals following the principle of think aloud protocols and given a short interview to measure their satisfaction. Results indicate that there is a usability issue of installing and balancing in novice users in both products. OSMO has simple buttons, which is easier for the novice, but users have to tap the screen of mobile phone to complete some tasks. On the contrary, MOZA enables users to operate with single hand all the time by more buttons, but it is too complicated for the novice.

Keywords: Mobile phone gimbal · Usability

1 Introduction

In present society, the high picture quality of mobile phones and the booming of mobile live broadcasting and short video industry have increased people's demand for the quality of mobile video shooting. This is true especially in terms of the stability and various photographic modes.

Products that are used in everyday life and that are not usable, that do not meet the requirements of users, cause frustration of users, and usually users no longer want to use these products [1].

According to ISO 9241-11, usability refers to the effectiveness, efficiency and subjective satisfaction of a product when it is used for a specific user in a specific environment [2]. Before embarking on the development of a new product, it may be beneficial to conduct evaluations of existing products in order to gain an understanding

© Springer Nature Switzerland AG 2020
A. Marcus and E. Rosenzweig (Eds.): HCII 2020, LNCS 12201, pp. 376–387, 2020.
https://doi.org/10.1007/978-3-030-49760-6_27

in terms of the usability of what is already available. This might form a baseline against which the usability of the new product can be judged [2]. Therefore, we chose two mainstream mobile phone gimbals in the market as research samples.

The purpose of this paper is to compare two Mobile Phone Gimbals from DJI and MOZA to investigate usability issues and access which product has better usability and provide iterative recommendations for Mobile Phone Gimbal. Because our usability scenario is comparing two products [3], task success, efficiency (time and steps) and self-report of satisfaction are chosen as metrics. Being able to complete a task correctly is essential for most products. By looking at efficiency, we will get a good sense of how much effort is required to use the product. Some self-reported metrics of satisfaction provide an overall user experience with the product, especially when comparing multiple products.

A mobile phone gimbal comprises a handle body, with the stabilizer and a fixing device for mobile phone on the stabilizer (see Fig. 1). The stabilizer includes three motors which are arranged at top of the handheld part and are orthogonal in a space, wherein the three motors are respectively an X-axis motor, a Y-axis motor, and a Z-axis motor [4], to guarantee the stability of mobile phone camera in all directions in space.

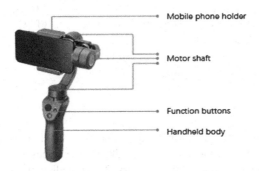

Fig. 1. The structure of a mobile phone gimbal (E.g. DJI OSMO MOBILE 2)

2   Materials and Methods

2.1   Materials

Two mobile phone gimbals from the Chinese brand DJI and MOZA have been chosen (see Fig. 2). In terms of the appearance, they are very similar in the size, shape and material. Relevant product data can be seen in Table 1. The significant difference between them is the button type on the handheld body. During the test all subjects will perform several tasks with both devices.

Fig. 2. DJI OSMO MOBILE 2 (left) and MOZA Mini MI (right)

Table 1. Product data

	OSMO	MOZA
Size (mm)	295 × 113 × 72	290 × 143 × 107
Weight (g)	458	543
Width of compatible phones (mm)	58.6–85	61–92
Max controllable speed (mm)	120°/s	Not given
App	DJI GO	MOZA Genie

2.2   Subjects

Seven subjects were recruited via online questionnaire. All subjects were between 20–24 years old and have basic video knowledge like shutter, focus and slow motion. They were divided into three groups (3 novice users, 2 intermediate users and 2 professional user) on the basis of familiarity and proficiency with the mobile phone gimbal, and we defined these three groups as one never used a mobile phone gimbal, used several times, used more than 10 times, respectively (see Table 2.). There was no prior training, and all subjects were only shown the product introduction (basis functions and modes) and notes on the products homepage.

Table 2. User grouping

Subjects	Feature	Number
Novice users	Never used: interested in recoding video; know this product	P1 P2 P3
Intermittent users	Used several times; short usage time	P4 P5
Expert users	Used more than 10 times	P6 P7

2.3   Task Design

Each case uses the same evaluation protocol. First, subjects will receive a short questionnaire (gender, age and field). Then, a concurrent think-aloud protocol is administered when they were given five tasks to complete using two products. One researcher will observe and record their emotions as they speak. At the same time, usability performance metrics (task success, time, satisfaction, steps, and errors) will be also assessed.

Subjects have five minutes to complete each task. If they could not complete within a limited time or do not want to proceed, they continue to the next task. The first task is to install the mobile phone on the gimbal and adjust it to the balance. Next is connecting Bluetooth and accessing the app for each product (task 2) to take a 2–5 s video, from left to right, and keep zoom in to maximum (task 3); Then they are asked to use slow motion mode to shoot a 2–5 s video (task 4); The final task is to adjust to self-timer mode of vertical screen and take a photo (task 5). After each task, the subjects will be given a short interview to measure task satisfaction. After carrying out all tasks, they fill out the questionnaire including 16 questions.

The usability tests will last around 60 min. The tests will be conducted in a cafe and each of them is performed in a closed room to minimize distraction. Audio and screen capture recordings will be made during the tests.

2.4   Task Analysis

In order to collect and measure the metric like efficiency more conveniently, we identify the actions of each tasks we want to capture. According to the common functions of smart phone gimbals, the tasks are divided into five aspects, including mounting and balancing, connecting, parameter adjustment, mode switching and working mode switching (landscape/portrait). The optimal steps for each task are defined according to the actual operations, in which are same in the task 1 and 2 for both products. In task 3–5 when it comes to the menu of apps, the operations of MOZA differ from OSMO, and the former is indicated by dashed lines. The task descriptions will be displayed to users at the start of each task.

3   Results

3.1   Effectiveness

Effectiveness refers to the degree of accuracy and completeness [1] of users when they complete specific tasks and achieve specific goals. Task success [3] is the broadest metric from it. All subjects were shown the end state in text clearly of each task before they started, and were told to give an oral self-report when they thought they have finished the task or wanted to give it up. We divided the success of tasks into three levels [3] (see Fig. 3).

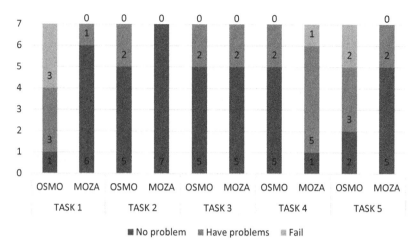

Fig. 3. Number of users with different levels of tasks success (No problem = Complete the task accurately without help; Have problems = Complete the task with some problems; Fail = Task failed or abandoned)

In general, the level of task success differs from types of users and tasks. When using OSMO, three novice users failed in task 1, and only an expert (P7) completed the task accurately, other users had the problem with balancing the gimbal, and repeatedly rotated the two knobs on the mobile phone holder and shaft. Similarly, there also were two novice users (P1 and P3) who failed in task 5 involving mounting and balancing. In task 4, there were some problems for two novice users (P1 and P2) in switching slow-motion mode. However, no significant differences between types of users were seen in task 2 and 3 when connecting and adjusting parameter.

For MOZA, the degree of task completion is generally better than that of OSMO, except for task 4, where a novice user (P1) failed to find the slow-motion mode due to a timeout, and five users completed the task with some other problems.

3.2   Efficiency

Efficiency refers to the amount of effort required to complete the task [1]. Task time [3] is an excellent way to measure the efficiency in the usability test. The time it takes a subject to perform a task says a lot about the usability of the product. Another way is measuring the number of actions or steps that subjects took in performing each task. In the steps of completing the task, the operation and cognitive errors of subjects will affect the performance of the task, so the number of error steps made during the interaction is also very revealing.

Task Time. In the task 1 and 5 which involve mounting and balancing, they took longer time than other tasks (see Fig. 4), and the effort novices made are two or three times as the experts' (see Table 3). It took longer time for subjects to use OSMO to complete the tasks (above two and three minutes respectively) comparing with MOZA, which has a greater experience in balancing. The bigger size of MOZA leads to a larger tolerance range and saving time.

There was no significant difference between types of users when completing task 2, while a marked difference can be seen in task 3 and 4. Two novice users (P1 and P2) spent more than two minutes to complete task 4 by OSMO, but the intermediate users and expert users took less than half a minute. It seems that the interactive ways of zooming in/out are different, and users can push up the zoom slider by OSMO or rotate the dial wheel by MOZA. The later has no obvious sign indicated that the dial wheel is used to zoom in and its finer scale and slower zoom speed cause lower efficiency.

Comparing the two products, the efficiency of using MOZA to complete the operation involving buttons and app interface (task 3 and 4) is lower than that of OSMO. Especially the novice users spend a lot of time to search for the position where the mode displays. However, as for Bluetooth connection (task 2), OSMO has more confusing feedback, so it takes more time than MOZA.

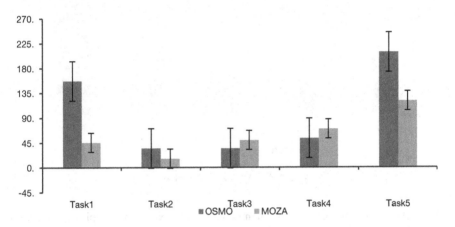

Fig. 4. Average task time of each task (shown in second)

Table 3. Task time (shown in second); "/" means the user failed in this task due to a timeout above 300 s, which is used to calculate the mean score

	TASK 1		TASK 2		TASK 3		TASK 4		TASK 5	
	OSMO	MOZA	OSMO	MOZA	OSMO	MOZA	OSMO	MOZA	OSMO	MOZA
P1	/	54	30	29	30	55	145	/	/	122
P2	/	80	54	10	68	77	150	34	211	224
P3	/	36	47	16	64	60	30	45	/	122
P4	87	44	46	18	40	60	10	60	190	146
P5	55	60	14	16	10	45	10	18	175	80
P6	37	15	44	10	17	27	15	20	220	80
P7	21	29	9	13	15	23	11	16	70	70

Task Steps and Error. From the optimal steps (see Fig. 5), when choosing a special shooting mode such as slow-motion and selfie mode, MOZA has two more steps than OSMO because of its functional structure which affects the user's efficiency. Users tended to make errors in task 4 and 5 by using MOZA, and there were six subjects except for P7 trying every icon on the first level of menu to search the slow-motion (see Table 3), as they considered that the basic mode switching should be on the first level of the functional structure as OSMO does. MOZO allows switching mode by the button on the handheld body, but a user (P5) regarded the record button which set in the middle of dial wheel as the menu button.

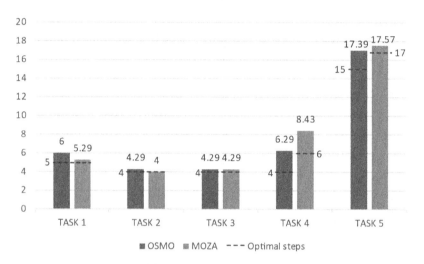

Fig. 5. Average task steps

Subjects are also prone to errors when mounting and balancing the phone, especially novice and intermediate users, because they are not familiar with the balancing principles and structure of gimbal. Five subjects thought they can adjust the balance by rotating the knob (which is actually used to unlock the arm-shaft and mobile phone holder), and it made them to spend more time trying to rotate each knob.

Another bigger error occurred in task 5 due to the smaller size of OSMO. There was no room for mobile phone to rotate, so subjects have to demount the mobile phone before rotating the mobile phone holder to the selfie mode. Four subjects expressed puzzle and they did not want to re-mount and balance again when they found it impossible to rotate the holder with mobile phone.

3.3   Satisfaction

Satisfaction refers to the degree of subjective satisfaction and acceptance that subjects feel in the process of using products [1]. After carrying out all tasks, the users were asked to fill out the questionnaire, which involve usefulness, learnability, satisfaction, ease of use [5] (see Table 4.), and given a short interview about their scores.

Table 4. Satisfaction questionnaire (5-point semantic ·differential scale, −3 = Totally disagree, 3 = Totally agree) Q1–Q3, Q4–Q7, Q8–Q10 and Q11–Q13 are related to the usefulness, learnability, satisfaction and fault tolerance.

	Mean score	
	OSMO	MOZA
Q1. I can improve the shooting effect of video with this device	2.67	2.50
Q2. I can save shooting time by using this device	0.33	1.33
Q3. This device meets my expected demand (shooting video)	2.67	2.67
Mean score of usefulness	**1.89**	**2.16**
Q4. The use process of my product is consistent with my cognitive operation	0.00	1.17
Q5. I don't think there is any confusion about the next step in the operation	1.16	1.67
Q6. I can learn to use it quickly	1.16	2.67
Q7. It is easy for me to remember how to use it	2.67	2.67
Mean score of learnability	**1.24**	**2.05**
Q8. I can skillfully finish my ideas very quickly	1.00	1.33
Q9. I am very satisfied with the use of product	1.50	2.00
Q10. I will recommend this product to my friends	1.50	1.83
Mean score of satisfaction	**1.33**	**1.72**
Q11. I can do what I want to do very quickly	1.50	0.83
Q12. My operation can hardly go wrong	−0.17	1.00
Q13. I easily recover from the wrong operation to the normal state	1.00	2.50
Mean score of ease of use	**0.77**	**1.48**

The average satisfaction of usefulness is 1.89 and 2.16 for OSMO and MOZA respectively, and the difference is shown in Q2, as the novice and immediate user thought them spend too much time on mounting and balancing.

For the experienced users, they use the mobile phone gimbal with ease, but in the operation of the other brands of mobile phone gimbal which they are not familiar with, is likely to be troubled by the existing experience, for example, an intermediate user (P4) who only used OSMO several times, felt confused and spent time to get used to the dial wheel to choose mode. However, the expert user (P6) who were used to use DSLRs (Digital Singular Lens Reflex) suggested some possible improvements to the product, such as "I think the wheel dial is more accurate (than the zoom slider)." While a few users (P4 and P5) thought "The zoom slider is better, as the zoom speed of dial wheel is too slow."

The average satisfaction of novice users is lower than that of other types of users. Compared with others, the novice users clearly showed confusion and uncertainty about the next step as they said "Is this balance?" and "Should I press this now?" (P1) "Now…is it shooting?"

The ease of learning scores are as low as 0.77 and 1.48, indicating that when using both gimbal, users cannot easily detect and correct their mistakes. In the user behavior analysis (including semantic analysis and operational process analysis), it is further concluded that the reason for the poor fault-tolerant data is more due to not knowing how to correct their own errors than finding them.

4 Discussion

In general, the task 1 and 5 which refers to mobile phone mounting and balancing takes longer time and results in more errors on both devices, as its low compatibility and consistency [3] with users' expectations based on their knowledge and other similar products in terms of two rotate knobs which used to unlock the adjustable arm and mobile phone holder to move horizontally and rotate respectively (see Fig. 6). In our tests, fives users were confused about two rotate knobs and their purposes, they considered it rotary to adjust balance, the reason is that there is no obvious sign on the arm that it can be retracted. Therefore, as the improvement for OSMO MOBILE 2, we keep only one knob behind the mobile phone holder which can be loosened to move mobile phone holder horizontally and rotate it to the self-timer mode (see Fig. 7).

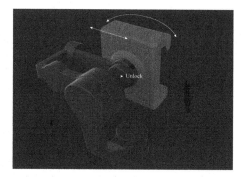

Fig. 6. OSMO MOBILE 2   Fig. 7. Improvement for OSMO MOBILE 2

We finished our test and developed our improvement for OSMO MOBILE 2 on June 10, 2019, it is worth noting that the DJI Technology Co, Ltd launched their new generation mobile phone gimbal OSMO MOBILE 3 on August 13, 2019 which removed two knobs and the adjustable arm. It needs to be balanced according to the adjustment position of the phone on the holder, and kept fixed by pressure and gear clasp [6], which is consistent with the structure of selfie stick. The similar proposal of keeping only the structure close to the phone be adjustable proved that the previous structure of adjustable arm leading to users' cognitive complexity.

Additionally, in our test we found that when installing the mobile phone to the gimbal, users have to operate the mobile phone holder and adjustable knob by hands, so a steady fulcrum is necessary. Both the table and body can be used as the fulcrum and that depends on the usage scenario. It is better to add a layer of anti-skid silica gel material on the bottom of handheld body.

The main features of mobile phone gimbal are shooting modes such as slow motion, time-lapse and panorama, so we took account of them in the task 4. There are differences in the interactive mode and functional framework between two apps of OSMO and MOZA. When switch the mode, OSMO can only complete the task through tapping the screen of mobile phone, on which the mode switch is on the first menu (see Fig. 8). It was similar to the camera interface on mobile phone, all users except for P1 could quickly and clearly complete the task of switching shooting mode within two steps. Conversely, MOZA can be operated both by tapping the mobile phone screen and buttons on the gimbal - Press the UP of dial wheel to enter the primary menu of setting, choose "camera mode" to the secondary menu (see Fig. 9) and users will find the slow-motion on the third level of menu with "photo" and "video" (see Fig. 10) by rotating the rotate wheel. The fact that MOZA puts the mode switch on the third menu below "setting" that associated with setting param, and the same level menu with "photo", leads to users' neglect when recording video. Actually, very few users tapped into secondary menu in our test. Remarkably, three intermittent and expert users (P4, P5 and P6) who used to use DSLRs (Digital Single Lens Reflex Camera) indicated a preference for buttons and dial wheel of MOZA, which was also adjustable to zoom in and out. Compared with the zoom slider of OSMO, the dial wheel is more accurate with its larger operating range and scale. Besides, they believed that operating the handle could prevent the damage of motors causing by the pressure generated by clicking on the screen. However, there was still a significant learning curve for the novices to get used to the complicated menu of MOZA. Future research could take account of the ease of learning. In response to this problem, we add a dial wheel around the original M button on OSMO, allowing users press the UP button on dial wheel to enter the first menu and select by rotating the wheel (see Fig. 11), which is easy to use with just one hand, providing more versatility and freedom of movement.

Fig. 8. Slow-motion on DJI GO app

Fig. 9. Slow-motion on MOZA genie

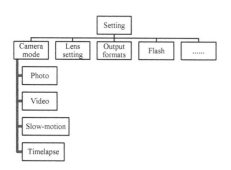

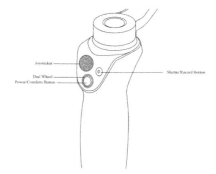

Fig. 10. Functional framework of MOZA Genie app

Fig. 11. Improvement for buttons

In addition to the basic functions involved in our tasks, users can quickly switch advanced functions with the M button on OSMO, which are not considered in our test due to their complexity and low frequency of use. As we can see, from DJI's newly released OSMO MOBILE 3, the implementation of these features has shifted to a trigger button behind the handle body [6].

5 Conclusion

This paper presented the result of a usability research of two Mobile Phone Gimbals from DJI and MOZA to provide iterative recommendations for Mobile Phone Gimbal. In order to measure the effectiveness, efficiency and subjective satisfaction, we chose four metrics of task success, time-on-task, errors and self-report. We recruited 6 users to complete five tasks with two gimbals following the principle of think aloud protocols and gave them a short interview to conduct the research.

The results revealed that there is a main usability issue of installing and balancing in novice users for both products. OSMO has simple buttons which is easier for the novice, but users have to tap the screen of mobile phone to complete some tasks. On the contrary, MOZA enables users to operate with single hand all the time by more buttons on the product, but it is too complicated to learn for the novice. Therefore, we iterate on the buttons and interaction mode of the gimbal products.

We designed a new gimbal on the base of OSMO Mobile 2. In the terms of the buttons, we keep only one knob which can be loosened to move mobile phone holder horizontally and rotate it to the self-timer mode. When users adjust the mobile phone on the gimbal, they need a steady fulcrum to support single-hand operation, so we add a layer of anti-skid silica gel material on the bottom of handheld body. Additionally, a wheel dial around the M button and a trigger on the back of the product are added to provide more efficient and interesting interaction experience between machine and the application.

With the improvement of technology, the access of short video has been increasingly convenient, and more people participate in the creation of video. In order to improve the shooting quality, there are many consumer products like OSMO mobile 2 coming into everyday life. As an innovative product in the emerging market, the mobile phone gimbal still needs constant usability tests to find problems and provide better experience. This is also the purpose of our research. The ease of operation on the machine and the efficiency of the interaction accessing with the application are both problems deserve our attention.

References

1. Bevan, N., Carter, J., Harker, S.: ISO 9241-11 revised: what have we learnt about usability since 1998? In: Kurosu, M. (ed.) HCI 2015. LNCS, vol. 9169, pp. 143–151. Springer, Cham (2015). https://doi.org/10.1007/978-3-319-20901-2_13
2. Jordan, P.W.: An Introduction to Usability, 1st edn. CRC Press, London (1998)
3. Albert, W., Tullis, T.: Measuring the User Experience: Collecting, Analyzing, and Presenting Usability Metrics, 2nd edn. Morgan Kaufmann, Waltham (2013)
4. DJI Technology. https://www.dji.com/sg/osmo-mobile-2. Accessed 27 Jan 2020
5. Measuring Usability with the USE Questionnaire. http://www.stcsig.org/usability/newsletter/0110_measuring_with_use.html. Accessed 27 Jan 2020
6. DJI Technology. https://www.dji.com/sg/osmo-mobile-3?site=brandsite&from=nav. Accessed 27 Jan 2020

Designing Games and Immersive Experiences

Augmented Reality Interface Design to Support Visualisation of 'Risk Landscapes'

Claire Ancient[1]([⊠]) [iD] and Richard Teeuw[2] [iD]

[1] University of Winchester, Winchester, UK
claire.ancient@winchester.ac.uk
[2] University of Portsmouth, Portsmouth, UK
richard.teeuw@port.ac.uk

Abstract. Climate change is producing an increase in the severity and frequency of hydro-meterological hazards, such as hurricanes, storm surges, flooding, landslides and debris flows. Small Island Developing States (SIDS) are particularly susceptible to such hazards because of their limited economic base. Furthermore, the inhabitants of SIDS tend to live near the coast and along river valleys: both are high-risk locations. The first priority of the UN's Sendai Framework for Disaster Risk Reduction is understanding disaster risk. To that end, the CommonSensing project is using satellite remote sensing data as the basis for an Augmented Reality application to support understanding of local "risk landscapes" for SIDS. This paper uses a systematic literature search to establish existing guidelines for Augmented Reality applications to support understanding of risk. There is very little recent research relating to developing interfaces for Augmented Reality applications, especially for risk reduction and management. Based on the results of this study, eight recommendations have been produced to support development of Augmented Reality applications. Additionally, suggestions have been made of how to apply these guidelines to an Augmented Reality for improved risk understanding and communication within SIDS.

Keywords: Augmented reality · Disaster risk · User interface · Usability

1 Introduction

Small Island Developing States (SIDS) are particularly vulnerable to natural hazards exacerbated by the changing climate [1]. Those hazards include: cyclones, flooding, coastal erosion, landslides and debris flows. According to the CommonSensing project, 29.3% of people in SIDS live less than 5 metres above sea level. This makes SIDS residents very exposed to a number of different natural hazards, with 18.8 million people being internally displaced due to disasters globally in 2017 [2]. In 2015, the Sendai Framework for Disaster Risk Reduction [3] aims to reduce disaster risks through four priorities: (i) understanding disaster risk, (ii) strengthening disaster risk governance to manage disaster risk, (iii) investing in disaster risk reduction for resilience, and (iv) enhancing disaster preparedness for effective response, and to "Build Back Better" in recovery, rehabilitation and reconstruction [3]. This particular study

© Springer Nature Switzerland AG 2020
A. Marcus and E. Rosenzweig (Eds.): HCII 2020, LNCS 12201, pp. 391–408, 2020.
https://doi.org/10.1007/978-3-030-49760-6_28

will be focusing on the first priority of understanding risk, to support the implementation of the other three priorities identified within the Sendai Framework.

The CommonSensing Project was established, via funding from the UK Space Agency, to help build the resilience of SIDS in response to an increasing frequency and severity of hydro-meteorological hazard events [1] in alignment with the Sendai Framework. Within the CommonSensing project, the Universities of Portsmouth and Winchester are focussing on improving understanding and communication of risk. As part of this, there is a drive to develop data presentation tools to enable people living in SIDS to better understand the hazard zones and vulnerable features that form the 'risk landscapes' in which they live. This study will contribute to that area of research within the CommonSensing project.

Azuma [4] defines Augmented Reality (AR) as allowing "the user to see the real world, with virtual objects superimposed upon or composited with the real world". This definition highlights the fact that AR should be designed to complement the real world and not replace it, as Virtual Reality (VR) would [5]. This aligns with the Reality-Virtuality (RV) Continuum developed by Milgram et al. [6], as shown in Fig. 1 whereby the Virtual Environment describes a fully immersive environment (provided by VR). The AR element of the continuum adds additional information to the real world rather than immersive experience provided by VR at the opposite end. Bai, Blackwell & Coulouris [7] extend Azuma's definition further to state that the reality and virtual elements must be combined in "meaningful ways".

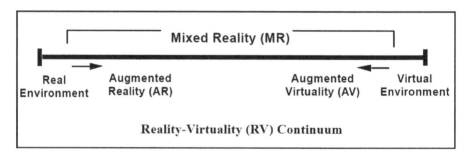

Fig. 1. A simplified representation of the Reality-Virtuality Continuum [6]

In recent years, AR has experienced a significant market growth [8], as demonstrated in Fig. 2, with AR spending predicted to continue to be a larger market than VR until at least 2021 [9]. del Amo et al. [10] highlight that until recently, AR has remained exploratory, but as Çöltekin [11] states, it has become more "mainstream". This growth can be attributed to increasing availability on mobile devices [12], increased ease of implementation for people who are not software developers [13], and the introduction of Apple's ARKit and Google's ARCore development kits [14].

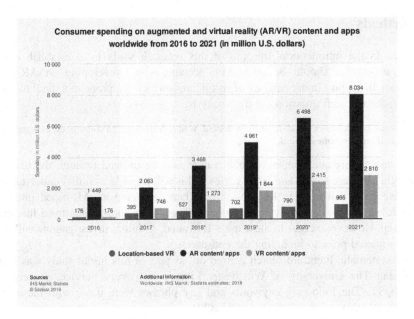

Fig. 2. Growth in consumer spending – Augmented Reality versus Virtual Reality [9]

AR has been utilized in a number of different arenas including: entertainment and gaming (e.g. [15–17]), education (e.g. [18–20]), medical and healthcare (e.g. [21, 22]), city planning (e.g. [23, 24]), and disaster management (e.g. [25]). As part of the CommonSensing project, the University of Portsmouth and University of Winchester team are proposing that AR is extended within the disaster preparedness arena to promote understanding of risk factors which may be prevalent in SIDS. The CommonSensing project is using satellite Earth Observation (EO) imagery and elevation models for the automated detection of many natural hazards over many decades (e.g. flood-prone areas, coastal erosion, landslides), with summary analysis-ready maps produced for emergency planners and policy makers [26]. The proposed AR application will make use of those analysis-ready map layers, for visualisation of 'risk landscapes' seeking to improve the viewer's understanding of risk.

Demir et al. [27] highlight that in AR, "poorly designed user interfaces may cause obstacles". As part of the development process for the proposed application, there is a need to consider the interface design to ensure that it does not introduce obstacles to use. Therefore, this study aims to establish design considerations that should be taken into account when developing an AR-based application to support understanding of risk in areas, which are prone to natural hazards.

This paper discusses the outcome of the study to achieve the stated aim. The paper is organised as follows: Sect. 2 discusses the methods used to inform the design considerations for AR interface design, Sect. 3 presents the results of the study based on the chosen methodology, Sect. 4 provides a discussion of some of the themes which emerged from the literature, and finally, Sect. 5 concludes this paper with some of the design considerations which were established.

2 Methods

As stated in the introduction, the aim of this research study is to establish design considerations that should be taken into account when developing an AR-based application to support understanding of risk in areas which are prone to natural hazards. As such, the research question for this study is:

> *"What design features need to be considered when designing AR interfaces to support increased understanding of risk?"*

To answer this question, existing literature will be utilized through the use of a systematic literature search and paper review. This will provide an initial understanding of the elements that need to be considered when designing an AR-based interface. Future research will aim to evaluate these findings, with participants from the target user group. However, access to these users is limited, so initial investigations will need to be completed prior to including the end-users.

The systematic literature search carried out as part of this initial study was facilitated using The University of Winchester Library Discovery Service, powered by EbscoHOST. The following keywords and key phrases were used, with the aim of capturing as many relevant articles as possible:

- "Augmented Reality"
- "Design Consideration"/"Design Considerations"
- "Design Implication"/"Design Implications"
- "Human-Computer Interaction"
- "Human Factor"/"Human Factors"
- "Interface Design"
- Usability
- Accessib*
- Risk
- Disaster

These key terms were chosen for their relevance to the topic to be considered as part of this research study – namely interface design considerations, AR, and the disaster risk landscape. In the case of accessibility, the wildcard character was utilized in order to obtain results which either used the word "accessible" or "accessibility". Boolean operators were used to combine the AR keyword with the other options for search terms. To assess the most recent research in the area of AR and interface design, the previous five years were chosen as limiting factors. In addition, in an attempt to ensure that peer-reviewed content was evaluated, it was decided to only view articles which have been published either in academic journals or within conference proceedings. Therefore, the following search criteria were utilized:

- Date Published: December 2014 to November 2019
- Publication Type: Academic Journals, Conference Proceedings
- Publication Language: English
- Search Categories: Abstract, Subject Terms, Title

Once the searches had been completed, a review of all the abstracts was conducted. This allowed the researcher to establish articles which needed to be read further, and which should be eliminated from the results due to irrelevance. Within this review, articles that did not discuss interface design and usability were eliminated. Subsequently, the remaining papers were read to highlight key information which would be relevant to designing interfaces and interaction of AR applications.

3   Results

A total of nine searches were conducted using the selection of keywords and the inclusion criteria demonstrated in Sect. 2. Table 1 demonstrates the results of these nine searches which were carried out, together with the number of articles which were isolated as possibly relating to the research question of current study, with their contents potentially containing suggestions for AR interface design.

Table 1. Results of nine searches carried out.

Keyword combination	Total results	Results which might relate to the research question
"Augmented Reality" AND ("Design Consideration" OR "Design Considerations")	4	3
"Augmented Reality" AND ("Design Implication" OR "Design Implications")	4	3
"Augmented Reality" AND "Human-Computer Interaction"	95	14
"Augmented Reality" AND ("Human Factor" OR "Human Factors")	20	7
"Augmented Reality" AND "Interface Design"	9	7
"Augmented Reality" AND usability	152	62
"Augmented Reality" AND accessib*	72	12
"Augmented Reality" AND Risk	123	18
"Augmented Reality" AND disaster	19	1
TOTAL	498	127

After the initial search and abstract review was completed, duplicates were removed and full text versions of the papers were downloaded, as demonstrated in Fig. 3. Unfortunately, due to restrictions on journal and database subscriptions, not all full-text versions of the papers were downloaded and read. As a result, this study considered 75 papers for full text review.

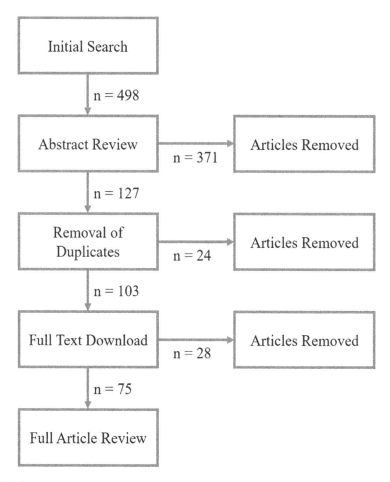

Fig. 3. Diagram to demonstrate process of reviewing and eliminating search results.

As part of the full-text review process, articles were grouped into whether they presented useful information relating to interface design (such as guidelines and/or recommendations) and those which did not. Only 28% of the 75 papers which were read were deemed to have information which is useful and relevant to the current study, as depicted in Fig. 4.

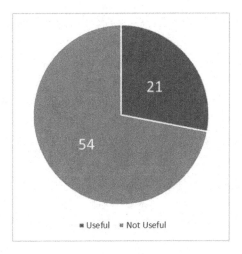

Fig. 4. Chart demonstrating proportion of articles which were established to contain relevant information for this study.

The high number of articles that were not useful for this study could be explained by two main factors: use of the word usability outside of interface design considerations, and focusing on quantitative outcomes rather than qualitative discussions of usability.

Firstly, a number of articles seemed to be directed towards defining usability as "fit-for-purpose", rather than focusing on the interface design implications. This was particularly prevalent in articles which focused on the potential medical uses of AR and those which were discussing acceptance of the application or devices.

Additionally, many articles claimed in their abstract to be discussing usability aspects of the interface, but ended up simply distilling this factor into either a yes or no statement, or a quantitative measure, with little discussion relating to the reasons for the high or low outcome. One interesting observation was in relation to the scale which was used to assess the quantitative usability of the system, with most papers opting to use the System Usability Scale (SUS). However, Kaur, Mantri and Horan [20] made use of the Handheld AR Usability Scale (HARUS) instead. It is interesting to see that whilst there is a scale which is dedicated to assessing usability of AR applications, most of the articles within this study still make use of the more generalized SUS. This may be a result of HARUS being a relatively new scale, which was developed in 2014 [28], and therefore, may not be adequately validated. It would be interesting to see whether the use of HARUS increases in the next few years – possibly in conjunction with the SUS until it has been rigorously validated.

Upon reading the articles, it was noticed that a number of different case studies were utilized to describe potential uses for AR. Figure 5 demonstrates the different case studies which were employed by the articles. Ramos et al. [14] highlighted that AR is mainly used within the entertainment and education field. This research seems to support and extend this assertion, with the majority of the useful papers using case studies from entertainment or gaming, workplace, education, and healthcare or medical arenas.

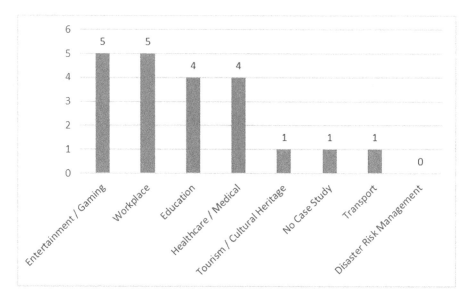

Fig. 5. Chart showing case study used within papers which were relevant for the research question.

It can also be seen from Fig. 5 that none of the articles that were found to contain useful information for AR interface design were focussed on disaster risk management. In fact, in all the articles which were read to establish whether they contained information relating to AR interface design only four considered case studies which related to disaster risk management, disaster risk reduction, or management of disaster events (5.33% of all articles read). This suggests that there is a lack of research in the area of using AR for disaster management. As part of this project, we are aiming to build an AR application which will support understanding of risk factors within SIDS. Therefore, as part of this activity, we will need to carry out usability research to establish how AR interfaces can be designed to support understanding of risk.

In the next section, further pertinent details will be discussed in relation to AR user interface design and related to the area of understanding risk factors in vulnerable areas.

4   Discussion

In this discussion, a number of key points that were highlighted within the articles read will be considered. These include the quality and timeliness of the information provided within the AR environment; the impact of cognitive load on the users; and impacts on the interaction with AR applications.

4.1   Quality and Timeliness of Information

The quality and timeliness of information and communications can have a significant effect on the quality of decisions made – especially when users are "in the field" or under emergency conditions [27]. AR has the potential to deliver information "just-in-time" [12, 29] which could support that decision making process. In this section, the following topics will be discussed: adequacy of the information delivered, the limitations associated with device choice, and implications of internet connectivity.

It has been highlighted that AR has the potential to provide additional information, providing supplementary data at the point of need [14, 22, 30]. In addition, Lazim and Rahman [31] imply that the use of AR allows people to access information quickly. This ability to provide information quickly and "just-in-time" has the potential to support the decision making process, especially when it comes to making decisions in relation to risk factors and their subsequent management.

Whilst AR does have the ability to increase the provision of pertinent information, Sugiura et al. [22] found that some of their participants became irritated with the time they had to wait for information to be displayed. This could be partly attributed to the devices which were in use during the study. Both Blut, Blut, and Blankenbach [24] and Kaur, Mantri, and Horan [20] found that the processing power of their chosen devices limited the implementation of their AR solutions. Bekaroo et al. [12] additionally found that the low resolution camera in the phones used for their device caused problems when reading the markers for their AR visualisation and also caused the device to become hot. Finally, both Laine and Suk [32] and tom Dieck and Jung [30] found that battery life was affected as a result of using the AR functionality. Therefore, care needs to be taken when choosing the appropriate platform for implementing AR. This is especially the case with SIDS, where funds may result in cheaper and lower resolution devices being chosen over more expensive devices.

In SIDS, it is common to find that the internet connection (including through the mobile network) is not stable or non-existent in some of the smaller islands. The United Nations (UN) Sustainable Development Goals (SDGs) highlight this need to ensure access to information and communications technologies as part of their 9th Goal: "Build resilient infrastructure, promote inclusive and sustainable industrialization and foster innovation" [33]. However, Blut, Blut, and Blankenbach [24] suggest that there is need for stable internet connections to be established to support AR activities. To support this, tom Dieck and Jung [30] highlight that it is possible to ensure that AR applications can be utilised through the use of offline storage. This highlights the need to consider the ability for AR applications to be cached for use offline, especially when trying to ensure people living in SIDS have an understanding of risk factors. However, this need to ensure content is available offline needs to be balanced against the specifications of the device utilized, with some devices not having adequate capacity to hold the information required.

4.2   Cognitive Load

Cognitive load can be defined as "the amount of information processing activity imposed on working memory" [34]. It is suggested that a higher level of cognitive load can reduce a person's ability to comprehend information – especially when the load is greater than the working memory capacity [35]. Deshpande and Kim [36] found that cognitive load when using their proposed AR solution was increased, however, they posited this could be related to usability factors. This suggests that cognitive load may be an important factor to consider when designing AR interfaces. In this section, the following factors will be considered: information overload, task switching, and distractions and inattentional blindness.

Information overload can have a significant effect on a person's performance when using AR applications [36–38], including leading to visual fatigue [39]. Demir et al. [27] highlights the need to "offer the right information when required, rather than having to create more information" especially in emergency settings. This has the potential to support ensuring that cognitive abilities are not overloaded with information. However, when Kim et al. [40] investigated whether information should be provided on-demand or always-on when using a head-worn AR display, users preferred the always-on approach. This has the potential to increase overload of information. However, this could be a context-dependent phenomenon, which may not apply to the emergency setting described in [27]. Therefore, it could be argued that further research needs to be carried out to define the fine line between adequate information provision and overload in various contexts, especially in case studies associated with emergency services and risk understanding.

Research conducted by Liefooghe et al. [41] found that task switching has a negative effect on working memory. When it comes to AR, Peleg-Adler, Lanir and Korman [42] suggests that cognitive load can be reduced due to less switching between tasks, especially in relation to switching between virtual and physical sources of information. This was also found by Ostendorp, Lenk and Lüdtke [38] where an AR-based system reduced the need for maritime pilots to switch between different viewpoints to obtain all the information required to guide the ship into port. By ensuring all the information required, whether that is in the physical or virtual domain, is presented in a single place, it is hoped that the cognitive load can be reduced with the hope that this will support assimilation of the risk factors in the local area.

In contrast, whilst AR has the potential to reduce the amount of task switching required, it can result in the user becoming distracted [37, 43], as they are focusing on the virtual elements of the interface rather than the real environment around them [30, 44, 45]. In a study conducted by Ma et al. [17], users were found to become distracted and experience inattentional blindness when interacting with AR, especially when carrying out specific activities using the devices. This led to increased risky behaviour when descending stairs. For this study, there needs to be a careful line drawn between providing appropriate information whilst minimising risks associated with inattentional blindness. In an open area, such as outside, there are a number of potential hazards which could cause additional harm to the users, such as uneven floors or roads. As the purpose of the proposed application is to increase understanding and awareness of risk factors, the developed AR solution should not expose the user to other hazards.

4.3 Impact of Interaction Techniques

Çöltekin et al. [11] highlight that traditional methods for interaction do not work for AR modalities. Therefore, consideration will need to be taken to ensure that appropriate interaction techniques are used for AR implementations. In this section, touchless interaction, information presentation mechanisms, ergonomics, and environmental factors will be considered. However, it is important to note this is not an exhaustive list of factors affecting interaction with AR devices and environments.

A key factor when considering the development of AR systems is how the user will be interacting with the system. A number of papers suggest using touchless interaction with gesture integration being offered as a potential solution [46–49], with AR being seen as an opportunity to "free up" the users' hands [37, 40]. However, when Caruso, Carulli and Bordegoni [50] compared remote control interaction with a gesture-based pointing mechanism, with participants preferring the tangible remote control to the touchless system. Voice has also been used as a touchless mechanism for interacting with AR devices [44, 51]. Condino et al. [44] obtained positive feedback in relation to a partially voice-based interface, suggesting that this may also be an appropriate mechanism for touchless interaction. This study has found that there are a few possible interaction techniques with AR environments. It could be argued that the interaction technique would be dependent on the potential users of the system and the context in which they are operating. Therefore, it would be beneficial to carry out further research within the risk areas to ensure that the interaction technique utilized is both appropriate for and accepted by the users.

Linked with the concept of touchless interaction is appropriate mechanisms demonstrating the information which is required by the user. del Amo et al. [10] suggest that there are three main mechanisms for providing feedback to the user: aural, visual, and haptic. In their article proposing Ecological AR, Raja and Calvo [52] suggest that using salience of visual elements within the interface could provide the user with feedback and information without increasing processing load on the user. They propose using highlighting to demonstrate routes rather than the traditional arrows which tend to be used in navigation. Ostendorp, Lenk, and Lüdtke [38] use this concept to show where the route has an adequate depth to facilitate maritime pilots to guide ships into harbour. However, rather than using the traditional shades of blue mechanism for showing depth [25], Ostendorp, Lenk, and Lüdtke [38] use a traffic light system – with green being adequate depth and red being too shallow. This overcomes the issue described by Macchione et al. [25] whereby various depths can be misinterpreted due to difficulty differentiating the increments of colour. Therefore, whilst Ostendorp, Lenk and Lüdtke [38] demonstrate that it is possible to utilise Ecological design within AR environments [52], it is important to ensure that appropriate colour schemes are utilised to ensure that the information is correctly interpreted, which is especially important when trying to understand risk factors.

The ergonomics of the device chosen to implement the AR environment have a key impact on their continued use. Many articles discussed the fatigue caused by using mobile devices, especially resulting from holding or wearing the device for long periods of time [5, 22, 37, 43, 46, 49]. In contrast, Gamberini et al. [39] concluded that over a short period of time (in this case, 5 min), there was no evidence of fatigue. Whilst this is not conclusive evidence that short term use of AR devices avoids the issue of tiring whilst using the device, it does suggest that this may be the case. In addition, research suggests that when glasses are utilized, consideration needs to be taken to consider the head position required to interact with the system so as not to cause further discomfort [40, 53]. In the case of understanding risk factors, care needs to be taken to ensure that overuse of the device which provides the AR is avoided, so as to avoid distracting from the task. If a user is experiencing discomfort from the device, they may be less likely to integrate the information being provided. The optimal length of time to utilize any AR device is yet to be established, therefore, further research will be required to make appropriate recommendations. However, it could be reasonably expected that these recommendations will be context-dependent, with some tasks (particularly those that produce higher levels of cognitive load) requiring less time within the AR environment to counteract other demands.

For this case study, it is anticipated that users will be engaging with the AR content to understand risk factors in outdoor environments. Therefore, factors associated with the environment will be a key consideration. A number of articles within this study discussed the need to consider the lighting conditions when developing interfaces [12, 18, 20, 54]. Efstathiou, Kyza and Georgiou [18] found that sunlight "limited the readability of the app information" a finding that was also experienced by other studies [20, 54]. Both Kaur, Mantri and Horan [20] and Bekaroo et al. [12] highlighted that the effect of lighting was particularly problematic when working with marker-based AR systems, with adequate lighting being required to identify the marker, but too much causing unexpected results. Therefore, when designing AR systems, particularly those which use markers or will be used in an outdoor environment (as the proposed CommonSensing project AR application will be), the lighting should be considered carefully.

5   Conclusion

This research study has found that there is limited research carried out within the area disaster preparedness and risk communication in relation to AR application development and interface design. With the importance of implementing both the Sendai Framework [3] and UN SDGs [33] to support resilience to climate change, it is important that future work tries to remove this gap in knowledge.

Based on the discussion within Sect. 4, a number of recommendations can be made. Table 2 demonstrates how these design considerations can be applied to generic case studies, as well as understanding of risk landscapes, with a particular focus on the CommonSensing project.

Table 2. Demonstrating application of the study recommendations to support understanding of risk landscapes

Design recommendation	Generic case study considerations	Applicability to understanding of the risk landscape
Consider the device that is to be used as part of the AR application interaction	Will the chosen device impact the user experience as a result of: low resolution cameras, poor processing power, or the battery capacity and associated consumption of charge?	Often in SIDS, technology utilized is of a lower processing power, and at times, using devices which are older than those normally used in developed countries. Therefore, the impact of this needs to be considered and accounted for when developing applications for understanding risk landscapes
Consider the availability of internet connections, if required	Does the application required an internet connection to support its running? Will the environment and/or device that this AR application is being run using support internet connections, through Wi-Fi or the mobile network?	SIDS are often located in remote areas – especially those which are partnered with the CommonSensing project. Therefore, often the internet connection is not to the same level of coverage or speed as developed countries – Honiara in the Soloman Islands have only recently obtained a fibre optic cable to support high speed internet. Therefore, applications which are heavily reliant on a stable internet connection may not function as anticipated within these areas
Avoid information overload	How can information overload be avoided in the context that the application is to be used in? At what point does the user become overloaded?	As this project is aiming to ensure that communities understand the risk in their local area, it is important that the information presented does not become overwhelming. If the users experience information overload, they may not be able to process the risk factors within their immediate location

(*continued*)

Table 2. (*continued*)

Design recommendation	Generic case study considerations	Applicability to understanding of the risk landscape
Consider a balance between reducing task switching, interface distractions, and information overload	What is the line between reduced task switching and information overload? Does the interface cause unnecessary distractions for the user when in use? What are the impact of the distractions? – e.g. stairs in the real world, etc.	If the risk application is being used outside, the user could become distracted whilst engaging in activities to improve their understanding of their risk environment which will be problematic if they are walking over an area which has an uneven floor
Establish the most appropriate interaction technique	What is the appropriate technique for the users, the task to be carried out, and the environment? – e.g. tangible versus touchless, gesture versus voice, etc.	For AR applications which are supporting understanding of risk landscapes, the interaction techniques need to be considered. The interaction technique should be appropriate for the device used as well as the environment it is being used in
Encourage use that reduces ergonomic fatigue	What device would be appropriate for the task to be carried out? What is the optimal amount of time to use the application without resulting in ergonomic fatigue?	When using AR to understand risk landscapes, the application should be developed to prevent overuse and fatigue associated with this. For example, if a tablet application is being used in AR mode, the user could become tired from holding the device in a particular position for a long period of time
Support salience of elements rather than using visual or text information	How can interface and/or environment highlighting be used to support understanding of information rather than simply relying on using textual or visual cues (such as arrows)?	In supporting understanding of risk landscapes, it is suggested that the use of salience and colour overlays (indicating relative levels of risk) could be used to avoid needing to process text information

(*continued*)

Table 2. (*continued*)

Design recommendation	Generic case study considerations	Applicability to understanding of the risk landscape
Consider the environment the AR application is due to be used in	Will the lighting in the environment have an impact on the interaction with the device? – this is especially the case if the AR application is due to be used outside as the sun can have a substantial impact on interaction	The proposed application is designed to be used in the external environment to help communities to understand risks associated with natural hazards within their local area. Therefore, this will need to taken into account as the weather within the South Pacific SIDS will more than likely impact their experience of using the AR-based application

As with all research, this study has several limitations. These include: small number of papers found by the searches, lack of consideration of the RV continuum, and a single research carrying out the evaluation.

It can be seen from Table 1 that only 25.5% of the articles returned by the search terms were potentially useful for the study. This suggests two things: either the search terms are not appropriate for what is trying to be achieved; or only a small amount of research has been carried out into interface design. Some of the articles reviewed implied that user interface design evaluations and guidelines had been developed prior to the beginning of the search range. Therefore, it would be appropriate in the future to extend the date range in an attempt to include these articles too. However, since 2014, there has been a huge growth in the AR market, due to a number of factors discussed earlier. Hence, it may be prudent to revisit these interface design guidelines with the aim of ensuring that they are relevant to the current AR implementations.

It is possible, due to the small number of searches that were conducted that not all the relevant keywords were captured. This could have resulted in many relevant papers not being found. Therefore, to support the development of this initial study, snow-balling of papers should be conducted together with a review of keywords associated with the papers which were found to be useful. This should result in further papers being established to add extra information and findings to the results of this study.

This particular research study is only focussed on the AR element of the RV continuum, however, it could be further extended to include other elements. These elements would include Mixed Reality (MR) and to some extent, the VR element too. The VR element could add further information which relates to the reality produced within the virtual elements to support the AR aspects of this project. In addition, the term Extended Reality (XR) has started to gain momentum describing the space which encapsulates AR, MR, and VR. Therefore, future research should endeavour to include all these terms in addition to just AR.

Finally, the literature review part of this study has primarily been carried out by the lead author, albeit within the CommonSensing team within the Universities of Portsmouth and Winchester. This opens the results of the literature review to potential bias. Therefore, future iterations of this study should involve more than just one member of the research team, to reduce the likelihood of this bias.

Acknowledgements. This study has been conducted as part of the CommonSensing project, which is funded by the UK Space Agency International Partnership Programme (IPP2).

References

1. CommonSensing – About Us. https://www.commonsensing.org.uk/about-us
2. Internal Displacement Monitoring Centre, Global Report on Internal Displacement 2018. http://www.internal-displacement.org/global-report/grid2018/
3. United Nations: Sendai framework for disaster risk reduction, 2015–2030 (2015)
4. Azuma, R.T.: A survey of augmented reality. Presence **6**(4), 355–385 (1997)
5. Escalada-Hernández, P., Ruiz, N.S., Martín-Rodríguez, L.S.: Design and evaluation of a prototype of augmented reality applied to medical devices. Int. J. Med. Inform. **128**, 87–92 (2019)
6. Milgram, P., Takemura, H., Utsumi, A., Kishino, F.: Augmented reality: a class of displays on the reality-virtuality continuum. In: Proceedings of SPIE, Telemanipulator and Telepresence Technologies (1995)
7. Bai, Z., Blackwell, A., Coulouis, G.: Using augmented reality to elicit pretend play for children with autism. IEEE Trans. Vis. Comput. Graph. **21**(5), 598–610 (2014)
8. Li, H., Gupta, A., Zhang, J., Flor, N.: Who will use augmented reality? An integrated approach based on text analytics and field survey. Eur. J. Oper. Res. **281**, 502–516 (2020)
9. Consumer spending on augmented and virtual reality (AR/VR) content and apps worldwide from 2016 to 2021. https://www.statista.com/statistics/828467/world-ar-vr-consumer-spending-content-apps/
10. del Amo, I.F., Galeotti, E., Palmarini, R., Dini, G., Erkoyuncu, J., Roy, R.: An innovative user-centred support tool for augmented reality maintenance systems design: a preliminary study. Procedia CIRP **70**, 362–367 (2018)
11. Çöltekin, A., Oprean, D., Wallgrün, J.O., Klippel, A.: Where are we now? Re-visiting the digital earth through human-centred virtual and augmented reality geovisualisation environments. Int. J. Digit. Earth **12**(2), 119–122 (2019)
12. Bekaroo, G., Sungkur, R., Ramsamy, P., Okolo, A., Moedeen, W.: Enhancing awareness on green consumption of electronic devices: the application of augmented reality. Sustain. Energ. Technol. Assess. **30**, 279–291 (2018)
13. Marques, B., McIntosh, J., Carson, H.: Whispering tales: using augmented reality to enhance cultural landscapes and indigenous values. AlterNative **15**(3), 193–204 (2019)
14. Ramos, F., Trilles, S., Torres-Sospedra, J., Perales, F.J.: New trends in using augmented reality apps for smart city contexts. Int. J. Geo-Inf. **7**(12), 478 (2018)
15. Wang, C., Chiang, Y., Wang, M.: Evaluation of an augmented reality embedded on-line shopping system. Procedia Manuf. **3**, 5624–5630 (2015)

16. Montero, A., Zarraonandia, T., Diaz, P., Aedo, I.: Designing and implementing interactive and realistic augmented reality experiences. Univ. Access Inf. Soc. **18**, 49–61 (2019). https://doi.org/10.1007/s10209-017-0584-2

17. Ma, H., Chen, P., Linkov, V., Pai, C.: Training or battling a monster of a location-based augmented reality game while descending stairs: an observational study of inattentional blindness and deafness and risk-taking inclinations. Front. Psychol. **10**, 623 (2019)

18. Efstathiou, I., Kyza, E.A., Georgiou, Y.: An inquiry-based augmented reality mobile learning approach to fostering primary school students' historical reasoning in non-formal settings. Interact. Learn. Environ. **26**(1), 22–41 (2018)

19. Herbert, B., Ens, B., Weerasinghe, A., Billinghurst, M., Wigley, G.: Design considerations for combining augmented reality with intelligent tutors. Comput. Graph. **77**, 166–182 (2018)

20. Kaur, D.P., Mantri, A., Horan, B.: Design implications for adaptive augmented reality based interactive learning environment for improved concept comprehension in engineering paradigms. Interact. Learn. Environ. (2019). https://doi.org/10.1080/10494820.2019.1674885

21. Monkman, H., Kushniruk, A.W.: A see through future: augmented reality and health information systems. Stud. Health Technol. Inform. **208**, 281–285 (2015)

22. Sugiura, A., Kitama, T., Toyoura, M., Mao, X.: The use of augmented reality technology in medical specimen museum tours. Anat. Sci. Educ. **12**, 561–571 (2019)

23. Haynes, P., Hehl-Lange, S., Lange, E.: Mobile augmented reality for flood visualisation. Environ. Model Softw. **109**, 380–389 (2018)

24. Blut, C., Blut, T., Blankenbach, J.: CityGML goes mobile: application of large 3D CityGML models on smartphones. Int. J. Digit. Earth **12**(1), 25–42 (2019)

25. Macchione, F., Costabile, P., Costanzo, C., De Santis, R.: Moving to 3-D flood hazard maps for enhancing risk communication. Environ. Model Softw. **111**, 510–522 (2019)

26. Teeuw, R.M., Leidig, M.: Uses of free geoinformatics for disaster risk reduction in small island developing states – a case study from Honiara, Solomon Islands. In: Khonje, H., Mitchell, T. (eds.) Strengthening Disaster Resilience in Small States, Ch. 1, pp. 1–12. The Commonwealth Secretariat, London (2019)

27. Demir, F., Ahmad, S., Calyam, P., Jiang, D., Huang, R., Jahnke, I.: A next-generation augmented reality platform for mass casualty incidents (MCI). J. Usability Stud. **12**(4), 193–214 (2017)

28. Santos, M.E.C., Taketomi, T., Sandor, C., Polvi, J., Yamamoto, G., Kato, H.: A usability scale for handheld augmented reality. In: VRST 2014, Proceedings of the 20th ACM Symposium on Virtual Reality Software and Technology, pp. 167–176 (2014)

29. Okimoto, M.L.L.R., Okimoto, P.C., Goldbach, C.E.: User experience in augmented reality applied to the welding education. Procedia Manuf. **3**, 6223–6227 (2015)

30. Tom Dieck, M.C., Jung, T.: A theoretical model of mobile augmented reality acceptance in urban heritage tourism. Curr. Issues Tour. **21**(2), 154–174 (2018)

31. Lazim, N.A.M., Rahman, K.A.A.A.: State-of-the-Art responses on augmented reality application in Malaysia. Alam Cipta **8**(2), 28–34 (2015)

32. Laine, T.H., Suk, H.J.: Designing mobile augmented reality exergames. Games Cult. **11**(5), 548–580 (2016)

33. United Nations: Transforming our world: the 2030 agenda for sustainable development (2015)

34. Cavanaugh, C.: Augmented reality gaming in education for engaged learning. In: Handbook of Research on Effective Electronic Gaming in Education. IGI Global, Hershey (2009)

35. Moody, D.L.: Cognitive load effects on end user understanding of conceptual models: an experimental analysis. In: Benczúr, A., Demetrovics, J., Gottlob, G. (eds.) ADBIS 2004. LNCS, vol. 3255, pp. 129–143. Springer, Heidelberg (2004). https://doi.org/10.1007/978-3-540-30204-9_9

36. Deshpande, A., Kim, I.: The effects of augmented reality on improving spatial problem solving for object assembly. Adv. Eng. Inform. **38**, 760–775 (2018)
37. Lukosch, S., Lukosch, H., Datcu, D., Cidota, M.: Providing information on the spot: using augmented reality for situational awareness in the security domain. Comput. Support. Coop. Work (CSCW) **24**, 613–664 (2015). https://doi.org/10.1007/s10606-015-9235-4
38. Ostendorp, M., Lenk, J.C., Lüdtke, A.: Smart glasses to support maritime pilots in harbor maneuvers. Procedia Manuf. **3**, 2840–2847 (2015)
39. Gamberini, L., Orso, V., Beretta, A., Jacucci, G., Spagnolli, A., Rimondi, R.: Evaluating user experience of augmented reality eyeglasses. Stud. Health Technol. Inform. **219**, 28–32 (2015)
40. Kim, S., Nussbaum, M.A., Gabbard, J.L.: Influences of augmented reality head-worn display type and user interface design on performance and usability in a simulated warehouse order picking. Appl. Ergon. **74**, 186–193 (2019)
41. Liefooghe, B., Barrouillet, P., Vandierendonck, A., Camos, V.: Working memory costs of task switching. J. Exp. Psychol. Learn. Mem. Cogn. **34**(3), 478–494 (2008)
42. Peleg-Adler, R., Korman, M.: The effects of aging on the use of handheld augmented reality in a route planning task. Comput. Hum. Behav. **81**, 52–62 (2018)
43. Janssen, S., et al.: Usability of three-dimensional visual cues delivered by smart glasses on freezing of gait in Parkinson's disease. Front. Neurol. **8**, 279 (2017)
44. Condino, S., et al.: How to build a patient-specific hybrid simulator for orthopaedic open surgery: benefits and limits of mixed-reality using the Microsoft HoloLens. J. Healthc. Eng. (2018). https://doi.org/10.1155/2018/5435097
45. Damala, A., Hornecker, E., van der Vaart, M., van Dijk, D., Ruthven, I.: The Loupe: tangible augmented reality for learning to look at ancient Greek art. Mediterr. Archaeol. Archaeo. **16**(5), 73–85 (2016)
46. Lv, Z., Halawani, A., Feng, S., ur Réhman, S., Li, H.: Touch-less interactive augmented reality game on vision-based wearable device. Pers. Ubiquit. Comput. **19**(3), 551–567 (2015). https://doi.org/10.1007/s00779-015-0844-1
47. Sun, M., Wu, X., Fan, Z., Dong, L.: Augmented reality based education design for children. Int. J. Emerg. Technol. Learn. **14**(3), 51–60 (2019)
48. Coughlan, J.M., Miele, J.: AR4VI: AR as an accessibility tool for people with visual impairments. In: 2017 IEEE International Symposium on Mixed and Augmented Reality (ISMAR-Adjunct), pp. 288–292. IEEE (2017)
49. Datcu, D., Lukosch, S., Brazier, F.: On the usability and effectiveness of different interaction types in augmented reality. Int. J. Hum.-Comput. Interact. **31**(3), 193–209 (2015)
50. Caruso, G., Carulli, M., Bordegoni, M.: Augmented reality system for the visualisation and interaction with 3D digital models in a wide environment. Comput.-Aided Des. Appl. **12**(1), 86–95 (2015)
51. Longo, F., Nicoletti, L., Padovano, A.: Smart operators in Industry 4.0: a human-centred approach to enhance operators' capabilities and competencies within the new smart factory context. Comput. Ind. Educ. **113**, 144–159 (2017)
52. Raja, V., Calvo, P.: Augmented reality: an ecological blend. Cogn. Syst. Res. **42**, 58–72 (2017)
53. Rochlen, L.R., Levine, R., Tait, A.R.: First-person point-of-view-augmented reality for central line insertion training: a usability and feasibility study. Simul. Healthc. **12**(1), 57–62 (2017)
54. Hall, N., Lowe, C., Hirsch, R.: Human factors considerations for the application of augmented reality in an operational railway environment. Procedia Manuf. **3**, 799–806 (2015)

Analyzing the User Experience of Virtual Reality Storytelling with Visual and Aural Stimuli

Burcu Nimet Dumlu[1]([✉]) and Yüksel Demir[2]

[1] Fatih Sultan Mehmet Vakıf University, Istanbul, Turkey
bndumlu@fsm.edu.tr
[2] Istanbul Technical University, Istanbul, Turkey

Abstract. Storytelling is an integral part of narratives relating to our daily events, news, personal experiences, and fantasies. While humans have long narrated their stories, the mediums they have used to do so have evolved over time through the effects of technological developments: initially, storytelling was solely oral, then written forms were added, and now, with the effects of new media, such narratives have also begun to employ photography and video. These new media tools are also undergoing their own processes of expansion and development. Today one of the most attention-getting are those using Virtual Reality (VR) technologies, a means that allows users to experience being-in-the-virtual-environments, with possibilities of becoming entirely immersed in a virtual environment. The ability to experience an environment with three-dimensional features enhances the experience in sensorial ways, with simultaneous stimulation of both the user's visual and auditory sensorial systems. The aim of this study is to gain a better understanding of what exactly the user experiences through VR storytelling. To this end we have conducted an experimental research based on an examination of the immersive experience in VR, which constructs the presence feeling. The experiment has been designed to study the effects on forty users. These participants used the HTC Vive head-mounted display to experience the contents of a story called "Allumette" (designed by Penrose Studios). User behaviors were recorded and observed by the tools used to collect data from both the physical world and the virtual environment. Users' physical movements were documented as coordinate data, while the behavioral reflections in the virtual environment were recorded as a video. Following this virtual experimentation, users were asked to answer a questionnaire that measured their responses to their VR storytelling experience. User experience was finally measured by analyzing both the behavioral outputs of the subjects and the questionnaire. "Cinemetrics" methodology was implemented to analyze the camera movements, which were considered as the user behavioral reflections in VR. The results of this study based on analyzing the behaviors and the reactions to visual and aural stimuli in the VR environment both lead to a clearer understanding of VR storytelling and uses these results to propose a design guide for VR storytelling.

Keywords: Virtual Reality · Virtual storytelling · User experience

© Springer Nature Switzerland AG 2020
A. Marcus and E. Rosenzweig (Eds.): HCII 2020, LNCS 12201, pp. 409–425, 2020.
https://doi.org/10.1007/978-3-030-49760-6_29

1 Introduction

Man has always used storytelling to relate his daily events, news, personal, or fantasies. According to Benjamin (2014), the story is one of the oldest forms of communication, one that differs from information passed down in the form of the relating of real events. Storytellers extract the story of their own experiences, or of experiences that have been narrated to them, and through their narration make the experience also that of those who listen to them (Benjamin 2014). The storyteller uses different environments as storytelling tools and by doing so creates original experiences that can trigger the imagination of his or her audience.

This story experience includes four kinds of narrative theory elements: characters, time, space, and storyteller. As Dervişcemaloğlu (2014) has explained, narrative theory studies are mostly focused on time. Lessing cites from Bucholz, Sabine, and Manfred Jahn relative to the fact that, especially prior to the 19th century, narration functioned more as a tool than as a purpose, and space was used primarily as just as a background or a décor (Dervişcemaloğlu 2014). Therefore, space was not as valuable as time in the construction of the plot. This situation changed with such advancements in the spatial arts as cinema, theater, or virtual arts. Now, developments in virtual environments allow for the stimulation of the audience in sensorial ways, thus leading space to become an element that proves to be more critical than other story environments. In this study, space was explored to understand the spatial sensory experience inside storytelling.

Virtual reality (VR) can be defined as media in which reality is reconstructed by computers (computer simulation). Baudrillard (2011) describes simulation as a hyperreality in which reality is reproduced through models. The spectator human is the one who builds his own reality, and this helps him to develop methods of understanding his own world. Heidegger's definition of "being-in-the-world" defines, as Ökten (2012) has stated, the individual who is conscious of "being-here" or "human existence." *Dasein*[1] in Baudrillard's hyperreality, on the other hand, is reinterpreted in the context of being "being-in-the-virtual-world" (Coyne 1994). In this study, the concept of virtual *dasein* has been defined as a virtual individual. In this context, the virtual individual is considered to be that individual who found and performed his spatial movements here.

VR creates an immersive experience by creating a virtual presence and stimulates both visual and aural perception. It creates real-life-like experiences through being-in-the-virtual-world features. Being inside the story and experiencing it with such body movements as turning around 360-degrees, watching 3D characters through 3D environments can serve to differentiate all the perception of the story. The three-dimensional possibilities of virtual reality enable the individual to immerse differently in media.

---

[1] Dasein means "being there" or "presence" with the German understanding of 'das' as "there" and sein meaning "being". This term is often translated into English with the word "existence". It is a fundamental concept in Martin Heidegger's existential philosophy and in his work 'Being and Time'.

While humans employ bilateral vision as they sense the physical world, VR uses head-mounted display (HMD) to create a phenomenon of vision that exists in the physical environment while extending to the virtual environment through augmentations of stereoscopic vision. The HTC Vive VR HMD was installed in a defined space which is called room-scale (see Fig. 1). The 360-degree vision (6DoF – six degrees of freedom) and spatial navigation possibilities provided by HMD parallels that of physical reality. Virtual space thus becomes a tool that allows us to measure physical behaviors and orientations while the user is watching the story unfold.

Fig. 1. HTC Vive Head Mounted Display (HMD) room-scale installation in a defined area in the physical environment.

This study aims to understand how VR affects the story experience of the user. The forty individuals who participated in this experiment were provided with VR HMD as the medium for their fifteen minute exposure to the contents of a story. Their behaviors as they watched this Allumette story content with HMD were recorded during the session. For the purposes of this study we defined user experience in terms of user behaviors, explorations, and their ability to remember the story line when presented within the VR medium. By doing so we were able to create meaningful data that can be utilized in the design of virtual reality storytelling spaces that can construct a three-dimensional user experience. Measuring the users' movements while using the VR head-mounted display and recording what they were seeing while watching the VR storytelling content allowed us to gain a better understanding of space perceptions and memory.

This study has been based on four fundamental goals to be gained on experiments on the subject: The first has been to understand how the role of architectural space changes when storytelling is integrated with VR technology. This understanding of the role played by space within the story demonstrates how narrative approaches can be affected. The results of this study lead to a clearer understanding of just how story space can be optimally designed. The second goal was to better understand just how the user explores the space within which s/he is immersed and to question if this exploration has an effect on perception. The third goal was to investigate the relation between the content of the visuals, the audio, and memory details. The fourth was to learn more about the kinds of effects on memory when VR is utilized as the medium of storytelling and to understand which narrative details were – or where not – remembered by the participants. Essential to this is to gain an understanding of the degree to which VR space exploration affects the memory.

2   Storytelling Mediums

Since the beginning of history, storytelling media have been advancing in ways that parallel man's technological advancements. Stories were first narrated in the forms of paintings and hieroglyphs, then oral story-telling traditions were instilled, followed by stories transmitted in written forms. Now, with the emergence of what we term as "new media," the range has widened to include photography and cinema. This widening of new mediums has given way to the emergence of mixed media. This development has been outlined by Blumenthal as he cites Henry Jenkins, the author of the book *Convergence Culture*, in his creation of a model he calls "transmedia storytelling" (Blumenthal 2016).

Today the still-developing technology utilizing VR as a technology is fast becoming another storytelling medium. This is an expected phenomenon for storytelling has always been an immersive experience and VR, which is based on such sensatory immersion, naturally emerges as a successful and preferred environment for such narration.

2.1   Conventional Storytelling

Extant cave paintings and certain religious rituals are proof that man has always felt the need to transmit his stories and that these needs even predate the invention of writing or even speaking. When we speak of conventional storytelling, we are referring to oral and scribed storytelling. We learn of a culture's history through the contents and forms of storytelling it employed. These stories were passed down through that culture's history as its populace both memorized and then retaught these narratives, sustaining and revealing its heroic figures and events (Leber 2017). Oral storytelling traditions thus function as conventional mediums as they serve as means of communication that construct reality conceptualizations for the *dasein* through narrative.

The new media, which includes such forms as photography, movies, multimedia, and computer games, have now become their own unique forms of storytelling mediums. While movies are passive forms of story narrations, computer games have evolved into a media that integrates the player into the narrative. As Zona (2014) cites from Stephen Heath's article of 1976, the notion of the narrative space, which is a theoretical term, is considered to function of an element of novels, films, video games, and also everyday mediums. She explains his approach as if grounded from a passive viewer of the film and Renaissance perspective rules, and relates that he defines narrative space as an element that controls the action during the story from the vantage point of the audience (Zona 2014). In this perspective, the story creates its own narrative space, one which Heath says is based on the observer's perspective, and is transformed into a reconstruction of the space in the minds of its audiences. (Heath

1976). Because the audience experiences the stories with the space, it can be argued that the story includes an architectural space, even in storytelling that is only transmitted in written form.

2.2 Virtual Reality Storytelling

As defined by Heim (1993), virtual reality is a broad term because it can be applied to its utilizations in all kinds of activities carried out during our daily lives. VR, however, creates an embodied effect that emerges as a new reality of its own, one that portends potentials for the futures of film, theater, and literature. In Ryan's (1999) mention of the ideas put forth by Pimentel and Texeira, the actual question is not whether this creation embodies a true physical space or not, but rather whether the user can believe it is true for at least some of the time. In this sense it is similar to reading and getting inside a good novel, and being captivated by a video game. Virtual reality (VR) creates a multi-sensory and unique experience. VR technology offers an immersive experience with three-dimensional (3D) features and interactivity. This technology offers its users the ability to watch and to move inside the scene by using HMD, listening to audio with headphones so that the audience can be isolated from the outside world. Users can see the virtual world through glasses, and they are not exposed to the voices of the outside world, which means that they cannot be distracted by anything external to him or her and the VR storytelling experience. The full isolation and the notion of being-in-the-virtual-world provides a new kind of experience for storytelling.

The three-dimensional story space of VR allows users to navigate freely and provides opportunities for non-linear storytelling. It is, therefore, the user who decides the storyline (Lau and Chen 2009). Also, VR has the capability of non-static storytelling with the characters, objects, so the story becomes active and dynamic based on the user's behaviors (Lau and Chen 2009). The last potential they describe is that the user can choose the flow of the story with non-linear storytelling (Lau and Chen 2009).

As defined by Ryan (2001), the VR medium is a kind of a digital wonderland which is an extension of the physical world, and sensorial stimulation that creates the illusion of leaving the body outside. The VR user becomes a new person, one who can experience the presented non-materialized reality with such senses as tactile and aural senses. The user is involved with the medium itself by using gestures or commands that provide such freedoms as that of visualizing imagination-originated thoughts without these thoughts becoming physically materialized (Ryan 2001). It is within such a "digital wonderland,", that the user is transformed into the protagonist of the story being presented by using this personalization and by watching and interacting with the content in three-dimensional space. One of the very first examples is Disney's *Aladdin*, which was designed as a VR storytelling experience. The team recorded the experiences of 45,000 users, leading to valuable primary findings. They found that regardless of gender and age, all of their viewers adapted to the reality of the simulation's space, and were able to bypass the actual reality that they were not truly in the space. Another finding of the research was that the content of the experience is vital for the immersive perception (Pausch et al. 1996).

Before VR, media designed to represent three-dimensional space, such as animations or motion pictures, occurred in the real world. Due to the limits of a two-dimensional screen, the audience could only see the story from a surface creating a two-dimensional perception. The notion of a 360-degree canvas that changes the user's passive role while watching the narrative inside a frame gives a chance for a real immersive experience that is hard to design as an experience (Anderson 2016). The linear storyline which is experienced with conventional storytelling methods changes when presented with VR. The storyline is developed within a three-dimensional space, one that offers the opportunity to explore. With this, every individual within the audience can focus on the story from their own unique perspectives within that 3D space (see Fig. 2). Such a personal perspective differentiates the experience in a way that fractures the linear storyline and leads the audience to create a personal storyline.

Fig. 2. Virtual reality storytelling (Allumette's boat scene) in room-scale installation.

Morgan says that VR has "frame-less scenes," which need to be designed to get the attention of the user by attracting them and leading them following all the story as an experience (Morgan 2017). He also adds that VR experiences have no limits or borderlines, which means the user does not have to follow the story. The user experience is thus an element that leads the user injection into the story, thus creating an experience that differs from that provided by film or theater (Morgan 2017).

Cotting says that the story narrated within a movie progresses within a passive environment, such that the audience does not have the power to influence what they are watching; they become passive observers of that which is presented to them. However, during a VR experience, the user becomes an active participant in the story and s/he decides where to look, what to do, or what or who to follow. In this way, the user creates his or her unique individual experience (Cotting 2016). Therefore, a well-designed VR experience means encouraging the user to get involved in the story for creating their personal experiences; it is not about telling the story passively (Cotting 2016).

3   Experiencing the Story in Virtual Reality

In this study the experiences and reactions of each participant were analyzed within a fifteen-minute long VR narrative exposure. At the end of the exposure, participants were asked to fill in an approximate ten-minute long questionnaire. This study was initiated by using 18 pilot experimental sessions. These pilot experiments both aided in the development of the questionnaire and also revealed what measurements would best lead to an understanding of the VR storytelling spaces. Following this pilot study and modifications to the methodology, the experiences of a total of forty participants were measured as they were exposed to the Allumette story with the HTC Vive HMD tool. Movement data were collected by utilizing the headset positional data tracking. A total of forty videos recorded both physical and virtual environments.

3.1   Pilot Experiments

The pilot study showed that participants were curious about the experience and tended to wander about the space, leading us to realize that the questions we were asking needed to be widened. Pilot study participants also displayed the tendency to explore all the places, thus demonstrating the need to measure spatial movements. When the participant had concerns about the spaces provided in the external world, s/he tended not restrict the movements he or she were making. It was thus revealed that the participants needed to acquire some familiarity with HMD itself. More experienced participants were better able to locate and react to spatial sounds. Some participants were more likely to expansively explore the story space. It was observed that such participants were more likely to create vantage points for the story.

3.2   Application of the VR Storytelling Experiment

The pilot experiments demonstrated the need for positional data, leading us to utilize the Brekel OpenVR Recorder software (Brekel OpenVR Recorder 2008). In addition to this we also used the Open Broadcaster Software during-experiment to record the videos of the virtual environment.

The experimentation started with a brief to the participants. Before wearing the headset, users were provided with information about the kinds of experience they would have and how they should move. Then both the Brekel OpenVR Recorder and OBS Studio Screen Recorder software were initiated at the same time so as to ensure data consistency between all the participants, for we realized that if the positional movement data does not start at the same time for each participant, the starting points would not be matched.

3.3   Data Analysis of VR Experiment

The video recordings, movement data, and the questionnaire were analyzed so as to understand the VR storytelling experience. Therefore, some methods such as audio analysis, visual analysis, movement data analysis, and the "Cinemetrics" (McGrath and Gardner 2007) were adapted to this methodology. At the end, analyses were super-posed to show all information together.

The first analysis was conducted on the video recordings of the virtual environment. Every user's individual screen recording was examined to detect the attractor points, and then the audio of the recording was analyzed. After that, the recordings were analyzed based on the visuals. Following this, "Cinemetrics" methodology, which is detailed below, was adapted to the VR storytelling analysis.

Definition of Attractor Points

Allumette represents a 15-min experience (Chung 2016). We determined which scenes performed as Attractor Points, thus permitting reliable analysis of the user experience. The screen recordings were then watched scene by scene so as to detect the reactions in which the participant was grasped by the story as evidenced by his or hers attempt to explore the environment to find some motions. The attractor points were identified as those in which some highlighted actions occurred in the story, such as the explosion of the ship. These points could be augmented both by sounds and by images. Fifteen attractor points, whether image only, sound only, or a combination of image and sound were detected from screen recordings.

One of the attractor points was the scene with "the interior" (see Fig. 3). While the participant was trying to look around the environment, one side of the flying ship opened, revealing the interior. With a change of the second scene, the sounds of a flying ship came from the left, and then the ship arrived and parked on the floating settlement. The mother takes control of the flying ship so as to stop it from falling onto the crowd in the town square. The ship explodes as she is flying it. This explosion constitutes the fourteenth attractor point: "the explosion" (see Fig. 3).

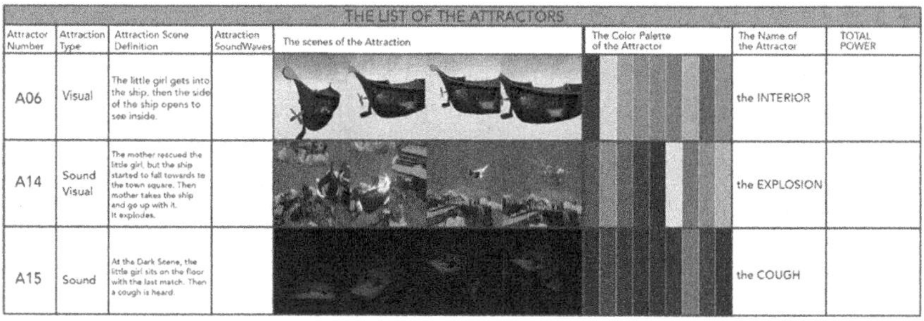

Attractor Number	Attraction Type	Attraction Scene Definition	Attraction Sound/Waves	The scenes of the Attraction	The Color Palette of the Attractor	The Name of the Attractor	TOTAL POWER
A06	Visual	The little girl gets into the ship, then the side of the ship opens to see inside.				the INTERIOR	
A14	Sound Visual	The mother rescued the little girl, but the ship started to fall towards to the town square. Then mother takes the ship and go up with it. It explodes.				the EXPLOSION	
A15	Sound	At the Dark Scene, the little girl sits on the floor with the last match. Then a cough is heard.				the COUGH	

Fig. 3. Descriptions of some of the attractors with their explanations, stimulant types, names, and color palettes.

In the last dark scene, as the girl was standing near the bridge the participant hears the sound of a cough. Here the user is stimulated by the sound. That was the last and the fifteenth attractor point: "the cough" (see Fig. 3).

Audio Analysis

The Allumette story audio consists of one musical piece used as the background along with the sounds of the characters and their gestures, and story elements. Because some of the attractors can function as aural perception stimulants, the story audio plays an essential role in the user experience. In some instances, these sounds gave rise to an increased user reaction to some of the attractor points.

Audio analysis commenced by converting the raw data of the ".wav (Waveform Audio File Format)" file to the numerical data by using python code. Sound waves drawn through a software script provides the flexibility to properly scale the sound waves. Every second included ten "sound-lines" because of the calculated soundwaves, meaning there was one sound-line for every millisecond, (see Fig. 4).

Fig. 4. The soundwave volume levels analysis of 'Attractor 10' from 09.24' to 09.40'.

Drawing the sound-lines allowed us to see which line serves as the starting line of the attractor point. We then determined the sound-lines for every attractor point, thus allowing us to see big scaled sound-lines on the attractor points. This proved to be valuable as it allowed us to define the real level of the sound from scaled sound-lines giving us the chance to compare with visual and the movement of the user for that attractor. We saw that the analysis of soundwaves and crosschecking them with the movements, visual stimulations, and reactions were essential to understanding the aural stimuli in VR storytelling (Fig. 9). Because the results showed that users were highly affected by the audio components, VR designers should carefully consider which parameters are essential, such as the position of the sound or volume of the sound.

The "Cinemetrics"

Cinemetrics methodology was applied to the screen recordings as a means of gaining a detailed understanding of user behaviors. This is a method that was designed by McGrath and Gardner (2007) so as to read the scenes from the movies and to create architectural drawings from the scenes. The origin of the study is based on Gilles Deleuze's cinema research studies.

Cinemetrics analyzes a scene by uses the metric system to show the movements of the camera. As Heath (1976) tells us, "The movements of the camera create the narrative space." Deleuze (1986) cited Bergson's hypothesis about "movement," and his claims that movement is different from the space covered. He added that covered space is related to that which is past and divisible, while movement is relevant to the present and indivisible (Deleuze 1986). This serves as a conclusion to a more complex idea that the "spaces covered" are the parts of a single, identical, homogeneous space, but "movements" are heterogeneous, irreducible through them (Deleuze 1986).

Assembling, comprehending, and combining images in daily life and work are commonplace (McGrath and Gardner 2007). These researchers defined daily life as a series of such events ranging from getting out of bed and continuing to unfinished drawings, but not waking up slowly or thinking about anything else, just finalizing the job that inspires us (McGrath and Gardner 2007). This narrative illustrates the morning time as a spatial form of "movement images," which are equivalent to regular daily progress – wake up and go to the work (McGrath and Gardner 2007). With this narrative approach, "continuous spatial moments are sequenced in time according to personal storytelling style" (McGrath and Gardner 2007).

McGrath and Gardner (2007) explained that the Cinemetrics drawing system was created to develop a personal architectural approach that corresponds to the dynamic nature of reality. They assert that linear thinking on architectural drawing is actually based on the perspective that developed during Renaissance Italy, one that started with the architect and the mechanical engineer, Filippo Brunelleschi.

This approach then continued to advance and to spread with Johannes Gutenberg's invention of the printing press (McGrath and Gardner 2007). However, in this day and age, this kind of linear thinking needs to change if it will be able to adapt to the "cybernetic" instruments, thus giving rise to the necessity of developing new methodologies (McGrath and Gardner 2007). Their research focused on how architects have expanded existing tools so as to create the ability to move topological architectural forms based on the suitability of the computers. These tools emerged to correspond to new "sensorimotor schema" based on how we sense and act. Cinemetrics was developed to serve as this new "sensorimotor schema" and to widen the architectural field by its tools and applications based on the schema (McGrath and Gardner 2007).

This methodology was developed to fulfill the new technology needs of architectural drawings with computer-generated systems. Architectural drawing systems are explanatory in nature and serve as abstractions of tangible objects such as buildings. New technological developments, however, are now expanding the use of these abstractions and surpass those of still images and tangible objects. Advanced technology has widened the definition of what we mean by the word image, taking it beyond that of a passive visual. Movement in and of itself has also become an important feature. It was towards this new requirement that advanced drawings have been developed. The Cinemetrics method used in films and architectural drawings are now overlapping with each other. Movement is rendering movies to become even more comprehensible and when utilized with architectural drawing methods the camera can render the scene more readable.

In VR applications, the HMD serves as the camera, with the user selecting the scene's vantage points. To this end, user behavior also functions as camera movement. This has revealed that by adapting Cinemetrics methodology to the space and the movement within virtual reality, drawing the scenes as the movie helps to reveal user behaviors.

In this study we adapted this methodology to the virtual reality medium. Three-dimensional environment scenes were created by using panoramic processing programs. After generating the panoramic image by the user's HMD screen recording video, the movements were processed from one image for every second. When the story flow came to the attractor point, users tended to turn towards the right because of the dynamic motion (the Flying Boat) (see Fig. 5). Then the user followed the boat with "pan right" three times more. Then s/he tended to tilt down. In the end, Tilt-Up did.

This method revealed whether the movement inside VR storytelling serves to verify whether the design of the content was served well or not. If the purpose of the story

SUBJECT 01 - ATTRACTOR 10

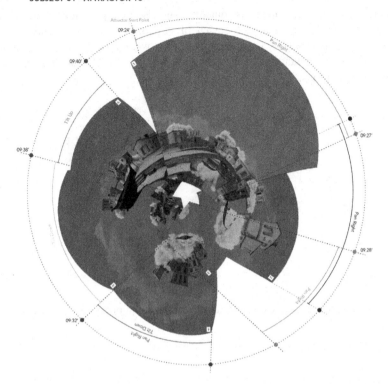

Fig. 5. Analysis of the Attractor Point 10 - "BOAT" for subject 01 based on "Cinemetrics."

content was directed towards increasing user experience, such movement analysis could reveal the expected results.

3.4   Movement Data Visualization

The data were collected from the recording software, which generated two outputs. The first one was the raw positional data file with the '.txt' (Text File) extension. The second one was the animation of the head-mounted display file with the '.fbx' (Filmbox) extension. Positional data were used to understand such user behaviors as how they react, and how much they explore, along with the measurements of their total paths, the measurements of the vertical path, and the measurements of the horizontal path.

The positional recordings included six-column data set for every second and the only three of these data, which are the positional coordinates (posX, posY, posZ) used for the analysis. Euler angles (rotX, rotY, rotZ) were not used. Positional data have been converted to the ".csv (comma-separated values)" file to import the file inside used software.

Software was also utilized to generate the movement paths, movement graphs, the horizontal and the vertical movement quantity, and also total path quantity (see Fig. 6). Movement paths were generated for each of the forty participants, and movement quantities were also calculated. After all the paths were generated, they were super-imposed so as to understand the total exploration (see Fig. 7). The movement data were calculated as quantities.

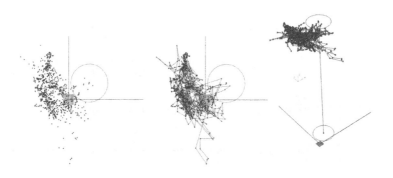

Fig. 6. The movement data as points, lines, and perspective view.

Fig. 7. The movement data plan for 40 participants (the gray circle represents the VR HMD).

3.5   Results

This experiment was conducted to understand the "user experience" of VR storytelling. This study led to the possibility of categorizing some estimations relative to user behaviors/reactions and memory. The study demonstrated that the behaviors were affected by both visual and aural stimulations. Also, memory was based on details, space, and story.

The behaviors/reactions of the user inside VR were examined; and this examination demonstrated that the users tended to react to the motions, sounds and the space of the story. If the scene had more than one motion, most of the users followed the movement that was more dynamic. If the users tracked the story, they demonstrated the most reactions to the stimulants, such as the attractors. Their tracking was affected by the motions' speed. If the story becomes slow and monotonous, the users tried to find other motions by looking around. If there is a more dynamic motion than the story scene, the user was attracted to motion instead of watching the story.

The behavioral data revealed that if the user was attracted to the space of the story, her/his reactions for motions and sounds tended to be weaker. Also, if there are more than one trackable motion, the user is attracted by the more animated one and tracks it.

Moreover, most of the participants tended to wander. Although most of them wandered through the space, some of the users who were not comfortable with the VR headset simply watched the story or displayed limited movements. The wanderer users tended to look around and wanted to see all the building details of the story space. This was an essential issue in order to design a story space, modeling it, and creating a story script.

Another interpretation is that if the current scene became slower than the previous scene, the user waited and looked for more, and he/she tended to wander around. This means that wandering tendencies were triggered by two different elements: the first is that the feeling of being present in the being-in-the-virtual-world of the story attracted people to wander. Also, if the users failed to catch the motion of the scene, they displayed an increased tendency to wander.

Furthermore, some of the attractor points, such as the "walk" were aural stimulants. These attractions were defined by the sounds of the gestures such as that of the little girl walking on the snow. The background music and the sounds of the story elements such as the sounds emitted by the flying ship's engine and the explosion of the ship were all defined as aural stimulants. These latter sounds were differentiated from the background music. If the user was stimulated by the sound, we noted three different possible reactions. The first reaction was that of noticing the sound. Also, some of the users looked about, trying to locate the origin of the aural source. Some users did not react to the sound and displayed no interest in either the sound itself or its origin.

The memory and recall of details, space, and the storyline were essential elements of this study. The colors of the matches were a small detail that most people could not answer correctly. They failed to answer correctly even if the colors were red, yellow, pink/purple, and the answer was mostly blue, which was the color of the blind man's suit in the same scene. Then, even if the users followed the story, their attentional degree cannot be sufficient enough to remember the details, such as the colors of the matches. It can be concluded from this situation that the highlighted components as the blind man can be remembered easier because there are so many distracting elements in the story space.

In general, the users' distance perception differed between two levels (the upper floating ground and the lower floating ground) (see Fig. 7). They can perceive the upper level better because this level serves as their vantage point. However, when it comes to the lower floating ground, their perceptions became fragmented and lost objectivity. One of the reasons for this fragmentation is that the users cannot directly approach the lower level and can only watch that level from a distance. Also, if the vertical movements of the users crosschecked with these answers, their distance perception of lower-level fractionation can be understandable. Although most of the users have a high number for the total path, their vertical path measurement is shallow. It can be concluded that if the user were able approach the lower level, a better distance perception and more vertical movements could be created (Fig. 8).

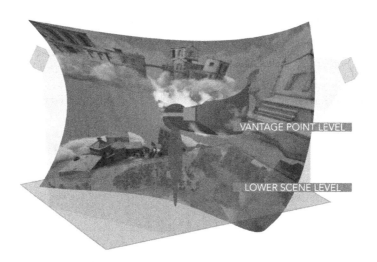

Fig. 8. The user vantage point of two levels in story space.

The questionnaire about the space included questions about the architectural styles of the space and the house. This question had a high correlation of correct answers. Very few wrong answers were given to the questions, which were about the architectural styles and the specific space details. One of the questions is the architectural type of the bridge, and the 99% of the users gave the right answer to the arched bridge. Also, 90% of the users provided correct answers to the question regarding the low-rise buildings. This leads us to understand that virtual individuals have a better memory of more general questions while question regarding small details proved more difficult to remember.

Remembering the storyline was the last part of the analysis. The story summaries as provided by the users were examined through the VR space movements (Fig. 9). So, if the user did not track the story, her/his summary would not be sufficient. If the user explored a lot, he/she could not catch the storyline details.

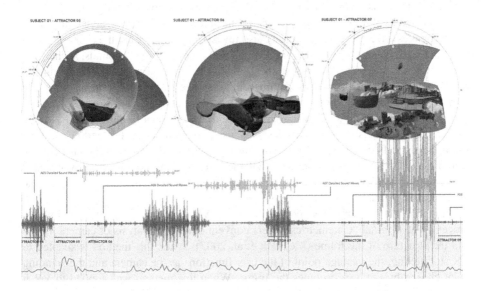

Fig. 9. Subject 01 Attractor 05-06-07 and audio analysis with movement graph (bottom).

The final step was to crosscheck and discuss the behavioral and the mnesic examinations. These estimations may prove to be a simple guide to understanding what the designer should do so as to elicit specific reactions. While designing the storytelling inside the VR environment, these data can support the design decisions. As an example, if the designer aims to attract the user with a story element, he/she can highlight the element and thus achieve the intended reaction.

4   Conclusion

The behavioral analysis and the other measurement analysis were conducted to attain the purpose of understanding the user experience by measuring space perception and memory recall of a story inside VR storytelling. The following methodologies were used, such as the audio analysis, the visual analysis, Cinemetrics, and the movement data analysis.

The quantitative and the qualitative data were collected and analyzed, along with the personal perceptional database having an effect on the experience. With this simple guide, a VR designer can predict what will happen if the user engages the story or not engage the story, and then s/he can direct the user with some moves. As an example, if some motions are meaningful for the designer, the designer can highlight that motion to get the attention of the user and lead them to track that motion. One of the findings of this study was that motions have a hierarchical influence order for the user. That means the more dynamic motion gets the more attention is given to them.

Users who follow the story display a greater reaction to both visual and aural stimulants. If the user is wandering about the space and/or not watching the story, s/he is not affected by the stimulations provided. The audio analysis demonstrated how such audio changes affect the user. The study also revealed whether or not the user reacted to the sounds. The result showed that most of the users did react to the sounds, such as the attractor point, the walk. When a sound started, users tended to look about trying to determine the source. Users also identified the distance and the location of the sound source. This study determined that aural stimuli plays a significant role in VR storytelling. While designing a VR storytelling content, the user can be stimulated easily by spatial aural features. Visual analysis was used to gain an understanding of how vantage points affect the experience. After the comparison of the 40 participants' screen recording videos, the results showed that the outcomes differentiated between each other, so everybody creates their unique experiences. That means the user becomes the director, and perhaps even the screenwriter.

Adapting the Cinemetrics methodology for VR storytelling is an experimental process. The original "Cinemetrics" offers conventional film analysis of camera moves and the structure of the frame (McGrath et al. 2007). When this method is adapted to VR storytelling, the vantage point of the user functions as the camera and the standing point chosen by the user becomes the frame. When this method was applied to VR it revealed the points towards which users tended to look, thus unveiling detailed information of design needs. The VR medium gives the user the opportunity to navigate within a three-dimensional story space. Therefore, the designer should decide that story and space dominance balance for VR storytelling.

The movement data analysis was evaluated together with all other data, such as the audio and visual analysis, so as to gain a more proper understanding of the user experience. An increase in totals of movement path correlated with a higher degree of user exploration. Similarly, if the vertical movement degree was low, the "one-point view" degree tended to be very high.

Designing storytelling for the VR environment is a new way of thinking because three-dimensional space and using an "undefined frame" for watching as a movie differentiates the "scenes." Unlike this, traditional designs of a movie (an animation or real footage movie), all called for design decisions to be based on the selected frame.

All these approaches demonstrate that the user, now serving as virtual individual within the story, becomes an actor for a VR storytelling; s/he is an active element of the story. So, if a user experience designer aims to craft VR storytelling properly, the designer needs to consider how the user will potentially respond to the story. This study was conducted to support these concerns, so this simple guide to understanding user behaviors inside VR storytelling can corroborate the user experience design.

Acknowledgments. This research was conducted to serve as a master thesis at Istanbul Technical University Architectural Design Computing Program. The study was conducted with the support of Istanbul Technical University Rectorate, which supplied the HTC Vive Head Mounted Display. We would like to thank our vice-rector Prof. Dr. Alper Ünal, Scientific Research Project Coordinator Behzat Şentürk, and Mehmet Kara.

References

Anderson, A.T.: VR Storytelling: 5 Explorers Defining the Next Generation of Narrative. Ceros Blog - Interactive Content Marketing & Design Tips. https://www.ceros.com/blog/vr-storytelling-5-explorers-defining-next-generation-narrative. Accessed 30 Aug 2016

Baudrillard, J.: Simulacra and Simulation, 3rd edn. (2011)

Benjamin, W.: Son bakışta aşk: Walter Benjamin'den seçme yazılar, pp. 81, 171. Metis Publications, İstanbul (2014)

Blumenthal, H.: Storyscape, a New Medium of Media. Georgia Institute of Technology, Atlanta (2016)

Chung, E.: Allumette. Penrose Studios (2016)

Cotting, D.: Storytelling vs. Story Enabling: Crafting Experiences in the New Medium of Virtual Reality. https://medium.com/shockoe/storytelling-vs-story-enabling-crafting-experiences-in-the-new-medium-of-virtual-reality-8b982359d3b8. Accessed 02 Nov 2019

Coyne, R.: Heidegger and virtual reality: the implications of heidegger's thinking for computer representations. Leonardo **27**(1), 65 (1994)

Deleuze, G.: Cinema I: The Movement Image. (H. Tomlinson, & B. Habberjam, Trans.). University of Minnesota, Minneapolis (1986)

Dervişcemaloğlu, B.: Anlatıbilime Giriş, 1st edn. Dergah Yayınları, Istanbul (2014)

Heath, S.: Narrative space. Screen **17**(3), 68–112 (1976)

Heim, M.: The Metaphysics of Virtual Reality. Oxford University Press, New York (1993)

Lau, S.Y., Chen, C.J.: Designing a virtual reality (VR) storytelling system for educational purposes. In: Iskander, M., Kapila, V., Karim, M. (eds.) Technological Developments in Education and Automation, pp. 135–138. Springer, Heidelberg (2009). https://doi.org/10.1007/978-90-481-3656-8_26

Leber, R.: The History of Storytelling: Part I: The Invention of Story. IndiePen Ink. http://indiepenink.com/research-a-torium/the-history-of-storytelling-part-1-the-invention-of-story/. Accessed 21 Apr 2018

McGrath, B., Gardner, J.: Cinemetrics. Wiley-Academy, Chichester (2007)

Morgan, A.: Virtual Reality: The User Experience of Story | Adobe Blog. from Adobe Blog. https://theblog.adobe.com/virtual-reality-the-user-experience-of-story/. Accessed 28 Apr 2018

Ökten, K.H.: Heidegger'e Giriş. Agora Kitaplığı, İstanbul (2012)

Pausch, R., Snoddy, J., Taylor, R., Watson, S., Haseltine, E.: Disney's Aladdin: first steps toward storytelling in virtual reality. In: SIGGRAPH 1996 Proceedings of the 23rd Annual Conference on Computer Graphics and Interactive Techniques, pp. 193–203. Association for Computing Machinery, Inc., New York (1996)

Ryan, M.-L.: Immersion vs. interactivity: virtual reality and literary theory. SubStance **28**(2), 110 (1999)

Ryan, M.-L.: Narrative as Virtual Reality: and Interactivity in Literature and Electronic Media. The Johns Hopkins University Press, Baltimore (2001)

Zona, M.: Narrative Space? https://mineofgod.wordpress.com/2014/01/08/narrative-space/. Accessed 20 Mar 2018

Automatic Emotional Balancing in Game Design: Use of Emotional Response to Increase Player Immersion

Willyan Dworak[1,3(✉)], Ernesto Filgueiras[1,3,4], and João Valente[2]

[1] University of Beira Interior, Covilhã, Portugal
wyworak@gmail.com, ernestovf@gmail.com
[2] Instituto Politécnico de Castelo Branco, Castelo Branco, Portugal
valente@ipcb.pt
[3] CIAUD - Research Centre for Architecture, Urbanism and Design,
Lisbon, Portugal
[4] Communication Laboratory – LabCom, University of Beira Interior,
Covilhã, Portugal

Abstract. This research aims to propose a theoretical model for the automatic balancing of games using the emotional state of the players. When launching a new game on the market, companies want to reach the largest number of people who are interested in playing the released title and for that they spend a large volume of resources to balance the games and deliver a good experience to the players. But this is not always possible because there are several types of players and each one has an expectation regarding the game. Some like a more difficult game, others prefer to just enjoy the narrative, but this, if defined statistically, limits the player to having multiple experiences, because the person may prefer to focus on the narrative and at the same time enjoy some moments with more action that, in a static configuration would be blocked. Given these assumptions, if the game can identify in real-time players' emotions, it may be able to make changes to the game design, manipulating the narrative and elements of the gameplay. One way to increase the player's involvement could be done through the monitoring of physiological signals and using AI algorithms to classify emotional states that potentiate changes in the scenarios and narrative of the story. In this study an approach based on biofeedback is explored, the measured physiological signals are used to make inferences about the emotional state of the player and this information is used to inform the game.

Keywords: Emotional game balancing · Adaptative videogame · Affective videogames · Emotion detection and gameplay biofeedback

1 Introduction

In the first decade of the 21st century, hardware development has been transcending the needs of videogames far beyond offering support for large resolutions and refresh rates above 60 Hz, reaching the point that new releases simply do not present innovations in the interaction, repeating the successful features from known franchises.

© Springer Nature Switzerland AG 2020
A. Marcus and E. Rosenzweig (Eds.): HCII 2020, LNCS 12201, pp. 426–438, 2020.
https://doi.org/10.1007/978-3-030-49760-6_30

The balancing in videogames exists to control the difficulty that the player will encounter, thus avoiding giving up and at the same time trying to keep the player's interest for as long as possible [13]. This control is done by changing various elements of the game, such as scenarios, music, artificial intelligence behaviours and parameters such as the character's resistance to damage, among several other items.

Currently, with the high processing power of graphics cards, videogames are with graphics increasingly closer to reality. They can have narratives that, in some cases, surpass the most complex films, but even so, sometimes they turn out to be just another game among so many and does not offer the entertainment expected by the players.

Another point is that, given the large amount of information that people have at their disposal, creating a media that can keep people's attention is becoming an arduous task for videogame developers. Thus, apart from the competition that videogame studios have among themselves, seeking to expand their Market Share, they also face competition from the internet, which offers to people, videos and social networks to compete for their time with games. So, these companies need to look for ways on how to develop a videogame with characteristics that are capable of offering entertainment and immersion to the largest number of people without dividing them into groups, such as professional players and casual players, that is, looking for a way to make a video game that can be played by anyone and in turn, the player stay with feeling that has received a custom videogame.

Video games are beginning to incorporate adaptive game mechanisms. In the traditional model, the game is linear and will always be presented in the same way to all players. Adaptive games evolve game design according to the player's choices and with that, offering a unique gaming experience for each person [9]. Currently, in some video games, the player has the false feeling that he is choosing the future of the narrative when making choices about which path to take. This can increase players' involvement and immersion, yet it does not guarantee that the player does not feel bored during certain points of the game. This is because the game may be poorly balanced and in some moments - it is very difficult to go through a level, while in other moments there is not much to do besides walking around the scenery without any resistance. When launching a new videogame, companies have in mind the desire for success. But, what guarantees the success of a video game? The success of a video game consists of four basic elements, which are: Mechanics, History, Aesthetics and Technology [22].

Despite the precise indications of Schell (2018) [22], the failure in sales and consumer adhesion in many video games that presented significant developments in each one of the highlighted areas or maintained successful recipes, some of them with recognition and prizes, demonstrate that there is no guarantee that success can be achieved only following technical criteria.

Another very common problem in videogames' development is their balancing. Nowadays, big companies invest millions of dollars to balance their games passively and, even so, there is no guarantee that the game will be pleasant to every player. With that, two accessory problems were formulated, which guide this study:

- P1 - Videogames do not have an automatic mechanism to help keeping players motivated and emotionally involved.

- P2 - Videogames are not able to make a personalized balance, to present a unique experience for each player.

With these problems in mind, knowing that there is a hidden ingredient to the success of videogames, and that their balance needs something more to be efficient, some questions arise: "What is behind all this? How to make people want to play a videogame and how to create an ideal balance for each person to offer a unique experience?"

For the development of this study, it is considered that the fundamental piece for the success of videogames is related to individual emotions [4]. When a videogame is able to produce different emotions, and those emotions being what people expect to have while playing, the videogame will certainly be successful.

Throughout the history of videogames, many examples show that the technical criteria alone is not the key factor for a successful videogame. How to explain the case of Minecraft? A videogame that does not have an in-depth narrative, aesthetically it doesn't have sophistication, technologically it does not have any advancement, as it is possible to play it on machines with simple hardware configurations and its mechanics are common among several games. While some studios are investing heavily in graphic quality to create games that look like real playable movies and are unsuccessful. One possible explanation for the Minecraft case could be in the way that each person can imagine their own world and do whatever they want within the game universe. Each game elicits a set of different emotions in each player and, consequently, has a unique experience in the game. But, how can this be reproduced in videogames where there is a defined narrative and the player must follow a path established by the game designer? It is already known from literature [4], that personalized emotions are the only way to guarantee the success of an entertainment medium, especially in videogames, that are the most immersive multimedia. An alternative is to provide game designers a model in which they can use the emotions of the players so that these emotions can influence the game design, making the game self-adaptable.

This study seeks to analyse how to use the emotions experienced by players in videogames to evolve game design. For this, the focus of the studies is on how to measure physiological signals, and identify emotional patterns, so they can be used as input patterns to a decision-making algorithm when advancing the game. It is important to note that a game can be adaptive only using AI (Artificial Intelligence) to learn from the player using Machine Learning [14] techniques and make changes, without needing to know player's emotion, but the focus here is to add emotion to the equation. Thus, with the wide variety of biosensors currently available on the market, and with relatively low prices, finding a way to use them in videogames can be a solution to the problem of balance and motivation of players. Seeking to offer even more immersion to the players so that they can fully uniquely enjoy each videogame, the following research question was raised:

- Is it possible to increase the involvement and attention of the players by making the game design adapt to the emotions of those who are playing?

The following research hypothesis was created after the research question was established:

- Assuming that it is possible to identify in real-time the emotions experienced by the players, it will be possible to make changes to the game design, manipulate the narrative and gameplay elements through the use of AI algorithms and thereby increase the player's involvement.

Thus, if the player is on a mission where, for example, he must keep collecting items around the scene and in the meantime, there is nothing that generates action, the player may end up getting bored and even closing the game. But if the video game can identify this, it can insert some enemies via AI to make the mission more difficult. And in case the player is facing a very strong opponent and the game identifies that the player is starting to feel angry for not being able to win, then it can adapt to decrease the resistance of the opponent character so that the game stays balanced with the player and still be interesting.

2 Emotional Envelope in the Gameplay

Currently, measuring emotions and interpreting them is not a simple task. Additionally, measuring emotional reactions through biofeedback is not yet consensual, despite having evolved a lot in the last 13 years [7, 18, 20]. Measuring the right emotions is still complex and inaccurate. Complex because for a more accurate reading of the biosensors, the necessary physical conditions of the environment still need to be very controlled due to the sensitivity of the biosensors.

Regarding interpretations, there are also conflicts of opinion between authors, since the terms emotion and feeling are sometimes confused [24]. Inaccurate because an emotion considered negative on emotion maps such as anguish and fear, can be good in videogames, as long as that is the goal of the game designer. One option offered as a solution is the creation of a model that involves obtaining physiological reactions from the players, making a subjective assessment and automatic repetition in the gameplay.

2.1 How to See Emotions?

Before talking about how emotions can be represented, first is needed to define what an emotion is. An emotion can be defined as an episode that causes interconnected and synchronized changes in the states of all or most of the five subsystems of the organism in response to the evaluation of an external or internal stimulus event as relevant to the main concerns of the organism [23].

To be able to visually represent emotions, some researchers over time have created some graphic models, in which each one defines sets of emotions and how is the interpolation between them. Among the main models are:

1. **Russell's Circumplex Model of Affect**: a person's affective state can be represented in two dimensions, excitement and valence. Where excitement represents the response to stimuli and the person's alertness level and the valence represents the level of feeling on a scale between pleasant and unpleasant [21].
2. **Plutchik's Wheel of Emotions**: in this model, the emotions are represented by the three-dimensional shape of a cone, the basic emotions are eight and, in this model,

the base of the cone represents these basic emotions that are arranged in a circle, organized in four pairs of opposites according to their similarities [19].

2.2   How to Measure Emotions?

When trying to measure and interpret people's emotions in an experiment, it is necessary to use a tool where the volunteer can identify or describe their emotions. For this research, two tools were considered, Self-Assessment Manikin and PrEmo.

Self-Assessment Manikin (SAM): is a non-verbal pictorial assessment technique that directly measures pleasure, excitement and dominance associated with a person's affective reaction to a wide variety of stimuli [15]. To facilitate reading, in this document the Self-Assessment Manikin technique will be simplified for the SAM Scale. This technique consists of a questionnaire that was developed to measure three characteristics of an emotional response that were identified as the main ones for measuring emotions, which are valence, excitement and dominance [15].

PrEmo is a tool that aims to indicate, through images and animations, the emotional state of a person on a given situation or subject. It is a non-verbal instrument in which the person makes a self-assessment of his emotions using images. PrEmo measures 14 emotions that are usually provoked by the design of a product [6]. The commercial version of the tool presents an option for respondents to be able to report their emotions using expressive cartoon animations. In this version, each of the 14 measured emotions is portrayed by an animation through dynamic facial, body and vocal expressions, so there is no need to rely on the use of words [16].

3   Biofeedback

Biofeedback is a technique that provides biological information in real-time [8]. With this, the use of biofeedback can help so that it is possible to understand and look for ways to interpret people's emotions with the use of computer algorithms. Currently, precisely defining emotions using biofeedback is still a task to be defined. Even with advances in research and attempts to create automatic systems for recognizing emotions, it is still very difficult to identify emotions using biological signals [10, 12]. Some studies show the difficulty in interpreting emotions. According to them, there are many interindividual differences when it comes to interpreting emotions using biosensors, since the same emotion can lead to different patterns of physiological reactions, which causes great difficulties in finding patterns in the data and thereby training classifiers [12].

In another study based on data from biosensors [11], the objective was to classify users' emotional experience when interacting with embedded conversational agents, that is, a virtual character. The study was carried out in two phases, where the first objective was to be able to train the classifier and the second to apply the classifier to human-agent interactions. In the first phase, images with known values of valence were used to be displayed to participants who used the SAM Scale [3] to evaluate these images. At the same time, they collected data from biosensors to train classifiers. During the second phase, the participants were placed to interact with a virtual agent and meanwhile their physiological data was collected, and the classifiers trained in the first phase were applied to that data.

One difficulty pointed out by the authors is the limitation in the use of subjective classifications for the training of classifiers for physiological signs. As this classification was acquired from satisfaction questionnaires carried out at the end of the interaction session, this can cause some problems because people may not remember exactly how their emotional experience was during the experiment. Another point is that the questionnaires provide measures only at the end of the interaction and this generates a single measure for the entire interaction [1, 17]. The conclusion was that making automatic recognition of emotions by distinguishing emotions with respect to valence is a difficult task. The study obtained good results for image evaluations, on average above 90% of correct answers, but for tests with virtual agents, the data were not satisfactory.

3.1 Biosensors

A biosensor is an analytical device that measures biological or chemical reactions and converts them into an electrical signal. Currently, biosensors are present mainly in biomedical diagnosis. They are used in applications such as disease monitoring, drug discovery and pollutant detection, disease-causing microorganisms and markers that are indicators of a disease in body fluids such as blood, urine, saliva and sweat [2].

The term biosensor is often used to refer to sensors used to determine the concentration of substances and other parameters of biological interest, even when they do not directly use a biological system [5]. Currently, these biosensors are accessible for research, mainly because low-cost equipment, such as Bitalino, can be used. Bitalino is a board slightly larger than a credit card that enables the acquisition of physiological data. It is a very versatile hardware and was designed in a way that allows anyone, from students to professional application developers, to be able to create projects and applications using physiological sensors [25].

However, to study emotions in videogames it is not enough to have the equipment. It is necessary to create experimental paradigms to study the players' behaviour, integrating for this purpose the synchronized reading of physiological signals, filtering algorithms and data treatment to use this information in the identification of emotional patterns generated during the execution of the games. In this sense, an online platform accessible at brainanswer.pt was used. With this platform, it is possible to develop experimental test paradigms while measuring various physiological signals, collecting forms and self-assessment scales from players. In this platform, tools are made available that allow the replay of the game while the physiological signals are visualized, and comments or markings can be made at the moments of greatest emotional involvement of the player. Another possibility is the crossing of the players' responses with the generated signals making it possible to investigate changes in physiological signals at key moments in the games.

The BrainAnswer platform works like an online laboratory for studying emotions. However, the ease with which it is possible to identify changes in some physiological signals through the platform, should not be accepted in any way, normally requiring interpretation by experts. This is because the changes can occur due to several factors: poor placement of the sensors, inappropriate collection environment, involuntary movement of the participant, electromagnetic noise in the room, external interference, great variability of signals between individuals, the stress associated with the monitoring experience and even the existence of some pathology. All of these are factors that escape inexperienced researchers and that are a factor of success or failure in the study of emotions. However, it is necessary to develop an API (Application Programming Interface), to integrate the game variables with the emotional parameters measured on the Brainanswer platform.

4   Emotional Gameplay Through Application Programming Interface - API

One way to solve these problems seen so far related to the interpretation of emotions in videogames is using an API, which receives data from three sources: Biosensors, Gameplay Telemetry and the Emotion Patterns expected to be found in that game. These three sources are important because from the biosensors' data it is possible to find the physiological variation of the players to the stimuli of the game at a given moment or event, but this information alone is not enough, because it is necessary to know the game data at the moments when these variations occur so that the interpretation of emotions is more accurate. These data can be acquired from the telemetry of the game, which must be done during the development of the game, so that it is possible to recover the value of the variables that are of interest for analysis, as well as events that the game designer considers important to generate emotions in players. And the third source of data is the emotional patterns expected for the game events, because by correlating the expected emotion with the player's emotion for a given game event, one can guarantee that the emotions obtained are the ones expected and so they are evaluated correctly. That way the API may be able to make more assertive decisions when it comes to predicting the next level.

4.1   API Training Model

To present an application that can perform these tasks, a model called the Emotional Game API was developed, which was divided into two stages. The first is responsible for training the API so that it can recognize emotional patterns. And the second stage is the application of the API for creating settings for a videogame based on the input data. Figure 1 shows the steps for training the API.

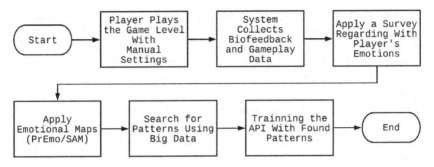

Fig. 1. Activity flow to API training.

1. **Player plays the game level with manual settings**: the first step for training the API is to prepare the game settings manually, that is, all the variables that define the difficulty of the level must be defined by the game designer so that it is playable by anyone, even if they do not have previous knowledge about the game.

2. **System collects biofeedback and gameplay data**: the player's biofeedback data, such as Electrodermal Activity (EDA), Blood Volume Pulse (BVP), Electrocardiogram (ECG) and Respiration, must be collected in a synchronized manner with the game's telemetry data. This facilitates the process of interpreting the data when placed in Big Data systems.

3. **Apply a survey regarding with player's emotions**: at this stage, it is important to survey with the player so that it is possible to understand what his emotions were during the gameplay. This step is important because if the evaluation is performed only considering the maps of emotions, wrong conclusions can be reached. An emotional pattern can be defined as positive or negative by the user without having to know whether or not it is positive or negative on the map of emotions. It happens because, in a game interaction, the player may like fear or anguish and hopes for it, but these types of emotions are considered negative on the scales of emotions. Therefore, the game designer needs to know what emotions are expected for the game's events.

4. **Apply emotional maps (PrEmo/SAM)**: with the utilisation of the two emotion maps, PrEmo [16] and SAM [15] together, the strengths of both can be added. With the use of PrEmo it is possible to identify the emotional state of the player during the gameplay and with the use of the SAM map it is possible to measure the intensity of that state, as well as to verify the levels of Pleasure, Arousal and Dominance, considering player's opinion. The utilisation of these maps helps in the API validation process, because based on the players' inputs it is possible to know if the changes made by the API have shown good results or not.

5. **Search for patterns using Big Data**: as the data acquisition process generates a very large volume of data to be analysed, the best way is to apply Big Data systems to extract information. At this stage, it is important to analyse recurring events in the game, for example, when the character receives a bonus, when he levels up, when he dies, when he is under pressure. These events can be defined in the game's telemetry, or if the analysed game is already existing and offers the option of

collecting the telemetry, these events must be defined manually. For this stage it is also important to have recordings of the gameplays, this helps to identify patterns of behaviour of the player as well as it is possible to know what he was doing before and after the event. These patterns can be simplified to positive and negative. Positive when the event pleases the player and negative when the event displeases the player.

6. **Training the API with found patterns**: after having found these patterns, these values can be used to train an Artificial Intelligence (AI) using Machine Learning. That way, when the API is in a production environment, it will only be necessary to input the biofeedback data, game telemetry and expected emotional patterns, that the API should be able to interpret these values and with them to create configurations for the next level of the game. In this way, each new level of the game may present a different configuration, based on the emotional state of the player and thus increase the engagement of players with the game.

An important point to be highlighted during the process of evaluating the emotional state of the players is to know what the player was doing before and after each analysed event. This information may not be found by Machine Learning systems, because they can only observe that there were changes in the data of the biosensors, but without knowing the reason for this change. Players can experience physiological changes while mentally creating a strategy. These changes also occur when players see that they will be in danger shortly. Therefore, in the initial evaluations, it is important to observe the gameplay recordings to remove these critical points.

4.2   API Application Model

The API usage model is like the training model. This model is indicated to be used as a continuation of AI training, because with it, the player will play the same level several times with different configurations suggested by the API. In this model, the player continues to starting the first level with a manual configuration suggested by the game designer, the procedure for collecting the game's biofeedback data and game telemetry data remains the same, as well as the application of emotion maps at the end of the level played. The flow of activities for using the API can be seen in Fig. 2 and the added points are presented subsequently.

1. **Game designer defines the expected emotions**: as stated earlier, the interpretation of an emotion can presents incorrect values for the prediction systems if they are evaluated only based on the maps of emotions. That is why the game designer needs to define the emotional pattern he intends to meet for each game event. This data must be sent to the API to be correlated with the data received from the biosensors and game's telemetry data. This is important because, for example, if the game designer expects that the player feels angry at a certain point in the game and then starts a battle with a desire to revenge, this emotional pattern will be interpreted as positive by the API, contrary to what it would be if analysed only based on emotion maps.

2. **API receives the biofeedback data, gameplay data and expected emotions**: each of these three data sources is a fundamental part of a successful API result. In the

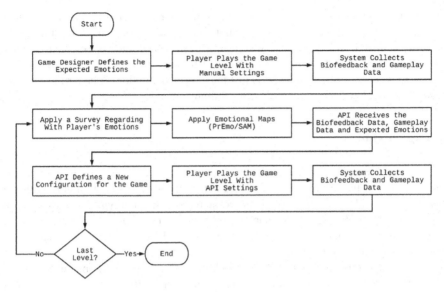

Fig. 2. Activity flow to use the API.

biofeedback data, there are the physiological changes of the players, in the gameplay data, there is all the game's telemetry with the relevant game data, such as the character's position, life level, distance between the character and the players, enemies, among others that the game designer considers important. And finally, there are the emotional patterns that the game designer hopes to meet for the game's events.

3. **API defines a new configuration for the game**: with all three data sources ready and the AI previously trained, the API may be able to predict configurations that are in line with the players' expectations. For this, at each event considered important by the game designer, the API must correlate a range of data from the biosensors, which in turn must be synchronized with the telemetry data of the game and thereby seek the standards previously defined in the training process, then, this result must be correlated with the emotional pattern established by the game designer so that it is possible to identify whether or not the player is involved with the game.

4. **Player plays the game level with API settings**: This step helps to test whether the API was efficient in creating a game configuration in a way that pleases the player. This is a feedback system process and also helps for AI training, because if it is identified that the settings did not satisfy the player, for the next level the API should be able to identify whether the game was too easy or too difficult, resulting in the player's disinterest and thereby adapting. If the result was positive and the player liked the game's difficulty settings, for the next level the API can be configured to offer the player more challenge.

With this model, for the realization of experiments, the game designer can define how many levels the player will play. So, in Fig. 2, there is the decision component called Last Level, it assists to direct the experiment, where the player will repeat the level with the settings suggested by the API until reaching the defined value and then the experiment is finished. For the "emotional pattern established by the game designer", it is understood that for a given game event, an emotion is expected. A point to be highlighted is that when starting the API training process there is still no data pattern, so what are needed to know is just the expected emotion. A pattern in the data is something that will be found only after training.

5 Conclusion

The model presented in this paper is being applied in a field study, in the final stage, with a sample of players (n = 40). The API behavior has revealed an affinity with the players' emotional envelopes, and it can be increased the emotional game experience between matches. The model has managed to combine the biofeedback elements with the predefined gameplay characteristics. The first results have shown that there is an expected viability for this model.

A point that must be observed in research that intends to use the model presented here is using an authorial videogame, where it is possible to test specific events without the influence of others. In general games, even though it is a simple game, have a very fast transition between events. So, it can be difficult to know what the exact reason for an emotional trigger was. Thus, being able to test events separately that cause joy, sadness, anger, fear, among other emotions, it becomes more evident if a person had an emotional shot because he was in danger or because he received a reward. Thus, creating a videogame where all people go through the same events and between these events there is an interval to calm down, it will probably be easier to identify patterns and thereby teach AI.

It is indicated that in the self-assessment forms that are presented to players when completing the level. That forms need to have a question that inspire the player to express in writing their experience during that game, because with that, in the initial stages of creating the API, where the pattern search process requires manual intervention and analysis, making it easier to remove misinterpretations. This is also one of the reasons for doing separate event tests, because when playing a full level and only at the end make an evaluation of the experience as a whole the player can consider only isolated cases that occurred during the gameplay and thereby hamper the process of the search for emotional patterns.

As seen in the literature, finding emotional patterns in the data is still difficult, but this can be simplified if the analysis was made to verifying whether the event caused an activation in the player or not. This can be found by correlating the game telemetry from a certain event with the biosensors data, mainly with the EDA and heartbeat rate curves of the player. This does not guarantee knowing the emotion of the player, but it does provide information on whether that event satisfied the player. This topic is under study and will be discussed in more detail in future research.

However, the model presented in this research aims to be a starting point for the search for emotional patterns of players in commercial games. As it has a Deep Learning and Machine Learning process, it is indicated that it is initially used in simple games, with levels that can be played again, because this way it is easier to search for emotional patterns when compared to complex games that have several forms of player activation.

References

1. Benedek, J., Hazlett, R.L.: Incorporating facial EMG emotion measures as feedback in the software design process. In: Proceedings of Human Computer Interaction Consortium (2005)
2. Bhalla, N., et al.: Introduction to biosensors. Essays Biochemistry **60**(1), 1–8 (2016). https://doi.org/10.1042/ebc20150001
3. Bradley, M.M., Lang, P.J.: Measuring emotion: the self-assessment manikin and the semantic differential. J. Behav. Therapy Exp. Psychiatry **25**(1), 49–59 (1994). https://doi.org/10.1016/0005-7916(94)90063-9
4. de Byl, P.: A conceptual affective design framework for the use of emotions in computer game design (2015). https://doi.org/10.5817/CP2015-3-4
5. Chaplin, M.: Enzyme Technology: What are biosensors? http://www1.lsbu.ac.uk/water/enztech/biosensors.html. Accessed 09 Nov 2019
6. Desmet, P.: Measuring emotion: development and application of an instrument to measure emotional responses to products. Hum.-Comput. Interact. Ser. **3**, 111–123 (2004)
7. Egger, M., et al.: Emotion recognition from physiological signal analysis: a review. Electron. Notes Theoret. Comput. Sci. **343**, 35–55 (2019). https://doi.org/10.1016/j.entcs.2019.04.009
8. Giggins, O.M., et al.: Biofeedback in rehabilitation. J. NeuroEng. Rehabil. **10**(1), 6–19 (2013). https://doi.org/10.1186/1743-0003-10-60
9. Gilleade, K.M., Dix, A.: Using frustration in the design of adaptive videogames. In: Proceedings of the 2004 ACM SIGCHI International Conference on Advances in Computer Entertainment Technology, pp. 228–232. ACM, New York (2004). https://doi.org/10.1145/1067343.1067372
10. Haag, A., et al.: Emotion recognition using bio-sensors: first steps towards an automatic system. In: André, E., et al. (eds.) Affective Dialogue Systems, pp. 36–48. Springer, Berlin (2004). https://doi.org/10.1007/978-3-540-24842-2_4
11. Hristova, E., et al.: Biosignal based emotion analysis of human-agent interactions. In: Esposito, A., Vích, R. (eds.) Cross-Modal Analysis of Speech, Gestures, Gaze and Facial Expressions, pp. 63–75. Springer, Berlin (2009). https://doi.org/10.1007/978-3-642-03320-9_7
12. Kim, J., André, E.: Emotion recognition based on physiological changes in music listening. IEEE Trans. Pattern Anal. Mach. Intell. **30**(12), 2067–2083 (2008). https://doi.org/10.1109/TPAMI.2008.26
13. Koster, R.: Theory of Fun for Game Design. Paraglyph Press, Hilo (2004)
14. Langley, P.: Machine learning for adaptive user interfaces. In: Brewka, G., Habel, C., Nebel, B. (eds.) KI 1997. LNCS, vol. 1303, pp. 53–62. Springer, Heidelberg (1997). https://doi.org/10.1007/3540634932_3
15. Lang, P.J., et al.: Looking at pictures: affective, facial, visceral, and behavioral reactions. Psychophysiology **30**(3), 261–273 (1993). https://doi.org/10.1111/j.1469-8986.1993.tb03352.x
16. Laurans, G., Desmet, P.M.A.: Developing 14 animated characters for non-verbal self-report of categorical emotions. J. Des. Res. **15**(3–4), 214–233 (2017). https://doi.org/10.1504/JDR.2017.089903

17. Mandryk, R., Atkins, M.: A fuzzy physiological approach for continuously modeling emotion during interaction with play technologies. Int. J. Hum.-Comput. Stud. **65**, 329–347 (2007). https://doi.org/10.1016/j.ijhcs.2006.11.011
18. Marci, C.D.: A biologically based measure of emotional engagement: context matters. J. Adv. Res. **46**(4), 381–387 (2006). https://doi.org/10.2501/S0021849906060466
19. Plutchik, R.: The nature of emotions: human emotions have deep evolutionary roots, a fact that may explain their complexity and provide tools for clinical practice. Am. Sci. **89**(4), 344–350 (2001). https://doi.org/10.1511/2001.4.344
20. Poels, K., Dewitte, S.: How to capture the heart? Reviewing 20 years of emotion measurement in advertising. J. Adv. Res. **46**(1), 18–37 (2006). https://doi.org/10.2501/S0021849906060041
21. Russell, J.A.: A circumplex model of affect. J. Pers. Soc. Psychol. **39**(6), 1161–1178 (1980). https://doi.org/10.1037/h0077714
22. Schell, J.: The Art of Game Design: A Book of Lenses. Elsevier/Morgan Kaufmann, Boston (2008)
23. Scherer, K.: Appraisal Processes in Emotion: Theory, Methods, Research. Oxford University Press, Oxford (2001)
24. Scherer, K.R.: What are emotions? And how can they be measured? Soc. Sci. Inf. **44**(4), 695–729 (2005). https://doi.org/10.1177/0539018405058216
25. da Silva, H.P., et al.: BITalino: a novel hardware framework for physiological computing. In: PhyCS 2014 - Proceedings of the International Conference on Physiological Computing Systems, pp. 246–253 (2014). https://doi.org/10.5220/0004727802460253

A Comparative Usability Analysis of Handheld Game Consoles

Weiting Gao$^{(\boxtimes)}$, Yun Wang, Wenzhuo Zhang, Chuan Qin,
and Marcelo M. Soares

School of Design, Hunan University, Changsha, People's Republic of China
gao_weiting@163.com, 2649250006@qq.com,
zhangmaotou@gmail.com, 980491901@qq.com,
soaresmm@gmail.com

Abstract. A handheld game console is a small and portable video game console with a built-in screen, game controls and speakers. Playing a handheld game console involves multiple operations and buttons. The usability of game consoles is influenced by users' expertise and skills. In this study, we mainly focused on testing the usability of products instead of video games and we adopted three variables from Leventhal and Barnes' usability model (reference) to analyze two game consoles (Switch and 3DS-LL) on three variables: task match, the ease of learning, and the ease of use. We recruited novice users and compared the usability of the two-handle mode and single-handle mode of Switch, and of Switch and 3DS-LL. Finally, we raised some suggestions for the design of handheld game consoles regarding usability.

Keywords: Handheld game console · Usability · Consoles

1 Introduction

The global gaming console market is expected to witness high growth over the forecast period [1]. In order to make gaming experience more enjoyable and win more customers, companies need to take usability into consideration when designing products. While many standard usability testing procedures and doctrine may not be applicable to video game design [2], we focus more on the usability of products themselves instead of video games.

Handheld game consoles contain the console, screen, speakers, and controls in one unit, which allow people to carry them and play them at any time or place. Playing handheld game consoles offers users different experience compared to PC or mobile games and can make playing games more active and flexible [9–11]. The first handheld electronic game can be dated back to 1976, when Mattel released Auto Race and the oldest true handheld game console with interchangeable cartridges is the Milto Bradley Microvision in 1979. Currently, Nintendo dominate the handheld console market.

Our study consists of two main experiments. In the first experiment, we made a comparative usability analysis of Nintendo Switch (Fig. 1) and Nintendo 3DS (Fig. 2), which are both Nintendo's star-products while Switch, the later-released product,

© Springer Nature Switzerland AG 2020
A. Marcus and E. Rosenzweig (Eds.): HCII 2020, LNCS 12201, pp. 439–451, 2020.
https://doi.org/10.1007/978-3-030-49760-6_31

enjoys a better sale currently [3]. Switch is a portable hybrid console that merge the handheld and home console experiences while 3DS is a handheld game console. We only compared the handheld mold of Switch to 3DS and test task match, the ease of learning, and the ease of use respectively.

In the second experiment, we focus on testing Switch and compare task match, the ease of learning, and the ease of use of two gaming modes of Switch: two-handle mode and single-handle mode. Switch has two detachable handles attached to the main product and can be used with both two handles or only one. The operations of two handles are different from the operations of one handle, which may cause confusion to new users.

Fig. 1. Switch is a video game console developed by Nintendo and released on March 3, 2017.

Fig. 2. The Nintendo 3DS is produced by Nintendo and is officially unveiled in June 2010. The one that we analyze in the study is Nintendo 3DS-LL, which was released in July, 2012 in Japan.

The aim of the study is to compare the usability of two different handle modes of Switch and of Switch and 3DS, as well as raise proposals and suggestions of designing video game consoles.

2   Methodology

The variables of the study are adopted from Leventhal and Barnes' usability model [4], which contains the ease of learning, the ease of relearning, the ease of use, task match, flexibility and user satisfaction. Since many operations of the consoles vary from game to game, we only tested basic universal operations which did not involve flexibility. We learned from pilot experiments that there was no apparent difference regarding relearning and users' satisfaction, so we ruled out these three variables. The ease of learning was measured by perform variables of accuracy, and quantitatively rating scales as a supplement while task match and the ease of use were measured by quantitatively rating scales and qualitatively subjective opinions.

We also conducted the method of 'Thinking Aloud Protocol'. According to Nielsen, this valuable usability test refers to the users' narrative about the actions performed, the decisions made, their opinions and their feelings while interacting with the evaluated product (or prototype).

We recruited 12 users in total to participate in the two tests. They were all students aged from 19 to 21 in Hunan University and had no previous experience in playing Switch or 3DS-LL. They were asked to perform several tasks with Switch or 3DS-LL independently. If one failed to complete a task, he or she would be given standard instructions only once and be asked to try again. We recorded the performance of users' every operation in the tasks and after they completed all tasks, we asked them to fill in a five-point scale rating table regarding the three variables to evaluate each operation and conducted semi-structured interviews to collect users' opinions and feelings. During the experiments, a facilitator facilitated the tests, a recorder recorded and wrote down users' words and opinions, another recorder shoot videos, and an observer observed users' operations. The recordings and videos were recorded by two smartphones (Huawei Mate10 and Huawei Mate 10 Pro) respectively.

2.1   Test One

The first test was a controlled experiment [6, 7] to evaluate the usability of the handheld mode of Switch and 3DS-LL. We recruited 3 males and 2 females in the test. The pre-test hypothesis [6, 7] was that the overall usability of Switch when playing games was higher than 3DS-LL for college students. The independent variable was Switch or 3DS-LL while the dependent variables were task match, the ease of learning, and the ease of use. The sequence of tasks, the environment, instructions and machine conditions were rigidly controlled during different users' testing.

The four tasks that users needed to perform in the experiment were listed below.

1. Powering on the evaluated product. Users needed to identify the power button and pressed it to power on the product.
2. Entering the game. Users needed to operate the joystick to choose the game we required.
3. Performing four main gaming operations: using the joystick to move, pressing the attack button to attack, pressing the shield button to shield and pressing the catching button to catch.
4. Operating to pause the game. Users needed to recognize the menu button and press it.

Nearly all buttons on the products are tested. During the test, users were encouraged to speak out their feelings and opinions towards the product and after which, they were asked to fill in the rating scales. Table 1 shows some example rating scales and questions for each operation are the same. After filling the scales, an interview about the usability of evaluated products was held to collect opinions and feelings. The goal of the experiment was to evaluate the usability of the same operations of Switch and 3DS-ll respectively and make a comparison.

Table 1. Sample questions from the rating table of the first experiment

Task	Operation	Rating scale
No.	**Operation**	**Five-point Likert scale**
1	Powering on (Fig. 3)	This operation is easy to understand 1 2 3 4 5 This operation is easy to learn 1 2 3 4 5 This operation is comfortable and effortless to do 1 2 3 4 5
2	Entering the game (Fig. 4)	This operation is easy to understand 1 2 3 4 5 This operation is easy to learn 1 2 3 4 5 This operation is comfortable and effortless to do 1 2 3 4 5
3	All tested operations	The overall operation of the evaluated product is easy to understand 1 2 3 4 5 The overall operation of the evaluated product is easy to learn 1 2 3 4 5 The overall operation of the evaluated product is comfortable and effortless 1 2 3 4 5

Fig. 3. Powering on

Fig. 4. Entering the game

2.2   Test Two

The second test aimed to evaluate the usability of Switch with a focus on the use of its handles. It contained an experiment to test some basic operations of the handles and a controlled experiment to comparatively test the usability of the two-handle mode and single-handle mode of Switch. Users (4 males and 3 females) were asked to perform the same tasks with two handles and one handle respectively after standard instructions. The pre-test hypothesis of the controlled experiment was that the overall usability of Switch's two-handle mode is higher than single-handle mode when playing games for college students. The independent variable was playing Switch with two handles or one while the dependent variables were task match, the ease of learning, and the ease of use. The sequence of tasks, environment, instructions and machine conditions were also rigidly controlled. Similarly, the ease of learning was measured by perform variables of accuracy and quantitatively rating scales, while task match and the ease of use was measured by quantitatively rating scales and qualitatively subjective opinions. Also, users' words, operations and facial expressions are recorded.

The tasks that users were asked to complete in the second test were as below.

1. Unlocking the product. Users needed to identify the unlocking button and press it.
2. Detaching the handles from the product. Users needed to press a certain button and taking the handles away from the console.
3. Fitting the handles to the handle holder.
4. Entering the game with two handles. Users needed to operate the joystick to choose the game we required.
5. Performing the four gaming operations same to the first experiment with two handles.
6. Cutting the connection between handles and the product. Users needed to recognize the connection button and pressed it.
7. Connecting one handle to the product. Users needed to recognize the two connection buttons and pressed them simultaneously.

8. Fitting the single handle to another handle holder.
9. Entering the game with one handle.
10. Performing the four main gaming operations same to the first experiment with one handle.

Table 2. Sample questions from the rating table of the second experiment

Task	Operation	Rating scale
No.	**Operation**	**Five-point Likert scale**
1	Unlocking the product (Fig. 5)	This operation is easy to understand 1 2 3 4 5 This operation is easy to learn 1 2 3 4 5 This operation is comfortable and effortless to do 1 2 3 4 5
2	Detaching the handles from the product (Fig. 6)	This operation is easy to understand 1 2 3 4 5 This operation is easy to learn 1 2 3 4 5 This operation is comfortable and effortless to do 1 2 3 4 5
3	Fitting the handles to the handle holder (Fig. 7)	This operation is easy to understand 1 2 3 4 5 This operation is easy to learn 1 2 3 4 5 This operation is comfortable and effortless to do 1 2 3 4 5
4	Entering the game (Fig. 8)	This operation is easy to understand 1 2 3 4 5 This operation is easy to learn 1 2 3 4 5 This operation is comfortable and effortless to do 1 2 3 4 5
5	Using the joystick to move (Fig. 9)	This operation is easy to understand 1 2 3 4 5 This operation is easy to learn 1 2 3 4 5 This operation is comfortable and effortless to do 1 2 3 4 5

The tasks 4), 5) are comparative to the tasks 8), and 9). After completing all the tasks, the users were given rating scales to rate the understandability, ease of learning and comfort of each tested operation as well as the overall understandability, ease of learning and comfort of the two-handle mode and single-handle mode. Table 2 shows some example rating scales and questions for each operation are the same. After filling the scales, an interview was held to collect more subjective opinions and feelings from users. Nearly all buttons on the products were tested. This experiment aimed to analyze the usability of basic operations related to handles of Switch and compare the usability of the two-handle and single-handle mode regarding the operations of entering the game and performing four main gaming operations.

Fig. 5. Unlocking the product

Fig. 6. Detaching the handles from the product

3 Results

The problems identified were categorized by the variables: task match, the ease of learning, and the ease of use. Regarding the quantitative results obtained in the first usability experiment, the average overall rating of Switch's ease of learning is 4.20/5, while the ease of understanding and comfort is 4.40/5 and 4.00/5 respectively. Generally, subjective ratings present a similar trend with users' objective task performance and serve as a strong supplement. The average overall rating of 3DS-LL's ease of learning is equal to Switch (4.20/5), while its ratings of the ease of understanding and comfort are around 0.5 points lower. The ratings of powering on, entering the game, pressing the 'a' button to attack and using joystick to move are relatively high (all average ratings of the three variables are over 4.00/5) and are similar between the two products, while the pausing operation of both products receive relatively low ratings in the three variables (most are around 3.00/5).

Fig. 7 Fitting the handles to the handle holder

Fig. 8 Entering the game

About the first variable, task match, the operations of 3DS-LL were better understood by the users. An apparent problem of Switch is that none of the tested users (100%, n = 5) could understand the metaphor behind the '+' button, the one to call up the menu. One participant mentioned that the '+' button is small and not salient enough, making it looks like an ornament instead of a button. He also suggested that a

Fig. 9 Using the joystick to move

round shape would make it more like a 'button'. Additionally, it is reported that the corresponding '−' button also brings great confusion since it has no clear function, unlike '+'. Additionally, the average ratings of shielding and catching of Switch are lower than 4.00/5). It is largely because that Switch has four similar oblong buttons on the top for catching and shielding (while 3DS-LL only has 2), which made users' cognition load heavier and caused confusion. Other operations of Switch are easy to understand generally. As for task match of 3DS-LL, the main problem is that the average rating of pausing is only 2.80/5 and one participant mentioned that the menu button for pausing is not obvious enough.

Regarding the second variable, the ease of learning, feedbacks are generally good. All ratings of Switch and 3DS-LL are over 4.00/5 except the pausing operation of Switch and all users (100%, n = 5) finally completed all tasks successfully after receiving standard instructions. Users' opinions towards the ease of learning of both products are optimistic, one user mentioned that 'even some operations may not be easy to understand, they are basically easy to learn'. Nevertheless, three users (60%, n = 3) failed to complete the task of 'pausing the game' with Switch and two users (40%, n = 2) failed to complete the same task with 3DS-LL at the first time.

On the third variable, the ease of use, several problems emerged. For Switch, two users (40%, n = 2) mentioned that the powering button of Switch is a bit small for their fingers to press. Two male users (40%, n = 2) mentioned that the oblong buttons on the top for catching and shielding are too close to each other while the four buttons for gaming operations on the front of Switch are also in close proximity, which may result in their mistaken triggering. As for 3DS-LL, three users (60%, n = 3) reported that the feedback of the menu button is ambiguous, which made them question whether they press the button successfully and one user (20%, n = 1) mentioned that the powering button of 3DS-LL is small and the surface is a bit concave, which makes it difficult to press. Interestingly, users' opinions vary on the joysticks. Two users (40%, n = 2) showed apparent preference to the joystick of Switch while another two (40%, n = 2) loved the joystick of 3DS-LL. The reasons for choosing Switch's joystick are that it is more comfortable to touch, its control and orientation is more acute and effortless (especially when performing two successive movements towards the same direction), and it gives users a strong feeling of operating since it likes a plane rocker. However, the reasons for preferring 3DS-LL are that the joystick has larger damping and can control the movement more accurately while the joystick of Switch is too acute and slippery to operate.

Regarding the first experiment of basic operations of Switch's handles in the second test, the rating of 'detaching handles from Switch' on test match is the lowest (2.57/5) and three users (43%, n = 3) rated lower than 3. Two participants (29%, n = 2) first thought that handles should be pulled horizontally to both sides while they actually need to be pulled vertically. The rating of 'fitting the handle to the single-handle holder' is the second lowest (3.00/5) and all participants (100%, n = 7) installed the single handle upside down without noticing the hint provided by the product. Another two operations rated lower than 4 are 'cutting the connection between handles and the product', and 'fitting the single handle to the single-handle holder'. When performing 'cutting the connection between handles and the product', one user said that the cutting-off button is too hidden and small, making it unlike a functional button, while the blue ornamental salient cube next to it is more like a functional button. It is also worth noting that when completing 'fitting the handles to the handle holder' two participants (29%, n = 2) tried to press the handles on the handle holder instead of inserting the handle into the handle holder. Besides, when doing 'entering the game', one user reported confusion since the joystick is used to choose instead of the up, down, left and right buttons.

As for the ease of learning, results are also generally optimistic, except 'detaching handles from Switch' and 'fitting the handle to the single-handle holder' (3.57/5 and 3.86/5 respectively). Users' task performances are consistent to the ratings since two users failed three time when completing 'detaching handles from Switch' and four users failed one or two times when completing 'fitting the handle to the single-handle holder'.

On the third variable, the ease of use, all operations receive relatively low ratings (all lower than 4/5 except 'connecting one handle to the product'). The lowest average rating is 'unlocking to product' (2.86/5) since it requires users to press any button three times and all participants (100%, n = 7) believed that there is no need to do so. The second lowest is 'detaching handles from Switch' and three male users (43%, n = 3) all reported that the button for detaching is too small to press and one female user mentioned that the operation requests great efforts. Besides, two users (29%, n = 2) reported that the button for 'cutting the connection between handles and the product' is too small and hidden, making it difficult to press. Additionally, three users (43%, n = 3) held that the positions of buttons and the joystick on the handles of Switch are biased to one side, making it uncomfortable to use with a single handle.

As for the compared experiment of the second test, generally, the ratings of the single-handle mode are higher than the two-handle mode. On the first variable, task match, the ratings of 'catching' and 'shielding' of both modes are relatively low, corresponding to the first experiment. About the two-handle mode, the average rating of 'catching' with two handles is 3.57/5 and four participants (57%, n = 4) rated 2 for 'shielding'. Regarding the single-handle mode, the average rating of 'attacking', 'catching', and 'shielding' all equal 4.14/5. Two novice users (29%, n = 2) reported that the different functions of the same buttons between the two modes caused their confusions. On the second and third variables, all ratings are above 4/5 except the 'catching', and 'shielding' operation of the two-handle mode. Similar to the first experiment, it is largely because the four similar oblong buttons on the top of Switch's handles (two on each handle), which results in confusion and inadvertently triggering. However, when using the single-handle mode, there are only two oblong buttons on the top, which reduces users' cognitive load and makes these two operations easier to understand and operate with one handle.

4 Limitations and Discussions

We analyzed the usability of Switch and 3DS-LL and received many opinions and suggestions from the users. However, there are some limitations of our study:

1. The tested users are all aged from 19–21 while Switch and 3DS-LL are designed for a much larger range of age.
2. When doing the compared experiment in the second test, the tasks of the two-handle mode and the single-handle mode were the same. However, the basic operating rules of the two modes are similar and users completed operations with two handles before one handle, which may make the performances of the one handle mode better. This may partly explain why generally, users rated higher scores of the single-handle mode than the two-handle mode, while they prefer using two handles instead.

Discussions that require further research are listed below:

1. One participant reported that the round salient point above the screen of 3DS-LL seemed like a powering button to her. However, this may not be changed because the two points served as shock absorbers.
2. The positions of buttons and the joystick on the handles of Switch are biased to one side, making operating with single handle uncomfortable. However, this may not be changed because it is to compromise the usability of the two-handle mode, which is a more common mode.
3. Two users mentioned that the functions of the same button are different when shifting between the two-handle mode and single-handle mode of Switch, which caused their confusions. However, this is also hard to fix since the handle is used horizontally when using the single-handle mode while the handles are used vertically with the two-handle mode, which change the buttons' relative position.
4. Two male participants thought the four oblong buttons on the top of Switch and the four functioning buttons on the front of Switch are in close proximity and are easy to trigger one or another mistakenly. However, they are all male adults above 175 cm in height while users of Switch also include kids.
5. All participants preferred to use two handles of Switch because they thought the single one handle was too small for their hands. However, they are all adults above 155 cm in height while users of Switch also include kids.

5 Recommendations

There are also more general problems and practical suggestions we would like to give to the design of Switch and 3DS-LL regarding usability. The recommendations for Switch are as below:

1. Make the powering-off button of the handle bigger and more salient.
2. Make the powering-on button of the product bigger and more salient.
3. Make the direction symbols for handle installation clearer.
4. The four oblong buttons on the top can be discriminated by different textile.
5. Add symbols to hint that the handles should be pulled vertically in order to be detached from the product instead of being pulled vertically.
6. Make the '+' and '−' buttons more salient or change their shapes to round, enabling them to look more like functional buttons.

The recommendations for 3DS-LL are as below:

1. Make the tactile feedbacks of the three buttons below the screen clearer.
2. Two touch screens of 3DS-LL may make users feel confused and dizzy. Reducing to one screen should be considered.

6 Conclusions

Despite the success of Switch in the handheld game consoles' market, several still needs to be improved in order to ensure a better gaming experience for users, especially for adult users. Since Switch intended not for the children but also for adults, results from our study are valuable references. Most problems of Switch and 3DS-LL obtained from the study regarding the ease of use and task match while the level of ease of learning is relatively high. It implies that as game consoles, Switch and 3DS-LL's basic operations are generally easy to learn, which is good to novice users. However, task match and the ease of use of both products should be improved.

References

1. Grand View Research, Inc. [US]. https://www.grandviewresearch.com/industry-analysis/gaming-console-market. Accessed 27 Jan 2020
2. Timothy Ballew, M.A.: Usability Testing and Video Games: Designing for Fun, 28 January 2020
3. Wei, Y.: The Evolution of Nintendo Company (2018)
4. Leventhal, L., Barnes, J.: Usability Engineering: Process, Products and Examples. Pearson Education, Inc., New Jersey (2008)
5. Nielsen, J.: Usability Engineering. Academic Press, San Diego (1993)
6. Harrison, R., Flood, D., Duce, D.: Usability of mobile applications: literature review and rationale for a new usability model. J. Interact. Sci. 1(1), 1 (2013)
7. Cabrejos, L.J.E.R., Kawakami, G., Conte, T.U.: Using a controlled experiment to evaluate usability inspection technologies for improving the quality of mobile web applications

earlier in their design. In: 2014 Brazilian Symposium on Software Engineering, pp. 161–170. IEEE (2014)

8. Pontes de França, A.C., Vitorino, D.F., de Oliveira Neves, A., de Lima, C.N., Soares, M.M.: A comparative usability analysis of virtual reality goggles. In: Marcus, A., Wang, W. (eds.) DUXU 2017. LNCS, vol. 10289, pp. 565–574. Springer, Cham (2017). https://doi.org/10.1007/978-3-319-58637-3_44

9. Simple Usability, Inc. [UK]. https://www.simpleusability.com/inspiration/2017/03/nintendo-switch-new-gaming-user-experience. Accessed 27 Jan 2020

10. Anunpattana, P., Khalid, M.N.A., Iida, H.: User-centered Entertainment Factors for Platform Transformation and Game Development (2019)

11. Lee, S.H., Song, D.H.: Functional usability analysis of top Korean mobile role playing games based on user interface design. Indones. J. Electr. Eng. Comput. Sci. **13**(1), 1 (2019)

Real-Time Interactive Online 3D Graphical User Interface (GUI) Technical Implementation and Usability Test for Architectural Technical Teaching

Zhen Liu[1]📷 and Yifang Wang[2](✉)

[1] School of Design, South China University of Technology,
Guangzhou 510006, People's Republic of China
[2] School of Art and Design, Guangdong Industry Polytechnic,
Guangzhou 510300, People's Republic of China
evawangyf@hotmail.com

Abstract. The development of a real-time GUI (graphical user interface) is considered to be an important factor in the future success and growth of the Internet for products and services towards entrepreneurship. However, there is lack of technical implementation and usability test for real-time interactive online 3D GUI for architectural technical teaching in terms of software and development of GUI, which is the aim of this study that covers the use of physical algorithms, programming, graphical programming, and conventional and traditional experimental design. These work resulted in the development of a complete process road map for implementation and testing, highlighting the many variables that can affect the success or failure of the GUI development process. Through the design of the online real-time 3D interactive GUI, there are five novel discoveries in key software platforms, which are (1) optimizing file download time, (2) optimizing baking to maximize visual quality, (3) optimizing the overall texture size of the GPU, (4) optimizing the relationship between the number of surfaces, and (5) optimizing the file size and understanding the impact of copied surfaces and textures. The results of the technical section lead to the conclusion that real-time 3D Interactive online GUIs are possible and may lead to a new 3D internet browsing experience in the future.

Keywords: Graphical User Interface (GUI) · Online 3D · Real-time interaction · Technical implementation · Usability test · Education · Entrepreneurship

1 Introduction

The Internet is becoming a central pillar of modern education, commerce, manufacturing and supply across multiple sectors. The theme and technology behind the project - the development of a real-time GUI (graphical user interface) is considered to be an important factor in the future success and growth of the Internet towards entrepreneurship [1], since it is the point in time at which major users interact with the World Wide Web and the products and services advertised or displayed on it.

© Springer Nature Switzerland AG 2020
A. Marcus and E. Rosenzweig (Eds.): HCII 2020, LNCS 12201, pp. 452–469, 2020.
https://doi.org/10.1007/978-3-030-49760-6_32

In terms of academic research related to software technology, most research has focused on the development of graphics engines or "kernels" and their applications. The notable authors are Doyle [2] and Simon et al. [3], whose work in creating virtual theaters has been widely discussed, although these authors are using different techniques from those of interest here. In the development of GUI, other researches also become very important, because GUI design includes HCI (human-computer interaction), psychology, and sociology. Academic research in these areas is concentrated including Byrne et al. [4] working on human factors in computing, which topic covers all of the above areas of expertise. However, there is lack of technical implementation and usability test for real-time interactive online 3D GUI for architectural technical teaching in terms of software and development of GUI, which is the aim of this study that is implementation and testing - combining the body of work, complex multi-step procedures, and built-in embedded design and development iterations to hone and refine the end result - has semantics similar to traditional design processes. The study covers the use of physical algorithms, programming, graphical programming, and conventional and traditional experimental design. These work resulted in the development of a complete process road map for implementation and testing, highlighting the many variables that can affect the success or failure of the GUI development process.

2 Technical Implementation and Testing

2.1 Introduction

This chapter combines the body of work, a complex multi-step program with embedded design and development iterations to improve and refine the end result that is semantically similar to the traditional design process. This section covers the use of physical algorithms, programming, graphical programming, and conventional "traditional" experimental design. This effort resulted in the development of a complete process road map for implementation and testing, with a strong emphasis on the many variables that can affect the success or failure of the 3D GUI development process.

2.2 The Importance of Understanding Variables

The following variables are important for the real-time 3D Interactive GUI in architectural technical teaching, which will be explained in turn:

1. Number of surfaces and facets
2. Graphics: total pixel dimensions of pictures
3. Graphics: best image types
4. Graphics: use of externally loaded files versus internal loading
5. Anti-aliasing
6. MIP mapping versus none
7. Zoning
8. Time delay of loading of textures
9. Camera parameters

10. Collide-able objects with respect to calculation reduction
11. Lighting type
12. Baking of textures
13. Unwrap UVW Map
14. Low polygon modeling.

Number of Surfaces and Facets. First, for a 3D scene, the number of surfaces and facets will determine the size of the 3D scene file. Second, the number of surfaces and facets will determine the size of the final export file based on 3D modeling packages. Finally, they have a direct impact on how fast the user moves while browsing the real-time 3D Interactive scenario.

Graphics: Total Pixel Dimensions of Pictures. Each texture used will flow the texture rule as shown in Table 1. When the user browsed a live 3D interactive scene, the wrong use of texture resolution increased the use of video memory.

Table 1. Texture Graphics Processing Unit (GPU) memory consumption.

		Height (pixels)								
		512	256	128	64	32	16	8	4	2
Width (pixels)	512	1024	512	256	128	64	32	16	8	4
	256	512	256	128	64	32	16	8	4	2
	128	256	128	64	32	16	8	4	2	1
	64	128	64	32	16	8	4	2	1	0.5
	32	64	32	16	8	4	2	1	0.5	0.25
	16	32	16	8	4	2	1	0.5	0.25	0.125
	8	16	8	4	2	1	0.5	0.25	0.125	0.0625
	4	8	4	2	1	0.5	0.25	0.125	0.0625	0.03125
	2	4	2	1	0.5	0.25	0.125	0.0625	0.03125	0.015625

Graphics: Best Image Types. PNG (portable network graphics) is a static image file format developed for the Internet and World Wide Web. JPEG (joint photographic expert group) uses a variable compression method called loss compression because image quality degrades as compression increases. As shown in Table 2, it is clear that PNG is better than JPEG in web applications such as faster download speed, alpha channel support and decompression.

Graphics: Use of Externally Loaded Files versus Internal Loading. As shown in Table 3, the use of externally loaded files is better than the internal loaded files.

Anti-aliasing. When exporting a scene to a 3D GUI file, anti-aliasing improves the quality of the 3D real-time interactive environment.

Table 2. PNG versus JPEG file.

Aspects	PNG	JPEG
Optimized palette (256)—8-bit color file	Yes	Yes
RGB 24 bit (16.7 Million)—a true color (24-bit) file	Yes	Yes
RGB 48 bit (281 Trillion)—a 48-bit color file	Yes	Yes
Gray scale 8 bit (256)—a gray scale image with 256 shades	Yes	Yes
Gray scale 16 bit (65,536)—a gray scale image with 65,536 shades	Yes	Yes
Alpha Channel—an alpha channel with the file	Yes	No
Interlaced—the file interlaced for faster display in Web browsers	Yes	No
Compression	No	Yes

Table 3. The use of externally loaded files versus internal loading.

Aspects	Externally loading	Internal loading
3D GUI file size	Small	Big
Download speed	Fast	Slow
Texturing	Good	Normal
Texture modification	Yes	No

MIP Mapping versus None. MIP mapping [5] is a texture mapping method in which the original high-resolution texture map is scaled and filtered into multiple resolutions before being applied to the surface, which means a lot of things in a very small space. When using MIP to map the texture in 3D rendering or real-time 3D display, if the texture is seen in 3D rendering, the full details can be displayed. A close-up, or when the object looks smaller or farther away, can be rendered quickly and smoothly from the lower MIP level. MIP mapping saves processor time and improves the anti-aliasing effect by allowing the computer to start with pre-filtering and pre-scaling the texture at a resolution that best suits each frame. Typically, the MIP mapping level uses powers of 2, so if the highest resolution is 1024 by 1024, the next level will be 512 by 512, 256 by 256, 128 by 128, and sometimes all the way down to 8 by 8 or 1 by 1 images. MIP mapping can get rid of tiling map noise. It can make 3D real-time interactive environment look real.

Zoning. Zoning is a convenient way to make 3D real-time interactive environments run smoothly. When the user reaches a very complex area, the zoning feature makes it easy for the user to reach the target location.

Time Delay of Loading of Textures. When the user arrives at the new 3D real-time interactive scene, all scenes will be downloaded, along with all external textures. So the user feels the time lag. A better way to eliminate this negative impact is to add a nice download interface.

Camera Parameters. Camera parameter determines which view the user will use and which real feeling the user will get. As shown in Fig. 1, the 17 mm setting of the

camera lens is better than the 35 mm setting of the camera lens. A 17 mm camera lens
will make the user feel real.

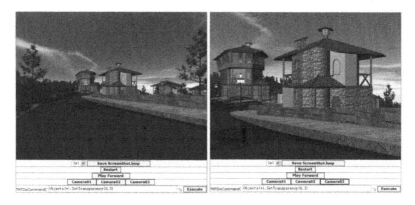

Fig. 1. Camera lens with 17 mm and 35 mm within online 3D GUI.

Collide-Able Objects with Respect to Calculation Reduction. Collision-able objects
are physical property objects that can be checked interactively, as shown in Fig. 2.
Performance can be gained by optimizing the collision objects. In general, a simple
geometric box or plane can handle most of the collisions in a scene. This saves a lot of
computation. Complex shapes can be easily handled in a box that is collision-able and
permanently invisible.

Fig. 2. Scene without and with a collide-able and permanently invisible box in online 3D GUI.

Lighting Type. The 3D real-time interactive online engine, such as Turntool, can
support many kinds of lights, such as omni. But they are all treated as omni within the
GUI. When there is no light in a 3D real-time interactive scene, all objects are with the

default material color, excepting texture maps, reflection maps, baking maps, and transparent objects, as shown in Fig. 3.

Fig. 3. Scene lighting off (left) and lighting on (right) within online 3D GUI.

Baking of Textures. The purpose of baking textures is to flat out render effects including lighting, shadows, textures, noise, bump, and even ambient light shading into texture files. Using baked textures to light up the scene allows for faster re-rendering of the scene and less memory consumption since all these calculations are not involved. But it's important to adjust the size of the baking texture. This is useful for 3D real-time interactive applications, as re-sizing textures typically reduces video memory in the 3D online GUI. For example, the original baked map had a resolution of 2048 by 2048 pixels and used 25.375 m of video memory, or 10.375 m if adjusted to 512 by 512 pixels. The total reduction is 15 million. But the quality of the scene is only slightly different, as shown in Fig. 4.

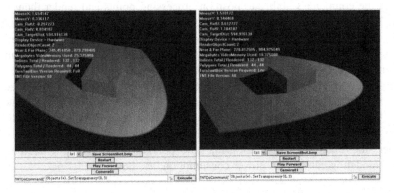

Fig. 4. Baked texture 2048 by 2048 with video memory 25.375 M versus 512 by 512 with 10.375 M within online 3D GUI.

Unwrap UVW Map. The UVW expand map is used to assign plane maps to sub-object selections and edit the UVW coordinates of those selections [6]. Existing UVW coordinates on the object can also be expanded and edited. Maps can be adjusted to fit Mesh, Patch, Polygon, HSDS, and NURBS models. The UVW expand map can be used as a separate UVW mapper and UVW coordinate editor. However, a very useful application is mapping complex objects. Expanding the UVW map makes it easy to map every detail texture to the object. It can support 3D real-time interactive online GUI very well. For example, it is difficult to map the Chinese terracotta warriors using UVW mapping. But the UVW map can make the warriors look real and stable, as shown in Fig. 5.

Fig. 5. Chinese terracotta warriors by unwrap UVW map within online 3D GUI.

Low Polygon Modeling. In order to achieve real-time rendering of the world, a technique called low-polygon modeling must be used [7]. In fact, where the shape of an object consists of many very fine details, this complexity can often be reduced by ignoring the complex details. Ignoring details reduces the realism of the world, but increases the computer's ability to position processing points and render them on the screen. Taking a low-poly model and texturing it with a digital image that can be cleverly mapped to the face of the object can replace the information lost when simplifying the grid. This gives the appearance of the detailed model while retaining the low computational requirements. This modeling method can effectively improve the working speed of 3D real-time online interactive GUI. In addition, it can reduce load time and 3D GUI file size. When there are large objects in a 3D scene, low poly modeling shows their navigation. For example, conventional modeling methods were used to model the Chinese terracotta warriors, resulting in a final face of 16,758. However, the final face modeled using low polygons was 4191. Therefore, low polygon modeling can reduce power consumption, as shown in Fig. 6.

2.3   Technical Implementation Process

As shown in Fig. 7, technical implementation refers to the process of constructing 3D geometry and implementing it in a 3D real-time interactive online GUI environment. There are three main stages with 10 steps that form a design process, which are:

Stage I. 3D and program Operations: 1) 3D modeling or translation of existing 3D model; 2) Optimization (reduction of surfaces); 3) Build environment to contextualize; 4) Apply lighting and textures; 5) Apply camera details; 6) Export to graphics engine; 7) Apply activity behavior components, i.e. interaction content (physics, collide-able surfaces, zoning, clickable icons, motion, and select-able objects); 8) Scripting including combination effects.
Stage II. 2D Graphic Design: 9) GUI visual design.
Stage III. Test: 10) Upload to test site.

Fig. 6. Chinese Terracotta Warriors modeling by normal method (left) versus low polygon (right).

1) **3D Modeling or Translation of Existing 3D Model.** In general, there are two ways to introduce the model into a 3D real-time interactive online GUI. One is to model objects in a 3DS Max, and the other is to convert existing CAD (such as Pro/Engineer, Rhinoceros, and Auto CAD) into a common file.
2) **Optimization (Reduction of Surfaces).** When making models in 3DS Max, low polygon modeling is used to make models efficiently. After converting from other existing CAD models, these models must be optimized. The optimized modifier in 3DS Max can be used to reduce surfaces. An iterative loop sometimes occurs from optimization to 3DS Max modeling to ensure that all the final models can be effectively used in subsequent operations.
3) **Build Environment to Contextualize.** Once the modeling is complete, the environment needs to be built so that all models look like real-world models.

4) **Apply Lighting and Textures.** Lighting and texture will be applied to the finished environment. Each setting must be carefully chosen to make the environment look like the real world. An iterative loop from applying lighting and textures to the built environment will occur to ensure that all final environment elements look realistic.

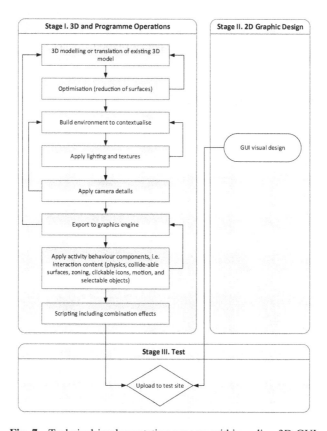

Fig. 7. Technical implementation process within online 3D GUI.

5) **Apply Camera Details.** Camera preferences determine which view the user will use and which real feeling the user will get. The camera animation will guide the user to explore the 3D scene. The iterative loop from applying camera details to the built environment will ensure that all camera parameter settings are appropriate for all environments.

6) **Export to Graphics Engine.** When modeling, lighting, texture, and environment is completed, all 3D scenes will be exported to the 3D real-time interactive engine. In the engine, all models, lights, textures, and environment objects can be double-checked to make sure they run smoothly. The iterative loop from exporting to the graphics engine to modeling will ensure that all models run smoothly in the engine.

7) **Apply Activity Behaviour Components, i.e. Interaction Content (Physics, Collide-able Surfaces, Zoning, Clickable Icons, Motion, and Select-able Objects).** The active behavior component is the link object between 3D modeling package and the 3D real-time online interaction engine. These components allow the user to move around in a 3D real-time online interactive GUI environment and assign special functions that allow the user to perform activities. The iterative loop from the export to the graphics engine to modeling ensures that all behavior components run smoothly throughout the model environment.

8) **Scripting Including Combination Effects.** The JAVA script will be used to add special features such as numeric counting and color swapping and playing objects in a 3D real-time online interactive GUI environment. It's the background controller.

9) **GUI Visual Design.** GUI visual design can begin with the first step, i.e. 3D modeling or translation of an existing CAD model, and can end with a JAVA script. This saves the overall processing time. The GUI visual design must fit the user's needs and make it easy to use.

10) **Upload to Test Site.** All completed files and links are uploaded to the test site to test their availability. If the download and virtual walk are too slow, all the previous steps are re-examined to find a solution to speed up the response. Unfortunately, there is no one formula for all geometries, only rules of thumb.

2.4 Testing Process

The whole testing process involves in three main stages, as shown in Fig. 8, which are:

Stage I. Primary usability test: 1) Online files size; 2) Downloading textures; 3) GPU (graphics processing unit) video memory; 4) Visual test – quality of aesthetic.
Stage II. Secondly usability tests of physics, programming and functionality: 5) Physics test 1 – usability; 6) Physics test 2 – realism; 7) Physics test 3 – collisions; 8) Physics test 4 – zoning; 9) Programming 1 – script performance; 10) Programming 2 – overcoming software bugs; 11) Functionality 1 – clickable objects functionality; 12) Functionality 2 – connections and hyperlinks.
Stage III. Finally usability test of accessibility: 13) Accessibility 1 – privileges and security; 14) Accessibility 2 – firewalls; 15) Accessibility 3 – custom configuration.

Stage I. Primary Usability Test. Online file size will directly affect file download time. As such, it must be as small as possible. Downloading textures also directly affects file download time. Therefore, the texture must be as small as possible in the scene. However reducing the size of the texture reduces the quality of the scene. GPU video memory will affect the browsing speed, where the GPU video memory has a special relationship with the size of all textures and the number of object surfaces. As the texture size increases, GPU video memory increases. Appearance testing is related to aesthetic quality that must be balanced between quality and texture size.

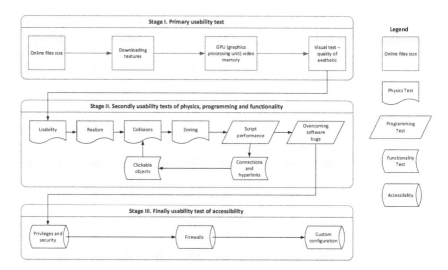

Fig. 8. 3D real-time online interactive GUI testing process.

Stage II. Secondly Usability Tests of Physics, Programming and Functionality

Physics Test. Usability: All GUI elements will be tested from the user's perspective. Realism: All objects and environments must feel real to the user, which is the spirit of the 3D real-time interactive environment. Collisions: Collision checking prevents illogical things from happening, such as walking over a wall, falling out of a virtual sky and jumping high into the sky, which enables 3D real-time interactive environments to run smoothly by adding low-surface collider-able objects. This usually reduces the use of the GPU. Zoning: Zoning testing will allow users to walk easily. When a user walks to a zoning area, the user will be automatically taken to the next point or scene. The zoning feature lets user narrow down the scene by changing and loading the new scene.

Programming Test. Script performance is important for 3D real-time online interactive GUI design. Because all the function ICONS are linked through the script. Overcome software errors: Sometimes software errors occur: A) read error. The GUI file created by the latest version engine cannot be recognized by the previous version viewer. Solution: install the new version view; B) white line. When running a file on a computer with a graphics card, some white lines appear. Solution: run the file on a computer with other brand graphics cards; and C) lack of texture. When exporting a file from a scene with a baking texture, the texture is sometimes lost. Solution: re-export the file.

Functionality Test. Clickable object. Clickable objects make the clickable object functional environment interesting. In fact, clickable objects are interactive objects. When the user clicks on them, functions such as object movement, attaching windows, and opening doors occur. Links and hyperlinks that are connections linking each external texture and the GUI file, and these connections combine everything together. When the user clicks the link, the hyperlink keeps the different files and documents linked. In some ways, connections and hyperlinks are joints of structure. The iteration loop occurs between collisions, partitions, script performance, connections and hyperlinks, and clickable object functionality. Hence, they all deal with 3D real-time interaction to form a function circle.

Stage III. Finally Usability Test of Accessibility. Privileges and security. Privileges and security are key elements of an online enterprise 3D real-time interactive environment. When users use 3D real-time interactive environment, all information and operation data should not be lost and error. The firewall. Some computers with firewall software can automatically block a 3D real-time interactive environment GUI with some special scripting. Custom configuration. The custom configuration will configure the GUI file and internet browsing to run properly.

3 Results and Discussion

3.1 Optimizing File Download Time

When exporting a 3D online GUI file from 3D modeling package, the default setting is to merge all the models and textures into one file. These textures are called internal textures. The final GUI file is large because it contains all the compressed internal textures. The file is difficult to download. This will take a long time, especially for large scenes. Figure 9 shows the relationship between them.

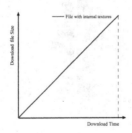

Fig. 9. File with internal textures downloading time within online 3D GUI.

The 3D online GUI file can be made smaller by using external textures. This method allows the engine to separate the file from all textures. This is an important way to optimize file and increase download speeds. Figure 10 indicates a significant change.

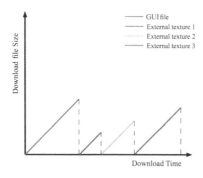

Fig. 10. 3D online GUI file with external textures downloading time.

3.2   Optimizing Baking to Maximize Visual Quality

When baking textures are used in 3D real-time online interactive GUI environments, problems related to visual quality often arise. As shown in Fig. 11, the biggest problem is using internal textures. The dark texture parting line becomes apparent and has noise in the scene. When using external textures, the visual quality, parting lines, and noise are not apparent.

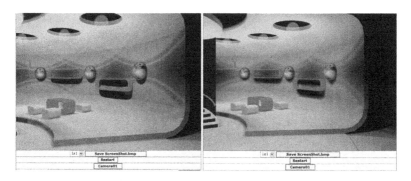

Fig. 11. Visual quality between internal and external textures within online 3D GUI.

Since 3D real-time interactive scene will be published on the web, the texture and 3D online GUI files must be as small as possible. But the visual quality of the scene must be as good as possible in order to show a trade-off. The principle of optimizing baking to maximize visual quality is applied and requires re-sizing the resolution of external textures in a photo editing package. This is a convenient way to get the best solution for the desired visual quality.

Images have little meaning for the visual quality of the human eye. But a scene that uses a 128 by 128 pixel texture document size has the smallest file size and is therefore more suitable for a 579 KB (kilobyte) web, as shown in Fig. 12. In addition, the video storage is only 10.94 MB, which is enough to run on the most common PC, as shown in Table 4.

Fig. 12. External textures from left to right with 512 by 512 (pixel), 256 by 256 (pixel), 128 by 128 (pixel), and within online 3D GUI.

Table 4. Relationship among external textures resolution, GUI and texture size and video memory.

External textures resolution	3D GUI and textures size	Video memory
512 by 512	1.1 MB	18.56 MB
256 by 256	773 KB	13.03 MB
128 by 128	579 KB	10.94 MB

3.3   Optimizing Total Texture Size Versus Graphics Processing Unit (GPU)

The textures used by the 3D real-time online interactive engine must follow the texture Settings. If the texture resolution does not meet this requirement, the engine will automatically resize the texture resolution to suit the engine's needs. Automatic resizing increases GPU usage.

As can be seen from Table 1, when the resolution of the texture is 512 by 512 pixels, the GPU utilization rate is 1024 K (kilobytes), equal to 1 M (megabytes). In order for the GPU to be acceptable, the texture resolution must be a multiple of 512 by 512 pixels.

3.4   Optimizing Relationship Between Number of Surfaces and File Size

Interestingly, the surface increases the size of the 3D online GUI file, but the video memory usage remains the same when no texture is present, as shown in Fig. 13. In 3D real-time interactive applications, the final size of the file is important for Web downloads. The amount of surface must be well controlled in GUI design. The reasonable number of surfaces is 30,000, which runs smoothly on most computers.

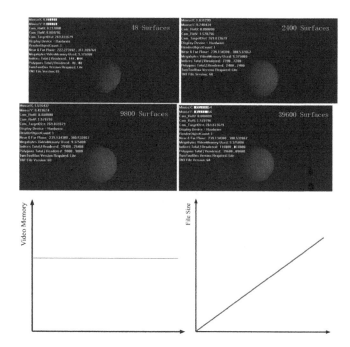

Fig. 13. Relationship between number of surfaces and file size.

3.5 Understanding the Impact of Copied Surfaces and Textures

If the copied surface only has no texture, the copied surface and texture scenes use the same 3D online GUI file size and video memory. If they have textures, the file size and video memory are greater than no textures. But under the same conditions, the file size and the video memory used are the same. These are shown in Fig. 14.

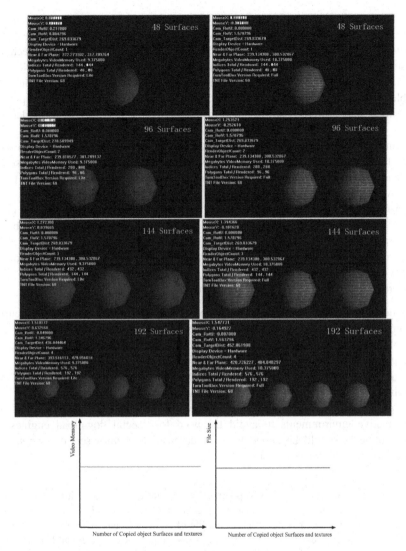

Fig. 14. Relationship between copied surfaces and texture.

4 Conclusion

Experience with 3D game design allows for elaborate 3D real-time interactive GUI design, as well as 3D real-time interaction. Real-time 3D interactive GUI design for architectural applications has many market advantages, such as the ability to let users experience the proposed environment and inform purchase decisions. The interaction area on the GUI is a key role in the GUI layout design phase and requires a lot of end-user consideration to make it right. It has been found that because all applications are different, there is no simple GUI design solution.

Technology implementation and testing results in many learning outcomes involve the use of physical algorithms, programming, graphical programming, and generally "traditional" experimental design. The first learning result is that it is a high-tech skill that cannot be mastered quickly. The work on this project resulted in the development of a complete process road map for implementation and testing, highlighting many variables that could affect the success or failure of the GUI development process. Following a standardized road map will eventually result in a universally understood process similar to that of the production line in traditional manufacturing. The importance of constructing exactly the files, the number of surfaces, the types of images and textures, and the importance of considering firewall issues when consumers download 3D Interactive content has generated important knowledge relevant to this future market.

Through the design of 3D interactive GUI, there are five novel discoveries in key software platforms, which are (1) optimizing file download time, (2) optimizing baking to maximize visual quality, (3) optimizing the overall texture size of the GPU, (4) optimizing the relationship between the number of surfaces, and (5) optimizing the file size and understanding the impact of copied surfaces and textures.

There are three suggestions for further study.

1) to develop a more efficient 3D real-time interactive engine, because the current technology is limited to scenes of a certain size and requires multiple scenes to be "spliced" together (similar to the level of detail (LoD) in computer games), so a large number of scenes can be well managed;

2) to develop an advanced 3D real-time interactive engine to support real-time lighting shadows computed on the GPU; and

3) to develop a new management structure for Web downloads in 3D real-time interactive environments to avoid the need for special download engines. All requirements should be added to a standardized Web browser, but for security reasons they do not yet exist.

Acknowledgements. This paper is supported by "South China University of Technology Central University Basic Scientific Research Operating Expenses Subsidy (project approval no. XYZD201928)". This paper is dedicated to the life of author LZ and his team to the dream of virtual reality, online interaction, game, entrepreneurship and success of all at T2L Mansfield, England 2005-2007.

References

1. Blumenthal, M.S., Clark, D.D.: Rethinking the design of the Internet: the end-to-end arguments vs. the brave new world. ACM Trans. Internet Technol. (TOIT) **1**(1), 70–109 (2001)
2. Doyle, P.: Believability through context using" knowledge in the world" to create intelligent characters. In: Proceedings of the First International Joint Conference on Autonomous Agents and Multiagent Systems: Part 1, pp. 342–349. Association for Computing Machinery, New York (2002)

3. Simon, H.A., et al.: AI's greatest trends and controversies. IEEE Intell. Syst. Appl. **15**(1), 8–17 (2000)
4. Byrne, M.D., John, B.E., Wehrle, N.S., Crow, D.C.: The tangled web we wove: a taskonomy of WWW use. In: Proceedings of the SIGCHI Conference on Human Factors in Computing Systems, CHI 1999, pp. 544–551, Pittsburgh (1999)
5. MIP Mapping. http://www.3drender.com/glossary/mipmapping.htm. Accessed 20 Jan 2020
6. 3ds Max Help_ Unwrap UVW Modifier. http://docs.autodesk.com/3DSMAX/16/ENU/3ds-Max-Help/index.html?url=files/GUID-EA10E59F-DE7F-497E-B399-6CF213A02C8D.htm, topicNumber=d30e263547. Accessed 20 Jan 2020
7. Melax, S.: A simple, fast, and effective polygon reduction algorithm. Game Dev. **11**, 44–49 (1998)

An Exploration of Low-Fidelity Prototyping Methods for Augmented and Virtual Reality

Martin Maguire[(✉)]

School of Design and Creative Arts, Loughborough University,
Leicestershire LE11 3TU, UK
m.c.maguire@lboro.ac.uk

Abstract. Low-fidelity prototyping is well-established method of developing concepts for traditional two-dimensional user interfaces. This paper considers the techniques and methods that can be used for simulating and early testing of augmented and virtual reality applications. It covers techniques such as body-storming, storyboarding, and mocking up prototypes using a variety of materials such as: sheets of paper, cardboard, sticky tape, straws, pin-boards, Lego bricks, etc. It describes the role of each method within the design process and provides practical advice for its application. The paper draws upon two student workshops that were organized to teach and practice several of these techniques for the design of augmented reality and virtual reality prototypes. Feedback from the participants is reported.

Keywords: Virtual reality · Augmented reality · Low-fidelity prototyping · Rapid prototyping · User-centred design · User interface design · User experience design

1 Introduction

Augmented reality (AR) is an experience where users see and interact with the real world while digital content is added to it. Typically, the real world is presented on a mobile device through the device's camera. Pokemon Go is a famous example of this application where the player searches for small virtual creatures that appear overlaid on the real scene. A different way to experience augmented reality is through an AR headset, such as Google Glass, where digital content is displayed on a very small screen in front of the user's eye. Applications of augmented reality can include entertainment (i.e. video games), enhanced shopping experiences, and head up displays for drivers and pilots.

Virtual reality (VR) immerses users in a completely virtual environment that is generated by a computer. Advanced VR experiences provide freedom of movement so that users can move in a digital environment and hear sounds. Moreover, special hand controllers can be used to enhance VR experiences. Applications of virtual reality also include entertainment (i.e. video games) and education (school teaching, medical training or military training). It is believed that the participants of such training not only learn faster, but also retain new information longer and are more motivated and attentive during classes.

Low-fidelity prototyping is a well-established method of developing concepts for traditional two-dimensional user interfaces [1]. This paper considers the techniques and

© Springer Nature Switzerland AG 2020
A. Marcus and E. Rosenzweig (Eds.): HCII 2020, LNCS 12201, pp. 470–481, 2020.
https://doi.org/10.1007/978-3-030-49760-6_33

methods that can be used for simulating and early testing of augmented and virtual reality. It also reports the feedback from two master's student workshops organized to teach and practice different rapid prototyping methods for AR and VR.

2   User Research

The first stage in a user-centered design process is user research [2]. This involves identifying the target audience, understanding the user's context, and identifying their needs. Achieving empathy with the user is a key aspect of these activities. The research process is completed with a definition of the specific problem to be addressed by the design team. In deciding whether to employ AR or VR technology, it is worth considering the pros and cons of each (Table 1):

Table 1. Advantages and disadvantages of augmented reality and virtual reality

	Advantages	Disadvantages
Augmented reality	Real world experience can be enhanced with additional information e.g. objects appearing when reading a book, or shop names popping up when viewing a town high street	Can diminish real world reality or lead to people becoming more dependent on devices which may cause health-related issues
	Possible to visualize the object in a more effective form e.g. item of clothing being worn before making an actual purchase	Open architecture of the augmented reality applications leaves it vulnerable to cyber-attacks and threats
	Can be applied to parts of training programs so that overall productivity is increased	Potentially expensive to develop an AR based system
	Can reduce risk when performing an activity e.g. of an operation by giving user improved sensory perception	Maintenance of an AR system can also be expensive unless designed to be easily updated or customised
	Can provide a framework so that users interact in a synchronized manner e.g. to enhance teamwork	
Virtual reality	Immersive – can create involving immersive experiences	Can be expensive to produce or update
	Interactive nature means it improves retention and recall	Health effects – can lead to spatial awareness, dizziness, disorientation, and nausea
	Can simulate a dangerous environment for training purposes	If a person relies more on virtual reality for social interactions, can ultimately lead to depression and disassociation
	Can facilitate a meeting situation in a realistic way saving time and money	
	Simplifies complex problems or situations	
	Suitable for different learning styles	

3 Bodystorming

Bodystorming is a technique used to quickly generate and evaluate design ideas that are vague or too early stage to prototype [3, 4]. The design team members act out scenes imagined in an AR or VR application. The purpose is to ideate quickly and efficiently by encouraging participants to think spatially.

If the application is AR, then the method can use a single cardboard frame to act as a window to the real world. As the user walks around, others in the team can point to items and voice the information that is presented as the user approaches it. During this process, there can be discussion as to what information would be useful to present.

If the application is VR, a similar effect can be achieved by asking one person (the user) to put on a makeshift headset e.g. a simple box with a viewing hole [5]. This helps to build user empathy, allowing the design team to understand how the user feels when they have a limited field of view. A second person then pretends to be the object the user is interacting with and can respond to the user's gestures accordingly. Alternatively, they can manipulate objects (imagined or made of cardboard or paper) that the user indicates. The pair act out what the user's task or mission including what they see and hear, and their actions through gestures and voice. This helps the designers to see users to interact with menu systems and which interactions are essential and intuitive, and which are not. It will also help understand how to improve the clarity of the experience from the user's perspective.

4 Storyboards

Storyboards are an effective tool for capturing and conveying ideas and concepts for a proposed experience [3]. A storyboard is a sequence of sketched images to show a set of scenes that a user might follow whether in AR or VR. The method, commonly used in the entertainment industry, helps to convey both the overall flow of an experience (at low fidelities) as well as the aesthetic look and feel (at high fidelities). Understanding the fidelity needs of your storyboard is key to gathering the right kind of feedback and avoiding counter-productive discussions.

Low-fidelity storyboards are appropriate for quick discussions, especially when conveying high-level ideas. These can be as simple as stick-figure drawings and primitive shapes to denote virtual elements in a scene or the proximity of interactive components (both physical and virtual). High-fidelity storyboards are useful when bringing in new stakeholders or combining insights from a bodystorming session with the proposed aesthetic direction of the experience. Generally, it is helpful to include captions to explain the action within each scene and possibly speech or thought bubbles (as in a comic-book) to indicate speech interaction or thought processes.

As the design develops, it may be useful to sketch out the story in third person and first person [4]. Sketching in third person allows the design team to view the experience at a distance and can help describe the big picture components of the experience being created. Sketching in first person allows the team to understand the field of view of the device and allows the team to make sure that they are including everything that is needed in the user's line of vision. Both perspectives allow each element of your experience to be laid out in a thoughtful way, especially if designing an application allowing 360 movement.

5 Testing Scenarios with Low-Fidelity Physical Prototypes

The next part of the UX process is to envision the design using low-fidelity prototyping methods so that design team members can share the concept and allow it to be tested with users. Using the ideas developing during bodystorming, scenarios can be developed to walk through. This involves staging how a user would move through the experience and use physical props [3]. This allows participants to not only experience the thinking through the perspective of the user but allow outside observers to see how events play out.

It may also be useful to include a wider audience of team members or stakeholders who are able to provide specific 'expert' feedback. For example, when exploring an augmented or virtual experience designed for hospitals, acting out the team's thinking to a medical professional to show how the experience might unfold and can provide invaluable feedback. Having a technical developer present might also give them heads up on the kinds of challenges they might face in creating the application or trading off visual quality for performance or deciding what assets are needed for application development.

For an AR application, a suitable way to develop a low-fidelity prototype is to create a cardboard frame to represent the mobile device, while objects such as information labels or miniature figures can be placed behind it to provide the augmented elements. The user can hold the frame and view the real world through it (although this may be a hand drawn scene) while the support team hold up the augmentations attached to straws or sticks or attach Post-Its to real world objects as the user views them. Another form of Augmented reality relating to retail clothes shopping is to use a projector to show an image of the augmented mirror which, with pre-prepared images can show the customer wearing their chosen garment as a digital representation (see Fig. 1).

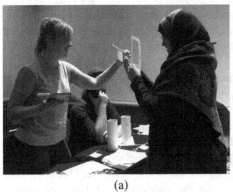 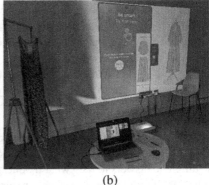

(a)   (b)

Fig. 1. Augmented reality prototyping (a) using frame and post-its, and (b) mock-up of mark mirror using short-throw projector

In one study, the authors developed an idea for an app for people watching a rugby match [5]. While waiting for a spot kick to be taken on the field, the user could try and score themselves by viewing the real posts through the app and swiping a digital ball on screen. A physical prototype of the AR design was created and tested using a cardboard frame for viewing a model of the rugby posts, and flicking a cardboard ball, mounted on the frame, over them.

For VR, it is possible to create an impression of immersion by projecting large images onto a wall or perhaps by setting up a sequence of display boards with a large sheet of paper displayed on each. If the boards are set up in fanfold fashion, this could simulate a sequence of VR locations. However, a more effective simulation could possibly be achieved by drawing an image on a paper template that is distorted similar to a projection of the world map. If photographed and uploaded to a suitable online tool and viewed on a mobile phone a 3D simulation is created allowing swiping motions on screen to explore the space. This can be enhanced further if the image is displayed as two images and viewed using a VR viewing headset in which a mobile phone can be inserted e.g. Google Cardboard. A walkie-talkie can be employed to simulate speech interaction, or a speaker nearby can be used to simulate sound.

Consideration of should be given for the input device that will be used within the application. Virtual reality systems with three degrees of freedom (3DOF) allow input by pointing and activation without letting the user reach out and interact with objects. Immersive VR experiences with six degrees of freedom (6DoF) add the ability to reach out and interact with objects in a 3D space. Tracking the user's fingers e.g. if wearing a data glove, allows for more control and flexibility e.g. to let go of the controller without it falling from the user's hand. The characteristics of the input device need to be included within the prototype. While the device may have constraints, the design should try to look for creative solutions within them, while also playing to a device's strengths.

6   Creating Digital Prototypes

Currently there are few easy to use prototyping tools for VR and AR, so it can take a lot of effort to create rapid digital prototypes for use within an iterative user-centred design cycle. Tools such as Google Expeditions can be used to create virtual experiences using a collection of 360° scenes and 3D objects. The ease with which such tools can be used means that they can be used for low-fidelity prototyping. Digital prototyping in 2D useful for determining flow.

Creating a clickable prototype for either AR or VR in an app like Marvel App makes it more realistic [6]. While bodystorming helps to design user feelings, a clickable version helps to design for usability. The elements that the user can interact with can be equivalent to the touchpoints available in the design. When there is audio or text, this can be written out in the window. Even if this clutters the window, this is okay since the aim is to make the user experience and flow clear and planning for all the different answers to the "what if" questions that the design team have been working with. The 2D prototype serves as a roadmap for the developers to follow and lessens the chance that there will be major mistakes or communication errors.

Multimedia prototyping may use a mixture of digital and physical elements to test and validate design solutions for interacting with menu systems in AR or VR in a way that is interactive, immersive, and easy for users to observe [6]. One relatively easy way to create a series of 3D scenes that a user can explore is to create a series of images in Microsoft Paint 3D and then import them into PowerPoint. Another technique is to create a cardboard model of virtual scene and to place a 360° camera within it. A still image taken with the camera will provide an all-round scene while a video taken on small figure moving around the scene can show interactions. The camera can also be moved around to show the layout of the virtual environment.

Other tools such as Google Expeditions can be used to create virtual experiences using a collection of 360° scenes and 3D objects. The ease with which such tools can be used means that they can be used for low-fidelity prototyping. When 3D environments need to be produced in higher fidelity, then specialist tools such as Unity are needed. This can take a lot of effort for easy integration into an iterative user-centred design cycle, although the creation, beforehand, of 3D assets for the developer can speed up the production time.

7 Design Principles

General design principles such as those produced by Don Norman [7] are just relevant to AR and VR applications as to traditional interfaces. Table 2 lists Norman's six principles and their interpretation for AR and VR which should be followed when designing the prototype application:

Table 2. Norman's design principles applied to AR and VR

Design principle	Augmented reality	Virtual reality
Visibility	Augmented elements such as labels, text boxes and highlighting should be clear and readable on the device on which the AR application is running at a normal viewing distance. It should be clear what elements the annotations relate to	Virtual elements should be clear and visible to the user, enabling them to interact with them easily. Try to avoid using big text blocks and highly detailed UI elements. Consider what is the optimal distance that the VR screens were intended to be viewed from which will inform the size of the screen in addition to the size and density of the content therein [8]. Having a way to enlarge text is helpful for people with reduced vision
Feedback	When the user selects an item to manipulate in AR, it should be clear that it has been selected with suitable	When the user selects an item or location in the virtual world, the selection should be clear and the

(continued)

Table 2. (*continued*)

Design principle	Augmented reality	Virtual reality
	feedback. The result of the action e.g. choosing an ornament from an online shop for viewing in situ, should be clear	result of the action performed on the object should also be evident
Constraints	Constraints is about limiting the range of interaction possibilities for the user to simplify the interface and guide the user to the appropriate next action. It should be made clear in the AR environment which objects can be selected	In the virtual world, while it may seem that the user can select any item, it may be helpful to provide some guidance as to what can be selected. This can be achieved through highlighting of items, showing they are selectable, as the user moves a pointer around
Mapping	Mapping is about having a clear relationship between controls and the effect they have on the world. Actions such as swiping on the device to perform an action should match user expectations e.g. swiping speed and direction should be reflected in the power and direction of a golf swing	In VR the user will have a controller to move around. Clicking the pointer to indicate relocation is useful for larger movements around a space e.g. a museum. Using a joystick type action may be easier for smaller movements e.g. walking arounds a particular museum exhibit
Consistency	Consistency refers to having similar operations and elements for achieving similar tasks to provide the user with a smooth, clean experience. Thus, for example, text labels and text sizes should be consistent throughout the AR application	Visual elements in VR such as label should have a consistency of appearance. Interaction should be consistent e.g. if an object can be selected via an air tap, make it also selectable via a voice command [6]. This not only provides consistency but improved user accessibility
Affordance	Affordance refers to an attribute of an object that allows people to know how to use it e.g. the recycle bin. While modern interfaces have tended to remove the affordances, it is important to ensure that it is still clear what are clickable elements. Thus, UI elements should be designed to mimic, to a reasonable extent, the shape of real-world objects (skeuomorphism)	Familiar environments and objects help new VR users feel more comfortable and present in the virtual space. It also gives a feeling of control by associating familiar knowledge and behaviours with objects and their corresponding physical reactions. For example, to open a door, the user might pick up a key put it in the lock and turn it as they would in the real world

8 Case Study: Workshops on AR and VR Prototyping

A workshop was run for 36 master's students on a design course. It was divided into two parts. In part 1, students were required to develop an application in augmented reality. They were shown an idea for low-fidelity prototyping using a cardboard frame as a screen. As the user, holding the cardboard frame, moved it around the scene, others held out tabs of paper attached to short sticks with additional information.

Users learned the technique of bodystorming with paper annotations and used them easily. Some comments made are shown in Table 3 (Fig. 2):

Table 3. Comments from students regarding augmented reality

Positive comments	Problems of suggested improvements
We designed a diet app to introduce snacks energy to users. it's a very fresh experience	User had issues with dimensions - hands not big enough
We got the sense of how easy and cost effective can be AR prototyping with using simple tools like post-it notes and wood sticks. We have created AR navigation of the building which was interesting	Problems: simulation object size/incomplete user journey
I've learned some ways to simulate AR experience in the real-world and it's pretty cool and useful	For interfaces that are far away, it is hard to create big enough labels to read
Easily and quickly created the prototype, therefore the experience	Problem might be that we don't know if it is feasible
Learn: the journey can really be simulated with diverse methods	Provide technology which can lead to high fidelity period
It's really fun to experience the journey of ordering food by AR	Spending more time on mocking up design concepts
Got to know how the context suitable for AR. Worked out some ideas based on the AR	Seeing the workflow on AR/VR and what it can do might be more useful
I've learned that I don't need to use fancy and expensive devices all the time. We can just use simple papers or applications	Offer digital prototyping lessons e.g. Adobe After effects
The people in my team were imaging different things from our initial concept. So it's useful to quickly compare our ideas in concrete	I would like to know more about techniques aspect. How to make idea become a reality

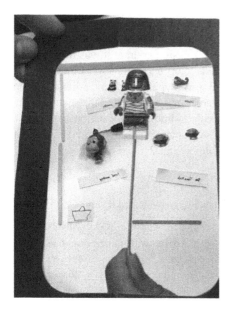

Fig. 2. Use of props to create AR effects within two prototypes (an augmented restaurant menu and room finder app)

One problem that users faced was being able to line up the AR elements behind the cardboard frame with the object being annotated. Another was creating annotations that were a suitable scale for the frame without obscuring the object being viewed.

For the second part of the workshop, the participants were asked to translate their AR prototype into VR. Some comments from the exercise are shown in Table 4.

Table 4. Comments from students regarding Virtual Reality

Positive comments	Problems of suggested improvements
Had fun creating the user experience using props, some big functions were missing due to the lack of time	I don't know whether there should be a trigger.. such as wearable glasses to put the user into the VR environment
A little confused about perspective and transferring photos to stereoscopic version	I'm not good at painting… so I don't know how to draw 3D objects into 2D pictures
Unsure at first. After seeing it demonstrated it was finally clear	Have no idea how to transform AR wayfinding to VR
It was a very interesting experience to let me practice and feel about the VR	It wasn't as close [as I would like] to actual VR
Useful, learned how the perspective will be changed	It's a bit hard to imagine it in the real world

(continued)

Table 4. (*continued*)

Positive comments	Problems of suggested improvements
The difference was about the use of buttons. It wasn't difficult to move from AR to VR	I would like to experience more devices or [ways to prototype in VR]
It's good to quickly understand the application of VR. But the time was short and limited to gain more knowledge	For VR to design, we need a device such as a VR headset or 3D camera
We can share the prototype with other people to play with	For VR to design, we need a device such as a VR headset or 3D camera
Impressive and motivational. Learn lots of new things. I now know how to design a virtual reality prototype. Amazing	It was more difficult than augmented reality because it is something very new. Wasn't sure how to do it, how it works
What's different is that the products will be floating in the middle of the air for the user to choose. It was very helpful for me to learn VR prototyping	It needs a VR wearable device and something can interact with

Generally, the students felt positively towards the workshop in terms of learning how to construct low-fidelity prototypes for AR and VR (see Fig. 3)

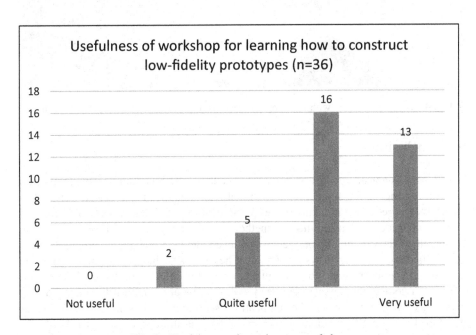

Fig. 3. Usefulness ratings given to workshop

Some of the key outcomes were that while students found the VR prototyping enjoyable, they felt they needed a structure similar to the AR session where the user was looking through the cardboard frame. A laser pointer was also available to use for indicating an item remotely (like an VR pointing device).

A second student workshop focused solely on VR prototyping was run where further techniques for rapid prototyping tested. Working in groups, the 6 participants each created four scenes on large sheets of card for a chosen application (create a garden and Mars mission). They then navigated through the 'environment' by either wearing a cardboard set of Goggles or by manipulating a cardboard overlay with a viewport for viewing the scene. It was felt that both the goggles and the viewport were reasonably effective with the viewport being marginally preferred. Participant feedback on the workshop experience was generally positive. One comment was: "It was an interesting journey. I enjoyed the process of drawing scenarios and creating a story board. It is a challenge to make a vivid and contextual scenarios" (Fig. 4).

Fig. 4. Using 2D scenes with a cardboard mask with viewport to simulate virtual reality

9   Conclusion

This paper has considered how different user-centered methods can be used to develop the user experience for augmented and virtual reality applications. Yet they are not in themselves novel and could equally well be applied to traditional types of applications. The essential idea is that low-fidelity methods combined with a good imagination can be an efficient way to explore ideas and even develop the basic structure of an application and the user flows through it. They can also help to try and mimic the emotional experiences that it the design team hope to achieve with the final developed system. Of course, the development team will only be able to tell it the intended user experience is mirrored when the application is programmed using AR software or developed using a VR development kit and presented through the headset. However, low-fidelity techniques should enable to design team to save a lot of time an effort in designing an application that offers a usable design and an enjoyable user experience.

References

1. Mobgen, Accenture Interactive: Low-fi prototyping: what, why and how? https://www.mobgen.com/low-fi-prototyping/. Accessed 24 Feb 2020
2. ISO 9241-210 Human-centred design processes for interactive systems, Ergonomics of human-system interaction, International Organization for Standardization, Geneva, Switzerland (1999), (2019)
3. Microsoft, case study expanding the design process for mixed reality. https://docs.microsoft.com/en-us/windows/mixed-reality/case-study-expanding-the-design-process-for-mixed-reality. Accessed 24 Feb 2020
4. Jaime, S.: Rapid prototyping methods for AR & VR (2017). https://medium.com/@oneStaci/vr-ar-prototyping-8e6d59cb260c. Accessed 24 Feb 2020
5. Thompson, A., Potter, L.E.: Taking the 'A' out of 'AR': play based low fidelity contextual prototyping of mobile augmented reality. In: CHI PLAY 2018 Extended Abstracts: Proceedings of the 2018 Annual Symposium on Computer-Human Interaction in Play Companion Extended Abstracts, pp. 647–653 (2018)
6. Prototypr, Creating user flows with mixed reality. https://blog.prototypr.io/creating-user-flows-for-mixed-reality-1986f8b85247. Accessed 24 Feb 2020
7. Norman, D.: The Design of Everyday Things: Revised and Expanded. Basic Books, New York (2013)
8. Purwar, S.: Designing user experience for Virtual Reality (VR) applications. https://uxplanet.org/designing-user-experience-for-virtual-reality-vr-applications-fc8e4faadd96. Accessed 24 Feb 2020

Other Worlds. When Worldbuilding and Roleplay Feed Speculation

Ilaria Mariani[(✉)]

Department of Design, Politecnico di Milano, 20158 Milan, Italy
ilaria1.mariani@polimi.it

Abstract. Games inherently deal with exploring alternative worlds. Worlds where players can experience other roles and have in-game, first-hand experiences by suspending our disbelief. This chapter digs into those features and peculiarities that make games and game design such good spaces where to imagine alternative pasts, presents, and futures for triggering reflection and imagining possibilities.

Being situated in the trend of future-oriented design practices, where fictional worlds, what-ifs, and their surroundings nurture design, the reasoning frames the game' worldbuilding activity and its potentialities in terms of envisioning and speculation from a twofold perspective—that of players and game designers. In doing so, it investigates the peculiar traits that make this practice compelling, challenging, and fruitful for feeding innovation. *Relying on which features and strategies can games embed reflections on the complex challenges we are facing today, will face tomorrow, or in the long run? How can the game design activity stimulate designers towards more aware, responsible, inclusive and diversity-oriented processes of envisioning, speculation, creation?*

Keywords: Game design · Wicked problems · Worldbuilding · Fictional world · Speculative design

1 Games and Worldbuilding for Future-Orientated Studies

> *«From the beginning, play is a symbolic act of representation,*
> *in which human life interprets itself.*
> Eugene Fink, The Ontology of Play, 1974, p. 107

Games inherently deal with exploring alternative worlds. Worlds where we can suspend our disbelief and experience other roles, dealing with choices and being open towards possibilities.

It is getting more and more frequent to run into games designed to be spaces that empower people to explore scenarios representing possible, plausible, or simply alternative presents, but also to speculate about preferable, probable or even undesirable futures [1, 2]. Moreover, the practice, both in terms of literature stream and case studies, transversally interest various typologies of games, showing a consistent interest. From digital games and interactive narratives [3, 4], to LARP and board games [5, 6], the state of the art reinforces that games can be a powerful and engaging medium for speculation.

© Springer Nature Switzerland AG 2020
A. Marcus and E. Rosenzweig (Eds.): HCII 2020, LNCS 12201, pp. 482–495, 2020.
https://doi.org/10.1007/978-3-030-49760-6_34

In the light of this reasoning, this chapter digs into those features and peculiarities that make games and game design such good spaces where to imagine alternatives, and above all, where to trigger reflection and imagining possibilities. Extending the rumination to a broader design perspective, it investigates the peculiar traits that make this practice compelling, challenging, and fruitful for feeding innovation. That said, *relying on which features and strategies can games embed reflections on the complex challenges we are facing today, will face tomorrow, or in the long run?* And secondly, *how can the game design activity stimulate designers towards more aware, responsible, inclusive and diversity-oriented processes of envisioning and speculation?*

The utilization of game design as an approach for addressing issues is growing, reaching out to various disciplines, beyond the Game Studies. The matters at stake become the speculation of futures and of those issues that cannot be easily reduced or solved. Complex matters of investigation that often take the shape of "wicked problems" [7–10]. Bridging the real and the fictitious into novel, often unexpected fictional worlds make the game world-making process emerge as a powerful practice for exploratory processes and scenario building. However, in parallel to the worldbuilding process, which takes a designerly point of view, it is also vital to consider that the play activity makes such fictional worlds experienced by players, boosting them to form judgments about such worlds and the systems they represent and reduce [11–13]. Such a perspective requires to deal with several key concepts, as representation, simulation, identification and interpretation/negotiation of meanings [14].

Hence, this reasoning frames the game' worldbuilding activity and its potentialities in terms of envisioning and speculation from a twofold perspective: that of designers who meaningfully and wisely craft games and their fictional world, and that of players who play and interpret them.

As a consequence, the rumination here presented reaches out to future-orientated Design Studies, as Speculative and Critical Design [2, 15, 16] from a Game Design perspective, while counting on the reasoning advanced on current design practices in the Game Studies field, as ethical gameplay [17–19], Flanagan's critical play [20, 21], Bogost's persuasive games and procedural rhetoric [22], Sicart's counter-analysis of proceduralism [23]. Further knowledge comes from a broader stream of literature, situated between narrative theory and media studies, where it is explored how to build meaningful narratives, and the features they should have to engage users [24–29].

2 Research Methodology

The hereby reasoning originates from an interdisciplinary theoretical background as well as empirical research conducted in the higher education context of Politecnico di Milano, School of Design, in the shape of specific experimentations carried on in the MSc programs of Communication Design, Digital and Interaction Design, and Design for the Fashion System, and in the BSc programs of Communication, Fashion, Product and Interior Design. An additional workshop was held in Potsdam, University of Applied Science.

The knowledge hereby presented relies on a line of research that started in 2012, and is still running. Over the years it involved several BSc and MSc classes in the

School of Design, Politecnico di Milano in worldbuilding activities for games or interactive narratives. In particular:

- The elective BSc course "Augmented Reality and Mobile Experience" (a.y. 2013/14, 2014/15, 2015/16), involving a total amount of 180 students who were asked to design LBMGs as engaging communication systems able to investigate and raise awareness on societal problems [30, 31].
- The Communication Design and Digital and Interaction Design MSc course "Complex Artefacts and System Design Studio" (a.y. 2015/16, 2016/17, 2017/18, 2018/19), involving a total amount of 223 students who developed complex interactive narrative systems and artefacts on matters of societal interests [32, 33].
- The Design for the Fashion System MSc module "Advanced Interactive Narratives" (a.y. 2019/20), which involved 39 students in crafting storyworlds and interactive narratives dealing with values and issues of the fashion domain.
- The elective MSc course "Game Design" (a.y. 2015/16; 2016/17; 2018/19), which involved each year from 30 to 40 students in designing board games as communication systems, covering global challenges.
- A one-day workshop in Digital and Interaction Design that involved 64 students in developing future scenarios starting from game-based mechanics.
- A series of 4 five-day workshops (a.y. 2014/15, 2015/16; 2016/17; 2018/19) that involved an amount of about 210 MSc students of Communication Design in developing LBMGs for social change.
- A five-day workshop where 54 MSc students in Communication Design (a.y. 2018/19) developed playful interactive narratives for speculative design research.
- A five-day workshop where 45 BCs students in Communication Design envisioned post-digital challenges as game-based experiences.
- An additional workshop was held at the Potsdam University of Applied Science (a.y. 2019/20), involving about 20 students in developing speculative interactive narratives on global challenges.

In such a context, the practice of designing games became a way to understand and rehearse the present, envision alternative presents, or imagine, speculate, frame possible futures. This framing ensued from the reflective practice of research through design [34, 35], also recalling the concept of constructive design research [36] as a way to translate the know-how gained through hands-on activities into theory.

By tapping into games from the twofold perspectives abovementioned, the aim is to explore the possibilities and implications respectively entailed in the worldbuilding and playing activities. In particular, it is paramount considering how they require both designers and players to translate wide ranges of information, concepts, and possibilities, which designers need to frame into game-experienceable worlds, and players should unpack, negotiating their meaning.

Conducting ethnographic analysis (participant observation, [37]) and interpretative research, this study examined design as a process of enquiry and the play activity as a way to gain knowledge. Data was collected applying a triangulation of different methods, acknowledging that each research method has its limits, biases, and weaknesses [38, 39]. In particular, the mixed methods used were: rapid ethnographies, participant observation, questionnaires, and informal interviews with students.

Aiming at unpacking how games can sustain and feed speculation, the following reasoning privileges the use of renowned games as case studies that point out the role that different game features, logic, mechanics or rhetorics play.

3   Worldbuilding: Immersion, Make-Believe, and Meaning-Making

Games can be framed as systems where players enter other worlds, where to struggle for overcoming unnecessary obstacles [40], facing conflicts that are "not real", but half [41]. In the Game Studies literature, games are archetypically framed as closed systems that involve players in a form of activity that separates and differentiates from everyday life in terms of time, space, and sociality [42, 43]. By one of its very first definition, that of Huizinga [42], the game-playing activity stands outside from ordinary life, in an area that is known as *magic circle*. This concept, conventionally used to identify the *other space* where players can operate following specific formal rules, was first proposed by Huizinga [42], then reframed by Caillois [44] and later formalized and actualized by Salen and Zimmerman [43] who contributed to its establishment and extensive dissemination. New forms of experimentations in the gaming field led indeed to the introduction of games—and games typologies—that question the perimeter itself of this definition [45–50]. This change originated in consequence of the technological advances that extended the game space with games that became pervasive [47] and hybrid [51, 52], and also because of the socio-cultural and ethical topics that games started to address and represent.

3.1   A Representational Space Where to Immerse and Suspend Disbelief

The very concept of *other space* and its features are central when it comes to discuss how games can impact our frames of reference, activating processes of critical-thinking and meaning-making [14]. Echoing Van Gennep's concept of *liminality* [53], games can be seen as *liminal spaces* wherein players can experience possibilities.

For unpacking the potentialities of designing and playing games as ways for envisioning and speculating, and understanding how they can nurture the design practice, the concept of game as representation is paramount. To explain the concept, it is necessary to consider games as representations of a broader reality, in which imagination as *mimicry* and *make-believe* are access conditions [44]. Introduced by Crawford in the early eighties [11], the concept of representation is tied up with the ones of interaction, conflict, and safety. Playing a game, players metaphorically enter a fictional world that is a fictitious, protected representation separated from reality. Within the figurative space of the magic circle, players can temporarily take the distance from everyday life and safely experience other worlds. Although typical and well-established game definitions do not formally include the fictional world as their definitional features, the concept serves a primary function. It is one of the reasons that make games a fertile ground for simulation, speculation and envisioning. From a design perspective, the worldbuilding activity as the act of defining its features, fundamentals, rules, and mechanics consists in designing what to explore, question and challenge, as well as the range of possibilities that the player should enquire through an act of playing, and then interpret [14, 54].

If Huizinga [42] mainly links games to being separated in time and space from everyday life, Caillois [44] establishes the play activity on *make-believe*. The expression identifies the status of *suspension of disbelief* that occurs when the player's engagement in a fictional world is such to spur a high level of pleasure. This state, known as *immersion* [26, 55, 56], can cause the player to lose awareness of the surrounding. Although the player is not rejecting reality, it occurs a sort of detachment from the real, primary world.

Indulging in a game of make-believe, the attention turns to the fictional world—also called secondary or imaginary [29]. Since human beings' attention is limited [57], being focused on the fictional world implies a reduction of attention on something else, namely the primary world. For this condition to occur, and get the player somehow lost within the world portrayed, it is necessary that s/he is absorbed in the story that is unfolding, which presupposes that the fictional world and its story are built coherently and completely [29], and therefore featuring established consistency as a solid logic ruling the world activities. To allow and encourage immersion, the fictional world should be *believable*.

The fictional world and the meanings it entails can be seen as a frame within which the fictitious makes sense: a frame where possibilities can be explored, and imagination is fed and can run. However, the fictional world is also the space where the player can move and take action. If immersion depends on the player's ability to suspend disbelief [58], *agency* [59] identifies the player's ability to partake in the game as a simulation, where intentional actions produce results and imply consequences shown by/in the fictional world. Central in this reasoning is that the player can perform significant actions and see their results [56], feeling effective in the interaction with the environment [60]. From a design point of view, players' in-game actions should be encouraged as if they were advocated and suggested by the world itself. This spurs players to engage in judgment- and meaning-making [27].

A well-known example for discussing how immersion, make-believe, and agency are intertwined in a challenging and engaging fictional world is *The McDonald's Videogame* (Molleindustria 2005) [61]. This digital game by the Italian social critic collective Molleindustria proposes a simulation that is a straight critique and satire of the fast food business practices. As stated by Bogost [22], *The McDonald's Videogame* uses procedural rhetoric to show how deeply corrupt the fast food business is. To do that, the game presents four scenarios: (1) the third-world farmland where cattle are cheaply raised, (2) the slaughterhouse for fatten the cattle in view of an approaching slaughter, (3) the fast food restaurant where burgers are sold, (4) and the corporate headquarters where lobbying, PR, and marketing take place. In every sector, the player is required to make choices considering what is best for the business. In this process, the logic and mechanics of the McDonald's system are exposed, while a variety of questionable moral choices are encountered, shaking the player towards some reflection.

The game system is designed for giving players the chance to experience alternatives. It quickly pops up that a politically-correct behavior is not paying back the efforts while being a clear non-winning strategy. Hence, by providing alternatives, the game system itself encourages the player to experiment with other possibilities. In particular, it is easy to recognize that acting corruptly and unscrupulously largely rewards. When managing the natural environments where soy is grown, it is possible to plow over rainforests and razing villages to turn them into terrains. In raising cattle to maturity, the player can choose to feed it with genetically altered grain, with other cattle, or growth hormones for a faster fattening. The third section is the fast food restaurant where to control employees and sandwich production. However, this corrupted system can be claimed and exposed by third parties as indigenous or antiglobalization groups that sue McDonald's for violations, requiring the headquarters to take care of the situation, limiting damages.

Although simplified and reduced to the essentials, *The McDonald's Videogame* uses procedural rhetoric to argument the fast food industry and its behavior. In particular, what is remarkable is that the game system is designed for challenging the player to do better, by doing worse, in a clearly rotten situation. Especially the concept of agency as a way of empowering the user to interact with the fictional world is wisely used to make first-hand, in-game experiences of specific alternatives. As a result, in this game as a simulation system, the player can gain knowledge on how the system portrayed works while experiencing the dark side of playing [62].

3.2   In Someone Else's Shoes

Man is least himself when he talks in his own person.
Give him a mask and he'll tell you the truth.
Oscar Wilde

A further concept to consider, since it serves a fundamental function in raising awareness is that of *identification* [63]. According to the literature, the term relates to identification as a member of a group, and with a character. However, because of the reasoning hereby addressed, the focus is on the latter. Ruminating on the topic, Gee [64] argues that games can fuel a tripartite play of identities. The player can identify (1) with his/her real-world identity, (2) with a virtual identity, as a member of a group, and (3) with the in-game character, as an identity provided with specific aims that may even largely differ from the players' ones. Considering the reasoning here presented, the third typology of identification is the one most at stake. Being linked to the concept known in the literature as *projective identity* [64–66], identification is at the core of the processes of fantasy and *mimicry* [44]. It is fundamental for establishing connectivity with the world represented and its stories, meanings, and values, and with the character of which the player takes the perspective and shares the in-game mindset [63, 67].

Sustaining and encouraging identification and projection [67–69] characters largely contribute to foster the player to vicariously enter a storyworld. Characters are in charge of turning a passive telling in a personal, shareable experience. Well-built fictional characters can be designed as repositories of stories and values, triggering understanding and even empathy. Therefore, not just the world-making activity, but also the act of building its characters(s) [33] is based on a practice of reduction [13], where the values, perspectives, drivers, and goals of an entire socio-cultural context can be embedded in a fictional world and its characters [70–72].

For example, contrary to the most war-themed video games that address the front line combat putting players in the shoes of soldiers, the war survival video and mobile game *This War of Mine* (11 bit studios, 2014) [73] proposes the civilian side of war. Players strive to make one to four characters survive everyday dangers, making a series of difficult decisions. During daytime and nighttime, the player is responsible for maintaining the characters alive, dealing with their physical and mental health. The game provides several options for taking action, where each of the player's actions and choices impacts the game resulting in several possible endings for each survivor. In the fictional world as a representation and simulation, the player in charge of considering possibilities and their implications related to the overall world, and make possibly shrewd moves accordingly.

As argued by Papale [66], "the notion of identification grants agency to the video game and its characters, that is the ability to operate on, to influence, to manipulate, to persuade the subject player, at the point of altering the player's personality". Playing, the player is actively involved in processes of decision-making and meaning-making. The alleged tendency to identify with the characters played can be wisely and conscientiously used to put players into someone else's shoes, experiencing perspectives that differ from their usual, ordinary ones. Echoing Turner's analysis of *liminality* [74, 75], the fictional world of the game becomes the space where players can temporarily overcome and break social hierarchies and relationships, even subverting "the usual".

In the liminal space of the game, players can experience diversity. Here the transgression of the ordinary is not just allowed but encouraged. This condition constitutes an opportunity for the designers who can invent coherent and complete [29] fictional worlds where to explore alternatives, independently from their being related to the past, the present, or the future, and see the show how each choice or actions implies consequences to consider.

3.3 Across Worlds: Choices, Failure, Alternatives

Agency, along with immersion and identification, is fundamental in leading players to process and reconstruct the world logics and its features. This process is responsible for fueling the comparison between the fictional world and the physical one [26, 76]: a nodal condition for speculation and experimentation of what-ifs.

Transcending the straightforward, functional, and solution-oriented approach typical of the design discipline, fictional worlds can be conceived and built for triggering meaning-making. Not only the game elements but also the world features concur in conveying messages. The world and its rules, its characters and objectives, the objects, context and environment, the story, the game mechanics and rhetoric: as an ecosystem they all contribute to creating a meaningful space where alternatives can be explored [31]. Such a space, that is fictional by definition, can host and be ruled by its own ideologies and practices. Moreover, it can use its own timeline and historical events, portraying a space where other technological evolutions took place, following the logic of the counterfactual history. A fictional world can be built to be believable and consistent, independently of its being based on an alternative past, present or future—ranging from probable to plausible, possible, or even impossible [1, 3]. From a broader design perspective, the possibility to encompass potentials and possibilities is what makes games and their fictional world challenging and powerful. In this alternative space, particular issues or situations can be addressed, peculiar or relevant points of view can be adopted to involve players in an experience that leads to consider options when attempting to raise awareness or fuel invention and creativity.

A renowned example both in the game and speculative design field is the serious alternate reality game *World Without Oil* (2007) [77]. Following the claim "Play it – before you live it.", the game invites players from all over the world to play in order to change the future. Aiming at calling attention to the economy, climate, and quality of life risk connected to our use of oil. The game simulates the first 32 weeks of a global oil crisis. In a span of a few months, a diffused and rich community of players started to explore the what-ifs for our future that oil poses, unpacking possibilities and providing forecasts about how the(ir) everyday life would be. This game creates a scenario for speculation, where players are involved in a make-believe process that relies on roleplay and identification. To speculate about a plausible future without oil, the game makes a call for participation to the Web. People's collective imagination becomes a way for exploring possibilities, valuing diversity and variety of perspectives. From its start to its end, *World Without Oil* welcomes everybody to play by creating a personal story that can take the shape of an email or voicemail, blog post or podcast, video or photo, twitter messages: whatever that can be used to chronicle and imagine a future in which we run out of oil. When the game ended, on June 1st 2007, it collected about 1500 personal entries posted across the Web, with about 68000 viewers that increased to over 110000 by the end of 2007 (http://writerguy.com/wwo/metaabout.htm).

Although it is evident that a straight separation between the fictional, secondary word and the primary world cannot exist, it persists a dichotomy. Being aware that some games belonging to the category of games for social change may be an exception [14], it is certain that when playing, the player is partaking in an act of play that is separate from reality [42]. The in-game actions impact on the fictional world, but not on the real world, and the player is aware that "this is a play" [78]. This context evokes a condition of openness toward possibilities and safety [11] that empowers players to put themselves to the test, as well as to test the game as a system that responds to their actions. In doing so, players are also testing the game as a system of representation, which portrays a specific context, with its mechanics and rules, possibilities and limits. It is natural to connect such a feature with the potentialities in terms of speculation. The game world becomes the space that welcomes what-ifs, alternatives, and their experimentation. Considering that, both worldbuilding and game design can be to various extent ethical activities that nurture ethical gameplay—as the outcome of a game sequence in which players rely on their moral thinking to make choices [10].

The ever-present ethical dimension of design [79] is particularly relevant in those games where societal issues wicked problems are addressed. The game design process becomes a combination of interpretations and decisions that leads to ethical gameplays able to affect in-game players' choices, but also their real attitudes towards the topic addressed. As such, the game design activity gathers, systematizes, and interprets values and ideals for representing them through the fictional world, its features, stories, characters, logic, and mechanics.

Independently from the fact that the player is aware and receive feedback related to how in-game actions bring more or less subtle changes in the gameplay and/or the game narrative, moral choices must have consequences on the game. Such consequence should be intelligible and also related to the choices made when playing. Moreover, when a choice is made in a game sequence, it is not possible to return—or reload in case of digital games [80]—a state that is prior to that choice. Such a game space as a fictional world that simulates how a system works [22] with its own rules and logic should not be built to welcome a sort of in-game trial and error, as the process of experimenting through different choices and attempts what happens if specific choices/actions are made. Since all decisions matter and have consequences, once a choice is made, it locks the player into a new state of the game and going back is impossible [80]. Sometimes this applies to a game sequence; other times it is permanent, as to say that once a choice is made, there is no way back. Decisions bind players to the path they chose.

Such games more and differently than others are based on the concept of failure as a trigger for reasoning. Since wicked problems have no given alternative solutions [7, 81]. There may be no solution at all, and/or there may be a solution that no one has ever thought of before. Moreover, when addressing wicked problems, the world is not meant to share or propose solutions, on the contrary, it is aimed at portraying complexity [14]. On the contrary to what happens in *The McDonald's Videogame* [61] where the game uses procedural rhetoric for forming the player's judgment and showing what is wrong, such games chose to show possibilities. Aiming at opening up reasoning and discussion about specific topics, games addressing wicked problems [7, 10, 81] are designed to involve players in ethical gameplays that underline how certain issues cannot be solved because of their complex nature.

September 12th (Newsgaming, Frasca 2003) [82], is a political digital game with "deadly simple rules": You can shoot or not. The game is a simple model aimed at making players explore some aspects of the war on terror. The player controls a weapon for launching missiles on a marketplace where terrorists are mingled with civilians. Here the player can shoot or not. Conveying the timeless maxim "violence begets more violence," the game system asks players to unconsciously contribute to creating more terrorists, by acting as unaware terrorists. By shooting, the player generates collateral damage among civilians, and the surrounding bystanders mourning for the innocent dead persons quickly turn into as many terrorists. This controversial game is an unwinnable game. Whatever actions the player does, failure is the outcome, and as such, it is extraordinarily meaningful in raising awareness.

Here the player can safely experience conflict, and above all failure. Being a fundamental feature of the medium [43], the possibility of failing is what makes games what they are: challenging and meaningful. In essence, failure provides motivation to play, and it provides the possibility to explore possibilities, failing over and over again [83]. However, when dealing with wicked problems, failure cannot be avoided. Hence it has a different meaning.

Especially games dealing with wicked problems designed to be unwinnable force players to repeat over and over again the same regrettable actions. The failure, the gameplay and the game narrative as a whole contribute to generating awareness.

That said, if on the one side entering and becoming immersed in the fictional world may result in a sort of escapism from reality, on the other, it allows to go through what is represented in a detached and unbiased way. As a consequence awareness and knowledge on the system represented can be gained through a form of reflective criticism, fed by an in-game, first-hand experience.

4   Discussion Envision, Speculate and Frame

Challenging the distinction between seriousness and playfulness, the activity of world-building becomes a way for envisioning, speculating and framing possibilities and alternatives. Games can welcome interactive representation of the past, present or of futures that can be possible, probable, plausible, preferred [2], being it likely or unlikely, desirable or undesirable. Providing a context in which to experience specific situations and see the results of the choices made, in-game events can influence who plays to challenge existing positions, frames and recognizes biases as such. Capitalizing on the affordances of the medium, players are invited to experience and understand the systems represented, even questioning their logic.

Especially by providing a space where to break existing timelines and technological evolutions, and in general practices akin to counterfactual histories, game's fictional worlds are fertile ground for introducing deliberate provocations, challenging established perceptions or habits, and applying alternatives. A wide range of complex issues and even wicked problems can be fully explored within the safer space that games create. From ideologies to what-ifs, or historical events that never happened: games fictional worlds became spaces that host explorations while problematizing and opening the debate. The reasoning hereby presented is rooted in the potential coming from building fictional worlds where players can vicariously immerse and can go through extraordinary experiences. Capitalizing on the benefits that come from make-believe and immersion, such fictional worlds can be specifically designed as unbiased apertures, where players can experience other roles and situations, going through the processes of identification and mimicry [84]. Fictional worlds can host complex concepts and present situations where causality is reverted, welcoming players to safely play and replay scenarios that differ from reality. The inherently potential of being subversive and irreverent makes games and their fictional worlds highly relevant in the for speculative design. Within their magic circle [42, 43, 46], they encourage considerable exploration. In doing so, designing such fictional worlds is a way to pose questions, as well as to provoke and inspire [3].

Since the late'90 s, games started to address topics of social and cultural matter, exploring how the medium can capitalize on its unique features for approaching coeval topics of societal relevance. Nowadays, such a trait is more and more evident.

However, what is today vital is to nurture reflections on how fictional worlds and the world-building activity itself can contribute to creativity and to the development of innovative ideas.

Taking the distance from the game design and game studies fields, and moving to a broader design perspective, such worlds can be built to invite the player to participate in a game of make-believe, where to explore alternative presents and imagine far away futures. Stepping away from the idea of designing for specific and identified needs emerged from the marketplace, design can look ahead of our current times and broaden its horizons. To pursue a design-driven innovation, entering the realm of the fictional, the unreal is a way to explore ideas and issues leveraging creativity and opening up new design possibilities [2, 85].

From design itself to technology research, and large-scale social and political issues, the areas of application can be varied and broad. Regarding such topics, building fictional worlds where to explore possibilities can provide a fertile ground for considering its social, cultural and ethical implications [86].

To address the topic of how gaming can contribute to speculation and envisioning futures, this chapter reached out to various fields, as game studies and game design, speculative design, interaction design, and media studies. In particular, the hereby rumination focused on how the game and fictional world features can be leveraged for designing safer spaces of explorations. This reasoning can be easily advanced and turned into practice, by creating a ground where identification and make-believe, failure and meaning-making, provocation and fictitiousness are wisely used in a worldbuilding and game design activity aimed at speculating for designing innovation.

References

1. Coulton, P., Burnett, D., Gradinar, A.I.: Games as speculative design: allowing players to consider alternate presents and plausible futures (2016)
2. Dunne, A., Raby, F.: Speculative Everything: Design, Fiction, and Social Dreaming. The MIT Press, Cambridge (2013)
3. Coulton, P., Jacobs, R., Burnett, D., Gradinar, A., Watkins, M., Howarth, C.: Designing data driven persuasive games to address wicked problems such as climate change. In: Proceedings of the 18th International Academic MindTrek Conference: Media Business, Management, Content & Services, pp. 185–191. ACM, New York (2014). https://doi.org/10.1145/2676467.2676487
4. Ruggiero, D.: Persuasive games as social action agents: challenges and implications in learning and society. Int. J. Gaming Comput.-Mediated Simul. (IJGCMS) 5, 75–85 (2013). https://doi.org/10.4018/ijgcms.2013100104
5. Bertolo, M., Mariani, I., Alberello Conti, E.: Discrimination: a persuasive board game to challenge discriminatory justifications and prejudices. In: Gray, K.L., Leonard, D.J. (eds.) Woke Gaming: Digital Challenges to Oppression and Social Injustice. University of Washington Press, Seattle (2018)
6. Schouten, B., Ferri, G., de Lange, M., Millenaar, K.: Games as strong concepts for city-making. In: Nijholt, A. (ed.) Playable Cities. GMSE, pp. 23–45. Springer, Singapore (2017). https://doi.org/10.1007/978-981-10-1962-3_2
7. Bosman, F.G.: There is no solution!: "wicked problems" in digital games. Games Cult. 14, 543–559 (2019). https://doi.org/10.1177/1555412017716603
8. Buchanan, R.: Wicked problems in design thinking. Des. Issues 8(2), 5–21 (1992)
9. Churchman, C.W.: Guest Editorial: Wicked Problems (1967)
10. Sicart, M.A.: Wicked games: on the design of ethical gameplay. Presented at the Proceedings of the 1st DESIRE Network Conference on Creativity and Innovation in Design (2010)
11. Crawford, C.: The Art of Computer Game Design. Osborne/McGraw-Hill, New York (1984)
12. Geertz, C.: The Interpretation of Cultures: Selected Essays. Basic books, New York (1973)
13. Goffman, E.: Frame Analysis: An Essay on the Organization of Experience. Harvard University Press, Cambridge (1974)

14. Mariani, I.: Meaningful negative experiences within games for social change. Designing and analysing Games as Persuasive Communication Systems (2016). http://hdl.handle.net/10589/117855
15. Bardzell, S., Bardzell, J., Forlizzi, J., Zimmerman, J., Antanitis, J.: Critical design and critical theory: the challenge of designing for provocation. In: Proceedings of the Designing Interactive Systems Conference, pp. 288–297. ACM (2012)
16. Tharp, B.M., Tharp, S.M.: Discursive Design: Critical, Speculative, and Alternative Things. The MIT Press, Cambridge, MA (2019)
17. McDaniel, R., Fiore, S.M.: Applied ethics game design: some practical guidelines. In: Ethics and Game Design: Teaching Values Through Play, pp. 236–254 (2010)
18. Schrier, K.: Ethics and Game Design: Teaching Values through Play, IGI Global (2010)
19. Sicart, M.A.: Beyond Choices: The Design of Ethical Gameplay. The MIT Press, Cambridge (2013)
20. Flanagan, M.: Making games for social change. AI Soc. **20**, 493–505 (2006)
21. Flanagan, M.: Critical Play: Radical Game Design. The MIT Press, Cambridge (2009)
22. Bogost, I.: Persuasive Games: The Expressive Power of Videogames. The MIT Press, Cambridge (2007)
23. Sicart, M.A.: Against procedurality. Game Stud. **11**, 209 (2011)
24. Campbell, J.K.: The Hero with a Thousand Faces. Princeton University Press, Princeton (1949)
25. Rouse, R., Koenitz, H., Haahr, M.: Interactive Storytelling: 11th International Conference on Interactive Digital Storytelling, ICIDS 2018, Dublin, Ireland, December 5–8, 2018, Proceedings. Springer, Cham (2018). https://www.springer.com/gp/book/9783030040277
26. Ryan, M.-L.: Narrative as Virtual Reality: Immersion and Interactivity in Literature and Electronic Media. Johns Hopkins University Press, Baltimore (2001)
27. Spallazzo, D., Mariani, I.: Keeping coherence across thresholds: a narrative perspective on hybrid games. In: De Souza e Silva, A., Glover-Rijkse, R. (eds.) Hybrid Play Crossing Boundaries in Game Design, Player Identities and Play Spaces. Routledge, New York (2020)
28. Vogler, C.: The Writer's Journey: Mythic Structures for Screenwriters and Storytellers. Michael Wiese Productions, Studio City (1992)
29. Wolf, M.J.P.: Building Imaginary Worlds: The Theory and History of Subcreation. Routledge, New York (2012)
30. Mariani, I., Spallazzo, D.: Game-design-driven knowledge: when prototypes unpack and reframe conventions. In: DRS Learn X Design 2019: Insider Knowledge, pp. 607–616. METU Department of Industrial Design (2019)
31. Spallazzo, D., Mariani, I.: Location-Based Mobile Games: Design Perspectives. Springer, Cham (2018)
32. Mariani, I., Ciancia, M.: Building interactive narratives: characters, stories and in-betweens. Experimentations and critique. In: Proceedings of the EDULEARN 2019, pp. 6844–6853. IATED (2019). https://doi.org/10.21125/edulearn.2019.1643
33. Mariani, I., Ciancia, M.: Character-driven narrative engine. Storytelling System for building interactive narrative experiences. In: Proceedings of the 2019 DiGRA International Conference: Game, Play and the Emerging Ludo-Mix, pp. 1–19. DiGRA (2019)
34. Frankel, L., Racine, M.: The complex field of research: for design, through design, and about design. In: Proceedings of the Design Research Society (DRS) International Conference (2010)
35. Frayling, C.: Research in Art and Design. Royal College of Art, Research Papers, vol. 1 (1993)
36. Koskinen, I., Zimmerman, J., Binder, T., Redstrom, J., Wensveen, S.: Design Research Through Practice: From the Lab, Field, and Showroom. Elsevier, Burlington (2011)

37. DeWalt, K.M., DeWalt, B.R.: Participant Observation: A Guide for Fieldworkers. AltaMira Press, Walnut Creek (2010)
38. Creswell, J.W.: Research Design: Qualitative, Quantitative, and Mixed Methods Approaches. Sage, Beverly Hills (2008)
39. Denzin, N.K., Lincoln, Y.S.: The discipline and practice of qualitative research. In: Handbook of Qualitative Research, vol. 2, pp. 1–28 (2000)
40. Suits, B.: The Grasshopper: Games Life and Utopia. University of Toronto Press, Toronto (1978)
41. Juul, J.: Half-Real: Video Games Between Real Rules and Fictional Worlds. The MIT Press, Cambridge (2005)
42. Huizinga, J.: Homo Ludens. A Study of the Play Element in Culture. Routledge, Kegan Paul, London (1949)
43. Salen, K., Zimmerman, E.: Rules of Play: Game Design Fundamentals. The MIT Press, Cambridge (2004)
44. Caillois, R.: Les jeux et les hommes: le masque et le virtige. Gallimard, Paris (1958)
45. Consalvo, M.: There is no magic circle. Games and culture 4(4), 408–417 (2009)
46. Klabbers, J.H.: The Magic Circle: Principles of Gaming & Simulation. Sense Publishers, Rotterdam (2009)
47. Montola, M.: Exploring the edge of the magic circle: defining pervasive games. Presented at the Proceedings of DAC (2005)
48. Stenros, J.: In defence of a magic circle: the social, mental and cultural boundaries of play. Trans. Dig. Games Res. Assoc. 1, 1–39 (2014). https://doi.org/10.26503/todigra.v1i2.10
49. Taylor, T.: Pushing the borders: player participation and game culture. In: Structures of Participation in Digital Culture, pp. 112–130 (2007)
50. Taylor, T.L.: Play Between Worlds: Exploring Online Game Culture. The MIT Press, Cambridge (2009)
51. DeSouza e Silva, A.: Hybrid reality and location-based gaming redefining mobility and game spaces in urban environments. Simul. Gaming 40, 404–424 (2009). https://doi.org/10.1177/1046878108314643
52. De Souza e Silva, A., Sutko, D.M.: Theorizing locative media through philosophies of the virtual. Commun. Theory 21, 23–42 (2011)
53. van Gennep, A.: The Rites of Passage. University of Chicago Press, Chicago (1909)
54. Mariani, I., Gandolfi, E.: Negative Experiences as learning trigger: a play experience empirical research on a game for social change case study. Int. J. Game-Based Learn. (IJGBL). 6, 50–73 (2016)
55. Csikszentmihalyi, M.: Flow: The Psychology of Optimal Experience. HarperCollins, New York (1990)
56. Murray, J.H.: Hamlet on the Holodeck: The Future of Narrative in Cyberspace. The MIT Press, Cambridge (1997)
57. Holland, N.N.: Literature and the Brain. PsyArt Foundation, Gainesville (2009)
58. McMahan, A.: Immersion, engagement and presence. In: Wolf, M.J.P., Perron, B. (eds.) The Video Game Theory Reader, pp. 67–86. Routledge, London, New York (2003)
59. Frasca, G.: Rethinking agency and immersion: video games as a means of consciousness-raising. Dig. Creativity 12, 167–174 (2001)
60. Buckles, M.A.: Interactive Fiction: The Computer Storygame "Adventure" (1986)
61. Molleindustria: The McDonald's Videogame (2005)
62. Mortensen, T.E., Linderoth, J., Brown, A.M.: The Dark Side of Game Play: Controversial Issues in Playful Environments. Routledge, New York (2015)
63. Shaw, A.: Identity, identification, and media representation in video game play: an audience reception study (2010)

64. Gee, J.P.: What Video Games Have to Teach Us About Literacy and Learning. Palgrave Macmillan, New York (2003)
65. Hart, C.: Getting into the game: an examination of player personality projection in videogame avatars (2016)
66. Papale, L.: Beyond identification: defining the relationships between player and avatar. J. Games Crit. **1**, 1–12 (2014)
67. Cohen, J.: Defining identification: a theoretical look at the identification of audiences with media characters. Mass Commun. Soc. **4**, 245–264 (2001)
68. Klimmt, C., Hefner, D., Vorderer, P., Roth, C., Blake, C.: Identification with video game characters as automatic shift of self-perceptions. Media Psychol. **13**, 323–338 (2010)
69. Yee, N.: Motivations for play in online games. Cyberpsychol. Behav. Soc. Netw. **9**, 772–775 (2006)
70. Boal, A.: Legislative Theatre: Using Performance to Make Politics. Routledge, New York (2005)
71. Schechner, R.: Performers and spectators transported and transformed. Kenyon Rev. **3**, 83–113 (1981)
72. Schechner, R.: Between Theater and Anthropology. University of Pennsylvania Press, Philadelphia (2010)
73. 11 bit studios: This War of Mine (2014)
74. Turner, V.W.: From Ritual to Theatre: The Human Seriousness of Play. Paj Publications, New York (1982)
75. Turner, V.W.: The Anthropology of Experience. University of Illinois Press, Chicago (1986)
76. Ryan, M.-L.: Possible Worlds, Artificial Intelligence, and Narrative Theory. Indiana University Press (1991)
77. Eklund, K., McGonigal, J., Cook, D., Lamb, M., Senderhauf, M., Wells, K.: World Without Oil (2007)
78. Bateson, G.: The message "this is play". Group process. **2**, 145–241 (1956)
79. Löwgren, J., Stolterman, E.: Thoughtful interaction design: a design perspective on information technology. The MIT Press, Cambridge (2004)
80. Sicart, M.A.: Moral dilemmas in computer games. Des. Issues **29**, 28–37 (2013)
81. Rittel, H., Webber, M.: Wicked problems. Man-made Futures **26**, 272–280 (1974)
82. Frasca, G.: September 12th (2003)
83. Juul, J.: The Art of Failure: An Essay on the Pain of Playing Video Games. The MIT Press, Cambridge (2013)
84. Caillois, R.: The Mask of Medusa. Clarkson N. Potter, New York (1964)
85. Auger, J.: Speculative design: crafting the speculation. Dig. Creativity **24**, 11–35 (2013)
86. Barbrook, R.: Imaginary Futures: From Thinking Machines to The Global Village. Pluto Press, London (2007)

UX Criteria Risk in Digital Product Investment: Literature Review

Larissa Rios[1]([envelope]), Ernesto Filgueiras[1,2,3],
and Farley Millano Fernandes[1,4]

[1] University of Beira Interior, Covilhã, Portugal
larissarios93@gmail.com, ernestovf@gmail.com,
farleymillano@gmail.com
[2] CIAUD - Research Centre for Architecture, Urbanism and Design,
Lisbon, Portugal
[3] Communication Laboratory – LabCom, University of Beira Interior,
Covilhã, Portugal
[4] UNIDCOM/IADE, Lisbon, Portugal

Abstract. The adoption of digital technology in the industry and its significant commercial outcomes underline the innovative potential of digital products and services and draw investments in search of technological breakthroughs. Usually, independent developers place their bets on the wishes and dreams of its creators. This behaviour results in unilateral decisions and a team of developers that is not prone to analysis or confrontation of its concepts and visions – in contrast with a business endeavour that should seek the product's success and return for investors. This kind of behaviour can bring about huge losses and failure for investors.

This article correlates the following subjects: (1) investment and digital entrepreneurship, (2) investment risk criteria; (3) principles of user experience in game design. The work focuses on the risk factors associated with investment in videogames – one of the most relevant digital products nowadays due to market dimension, the growing complexity of its projects and the rise in the number and value of investments. This process favours the use of corporate improvements techniques, such as digital evolution scanning, user experience, skills, value proposition and improvisation. At the same time, it brings about risks associated to factors such radical and incremental innovation, digital technology generativity and maladaptation. This article presents a literature review shining a light on the dramatic absence of key elements in the investment models for digital products. One of these elements is the lack of command in modern techniques that test the concepts and ensure the satisfaction of future users, for instance UX methodologies or the mere consultation and interaction with potential users.

Keywords: Investment risk · UX risk factor · UX in game design method · Game design method

© Springer Nature Switzerland AG 2020
A. Marcus and E. Rosenzweig (Eds.): HCII 2020, LNCS 12201, pp. 496–505, 2020.
https://doi.org/10.1007/978-3-030-49760-6_35

1 Introduction

The adoption of digital technology in the industry and its significant commercial outcomes underline the innovative potential of digital products and services and draw investments in search of technological breakthroughs. This process favours the use of corporate improvements techniques, such as digital evolution scanning, user experience, skills, value proposition and improvisation. At the same time, it brings about risks associated to factors such as radical and incremental innovation, digital technology generativity and maladaptation.

This article correlates the following subjects: (1) investment and digital entrepreneurship, (2) investment risk criteria; (3) principles of user experience in game design. The work focuses on the risk factors associated with investment in videogames – one of the most relevant digital products nowadays due to market dimension, the growing complexity of its projects and the rise in the number and value of investments.

Current investment models are based on market projections developed for physical products, which define the main criteria for investment risk. Some criteria, for example the developers' experience and the mastery of development tools, do help investors in their risk assessment. However, these variables are not the only ones and will certainly no longer be the most important to anticipate the investment risk associated with the guarantees and return for investment in videogames. There are examples of large investments in indie videogames that were never actually produced as originally presented due to factors such as the personality of team members and the absence of a process for consultation and evaluation of its concepts with real users.

Usually, independent developers place their bets on the wishes and dreams of its creators. This behaviour results in unilateral decisions and a team of developers that is not prone to analysis or confrontation of its concepts and visions – in contrast with a business endeavour that should seek the product's success and return for investors. This kind of behaviour can bring about huge losses and failure for investors.

This article presents a literature review shining a light on the dramatic absence of key elements in the investment models for digital products. One of these elements is the lack of command in modern techniques that test the concepts and ensure the satisfaction of future users, for instance UX methodologies or the mere consultation and interaction with potential users.

Having analysed this material, we will develop UX Risk Criteria in Digital Product Investment that bring together: a) a combination of internal collaboration techniques, b) the sensibility towards the efficiency of these methods in the production of videogames, and c) the association with traditional mathematical models that quantify and assess the investment risk percentage of an independent business.

Our goal is to grasp the state of the art when it comes to approaches that deal with UX risk in the process of digital products and to acknowledge the level of practical development to answer the following research question: Which principles of UX risk criteria can be applied when it comes to investment in digital products?

The documents were assessed and segmented in the following way: 1) identification of processes, practices, people/teams and technology in independent businesses; 2) correlation of the main findings of the bibliographical research with the principal foundations for the composition of investment risk; and 3) the basic characteristics of the future implementation of UX Risk Criteria in Digital Product Investment.

This work contributes to the understanding and development of risk criteria that make use of UX services (1), allowing an overall vision of publications related to this field (2), through the identification of combined basic characteristics of User Experience (3), and to associate these characteristics with the practices and processes of investment.

2   Literature Review

The implementation of digital technology in industries and its important commercial results motivate the potential for innovation of digital products and services and attract investments in search of technological advances (Nylen and Holmström 2015). Video games are part of the most consumed digital entertainment, technology and innovation products today (Cardoso 2007). Created in the mid-1950s, their development allowed new models of interaction between human and machines. Since then, its market growth has aroused interest in many developers of technology, art and design, resulting in the creation of startups and small companies around the world. With reduced teams and many hours of work, professionals create the first game projects and exhibit at fairs and industry events, looking for partnerships and investors who are interested in the concepts presented. Considering the vast competition in the search for capital through investment, keeping up with technological innovations of products and processes that can be implemented in video games can become a competitive advantage (Porter 1980).

Considering innovation as part of production is an act that contributes to the progress of the development of qualified and effective products (Abreu et al. 2018). This thought goes along the interests of those who invest, who are willing to risk resources in the hope of obtaining success and greater return on what has been invested.

Current investment models are based on market projections for physical products, which define the main investment risk criteria.

2.1   Digital Investment Market

Companies are being created all the time around the world. Companies that, regardless of the sector in which they operate, usually recognize the power of innovation for the development and survival of the business. Nowadays, business investment in digital initiatives is one of the most important actions in the pursuit of achieving goals (Nylen and Holmström 2015). The innovation of processes, products and services of companies involves managing the effort given to the application for a satisfactory result. Nylen and Holmström (2015) identified five main areas to be evaluated for good management of digital innovation: user experience, value proposition, digital evolution scanning, skills and improvisation. These skills support the decision-making process regarding innovation and what tools will be applied and invested.

It is possible to find companies and individuals that invest in digital innovation and do not obtain the expected return. Among the points that can result from this situation, the difficulties in creating IT value can be an aggravating factor. Short-term demands for new concepts in industries have become recurrent, making this a constant challenge for companies to deliver orders in a timely manner. For this reason, it is possible to find companies that seek to outsource the demands to other companies. Recent research (e.g., Grover and Kohli 2012) has highlighted how collaboration between companies can encourage the creation of value for digital products and services, equity in the allocation of risks and complementary investments.

The digital transformation that happens in institutions is the result of the implementation of conditions for innovation in processes, products, services and people. Organizational alignment is an important step towards effective optimization of this investment (PWC 2016). The digitalization process of industries impacts the entire world and increases the interest of companies and individual investors to find products that economically results the most (PWC 2016). Within digital world spectrum, video games stand out as a source of revenue in entertainment industry. Its cycle of innovation, interaction and globalization reaches different audiences, with the ability to keep them engaged to the product. Currently, video games are increasingly sought after by investors who support the industry, in order to enjoy medium to long term profits.

2.2   Independent Games Investment Market

The video game private investment market, which comes from angel investors, private companies and publishers, raises millions of euros annually, applied to startups, small and medium-sized companies (SMEs). The services are made available to society. Independent video game studios often rely on the private investment model as the primary source of capitalization. Its objectives include joint ventures and strategic partnerships in order to leverage business and possibly take on projects for the main foreign markets.

Through business rounds, as meetings with investors and producers are known, developers present their proposals, and, in return, evaluators agree on possible funds applications in such businesses. For decision-making, investors follow requirements and respective assessment processes that determine the interest in supporting and promoting this sector.

The evaluation of a business model is an important step towards supporting a specific business. Mahadevan (2000) defines a business model as the set of organizational flows, revenue, logic and value. The flow of value being the point of greatest interest, since it contains proposals for buyers, sellers and market makers. Mahadevan (2000) also points out the importance of companies that take into account the long-term viability of the business. Thus, the risk assessment model is part of the requirements analyzed by investors (Abreu et al. 2018).

Some criteria, such as the experience of the developers and the mastery of development tools, assist in the assessment of investor risk. However, these factors are not the only ones and will certainly not be the most important to predict the investment risk associated with the guarantees of a video game and the resulting return on investment. There are cases of large investments and indie video games that were never produced as presented due to factors such as the personality of the team members and the absence of assessment and concept evaluation processes with real users.

In general, independent producers bet on dreams, on particular desires of their creators. This behavior makes decisions unilateral and produces a team of developers reactive to the analysis and confrontation of their individual concepts and views, different from a commercial production that aims at the return of investors and the success of the product. This type of business behavior can generate big losses and accumulate huge failures for investors.

2.3   Risk Factors in Digital Initiatives Investment

Digital and innovation market productions, even though they can be perceived as economically advantageous, are still considered fickle and uncertain. Digital products go through evaluation criteria, known as risk factors, which identify external and internal aspects of the business, mapping opportunities and threats that may compromise a project's success (Purdy 2010). For Purdy (2010), the risks derive from attitudes generated by organizations. For him, it is possible to create and change these risks according to the decisions taken in internal and external events of the business. Risk has the important role of assessing the probability of losses and possibilities of gains (Wysocki 2009).

In their research, Abreu et al. (2018) elicit seven types of risks, which are:

- **Market risk** - uncertainties regarding the acceptability of the product or service by the market;
- **Regulatory risk** - uncertainties regarding aspects of the legal environment in which the company, its product or service is subject to laws, rules and regulations that can affect the business positively or negatively;
- **Economic and financial risk** - uncertainties related to the company's ability to generate revenue to cover its costs and provide return on investment;
- **Human resources risk** - uncertainties regarding the technical and managerial capacity of the project/enterprise team to provide the necessary competences to conduct the business;
- **Technological risk** - uncertainties regarding the degree of innovation, mastery of technology and the secrecy or protection of intellectual capital;
- **Environmental risk** - uncertainties regarding the environmental impact of the product or service;
- **Social risk** - uncertainties regarding the social impact of the product or service.

The categories involve subjective and objective risks (Zhang 2011), balancing the capacity for analysis. Risk assessment goes through three stages: identification, analysis and risk assessment (ISO 31000: 2009). The result of this process can positively or negatively impact aspects of cost, scope, quality and schedule of the evaluated business (Abreu et al. 2018).

In this point, some disagreements between entrepreneurs and investors arise regarding the importance of a particular identified risk. Polzin et al. (2018) determine some aspects generally discussed between parties: misalignment of risk perception, degree of importance to risk, partnership recruitment channels and risk assessment criteria that involve product innovation and professional skills of the team. User Experience is a knowledge field that, among other activities, includes the risk assessment of products and human resources.

2.4   User Experience in Videogames

Among the factors considered in the evaluation of digital products, the user experience (UX) is an important component (Gothelf 2013). This model analyzes the beginning, middle, end and their market projections. (Garrett 2011) This means that investors take into account the studio's internal behaviors and experiences when creating the product. This assessment is important to measure the team's alignment and consider its results in relation to the activities performed (Abreu et al. 2018). The role of User Experience in the internal development of a company is fundamental for the construction of effective and qualified projects. For Moule (2012), UX can be defined by the user's interactions with the tested product. This field generates results that can prove, change or invalidate decisions made during the production of the device. Good UX practices can fulfill objectives expected by those who apply them (Moule 2012). It is a good measure of technological advances and consumer acceptance (McNamara and Kirakowski 2006). The tool is sometimes only recognized for the purpose of aligning product user preferences. This thinking eliminates all possibilities of applying the experience ("X"), which allows experiences in the production process.

Creating a risk factor that involves User Experience for video game projects is important, as the market is constantly rebuilding itself, with new desires and consumption audiences. It is noted that the User Experience is practiced in several startups, but behavioral/human factors are often ignored. As previously presented, this category is consistent with the set of risks assessed by industry investors. Evaluation of experience, usability and functionality are part of User Experience process as well as professional and behavioral skills of the development team, which can define the direction of investment within the evaluated business.

The Mechanics, Dynamics and Aesthetics (MDA) Framework, proposed by LeBlanc (2004) illustrates well the iterative processes that must be considered and constantly evaluated by a video game development team (Fig. 1).

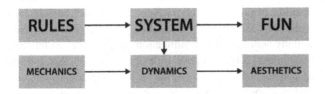

Fig. 1. MDA Framework, LeBlanc (2004)

Mechanics is responsible for building all possible actions within the game. The Dynamics component involves the relationship between mechanics, time and execution made by players during a match, through challenges. Aesthetics represents the

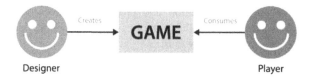

Fig. 2. MDA: Designer, Game and Player, LeBlanc (2004)

sensations caused to the player during a video game match. Its function is to engage the player through sensitivity. That said, it is important to consider the complementary perspectives between developer and player regarding a game artifact (Fig. 2).

LeBlanc (2004) points out that the unpredictable consumption of video games is part of the gameplay process, where the result is unknown and only tested in the final stage of the product and/or at market launch. The aesthetics element describes the emotions and sensations that a video game provokes in the player during a game. It is used in User Experience to measure consumption preferences for results with greater market impact. To achieve results that involve the desire to consume video games, it is necessary to build a structure rich in conceptual elements. Luban (2001) proposes a method that involves four phases for the realization of the final concept of a project, characterized by: multidisciplinary team, value proposal, filtering and definition of ideas and the combination of hypotheses and priorities of the project. Luban (2001) points out that the disorganization of ideas without the support of processes makes the project biased, meeting individual desires and elements.

Huntsman (2000a, b, c) states in his study that the game designer must consider, from the beginning of the project's development, the needs of the market and of its sponsors and financiers. Thus, by paying attention to these factors, risks can be minimized.

Considering the needs of the market involves finding alternatives to make the interface more pleasurable, helping its users to achieve enough engagement. Tim Skelly (1994) calls this state of mind "flow". It is only possible to reach the flow of a player if there is a direct interaction of the final audience with the product, and this is accompanied by highlighting the main element of a video game: fun.

Raymen (2006) states that the lack of interaction is one of the main problems in product development and recommends that the developers move away from the project so that there is fluidity in product creation. Another common mistake is to find teams that confuse players' and developers' role, taking into account personal development wishes, while actually ignoring the identification of the target audience's profile.

Adams and Rollings (2006) propose a design approach that is oriented towards players and that considers the target market as a fundamental element for the production of successful games. For that, it is necessary to take into account the empathy of the developers for its users. Empathy is a fundamental dimension to observe and understand the environment and the needs and desires of its customers and thus adapt your project to these situations (Cooper 2008; Cooper 2014), considering all its elements (Fig. 3).

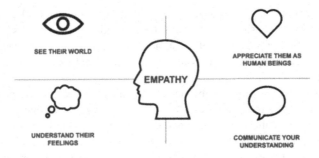

Fig. 3. Model of Empathy, Interaction Design Foundation (2019)

Using methods of empathic approach through the element "fun" can help the user's engagement to sympathize and wish to interact with the product.

3 Stream and Social Communication

Although the answer to the success of a video game lies in the interaction and emotion that it can provoke in its users, not all game developers have the sensitivity or training to observe and perform these characteristics for the product under development. The lack of developer-needs-consumer interaction can cause projects to fail during investment. Technically feasible proposals can receive large amounts of funding and thus win partnerships at a global level.

The absence of a model that assesses the investment risk regarding the UX components practiced by the team (involving the MDA model), is a threat that can cause a high risk of failure after its launch. In order to bring interaction and emotion to the

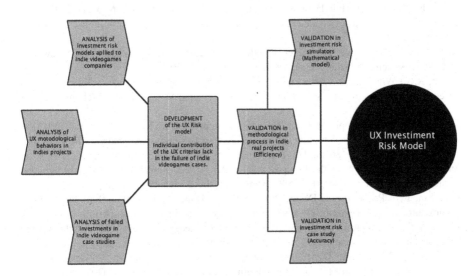

Fig. 4. UX used as part of investment risk assessment model

center of risk assessment, we present a structure (Fig. 4) that considers User Experience and its dimensions of sensitivity generated through video gameplay. Its guidance can help investors to find probabilities of losses and possibilities of gains through elements involving UX, facilitating the connection between the target market and the evaluated company or game.

As shown in our structure, many factors influence the decision process regarding investment in a digital product. Risk factors help to observe the business's capacity for growth and future valuation. For video games, a risk assessment of UX components is necessary, through engagement, interaction and emotion that can help identify possible failure or success of a specific game. Our structure focused on prioritizing essential elements for the production of a model that involved properties in the technology, investment and innovation segment.

The creation of such a model highlights the importance of understanding aspects of engagement and interaction of digital products as an important decision-making element regarding investments in the sector. With appropriate models for assessing these risks, investors will be able to find qualified companies that are better prepared to receive their investments. Given the lack of a model that involves UX risk criteria, our model will serve as an important contribution to technology investor community and opens up new opportunities for more solid investments. Finally, it is expected that this model will also promote a significant change in User Experience practices applied from the concept to the final product, increasing the investment attractiveness for indie video game companies.

References

Abreu, W.R.A., Zotes, L.P., Ferreira, K.M.: Gerenciamento de risco na avaliação de projetos de investimento em Startup. Sistemas & Gestão **13**(3), 267–282 (2018)

Adams, E., Rollings, A.: Fundamentals of game design, 3a edn. Pearson, New Jersey (2006)

Cardoso, G.: A mídia na sociedade em rede: Midias redes e vitrines, p. 526. Editora FGV, Rio de Janeiro (2007)

Cooper, R.G.: Perspective: the stage-gate idea-to-launch process – update, what's new, and NextGen systems. J. Prod. Innov. Manag. **25**, 213–232 (2008)

Cooper, R.G.: What's next?: After stage-gate. Res.-Technol. Manag. **57**, 20–31 (2014)

Garrett, J.: The Elements of User Experience: User-Centered Design for the Web and Beyond, vol. 2 (2011)

Gothelf, J.: Lean UX: Applying Lean Principles to Improve User Experience, vol. 1 (2013)

Grover, V., Kohli, R.: Cocreating IT value: new capabilities and metrics for multiform environments. MIS Q. **36**(1), 225–232 (2012)

Huntsman, T.: A Primer for the Design Process, Part 1: Do. Gamasutra (2000a). http://www.gamasutra.com/view/feature/131558/a_primer_for_the_design_process_.php

Huntsman, T.: A Primer for the Design Process, Part 2: Think. Gamasutra (2000b). https://www.gamasutra.com/view/feature/131559/a_primer_for_the_design_process_.php

Huntsman, T.: A Primer for the Design Process, Part 3: Need. Gamasutra (2000c). https://www.gamasutra.com/view/feature/131560/a_primer_for_the_design_process_.php

LeBlanc, M.: Mechanics, Dynamics, Aesthetics: A Formal Approach to Game Design. Northwestern University (2004). http://algorithmancy.8kindsoffun.com/MDAnwu.ppt

Luban, P.: The right decision at the right time: selecting the right features for a new game project (2001). http://www.gamasutra.com/features/20010926/luban_01.shtml

Mahadevan, B.: Business models for internet based e-commerce an anatomy. Calif. Manag. Rev. **42**(4), 7–9 (2000)

Moule, J.: Killer UX Design. SitePoint Pty. Ltd., Melbourne (2012)

McNamara N., Kirakowsk, J.: Functionality, Usability, and User Experience: Three Areas of Concern (2006)

Nylen, D., Holmström, J.: Digital innovation strategy: a framework for diagnosing and improving digital product and service innovation. Bus. Horiz. **58**(1), 58–59 (2015) (2019)

Polzin, F., Sanders, M., Stavlöt, U.: Do investors and entrepreneurs match? Evidence from The Netherlands and Sweden. Technol. Forecast. Soc. Change **127**, 112–126 (2018)

Porter, M.: Competitive Strategy. Free Press, New York (1980)

Purdy, G.: ISO 31000:2009 - setting a new standard for risk management. Risk Anal. **30**(6), 881–886 (2010). https://doi.org/10.1111/j.1539-6924.2010.01442.x. Accessed 17 July 2018

Reymen, I., et al.: A domain-independent descriptive design model and its application to structured reflection on design processes. Res. Eng. Des. **16**, 147–173 (2006). https://doi.org/10.1007/s00163-006-0011-9

Skelly, T., Pausch, R., Gold, R., Thiel, D.: What HCI designers can learn from video game designers. In: Conference Companion, Boston, Massachusetts, USA (1994)

Wysocki, R.K.: Effective Project Management: Traditional, Agile, Extreme, 5 edn. Wiley, Hoboken (2009)

PWC: Industry 4.0: Building the digital enterprise. 2016 Global Industry 4.0 Survey (2016)

Zhang, H.: Two schools of risk analysis: a review of past research on project risk. Proj. Manag. J. **42**(4), 5–18 (2011)

eSports: How Do Video Game Aspects Define Competitive Gaming Streams and Spectatorship

Eulerson Rodrigues[1,3] and Ernesto Filgueiras[1,2,3(✉)]

[1] University of Beira Interior, Covilhã, Portugal
eulerson.pedro@gmail.com, ernestovf@gmail.com
[2] CIAUD - Research Centre for Architecture, Urbanism and Design, Lisbon, Portugal
[3] Communication Laboratory – LabCom, University of Beira Interior, Covilhã, Portugal

Abstract. On the last decade, videogames streams have reached incredible numbers and are becoming more important every day. With the advancements of the internet, videogames are no longer local and can be played by people in different places as long as there is an internet connection between them. In this field, we have seen the recent innovations in videogames, especially in the so-called eSports category, with the growing adherence of fans worldwide and several events of great magnitude. In this study, we analysed and selected eSports aspects based on the related literature and videogame development specialists. The selected aspects are Objectives and Rules, Competitiveness, Interface Information, Visual Identification in Players and Teams, Stream Content and Communication Groups. Through a social network (LinkedIn), indie videogame developers were consulted (n = 11), thus answering 10 questions about how the above aspects should be addressed, and whether changes should be made to improve videogames in a general context. We found out that the presentation of the objectives and rules of the game may need changes across different game genres and developers **may use** competitiveness to entertain players and spectators. About interfaces, customizable and increase the viewer's experience is crucial to keep differences between playing and watching screens. The use of external groups and media is important to improve the communication between viewers, players and developers, as the use of visual elements can be useful to create marketing identities with customers.

Keywords: eSports · Game developer strategy · Stream content · eSports spectator behaviour · Player's interfaces

1 Introduction

Digital games evolve and change every year. Nowadays, games are no longer exclusive object of the fans as they became part of the lives of people who come from the most different contexts. Families play and watch together, friends compete with each other, as do all types of people regardless of their social or cultural context. Taking into

A. Marcus and E. Rosenzweig (Eds.): HCII 2020, LNCS 12201, pp. 506–516, 2020.
https://doi.org/10.1007/978-3-030-49760-6_36

account that games formerly had few tools that encouraged disputes, what we see today are scenarios completely focused at the competitive public. If before we ran rankings and lists to know who were the best players in the neighbourhood or the city, nowadays we can access dedicated websites that expose as real heroes players who stand out in their area, making them celebrities known worldwide. In this study, we will focus on competitive multiplayer online games, which are the base of the electronic sports (also known as eSports).

There are recent studies that focus on improving eSports streams in order to retain spectators or attract new public (Hamari and Sjöblom 2017; Pizzo et al. 2018). Some discuss about general video game aspects, which are useful to the eSports scenario, such as escapism, virtual world association and physicality (Weiss and Schiele 2013). Other authors aim the motivation for consume and the competitiveness that lead players and spectators to have fun while playing video games (Kaye 2012).

In addition, there is also extensive discussion about whether or not eSports are part of the sports world. Hamari and Sjöblom (2017), Lee and Schoenstedt (2011) and Pizzo et al. (2018) use the consumption motivation of sports and eSports viewers as research point, thus searching for differences and similarities between the areas.

Some authors try a more marketable approach to the study of eSports, using the customers (players and spectators) as focus. These studies include the involvement and participation of developer teams in the final product, trying to find the level of attention given to users, the creation and maintenance of tournaments, players and teams sponsorships, tournament and event broadcasts, and athletes who are also streamers (Johnson and Woodcock 2019; Sjöblom and Hamari 2017; Sjöblom et al. 2017; Wulf et al. 2018).

The preference in choosing players and spectators as the focus of this study is due to their importance the area as they are responsible for the viability of economic activities. This significance is shown in the number of individuals attending events and buying merchandising products and the great number of eSports athletes that compete on recent tournaments.

The main propose of this paper is to identify eSports aspects that need to be improved in order to attract more consumers and increase the experience of those who already spend time watching eSports streams.

2 Literature Review

2.1 Videogames as Competitive Sports

Beck and Bosshart (2003), argue that sports activities were developed along with the human race. Hunters and collectors had to improve their mental and motor skills in order to get more food, protect themselves and gather other resources to survive on dangerous environments. Those skills are used nowadays in sports competitions, such as athletics, fighting or swimming.

There are some key concepts that may be used to define sports, as stated by McKibbin (2011). According to the author, excellence concepts described as discipline, organization and competition dominate sports and are used by people who practice physical activities. On the other hand, creativity, freedom and spontaneity are aspects related to people who seek recreational and fun activities. Sports athletes use competition as motive to improve their performance throughout the practice. To exemplify this, we can say that there is a difference between running for pure pleasure and running on a field in order to reduce the time spent on each lap.

In order to define videogames, we can use Esposito (2005) concepts that involve game, interactivity and narrative. Putting together the playful part of the activity, the player-machine interactions and a storytelling that presents the world and characters to anyone who is playing or watching, we have a raw definition of what a videogame is. Therefore, by combining sports concepts with videogame concepts, we can get what would be an early definition of eSports.

Many sports elements are nowadays a part of the videogames world. As mentioned by Pizzo *et al.* (2018), those concepts involve rounds/turn based activities, score keeping, field rules, professional players and teams, managers, organized leagues, international competitions and events, high value contracts and student scholarships. According to Funk *et al.* (2018), to categorize a game as eSports, developers must implement a set of rules and enforce their fulfilment by the players. Therefore, the outcomes of a match must clearly identify winners and losers.

2.2 Competitiveness as Consumption Motive

From the beginning, videogames have sought to promote conflict during their gameplay, either in a player-machine relation or between players, and it allows game designers to use these conflicts to force the players and groups to chance their strategies, thus becoming a more cooperative or more competitive environment, as maintained by Vegt *et al.* (2016).

To Kaye (2012), competitiveness is an essential part of sports games, and this aspect can be appealing to players and viewers interested in their content. For Weiss and Schiele (2013), competition encourages eSports players to find teams so they can also compete internally; showing that while competitive virtual worlds are a source of competition, competition itself leads players to seek competitive virtual worlds.

2.3 Spectator's and Player's Interfaces

An important part of videogames is the interface. The main purpose of an interface is to connect the player with his or her avatar on the digital world. According to Ruch (2010), the usage of heads-up display (also known as HUD) makes the game playable while trying not to interfere with the players actions, even though sometimes the amount of information that is being displayed on the screen can be distractive.

The interface can also be informative to the player about possible functions, such as showing a door that can be opened, a tool that can be picked up, or a dead body that can be looted. As stated by Ruch (2010) the interface also transforms the player input into codes, so the game can understand it as an action. The author also mentions two other uses of the interface: the first one is showing the characters status, such as health and mana points, weapon status, ammunition and available abilities and skills. The second one is the minimap, which is used as a highly technological GPS to inform the player of his current position in the game world.

Even though the interface has such high importance to videogames, it is often left aside by games developers, even on eSports that has narrators/commenters constantly using interface information to communicate statistics and data to the audience. Sher *et al.* (2018) on their research, studied 20 popular eSports games and their spectator mode, as they show that different games have problems not only related to the interface but also to the spectator mode in the game client, and that those problems may disturb the user experience. To summarize those problems, they point out the lack of clear indication on how to spectate games, where you simply cannot find any option that leads to the spectator mode from a menu or social interface. Limited control and information is also mentioned, which means that the spectator sometimes does not have total control of the selected camera, and in the rare cases that this option is available, it is hard to be used. The information shown often does not provide additional content to who is watching in terms of statistical information, and sometimes HUD items overlaps with other essential elements.

2.4   Stream Content

There are recent studies that discuss about knowledge acquisition while watching eSports. It means that one may learn about tactics, tools and other gameplay related activities during a stream (Hamari and Sjöblom, 2017; Pizzo *et al.* 2018). To Hamari and Sjöblom, knowledge acquisition is one of the main reasons for eSports consumption. On their study, they also point that eSports developers should invest more time and money to develop better spectator interfaces (also pointed by Sher *et al.* 2018), thus making easier for newcomers and unexperienced players to understand what is going on during different game stages.

To Pizzo *et al.* (2018), the skill of athletes in eSports is an even bigger consumption motive then on traditional sports. They discuss that the appreciation of the eSports players skills increase event attendance, while Seo and Jung (2016) argue that watching eSports requires some skills and competencies from the spectators. To summarize that, they say that a basic comprehension of how the game works is important to who is watching, and this may explain why many eSports spectators are also game players (see also: Ditmarsch 2013, p. 21);

2.5   Stream and Social Communication

The most diverse public with different kind of objectives use streaming platforms. Wulf *et al.* (2018) define Twitch[1] as a sportscast, social network, videogame and teaching video platform. According to the authors, Twitch users may find streamers who best suit their interests, doing a bunch of activities such as playing for entertainment, showing off in-game skills, or chatting/cooperating with their audience. As motives for

---

[1] Twitch is a video live streaming service operated by Twitch Interactive, a subsidiary of Amazon (twitch.tv).

streams consumption, the authors list membership, influence, need fulfillment and emotional connection to others.

Sjöblom and Hamari (2017), emphasize the social aspects presents on streaming. On their study, they discuss that platform developers, game developers and streamers should focus on increasing the social fulfillment of the spectators, thus attracting more viewers and subscribers, in order to increase the revenue. The social aspect is currently mainly represented on those platforms by chat tools. By using the chat, users can sent text messages that are shown to everyone who is watching at the moment plus the streamer himself. Wulf *et al.* (2018) point out that the communication between users can be used to discuss about what they are watching, share knowledge and impressions, and even give hints or advice to the streamer.

3   Methodology

Based on the discussed literature, we selected 6 videogame aspects that demonstrated potential interaction between the game and players or spectators. These aspects might be useful to help us understand how experts contemplate those ideas when developing a game (Table 1).

Table 1. Selected videogame aspects and the study objectives.

Videogame aspects	Study objectives
Objectives and rules	Understand how developers can leverage the creation and presentation of these aspects for the benefit of eSports streams
Competitiveness	Understand how viewers and supporters consume competitiveness in eSports and how this aspect can be used to attract more players and spectators
Interface information	Understand how the amount of interface information can turn the stream content into a more enjoyable experience for players and spectators
Visual identification in players and teams	Understand how players and spectators absorb visual identification elements and create marketing identities with customers
Stream content	Increase spectator's knowledge acquirement through streams and external media consumption
Communication groups	Understand the utility and increase outreach to communication groups by improving communication between players, spectators and videogame developers

In total, 11 videogame developers formed an expert panel. We asked experts to answer (through an open questionnaire) 8 questions about videogame development and players/spectator interactions with the game.

Through a business and job-oriented social network (Linkedin), the authors contacted several game developers in search of potential participants. For the final group composition, we adopted two selection *criteria*: professionals must have at least 3 years of experience on the videogame development area and must have developed at least one competitive videogame during this time. Questionnaires were distributed via e-mail between July and August 2019. Due to restrictions imposed by some companies that have games under development, we removed participants' names and replaced them with identifying numbers (Table 2).

Table 2. Expert panel functions and experience as game developers.

Specialist	Function	Experience	Relevant genres
#1	Game Designer	9 years	Educational
#2	Programmer	4 years	Puzzle
#3	Developer	3 years	Adventure
#4	Game Designer	7 years	Educational
#5	Creative Director	8 years	Puzzle
#6	Producer	3 years	RPG
#7	Programmer	14 years	Roguelike
#8	Developer	4 years	Platform
#9	Professor	8 years	Educational
#10	Level Designer	8 years	MOBA
#11	Game Designer	3 years	Adventure

As we had some issues trying to get a sufficient number of participants, we decided to change the second *criterion* by removing "competitive" from the requirements, which resulted in "having developed at least one videogame during this time".

Although the lack of competitive videogame developers was an obstacle to the study, we decided to continue the research by focusing on previous mentioned aspects of videogames such as objectives and rules, interface information, player and team visual identification, stream content and communication groups. These aspects are also presented in various non-competitive genres and may be used on our research. The expert panel was instructed to respond according to their experience in the videogame development area (Table 3).

Table 3. Study phases and activities.

Phase	Researchers activities	Experts activities
Phase 1 – Preparation	• Select related videogame aspects • Contact available game developers to compose the panel • Preparation of the first questionnaire	• Answer the first questionnaire
Phase 2 – Results	• Analysis of experts' answers • Results discussion and presentation	

4 Results

Expert panel opinions were related to predefined topics for response analysis. The creation of the topics was based on the previously discussed videogame aspects and adapted to the expert panel (Table 4).

Table 4. Predefined topics and expert panel opinion.

Predefined topics (game aspects)	Topic description	Expert panel agreement (%)
Q1 - How should the game objectives be set (i.e.: Destroy all enemies.)?		
Introducing game objectives	Inform in a direct and clear way	41.2%
	Inform through tutorials	17.6%
	Inform during gameplay	41.2%
Q2 - How should the game rules be set (i.e.: Each team should consist of 5 units.)?		
Introducing game rules	Inform in a direct and clear way	20.0%
	Inform through tutorials	33.3%
	Inform during gameplay	46.7%
Q3 - Can competitiveness be used to attract new viewers and players?		
Using competition as consume motivation	It is possible	80.0%
	It is NOT possible	0.0%
	It is possible, but only partially	20.0%
Q4 - How the amount of information displayed on the interface should be managed?		
Defining information to be displayed on the interface	Minimalist interface	61.5%
	Detailed interface	7.7%
	Merged interface	30.8%
Q5 - Can a player acquire knowledge about the game by watching matches?		
Knowledge acquisition through consumption	It is possible	90.0%
	It is NOT possible	0.0%
	It is possible, but only partially	10.0%
Q6 - How other media (blogs, forums) may be used as external content?		
Use of external media	Use to inform about the game	83.3%
	Use it to inform about the company	8.3%
	No functionality/limited functionality	8.3%
Q7 - What is the use of communication groups?		
Use of communication groups	Information exchange between players	23.5%
	Information exchange between devs and players	64.7%
	Create social groups between players	11.8%
Q8 - What is the impact of using identifying elements on teams/players?		
Use of visual identity elements	Get teams recognized	22.2%
	Get players recognized	66.7%
	No functionality	11.1%

4.1 Introducing Game Objectives and Rules

The expert opinion are divided while discussing the introduction of objectives. In the question, the example used to describe such activity was "destroy all enemies". Passing simple and clear information summarizes the opinion of 41.2% of experts, and the same percentage agrees to introduce those aspects during gameplay. Other experts demonstrate a preference for using tutorials.

Experts #6 and #10 argue that some games use the narrative to introduce the objectives, but as narrative is often eclipsed by the competition on eSports, maybe we need to find more direct forms to introduce these objectives, so spectators can situate themselves in a faster and easier way, as stated by expert #4.

When talking about rules (i.e.: each team have a maximum of 5 units), 46.7% of the experts agree that rules should be introduced during gameplay, while 33.3% prefer using tutorials and 20% chose a simple but direct approach.

Also, expert #1 reminds us that some games rules (i.e. sports games, such as FIFA or NBA) are common knowledge (depending on the local culture), so the players/spectators background should be taken into consideration. Another thing to keep in mind is that eSports are constantly receiving updates that may change the rules (Witkowski and Manning 2017), thus making it difficult for people who have been away for a while.

4.2 Using Competition as Consume Motivation

The use of competitiveness as a motivation for consumption is almost unanimous among experts. While 80% agree that implementing competition has a great appeal to customers, 20% argue that some preventive actions must be taken while preparing competitive scenarios.

Experts #3 and #10 suggest the implementation of competitive game modes on non-competitive games. Therefore, to expert #3, rankings can boost competitiveness, even on game modes that players do not compete directly.

4.3 Defining Information to Be Displayed on the Interface

A big percentage (61.5%) of the experts agree that the interface should be minimal, and show only important information. We point out that 30.8% of the experts defend a merged, customizable interface that let the user choose, edit and combine elements in order to have something personal.

Said that, we argue that the displayed information on the interface of a videogame should be carefully controlled and only informational data of the utmost importance should be shown to viewers. Six different experts stressed the importance of different interfaces for players and spectators, as the purpose and form of consumption are different. By reducing the amount of information available in the interface, we can notice an approximation of eSports with Sports, where the information is carefully measured so as not to interfere with the viewer's immersion.

4.4   Knowledge Acquisition Through Consumption

Another topic that was almost unanimous among the panel. A total of 90% of the experts agree that is possible to learn about game content during gameplay, but 10% agree that watching a game can only take the player to a certain point, and to get beyond that, a deeper research is needed.

4.5   Use of External Media and Communication Groups

About external media, the experts seem to agree (83.3%) that it can be useful to inform players about the game content. The two other options had 8.3% agreement each, the first one being to inform players about the company or developer group, and the second one being no utility at all.

This point of view may change when we talk about communication groups. Most experts concur that these groups may be used to exchange information between players and developers, they also include discussions about updates feedback and new ideas.

Using external media may be the solution to narrative problems in competitive videogames. Some games like Dota 2, League of Legends already post extra content on their blogs, forums or different contexts. By doing that, little narrative is left inside the game. One of the problems, however, is that there is a possibility that this content is difficult for players to access, which may require more disclosure from developers.

Keeping in touch with spectators is also present in Sports, with entities such as FIFA and the NBA maintaining active social networking accounts on Facebook and Twitter. In addition, six experts highlighted the identification of bugs and cheats within the information exchange with players/viewers.

4.6   Use of Visual Identity Elements

Using identification elements may turn players (66.7%) and teams (22.2%) into well-known parts of the scene, as stated the experts. Only 11.1% disagree with those elements usage.

These identification elements may include medals, rankings, insignia, flags and other visual elements present in the player/team profile. Experts #2 and #11 emphasize that these elements should be cumulative, while experts #5 and #10 emphasize the importance of self-identity for each user, including items such as nationality flags and preferences within the videogame.

5   Conclusion

This study showed us that even though some of the presented aspects are carefully treated on commercial success games, some of those aspects need to be changed in order to improve spectatorship on the eSports scene.

Regarding the objectives, we argue that some common ways of presenting the objectives of the videogame may be efficient in non-competitive videogames, but may be inefficient in eSports. This can be detrimental since unlike sports, not all video games have goals that are easy to understand.

Some video games tutorials may not be of interest of the spectator, or may be inaccessible due to third party broadcasts (such as streams or gameplay videos).

A viewer may not be interested in watching or may not have access to the game tutorial, especially if we consider third party broadcasts (streams or gameplay videos, for example). Also, explaining the goals at the start of the match (albeit simply and clearly) can be ineffective in eSports where there is a possibility for the match to last long periods of time, as new spectators arrive or current spectators may forget if there are no updates on the displayed information.

A possible solution would be to switch between display methods, with simple instructions at the start of matches, reminders during the match, and the use of external media as a tutorial and narrative insertion (introduction videos, for example).

Meanwhile, having a clean interface may be useful to spectators, probably because they are used to Sports broadcasts. As stated by Sher *et al.* (2018), many videogames have two interfaces: the first one being designed for players while the second one focus on spectators, but it may be interesting to open the possibility of customizing the interface so that spectators can hide or show items according to their own interests.

Profile customization is also an important point. Whether for famous player identification, skill level or regionalism, the profile is the identity of the player and the spectator, and we need to let each individual express themselves in their own way. In addition, associating spectators with brands and organizations is a strong aspect of sports, showing marketing identities are important when it comes to retaining customers.

We also emphasize the importance of communication groups, both between players and spectators as well as spectators and developers. While players and spectators exchange information, stories and videogame content with each other, developers can benefit from this communication, just as sports organizations use social networks and other media to get their spectators opinion.

This study will be continued. However, the next research aspects will discuss less about developers and more about players and viewers, especially issues related to the emotions and behaviours of these individuals within the scope of eSports.

References

Beck, D., Bosshart, L.: Sports and media. Commun. Res. Trends **22**(4) (2003)

Esposito, N.: A short and simple definition of what a videogame is (2005)

Funk, D.C., Mahony, D.F., Nakazawa, M., Hirakawa, S.: Development of the sport interest inventory (SII): implications for measuring unique consumer motives at team sporting events. Int. J. Sports Mark. Sponsorship **3**(3), 38–63 (2001)

Hamari, J., Sjöblom, M.: What is eSports and why do people watch it? Internet Res. **27**(2), 211–232 (2017)

Johnson, M.R., Woodcock, J.: 'It's like the gold rush': the lives and careers of professional video game streamers on Twitch. tv. Inf. Commun. Soc. **22**(3), 336–351 (2019)

Kaye, L.K.: Motivations, experiences and outcomes of playing videogames. Ph.D. thesis, University of Central Lancashire (2012)

Lee, D., Schoenstedt, L.J.: Comparison of eSports and traditional sports consumption motives. ICHPER-SD J. Res. **6**(2), 39–44 (2011)

McKibbin, R.: Sports history: status, definitions and meanings. Sport Hist. **31**(2), 167–174 (2011)

Pizzo, A.D., Na, S., Baker, B.J., Lee, M.A., Kim, D., Funk, D.C.: eSport vs. sport: a comparison of spectator motives. Sport Mark. Q. **27**(2) (2018)

Ruch, A.W.: Videogame interface: artefacts and tropes. In: Videogame Cultures and the Future of Interactive Entertainment Global Conference (2010)

Seo, Y., Jung, S.U.: Beyond solitary play in computer games: the social practices of eSports. J. Consum. Cult. **16**(3), 635–655 (2016)

Sher, S.T.H., Kempe-Cook, L., Cordova, E.N: A Better Lens: Refining Esports Spectator Modes (2018)

Sjöblom, M., Hamari, J.: Why do people watch others play video games? An empirical study on the motivations of Twitch users. Comput. Hum. Behav. **75**, 985–996 (2017)

Sjöblom, M., Törhönen, M., Hamari, J., Macey, J.: Content structure is king: an empirical study on gratifications, game genres and content type on Twitch. Comput. Hum. Behav. **73**, 161–171 (2017)

van Ditmarsch, J.L.: Video games as a spectator sport. Master's thesis, MA New Media & Digital Culture, Utrecht University (2013)

Vegt, N., Visch, V., Vermeeren, A., de Ridder, H.: Player experiences and behaviours in a multiplayer game: designing game rules to change interdependent behaviour. Int. J. Serious Games **3**(4) (2016)

Weiss, T., Schiele, S.: Virtual worlds in competitive contexts: analyzing eSports consumer needs. Electron. Mark. **23**(4), 307–316 (2013)

Witkowski, E., Manning, J.: Playing with (out) power: negotiated conventions of high performance networked play practices. In: Digital Games Research Association Conference, pp. 1–18 (2017)

Wulf, T., Schneider, F.M., Beckert, S.: Watching players: an exploration of media enjoyment on Twitch. Games Cult. (2018)

Spectator Experience Design for AR Sport Events from a Service Design Perspective – Using HADO as an Example

Pei-Ling Shih[1]([⊠]), Hsien-Hui Tang[1], and Shu-Yi Chen[2]

[1] National Taiwan University of Science and Technology, Taipei, Taiwan
{ml07l0902,drhhtang}@gapps.ntust.edu.tw
[2] Ming Chuan University, Taipei, Taiwan

Abstract. Augmented reality (AR) has been used to improve spectator experience in traditional sport events. For the first AR sport in the world, Meleap's HADO, the discussion of spectator experience is lacking. To understand the problems in the spectator experience of AR sports, we have conducted a two-phase investigation into HADO match. The first phase investigated HADO's live sports events, while the second phase examined their online sports events. We conducted an integrated analysis based on the quantitative and qualitative results to determine how to optimize HADO's spectator experience. To help designers and researchers of AR sports in the future, we summarized challenges and issues found in spectator experience within integrated AR sport. Moreover, six interdisciplinary designers were invited to a co-creation workshop to identify related design concepts. These concepts were further provided to and discussed with stakeholders from Meleap. Finally, we suggested building digital channel tools in AR sports events to connect online and offline spectator. or even establish a link between the event and the spectator for better user experience.

Keywords: Augmented reality · Service design · User experience design · Co-creation · Spectator experience

1 Introduction

The development of augmented reality (AR) has brought numerous innovative applications to the sports industry, creating brand new user experience designs for those participating in or watching the games. Most cases in the past tried to change the way viewers watching traditional sport, but few touched the topics of integrating AR within sport events. Needless to say, for the first AR sport in the world, Meleap's HADO, the discussion of spectator experience is lacking. This study explored these issues from principles of service design, including user-centered perspective, co-creative process, and holistic evidencing and sequencing (Stickdorn and Schneider 2013). With the user-centered principle—this study focused on spectator's experience of both online and offline live event, also explored the pain points and design opportunities. The research process is based on a multidisciplinary, co-creation spirit and maintained communications with Meleap and stakeholders to ensure aligned objectives.

© Springer Nature Switzerland AG 2020
A. Marcus and E. Rosenzweig (Eds.): HCII 2020, LNCS 12201, pp. 517–531, 2020.
https://doi.org/10.1007/978-3-030-49760-6_37

The case chosen is HADO from Meleap, a Japanese startup that develops AR games. Meleap created Techno-Sports, which combined AR with traditional sports, and HADO became the first AR sport in the world. One of the researchers is a designer from Meleap and has real experience playing HADO. Therefore, this is an action research. HADO was created to shape the competitive sport of the future. HADO is a 3-on-3 team sport that combines AR and dodgeball. In a HADO match, players can shoot energy balls and block the other team's attack with a shield. At the end of the match, the team with the higher scores wins. All the AR special effects are not visible to the naked eyes; the only way for the spectators to see the effects is by looking at the projector screen, where game footages are played with added effects (Fig. 1).

Fig. 1. How the spectator watches the game in the venue (left) versus what the game looks like on the projector screen and online (right).

2   Literature Review and Related Work

2.1   Augmented Reality and Its Applications to the Sports Industry

AR applications in the sports industry are divided into two categories: watching and participating. In terms of watching, AR has been widely adopted in sports broadcasting. Ericsson, for instance, introduced *Piero AR* in 2016, which allows broadcasters to overlay 3D graphics in real time during live studio productions and sports games. AR has changed the way people watch and participate in sports games; we are now officially in the "AR competitive sports era". In the past, AR was mostly used to improve the connection and interaction between the spectators and the events. However, there has not been enough discussion about the spectator experience within a traditional sports event combined with AR, indicating that there are still challenges to overcome when it comes to AR sports games' spectator experience, which also requires innovation.

2.2   Service Design

In the competitive service industry, products alone can no longer satisfy picky consumers (Pine and Gilmore 1998). Currently, academia and the industry do not share a definition for *service design*. Essentially, service design is a newly emerging design that adopts a holistic, multidisciplinary and integrative approach (Ho and Sung 2014).

By understanding the users and their backgrounds, service providers and social practice, then transforming such insight into the interactive development of evidence and the service system. Service design is also considered an explorative process to create new valuable relationships among different participants and develop and integrate proper design capability as its core competence (Kimbell 2011; Holmlid and Evenson 2008). The principles for service design include user-centered, co-creative, holistic, evidencing and sequencing (Stickdorn and Schneider 2013).

With the user-centered principle of service design and the assistance of a service design tool—customer journey map—this paper will focus on spectators' experience and explore its pain points and design opportunities. This research adopted the value of multidisciplinary and co-creation from service design, communicating with the Company to ensure consistent objectives.

3   A Discussion on Spectator Experience of HADO Matches

To understand the problems and flaws in the spectator experience of AR sports events from both physical and virtual perspectives, we have conducted a two-phase investigation into Meleap's HADO. The first phase investigated HADO's live sports events, including participating in the entire HADO Summer Cup event in Tokyo during August 2019. The second phase examined HADO's online sports events. Questionnaires and semi-structured interviews were conducted to obtain qualitative and quantitative data. These data then help pinpoint the factors that affect spectator experience, and at the same time give us a clear direction on how to optimize HADO's spectator experience effectively (Fig. 2).

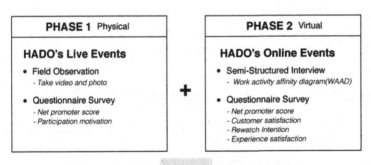

Fig. 2. Research process and methods

3.1   Discussion on the Issues in the Spectator Experience of HADO's Offline Live Event

One of the researchers participated in the entire 2019 HADO Summer Cup event in Tokyo during August 2019. The content and procedures adopted in this research had previously approved by the company. We conducted questionnaires with the spectator at the game to obtain their feedback on their experience of the event. Finally, based on our field observation and the results from the questionnaires, we constructed a customer journey map to pinpoint the pain points and later explored design opportunities in the spectator experience.

3.2   1 Questionnaire Survey and Result

82 questionnaires were collected and the results were compiled and presented in Fig. 3. The results show that most of the spectator attended the event out of curiosity toward AR sport events, and that approximately 60% of them attended the event for the first time. Since they had just learned about the game, they had to observe the game to understand its format. In addition, most spectator members pointed out that having to watch the game on a projector screen to see the AR effects is the part that needs to be improved the most. The overall NPS score of 10 points is a clear indicator that the current spectator experience does need to be improved.

Question	Results
NPS Score	NPS 10
Where did you hear about the event?	**70%** by referral. The rest either have participated in HADO events before or heard about it on the social media.
Why did you come to see the event?	Most of them came to the event out of the curiosity for AR sports events.
Have you seen or participated in a HADO event?	Approximately **60%** of them came to see the game for the first time. **30%** of them has played and watched HADO before. **10%** of them has never played HADO but has been to an event before.
Past HADO experience	Only **30%** of the audience has experienced HADO before.
Understanding of the format	**50%** learned about the format by watching; **20%** by reading the event brochure and the last **30%** already knew about the format in advance.
What are the improvements you would like to see about this event?	Most of the respondents pointed out that having to **watch the game on the projector screen** needs to be addressed. Other parts that need to be improved are: event schedule, performances, activities and merchandise store.

Fig. 3. Survey results from offline live event spectator

The spectator was divided into different groups based on the feedback from the survey (having played or participated in HADO events), combined with the respective NPS. The result is shown in Fig. 4. The first quadrant is the target spectator of this event—those who have never played HADO, with this event being their first. These accounted for more than half of the respondents and yet only had an NPS of 4, which is less than ideal, and a clear indicator that spectator experience needs to be optimized. The third quadrant shows the spectator who had played and participated in HADO events before, and the number of respondents is second only to the target spectator.

However, this group is more willing to recommend HADO events to others. It is plausible that spectators may be more willing to recommend HADO events if they have played HADO themselves.

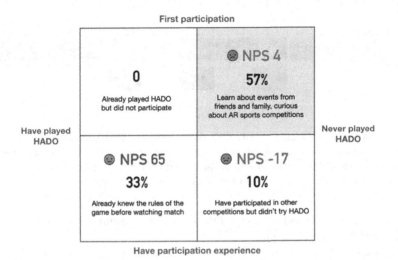

Fig. 4. HADO event live spectator group analysis

3.3 2 Customer Journey Map

A customer journey map visualizes different stages of a user's experience or interaction with a product or service, allowing each detail of the journey to be reviewed. The map shows a customer's characteristics, emotional responses and problems while interacting with the product or service; this information can be reviewed and used to improve user experience (Ho and Sung 2014). Based on the abovementioned field observation and insights from the survey, a customer journey map was constructed and illustrated in Fig. 5. The map details the pain points of the spectator before, during and after watching the event.

From the emotional lines in the customer journey map, we can perceive that sspectator's unpleasantness occurs when they entering the venue, watching game through the projector screen, waiting for the game to begin. However, these problems are independent events. We found that before watching the game, the spectator felt interested and excited about the AR sport event at first, this sense of surprise and excitement would reduce as watching time went by. Whether it's a lack of understanding about the game or the way of watch the projection screen, etc., it causes the overall experience of watching the game to be even more dull. Based on the above discussions and findings, this study summarized how the service would be optimized in the following 3 points:

1. Lack of understanding of the game and ruleset before watching the event: As most spectator members had never played HADO before, it was difficult for them to

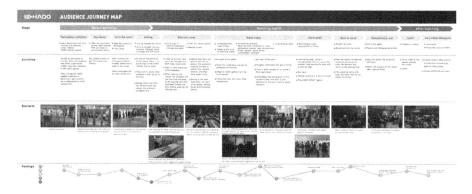

Fig. 5. Customer journey map of a HADO event, which includes users' actions, interaction scenarios, emotions, pain points, touchpoints and stakeholders before, during and after watching the game, presents a clear picture and the problems and issues in the spectator experience. (Visit the following link for a larger version of the CJM: https://reurl.cc/qD4zbN)

understand the skill and difficulty of the game, not to mention imagining a player's perspective with AR goggles on.

2. User experience issues resulting from the way the game is watched: Spectator members who had never been to an AR sports event became very excited at the beginning of the event. However, the excitement gradually faded as time went on, especially when people experiencing frustration while watching the game. The greatest pain point in watching the game was that the spectator had to look up at the screen to see what was happening in the game, even though the players were playing right in front of them.

3. Lack of interaction during the game: there was no interaction among the spectator members or between the spectator and the players during the game, which meant that the sense of engagement might be absent while the audience was watching the game.

3.4 Discussion on the Issues of Spectator Experience in HADO's Online Event

The survey conducted at the physical event provided the researchers with a certain level of understanding of the issues within spectator experience in HADO events. Afterwards, the focus shifted to the live streaming content of the 2019 HADO Summer Cup. We used questionnaires and semi-structured interviews to obtain both qualitative and quantitative data, so as to discover the factors that truly affect spectator experience, in the hope of finding a clear direction on how to optimize HADO's spectator experience effectively.

Investigation Process

Since HADO combines e-sports and traditional sports, the researchers would like the interviewees to have at least one year of experience of watching sports or e-sports online. A total of 29 interviewees were interviewed.

First, we tried to understand the interviewees' past experiences in watching HADO events, and asked them about their understanding of AR and their imagination, as well as expectations towards AR sports events. Next, we introduced the basic game details and rules of HADO to the interviewees. All the provided information is according to official information from HADO. Then we conducted interviews to discuss their opinions and expectations towards HADO events. Lastly, we asked the interviewees to watch 2019 HADO Summer Cup online to simulate a real situation of watching an actual game and then asked them to fill out a questionnaire. Once completed, we continued the interviews, in which we provided them with video clips taken directly from the game venue and solicited their opinions to obtain more feedback on watching the game in person, in addition to their online spectator experience (Fig. 6).

Fig. 6. Interviewees watching the event online and getting interviewed.

Contextual Analysis

In the second phase investigation, we had interviews with spectators to explore problems in game watching experience. In addition, it was a simulation of watching the game online, and the process at this stage was relatively simple, a customer journey map of online spectator wasn't really necessary. Contextual analysis was adopted in the process of interpreting, consolidating and communicating a user's work activity data (Beyer and Holtzblatt 1998). In this study, the interviews were transcribed, and the transcription was checked for correctness before being encoded. During the analysis process, the field notes and transcription were compiled into a WAAD (work activity affinity diagram) to discover the problem categories, insights and opportunities. The results were further sorted according to different stages in game watching, as shown in Fig. 7.

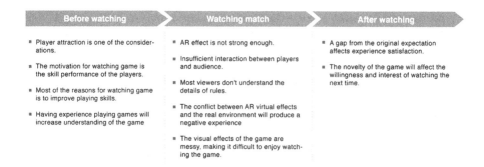

Before watching	Watching match	After watching
• Player attraction is one of the considerations. • The motivation for watching game is the skill performance of the players. • Most of the reasons for watching game is to improve playing skills. • Having experience playing games will increase understanding of the game	• AR effect is not strong enough. • Insufficient interaction between players and audience. • Most viewers don't understand the details of rules. • The conflict between AR virtual effects and the real environment will produce a negative experience • The visual effects of the game are messy, making it difficult to enjoy watching the game.	• A gap from the original expectation affects experience satisfaction. • The novelty of the game will affect the willingness and interest of watching the next time.

Fig. 7. Online spectator's WAAD result.

Questionnaires and Quantitative Analysis Results

The questionnaires for the satisfaction toward the HADO's online event in this study sought for customer loyalty indicators, experience satisfaction and other factors that interviewees believed were crucial to their spectator experience. The results from the questionnaires were analyzed and compiled using the slope of linear regression to understand the correlation between loyalty indicators, experience satisfaction and the driving factors. With the exception of NPS, the questions in the questionnaire all used the Likert scale (Fig. 8).

Loyalty Indicators		Driving Factors	Experience Satisfaction	
Item	Average satisfaction	First key sort order R^2 0.56	Item	Average Agreement
• Rewatch Intension	3.1	→ O	R^2 0.51 Augmented Reality Effect	3.4
• Coustomer Satisfaction	3.4	→ X Game Excitement Average satisfaction 3.5	R^2 0.49 Expectations of playing HADO	4.3
• Net Promoter Score	-34	→ X	R^2 0.43 Sight and Sound Effects	3.2
		Linear Regression Linear Regression		

Fig. 8. Questionnaires and quantitative analysis result.

The result shows a - 34 of overall NPS, average 3.4 in overall customer satisfaction and an average 3.1 in rewatch intention, a clear indicator that customer loyalty needs to be improved. The interviewees considered game excitement as the most important driving factor, for which HADO scored a mediocre 3.5. The slope in linear regression was used to find the correlation between customer loyalty indicators, experience satisfaction and driving factor satisfaction. We found that enhancing game excitement will effectively boost the spectator's rewatch intention. To understand factors that affect game excitement satisfaction, we analyzed game excitement and game watching satisfaction and discovered the three aspects with the highest correlation to game excitement: expectation of playing HADO, sight and sound effects, and augmented reality effect. Optimizing these three factors will elevate the spectator's satisfaction toward game excitement, which will in turn affect rewatch intention.

4   Results from the Survey of HADO

4.1   Problem of Spectator Experience of HADO Matches

After comparing the questionnaires and contextual analysis of both live and online HADO events, we verified that the issues are consistent. By combining qualitative and quantitative data, we were able to pinpoint the factors that truly affect spectator experience, with a clear direction on how and where to allocate resources to effectively improve and meet users' expectations.

A lack of understanding of the game rules and without prior HADO experience resulted in poor understanding of the game, which was the main issue for the spectator before watching. Therefore, it is necessary to help the spectators to understand the game. However, HADO cannot be played at home; we can only play it at some of the HADO stores. Thus, it is suggested that Meleap should utilize other contact points (website, mobile app, etc.) to allow users to get a glimpse of what it is like to play HADO, which will help them understand the game better while watching.

AR is a technology that provides unique visual experience; however, some spectator members believed that the AR effects in the game, as well as the light and sound effects, were not impressive enough, and deteriorated their satisfaction of in-game excitement. Moreover, we found that a lack of interaction during the game left so most spectators without memorable or interesting experience.

4.2   Challenges and Issues of AR Spectator Experience

Although we pointed out the problem of lacking understanding of the game rules in the previous discussing on HADO, it's actually a problem that all games will face. Therefore, it won't be discussed in this section. Based on the discussions and analysis on the issues of spectator experience in HADO events, this study categorized the challenges and problems of AR spectator experience into two aspects: user expectation and AR characteristics. These can serve as reference for any future studies involving AR event spectator experience (Fig. 9).

Fig. 9. Challenges and issue in AR spectator experience.

1. Challenges and issues of AR spectator experience as a result of high user expectations: for most users, watching an AR sport event is a completely brand-new experience. They base their understanding of AR on the special effects they have

seen in animations, movies, anime and videogames—which have very sophisticated effects. Being used to such high-quality visual and sound effects, they have very high expectations and standards toward AR effects.

2. Issues and challenges from AR sports events: compared to traditional sports events, the biggest difference with AR sports events is that the special effects on balls or other objects can only be seen on screen. However, this combination of real and virtual worlds restricts the spectator's interaction with the players. In a traditional sports event, live spectator members can see the game with their own eyes, and the players can hear and respond when the spectator cheers for them. However, in an AR sports event, the players are in a mixed (virtual and real) environment once they put on AR goggles. Even though they can see the real environment, a wall still exists between them and the reality. This relegates the players and the spectator in two different environments with little to no connection or interaction.

5 Optimization Design Concept Developing

Based on the key problem of spectator experience of HADO that we found in previous stage. We further explored design strategies to optimize the experience of watching AR sports events and sought for the best solution by multidisciplinary co-creation. Co-creation is one of the foundations of Service Design and it's in the key position in the strategy for innovation. By including users, user experience designers, AR engineer and stakeholders, six participants with different backgrounds and roles as partners in ideation and design, we can ensure the creation of truly customer-centric new products and services that reflect the needs of each sides of stakeholders.

5.1 HADO Co-creation Workshop

The co-creation workshop for this study was held at Taiwan University of Science and Technology. Total of 6 cross-disciplinary members were invited to participate, including 3 designers with experience in user experience design, 1 user, 1 stakeholder from Meleap, 1 engineer who is working in the field of AR and VR (Table 1).

Table 1. Co-creation workshop participants

Gender	Occupation	Role in Co-Creation Workshop
Female	Service Designer	Designer with UX Design Experience
Female	Visual Designer	Designer with UX Design Experience
Female	Research Assistant	Designer with UX Design Experience
Male	Sr. Industrial Designer	Stakeholder
Male	Director of IP License Business	Spectator
Male	Manager of a VR company	Professional in AR and VR field

The host first introduced the background of the participating members and explained the purpose of the workshop. Because the participating members have a certain degree of understanding of the HADO competition, this activity only leads the participating members to quickly review the current status of the competition and refer to the brainstorming rules form IDEO. Subsequently, a brainstorming meeting for four design opportunities was launched. The four design opportunities were:

1. Helping the spectator understand the rules of the game, simulate the experience of playing HADO.
2. Enhancing the interaction between spectators and players during the game.
3. Diversified and customized ways of watching for the spectator. In addition to watching projection screens, providing other ways for the spectator to watch the game.
4. Optimizing the visual effects to meet users' expectations.

Before starting to think of ideas, each member has to speak out loud content of content cards to other members. The content card is a little card which is printed interviewee's feedback text. It's helpful to increase the sense of participation among participating members, rather than simply reading the text. it can deepen the members' understanding of the user's pain points or expectations.

After participating members understood the problems, design opportunities and feedback from research, every design opportunity that inspires innovation has 20 min to think and discuss. We prepared a model that can simulate the live venue of HADO, online and offline live event photos to stimulate participants to think and discuss the details of the operation of the idea. After the design solution is developed, members have 10 min to discuss and select the better solution (Fig. 10).

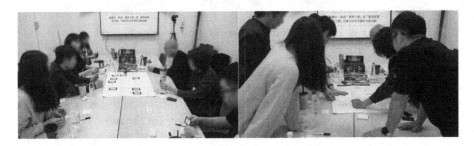

Fig. 10. HADO co-creation workshop, participants are discussing ideas.

5.2   Design Concept

Combined with the solutions selected by the co-creation workshop and the initial concept from researcher, this study proposes design concepts for optimizing HADO game watching experience and corresponding to online and offline scenario. We also have discussed these ideas with stakeholders from Meleap to ensure its feasibility and innovative. Selected design concepts are described as follows:

In order to solve the problem of lack of understanding of game rules and details, and provide opportunities to play HADO. Before watching the game, spectator learned about the game related information on the official HADO website, including the game introduction video, game rules introduction graphics. We suggested publishing a game watching application (App) and provide its download information on the HADO official website. In addition, we can add the page for downloading information and introduction of the App in the paper manual from HADO offline live event. This App Includes AR scanning function, spectator can find the scanned QR code introduced by the game rules on the official website of the HADO tournament for scanning. The information obtained after scanning can be divided into two types: 1. Introduction to gameplay rules animation, 2. Experience the game of HADO from the perspective of the first player (Fig. 11).

Fig. 11. Concept diagram of AR camera scan effect.

After the spectator has a certain understanding and interest in the event, they can go to the official website of HADO to participate in the voting activities of the team's uniform and establish an initial connection between the spectator and the players. Before the start of the competition, the introduction video of the rules will be played. And add a link card on YouTube live video, provide online viewers to link to the official website of HADO to review the rules of the game. When introducing the team at the beginning of the game, we recommend that players go to the spectator seat in live match event to interact with the spectator to enhance the spectator's impression and understanding of the players. The spectator seat of the live game is set with a lottery code. Spectator is drawn to challenge the champion team after match. It's increased the chance to experience playing HADO and the chance to contact with players. Moreover, to enhance the interactive between spectators and players during the watching game process, the functions of the App designed for the spectators contain the following:

1. Learn about game rules and information.
2. Provide spectator with a variety of game watching perspective to choose.

3. Spectators can vote to predict the winning team, and if the prediction is correct, they can accumulate points. Spectators with the highest accumulated points in this season's event can participate in the prize draw.
4. During the competition, a celebrity is placed as a masked player. Several tips about the celebrity are given on the spot. The spectator can guess, correct answering will accumulate points.
5. In each match, the spectator can choose one option to attack or support the team. Options are: support red team, support blue team, attack red team, attack blue team, attack both teams. The game lasts for 80 s, and spectator can vote between 40 and 50 s. The match will count the option to get the highest turnout in these 10 s. If a team has a high number of attacks, virtual obstacle will block the player during the game, such as a virtual snowball, barriers, etc. If a team gets a higher number of supports, it will get the highest intensity energy ball attack in the game. The significance of this interaction is to provide the influence that the spectator can involve the game.

In order to make the visual effects of HADO in the match meet the expectations of the spectator and helping them to understand the match information. We suggested optimizing the sound, light and visual effects of players in the game:

1. Adjust the player number in the game interface to the player's role, such as attacker, defender, etc.
2. Enhancing the effects of KO, such as adding cracks on the shield when it got hit, and when player is about to be knocked down, the player gradually becomes transparent, and appears again in the screen after resurrection.
3. Add sound effects when the player got K.O., and distinguish the sound settings according to the number of hit points.
4. Add the visual design of the players attacking skill and show it in the game interface to help spectator notice the great performance of players.
5. Enhance the visual design segmentation of the differences setting in parameter point.

In order to strengthen the connection between the spectator and HADO match and the discussion of the match. After watching the game, HADO official website provides endgame games for several key games of the season. Spectators can simulate different match results by choosing options, helping them to understand HADO gameplay and strengthen players' skills Identity. Furthermore, spectator can use the QR code picture which provided in the game manual and hold it in their hands for taking a photo. Through camera shooting from the App, the HADO elements such as energy ball or shield game appears. Live spectators can take picture with the photo wall in the venue square, online spectators can download QR code picture on HADO website and print them for selfies. This activity combined with HADO elements can be shared on social networking sites, increasing the continuity and topicality of discussions on the event (Fig. 12).

Fig. 12. Concept diagram of AR photoshoot effect.

5.3   Discussion of Design Concept

Through the creative ideas of the co-creation workshop, and the discussion of design solutions with case companies, we found that improving the AR game watching experience requires digital channels to connect online and offline physical event interactions, and establish event and links between spectator (Fig. 13).

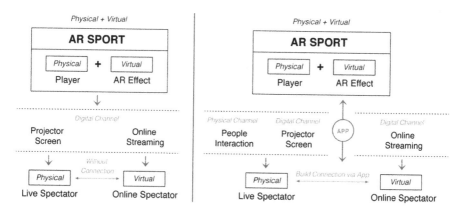

Fig. 13. AR match interaction scenario: left one is current existing scenario, right one is scenario with digital channel of design concept.

Due to the current technical limitations, the spectator has not been able to use the AR glasses to watch the game, so a layer of barriers between the match and the spectator. The main element of the match is virtual object, it only interacts directly with players. That's why the match and spectator have to be connected through digital channels. For example, using a projection screen and online live broadcast platform.

Therefore, the spectator is indirectly receiving information of the match, and there is no direct channel to interact with it.

In order to overcome the above problems, we propose to increase the digital channels to establish contact for direct interaction between the spectator and the match. Through app-related interactions, for example, the spectator can predict the winning team and accumulates award, or they can influence the outcome of the game by using attack or support function in App. These interactions are not limited to the participation of online or offline spectators, so that a deeper relationship between them can be established.

In addition, physical activities can also be used. However, the use of physical activities in AR events is relatively limited. The content of the match is generated by virtual object and physical players, so a medium to build a digital channel between the match and spectator is indispensable.

6   Future Work

This study is the first to explore and discuss user experience design in watching AR sports events. With a unique case study, this research conducted an in-depth analysis of the current issues facing the experience of watching AR sports events, and proposed design concept for optimization through a co-creation workshop which is based on one of the service design core value. We will continue to explore other design solutions to optimize the experience of watching AR sports events and seek the best ideas by multidisciplinary co-creation. We will then test and verify these design concept to determine an appropriate method to test service design prototypes in spectator experience.

Acknowledgments. We thank all the participants and Meleap Inc for the support.

References

Beyer, H.R., Holtzblatt, K.: Contextual Design: Defining Customer-Centered Systems. Morgan Kaufmann Publishers Inc., San Francisco (1998)

Pine II, J., Gilmore, J.H.: Welcome to the experience economy. Harvard Bus. Rev. **76**(4), 97–105 (1998)

Stickdorn, M., Schneider, J.: This is Service Design Thinking. Basics - Tools – Cases (2013)

Ho, S.-S., Sung, T.-J.: The development of academic research in service design: a meta-analysis. J. Des. **19**(2), 45–66 (2014)

Holmlid, S., Evenson, S.: Bringing service design to service sciences, management and engineering. In: Hefley, B., Murphy, W. (eds.) Service Science, Management and Engineering Education for the 21st Century. SSRI, pp. 341–345. Springer, Boston (2008). https://doi.org/10.1007/978-0-387-76578-5_50

Kimbell, L.: Designing for service as one way of designing services. Int. J. Des. **5**(2), 41–52 (2011)

VR Appreciation System for Fountain Pens and Analysis of User Behaviors in Museum Exhibition

Asako Soga[1(✉)] and Takuzi Suzuki[2(✉)]

[1] Ryukoku University, Otsu, Japan
asako@motionlab.jp
[2] National Museum of Japanese History, Sakura, Japan
suzuki@rekihaku.ac.jp

Abstract. In this research, we developed a VR appreciation system for fountain pens using a head-mounted display (HMD) and a pen-type device. The purpose of this system is to allow museum visitors to view Maki-e fountain pens more freely. This system allows users to preview 3DCG of fountain pens displayed in VR space using the HMD while operating the pen-type device. In order to intuitively operate the 3DCG of the fountain pen, the 3DCG is rotated based on the angular velocity detected with a gyroscope sensor mounted on the pen-type device. In addition, the system allows users to select a fountain pen to view using only head motion by displaying the cursor at the center of the HMD screen. The system was used at a special exhibition of the National Museum of Japanese History for eight weeks. Moreover, to clarify the requirements of museum exhibition systems and the types of knowledge used to appreciate an exhibition, we analyzed user behaviors from the log data of a system deployed at a museum. As a result, when the users wore the HMD, fountain pens in the center of the screen were often browsed regardless of their features.

Keywords: Fountain pens · HMD · Museum · User behavior · 3DCG

1 Introduction

In recent years, information technology has been adopted in museum exhibitions. In actual museums, many systems visualize digital content to support visitors who are interested in appreciating exhibits, some of which can be interactively manipulated by visitors. For example, the Natural History Museum in London [1] uses augmented reality to take visitors on a virtual journey back through human's evolutionary past, and interactive stereoscopic content has been used at the Nagoya City Science Museum [2]. Many museums have prepared space to increase visitor comprehension of certain exhibits.

In addition, as consumer-level virtual reality (VR) devices have become freely available to the public, VR technologies are present at museums. For example, the British Museum held a two-day event in 2015 [3], where users could use a Samsung Gear VR to view 3D-scanned exhibit artefacts. McSheery et al. developed Aquarium Earth [4], which is a short VR experience system that also uses Gear VR. This system

© Springer Nature Switzerland AG 2020
A. Marcus and E. Rosenzweig (Eds.): HCII 2020, LNCS 12201, pp. 532–541, 2020.
https://doi.org/10.1007/978-3-030-49760-6_38

allows users to observe and interact with a virtual representation of a coral reef that is being destroyed even they are not in an actual aquarium. However, since obtaining visitor feedback by surveys is discouraged, analyzing how a given system is actually used is difficult.

Many digital museums have been using VR and Augmented Reality (AR) technologies since the 2000s [5]. For example, Wojciechowski [6] suggested in 2004 that VR and AR museum exhibits should access web browsers. Most works proposed digital contents that can be accessed from networks without visiting actual museums. Some VR or AR systems were temporarily used in actual museums for a few days as trials. Our purpose is to support the actual exhibitions of museums for a few months by recommending permanent systems that can be used in conjunction with actual cultural properties to support exhibit comprehension.

In this study, we developed an exhibition-support system for fountain pens using a head-mounted display (HMD) and a pen-type device to intuitively operate their 3DCG. Our system allows museum visitors to view Maki-e fountain pens more freely. Maki-e fountain pens are degraded by light and humidity, so they are unsuitable for permanent exhibitions. Some fine patterns are also difficult to see with the naked eye. To clarify the requirements of museum exhibition systems and the types of knowledge that can increase an exhibition's appreciation, we analyzed the user behaviors from the log data of a system deployed at a museum.

2 VR Appreciation System of Fountain Pens

2.1 System Overview

We developed a VR appreciation system for fountain pens using an HMD and a pen-type device to support museum exhibitions. Figure 1 illustrates the concept of our VR appreciation system. It allows users to preview the 3DCG of the Maki-e fountain pens in the collections of the National Museum of Japanese History that are displayed in VR space by an HMD while they are being manipulated. This system uses Oculus Rift CV1 as the HMD and Wii-remote plus as the pen-type device. For intuitively operating the fountain pen's 3DCG, the 3DCG is rotated based on its angular velocity detected with a gyroscope sensor mounted on the pen-type device. With a 4K monitor, this system also allows visitors without an HMD to appreciate the 3DCG of the fountain pens. We reproduced the 3DCG of the fountain pens using their existing radius data and rollout images [7, 8].

To analyze user behaviors at museum exhibition, this system records log data, which are used to calculate the number of browsings and the browsing times per fountain pen.

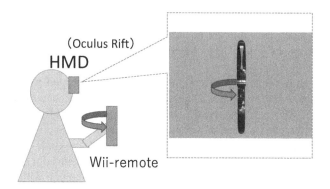

Fig. 1. VR appreciation system of fountain pens

2.2   Interface

This system is designed for use in actual museum exhibitions. We made a monitor and a special board with manipulation buttons without VR devices because operator supervision is required to use them and constantly assigning an operator is difficult.

Table 1 shows the system's functions and manipulation methods. When the system runs with VR devices of HMD and Wii-remote, the 3DCG is rotated based on the angular velocity detected with a gyroscope sensor mounted on the pen-type device. Users can switch and zoom in/out of the fountain pen to browse by buttons on the Wii-remote. They can also switch the fountain pen by pushing the buttons on the Wii-remote. To select one pen from multiple fountain pens with the HMD and to switch among them easily, the system allows users to select a fountain pen for viewing with just a head motion by displaying a cursor at the center of the HMD screen. Figure 2 illustrates switching fountain pens using HMD.

When the system operates without any VR devices, visitors can use a manipulation board (Fig. 3) that has buttons that provide simple explanations for easy system use. Each button has functions, including switching fountain pens and zooming in/out. Figure 4 shows the GUIs of both systems. The users can see all the thumbnails of the fountain pens arranged in four rows and five columns with the VR device. Without it, the thumbnails of the fountain pens are continuously arranged in one row, and five of the 20 thumbnails are shown on the monitor (Fig. 4(b)). To switch among fountain pens with the board, users can select their thumbnail by right or left buttons. Then 3DCG of the selected fountain pen is displayed on the monitor.

Table 1. Functions and manipulation methods of system

Function	Manipulation with VR devices (HMD and Wii-remote)	Manipulation without VR devices (with manipulation board)
Orientation of CG model	Rotate Wii-remote	Up/Down/Left/Right buttons
Reset of viewpoint	Reset button on Wii-remote	Reset button
Zoom in/out	Up/Down keys on Wii-remote	Zoom in/out buttons
Displaying menu	"B" button on Wii-remote	Menu button
Fountain pen selection	"A" button on Wii-remote, or gazing thumbnail of pen by HMD	Left/Right buttons and then select button

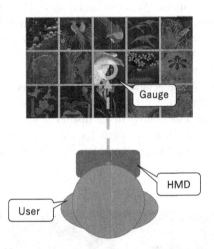

Fig. 2. Switching fountain pens using HMD

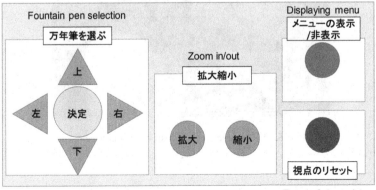

Fig. 3. Buttons on manipulation board

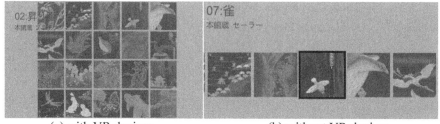

(a) with VR devices   (b) without VR devices

Fig. 4. System GUI

3 Museum Exhibition

We demonstrated our system for eight weeks from March 14 to May 7, 2017 at a special exhibition of the National Museum of Japanese History: "Explore the digital world of historical materials!" [9]. On weekends and holiday afternoons, an operator was assigned to the exhibition, and visitors played the VR appreciation system for fountain pens with the VR devices. On weekdays, we used a monitor and the manipulation board with buttons.

Figure 5 shows the VR appreciation system for the fountain pens. Figure 6 shows the exhibition area. We placed the VR appreciation system with a chair to the left of the area. On the right, ten actual fountain pens are displayed in a case that can control light. The displayed fountain pens were switched for the first and second exhibitions. We created identical 3DCG of 20 fountain pens: ten for the first exhibition and ten for the second.

Fig. 5. VR appreciation system of fountain pens

Fig. 6. Scene of special exhibition

4 Analysis of User Behaviors in Museum Exhibitions

4.1 Method

We analyzed the user behaviors from the log data of a system that was actually being deployed at a museum based on the differences between the user interface and the contents. For the interface difference, we compared the number of gazes at each pen with/without the HMD and the Wii-remote. For the content differences, we analyzed the gazing time of each pen to determine which fountain pens were more frequently previewed among all twenty of them.

In the exhibitions, log data of 22 days from April 16 to May 7 were recorded, and VR devices were used on 11 of those days. Some hours provided no VR devices because they were only available on weekend afternoons and holidays. In this analysis, we used the log data of seven days on which the VR devices were used in the afternoon to compare the interface difference. Moreover, the most frequently viewed two days were selected from the seven days to compare the content differences.

4.2 Log Data

In the log data, the system recorded the time, the event type, and such additional event information as pen ID and input key. Table 2 shows an example of the log data. After the Wii-remote starts to move, the "start moving" event type is recorded with the fountain pen ID and the key. The time represents the elapsed time from the beginning of the exhibition. The key corresponds to the input button. We also recorded whether the user used the HMD.

When the HMD was used, the number of browsing times per fountain pen was counted when users successfully selected a pen by gazing at its thumbnail by the HMD. Without the HMD, we counted when over four seconds were required before changing to another fountain pen, or a zoom-in/out event occurred after selecting a fountain pen.

We calculated the browsing time as the elapsed time from the "start moving" to the "stop moving" of the pen. Without the HMD and the Wii-remote, when there is no input over four seconds, we defined it as "stop moving" because this is probably idle time.

Table 2. Example of log data

Time	Event	Pen ID	Key
1493945500968	Start moving	02	Z
1493945503784	Key input		Z
1493945505661	Stop moving		

4.3   Analysis Based on Interface

We used the log data of seven days to compare the number of browsings of each pen with/without the VR devices of HMD and Wii-remote. Figures 7 and 8 illustrate the number of browsings at each fountain pen. The horizontal axis of each graph shows the fountain pen ID; the vertical axis shows the number of browsings for each fountain pen. Figure 7 shows with the VR devices. Figure 8 shows without them and where visitors used the special panel with control buttons.

Figure 7 shows that pen IDs 14, 17, 30, and 32 were frequently browsed. Pen IDs 02, 04, 11, 23, 34, and 44 were less viewed with the VR devices. Figure 9 shows the arrangement of the fountain pens and the result of the number of browsings. The fountain pens were arranged from upper left to lower right lower by pen ID. The number on the thumbnail indicates the number of browsings. As shown in Fig. 9, when the user wore the HMD, the fountain pens in the center of the screen were more often browsed regardless of their features, and those on the left edge of the screen were less often browsed. Based on questionnaires from visitors who used our VR systems on the other days, 12 of 36 (33%) had never used HMD before. Therefore, we believe that the main cause of this result is that many visitors were unfamiliar with VR devices and might have experienced difficulty selecting fountain pens by gazing at thumbnails.

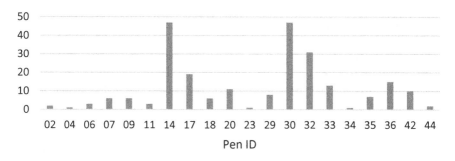

Fig. 7. Number of browsings for each fountain pen with VR devices

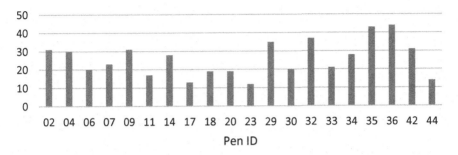

Fig. 8. Number of browsings for each fountain pen without VR devices

Fig. 9. Arrangement of fountain pens and number of browsings

On the other hand, almost all the fountain pens were equally browsed without the VR devices (Fig. 8). When viewing a specific item among many with HMD, the most centrally positioned one is often the most browsed.

4.4 Analysis Based on Contents

We used the log data of two days to compare the browsing times of each pen based on the contents. Figure 10 illustrates the browsing times of each fountain pen. The horizontal axis of each graph shows the fountain pen IDs, and the vertical axis shows the amount of browsing time (seconds) for each fountain pen. Pen IDs 02, 35, and 36 were browsed longer than the others, and pen IDs 04, 17, and 23 were shorter. Our observations suggest that the main reason is that many visitors browsed by rotating the fountain pens because the frequently browsed fountain pens had bigger illustrations and were more colorful than the others. On the other hand, we did not find any common reasons for shorter browsing times.

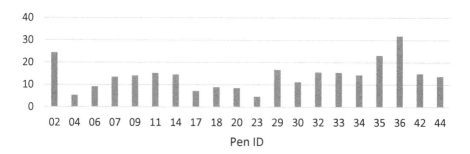

Fig. 10. Browsing times of each fountain pen

5   Discussion and Conclusion

We developed a VR appreciation system for fountain pens using an HMD and a pen-type device. Our system allows users to preview the 3DCG of fountain pens displayed in VR space using the HMD while operating the pen-type device. Our system was used for eight weeks at a special exhibition of the National Museum of Japanese History.

To clarify the needs of museum exhibition systems and the types of knowledge for appreciating an exhibition, we analyzed the user behaviors from our system's log data at a museum. When they wore the HMD, they more often browsed the fountain pens in the center of the screen regardless of their features. We found that when viewing a specific item among many with HMD, the most centrally positioned one is often the most browsed. Perhaps the main reason is simply that the visitors were unfamiliar with VR devices. This observation suggests that a detailed user manual or demonstration might be required.

From general questionnaires during the eight-week exhibition, 13 of 134 visitors wrote that our proposed fountain pen and VR usage system was an impressive point of the special exhibition. We got the following positive comments about using 3DCG and VR: "Viewing the fountain pen from many different angles in 3D was helpful because that flexibility is usually unavailable"; "I could see the brilliant colors of the pens in VR better than from the actual pens"; and "I want more exhibits using VR." We verified that the concept of our system was acceptable by museum visitors.

In future works, we will analyze our system's log and continue to explore its possibilities. For example, considering the head position and orientation for the VR device in the logs allows us to analyze to which pen features the users are paying more attention. This system can also be extended to other virtual museum applications. We will apply its techniques to other exhibitions.

Acknowledgements. We wish to thank Shuhei Tomita and Yuho Yazaki for their support in developing the system. We also wish to thank Atsushi Asai for his support in analyzing the log data. This work was partly supported by JSPS KAKENHI Grant Number 17K01213.

References

1. Natural History Museum. http://www.nhm.ac.uk. Accessed 31 Dec 2019
2. Mizuno, S., Tsukada, M., Uehara, Y.: A stereoscopic CG system with motion parallax and its digital contents for science museums. In: Proceedings of SITIS 2013, pp. 378–384 (2013)
3. Rae, J., Edwards, L.: Virtual reality at the British Museum: what is the value of virtual reality environments for learning by children and young people, schools, and families? In: Proceedings of Museums and the Web 2016 (2016)
4. McSheery, T., Yim, K., Thompson, M., Young, B.: Aquarium earth. In: SIGGRAPH 2016 VR Village (2016)
5. Styliani, S., Fotis, L., Kostas, K., Petros, P.: Virtual museums, a survey and some issues for consideration. J. Cult. Heritage **10**(4), 520–528 (2009)
6. Wojciechowski, R., Walczak, K., White, M., Cellary, W.: Building virtual and augmented reality museum exhibitions. In: Proceeding of the 9th International Conference on 3D Web Technology, pp. 135–144 (2004)
7. Soga, A., Suzuki, T.: 3DCG reproduction of fountain pens utilizing museum's existing archives. IPSJ SIG Technical Report, vol. 2018-DCC-19, no. 4, pp. 1–7 (2018). in Japanese
8. Suzuki, T.: Development of the technique for multi-angle image capturing and rollout image composition of maki-e fountain pens collection. Bull. Natl. Mus. Jpn. Hist. **206**, 39–59 (2017). in Japanese
9. Explore the Digital World of Historical Materials! National Museum of Japanese History. http://www.rekihaku.ac.jp/english/exhibitions/project/old/170314/index.html. Accessed 31 Dec 2019

Reflecting on New Approaches for the Design for Behavioural Change Research and Practice: Shaping the Technologies Through Immersive Design Fiction Prototyping

Mila Stepanovic[✉] and Venere Ferraro[✉]

Politecnico di Milano, 20158 Milan, Italy
{mila.stepanovic,venere.ferraro}@polimi.it

Abstract. This position paper is founded on an on-going research aimed in developing new approaches for the design for behavioural change research and practice, based on design fiction principles considered able to trigger critical thinking related to the use of technologies. The focus of this research is on the role of disruptive technologies in fostering the behavioural change, and on the importance of critical thinking related to the societal, and ethical issues when designing for these technologies. In regard, this paper proposes to reflect on the implementation of virtual reality (VR) as a tool for prototyping the design fiction for the technologies able to tackle the behavioural change. The VR can be a powerful tool for creating the context and experiences related to these technologies, especially when it gets about the near future scenarios, and not-yet-existing products and services. Besides, VR technology is used as a tool in different applications with a purpose to influence human behaviour and perception (i.e. safety training, psychological therapy, rehabilitation, etc.). This paper will discussed the benefits of virtual design fiction prototyping in relation to the near future technologies able to tackle behavioural change. How this kind of approach might evoke critical thinking in a work of designers and researches, and also help in testing of the not yet existing technologies with users, is the question of this paper. In conclusion we will introduced the further development of the research that considers the implementation of VR as a medium for prototyping the design fiction scenarios and artefacts.

Keywords: Design fiction · Disruptive technologies · Design for behavioural change · Virtual Reality (VR)

1 Introduction

This position paper is based on the first results emerged from an on-going research, aimed at proposing the new approaches for the design for behavioural change research and practice, based on design fiction principles considered able to trigger critical thinking when using disruptive technology to foster behavioural change.

© Springer Nature Switzerland AG 2020
A. Marcus and E. Rosenzweig (Eds.): HCII 2020, LNCS 12201, pp. 542–560, 2020.
https://doi.org/10.1007/978-3-030-49760-6_39

Critical thinking related to the use of disruptive technologies, and especially in behavioural change interventions consider different societal and ethical implications. Design as a discipline is getting always more interested in critical practices, especially when it comes to new disruptive technologies and its role in persuading users. Design Fiction, Speculative Design, Critical Design, are just some of the branches of design emerged recently to support the critical thinking and critical inquiry in design research and practice [1]. Bleeker (2009) explains design fiction as a different genre of design, that is not realism, but rather a genre that is forward looking, beyond incremental and makes an effort to explore new kinds of social interaction rituals [2].

In particular, design fiction is an emergent field in Human-computer interaction (HCI) and Interaction design research and practice [3]. The fields of HCI and Interaction design are those that draw upon the creative, generative and experimental approaches and methods [4, 5], as McVeigh-Schultz J. (et al.) explain: "Human-Computer Interaction (HCI) is a field-oriented to the future through both discursive and experiential methods" [6].

On the other side, ubiquitous computing and pervasive development, use and miniaturization of technologies inspired the human-computer interaction researchers to design increasingly for behavioural change applications [7]. These technologies are able to persuade users toward a healthier lifestyle, safe behaviour, making better sustainable choices, and many other kinds of behaviour [8]. These technologies can persuade users in many ways and help them maintain behaviour long in time. But do these technologies impact only individuals, or also the society and environment. And how its development is related to other social and technological transformations? According to Grand and Wiedmer (2010): "Our world is increasingly involved and engaged in complex, collective political and economic debates and experiments [...] in which different actors [...] are engaged [...] design and design research should make its particular practices, tools, and methods relevant to those debates [...] which are important for collectively dealing with possible futures in a complex world." [9].

Design fiction, as an alternative research tool, can help in envisioning and illustrating not-yet-existing technological devices, and help in understanding technological opportunities, while helping the researchers and practitioners suspend the disbelief about the future.

Here we introduce the first experimentation of this research aimed in exploring the narrative - "text as world" - dimension of design fiction, aimed at developing the near-future scenarios about the not-yet existing disruptive technology (products and services) able to tackle the behavioural change, concerning the specific societal challenge.

Building on results emerged from the experimentation, we recognize the necessity to increase the experiential dimension when designing for the near future technologies. Taking the cue from the McVeigh-Schultz J. (et al.) research on immersive Design fiction where they define the Immersive design fictions (IDFs) as the medium able to "extend methods of VR prototyping by placing speculative interfaces and interaction rituals within virtual narrative contexts", we propose in this paper the implementation of the Virtual Reality (VR) as a medium for prototyping near-future scenarios about the not-yet-existing technologies able to tackle behavioural change.

We want to exploit those benefits of VR as a medium for visualization and communication, that Abbas and Ryan (2004) define as: "computer-generated three-dimensional landscape in which we would experience an expansion of our physical and sensory powers; leave our bodies and see ourselves from the outside; adopt new identities; apprehend immaterial objects through many senses, including touch; become able to modify the environment through either verbal commands or physical gestures; and see creative thoughts instantly realized without going through the process of having them physically materialized" [10]. Virtual Reality (VR) is a well- known as a technological medium of experience design as well as a site of accelerated user experience innovation.

2   Theoretical Background

The background of the research described in this paper relies on different theoretical backgrounds. From the one side, it borrows the knowledge from the design for behavioural change literature and practice, and on the other side, it researches the critical theories and practices used in design research. This research is focusing on the role of technologies in changing human behaviour, and related ethical and societal issues. We start from the consideration that it is very important for design researchers and practitioners to be critical when designing for behavioural change and disruptive technologies, and we suggest that the implementation of the design fiction principles might help in triggering the critical thinking. In the text below there will be introduced the concept of the background research, and we will make a reflect on the potentialities of design fiction as a tool for critical inquiry.

2.1   Why Do We Need a More Critical Approaches When Dealing with the Technology for Behavioural Change?

We are living in a very complex world, in which we testimony the great transformations, such as environmental, technological, economical, etc. In a changing world, also design research and practice have to adopt, and propose new approaches, methods, solutions [9]. Design for behavioural change research is trying to propose new reflective approaches and different kind of techniques able to trigger critical thinking regarding the technological impact on individuals, society, and natural environment. Rapp (2019) is proposing the design fiction as a possible alternative tool for designing for behavioural change: "Design fictions, therefore, could represent a tool for reasoning on how current behaviour change designs embed values, opportunities and threats that may not be immediately visible through the lens of traditional evaluation techniques." [11].

In our research we are focusing on the disruptive technologies (i.e. artificial intelligence, wearables, smart materials, etc.) as persuasive tools able to tackle the behavioural change, without coherence, and motivate and help users maintain the target behaviour [7, 13–15]. Advantages of the use of technology for persuading the users is in its capability to relate to the users in engaging but not on emotional level as it happens in human-human relationships, the second is that these are capable of providing the objective and real-time feedback, and maintain the level of motivation constant [15, 16]. There are of course, many other recognized benefits from the use of technologies as persuasive tools, such as possibility to adopt to the needs of the person (personalization), possibility to have a history of our behaviour, possibility to create the community, and many other. There is a high demand when it is about the societal and ethical issues and implications when designing for this kind of technologies and applications. Thus, the considerations to take in account when designing for these technologies are whether these technologies always persuade ethically; where our data is stored, which are the limits and critical points in relationship between the user and technology; how sustainable is the technology; and how all these issues are evolving with the societal and technological transformation.

The process of behavioural change through the use of persuasive technologies is not only a matter of technological performance, these technologies embed the experiences. This is the reason why interaction designers have an important role in designing for these technologies and experiences. Stienstra, J., Alonso, M. B., Wensveen, S., and Kuenen, S. (2012) state that nowadays interaction design moved away from productivity and efficiency towards designing for experience, where they explain: "An experience cannot be designed directly, but may be approached through the role that artefacts play in affecting our behaviour [...] persuasive computing is becoming relevant to interaction designers who want to explore how design can address societal issues by transformation of behaviour." [18].

Today there is a high demand on social and environmental issues, and on awareness regarding the possible future consequences of human actions. Technology by its own cannot suffice in achieving the desired and more sustainable behaviours. Ilstedt and Wangel (2014) explain: "Sustainable lifestyles are today however often depicted through a sacrifice-based cultural narrative, in which losses, rather than gains stand in focus" - and acknowledge that thinking about the future may help us rethink our present - "These ideas, or expectations, about the future thus provide an opportunity for intervention." [16].

In conclusion of this part, we believe that reflecting about the plausible future might help us re-think our present, and make us design in a more reflective and critical way for behavioural change and the use of disruptive technologies [16, 18]. Thinking about the behaviours that the user will adopt in the future, trying to imagine the context of the future and the technological opportunities, can help us rethink our current approaches in research and practice of designing for behavioural change.

2.2 Design Fictions as a Trigger for Critical Thinking

Design fiction as a term was the first time pronounced by the Science Fiction (SCI-FI) writer Bruce Sterling in 2005, almost by accident at that time, while he was trying to figure out how design thinking was impacting his literary output [3, 5, 19]. Initial Sterling's concept about design fiction was later on used as a foundation for many papers and researches aimed at defining better this concept, commonly concerning the technologies, or rather the development and anticipation of a technologies in SCI-FI films and its impact on the real world innovations. Sterling's concept builds on Kirby's definition of "diegetic prototypes", as: "cinematic depictions of future technologies [...] that demonstrate to large public audiences a technology's need, benevolence, and viability" [20]. Kirby defines "diegetic prototypes" as "performative artefacts", explaining: "The performative aspects of prototypes are especially evident in diegetic prototypes because a film's narrative structure contextualizes technologies within the social sphere." [20]. The artefacts present in the fictional world, are becoming socially relevant in that worlds, and this coexistence of the context, actors, social norms, politics, in the fictional worlds, makes us look at that technology as if it was already real. Bleeker (2010) explains that design fiction happens when you tie together fact and fiction and play comfortably and happily in the between. For him, the design fiction outputs "are projections and extrapolations meant to explore possible near futures. They are speculations on what the next "now" will be like, always remembering "no possible future is out of the question." [2]. Bleeker explains design fiction prototyping for technological products, as an alternative to the canonical engineering prototyping that offers the solutions instead opening the space for alternative transformations and inquiry: "These design fiction props and prototypes would be things that help one imagine and tell stories about new near future objects and their social practices." [2].

Design fiction can have different dimensions, as narrative (intangible) or for instance tangible (fictional prototypes). Even though the design fiction as output is often considered as something immaterial, intangible, probably because of its narrative nature and tight relation to the literature, there are some suggestions on how to illustrate or prototype design fiction in design research and practice. Besides the textual form, design fiction is often expressed through the traditional techniques such as those already used in design practice, like sketching, mock-ups, mood boards, collage, videos, photo-montage and rendering, three-dimensional models, and other [21]. The techniques, as we can notice are generally rapid and very flexible because they are not supposed to represent the *solution* - at this stage researchers and practitioners can stay very conceptual, and the nature of these kinds of artefacts is supposed to be easily transformable and simple to suggest the possible alternatives [22]. Envisioning the not-yet-existing, future technologies through the fantasy prototypes or scenarios, is opening the new spaces - the spaces in which things exist only for the exploration and inquiry [23]. These fantasy prototypes or artefact, often called the Post-optimal objects, are used in critical practices with a purpose to provoke and create a discursive space [23]. This idea of not dealing with commercial products is helping design researchers and practitioners focus on the new methods and applications through which they produce a piece of new knowledge [22].

The fictional worlds we create to provoke the critical inquiry have to be persuasive and credible. Design fiction is a useful tool for illustrating and testing the public opinions, and create debates about the topics such as technologies, sustainability, and other. For this reason the technologies we design in a fictional world have to be experienced realistically, both by the researchers and designers, and by the potential users. Kirby is calling this kind of experience "technological sincerity".

We analysed different papers describing the different design fiction based studios and workshops, to understand how it is the most commonly practiced in design research and practice. The SCI-FI stories are often used in design fiction experiments as a reference for creating the scenarios about the products and technologies for the future. An example on that is the case of the paper "The poetics of design fiction" by Markussen and Knutz, where they introduce the design workshop based on the question: "How can we prototype the future?"- where the participants were given the un-published manuscript of Kaspar Colling Nielsen's next novel "The Civil War in Denmark" as a starting point for building the new worlds and solutions which make sense in that kind of context, considering the new social, economic, and cultural structure of Denmark [3]. The participants were supposed to materialize (graphical illustrations, videos, and worlds build up from a set of objects) design fiction scenarios, representing the worlds and solutions for the future, through the process based on the following typology: (1) "What if"-scenarios being the basic construal principle of design fiction; (2) the manifestation of critique; (3) design aims; (4) materializations and forms; and (5) the aesthetic of design fictions.

When we come to the materialization of design fiction scenarios and objects, Tina Kymäläinen draws upon the importance of experience design research in science fiction prototyping, as she explains: "[…] science fiction prototypes have nevertheless touched upon the experiences people will have towards the technologies in the future settings." [24].

What happens when we need to unify the narration to the experience in design fiction projects is a sort of "experiential gulf" - as McVeigh-Schultz J. (et al.) explain - between our ability to imagine the future and our ability to experience it. Here emerges the necessity to transform the ideas about the near future artefacts in embodied experiences in which the participant becomes a character of the fictional world. The Immersive design fiction is the approach that uses Virtual reality technology as a medium for prototyping the net yet existing scenarios and products. The VR enable practitioners to explore aspects of not-yet-existing technologies and related experience, such as new interaction modalities, applications, aesthetics, and other.

We believe that the journey in the future may help us reason more critically about the technologies for behavioural change in present. To understand how this can be done, we conducted the first experimentation, with participants actively involved in design research, aimed at understanding whether the creation of the envisioning near-future scenarios about the not-yet-existing technology able to tackle the behavioural change can make us reason more critically toward the role of technology and related societal and ethical implications. The objective of the experimentation was to create the envisioning near future scenarios, which we defined as explorative intangible artefacts. In the following text, we will introduce the insights from this experimentation and results.

3   Speculate4Behavioural Change: Insights from the First Experimentation

In this section, we want to introduce and describe the first experimentation developed within our research, that aims in suggesting the new approaches for designing for behavioural change research and practice. This research is funded on design through research approach, within which we conduct different experimentations, involve design researchers and practitioners, and investigate different dimensions of design fiction and its influence on designing for behavioural change.

The first experimentation investigates how the near future scenarios can open new spaces for inquiry and creative exploration. In particular, we analysed the influence of science fiction genre on inspiring the near-future scenarios about the not-yet-existing disruptive technology able to tackle the behavioural change. We organized the experimentation in a form of the one-day workshop, titled "Speculate4Behavioural Change", that gathered together the participants actively involved in design research (7 Ph.D. students, and 2 research fellows). The participants we involved come from different design fields, as product design, interaction design, communication design, smart materials, fashion for sustainability, and cross-cultural teamwork in design-based learning. The workshop was funded on the question: How can we trigger critical thinking in design for behavioural change research and practice? The objective of the workshop consisted of creating the envisioning near future scenarios that describe the context, technology, behaviour related to the specific societal issue. These scenarios, we defined as explorative artefacts – narrative and intangible – that can be used by researchers and practitioners for reflecting on the ethical and societal issues concerning disruptive technologies.

The activity was organized in the several stages, where the participants had to select the (1) societal challenge topic, (2) identify the human behaviour influence for the selected topic, (3) identify the design for behavioural change strategies and target behaviour, (4) use the SCI-FI contents to inspire they scenarios for the near future, and finally (5) deliver the scenario.

We founded the approach of this experimentation on the PPPP model developed by Dunne and Raby, which stands for "Present, Plausible, Possible and Preferable futures". This model aims to define different kinds of future and different levels of likelihood [1]. Besides, we selected some already existing tools to support the activity – Design with Intent Tool for designing for behavioural change, and Fogg's triad for defining the role of technology. Additionally, we developed a support tool with a purpose to inspire designing of the disruptive technologies through SCI-FI genre (cinematography).

In the text below we will describe more precisely the activities and results of the experimentation.

3.1   Methodology and Activities

Approach of the first experimentation was founded on the PPPP model for defining different levels of the future [1]. We created the map based on this approach, with a purpose to help the participants organize the output of each activity and make more fluid the process of transferring from the present state (Actuality zone) to the preferable future ("What if" zone) (see Fig. 1).

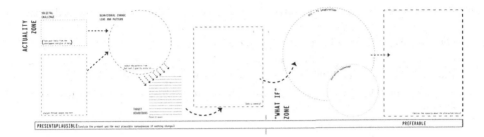

Fig. 1. Approach based on PPPP [1]

The first activity within the zone of actuality (Present and Plausible) consisted in selecting of the starting societal challenge topic. We defined three macro areas of societal challenges with different topic within each: (1) Environmental sustainability (Air pollution, Energy consumption, and pollution, water consumption and pollution, Waste management and recycling), (2) Health and wellbeing (General health prevention, Ageing, Occupational health), (3) Urban safety (General urban safety, Urban mobility safety, Cyber-safety) [25]. The topics collected from the various scientific and popular literature on current societal issues, facts, and future risks forecasts, were provided in a form of a short texts to the participants. The participants were asked to analyse the selected topic and reflect on the human influence, or rather which are the negative behaviours that might provoke the negative consequences in the future.

After the first analysis, remaining always in the zone of actuality (Present and Plausible), the participants were asked to use Design with the Intent (DwI) tool that offers numerous strategies for behavioural change, aimed in helping designers create more empowering design briefs and describe the products, services, interfaces, environments, and design strategically with the intent to influence how people use them (Dan Lockton 2010). [8] This tool is based on eight lenses, each of these proposing a different strategy for designing for behavioural change. For our activity, narrowed the selection on 5 lenses[1], those that we found the most suitable strategies to use for the objective of the workshop: Cognitive, Perceptual and Machiavellian lens as mandatory to use, or combine, while the use of the Ludic and Interactive lens was facultative. The participants had to select the lenses (strategies) and the patterns offering specific examples on how to achieve the desired behaviour through design. The exploration of DwI tool was supposed to serve for defining the target behaviours regarding the starting topic they selected.

---

[1] (1) The Cognitive lens takes inputs from the behaviourist economy and cognitive psychology. (2) The Perceptual is combining the concepts of gestalt psychology and product's semantic. (3) The Machiavellian is proposing solutions based on the thought that "end justifies the means". (4) The Ludic proposes the strategies that can engage the user long in time, while (5) the Interactive lens is using the interaction modalities and interfaces to stimulate the user's behaviour.

To summarize the first two activities within the actuality zone, we asked the participants to write the design brief in which they describe the current state related to the societal issues, propose the strategy and possible solution to help users achieve the target behaviour in the near future, in which disruptive technologies evolved and they can tackle the behavioural change for the new social contexts and structures.

The third activity consisted of the use of the tech inspiration cards and library that we developed for this occasion (see Fig. 2).

Fig. 2. Sci-fi content library

The selection of the films was done by using two different tools: (1) Seealsology[2], and (2) InData. The Seealsology was used to explore the phenomenology, the semantic area of disruptive technologies, and to subsequently individuate the keywords which represented again different technologies and technological devices within the macro categories. In this way we individuated four categories of disruptive technologies: (1) Simulated reality, (2) Wearables, (3) Artificial Intelligence, and (4) Smart materials. We used the Seealsology results also for clustering the keywords related to the disruptive technologies, which we subsequently applied in the InData[3] tool for scraping and plotting cinematographic content, with a particular focus on SCI-FI genre [25]. The cards we created as a result of the use of these two tools, are suggesting the technologies used in films and the plots for describing the context (see Fig. 3).

---

[2] Seealsology is an open access tool that allows quick exploration of the semantic area related to any Wikipedia page, by extracting of the all links in the "See also" section producing a graph.

[3] InData is an open access tool developed at Politecnico di Milano. This tool scrapes data from the open-access on-line repositories, in particular, Internet Movie data Base (IMdB) and it produces the plots with different films, episodes, games and other content, regarding the relevance to the inserted keywords.

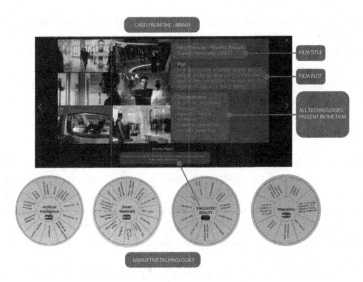

Fig. 3. Sci-fi tech card from library

We asked the participants to individuate some films that they consider inspiring for the development of their scenarios and to write down the technologies that they want to apply.

The last activity was writing of the near-future scenario in the form of a story, that describes the context, target behaviour, and the shape and the role of technology in tackling the behavioural change. To help participants define the role of technology we gave as a reference to the Fogg's triad, which describes the role of computers in persuading the users: (1) Computer as the mediator, (2) Computer as Tools, (3) Computer as Social actors [7]. The near future scenarios were requested in a textual form and we suggested participants support the scenarios with sketches, user journeys, images, and any other material that might help in describing better the scenario (see Fig. 4).

Fig. 4. Near future scenarios developed by the participants in the first experimentation

The method we used for evaluating the activity and collect the feedback is questionnaire and direct observation. The questionnaire was framed in general information collection and evaluation of the activities. The questionnaire aimed in understanding the participant's perception of understanding whether and at which stage he was thinking more critically about the behavioural issues and technologies, and if they were able to relate different topics of the workshop.

3.2   Results

The final output of the activities were three (3) near future scenarios in a form of the story, describing the near-future context, behavioural issues and the strategy, disruptive technology and the role of technology able to tackle behavioural change. The participants were free to use also other techniques beyond the textual form, like sketching, making the user journey, using the images, etc. Scenarios produced by the participants were structured differently one from another, from textual form to combining the text with schemes and sketches.

The questionnaire results confirmed that all of the participants find very important to think critically both when designing for behavioural change and for disruptive technologies. All of them were able to relate the different topics of the workshop, but not all of the participants did it with the equal facility. They stated that the activity in its whole triggered very much the critical thinking related to design for behavioural change. The use of the SCI-FI content, for those already familiar with the SCI-FI genre, was easier respect to those that have never seen the offered films. Most of the participants said that the film plot on the cards was too short and they did not have enough time to go online and make ulterior research. Also, they found the images poorly clear and evocative, considering that some are very abstract or maybe not easy to relate them to the context of use, and to the overall experience of the plot.

From what emerged we realized that the SCI-FI cards and library have to be improved, in order to provide a broader or more precise description of the plots, and consider a larger and more evocative selection of the images that describe the technology and context of use.

Most of the participants claimed that speculating about the near-future through the use of envisioning scenarios can be useful to identify the strategies to deal with current challenges and be more aware of the potential future consequences in our research. Still, there was a sort of disbelief in their experience about the written scenarios – intangible narratives - in a function of explorative artefacts. The participants stated that the medium (video, written story, infographics, and other) used for expressing the scenarios may play an important role in this kind of activity, in sense how can we illustrate, reproduce the fictions.

Building on these findings, we believe that providing a medium that can enhance the experience, related to the perception of the future and its context, might increase so called "technological sincerity" and as a consequence increase the critical inquiry [18]. Immersive and multisensory experience can expand our physical and sensory powers by increase the sense of presence in the fictional worlds and interaction with fictional objects [36]. Another important factors when dealing with not-yet-existing scenarios and objects is the temporal dimension and a narration that lays behind. Tanenbaum

(2016) explains the importance of the narration when dealing with technologies in our designs in the following way: "Situating a new technology within a narrative forces us to grapple with questions of ethics, values, social perspectives, causality, politics, psychology, and emotions." [11].

The results of the first experimentation are the starting point for the setting of the theoretical background and the next experimentation, with a focus on exploring the design fiction prototyping and its influence on triggering the critical thinking in design research and practice.

4 Virtual Reality: A Space-Time for Inquiry

We analysed the results of the first experimentation that was investigating the narrative, intangible, dimension of design fictions, for envisioning the near-future disruptive technologies able to tackle the behavioural change, in a function of explorative artefacts. From the analyses emerged, that the use of the SFI-FI context as we suggested was not inspiring for everyone, considering that the provided plot was too short, images sometimes too abstract and not enough evocative especially for those that were not familiar to the films.

Our reflection at this point is that the engagement between the participants and the future was not reached at the right level. Without the realistic perception of the context of the future, it is hard to be confident and comfortable with what is designed. According to us, the participants were missing a multisensorial and temporal experience related to the context of the future, and as a consequence, the realistic perception about the technology existence was lacking.

This brought us to the idea that it would be opportune to investigate the field of Simulated Reality (SR) for our research, where in specific Immersive Virtual Environments. We believe that Virtual Reality (VR) might be the appropriate medium for enhancing the multisensorial experience and for the improvement of the perception about the behaviour and technology influence on behaviour. The immersive virtual environment here could become a kind of "space-time" for inquiry, a medium that can give us the experiences related to our senses but also make us "travel in time"- going in this fictional future, and on our way back make us reflect about the present.

For this purpose, we investigated the fields of application of VR, both in the context of behavioural change application, and design and architecture. The following text is just a short introduction about the applications we identified as useful for creating our future case.

4.1 An Overview of VR Field

VR technology emerged as a very helpful and efficient tool in different fields of research, from neurosciences and psychology, engineering, architecture and design, medicine, etc. Recently, the number of applications of the VR within different research fields is in growth. VR as a visualization and communication tool experienced an important boom both in academic and professional literature and purposes [3]. This technology found its purpose in numerous fields, such as neurosciences and psychology, physical therapy, education and training, interior design, architecture and urban planning, etc. Some of these we will introduce in the text below.

Starting from the neurosciences and psychology, this technology found different purposes when it is about the modification of human behaviour. The use of VR in this field is often related to the cognitive and psychological therapies on different levels. For instance, the cognitive-behavioural therapy the VR is used for the person suffering from autism, but also for overcoming phobias or helping us reduce the level of anxiety as the one of public speaking and relating to other persons in general [27]. Beside the therapies and motivation influence, there are also some other behaviours that can be stimulated through the VR environments, for instance awareness toward the climate change issues. These environments have as a purpose to raise the perception about the negative consequences of the climate change and motivate the people behave more responsibly toward the planet [28].

Medical applications are mostly focused on training, as in the case of doctors, and patients' rehabilitation. Medical training in VR helps doctors simulate real-life situations and practice on the virtual body. While the rehabilitation of patients in VR is very typical for the motor skills repairmen, such as post-stroke therapy. Besides stroke therapy, there are also applications for different typologies of paralysis. These applications are often exploiting the robot technologies and other wearable accessorize (i.e. Cyber Glove) [29].

Virtual reality is becoming quite common in the industrial and engineering sphere where it is used for different purposes, such as safety training, training for the maintenance of the machines, etc. Also it becomes common the use of software visualization in engineering modelling and analysis [30, 31].

Another field that exploits VR technology and in general Simulated Reality is of course design and architecture. These fields are exploiting very often the Virtual Environments for testing the ideas with users, but also for creating interactive, engaging and immersive environments (i.e. interactive museums, entertainment), or experiences such as online shopping, etc. [29, 32, 33].

Here we mentioned just some of the examples on the fields exploiting the VR, but non the less VR offers numerous possibilities for engaging with the fictional spaces and object speculations, and we believe there are a lot of benefits that we can exploit from immersion for our application. First-person experience, sense of presence and multi-sensory experience are permitting us create realistic experiences related to the future, and have a perceptual illusion of interacting with the not-yet-existing technologies. These technologies are changing the way we understand the world through its being interactive, immersive, intensive, illustrative and intuitive (5 "i" of VR) [3].

4.2   Design Fiction Prototyping: What's New on the Horizon?

Previously we introduced that there are many ways to materialize design fictions and that there can be used different mediums for doing so. But what is actually the design fiction prototyping? Bleeker is defining the prototypes as: "a way to extend an idea into its materialization. Prototypes move ideas out of the mind off the page and into the hand. We prototype to render and materialize ideas so that they can be shared and tested and allowed to circulate. They are plastic and malleable and can be expected to change both themselves and the larger set of circumstances in which they exist." [2]. He distinguished different levels of prototypes, regarding their distance on the scale from functional to fictional. Those fictional, that he defines as Props[4] are those prototypes that lie on the extreme opposite respect to the traditional, functional engineering and technology materializations, that have as a purpose to justify the feasibility and functionality. Differently from the prototype in its traditional form on the one extremity, and a props on the other, the design fiction object speculates about what could be without expecting that the ideas in the fiction will materialize in the same pragmatic form as a prototype.

Coulton, P. et al., referring to Kirby's diegetic prototypes, explain that the design fiction scenarios: "invoke such worlds and prototypes through the crafting and sculpting of a miscellany of different media and forms." [34]. In design fiction prototyping, the designer becomes a storyteller, while the object becomes the actor [34].

Differently from the cinema where the focus is on storytelling, in design fiction the primary focus is often on the design fiction prototypes as objects.

In the last years, there is an emerging interest in the immersive and experiential dimension and potentialities of design fiction. We believe that the context, the world that we create to simulate the design fiction is of great importance. McVeigh-Schultz et al. studied the immersive design fictions, where the use of Virtual reality (VR) story world to speculate about the interfaces and interaction rituals. They suggest that the researchers and practitioners can explore embodied aspects of design fiction by situating speculative prototypes within an experiential story world in VR [5]. They propose a very novel approach able to provide the experience directly in the narrative context, and they believe that this kind of application may have broad applicability in implications for critical engagement. They develop narrative experimentations that start from the story world about the Virtual Design Workspace and develop different episodes in which they position the participants as if they were designer working in the near-future. The participants are experiencing three different virtual episodes that represent different stages of the design cycle, as they explain: "These episodes reimagine familiar practices of ideation, sketching, modelling, annotation, and review." This kind of approach help participants experiences the story world directly, where the narration is grounded with the fictional materialization.

Previously we made a brief overview of the VR field and its application and benefits. We acknowledge the VR as a possible medium to apply in our research, which may increase the persuasiveness related to the future, its social, ethical, and cultural structure, and reach the "technological sincerity" for designing for behavioural change [20]. In particular we refer to the sense of presence and immersion. The sense of presence is related more to the context in which our body is transferred while immersion is a more complex phenomenon that is considering both the spatial body transfer and agency [35, 36]. We believe this kind of approach can be used by the design researchers and practitioners dealing with design for behavioural change as a space-time for inquiry and reflection, and also it may help practitioners test the public opinion regarding the near-future technology and behavioural implications with users.

---

[4] "An object used by the actors performing in a play or film" (Cambridge Dictionary).

5 Further Development

The first intermediate step we will take in our research consist in improving the SCI-FI support tool content visualization and usability, while enriching the contents in the library. The improved tool will be once again implemented and teste in didactic activity in the Design Studio Lab entitled "Envisioning AI through Design" inside Master Degree in Digital and Interaction Design at Politecnico di Milano.

While, the further development of this research wants to go in direction of grounding the structure of the next experimentations that want to explore the materialization of design fictions through immersive design fiction prototyping, and investigate its influence on critical thinking in using the disruptive technologies able to tackle behavioural change, considering its societal and ethical implications. At this level, we want to consider the fictional prototypes as a three-dimensional, digital artefacts, for exploration and inquiry, that exist only in a fictional (virtual) world (environment).

Differently from the first experimentation that was exploring the narrative dimension of design fiction, in our future work we would like the switch from the textual and narrative form of design fiction to the development of digital models and contextualization of these in a physical, fictional world. Even though we are still lacking the clear idea of how exactly this will be realized, we suggest some possibilities here.

Multisensorial experience and sense of presence enabled by VR technology are the benefits that we want to exploit, in order to create the immersive and at the same time persuasive design fictions. Besides the multisensory experience, VR is a flexible medium that permits us to create and modify environments continuously.

From the results of the first experimentation emerged that there was lacking a real experience about being in the future when they were producing the scenarios. The scenarios produced by the participants were giving the impression to be a bit obsolete. According to Abbas and Ryan (2004): ""the text as world" is only one possible conceptualization among many others, not a necessary, objective, and literal dimension of literary language, but this relativization should be the occasion for a critical assessment of implications that have too long been taken for granted."

Building on this, we want to investigate the virtual environments, as a worlds in which to build and contextualize design fiction objects of not-yet-existing technologies for behavioural change. These environments can differ in genre, story (plot), aesthetics qualities, the social, ethical and cultural structure of the near-future. These environments can take inspiration from the SCI-FI cinematography and literature contents, such as the one we provided in the first experimentation. These environments can be supported by the written or vocal story, or with a voice-narrator. The participants could directly inspire for developing of the not-yet-existing technologies able to tackle the behavioural change (products and services). These design fiction prototypes could be a three-dimensional, digital models, placed in the virtual environment. At the advanced level, we could imagine that this world can be enriched and modified in order to represent the future context in the best way. Different VR software (i.e. Unity, Unreal Engine) offer a numerous libraries with ready to use elements, and they permit the importation of the other support elements to integrate in the virtual worlds, which can enrich additionally the environment and enhance the experience related to the future. We can also consider the creation of the ad hoc libraries that correspond to the fictional world we want to create, and that inspire on the societal contexts from different SCI-FI films.

6   Discussion

In this section we would like to discuss briefly the limitations, the potentialities of the approach we are proposing, and what eventual contributions we think might come out from this approach.

We identified some limitations in the use of the "text as world" approach for our application, regarding the scenarios participants produced in the first experimentation. Starting from those insights, we propose the second experimentation in which we would like to implement the Virtual reality (VR) as a medium for design fiction prototyping. In particular, we propose the virtual environments, inspired by SCI-FI cinema and literature, as a reference about the near-future, in which the researchers and practitioners can access to think and design for.

In conclusion of this part, we want to stress that we are aware of the critical points of a such approach. First of all this kind of approach can be implemented and tested only with researchers and designers skilled in three-dimensional modelling. Besides, the environments had to be designed in the way to provide the desired experiences which may be critical. Immersion can be an adventurous and invigorating experience, as Abbas and Ryan (2004) explain, but we have to consider that in virtual environments all sensory data must be simulated by the imagination, and here we stress the impor- tance of the narrative aspects in VR [36]. The sense of presence related to the context of the future, and to how this future is related to the reality, can be conducted by narratives "told as truth" as well as by stories told as fiction [38].

The narrative environments, we believe, may become a sort of space-time for inquiry. Entering in these worlds to analyse and coming back to the present to design for them might help researchers and practitioners trigger critical thinking. In this case the "space-time travel" would not be linear as in the first experimentation, but rather a dynamic activity than does not only engage our mind but also our body, by giving us the sensation of being actually present in that fictional world.

Speaking about the advantages, we find that near-future designs and context (design fiction) could be easily tested with the users in order to understand the public opinion about the technology for behavioural change and understand the possible behavioural implications and difficulties.

Another important demand in this kind of approach is time and instrumentation. If we want to go on the next level and test the story worlds and technologies with users this might consider additional time and would require the development of the specific methodology.

7   Conclusions

This position paper started from the foundations of the on-going research that researches the new approaches for the design for behavioural change research and practice, based on design fiction principles able to trigger the critical thinking related to the use of disruptive technologies.

Recently design and HCI research are getting always more interested in critical practices when it comes to designing of disruptive technologies. The same trend occurs in design for behavioural change research and practice.

In this paper, we introduced the research and theoretical background that is founded on theoretical and practical foundations of design for behavioural change and critical design practices. This research is based on design through the research approach and it uses the experimentations for researching and exploring the new approaches for the design for behavioural change research and practice.

The body of this paper is grounded on the findings emerged from the first experimentation aimed in exploring the narrative dimension of the design fiction, with the purpose to understand how near future scenarios open a new spaces for inquiry and creative exploration. The objective of this experimentation was to invite the participants to reflect on the current societal challenges and actual disruptive technologies and imagine an alternative world in which these technologies are shaped (i.e. products, services) and have a particular role to help humans to adapt and behave in the context of the near future. The results emerged from the experimentation showed that this kind of approach, based on the "text as world" form of narration, is neglecting in the experience related to the transportation in the future and related "technological sincerity".

In our further work, we want to investigate more potentialities of design fiction beyond the intangible explorative artefacts, by moving toward exploration of the VR technology as a medium for design fiction prototyping. We suggested that the use of fictional space (virtual environment) may emphasize the experience related to the perception of being in the near future, and in this way trigger, even more, the critical thinking related to the role of disruptive technologies able to tackle the behavioural change.

References

1. Antony, D., Raby, F.: Speculative Everything: Design, Fiction, and Social Deaming. The MIT Press, Cambridge (2013)
2. Bleecker, J.: Design fiction: from props to prototypes. In: Proceedings of the 6th Swiss Design Network Conference, pp. 58–67 (2010). https://doi.org/10.1002/glia.20282
3. Knutz, E., Markussen, T., Christensen, P.R.: The role of fiction in experiments within design, art & architecture - towards a new typology of design fiction. Artifact III(2), 8.1–8.13 (2014)
4. Elsden, C., et al.: On speculative enactments. In: Conference on Human Factors in Computing Systems - Proceedings, 2017-January, pp. 5386–5399 (2017). https://doi.org/10.1145/3025453.3025503

5. Lindley, J., Coulton, P.: Back to the future: 10 years of design fiction. In: Proceedings of the 2015 British HCI Conference on - British HCI 2015, pp. 210–211 (2015). https://doi.org/10.1145/2783446.2783592
6. McVeigh-Schultz, J., Kreminski, M., Prasad, K., Hoberman, P., Fisher, S.S.: Immersive design fiction: Using VR to prototype speculative interfaces and interaction rituals within a virtual storyworld. In: DIS 2018 - Proceedings of the 2018 Designing Interactive Systems Conference, pp. 817–830 (2018). https://doi.org/10.1145/3196709.3196793
7. Fogg, B.J., Cuellar, G., Danielson, D.: Motivating, influencing, and persuading users. In: The Human-Computer Interaction Handbook: Fundamentals, Evolving Technologies and Emerging Applications, pp. 133–146 (2008). https://doi.org/10.1201/9781410615862
8. Niedderer, K., et al.: Design for behaviour change as a driver for sustainable innovation: challenges and opportunities for implementation in the private and public sectors. Int. J. Des. 10(2) (2016). http://www.ijdesign.org/index.php/IJDesign/article/view/2260
9. Grand, S., Wiedmer, M.: Design fiction: a method toolbox for design research in a complex world. In: Proceedings of the DRS 2010 Conference: Design and Complexity, Montreal (2010)
10. Abbas, N.B., Ryan, M.-L.: Narrative as Virtual Reality: Immersion and Interactivity in Literature and Electronic Media. The Yearbook of English Studies, vol. 34 (2004). https://doi.org/10.2307/3509518
11. Tanenbaum, J., Pufal, M., Tanenbaum, K.: The limits of our imagination, pp. 1–9 (2016). https://doi.org/10.1145/2926676.2926687
12. Rapp, A.: Design fictions for behaviour change: exploring the long-term impacts of technology through the creation of fictional future prototypes. Behav. Inf. Technol. 38(3), 244–272 (2019). https://doi.org/10.1080/0144929X.2018.1526970
13. Ijsselsteijn, W., de Kort, Y., Midden, C., Eggen, B., van den Hoven, E.: Persuasive Technology. Springer, Heidelberg (2006). https://doi.org/10.1007/11755494
14. Fogg, B.J.: Creating persuasive technologies: an eight-step design process. In: Proceedings of the 4th International Conference on Persuasive Technology - Persuasive 2009, p. 1 (2009). https://doi.org/10.1145/1541948.1542005
15. Ananthanarayan, S., Siek, K.A.: Persuasive wearable technology design for health and wellness. In: 2012 6th International Conference on Pervasive Computing Technologies for Healthcare and Workshops, PervasiveHealth 2012, pp. 236–240 (2012). https://doi.org/10.4108/icst.pervasivehealth.2012.248694
16. Ilstedt, S., Wangel, J.: Altering expectations: how design fictions and backcasting can leverage sustainable lifestyles. In: Proceedings of the Design Research Society International Consortium (DRS), pp. 1–12 (2014). http://www.drs2014.org/media/654245/0265-file1.pdf
17. Bina, O., Mateus, S., Pereira, L., Caffa, A.: The future imagined: exploring fiction as a means of reflecting on today's Grand Societal Challenges and tomorrow's options. Futures 86, 166–184 (2017). https://doi.org/10.1016/j.futures.2016.05.009
18. Stienstra, J., Alonso, M. B., Wensveen, S., Kuenen, S.: How to design for transformation of behavior through interactive materiality. In: Proceedings of the 7th Nordic Conference on Human-Computer Interaction Making Sense Through Design - NordiCHI 2012, p. 21 (2012). https://doi.org/10.1145/2399016.2399020
19. Lindley, J.: A pragmatics framework for design fiction. In: 11th EAD Conference Proceedings: The Value of Design Research (2016). https://doi.org/10.7190/ead/2015/69
20. Kirby, D.: The future is now: diegetic prototypes and the role of popular films in generating real-world technological development. Soc. Stud. Sci. 40(1), 41–70 (2010) (2013). https://doi.org/10.1177/0306312709338325

21. Blythe, M.: Research through design fiction: narrative in real and imaginary abstracts. In: Proceedings of the 32nd Annual ACM Conference on Human Factors in Computing Systems - CHI 2014, pp. 703–712 (2014). https://doi.org/10.1145/2556288.2557098
22. Malpass, M.: Critical Design in Context: History, Theory, and Practices. Bloomsbury Academic (2017). https://books.google.it/books?id=QpGWDQAAQBAJ
23. Dunne, A.: Hertzian Tales. MIT Press, Cambridge (2005)
24. Kymäläinen, T.: An approach to future-oriented technology design - with a reflection on the role of the artefact. In: DRS 2016: Future-Focused Thinking, vol. 4, no. September (2019). https://doi.org/10.21606/drs.2016.87
25. Loughborough University Institutional Repository: Creating sustainable innovation through design for behaviour change: summary report, vol. 91 (2017)
26. Varisco, L., Mariani, I., Parisi, S., Stepanovic, M., Invernizzi, M., Bolzan, P.: InData envisioning and prototyping informed by data. A data scraping and visualization tool to support design scenarios. In: Ahram, T., Taiar, R., Colson, S., Choplin, A. (eds.) IHIET 2019. AISC, vol. 1018, pp. 441–447. Springer, Cham (2020). https://doi.org/10.1007/978-3-030-25629-6_68
27. Bowman, D.A., McMahan, R.P.: Virtual reality: how much immersion is enough? Computer 40(7), 36–43 (2007). https://doi.org/10.1109/MC.2007.257
28. Sheppard, S.R.J.: Landscape visualisation and climate change: the potential for influencing perceptions and behaviour. Environ. Sci. Policy 8(6), 637–654 (2005). https://doi.org/10.1016/j.envsci.2005.08.002
29. Jack, D., et al.: Virtual reality-enhanced stroke rehabilitation. IEEE Trans. Neural Syst. Rehabil. Eng. 9(3), 308–318 (2001)
30. Romano, S., Capece, N., Erra, U., Scanniello, G., Lanza, M.: On the use of virtual reality in software visualization: the case of the city metaphor. Inf. Softw. Technol. 114(June), 92–106 (2019). https://doi.org/10.1016/j.infsof.2019.06.007
31. Çakiroğlu, Ü., Gökoğlu, S.: Development of fire safety behavioral skills via virtual reality. Comput. Educ. 133, 56–68 (2019). https://doi.org/10.1016/j.compedu.2019.01.014
32. Lu, Y., Smith, S.: Augmented reality e-commerce assistant system: trying while shopping. In: Jacko, J.A. (ed.) HCI 2007. LNCS, vol. 4551, pp. 643–652. Springer, Heidelberg (2007). https://doi.org/10.1007/978-3-540-73107-8_72
33. Carrozzino, M., Bergamasco, M.: Beyond virtual museums: experiencing immersive virtual reality in real museums. J. Cult. Herit. 11(4), 452–458 (2010). https://doi.org/10.1016/j.culher.2010.04.001
34. Coulton, P., Lindley, J., Sturdee, M., Stead, M.: Design fiction as world building. In: Proceedings of the Research Through Design Conference, no. march, pp. 1–16 (2017). https://doi.org/10.6084/m9.figshare.4746964.Image
35. Slater, M., Lotto, B., Arnold, M.M., Sanchez-Vives, M.V.: How we experience immersive virtual environments: the concept of presence and its measurement. Anuario de Psicologia 40(2), 193–210 (2009)
36. Slater, M., Spanlang, B., Sanchez-Vives, M.V., Blanke, O.: First person experience of body transfer in virtual reality. PLoS ONE 5(5), 1–9 (2010). https://doi.org/10.1371/journal.pone.0010564
37. Abbas, N.B., Ryan, M.-L.: Narrative as Virtual Reality: Immersion and Interactivity in Literature and Electronic Media. The Yearbook of English Studies, vol. 34 (2004). https://doi.org/10.2307/3509518
38. Portman, M.E., Natapov, A., Fisher-Gewirtzman, D.: To go where no man has gone before: virtual reality in architecture, landscape architecture and environmental planning. Comput. Environ. Urban Syst. 54, 376–384 (2015). https://doi.org/10.1016/j.compenvurbsys.2015.05.001

Proposal of Perception Method of Existence of Objects in 3D Space Using Quasi-electrostatic Field

Kenta Suzuki, Koya Abe, and Hisashi Sato[✉]

Kanagawa Institute of Technology, 1030, Shimogino,
Atsugi, Kanagawa 243-0203, Japan
sato@ic.kanagawa-it.ac.jp

Abstract. In real space, it is possible to know if there is a person standing behind you without turning one's head. This is due to the quasi-electrostatic field, a type of electric fields that can be recognized by simulating body hair. However, a head-mounted display cannot recognize the presence of an object behind the user because it uses only visual and audio to interact with the environment. Therefore, we propose a system that promotes the perception of the existence of an object by generating a quasi-electrostatic field depending on the situation in 3D space.

Keywords: Quasi-electrostatic field · Perception of signs · VirtualReality

1 Introduction

In recent years, head-mounted displays (HMD) have become widespread as systems that can be easily immersed in 3D space. Among them, games using HMD have also appeared. Various genres of games such as action games, shooting games, and games that reproduce sport have appeared. However most of these things simulate and experience only vision and hearing. In order to further improve the immersive feeling of HMD games and increase the breadth of experience, it is important to stimulate sensations other than vision and hearing. TACTSUIT [1] developed by bHaptics et al. has succeeded in stimulating the skin sensation using a vibrator and presenting the sensation of being touched or being shot with a gun. The system developed by Nippon Telegraph and Telephone Corporation [2] has succeeded in presenting the feeling of walking even while sitting by applying vibration stimulation to the sole. In everyday life, you may feel someone's presence even without footsteps or touched sensations. This is thought to be due to the quasi-electrostatic field [3,4] discovered by Takiguchi et al. In this paper, we propose a system that promotes the perception of the existence of objects according to the situation in 3D space, which has not been realized so far. In addition, when urging the perception of the existence of an object, the quasi-electrostatic field is used to promote the perception of the existence of the object. In addition to aiming at practicality of perception of signs

© Springer Nature Switzerland AG 2020
A. Marcus and E. Rosenzweig (Eds.): HCII 2020, LNCS 12201, pp. 561–571, 2020.
https://doi.org/10.1007/978-3-030-49760-6_40

using quasi-electrostatic field with the subject wearing HMD, we exhibited at Entertainment Computing 2019 [5] to find further possibilities of this research.

2   Purpose

In this study, the team proposed a method of perceiving a sign in an HMD using a quasi-electrostatic field as a perception of a sign that does not depend on vision andhearing. As described in Sect. 1, most of HMD-based games simulate only the visual and audio, leaving users only able to experience 2 senses. Using a quasi-electrostatic field, which is one of the factors causing this sensation, the team proposed a new way of perceiving a sign to further enhance the immersion of the HMD game and increase the range of experience. For example, considering the operation in a horror game, when a ghost is slowly approaching, a quasi-static electric field can be used to encourage the perception of the invisible ghost. Also, the usefulness of presenting a sign by using a quasi-electrostatic field emitted from a CRT television was evaluated by comments from users.

3   Related Work

An immersive auditory display Sound Cask [6] developed by Ito is one of the systems that promote the perception of signs. In this Sound Cask, it is possible to know the space while moving the head under the same conditions as in real space by generating a 3D wavefront around the head. The generated 3D wavefront allows you to hear sounds that are almost the same as in real space, that is, breathing and walking sounds of people around you. As a previous study using quasi-electrostatic field, according to Odagiri et al. (1989), in humans, the electrostatic field is perceived by minute vibrations of body hair caused by the electrostatic field [7]. Chen et al. (2014) investigated changes in pedestrian behavior due to quasi-electrostatic field [8]. In this research, we are experimenting with quasi-electrostatic field emitted from CRT(cathode-ray tube) television. The average distance to feel the quasi-electrostatic field when using a CRT television was 43 mm, indicating that the distance felt by women was about 10 mm longer than the distance felt by men. Suzunaga et al. (2019) proposed the presentation of fear using quasi-electrostatic fields and cold air [9]. In this research, a handset-type device is charged to stimulate the vicinity of the inner ear, which is one of the organs that are susceptible to a quasi-electrostatic field when placed on the ear, to give a thrill.

4   Method

4.1   Selection of Direction

In this experiment, the body hair is directly stimulated by a quasi-electrostatic field and the object's sign is presented to the subject. Therefore, the presentation should be directed toward the feet where the skin is relatively easy to expose. In this paper, we adopted a method of stimulating using a CRT television used by Chen et al. (2014) as a transmitter that emits a quasi-electrostatic field [8]. Also, since it is necessary to distinguish between the quasi-electrostatic field emitted from the human body and the quasi-electrostatic field emitted from the transmitter, we created a mechanism as shown in Fig. 1 The servo motor can be used to turn on/off the transmitter so that the experiment can be performed without approaching the subject. In order to cut off the high-frequency sound generated from the transmitter, both subjects in experiments 1 and 2 were wearing headphones.

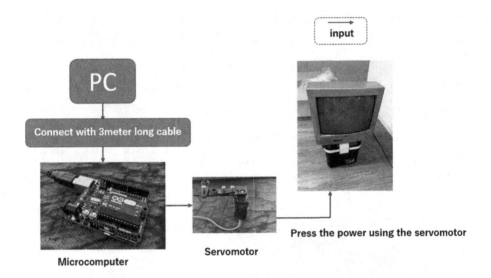

Fig. 1. System configuration

4.1.1 Purpose

In experiment 1, the quasi-electrostatic field generated from a CRT television is stimulated from the front, back, left, and right of the foot to determine whether there is a difference in how the foot felt different stimulations and from where is the stimulation most pronounced. At the same time, we confirmed how much the quasi-electrostatic field can actually be felt.

4.1.2 Experiment

The system shown in Fig. 2 and 3 was constructed. A transmitter was installed at a position 40 mm away from the test subject, and the operation of turning off the power in 3 s after turning on the transmitter in the front, back, left, and right, and turning on the power 3 s after turning off the power were repeated four times. As a measurement method, when the subject indicates feeling any change, the team would ask the subject to describe the state at that time in detail. Counting was performed when subjects mentioned specific phrases such as "tingling", "fluffy", and "felt something". In Table 1, we calculated the average of how many times subject could feel it during the 4th session, and the total average of the subjects and the sexes of the subjects and subjects.

Table 1. Ease of feeling of quasi-electrostatic field in front, back, left and right.

	Left on	Left off	Back on	Back off	Right on	Right off	Front on	Front off	Total average
Male1	50	25	0	0	100	100	75	75	53.1
Male2	50	0	25	0	50	25	75	50	34.3
Male3	25	25	75	75	100	50	0	25	46.8
Male4	100	75	25	75	0	0	25	25	40.6
Male5	0	0	25	0	0	0	0	0	3.1
Male6	75	75	50	75	0	25	75	75	56.2
Female1	25	75	75	50	100	100	75	25	65.6
Female2	0	0	0	0	0	0	0	0	0
Female3	100	75	75	50	75	75	0	75	65.6
Female4	0	0	0	0	50	25	0	75	18.7
Female5	25	0	0	0	0	0	0	0	3.1
Female6	50	75	0	0	75	75	0	0	34.3
Male average	50	33.3	33.3	37.5	41.6	33.3	41.6	41.6	39.0
Female average	33.3	37.5	25	16.6	50	45.8	12.5	29.1	31.2
Average of total gender	45.8	38.1	31.9	30.2	49.3	42.3	30.5	38.8	35.1

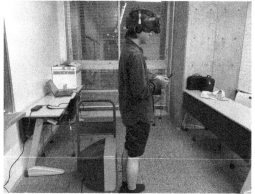

Fig. 2. State of experiment 1.

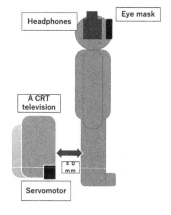

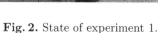

Fig. 3. Experiment 1 experience schematic diagram.

4.1.3   Results and Discussion

The experiment shows that the effect of the quasi-electrostatic field can be felt more often when the power is turned on the left and right of the foot. Some people could not feel it at all. This is due to the fact that when humans feel a quasi-electrostatic field as described in Sect. 2: Related Work, they are perceived by minute vibrations of the body hair, and it is thought that they cannot be felt when there is no body hair.

4.2   Generation of Quasi-electrostatic Field

4.2.1   Purpose

In experiment 2, the research team investigated whether a quasi-electrostatic field was generated when approaching an object in the 3D space displayed on the HMD, and the direction of the object could be perceived and directed. In Sect. 4.1.2, it was found that there were people who could not feel the influence of the quasi-electrostatic field. For that reason, in this experiment, the experiment was conducted on two men and women who were able to feel the effect of the electrostatic field in Sect. 4.1.2.

4.2.2   Experiment

The system shown in Fig. 4 was constructed. The research team prepared a 3D space with low traffic dim streets and a T-shaped road with objects hidden in the alley. The subjects walked down the alley using the controller and turned on the device when approaching the T-shaped road. During the experiment. the experimenter would explained that, "from now on, I'll have you walk in the alley. You might feel people's eyes and signs from somewhere. If you feel them, please look over there." Also, as in Sect. 4.1.2, the team asked the subjects to utter details of the situation at the time of occurrence. Figure 1 proved that stimulation of the left and right feet was effective, so the research team conducted experiments when placing the object on the left and on the right. When two males and two females were stimulated from the left and right of their feet, they performed the action such as they are directed to the direction of the object (the direction of stimulation), look around, and look into the T-shaped.

4.2.3   Results and Discussion

Since the stimulation to the left and right of the foot was found to be effective in Sect. 4.1.2, it was confirmed that the effect of the quasi-electrostatic field could be presented in this experiment as well, and that it could actually be presented. Also, the result of looking around and looking into the T-shaped despite stimulating the foot was obtained. I think this is what Gary R. VandenBos showed, due to visual superiority [10], which is "the tendency to become aware of visual stimuli even when auditory and other stimuli are presented simultaneously".

5   Application

5.1   System Configuration

5.1.1   Hardware Configuration

As a hardware configuration, the method of changing the power supply state using Solid State Relay was changed instead of the method (Fig. 5) of changing

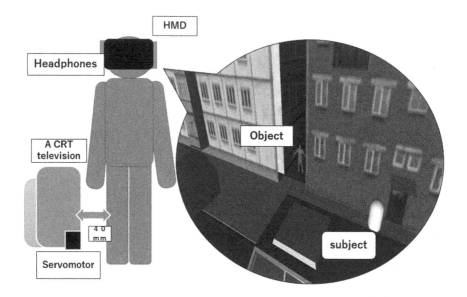

Fig. 4. Experiment 2 experience schematic diagram.

the power supply state by the servo motor implemented in Sect. 4.1. The reason for changing the configuration is that the method using the servo motor has problems such as the installation of the servo motor becoming unstable after being executed many times and the malfunction of the servo motor due to static electricity generated from the CRT television. Therefore, by using Solid State Relay to manage the power ON/OFF, the above problem was solved, and the software can be controlled stably from the software side.

5.1.2   Software Configuration

The application software was created using Unity, a game engine. Creation of stages and quasi-electrostatic field presentation gimmick were done with reference to Sect. 4.2.2. The team also prepared a long corridor model in Scene. The subject advances the corridor with one button on the controller. The hallway was made dark to prevent light from entering. The end result is a stage that looks like a night school corridor that can be navigated using a flashlight controlled by the controller. An invisible ghost is placed on the way of the corridor and appears when subjects illuminate the place with the flashlight. Some people have a hard to feel the quasi-electrostatic field, and as a countermeasure for when the position of the ghost is not known at all, a button that displays a mark using particles is prepared. By doing so, the team designed as much as possible to find ghosts. Also, when the subject approaches the ghost, the system detects the location of subjects and ghosts and turns on the television. This operation is repeated about five times at intervals and the state of the subjects is observed.

Fig. 5. Improved control device.

Within the experience, when the subject arrived at the end of the corridor, it automatically enters the door and loads the scene and ends the experience.

5.1.3 Application Configuration/Overview

Subjects wear HMD and sit on a chair with controller. Subjects start the experience with a CRT television installed on both sides of the feet. As an application story, subjects were instructed to go to the school classroom to collect forgotten items. There are many ghosts lurking in the school at night, so subjects get to

Fig. 6. Application configuration diagram.

safely collect forgotten items by searching for the ghost signs with their flash-light. Here, as described in Sect. 5.1.2, by presenting a quasi-electrostatic field where ghosts are to be present, it provides an experience where subjects can feel the ghosts that are invisible to the eye (Fig. 6).

6   Entertainment Computing 2019 Exhibition

To summarize the results and discussion of previous research, the research team actually exhibited what was created in Sect. 5.1.3 at Entertainment Computing 2019 to seek further opinions. Entertainment Computing 2019 is held every year as an academic conference since 2003. New technology for Entertainment Computing, new possibilities of Entertainment Computing, and relationship between Entertainment Computing and people and society, was a theme this year. Why the team chose Entertainment Computing 2019 was due to considering the operation of the game using HMD as the goal of this research. For that reason, because by presenting the research results at the famous Entertainment Computing Society in Japan, it was thought that the team could obtain valuable opinion from third parties about the possibility of further research and the problems of this research.

6.1   Experimental Result

6.1.1   Consideration

Positive feedback obtained throughout the exhibition include: "I could feel the quasi-electrostatic solution generated from the left and right a CRT television and perceive the direction in that direction" and "After feeling that sign, I was able to find a ghost quickly".

6.1.2   Bad Point

On the other hand, negative opinions such as "Despite feeling sign to the feet, ghosts appeared not from where the sign originated from", "Isn't it possible to have such a strong static electricity against an ambiguous thing?", "The ghost that comes out is too cute and scary", and "I didn't feel a quasi-electrostatic completely" were given.

6.2   Consideration

6.2.1   Good Point

While experiencing in state with only the HMD and controller attached, the subjects were able to feel the sign from a CRT television and notice the direction. From this result, the team felt that the presentation of the sign by a CRT television was useful.

6.2.2 Bad Point

The team thought that: "as a result of dragging the experiment in Sect. 4.2.2, there was a sense of incongruity due to the disagreement between the position of a CRT television and the appearance of ghosts in software", "The strength of the quasi-electrostatic field when the television is turned on and off is too great as a cause of tactile presentation that jumps over the image that it may be ghosted", "Some people thought of a scary ghost that just listen to the keywords ghost and sign", "After all, the presence or absence of body hair to resonated greatly with whether or not we felt quasi-electrostatic field, and there was a lack of countermeasures" against bad opinions.

6.3 Improvements

As an improvement point, I thought that it would be necessary to review the presentation method of the quasi-electrostatic field and create content that matches it. In particular, instead of using a CRT television as a presentation method, the team thought that it would be necessary to create a small device that can easily present a quasi-electrostatic field other than a foot. In content, I thought that the position when presenting a quasi-electrostatic field to the subjects and the position felt in the content should be matched to make it easier to understand the position where you feel the sign.

7 Conclusions and Future Work

In this paper, the place the presentation of the quasi-electrostatic field which uses aCRT television in the main research and made the experience for the purpose of perception of signs, such as feel something also to the part that made the presentation of quasi-electronic field in a state of wearing the HMD. Inside, subjects were able to feel the quasi-electrostatic field and said "I left an impression that I feltsomething like "spring" and "fluffing" as revealed in Sect. 4.1.2. Based on these results, itwas shown that it is useful to the quasi-electrostatic field on a CRT television to promote the perception of signs to subjects wearing HMD as described in Sects. 4.1.1 and 6.1.1. However, as discussed in Sect. 4.1.3, people with little body hair did not feel the quasi-electronic field at all and this appears to be the problem of this device. It is difficult to feel when there is no body hair on the legs because the quasi-electrostatic field was presented toward the foot without contact. Furthermore, the parameter of the quasi-electrostatic field changes depending on how the object walks as originally mentioned in Sect. 2. To solve the problem from these experimental results, it was concluded that there would be a need for a device that could vary the capacitance and present it. From these findings, the first is a device that can be compact and fit so that many people can feel it. For that reason, the research team believed that it is necessary to provide a presentation method that a position closer to the downy hair to adhere with human skin, research on quasi-electrostatic field generation methods and presentation methods other than a CRT television, to create a

Fig. 7. Future work

device that allows one to perceive a sign with or without hair. Also, the team believed it is necessary to make a device that can present a quasi-electrostatic field other than the neck, such as presentation on the neck and back.

Furthermore, it was found in Sect. 6.1 that there are many software problems. In order to present an immersive feeling, one of the important factors in creating VR contents, the five senses that account for more than 80% of the perception of information is important. Accordingly, as mentioned in Sect. 6.2.2, it is necessary to modify the design so as not to give a sense of incongruity of the difference due to the position shift of the perceived position of the sign in the real world and the perceived position of the sign in the software. Also, by improving the visual to match the content, it was thought that it can be improved to be more convincing. Based on these findings, thefinal concept is a visual and immersive experience that matches the content. It was thought that it was important to finish things that are not to a sense of incongruity by having many people experience it (Fig. 7).

References

1. bHaptics - Tactsuit, full body hapticsuit for VR. https://www.bhaptics.com/. Accessed 30 July 2019

2. Nippon Telegraph and Telephone Corporation: realize the feeling of walking even when sitting enables walking expression in VR space without actually walking. https://www.ntt.co.jp/news2019/1905/190530a.html. Accessed 30 July 2019

3. Takiguchi, K., Toyama, S.: Can dogs identify masters by electric field - Electric field generation and propagation of human body by walking. Int. Life Inf. **21**(2), 428–441 (2003)

4. Takiguchi, K.: Existence of unique patterns in walking, pp. 108–111. Nikkei Science, February (2002)

5. EC2019 Executive Committee: Entertainment Computing 2019, EC2019 Executive Committee. http://ec2019.entcomp.org/. Accessed 1 Dec 2019

6. Ito, S.: Sound design for auditory reality - the essence of reality brought about by the movement of people and things. Acoust. Soc. Jpn. **74**(11), 598–602 (2018)

7. Odagiri, H., Shimizu, K., Matsumoto, G.: Measurement and analysis of ELF electric field on human body surface. In: Proceedings of the International Symposium on EMC, no. 2, pp. 633–637 (1989)

8. Chen, S., Daiu, M., Kazuto, H., Hitoshi, W., Kenzi, K., Kiyoaki, T.: Pedestrian changes due to quasi-electrostatic field. In: Proceedings of the 37th Symposium on Computer Technology of Information, Systems and Applications H20(Dec), pp. 183–186 (2014)

9. Suzunaga, S., et al.: Call from merry. In: Proceedings of the 24th Annual Conference of the Virtual Reality Society of Japan, 2B–09, September 2019

10. CandenBos, G.R.: APA Psychology Dictionary. Translation, by Shigematsu, K., Yotsumoto, Y., September 2013

JigsAR: A Mixed Reality System for Supporting the Assembly of Jigsaw Puzzles

João M. X. N. Teixeira[1,2,3(✉)], Pedro J. L. Silva[1,2,3], Júlia D. T. de Souza[1,3], Filipe F. Monteiro[1,2], and Veronica Teichrieb[1,2]

[1] Universidade Federal de Pernambuco, Av. Prof. Moraes Rego, 1235 - Cidade Universitária, Recife, PE, Brazil
{jmxnt,pjls2,ffm,vt}@cin.ufpe.br, juliadtsouza97@gmail.com
[2] Voxar Labs, Recife, Brazil
[3] Maracatronics Robotics Team, Recife, Brazil
http://www.cin.ufpe.br/voxarlabs, http://www.maracatronics.com

Abstract. Augmented reality used to be only possible for science fiction. However, nowadays it is used in different areas for the improvement of human life. Even jigsaw puzzles could be improved by AR, and that's the purpose behind JigsAR: transforming a classic into something new. JigsAR is a web-based solution that is made with Javascript to improve the assembly of a jigsaw puzzle. JigsAR uses color quantization and image histograms to compare the piece with a database and indicate to the user the three most probable correct places. Two hypotheses were tested with twenty-five users to evaluate the tool effectiveness. In the end, the user test results are discussed from the point of view of ergonomics and technology usage.

Keywords: Jigsaw Puzzle · Augmented reality · Human-computer interaction

1 Introduction

The age of augmented reality (AR) is upon us. There have been AR headsets for a while now, with Microsoft pioneering the field with its Hololens. With other companies working in their solutions, such as Google (with the return of its Google Glasses) and Apple (with its AR Glasses estimated to be launched in 2022), this trend will lead to the popularization of a device now reserved to professionals. Augmented reality is not a new technology. Since Azuma's Augmented Reality survey [1] back in 1997, there is plenty of solutions focusing on different fields. Augmented Reality is known as a technology capable of modifying the real environment adding virtual content to it to indicate help the user perform a task.

Regarding physical/tactile games, while some solutions help users solve Rubik's cubes, others add virtual elements to the game instead of helping its

© Springer Nature Switzerland AG 2020
A. Marcus and E. Rosenzweig (Eds.): HCII 2020, LNCS 12201, pp. 572–585, 2020.
https://doi.org/10.1007/978-3-030-49760-6_41

players. This paper describes a solution capable of supporting the assembly of jigsaw puzzles using mixed reality. Since it is implemented in pure Javascript, it should be deployed to any of the existing devices with a browser or like a web app.

We make use of augmented reality techniques to highlight the correct place of the pieces in a board to the user and make him/her focus on a specific piece. The steps of the proposed algorithm are listed as follows:

1. Marker detection and perspective distortion correction;
2. Image quantization and piece identification using histogram comparison;
3. Highlight of the three most probable piece locations.

The remainder of this paper is organized as follows. Section 2 lists the works related to the solution proposed by the authors. Section 3 details how JigsAR, the Augmented Reality-based app that supports the construction of jigsaw puzzles on web browsers, was implemented. Section 4 describes the methodology used behind tests and JigsAR evaluation with the results obtained from the tests, along with some of the findings that emerged from the tests performed. At last, Sect. 5 concludes the work and points some future work directions.

2 Related Work

Augmented Reality techniques are vastly used by many user assistance solutions so that the user performs some activity in an optimized way. The utilization of these techniques allows highlighting elements in the screen to hold the user's attention or even guide him/her to a better solution.

One example of solution that assists the user to perform an activity in a better way is proposed by [6], which uses projective augmented reality to assist in the assembly of tracks for a line-follower robots competition, as shown in Fig. 1. According to the authors, the augmented reality usage decreases the assembly time significantly. However, to use the solution, a very large equipment setup is required. An advantage of the technology is that it runs on browsers, with no software installation required.

Another solution that makes use of augmented reality to assist the user is the Jigsaw Puzzle AR, proposed in [5] and [2]. This solution aims to track non-textured objects based on a shape discriminant using Depth-Assisted Rectification of Contours (DARC) and depth cameras. The solution was implemented using a puzzle and aimed to recognize and obtain the pose of planar objects in real-time. The proposed solution showed potential even for use in an educational environment to assist in teaching geography, as in Fig. 2, because a child could have access to content related to each region when assembling the map.

In [4] another augmented reality educational solution, called ARBlocks, was proposed to help the development of educational activities for children. Using generic blocks and projective augmented reality, as can be seen in Fig. 3, the solution proposes the tracking of blocks with specific markers where the contents to be worked playfully are projected, including puzzle applications. This solution

Fig. 1. ARena being used to help the assembly of line-following robots tracks. Source http://bit.ly/arenaTool

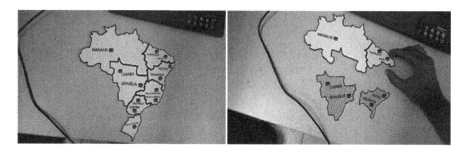

Fig. 2. AR Jigsaw Puzzle being used to teach Brazilian geography. Source: http://bit. ly/voxarPuzzle

requires an expensive and very large equipment setup that is difficult to assemble and not accessible to every user. Also, the solution requires camera calibration processes to be able to track objects.

Voxar Puzzle [7] is a puzzle game for children, where the main focus was the user interaction with the solution. With Voxar Puzzle, in Fig. 4, the user can manipulate real blocks similar to ARBlocks, in order to interact with the entire game interface, which is virtual. To ensure playfulness and attractiveness for the children, each block has a different character, which makes the piece unique. This solution had pre-registered puzzles that were displayed in the game environment.

In [3], the authors propose a solution that uses augmented reality as an assistive tool for the resolution of a $2 \times 2 \times 2$ magic cube using an iPad and

Fig. 3. Tangible pieces being highlighted using ARBlocks solution.

Fig. 4. Voxar Puzzle and interaction between blocks and game. Source: http://bit.ly/voxarPuzzle

Fig. 5. A solution that help users to solve a Rubik's cube.

2D markers to identify the position of the pieces, as in Fig. 5. After identifying where each part is, the software indicates a series of steps for solving the cube.

3   JigsAR

The proposed solution consists of a web app capable of running on any computer or mobile device and helping a person to assemble puzzles previously registered in the database.

The device must have Javascript support through a browser and a camera (webcam connected to a computer or integrated camera in case of a mobile device). Also, no image calibration process is necessary. The calibration is done automatically by the app itself using an Aruco marker present on the assembly platform. It is used to find the user work area in which the puzzle should be assembled as well to correctly highlight the location of the most probable place of the piece.

For the identification of each piece, a color quantization process was used. This process is quite common for obtaining histograms, which consequently were also used in this solution. The process consists of analyzing the intensity of each color in each pixel of a given image. For this, the total set is divided into sub-dimensions called *bins*. In this work, each RGB pixel (originally using 3 8-bit channels, 24-bit total) was quantized to only 6 bits, being 2 bits the most significant bits of each channel. This approach works well since we are dealing with Romero Brito's painting style, that uses colorful palletes and lacks soft color variations (gradients). Figure 6 illustrates the difference between the original image and the quantized one. Given the described characteristics, the difference between the images are almost nonperceivable by the human eye. A clear difference between the two images is that the quantized one is darker, since the six less significant bits are ignored (set to zero).

Once this is done, the process of classifying each pixel begins. It consists of analyzing the pixel intensity, as in Fig. 7 and adding a unit in the subset to which the value of that pixel belongs. Thus, it is possible to obtain a one-dimensional representation of the image such as Fig. 8, which allows processing for identification of the piece.

One advantage of using histogram information to detect pieces is that the piece image can be captured in any orientation. Since histogram information ignores pixel positions, the computed histogram for the same piece in different orientations should be very similar. It is also possible to capture pieces with different sizes since the computed histogram is normalized (the sum of all bins equals 1). The piece database only stores the 64 floating numbers regarding each piece histogram. The order in which they are stored already indicates their linear position in the jigsaw puzzle and is used as a piece index. For a 5×4 jigsaw puzzle, for example, only 1.25 KBytes are needed for storing all 20 pieces of information. The disadvantage of using histogram comparison is that despite it is a faster comparison method, it is not so robust to illumination changes and, before the usage, a histogram for each peace of the puzzle must be generated. A different approach (by detecting piece features and searching the complete puzzle image for them) is also possible, but more computationally intensive. Since the solution was proposed for mobile devices and browsers, the simplest one was used.

Fig. 6. Original images (left) versus quantized ones (right): Romero Brito's Mia garden painting (Puzzle #1, top) and Garden painting (Puzzle#2, bottom).

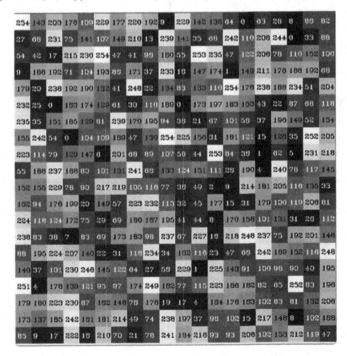

Fig. 7. Luminosity intensity of each pixel. Source: http://bit.ly/histoOpencv

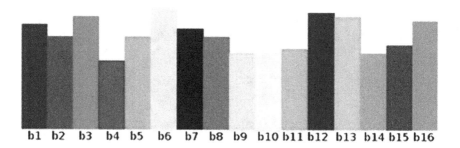

b1 b2 b3 b4 b5 b6 b7 b8 b9 b10 b11 b12 b13 b14 b15 b16

Fig. 8. Quantization final result. Source: http://bit.ly/histoOpencv

For each piece, its histogram is associated with its matrix position in the game and thus it is possible to indicate to the user where that piece should be placed on the board.

The algorithm illustrated in Fig. 9 was validated using two 5×4 jigsaw puzzles, as illustrated in Fig. 10.

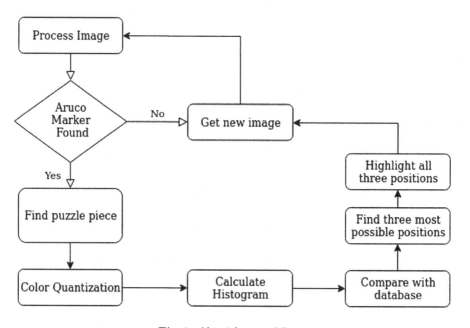

Fig. 9. Algorithm workflow.

The shape of the pieces came from The Jigsaw Puzzle website[1], to whom the original images were uploaded and a 20 piece classic cut was selected, as shown in Fig. 10.

---

[1] www.thejigsawpuzzles.com.

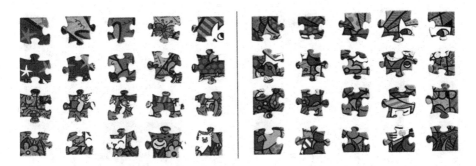

Fig. 10. Pieces of the two 5 × 4 puzzles used.

Figure 11 illustrates a possible outcome of the developed system, in which the three most possible positions of the evaluated piece are shown in the assembly area. The small squares in red, green and blue (in this sequence) are the locations with highest reliabilities, in which the red one has the most probability of being correct. It is important to note that the piece must be initially placed in the area bellow the ARuco marker in order to be recognized by the system. In all tests a Samsung S10 cellphone was used, running the solution inside the Google Chrome browser for Android.

4   User Tests and Analysis

4.1   Test Methodology

We performed user tests to estimate how much the solution improves the process of assembling a jigsaw puzzle, against the conventional assembly process with no additional help.

The tests were based on five separated groups, each with five people. In the first group, the users started the experiment using the JigsAR tool to solve Puzzle #1, after that, they were requested to solve Puzzle #2 with no additional help. The second group started with Puzzle #2 with no additional help and after that, they were requested to assembly Puzzle #1 using JigsAR.

The third and fourth groups used the JigsAR with Puzzle #2, in an analogous way to groups 1 and 2. This way all combinations were tested: J1C2, C2J1, J2C1 and C1J2 (where C means conventional and J means using JigsAR).

The fifth group used the same configuration as the first group, but the cellphone was placed in a support pedestal, removing the need of users to hold the phone in their hands, granting them more freedom to move.

Each group used one of Romero Britto's jigsaw puzzle presented in Fig. 10. Both puzzles had the same quantity of pieces (5 × 4) and a very similar difficulty, once they had a similar color set, drawings and cuttings.

Before using JigsAR, all users received a brief explanation about how the proposed solution works. For both scenarios (using and not using JigsAR), the

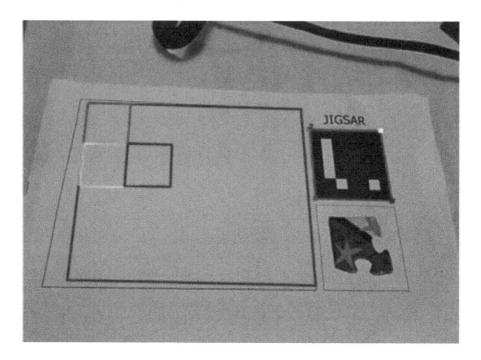

Fig. 11. Possible outcome of the proposed algorithm. (Color figure online)

timer started when the users moved the first piece and ended when the last piece was placed.

After the test, all users answered a brief questionnaire asking about their ages, previous experience with AR, if they liked to play with jigsaw puzzles and their scholarity. It is important to note that all tested users study or work in the same University. The users profile is detailed as follows.

4.2   User Profile

The test was applied to 25 users, of which eleven had previous experience with Augmented Reality and 16% were female. The average age of users was 25 years old and twelve were under-graduated students, two were graduated and other six are doing or did post graduation.

About 50% said they like to assemble puzzles, 25% said they like to assemble but they don't do this often. The remaining 25% said they do not like to assemble puzzles.

This user profile allowed a test with non-biased results due to the variability of users' characteristics. Another important point is the percentage of people who had previously experience with augmented reality, this value is less than 50% of all users. This fact could be a cause of a biased result due to their knowledge about AR challenges.

4.3   First Hypothesis Evaluation

The initial hypothesis was that JigsAR was an effective tool to shorten the assembly time of any jigsaw puzzle. Since the user would not take too much time to correctly guess where the pieces should be placed, we supposed that the system would diminish the time required to finish the task by a significant amount.

Table 1 details the time spent by each user as well the mean time for each group. The analysis of this data is presented in the next section.

Table 1. Time in seconds spent by the four groups.

User	Sequence	First time	Second time
1	J1C2	240	399
2	J1C2	258	288
3	J1C2	373	503
4	J1C2	305	450
5	J1C2	470	541
	J1C2 mean	**329.2**	**436.2**
6	C2J1	321	274
7	C2J1	452	454
8	C2J1	265	394
9	C2J1	269	212
10	C2J1	314	301
	C2J1 mean	**324.2**	**327**
11	J2C1	301	257
12	J2C1	301	230
13	J2C1	207	187
14	J2C1	395	515
15	J2C1	370	398
	J2C1 mean	**314.8**	**317.4**
16	C1J2	522	1083
17	C1J2	475	372
18	C1J2	436	758
19	C1J2	240	451
20	C1J2	531	825
	C1J2 mean	**440.8**	**697.8**

The analysis of the average time of experiments with JigsAR indicates an increase of time spent to assemble the puzzle in comparison with experiments without JigsAR for all tested groups. This fact indicates that using the tool in the first experiment does not impact the second experiment without the tool, and the opposite is true, too.

Only seven users of twenty, about 35%, had a result compatible with the initial hypothesis and had a decrease in time spent to assemble the puzzle with JigsAR in comparison to assembling the puzzle with no additional help.

Many users talked about the ergonomics of the solution. They said that the fact of having to hold the phone in one hand, as shown in Fig. 12, caused delays in putting the puzzle together and that it would be nice to be able to use both hands. Another problem was regarding the colors used to specify the most probable correct places to each part. Some users said that the colors used can cause confusion and it would be better if the most probable place was painted using the green color.

Fig. 12. Users testing JigsAR using one hand to hold the cellphone. (Color figure online)

The users also said the multiple possible places the tool indicated caused some confusion about the correct place, and some users said they just stopped using the JigsAR. But other users said the JigsAR tool helped so much and correctly indicated the piece probable locations.

This feedback was the main reason to test another hypothesis, one that would address the ergonomic challenges that many users mentioned.

4.4   Second Hypothesis Evaluation

The second hypothesis was that JigsAR use has ergonomic problems, and if we minimize such problems the tool could in fact reduce the assembly time of a jigsaw puzzle.

Table 2 details the time spent by each user as well the mean time for each group. The analysis of this data is presented in the next section.

Table 2. Time in seconds spent by the fifth group in the test with both hands free.

User	Sequence	First time	Second time
21	J1C2	325	430
22	J1C2	173	222
23	J1C2	233	300
24	J1C2	260	421
25	J1C2	235	381
	J1C2 mean	**245.2**	**350.8**

The solution was tested with a group of five extra users (group 5). In this test, we positioned the cellphone in a support pedestal, so that the users would not have to use their hands to hold the phone, as shown in Fig. 13.

This decision was made because many users complained that they would like to have both hands free to position the puzzle pieces. Although the users seemed to like the extra mobility, the time required to perform the task with the tool

Fig. 13. Cellphone with support pedestal.

did not improve significantly. We also realized that in this configuration, the accuracy of the tool improved, as the phone was in a fixed position, shown in Fig. 14.

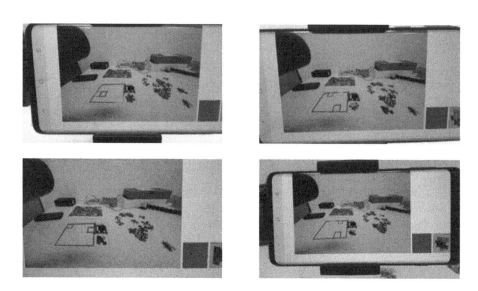

Fig. 14. JigsAR with better accuracy in the support pedestal.

5   Conclusion

This work detailed JigsAR, a web tool for supporting the assembly of jigsaw puzzles. The tests performed show that despite some limitations regarding illumination variations, the system was well accepted by users. Most of them considered JigsAR an interesting tool, but by using two simple jigsaw puzzles we were not able to confirm our hypotheses that the proposed tool would improve the time needed to assembly the puzzles. By using a simple approach (based on histogram comparison), we were able to get a good performance even if the solution runs on mobile devices, inside a web browser.

The use of histograms can cause some confusion in the system, making different pieces to be classified wrongly. One possibility would be to use, in conjunction with histogram analysis, an external contour analysis of the part, thus reducing the possibility of errors in identification. With the appearance of depth cameras on mobile devices, the use of algorithms such as DARC become closer to the proposal of this solution.

As future work, we intend to port the solution to different augmented reality headsets and evaluate its performance while being used in such devices (with both hands free). We also intend to verify the user performance gain while using JigsAR to assembly more complex puzzles (with more pieces). We believe that there will be a true gain in performance when applying the system to more complex puzzles (more than 100 pieces).

A live demo of JigsAR can be found in https://pedrojlsilva.github.io/jigsAR/, together with a video showing JigsAR in action in https://youtu.be/Prlbv0f5sMo.

References

1. Azuma, R.T.: A survey of augmented reality. Presence: Teleop. Virt. Environ. **6**(4), 355–385 (1997)
2. Lima, J.P., Teixeira, J.M., Teichrieb, V.: AR jigsaw puzzle with RGB-D based detection of texture-less pieces. In: 2014 IEEE Virtual Reality (VR), pp. 177–178. IEEE (2014)
3. Park, J., Park, C.: Guidance system using augmented reality for solving Rubik's cube. In: Stephanidis, C. (ed.) HCI 2014. CCIS, vol. 434, pp. 631–635. Springer, Cham (2014). https://doi.org/10.1007/978-3-319-07857-1_111
4. Roberto, R.A., de Freitas, D.Q., Simões, F.P.M., Teichrieb, V.: A dynamic blocks platform based on projective augmented reality and tangible interfaces for educational activities. In: 2013 XV Symposium on Virtual and Augmented Reality, pp. 1–9. IEEE (2013)
5. Silva, M., Vilar, E., Reis, G., Lima, J.P., Teichrieb, V.: AR jigsaw puzzle: Potencialidades de uso da realidade aumentada no ensino de geografia. In: Brazilian Symposium on Computers in Education (Simpósio Brasileiro de Informática na Educação-SBIE), vol. 25, p. 194 (2014)
6. Silva, P.J.L., Henriques, D.B.B., Lima, G.C.R., de Souza, J.D.T., Teixeira, J.M.X.N., Teichrieb, V.: ARena: improving the construction process of line-follower robot arenas through projection mapping. In: Marcus, A., Wang, W. (eds.) HCII 2019. LNCS, vol. 11584, pp. 291–308. Springer, Cham (2019). https://doi.org/10.1007/978-3-030-23541-3_22
7. Silva, V.E., et al.: Voxar puzzle: an innovative hardware/software computer vision game for children development. In: 2015 XVII Symposium on Virtual and Augmented Reality, pp. 147–153. IEEE (2015)

Analysis of Clustering Techniques in MMOG with Restricted Data: The Case of Final Fantasy XIV

Lucas Vanderlei Fernandes[1] , Mauricio Miranda Sarmet[2] ,
Carla Denise Castanho[1] , Ricardo Pezzuol Jacobi[1] ,
and Tiago Barros Pontes e Silva[1(✉)]

[1] Brasília University, Brasília, Brazil
lucas_v.f@hotmail.com, carladenisecastanho@gmail.com,
ricardojacobi@gmail.com, tiagobarros@unb.br
[2] Paraíba Federal Institute of Education, Science and Technology,
Paraíba, Brazil
msarmet@gmail.com

Abstract. One of the challenges in the Game Analytics field is to determine the type of information that can be obtained from a specific MMOG, as well as which data mining technique to use or develop depending on the peculiarities of its database. In this context, the object of study of this research is Final Fantasy XIV, a very popular MMOG that provides a limited amount of open data and also has been little researched in the literature. Therefore, this work studies the various clustering techniques as a game data mining tool. Different clustering methods are compared in order to find out the best results in the context of this game, which presents a narrow range of data for analysis. The following seven clustering algorithms were used: The k-means (partitional clustering), WARD (hierarchical), DBSCAN (density-based), spectral-based, BANG (grid-based), SOM (model-based), and Fuzzy C-means (Fuzzy Clustering). Regarding the identified player profiles by the clustering process, the results suggested the presence of five different categories: Beginner, Casual, Dedicated, Hardcore and Intermittent, characterized according to their behavior within the game. These results may contribute to a better understanding of the Final Fantasy XIV player groups and provide a basis for future work, as well as provide a case study on clustering techniques applied over a limited set of game data.

Keywords: Massive multiplayer online game · Game analytics · Final fantasy

1 Introduction

Digital games are one of the fastest growing segments in the recent years within the entertainment industry [1]. The MMOGs, or Massive Multiplayer Online Games, have benefited as a result of this growth. Nonetheless the genre of this games demands a wide player base to be profitable. Many MMOs have been created in recent years, but few have achieved success [2]. Unlike other genres, the financial success of such games relies on maintaining old players and attracting new ones. However, the dedication they

A. Marcus and E. Rosenzweig (Eds.): HCII 2020, LNCS 12201, pp. 586–604, 2020.
https://doi.org/10.1007/978-3-030-49760-6_42

require is time consuming and may be a problem for many individuals. Several players tend to stop playing in favor of other alternatives, a situation that may occur when the player loses interest in the game. Therefore, the continued interest of the player is vital to the survival of this kind of game.

Many developers use analytics to better understand the game's development and user experience in order to participate in this very competitive market. The analysis of data from digital games, or Game Analytics, is being adopted not only by the industry, but also by researchers as an easily adaptable investigation tool for many studies [3, 4]. The Game Analytics can be used in several stages of a game's life cycle, regardless of its genre. During the conception and design stage, its use can focus on finding elements of success in similar games, for example. In the development stage, optimizing performance and making decisions about game mechanisms are preferable targets for the Game Analytics. The tests stage can apply the techniques of this process to validate improvements and point out flaws in the game. Finally, when the game has already been released, the Game Analytics can provide valuable information on how to improve the product. The use and application of this type of analysis tool results in a product with more appeal to the player base.

One of the most frequently used techniques both in Game Analytics and in general data analysis is clustering [5–22]. This technique groups objects under analysis based on common characteristics, allowing the classification of large volumes of data. However, despite being a widely used technique, there is no single clustering algorithm that can be successfully applied to any type of data [23, 24]. Consequently, there are different approaches and algorithms for performing these groupings, thus generating the need for studies to establish the best approach for each situation.

In this competitive gaming scenario, the application of Game Analytics techniques requires an extensive collection of data about the behaviors of players. However, such information is not always easily available. The data source accessible to the developers consists of the database generated by the players' actions and the evolution of their characters throughout the game. While the company that produces the game has access to all the collected information, the data is not always publicly available. In addition to the restrictions on the type of obtainable information, another equally fundamental problem is the understanding of these data, which purpose is to generate useful information for the analysis.

In this context, the present study's object is Final Fantasy XIV, a very popular MMO game. Despite the large number of users, there is a limited amount of available open data for the researchers. Also, it has been little researched in the literature. Notwithstanding these restrictions, it has an expressive and growing number of characters that can currently rival even World of Warcraft, the most popular game of its kind [25]. Another peculiar factor of Final Fantasy XIV is the player's freedom to explore all the available classes in the game with the same character. It is a different approach from the one adopted by the World of Warcraft, which limits the character according to the chosen class, not allowing class changes as in Final Fantasy XIV. This freedom allows the person's playing style to be more precisely reflected in the character's actions, not requiring the creation of other characters to explore other classes, a common event in World of Warcraft. This peculiarity may benefit the data analysis in Final Fantasy for having a number of characters closer to the number of players, allowing the understanding of the complete behavior of each player from the available data.

Therefore, the main objective of this research is to determine the most adequate data clustering technique for the set of data provided by the Final Fantasy XIV game. Data from the characters of Final Fantasy XIV will be collected within a website that makes them available monthly [26]. Data is pre-processed in order to make it more adequate to clustering algorithms. Python will be used to perform the treatment of the data set aided by libraries recommended by the literature for cluster analysis. The results of the different clustering algorithms with be evaluated based on internal statistic tools. Player profiles will also be derived for comparison purposes.

2   Methods

The analyzed data comes from the game Final Fantasy XIV, grouped monthly by the FFXIV Census [26]. In this study, the following months were collected:

- 2017: June, October;
- 2018: February, June, October;
- 2019: February, June.

The existence of a standard period between the months allowed the organization of the data. The choice of using the months listed above was made looking for the lowest possible cadence among the months available within an expansion, resulting in a difference of four months between one analyzed month and the next. The SQL files for those related months were downloaded and executed with MySQL Workbench to create the Database with a table of characters for each month. Using the Python language, a code was developed to make the connection with the resulting Database and to collect the data of each character in the required month to apply the clustering.

2.1   Pre-processing

In this section, the procedures performed to deal with data pre-processing are presented. All listed treatments will be performed once for each analyzed month. Each clustering algorithm will be executed using the result of this step.

Missing Values. Classified as a data cleaning process, checking and correcting missing values analyzes each data object for any attributes that are not recorded. A Python algorithm was developed to connect with the studied database and performed a search for empty or null attributes. The algorithm finishes informing if there was any empty attribute. If so, the missing attributes are filled in manually in the Database with the minimum value related to the attribute domain.

Attribute Conversion. Processes that perform attribute comparisons are more efficient when using numerical values because their comparison is simpler than comparing non-numeric values. A conversion will be performed for each non-numeric value contained in the Database collected for analysis. Only the character's name will not be converted into a numeric attribute. The originally binary attributes will be converted to 0 for false and 1 for true. The gender attribute will be converted into the same binary representation because in the game they have only two genders. The race attribute and Grand Company will be converted using the data structure contained in Python, dictionary. From this structure, each option is converted into a numerical value. The representation of the players' clan was converted into a binary representation (0,1) using the attribute that references the clan's name.

Attribute Aggregation. The aggregation of attributes aims to improve the efficiency of the data mining process, as well as to make the result more easily interpretable. In this process, groups of attributes of the characters from the database were compiled into more general attributes. For example, the conversion of the attributes related to the levels of each class and job into attributes related to the experience were made through the sum of the experience necessary to reach each informed level. The conversion into experience was necessary because the amount of experience needed depends on the current level and increases exponentially. The attributes of class and job have been added according to their roles, due to the fact that each role characterizes a different playstyle. Such aggregations were performed by the Python algorithm created for the present study.

Normalization. Standardization techniques were applied to avoid dependence on the choice of measurement units. These techniques are necessary for cases where the attributes' units of measurement affect the result of the analysis [23]. Normalization involves transforming the original numerical data into a smaller, common range for all attributes, frequently between (0,1) or (−1,1) [23]. The technique applied in this work is Min-Max Normalization, a technique that preserves the relationships between the original values of the data [23]. The implementation adopted in this work is the one present in the Scikit-Learn library, with the name of MinMaxScaler [27]. The range that will be used will be (0,1).

Dimension Reduction. The structure of a real database may have dozens of attributes. Because of that there is a high possibility of occurrence of irrelevant or redundant attributes. Keeping these attributes can be disadvantageous to the analysis, causing confusion for the employed mining algorithm. A solution to this dilemma is the removal of such attributes. However, this task is performed with care as the removal of relevant attributes will result in low quality analysis [23]. The assistance of an expert in the field might be very useful in choosing the subsets of attributes. Nonetheless, such an activity can be complex and time-consuming, especially when the behavior of the data is unknown [23].

The adopted solution involves a correlation matrix using Pearson's Correlation with the attributes resulting from other pre-processing procedures [28]. The resulting correlation map will relate all variables to each other, calculating the correlation coefficient for each pair. The value of this coefficient varies in the range (−1, 1) [28]. The attributes that have low correlation with all other variables will be removed from the cluster analysis, since it won't help to build any profile. That is, those attributes that do not have correlations outside the range of (−0.5, 0.5) will be ignored. This filtering method was chosen for its simple implementation that allows the treatment of many attributes without higher costs and for its good performance with Exploratory Data Analysis [28]. The implementation was made with the Python libraries: Pandas, matplotlib [29] and seaborn.

Domain Size Reduction. The analysis of significant amounts of data may be costly for the hardware that will perform the experiment. Such difficulties stem from the need for large computational resources to carry out operations with the massive volume of data. Though, the available computational resources for this research are not able to analyze the complete set of collected characters. Therefore, the analysis was done with a sample of the studied domain. The selection of the sample members was randomly made through a command present in SQL to retrieve the sample arbitrarily. This choice is made to avoid a possible biased outcome. As a consequence of this selection, the analyzed characters in one month will not necessarily be those analyzed in another month, making it impossible to perform a temporal analysis of characters.

A tool was used to calculate the population proportion to determine the number of present characters in the sample. It is available at the Select Statistical Services website [30]. For this, the chosen number to represent the population is 16,000,000 as this is the smallest rounded valor that is higher than the population for any studied month. The proportion was estimated as 50% due to the lack of knowledge about the population profile. Finally, the margin of error and confidence levels were chosen as 1% and 99% to produce more reliable results. The obtained number was 16,571. Consequently, the chosen sample size was rounded to the upper bound 17,000.

Choosing the Number of Clusters. Some algorithms may need the number of clusters as an input parameter. k-means is an example of such kind of algorithms. Still, a wrong choice can result in a biased outcome, which consequently will generate unreliable scores. There are many ways in literature to achieve the "correct" number of clusters and there is no best way to make this decision [23]. The chosen approach for this study is simple, popular and effective, known as the Elbow Method.

The Elbow Method suggests that the ideal number of clusters is the largest possible number before the increase in clusters does not cause a significant reduction in the sum of variance within each cluster. This suggestion is based on the fact that although more clusters allow the capture of more refined groups of data objects, the effect of this increase in clusters on the sum of variances will be less and less significant. This decrease can actually be observed when dividing a cohesive grouping into two and both results will be similar to each other due to the cohesiveness of the original cluster [23]. In short, the heuristic of this method for selecting the right number of clusters is to use the turning point on the curve of the sum of the variances within the cluster in relation to the number of clusters [23].

2.2   Clustering Algorithms

This section will detail the clustering algorithms used in this research: k-means, WARD, DBSCAN, Spectral, BANG, SOM and Fuzzy C-means.

Partitional Clustering: k-means. The chosen algorithm to represent partial clustering methods is the most frequent algorithm in the related studies [5–14], the k-means. This can be justified by its simplicity and effectiveness [24].

Initially, the algorithm considers k random points in the dimension of the data in which the clustering will be applied. These will be the centers of each cluster in this first interaction [23, 24]. The second step assigns each data point to the nearest center. This approximation is based on a chosen distance measure, the n-dimensional Euclidean distance is used in this implementation [27]. Then, each cluster center is changed to the average of the values of its members. Subsequent interactions repeat the assignment of each data point to the new clusters. The algorithm will repeat such interactions until the center of the clusters does not change or it reaches some predetermined criteria [23, 24]. The implementation used will carry out such interactions until reaching the standard value of 300 repetitions or until the new centers are not distinguished from the previous centers [27]. This algorithm aims to minimize the sum of squares criteria within the cluster, that is, to decrease the general inertia.

Hierarchical: WARD. In addition to the partitional approach, one of the most popular methods in the literature is the Hierarchical methodology [13, 15–17]. This clustering model commonly relies on two alternative procedures: agglomerative or divisive. The agglomerative is a bottom-up method while the divisive is a top-down approach. Another common division between these algorithms is through the adopted similarity measure. Among the possible combinations of hierarchical algorithms, the most applied approach was the agglomerative one [13, 15, 16], with the use of Ward's criterion as the most frequent similarity measure [15, 16]. The Ward's criterion minimizes the sum of the squared differences across all clusters. Therefore, it is an approach that minimizes variance [27].

Density-Based: DBSCAN. The algorithm chosen to represent Density-based clustering is the DBSCAN algorithm (Density-Based Spatial Clustering of Applications with Noise) [14, 23]. This algorithm connects data objects and their surroundings to form dense regions as clusters [23].

The algorithm starts by marking each data object in a set as "not visited". Then the algorithm will perform a loop until all data objects are marked as "visited", ending the algorithm after these markings are closed. The first step inside the loop is the random selection of an "unvisited" object and its marking as "visited". After this markup, a check is made if the neighborhood of the point has at least MinPts objects. In negative cases, the point is marked as noise. In positive cases, a new cluster is created, and the point is added to it. Subsequently, another loop is made where each point within the vicinity of the point under analysis is evaluated if it has been "visited" before and if it belongs to any cluster. If not, it will be added to the created cluster. If it has not been visited, it will be marked as "visited" and if your neighborhood has at least MinPts objects, that neighborhood is added in the vicinity of the point under original analysis. After that, the outer loop will restart if "unvisited" points still exist [23].

Spectral-Based. This clustering methodology may not be considered one of the most applied techniques in recent studies. However, its growing popularity in recent years demonstrates the interest of the scientific community in these algorithms [5, 24]. This class of algorithms performs three steps in their implementations [24]. Initially, an affinity matrix is built for all data points. Then, the data points are incorporated into a sub-space, in which the clusters are more "obvious" using the Laplacian chart's eigenvectors. Finally, a classic clustering algorithm, such as k-means, is applied to partition the points in each sub-space.

Such algorithms can be summarized as a low-dimensional incorporation of the affinity matrix between the samples followed by a k-means in the low-dimensional space. The current implementation builds the affinity matrix using a Kernel function, such as the Euclidean distance Gaussian Kernel. It also requires the number of clusters as an input [27].

Grid-Based: BANG. The grid-based clustering approach was not applied in the related work. Therefore, an algorithm of this approach will be applied despite its lack of apparent popularity, this being the BANG algorithm [31]. Algorithms of this methodology use grid structures to group data objects. In this algorithm, a binary tree is used to store this multidimensional grid structure so that the search for neighbors can be done more efficiently. Then, a dendrogram is calculated from this tree in the grid directory and the density of classified blocks. Cluster centers are the densest blocks in the grouping phase [24].

Model-Based: SOM. Clustering based on probabilistic models have gained considerable popularity and expressed promising results in many applications [21, 22, 24]. Such algorithms are intended to optimize the fit of data objects to some mathematical model, adopting a probabilistic approach.

Presented in other researches in this field [21, 22], the clustering algorithm based on Self-Organizing Maps, or SOM, was applied in this study [31]. One of the advantages of this algorithm is its efficiency in data visualization. Its sequence of phases is similar to the sequence of the k-means algorithm, where each point is assigned to the cluster whose center is closest. However, during the stage of updating the center of each cluster, the neighbors of this central point are also updated. Upon completion, this algorithm generates a neural network, which exploration allows understanding of the relationships between the different involved objects in the cluster [24]. This algorithm can be summarized as being the neural network function implementation of the k-means algorithm [31].

Fuzzy Clustering: Fuzzy C-means. All previous algorithms had in their configurations a rule that each data element must belong to a single cluster. Nevertheless, the Fuzzy Clustering methodology algorithm does not have this rule and performs degrees of application for each data object in each cluster. This method arose for auxiliary data analysts in situations in which the execution of specific points assignments for clusters is not feasible as a result of complex data sets where there are overlapping clusters [24]. The algorithm that represents this method is the diffuse C-medium [31].

The implementation of this algorithm minimizes the SSE (Error Sum of Squares), followed by the update of the association weight of each point with every cluster, similarly to the k-means. Such interactions are repeated until the cluster centers converge [24].

2.3   Clustering Comparison

This section will approach the methods applied to evaluate and compare the results of clustering processes. These methods are Hopkins Statistics, Silhouette Coefficient, Calinski-Harabasz Index and Davies-Bouldin Index.

Hopkins Test. It is possible to have a homogeneous distribution in a random sample considering the lack of prior knowledge about the data. Such distributions invalidate any results obtained by eventual clustering. This invalidation occurs because in a homogeneous distribution, the divisions created by the clusters will be irrelevant. There is a method in literature that allows assessing the tendency towards clustering. The Hopkins Statistics [23] assesses how especially random a variable is distributed in a space employing the calculation of the shortest distances between neighbors in a data set and their randomly collected samples, resulting in a value in the range between 0 and 1. The employed implementation [32] will be applied in each analyzed month.

Silhouette Coefficient. The absence of external information to validate clustering results prevents the use of extrinsic means of validation, leaving only intrinsic methods to support the results. Intrinsic methods are used to assess how separate the clusters are from each other and how close are the elements within the same cluster. This study applies the Silhouette Coefficient [23] for such comparison.

The calculation is performed from the average distance between all objects belonging to the cluster for each object, representing the compactness of the cluster. In addition, the minimum distance from the objects to all other clusters is also averaged, representing how separate the object is from the clusters. The higher the average, the greater the separation between clusters [23]. With such definitions, the object's Silhouette Coefficient is calculated, generating a value between -1 and 1. The Silhouette Coefficient is computed using the average of the coefficients for each cluster. In turn, the coefficient of each cluster is calculated by the average of the Silhouette Coefficients of each of its members [23]. The implementation used to calculate this measure is contained in the Scikit-learn Machine Learning library [27].

Calinski-Harabasz Index. In addition to the Silhouette Coefficient, this study will apply the Calinski-Harabasz Index [33] to perform the intrinsic assessment of the resulting clusters. A higher value for this indicator suggests well-defined clusters [27]. The calculation of this index is performed using the sum of squares definitions between clusters and within them. After these calculations, the value of the Calinski-Harabasz index is obtained. Its implementation is contained in the adopted libraries [27].

Davies-Bouldin Index. Another available index for evaluating the resulting cluster model is the Davies-Bouldin Index [27, 34]. This index is defined as the average similarity between each cluster and its most similar cluster and is also contained in the adopted library [27]. Well-separated clusters result in values close to zero. The closer to zero, the better the separation between clusters, thus indicating a better data partition [27].

2.4   Profile Assignment

After the application of the clustering algorithm and the resulting groupings evaluated, there is only one step left to complete the data mining process: The inference of the result information. This work intends to analyze the properties of the resulting clusters in order to search for information about the player profiles that exist in Final Fantasy XIV. Nonetheless, if such profiles are not defined for a given clustering algorithm, this fact does not invalidate the algorithm.

The considered properties for profile assignment for each resulting cluster are composed of the following descriptive statistics:

- Number of Members;
- Average values;
- Standard deviation;
- Minimum Value Found;
- 1st, 2nd and 3rd Quartile;
- Maximum value found.

3   Results

3.1   Pre-processing Results

This section highlights the steps taken during the pre-processing of data from Final Fantasy XIV. The Missing Values, Attribute Conversion, Attribute Aggregation and Normalization processes took place as expected and did not require any deliberations.

Dimension Reduction. The execution of this step produced a heat map with the correlations between attributes for each month. When observing the result, the following attributes were removed from the analysis due to little correlation with other variables:

- Race: attribute that defines the player's race;
- Gender: attribute that defines the player's gender;
- Realm: attribute that defines the location of the server being used by the players;
- Grand Company: attribute that defines the Grand Company in which the player is a member;
- Legacy Player: attribute that defines whether the player played the version released in 2010;
- PreArr: attribute that defines whether the player purchased the game prior to launch the second version of the game;
- PObject: attribute that defines whether the player bought a game-related item in the real world.

After the removal, the player will be represented by the following attributes:

- Free Company: Identifier if the player belongs to a group of players;
- Physical Melee: Sum of the experiences of jobs that physically attack melee;
- Physical Ranged: Sum of the experiences of jobs that physically attack distance;

- Tank: Sum of job experiences that focus on defending the team;
- Magic Ranged: Sum of the experiences of jobs that attack with magic;
- Healer: Sum of job experiences that focus on healing allies;
- Arcanist: Sum of the experiences of the job Arcanist, which can heal or attack;
- Crafter: Sum of the experiences of jobs that focus on making items;
- Gather: Sum of experiences of jobs that focus on collecting materials;
- Lower Limit of Paid Months: Minimum amount of monthly payments;
- Heavensward Pre-Order: Identifier if the expansion was pre-purchased;
- Hildibrand: Identifier if the player did all missions contained in the comic story;
- Marriage: Identifier if the player married or was part of a virtual marriage;
- Complete Bestial Tribes: Identifier of the tribes that reached the highest level.

Domain Size Reduction Results. As a primary test, the pre-processing steps were applied to the total domain of characters contained in the least populous month without reduction. The program was unable to terminate since the process run out of memory. Thus, domain size reduction was shown essential to make the analysis feasible. Thereby this work performed the clustering in the totality of seventeen thousand characters chosen at random in each analyzed month. The choice of characters is made once a month, so the repetition of characters is possible, but unlikely due to the extensive amount of available data.

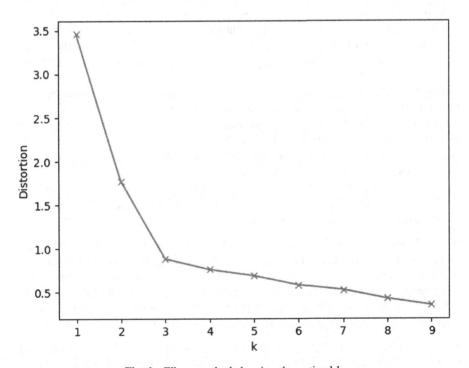

Fig. 1. Elbow method showing the optimal k.

Number of Clusters. The application of the elbow method made use of the graphs, as shown in Fig. 1. The conclusion reached when analyzing such graphs was the use of three clusters as an input value for the algorithms that require such pre-definition.

3.2   Clustering Algorithms Results

K-means Results. The first algorithm applied in the domain was *k*-means. As defined by the input value, each application generated three resulting clusters. The similarity of the averages of the attributes of the resulting clusters allows the identification between results. This shows that the algorithm produced the same clusters in all its applications, however, the order was not sustained. If the resulting clusters were not so different, the identification task would be more complex.

WARD Results. The second algorithm applied was the WARD. Like the previous algorithm, the execution generated three clusters for each month. The identification of clusters performed in the previous algorithm can be replicated in this result. However, Cluster 1 identified in the June 2017 application remains Cluster 1 in each subsequent application, also an observed characteristic in Clusters 2 and 3. This consistent feature of cluster generation can be used in sequential analyzes whose temporal distance from bases are so far as to make it difficult to identify each cluster formed in relation to a past state.

DBSCAN Results. After the execution of hierarchical clustering, the method applied was the density based. Unlike previous algorithms, DBSCAN does not require a number of clusters as input. This was the algorithm that generated the highest number of clusters for each of its applications. As the algorithm is not biased as to the number of clusters that will be formed in its result, this number varied throughout the applications.

Due to the large number of clusters shaped, the identification of a cluster resulting from one month in another month was made difficult. Only Clusters 1, 2, 3, 4 and 7 of June 2017 were listed in all subsequent months. In addition, the fact that made the analysis of the clusters even more difficult was the deterministic characteristic of the algorithm in conjunction with the random selection of characters, which did not allow the algorithm to generate the clusters in the same order.

Focusing on the Clusters that have been identified every month, despite the averages not showing consistent results, this algorithm still has frequently identified clusters not acknowledged by other algorithms so far.

BANG Results. The BANG algorithm was executed after applying the density-based procedure. Similar to the previous algorithm, the definition of a cluster number is not required. However, contrary to the result obtained with DBSCAN, the completion of this procedure did not result in multiple clusters. The algorithm was unable to identify different clusters in any of the applied months. One hypothesis for this result is the difficulty in generating grids for domains with many dimensions.

SOM Results. The clustering applied next represented the Model-Based approach. Like other algorithms, SOM required a number of clusters as input, so its execution created three clusters. When looking at the resulting clusters, it is notable that the averages of the first cluster formed in the first month are very similar to the averages of the first cluster of each month. This consistency is persisted in all clusters formed by this algorithm.

If we compare the result of this algorithm with the result of the k-means algorithm, the difference between results is the smallest of any other comparison. That is, both techniques identified the same clusters, but this algorithm produced results with greater consistency.

Spectral Results. The execution of the Spectral algorithm was performed after the model-based approach. This algorithm is part of the set of procedures that were started with the predefined cluster number. Consequently, the result for each month contains three clusters.

Analyzing the results, it was possible to identify the consistent existence of two clusters, the first and the third cluster created in June 2017. These were found in the following months, while Cluster 2 of that same month was not identified in the following months and was replaced by another cluster with similar means. One possible explanation is that the percentages for June 2017 were taken at the end of the second expansion of the game, so they may represent the final potential of Cluster 2 in subsequent months. The consistency of this algorithm was broken in June 2018, by identifying Cluster 3 from previous months as Cluster 2.

Fuzzy C-means Results. The last algorithm to be executed was the representative of the Fuzzy methodology, Fuzzy C-means. Like the previous algorithm, Fuzzy C-means resulted in three clusters due to the input value. Despite the characteristic that a data element can belong to more than one cluster, the result of this algorithm did not present any character in more than one cluster. This fact is evidenced by the sum of the members of all clusters in each month being equal to the size of the domain.

The similarity with the clusters formed by the SOM and k-means algorithms is evident. Another important peculiarity to note is the consistency present in the resulting clusters. As in other previous algorithms, Cluster 1 for the month of June 2017 is the same identified in Clusters 1 of each subsequent month. This Occurrence remained for Clusters 2 and 3.

3.3   Comparison of Clustering Results

Hopkins Test Results. The application of Hopkins' statistics was performed in each month to validate the distribution of data objects. The result of the statistic was constantly reported as higher than 0.965. These values show the high trend towards clustering of the explored domain. Therefore, such results confirm the hypothesis that the Final Fantasy XIV database contains great potential for cluster analysis.

Evaluation of Resulting Clusters. After domain validation with Hopkins statistics and the application of clustering algorithms, the result of the process must be evaluated. The average result of the Silhouette Coefficient for each algorithm was calculated. Observing the final values, it is noted that all algorithms achieved good numbers (higher than 0.8), with DBSCAN reaching the highest coefficient (0.85163). However, the difference between the results was small, indicating an equivalence when observing only the Silhouette Coefficient.

When examining the result of the Calinski-Harabasz Index, a greater disparity is perceived between the algorithms. The k-means (12011,91), SOM (11892,4) and C-means (11778,55) algorithms reported the best numbers, with the WARD (9786,81) in fourth place, with numbers approximately 20% smaller than the index of the best algorithm in this evaluation, k-means. The Spectral (4283,75) and DBSCAN (4362,94) algorithms resulted in the worst rates.

The last cluster assessment technique applied in this work was the Davies-Bouldin Index. All the algorithms achieved good results as well. However, the difference between the best (1.30766) and worst algorithm (0.98187), k-means and Spectral respectively, is considerably greater than the difference in Silhouette Coefficient.

3.4   Profiles Assignment Results

Players that present similar values for their attributes are grouped into clusters by the algorithms. By analyzing the common features, it is possible to build a profile for each cluster of Final Fantasy XIV players. Different algorithms may group players in distinct ways, producing alternative profiles.

The percentages were generated by dividing the average value of the attribute by the maximum possible for that attribute. Clusters were assigned to the same profile when their population percentages and more than half of the attributes have similar percentages.

Beginner. The Beginner profile, identified by all algorithms with the exception of BANG, includes the highest percentage of characters present in the database, with numbers exceeding 80% of the population. The most striking feature of this profile is the fact that it is the starting point for all players. Due to this characteristic, most of the attributes of the members of this profile have the lowest average values of any profile. This profile generally did not explore even more than 1% of any play style, with little participation in the activities of Bestial Tribes, Marriage or Hildibrand. Less than 10% committed to the purchase of the first expansion. Approximately 15% of the characters are part of a player clan and the average monthly fee is around three months. The sum of all players who started the game recently and who gave up playing after little experience make up this group. One of the most important challenges for MMO developers is to encourage players to migrate from this profile to more dedicated ones.

Casual. The next profile identified, called casual, gathers players with a greater experience in the game than the previous group, having an average between 5 and 12 paid monthly fees. These players overcame the challenges of the beginning of the journey and started an engagement with the game. This profile includes an average population less than 15%, but greater than 5%, of the domain. Their experiences with each way of playing surpassing the minimum values of Beginners, but still do not constitute even 10% of the maximum in any attribute of this type. Casual players, in general, are called as such due to the infrequent act of playing. His focus is usually on momentary entertainment, avoiding investing the time necessary to optimize his actions within any game. Although they are not avid players, they still invest in the game and can easily return when an update attracts them. One-third of casual players purchased the first expansion prematurely, while an average of 15% attended a wedding and completed Hildibrand's missions. Bestial Tribes missions have not been explored by this profile. An interesting feature is the high percentage of members belonging to clans, exceeding 75% of the members. This aspect is advantageous for the mass return of players, as casual players with a social aspect can return to investing time in the game if others join it. This phenomenon may be the explanation for this profile to have a high number of paid months and low experience, as many returns to play easily, but do not dedicate enough time to advance in their jobs.

Dedicated. In addition to Beginners and Casuals, another large group of players present in any game are those who invest considerably more of their time in the game. This group is represented by the Dedicated profile. The high engagement of this profile is evidenced by the use of 40% in some or most of the available means of play, a much higher value than the previous profiles. These values show a high probability of the player having jobs at the maximum level in the different means of play, revealing a characteristic of activities' exploration and optimization. Such characteristics are also seen in the high values of the attributes of Bestial Tribes, Weddings and Hildibrand missions, configuring a considerable interest of this profile in experiences outside the main mission. In addition to the expressive use of these players, the financial commitment is noticeably greater than other profiles. A margin of 55% to 79% of the players in this profile made the prior purchase of the first expansion and the attribute of paid monthly fees is the maximum seen in this database. The number of players in this profile is small, constituting only 5% to 2% of the characters present in the game. However, its existence influences and inspires other profiles to dedicate more to the game in order to be able to reach where this profile has arrived, thus helping the growth of the game.

The DBSCAN and Spectral algorithms identified clusters with percentages of population below the Dedicated profile identified by the other algorithms. Possibly ignored by the limitation of the number of clusters, the next two profiles are contained in the groupings of the algorithms that did not identify them.

Hardcore. The Hardcore profile can be seen as an extreme of the Dedicated Profile. Players of this profile seek to explore and optimize the maximum of each possibility offered by the game. The content of the End Game is the goal of these players, they seek to improve their character and equipment to the maximum level to be able to conquer the most complex and difficult challenges of this game. The reward of these achievements is commonly associated with a visual element, allowing these players to stand out among others. This prominence generates pride in Hardcore players, further increasing their engagement, and encourages other players to dedicate themselves more to the game. In contrast, the population of this profile is less than 1% of the domain, indicating the difficulty in achieving this result.

Intermittent. Finally, the last profile identified is the Intermittent, composed of clusters that have not been assigned to any other already mentioned profile. Only the DBS-CAN algorithm was able to identify it. The three clusters assigned to this profile have similar averages in almost all attributes. They report a high percentage of players who previously purchased the Heavensward expansion. However, there are four attributes where the clusters of this profile differ: FreeCompany, Monthly, Hildibrand and Marriage. In these attributes, the difference between percentages is greater than 50%. Although one of the clusters has a high average of paid monthly fees, their experiences are less than 10% of the maximum. One hypothesis for this behavior is the creation of characters for the benefit of another character. For example, creating an extra character to marry the main character and enabling the main character's wedding benefits without depending on another player, or even to purchase unique items with the second character and sell them for the main character's profit without him losing his unique item. Another hypothesis about the characters in this profile includes new players who knew another player who already belonged to a Free Company, so the character enters a clan right at the beginning of the game, purchases the first expansion before launch and immediately afterwards does not continue to play with the character.

3.5   Unidentified Profiles

Although the limited data available did not make cluster analysis impossible, the absence of important attributes for the study of MMORPGs made it difficult to identify derived profiles, or to classify characters that do not match the player's profile. Access to information about the character's game sessions would allow the classification of **Hardcore Specialists** profiles. A player profile that chose to specialize in just one job, playing concentrated and prolonged amounts of time, would probably be framed as Dedicated or Casual in the algorithms applied in this work, despite its characteristics being more similar to Hardcore.

Another profile that would be identified with this missing information is **Temporary Hardcore**. Unlike Hardcore, this profile focused on evolving the jobs available to the maximum and stopped playing, did not invest more time in the game and did not explore End Game content. Until a new expansion is launched and the maximum level is increased, these players will be classified as Hardcore by the algorithms that identified this profile. However, the engagement associated with the Hardcore profile are not present in the Temporary Hardcore profile in the same proportion.

These profiles include different types of gaming session, which are not identifiable by the available data. The frequency and volume of game sessions used in other studies [11] cannot be accessed due to the limited database, making it difficult to identify these profiles. To circumvent such adversity, an assessment of the player's equipment and items would make it possible to identify the type of content explored by the player as well as the frequency in which a new item is purchased. Unfortunately, such information is also outside the available domain.

Finally, a peculiar data that would provide interesting information about Final Fantasy XIV players would be the identification of the player who owns that character and what activities were done by him. In addition to improve the characters' classification in the clustering, knowing the player's activities allows the investigation of the Roleplay phenomenon. This phenomenon involves the simulation of a real life within the game, where the player aims to fulfill the responsibilities and activities that a person from the real world has, but in the virtual world. The identification of this profile was likewise not possible with the available data.

Player identification would also make it possible to study players who have more than one character. Regardless of the fact that a character has the ability to participate and execute any content in the game, there is the option of having more than one character. The study of the profile of these players has great relevance in understanding the success of MMORPGs.

4 Conclusion

4.1 New Database

The first expected contribution of this work is the introduction of the Final Fantasy XIV Database to the scientific community, thus expanding the diversity in studies about MMO games. The application of Hopkins' statistics revealed the high potential of contained grouping in this database.

This base has an aspect aimed at data analysis, the high dimensionality and size of the domain, which promote several combinations of analysis, allowing to overcome its limitations. It is expected a greater engagement of the scientific community with this base.

4.2 Algorithms' Comparison

The central contribution of this work is the result of the comparison of the different clustering techniques. This research applied seven clustering algorithms, each belonging to a different methodology, in seven databases referring to Final Fantasy XIV players, where each set corresponds to a specific month. After this application, the available clustering assessment methods were used in the result. Based on these evaluations and results, multiple conclusions were made.

No negative impact was observed in the result of the clustering due to the absence of more attributes or the availability of data more frequently. Therefore, the inherent restriction of this database did not affect the analysis of clusters. In agreement with the absence of a better clustering algorithm for any case, it was not possible to identify the best algorithm for the characters in Final Fantasy XIV. Still, the BANG algorithm was unable to cluster in any of its applications, configuring the worst result in addition to having the second worst performance.

The most classic clustering algorithm, k-means, achieved the best performance of all applied algorithms, characterizing it as a primary choice if the researcher has limits in terms of hardware. With highly similar clusters, the SOM algorithm obtained results almost identical to k-means. Nevertheless, the advantage of the SOM algorithm is identified in the consistency of the formed clusters, that is, the first cluster in a given month is the same first formed in any month subsequent. This consistency configures the SOM algorithm as a good choice when analyzing databases with a large temporal difference between them, facilitating the identification of possible profiles. The Fuzzy C-means algorithm achieved the same achievements as SOM, so its applications in this scenario are equivalent.

The Spectral algorithm obtained low evaluations, having the worst Davies-Bouldin and Calinsk-Harabasz Index. Also, the performance of this algorithm was the worst observed. One of the advantages of this algorithm was the identification of the Hardcore Profile, something unique in relation to the other algorithms, so its application can be made to complement the application of another algorithm.

The WARD algorithm did not achieve a better result in any evaluation and had the third worst performance. Despite having consistently identified clusters, it was not the only one to achieve this. Consequently, based on these results, its application is advised only in cases of results validation of other applications.

Finally, the last algorithm studied in this work, DBSCAN, obtained inconsistent evaluations, having the best Silhouette Coefficient and one of the worst Calinski-Harabasz Index. Its performance was reasonable, being the fourth best and worst performance. The peculiarity of this algorithm involves the lack of limitation on the number of clusters, so the final number of clusters is not known *a priori*. This characteristic impacts on the result's consistency, of which only five clusters were related to persistence. Another weakness of this algorithm is the categorization of data objects as noise, increasing the error in the final conclusion about the sample. Despite its weaknesses, the use of this algorithm is considered beneficial to discover new clusters and profiles.

4.3 Final Fantasy XIV Player Profiles

The third intended contribution of this work is the relationship of the resulting clusters with possible player profiles. The description of each profile was made by manipulating the averages of the attributes of each cluster, assigning a percentage margin for each one of them. In this way, five profiles were identified and pointed out: Beginner, Casual, Dedicated, Hardcore and Intermittent. A starting point for any research that will investigate Final Fantasy XIV players has been outlined by identifying these player profiles.

Also, confirming the existence of the identified player profiles will allow the developers to direct their actions to please the players of a given profile. On the other hand, the correlation with profiles found in other games has a wide value for the scientific community, allowing the creation of a generic profile. The validation of the identified profiles is valuable for developers, while the creation of the profiles has the potential to contribute to the broader understanding of the human being as a player.

4.4 Perspectives

Several aspects of the present study would benefit from further study. One of these aspects involves a more detailed consideration on each specific clustering methodology. Each clustering methodology has a wide range of algorithms. Exploring the differences between these solutions and extracting generalized conclusions for the problem in question has great potential for future research.

Another crucial topic for the next studies involves the temporal investigation of the clusters' behavior found on this data set, directing it to a predictive analysis of the custom of Final Fantasy XIV players. Unlike the random choice made in this research, observing the behavior of specific characters in their transitions between clusters should produce results of great interest to developers, helping them to design mechanics that facilitate the evolution of characters between profiles. Predictive analysis will allow the content planning among updates to match the number of estimated characters who will be able to enjoy the developed content. In addition to these aspects, we also suggest that the resulting clusters might be more deeply investigated.

References

1. Ell, K.: Video game industry is booming with continued revenue. https://www.cnbc.com/2018/07/18/video-game-industry-is-booming-with-continued-revenue.html. Accessed 27 Nov 2019
2. Florio, P.: The 15 biggest failures in MMO history. https://www.thegamer.com/the-15-biggest-failures-in-mmo-history/. Accessed 27 Nov 2019
3. Drachen, A., Seif El-Nasr, M., Canossa, A.: Game Analytics: Maximizing the Value of Player Data. Springer, Heidelberg (2013). https://doi.org/10.1007/978-1-4471-4769-5
4. Fernandes, L.V., Castanho, D.C., Jacobi, R.P.: A survey on game analytics in massive multiplayer online games. In: 17th Brazilian Symposium on Computer Games and Digital Entertainment (SBGames). IEEE (2018)
5. Bauckhage, C., Drachen, A., Sifa, R.: Clustering game behavior data. IEEE Trans. Comput. Intell. AI Games 7(3), 266–278 (2014)
6. Chen, C.W., Hsu, T.: Game development data analysis visualized with virtual reality. In: 2018 IEEE International Conference on Applied System Invention (ICASI), pp. 682–685. IEEE (2018)
7. Dheandhanoo, T., Theppaitoon, S., Setthawong, P.: Game play analytics to measure the effect of marketing on mobile free-to-play games. In: 2016 2nd International Conference on Science in Information Technology (ICSITech), pp. 125–130. IEEE (2016)
8. Benmakrelouf, S., Mezghani, N., Kara, N.: Towards the identification of players' profiles using game's data analysis based on regression model and clustering. In: Proceedings of the 2015 IEEE/ACM International Conference on Advances in Social Networks Analysis and Mining 2015, pp. 1403–1410. ACM (2015)
9. Yang, W., Yang, G. Huang, T., Chen, L., Liu, Y.E.: Whales, dolphins, or minnows? Towards the player clustering in free online games based on purchasing behavior via data mining technique. In: 2018 IEEE International Conference on Big Data (Big Data), pp. 4101–4108. IEEE (2018)
10. Drachen, A., Sifa, R., Bauckhage, C., Thurau, C.: Guns, swords and data: clustering of player behavior in computer games in the wild. In: 2012 IEEE Conference on Computational Intelligence and Games (CIG), pp. 163–170. IEEE (2012)
11. Siqueira, E.S., Castanho, C.D., Rodrigues, G.N., Jacobi, R.P.: A data analysis of player in world of warcraft using game data mining. In: 2017 16th Brazilian Symposium on Computer Games and Digital Entertainment (SBGames), pp. 1–9. IEEE (2017)
12. Sifa, R., et al.: Controlling the crucible: a novel PVP recommender systems framework for destiny. In: Proceedings of the Australasian Computer Science Week Multiconference, p. 39. ACM (2018)
13. Rodrigues, L.A.L., Brancher, J.D.: Improving players' profiles clustering from game data through feature extraction. In: 2018 17th Brazilian Symposium on Computer Games and Digital Entertainment (SBGames), pp. 177–17709. IEEE (2018)

14. Kwon, H., Jeong, W., Kim, D.W., Yang, S.I.: Clustering player behavioral data and improving performance of churn prediction from mobile game. In: 2018 International Conference on Information and Communication Technology Convergence (ICTC), pp. 1252–1254. IEEE (2018)

15. Saas, A., Guitart, A., Periánez, A.: Discovering playing patterns: time series clustering of free-to-play game data. In: 2016 IEEE Conference on Computational Intelligence and Games (CIG), pp. 1–8. IEEE (2016)

16. Hsu, S.Y., Hsu, C.L., Jung, S.Y., Sun, C.T.: Indicator products for observing market conditions and game trends in MMOG. In: FDG 2017, pp. 54:1–54:5. ACM (2017)

17. Anagnostou, K., Maragoudakis, M.: Data mining for player modeling in videogames. In: 2009 13th Panhellenic Conference on Informatics, pp. 30–34. IEEE (2009)

18. Jiang, J.R., Huang, C.C., Tsai, C.H.: Avatar path clustering in networked virtual environments. In: 2010 IEEE 16th International Conference on Parallel and Distributed Systems, pp. 845–850. IEEE (2010)

19. Bell, J., Sheth, S., Kaiser, G.: A large-scale, longitudinal study of user profiles in world of warcraft. In: Proceedings of the 22nd International Conference on World Wide Web, pp. 1175–1184. ACM (2013)

20. Ahmad, M., et al.: The many faces of mentoring in an MMORPG. In: Proceedings of the 2010 IEEE Second International Conference on Social Computing, pp. 270–275 (2010)

21. Rodrigues, L.C., Lima, C.A.M., Mustaro, P.N.: Clustering online game communities through SOM. In: 2009 International Joint Conference on Neural Networks, pp. 2699–2702. IEEE (2009)

22. Rodrigues, L.C., Lima, C.A.M., Oliveira, P.P.B., Mustaro, P.N.: Clusterization of an online game community through self-organizing maps and an evolved fuzzy system. In: 2008 Fourth International Conference on Natural Computation, vol. 2, pp. 330–334. IEEE (2008)

23. Han, J., Pei, J., Kamber, M.: Data Mining: Concepts and Techniques. Elsevier, Amsterdam (2011)

24. Aggarwal, C.C., Reddy, C.K. (eds.): Data Clustering: Algorithms and Applications. CRC Press, Boco Raton (2014)

25. Indvik, L.: The fascinating history of online role-playing games. https://mashable.com/2012/11/14/mmorpgs-history/. Accessed 27 Nov 2019

26. Final fantasy xiv census. https://ffxivcensus.com/. Accessed 26 June 2018

27. Pedregosa, F., et al.: Scikit-learn: machine learning in python. J. Mach. Learn. Res. **12**, 2825–2830 (2011)

28. Shetye, A.: Feature selection with sklearn and pandas. https://towardsdatascience.com/feature-selection-with-pandas-e3690ad8504b. Accessed 23 Oct 2019

29. Hunter, J.D.: Matplotlib: a 2D graphics environment. Comput. Sci. Eng. **9**(3), 90–95 (2007)

30. Services, Select Statistical: Population proportion - sample size. https://select-statistics.co.uk/calculators/sample-size-calculator-population-proportion/b. Accessed 24 Nov 2019

31. Novikov, A.: PyClustering: Data mining library. J. Open Source Softw. **4**(36), 1230 (2019). https://doi.org/10.21105/joss.01230

32. Kunaver, M.: Hopkins test for cluster tendency. https://matevzkunaver.wordpress.com/2017/06/20/hopkins-test-for-cluster-tendency/. Accessed 24 Nov 2019

33. Cengizler, C., Kerem, M.: Un: Evaluation of Calinski-Harabasz criterion as fitness measure for genetic algorithm-based segmentation of cervical cell nuclei. J. Adv. Math. Comput. Sci. 1–13 (2017)

34. Davies, D.L., Bouldin, D.W.: A cluster separation measure. IEEE Trans. Pattern Anal. Mach. Intell. **PAMI-1**(2), 224–227 (1979). https://doi.org/10.1109/TPAMI.1979.4766909

Possibility of Using High-Quality Bow Interface in VAIR Field

Masasuke Yasumoto[1(✉)], Kazumasa Shida[1], and Takehiro Teraoka[2]

[1] Faculty of Information Technology, Kanagawa Institute of Technology,
1030 Shimo-ogino, Atsugi, Kanagawa 243-0292, Japan
yasumoto@ic.kanagawa-it.ac.jp, s1623180@cce.kanagawa-it.ac.jp
[2] Department of Computer Science, Faculty of Engineering, Takushoku University,
815-1 Tatemachi, Hachioji, Tokyo 193-0985, Japan
tteraoka@cs.takushoku-u.ac.jp

Abstract. A game device that imitates a real object can provide a realistic experience. For example, a gun-type device and car-handle-type device can give players a realistic experience of shooting and driving, respectively. In our previous study, we proposed Physical e-Sports and developed extended reality con-tent that includes a bow-shaped controller device and gun-shaped controller devices. These two devices imitate a real bow or guns. The bow-shaped controller device consists of real bow components and sensors, enabling a player to feel the actual experiences of drawing and shooting. In this study, to improve the feeling of reality, we compared this bow-shaped controller device with a real bow by measuring a player's motions and gaze directions and confirmed the differences between them. We also investigated the relations between the amount of force applied the string and strain with this device. By using these relations, we integrated a mechanism of reducing shooting force into this device and improved the environment of measuring this force by using the strain gauges. From these experiments, we discuss the potential of using this bow controller device in Physical e-Sports.

Keywords: VR · Interface · Bow · Physical e-Sports

1 Introduction

Head-mounted displays (HMDs) offer virtual reality (VR) gaming that exploits visual and auditory senses. For example, "The VOID" [1] is a large-scale VR attraction that enables players wearing HMDs to play games while walking around a wide area. However, using HMDs can lead to problems including VR sickness or discomfort due to compression of the head, and HMDs are often not sanitary due to sweat when used by large numbers of people. Children under the age of 13 are also recommended not to use HMDs as wearing them may cause health problems.

Supported by the HAYAO NAKAYAMA Foundation for Science & Technology and Culture.

To solve these problems, we previously proposed Physical e-Sports, which differs from the current e-Sports [2] in that it enables players to feel the actions involved in the actual sport not only through computer graphics (CG) images but also through feedback to their bodies using extended reality (XR) technology without being concerned about physical limitations or age-restricted HMDs.

We developed VAIR Field, which is a mobile VR system composed of multiple VAIR devices and a server [2,3], as an application of Physical e-Sports. In this system, players use a bow- or gun-shaped controller device with a smartphone. The system tracks all device positions and shows images corresponding to the views from their positions on each smartphone's display. It enables up to ten players to play a game with such VAIR devices at the same time. In this application, we focused on improving the tactile sensation that players experienced rather than visual information.

Players wearing HMDs for VR generally cannot see information in the real world and their hand movements are limited to the range that can be acquired by the controllers. Also, they cannot see their handling of controllers directly. In fact, instead of real controllers, guns made with CG are displayed in much VR content. These images include the reality of using guns and enable the players to feel more comfortable due to their restricted movements. However, what these images show differs from the hand movements, and other movements cannot be expressed with the controllers. Players wearing transmission-type HMDs for mixed reality (MR) can see the actual controllers, but other problems with general-purpose controllers remain.

To solve these problems, in this study, we improved the quality our bow-shaped controller device, called VAIR Bow, for playing Physical e-Sport in VAIR Field. We also investigated whether players can experience the same operation of a real bow. Our approach is that device controllers will enable players to have the same feeling and handling as of real objects by specializing their shapes to bows or guns. By using bow- or gun-shaped devices, our XR content can use players' physical abilities for handling a bow or gun in the real world. Players with these devices can see their hands and controllers when wearing transmission-type HMDs for MR. Because our XR content for Physical e-Sports does not require HMDs, children can also play.

To improve the reality that players can feel, our controllers require the sense of real texture and operations. The controller materials, weights, and shapes have very important roles. It is difficult to make all the components of the controller real because since actual bullets, arrows, and explosives obviously cannot be used. Therefore, it is important to incorporate alternative stimuli and mechanisms for easy and safe use while coming as close to the real thing as possible.

We compared our bow-shaped device with a real bow and clarified the differences to get the device as close to the real one as possible.

Fig. 1. Bow-shaped controller devices. (Left: Light Shooter, Center: 3rd Electric Bow, Right: VAIR bow)

2   Related Work

Figure 1 shows three Japanese- and Western-style bow-shaped controllers that developed and improved.

First, the "Light Shooter" with the Electric Bow Interface [4] is based on a traditional Japanese bow and is used in combination with a projector. This controller includes a 6-axis sensor and can determine the shooting directions from the projected images. When a player draws this bow, the entire bow bends because the grip and limb are integrated. Considering this structure, we installed two strain gauges on the grip part for measuring the force required to pull the string, i.e. string-pulling force, by using a differential amplifier circuit with the Wheatstone bridge circuit. This controller detects the string-pulling force in 1024 steps and determines whether the player shot by measuring the change in the amount of string-pulling force over time. However, there is a problem in that the movable range is narrow because the image is projected on only one surface. Also, the player using this controller cannot move sufficiently due it only having 3 degrees of freedom (3-DoF).

The 3rd Electric Bow [5] is based on a western recurve bow and is a standalone system incorporating a mobile projector and computer. This controller can accurately detect the shooting directions of shooting virtual arrows by calculating information from a 9-axis sensor with the Kalman filter. It can also project the images on a wall, ceiling, or floor with the internal projector, and the images can create a 360-degree view. As with the Light Shooter, we installed strain gauges on its limb to measure the amount of string-pulling force. This controller consists of a PC, battery, and various sensors, which are all built-in, but the weight is about 1.5 kg. This is the same weight as an actual competition recurve bow. However, using this controller has only 3-DoF like the Light Shooter and cannot recognize player's movements. Because the light of the mobile projector in this controller is not sufficiently bright, this can only be used in a dark room with six white surfaces.

VAIR Bow [2,3] is a bow-shaped device for playing Physical e-Sports in VAIR Field. Instead of the 9-axis sensor in the 3rd Electric Bow, this controller uses a Vive Tracker for detecting 6-DoF positions and angles simultaneously. To measure the amount of string-pulling force, we installed four strain gauges on the metal parts on the grip of this controller. VAIR Field calculates the force by using a HX711 differential amplifier circuit. This controller can also be used in bright places because a smartphone attached to this controller displays images of XR content. From these features, VAIR Bow solves some of the problems we mentioned with the other con-troller; however, there is a new problem. Because the acceleration sensor in the Vive Tracker has a narrow detection range, the force of the returning pulled string can exceed this range. Therefore, when a strong shooting force is applied to this controller, the acceleration sensor may show abnormal values.

Several bow-shaped controller devices have been proposed and evaluated [6–9]. The bow device for VRHMD [6] is an example. The major difference between this bow device and our bow-shaped controller devices is that it uses a compound bow and arrow. However, the area where this bow device is used is restricted because it uses optical motion capture to detect the movement of strings and players by recognizing images with an external camera. Using a real arrow provides the real feeling of shooting, but there is a risk that the arrow may be actually shot from the bow. There-fore, this device is not suitable for competitive games with multiple players of Physical e-Sports players.

Our bow-shaped controller devices require "air shot" to shoot virtual arrows. The air shot means that a player draws and shoots without an arrow and is inherently dangerous for the player, but no accidents including bow breakage have occurred when using our controllers. This is because the bow is relatively weak and there is a mechanism to reduce string releasing force. Also, the timing of displaying the virtual arrow in images after releasing the string and shooting sounds improves the feeling of using a real bow; therefore, our basic policy is using a bow device without real arrows for Physical e-Sports. For this study, we investigated the differences between our VAIR Bow and a real bow.

3   Experiments

In this section, we describe two experiments and the results. First, we compared our VAIR Bow to a real bow by visualizing a player's drawing and shooting with each bow through biological measurements. We then investigated the relations between the amount of string-pulling force and degree of the strain gauges in the grip of VAIR Bow. To measure the force of drawing and shooting with high accuracy, the bow controller needs to prevent the sensor from causing errors due to shooting force. Therefore, we integrated a mechanism of reducing shooting force into this controller and improved the environment of measuring the shooting force by using the strain gauges.

3.1   Biological Measurements from Using Different Bows

In this experiment, a student, who is one of Japan's leading archery athletes, used his bow and VAIR Bow, and we measured his motions and gaze directions. He shot at a target for indoor practice in the three following patterns.

1. Using a 40-pound athletic recurve bow and shooting an arrow at the target
2. Using a 12-pound athletic recurve bow and shooting air at the target
3. Using our 12-pound VAIR Bow and shooting air at the target in MR

In pattern 3, a Vive Tracker was used instead of a target, and VAIR Field shows the target block at the tracker location in the same location on the smartphone (Fig. 2).

Fig. 2. Shooting experiments, upper left (40-lb bow with arrows), upper right (12-lb bow without arrows), and lower (10-lb VAIR bow without arrows)

We carried out three measurements simultaneously using an inertial motion capture Xsens MVN was used to capture the movement of the whole body, Pupil-Labs' PupilCore, an eyeglass-like eye-tracking device, and PLUX biosignalsplux to measure the surface electromyographic activity of eight muscles; left trapezius, left rhomboid, left pectoralis major, left triceps brachii, left forearm, right trapezius, right pectoralis major, and right forearm.

Body Motion. There was a difference in the time from preparing the bow for shooting to shooting. It took about 19.106 s for pattern 1, 7.995 s for pattern 2, and 6.389 s for pattern 3. This was mainly because it took time to actually set the arrow on the string. The time required to start pulling the string with the right hand and finish pulling it was 2.683 s in Pattern 1, 3.248 s in Pattern 2, and 2.672 s in Pattern 3, and there was no clear difference in terms of the existence of an arrow or strength of the limb of the bow.

From these results, there was no significant difference between the recurved bow and VAIR Bow when air shooting, although the time required for shooting varied depending on the existence of arrows. In the future, we will analyze the differences in movement in more detail by analyzing the amount of change in each joint and the difference in movement speed (Fig. 3).

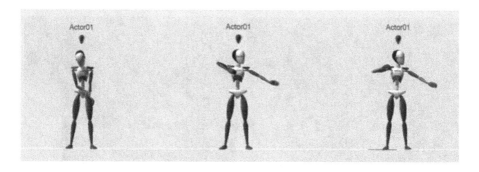

Fig. 3. Comparison of shooting motions, patterns 1, 2, and 3 from left; 7 s after the shooter's gaze point

Eye Tracking. For the eyeglass-type measurement, the position of the fixation point could be confirmed from an image, as shown in Fig. 4, and the image from the built-in video camera and fixation point at that time were displayed with a green dot. For pattern 1, since the arrow had to be set, the gaze was directed downward first, and the gaze point was at the hand setting the arrow to the string. The gaze point did not move from the approximate point when the bow starts to be held in preparation for shooting. In Pattern 2, the gaze point did not move much from the beginning to the end, and the gaze did not turn to the string or the missing arrow. Pattern 3 is also close to 2, but the point of interest is located at the target until the position of bow is fixed, then the point of interest is moved to the screen on the smartphone.

Surface Electromyography. Sensors were attached to each of the eight muscles, and the surface electromyography measurement was carried out. There was no significant difference in the weight of the bow, but Pattern 1 used a powerful 40-pound bow, so it was assumed that there was a difference in the movement of

Fig. 4. From left to right, patterns 1, 2, and 3; 7 s after the shooter's gaze point

the muscles during shooting. However, no beneficial results were obtained this time. It will be difficult for a weak bow limb to approximate the activity of a strong arm (Fig. 5).

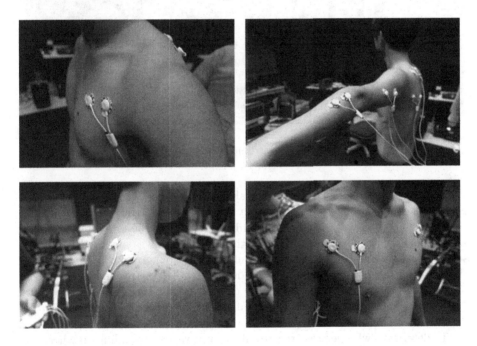

Fig. 5. Surface electromyographic sensors attached to eight muscles

3.2 Measurement of Bow

Two main approaches were taken to improve the accuracy of VAIR Bow. First, the relationship between the bow and the strain gauge was clarified. To do this, it is necessary to clarify the relationship between the string-pulling force and the strain gauge. The same 12-pound recurved bow used in the above experiment was used for this experiment.

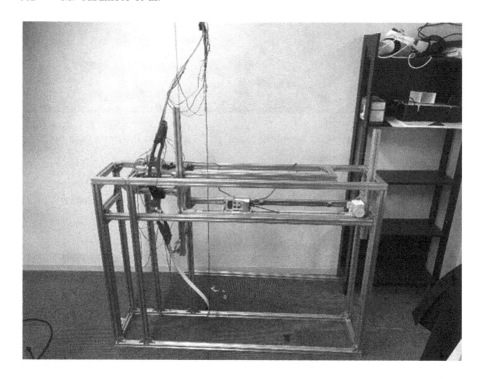

Fig. 6. Measuring instrument holding a 12-lb bow

First, the bow was fixed using an aluminum frame, and the apparatus in Fig. 6 was constructed for simultaneously measuring the string-pulling force and the strain. The bow was fixed to the aluminum frame with bolts where the strings are perpendicular. As shown in Fig. 7, the force gauge was attached where the string is pulled, and the string can be pulled using hook and any distance using the winding device at the rear of the device. The string-pulling force can be measured using a ruler attached to the device and the force gauge. The entire force gauge slider can be moved vertically, and a similar measurement can be done by changing the pulling position of the string.

To determine whether the string-pulling force varies depending on where one pulls the string, i.e., pulling the string at 5 cm intervals from the center of the string and 10 cm above and below that position. Figure 8 shows these results. The string-pulling force increased in proportion to the pulling position.

The grip of the bow is made of aluminum alloy and strain gauges are attached to the front and back of the limb. As shown in Fig. 9, two strain gauges were mounted on the front surface and four on the back surface. A preliminary experiment was carried out using four strain gauges in combination of two out of the four gauges on the back surface. The four strain gauges were integrated to the load cell amplifier module HX 711 and connected to the Arduino Uno R3, from which information was transmitted to the PC via a USB cable. The HX

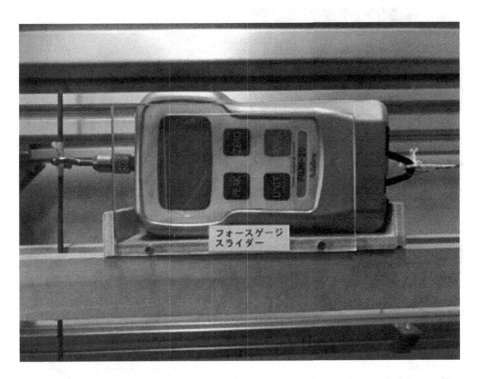

Fig. 7. Force gauge slider and ruler attached to measuring device, and string-pulling force can be measured

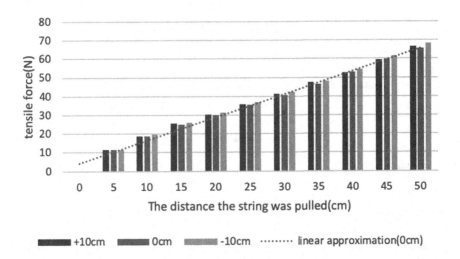

Fig. 8. Relationship between tensile force and string-pulling force 10 cm above and below center of string (red dotted line is linear approximation) (Color figure online)

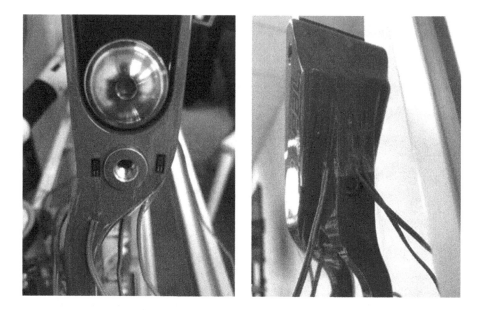

Fig. 9. Strain gauges attached over entire surface and back of upper and lower grips

Fig. 10. Measured strain values for each combination of back-surface strain positions

711 outputs were at 10 samples per second (SPS) based on the average of 1-s measurement at each position.

Figure 10 shows these results. The largest change appeared in the back surface using the strain gauges placed at two locations in the center. Therefore, the two positions in the center having the best resolution were used as measurement points on the back surface.

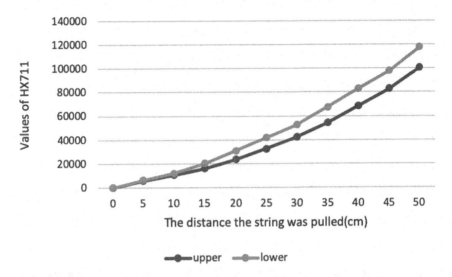

Fig. 11. Upper and lower distortion when center of string is pulled

Next, since the shape of the grip where the limb of the bow is attached is the same at the top and bottom, a strain gauge was attached to the top at the same position as bottom. To measure the strain values at these two points at the same time and con-firm whether the strain increases with the distance that the upper and lower lines are drawn in the same manner, the strings were drawn at intervals of 5 cm at the center of the strings, and the upper and lower strains generated at that time were measured.

Figure 11 shows these results. When the center of the string was pulled, The upper and lower strains similarly increased according to the pulling distance but did not match. Therefore, to determine whether there is a difference in the upper and lower values depending on where the strings are pulled, we measured the force applied when the strings are pulled 50 cm at intervals of 2.5 cm in the range of 10 cm from the center.

Figure 12 shows these results. If the string is pulled closer to the top, the upper distortion increases and lower distortion decreases. Therefore, it is possible to estimate which position of the string is drew by the ratio of the upper and lower distortion values. In this experiment, the string-pulling position was fixed at 50 cm, so it was necessary to confirm whether the same thing can be said when the string-pulling position is changed. According to the graph, since the upper and lower strains intersect at a position of 7.5 cm above the middle of the string, the string is then pulled at this position to measure whether the upper and lower strains agree with each other.

Figure 13 shows these results. The upper and lower strains agreed with each other for any amount of drawing and that the string-pulling force was proportional and could be estimated from the strain gauge affixed near the grip holding the limb and the value obtained through the load cell amplifier module. It was

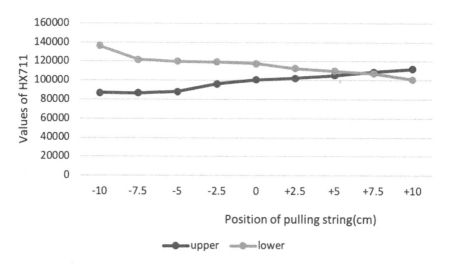

Fig. 12. Upper and lower strains when chord is pulled at different places and at 50 cm

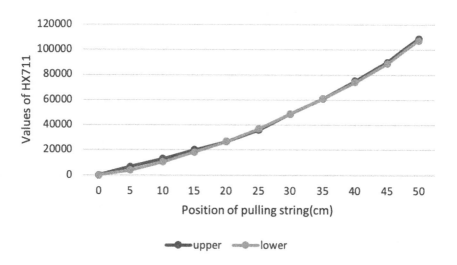

Fig. 13. Upper and lower strains when chord is pulled 7.5 cm above middle of string

also confirmed that it is possible to estimate the position where the string was pulled from the difference be-tween the strain gauges attached to upper and lower limbs.

3.3 Reduction of Force on Sensor

The bow position tracking uses a vive tracker. This is an outside-in system based on the lighthouse system, which enables high-precision and high-speed measurement. However, there is a problem that the sensor showed abnormal values when a strong force is received. The cause is thought to be the shooting force being transmitted directly to the sensor. This was solved using the VN 100, which can input the acceleration of 16 g and is excellent in the impact resistance in the conventional bow. However, it is difficult to replace the inertial sensor of the vive tracker because it is built in.

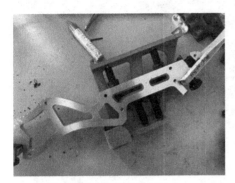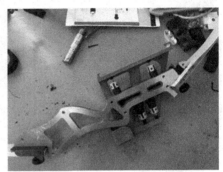

Fig. 14. Shock absorbers were fixed in 4 places between aluminum frame and base to fix vive tracker, and type of shock absorber was changed during experiment

Therefore, instead of fixing the shock absorber directly to the grip, as shown in Fig. 14, a shock absorber was attached between the aluminum alloy of the grip and the base to which the sensor was attached so that the shock would not be transmitted directly. The shock absorbers were installed in four places, and the experiments were carried out with different types of shock absorbers. However, even the shock absorber with a high-speed response up to 3 m/s could not cope with the force of the bow, and the sensor showed abnormal values.

Next, instead of the shock absorber, the system was changed to that in which two metal shafts are held by a linear bush. Under this condition, the occurrence of outliers decreased, but the position of the base changed every time a shot was fired, so the springs were sandwiched in four places (Fig. 15).

However, the outliers were still not completely prevented. This is because there is a possibility that there is a problem with these ways that can only be applied horizontally. In the future, we will measure the direction of the force on the bow during shooting. This may also change depending on the shape of the bow and the position of the string.

4 Discussions

From these experimental results, it was possible to clarify how to make the bow device feel more real and how to improve the accuracy of the bow device itself. However, there were limitations to this study. Only one person was tested because there were not many advanced archery athletes. We need to conduct an

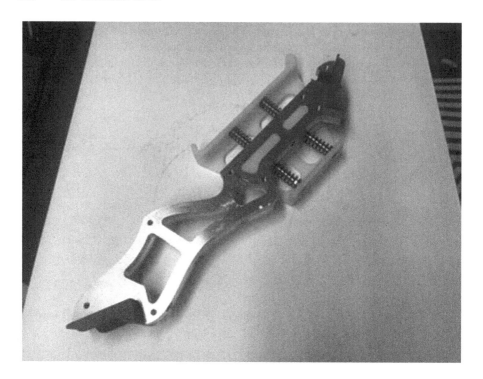

Fig. 15. Shock absorber consisting of shaft, linear bushing, and spring

experiment involving more athletes, even intermediate athletes, to increase the number of subjects. Although several types of biometrics were carried out, since the instruments were not synchronized, integrated evaluation could be carried out.

In the bow-measurement experiment, it was confirmed that the pulling position of the string could be estimated from the change in the upper and lower strains. However, the center of the string was not the center of the upper and lower strains. This is considered due to the fact that the position where the strain is applied does not completely match and the shape of the entire grip is not vertically symmetrical. In the future, we plan to conduct more accurate measurement but also measure the difference when the strength of the limb is changed. We were able to measure the strength of the string, but by clarifying the relationship between strain gauges and the speed and flying distance when the arrow is actually pinched, we hope to achieve a level of accuracy that can be used for bow simulation. Based on the results of these experiments, the position to pull the string, that is, the position to shoot the arrow, amount of force that will be exerted on the arrow, and not only the direction of the bow but also the direction of the arrow were more accurately estimated, and this allows the fabrication of a bow device that can predict the trajectory with high accuracy without using an arrow.

Although it was effective to some extent in reducing the impact of the bow, it was not perfect. There are several possible causes, including the direction of the force applied during shooting, the position of the string, the strength of the limb, and the shape of the bow device. Therefore, since the shape of the bow device cannot be determined from the bow or biometric measurements we carried out for this study, we will do this after these measurement are completed.

References

1. The Void. https://www.thevoid.com/
2. Yasumoto, M., Teraoka, T.: VAIR field - multiple mobile VR shooting sports. In: Chen, J.Y.C., Fragomeni, G. (eds.) VAMR 2018. LNCS, vol. 10910, pp. 235–246. Springer, Cham (2018). https://doi.org/10.1007/978-3-319-91584-5_19
3. Yasumoto, M., Teraoka, T.: Physical e-Sports in VAIR field system. In: SIGGRAPH Asia 2019 XR (SA 2019), pp. 31–33. ACM, New York (2019)
4. Yasumoto, M., Ohta, T.: The electric bow interface. In: Shumaker, R. (ed.) VAMR 2013. LNCS, vol. 8022, pp. 436–442. Springer, Heidelberg (2013). https://doi.org/10.1007/978-3-642-39420-1_46
5. Yasumoto, M., Teraoka, T.: Electric bow interface 3D. In: SIGGRAPH Asia 2015, Emerging Technologies (SA 2015), pp. 11:1–11:2 (2015)
6. The Fist Virtual Reality Archery. https://infinityleap.com/the-first-virtual-reality-archery/
7. Drochtert, D., Owetschkin, K., Meyer, L., Geiger, C.: Demonstration of mobile virtual archery. In: SIGGRAPH Asia 2013 Symposium on Mobile Graphics and Interactive Applications (SA 2013), pp. 62:1–62:1. ACM, New York (2013)
8. Göbel, S., Geiger, C., Heinze, C., Marinos, D.: Creating a virtual archery experience. In: Proceedings of the International Conference on Advanced Visual Interfaces (AVI 2010), pp. 337–340 (2010)
9. Zhao, Y., Salunke, S., Leavitt, A., Curtin, K., Huynh, N., Zeagler, C.: E-archery: prototype wearable for analyzing archery release. In: Proceedings of the 2016 ACM International Joint Conference on Pervasive and Ubiquitous Computing: Adjunct, pp. 908–913 (2016)

UX Studies in Automotive and Transport

Definition of People with Impediments and Universality Evaluation of Public Service in Airport Travel Scenarios

Miao Cui[1]([⊠]) [iD], Tao Wang[1] [iD], Zilin Pan[2] [iD], and Liyang Ni[1] [iD]

[1] Guangzhou Academy of Fine Arts, No. 257 Changgang Road,
Guangzhou, China
76742210@qq.com
[2] GAC R&D Center, No. 668 Jinshan Road East, Guangzhou, China

Abstract. This article is based on the Universal Design theory. Combining data of on-the-spot investigation and statistics from Guangzhou Baiyun Airport, it sorts out and compares the relevant definitions, terms, facilities, and services for people with disabilities (mainly takes pregnant women, mother and infant, and disabled people as examples) in major airports, airlines, and civil aviation organizations around the world. Based on this, the data of the three dimensions of the cognition, behavior and needs of the disabled in the airport travel scene are analyzed and summarized. Through analysis, this article extracts the core definitions and three levels of barriers in the airport travel scenario, and proposes an evaluation system for airport public service accessibility based on the *Universal Design PPP Evaluation* standard to improve service design in the airport travel scenario. It provides a general theoretical model and optimization ideas, and also provides an objective and strong basis for the development of airport public facilities that meet the needs of multiple users. It aims to improve the mobility and satisfaction of people with impediments, and promote the construction of an equitable, democratic, and friendly society.

Keywords: People with impediments · Public service · Accessibility · Universal design

1 Introduction

At the UN conference on sustainable development, the UN stated that "around the world, disparities in income, gender, age, disability, race and religion are common within and between countries. These inequalities threaten social and economic stability, impede the reduction of poverty, and at the same time undermine people's sense of achievement and self-worth, leading to more disease, conflict, poverty, and environmental degradation. The 2030 agenda for sustainable development, adopted by the United Nations general assembly in its resolution 70/1 of 25 September 2015 [1], states that we cannot achieve sustainable development if we exclude any part of the world's population. We can and should achieve equality for all to ensure a life of dignity for all. Political, economic and social policies need to be harmonized with a focus on the needs of vulnerable and marginalized groups. And in "sustainable development goal 11:

© Springer Nature Switzerland AG 2020
A. Marcus and E. Rosenzweig (Eds.): HCII 2020, LNCS 12201, pp. 623–639, 2020.
https://doi.org/10.1007/978-3-030-49760-6_44

Make cities and human settlements inclusive, safe, resilient and sustainable", it specifies that "By 2030, provide universal access to safe, inclusive and accessible, green and public spaces, in particular for women and children, older persons and persons with disabilities" [1].

In China, as early as the *12th five-year plan "national basic public service system* was formulated, "Advance equal basic public services is not only to ensure everyone will have access to basic public services, also includes the requirement of social fairness and justice" was highlighted, and put forward specific requirements in will intensify protection of basic public services, to the disadvantaged [2]. For the upcoming Beijing winter Olympic Games, the guidelines for barrier-free Beijing 2022 winter Olympic Games and Paralympics jointly issued by BOCOG, China disabled peoples' federation, Beijing municipal government and Hebei provincial government follow the basic principles of "fairness, dignity and applicability", take safety as the primary starting point, reflect the universal design concept, improve the accessibility details, and adapt to the characteristics of the country, strengthen the information accessibility, service accessibility and other weak links. It is the first time in China to set up the proportion of barrier-free sanitation facilities, that is, to provide one barrier-free urinal and one barrier-free urinal for every 15 people in need; The barrier-free requirements for seats at the venue include not only a certain number of seats for wheelchairs and accompanying seats, but also a certain number of seats for courtesy, to serve pregnant women, the elderly and other people who do not use wheelchairs. When entering the venue, waiting in line is inevitable, and the width, slope and rest seats of the queuing area are required [3]. Reducing inequality, raising basic living standards, and promoting equitable and inclusive social development have also become the mission of sustainable development for every country in this era.

In modern society, the developed interconnecting road network, air route and public space constitute the skeleton of the city, and also become the foundation of social development and operation. When public Spaces are under functioned, poorly designed, or not used fairly, cities become more isolated and crowd relationships become fragmented. The effective construction of modern street networks and open public Spaces will greatly promote urban productivity, people's livelihood and public services, and even expand employment and market development opportunities. In China, civil aviation, as an important part of the public transportation system, has developed rapidly in recent years. According to the statistics bulletin on the development of the civil aviation industry in 2018 released by the civil aviation administration of China in May 2019, the industry completed 611,737,700 passenger trips in 2018, an increase of 10.9 percent over the previous year. From 2014 to 2018, the number of civil aviation passenger traffic increased continuously, and the year-on-year growth rate remained above 10%. While the passenger throughput is increasing year by year, users' requirements for service quality are also improving. As the "special passengers" in the airport travel scene, the people with impediments have changed their cognition and attitude towards this group with the continuous improvement of social civilization, and more attention has been paid to the provision of barrier-free facilities and the construction of humanized services. According to the CAAC passenger satisfaction evaluation report released by CAAC, the score for 2018 has increased to 4.23, compared with 4.20 out of 5 for special passenger service in the second half of 2017 [4].

Through the official standardized survey statistics, people have a new perspective and standard to judge the level of airport service quality.

2 Situation of Airport Service for People with Impediments

Memphis International Airport, USA (IATA: MEM). MEM has teamed up with Aira technologies to provide amblyopia and blind travelers with smart glasses or a passenger's smartphone camera that can be used in conjunction with an Aira app to allow passengers to share views of their surroundings, crowd flow, signs and other objects from their perspective, and use augmented reality dashboards to provide passengers with a real-time narrative. They can assist with step-by-step navigation through the airport and assist with other tasks, such as finding flight information, finding and identifying baggage, and arranging transportation [5].

Shannon International Airport, Ireland (IATA: SNN). SNN focuses on autistic children, family travel passengers and the needs of passengers with travel anxiety. In March 2017, SNN established the first airport sensory room in Europe, which uses low color matching, low sensory lighting and bubble tube to create a calm and relaxed space, greatly alleviating the anxiety and anxiety of autistic children in the public variable environment, and changing the travel experience of family passengers with neurodevelopmental challenges such as autism [6].

Toronto Pearson International Airport, Canada (IATA: YYZ). YYZ provides a free and interesting application for autistic people, which introduces excellent game design and learning methods. It can help people with autism and other cognitive special needs to simulate the airport process online, get familiar with and refer to the upcoming new scenes, and cultivate users' ability to complete the travel independently [7].

Guangzhou Baiyun International Airport, China (IATA: CAN). CAN create "on time, convenient, friendly, smooth" service with the launch of the "spring breeze service" brand, the essence of the characteristics is cordial, warm, natural. The airport has set up more than 80 demonstration posts on the front line to answer passengers' questions, through the identification of "love stickers" to strengthen special passenger services, the "true feelings of service" to meet all kinds of special needs of passengers. Radiation population: old, weak, sick, disabled, pregnant and other passengers [8].

Pittsburgh International Airport (IATA: PIT). At PIT, the traditional service for the blind is that they are taken to the gate by an officer after checking in at the counter, but are still required to take care of themselves before boarding. By introducing the NavCog App, developed by the robotics institute at Carnegie Mellon university in the us, blind and visually impaired people can use the Bluetooth-based tool to navigate through airports and use the audio instructions provided by the program to get to all the places they want to go [9].

3 Definition of *People with Impediments*

3.1 Definitions from Airports or Airline Companies Worldwide

Civil Aviation Administration of China (CAAC). In CAAC, the concept of "special passenger service" is generally adopted, and it is basically defined as the passenger who needs the carrier to give special benefit or special care in the course of transportation, or to comply with the conditions of transport prescribed by the carrier and to make arrangements before the carrier can carry the passenger when necessary. The targets include important passengers, sick and disabled passengers (sick passengers, wheelchair passengers, stretcher passengers, blind people, deaf and mute passengers), pregnant passengers, unaccompanied children, infants, drunk, late arrival passengers, and extra passengers [10].

Narita Airport (IATA: NRT). Guided by the concept of universal design, NRT has adopted various measures to create an airport environment that all passengers can safely use. It has put forward the following 6 categories of special passengers:

1. Customers with Walking Disabilities.
2. Customers with Visual Disabilities.
3. Customers with Hearing and Speech Disabilities.
4. Customers Who Have Difficulty with Communication or Using Airport Facilities Due to Developmental or Intellectual Disabilities or Behavioral Disorders.
5. Customers with Illnesses and Injuries.
6. Customers Accompanied by Children, Expectant Mothers and Senior Citizens.

Through the above classification, NRT not only respects individual needs, but also provides public facilities and tools to meet the needs of as many people as possible, forming a characteristic and systematic universal design service facility contact matrix [11] (Table 1).

Table 1. An example of characteristic and systematic universal design service facility contact matrix.

Customers with walking disabilities	
Information counters	Priority seats
Car parks and parking discounts	Multipurpose restrooms and assistance dogs
Wheelchair rental	Electric walker
Special assistance and intercom services	Medical clinic
Elevators, moving walkways, ramps and handrails	Terminal shuttle bus
Baggage service	Electric carts
Other barrier-free facilities	Help strap

Japan Airline (JAL). Jal established Universal Design Service Facilities in its corporate philosophy, and proposed *JAL Special Assistance*, in which "We aim to create a society where everyone can enjoy traveling, sports and culture, who requests special assistance, and all customers can have a safe and comfortable journey." Is promised. Based on this concept, this paper defines 6 types of Available Assistance:

1. Assistance for mobility and wheelchairs.
2. Vision Assistance
3. Hearing or Speech Assistance
4. Cognitive and Developmental Assistance
5. Customers who are ill or injured
6. Customers with food allergies

Meanwhile, some assistance and services that requires advance notice are listed separately as follows:

1. Assistance dog
2. Customers who bring and use medical device
3. Customers who use a stretcher
4. Customers who use an oxygen bottle
5. Customers with sleep apnea syndrome
6. Customers for whom it is difficult to stay in a sitting position
7. Group tour customers
8. Disabled sports athletes
9. About medical certificates or consent forms [12]

Brief Summary. In terms of the definition of barrier passengers, the system definition of Japanese users is the most comprehensive and systematic compared with the airports of seven countries in Europe, America and Asia. This is the objective result of vigorously popularizing and deeply implementing the concept of universal design in Japan.

Although all major airlines, airports and institutions have proposed lists of UD objects based on the company's development philosophy and understanding of universal design, no classification has been made based on the individual status and characteristics of different types of users. This can enlighten the definition of civil aviation service users, but it is difficult to become the basis and reference standard for the construction of excellent services.

3.2   User Definition Based on Universal Design Concept

In the official website of Japan International Association for Universal Design, the research objects are well arranged and displayed. Among them, the data are clearly divided into five parts: sensory impediment, motion impediment, physical impediment, brain impediment and language skill disability. The user characteristics and state under the type are described in detail [13].

The data clearly show the results of the disorder caused by nature or nurture, and more of a normal state of functional impairment or loss. But at the same time, the UD experts in Japan also proposed that the universal design of the defined service should include the disabled, ordinary people obstacles. Panasonic company has taken the obstacles of ordinary people to the next level by defining universal design (UD) as the design of facilities, products and information that can be used regardless of the user's culture, language, nationality, gender, disability and ability. Ordinary people's obstacles include but are not limited to: Sick time, barriers of time, when injured, pregnancy, child along with the gender, worries ease, tired, when in a hurry, excess weight. This description clearly shows the types of impedimental state of users under abnormal conditions, such as pregnancy, injury and depression. Compared with the user state defined in Fig. 1, these users have periodic, sporadic and repairable deficits.

In addition, the author believes that the state of hurry, overload, exhaustion and children's wayward defined by Matsushita is not only occasional and repairable, but also affected by external forces in the environment and scene. It is in a specific situation, by the user's own active or passive behavior of the negative results, Panasonic for this kind of situation has also carried out a specific interpretation, such as: carrying a large number of fruits and vegetables home, cannot easily free hands open the door of the physical movement obstacle housewife; In the noisy market, due to the interference of the surrounding environment, the hearing impaired youth cannot get clear voice and so on. Such impediment is transient and triggered by the user's situation. This paper considers that it can be separated from the other two disorders and defined as:

1. Normal impediment
2. Periodic impediment
3. Scene impediment

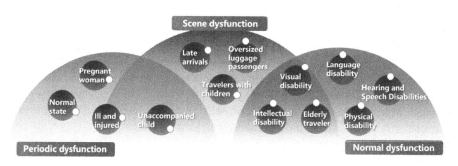

Fig. 1. Guangzhou Baiyun Airport "Special Passenger" user barrier classification

Through an in-depth study on the possible impediment in "Scene impediment" public transportation, combined with interviews with airport staff and field observation of users, it was found that "traveling with heavy burdens" and "anxiety emotion" were the key factors that hindered ordinary people from traveling. Among them, the load includes "carrying heavy luggage, carrying infants, group leader" and other different types of load state; In the process of taking a vehicle, factors such as the running condition of the vehicle, the emotional atmosphere of the riding environment, the service attitude and quality of the service personnel will induce emotional experience through sensory and perceptual information [14]. In this survey, users' anxiety mainly focused on "high-pressure environment, time pressure, information delay, waiting anxiety" and other aspects. Anxiety is excessive worry about the potential negative consequences of future events, accompanied by physical arousal and physical tension [15]. A large number of studies have also proved that individuals with high anxiety have processing bias when processing emotional information, especially negative information [16]. About the interaction between emotion and executive function "Two-Stage Competition Mode" [17] argues that emotional intensity is one of the important factors affecting the relationship between emotion and executive function, high intensity of emotion not only can lead to a stronger sense of perception, but need to take cognitive resources to priority processing to these stimuli, which hinder the executive function. Therefore, in the analysis path of scene impediment, both the obstacles caused by the physical burden and the obstacles caused by the emotional burden should become important indicators to judge the user's obstacle state (Fig. 2).

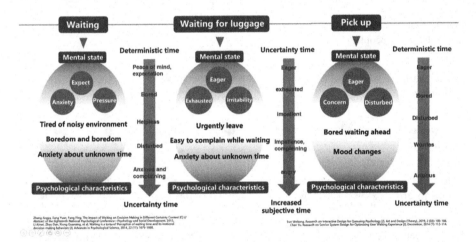

Fig. 2. Analysis of users' anxiety in public transport travel scenarios

4 Demands of People with Impediments in Airport Analysis

At the user research stage, 68 target users were first investigated by questionnaires, and the airport service scenarios and public facilities targets that users strongly expected were obtained (Fig. 3).

Fig. 3. Airport travel flow & touch points

Then, the high frequency use and high obstacle scenarios of user feedback were dismantled in detail, and the required environment, scale, temperature and other factors in the specific behavior process of users were analyzed to explore the deep causes of pain points of users (Figs. 4, 5 and 6).

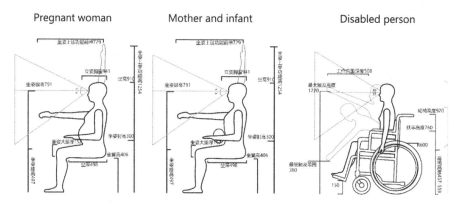

Fig. 4. Man-machine size chart of typical disabled peoples (Pregnant Woman, Mother and Infant, Disabled people)

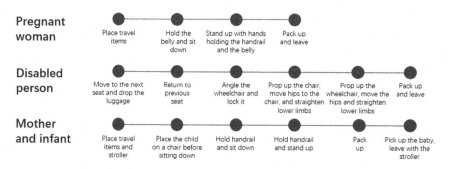

Fig. 5. Seating flow chart of typical disabled peoples (Pregnant Woman, Mother and Infant, Disabled people)

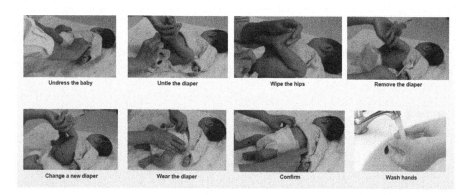

Fig. 6. Maternal and infant behavior disaggregation - Change the diaper

Four kinds of public facilities are selected to track the actual usage of various users for human-computer interaction scale mapping (Fig. 7).

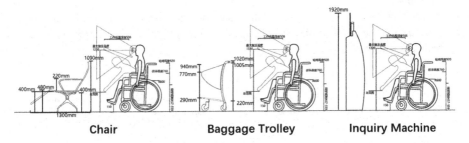

Chair   **Baggage Trolley**   **Inquiry Machine**

Fig. 7. Man-machine mapping of airport facilities for disabled people

According to the user journey simulation, draw the user journey diagram to explore the smoothness of the service link. Through the methods above, this paper tries to summarize behavioral characteristics, cognitive ability and emotional needs.

Pregnant Woman. Pregnant woman is a kind of identity of human society, they have a common psychological and physiological characteristic, and consumer demand. Pregnancy, also known as gestation, is the time when one or more offspring develop inside a woman's body. Pregnancy is divided into three stages: pre-pregnancy, the second trimester and the third trimester, each lasting about 3 months. Each stage of pregnant women's behavior, psychological and physiological needs will be different, according to the characteristics of each stage of care. Below 32 weeks pregnant according to the ordinary passenger transport; Pregnant women who are more than 8 months (32 weeks) pregnant but less than 35 weeks are required to obtain medical permission for the flight; Pregnant more than 35 weeks (including) cannot fly (Fig. 8).

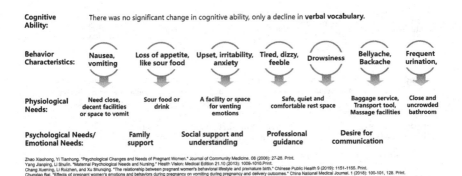

Fig. 8. Behavioral characteristics, cognitive ability and emotional needs of pregnant women

Disabled People. Disabled people include persons with long-term physical, mental, intellectual or sensory impairments that interact with disorders or may prevent persons with disabilities from participating fully and effectively in society on an equal footing with normal persons.

Airlines generally define people with disabilities as visual, hearing, speech, physical, intellectual, mental, multiple and other disabilities, and offer different services accordingly (Fig. 9).

Fig. 9. Behavioral characteristics, cognitive ability and emotional needs of disabled people

Mother and Infant. Mother and infant is an adult passenger who is age 18 or above and capable of civil conduct, carrying one or more babies under the ages of two (Fig. 10).

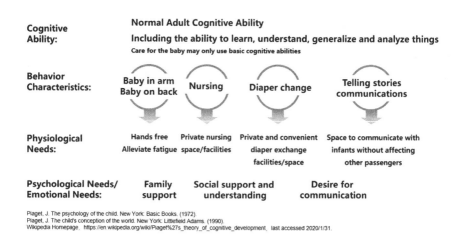

Fig. 10. Behavioral characteristics, cognitive ability and emotional needs of mother and infant

Late Arrivals. Late arrivals refer to those who arrive at the airport check-in counter 50 min before the flight departure time announced on the ticket due to bad weather, traffic congestion, etc., but the check-in time is less than 10 min.

Passengers who are less than 40 min from the departure time of the flight are considered as missed passengers and cannot check in principle (Fig. 11).

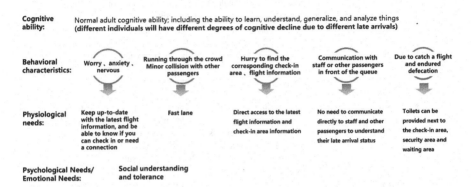

Fig. 11. Behavioral characteristics, cognitive ability and emotional needs of late arrivals

In view of the pain points in the use of various facilities and services by the above four types of typical people in the airport travel scene, this paper is summarized through the following table (Table 2):

Table 2. A high-frequency pain point summary based on 68 user in-depth tracking studies

	Pregnant woman	Disabled people	Mother and infant	Late arrivals
Ordinary seat	Hip and waist increase, size of ordinary seat is not suitable	1. The armrest prevents wheelchair passengers from moving to the seat 2. Seats are not compatible with wheelchairs	1. Not suitable sitting height and depth 2. Lack of protection for children when climbing	No time to use
Lounge chair	1. Large seat tilt 2. Lack of protective handrails	1. Large reclining seat 2. Lack of protective handrails	1. The space between recliners is too large for taking after children 2. Not suitable size for children 3. Lack of protection	No time to use
Water dispenser	Complicated operation interface, not clear how to operate the first time	1. Small space in the water intake area 2. Lack of knee space for wheelchair users when approaching	1. Travelers with children/infants cannot concentrate on operation 2. Lack of heating devices for milk or drinks	No time to use

(continued)

Table 2. (*continued*)

	Pregnant woman	Disabled people	Mother and infant	Late arrivals
Inquiry machine	Machine dimensions are not suitable to pregnant passengers	1. The machine scale is not applicable to disabled passengers 2. No knee space reserved for wheelchair users	1. Travelers with children/infants who need to be taken care is difficult to concentrate on the information or operation	Takes too much time to operate
Baggage trolley	When there is a lot of luggage, it is difficult to bend down	1. Wheelchair users have difficulty using trolleys at the same time	1. Lack of space for infants/young children, it is cumbersome to take care of both cars when used with a stroller	Not enough time to find one
Information desk	Normal use	1. Insufficient number of low counters 2. The low counter is beside the ordinary counter, which is difficult to identify	1. Travelers with children/infants with babies need to look after children, it is difficult to consult	Sometimes need to wait for a long queue
Floor-standing TV	Normal use	1. The TV is not located in a reasonable position, and the seat for the disabled is not taken into account	1. TV screen size is not enough for children to see clearly 2. Lack of children's program content	Important information cannot be read in time from the scrolling display
Terminal plan & flight information	There is a lot of content in the flight information, which is complicated and difficult to identify directly	1. The flight information is rich in content, complicated, and difficult to identify 2. Wheelchair passengers are unable to identify higher information 3. Visually impaired passengers cannot obtain information	1. Travelers with children/infants with babies need to look after children and have difficulty identifying information	Not enough time to read and distinguish carefully, Quick navigation is necessary

Public facilities are an important part of the airport service system. From entering the airport to completing different tasks to achieving different goals, users need to cooperate with the corresponding public facilities to realize. The adoption of the universal design PPP evaluation system, through the acquisition and analysis of the key contact evaluation with high or low user satisfaction, excavates the potential needs of users, which provides important basis for the insight into the problems in the service system chain and the provision of effective optimization schemes [18].

This research has used Universal Design of PRODUCT PPP evaluation model (PRODUCT PERORMAN PROGRAM). A systematic investigation was conducted on the accessibility of core public products (Barrier-free elevator, Self-service check-in machine, Baggage check-in desk, Barrier-free seats, Baggage security check desk, etc.) to people with impediments in the high-frequency scenes of "arrival", "check-in", "security check" and "waiting" in airport travel services. The public facilities of international airports in China's first-tier cities were selected as samples for the research, and the methods of field observation, data evaluation and behavior simulation were adopted for the sampling research. Investigate the use of facilities in airport travel scenarios for passengers with impediments (Disabled people, pregnant women, unaccompanied children, the elderly). And using the PPP evaluation model of 7 evaluation methods:1. Equitable Use; 2. Flexibility in Use; 3. Simple and Intuitive Use; 4. Perceptible Information; 5. Tolerance for Error; 6. Low Physical Effort 7. Size and Space for Approach and Use. Through these dimensions, product evaluation and data analysis are carried out to form the accessibility data matrix of airport core public facilities for people with impediments (Table 3).

Table 3. Airport service PPP model evaluation table.

PPP principles	Airport staff, users, designers co-create evaluation indicators	Problem raiser
1. Equitable Use		
Equal use	Whether any person, any ability situation can use fairly	Wheelchair users, crutches users
Elimination of discrepancies	Whether there is differential information representation or service	People with Impediments
Provide options	Run-in Heading in Bold. Text follows	Mutilated users, pregnant women, allergy patients
Eliminate anxiety and fear	Whether to consider the privacy needs of different individuals and states	Mother and infant, intubated person
2. Flexibility in Use		
Freedom of use	Whether there are multiple ways to achieve the goal	Disability, hearing impairment, language impairment users
The acceptability of left and right handers	Whether to satisfy left, right - handed, one - handed operation	One - handed operator in load - bearing travel
Proper use in emergency situations	Are there any emergency instructions and assistance	Late arrivals
Applicability under changing circumstances	Whether the use effect under the influence of environment can be considered	Mother and infant, intubated person, etc.
3. Simple and Intuitive		
Eliminate complexity	Whether structure and process are simple and clear	Old people, children, pregnant women, late arrivals
Intuitive to use	Can it be used smoothly without supplementary instructions	Old people, children, international passengers, late arrivals

(*continued*)

Table 3. (*continued*)

PPP principles	Airport staff, users, designers co-create evaluation indicators	Problem raiser
Simple method	Whether the operation is simple and easy to use	Old people, children
Tips and feedback in time	Whether giving dangerous and important information feedback in time	Late arrivals, visual disabled users
Intelligible Structure		Old persons, children
4. Perceptible Information		
Optional information transmission	Whether to provide information that can be received by multiple senses	Hearing disabled, language disabled, visual disabled, international passengers
Intelligible important information	Whether to strengthen the important information visualization and size	Old person, children, international passengers, late arrivals
5. Tolerance for Error		
Safety structures to prevent accidents	Whether there is a reasonable structure to avoid accidents	Children, wheelchair users, mother and infant
Usage errors can ensure safety	Whether misoperation will not produce personal harm	Children, visual disabled users
Errors can be quickly recovered	Whether a solution is provided to remedy the error	Disabled peoples, children
6. Low Physical Effort		
Use in a natural position	Whether to consider the health and comfort of users on different human-machine scales	Wheelchair users, pregnant women, children
Avoid repetitive motions	Whether to minimize the use of steps	Wheelchair users
Reduce physical burden	Whether it provides structure, function, and AIDS to reduce the burden on the body	Old persons, pregnant women, mother and infant, passengers with heavy luggage
Not tired after prolonged use	Whether it provides the scale, structure, and function to reduce the burden	passengers with heavy luggage, mother and infant
7. Size and Space for Approach and Use		
Convenient space and size	Whether or not to use the behavior is not limited by space and scale	Hearing disabled, language disabled users
Suitable for people of all sizes	Whether to provide enough reasonable scale, space and intensity	Wheelchair users, pregnant women, children
Can be used with caregivers	Whether the scale is consistent with the necessary number of people walking, sitting together	Mother and infant, family, Patients in need of care

(*continued*)

Table 3. (*continued*)

PPP principles	Airport staff, users, designers co-create evaluation indicators	Problem raiser
Annex 1: Ensure the Efficiency of the Operation		
The configuration of key contacts	Is the number and location of contacts properly configured	Late arrivals
Immediate access to itinerary information	Whether the key trip information is obtained at the first time	Late arrivals, anxious passengers
Necessary and effective shortcut recommendations	Whether to provide a reasonable shortcut path, tools	Late arrivals, pregnant women, wheelchair users, wounded passengers
Annex 2: Effective Relief of Anxiety		
Information traceability	Whether to provide real-time information about the trip	Late arrivals
Appropriate personnel service tracking	Provide facilities or paths to contact service personnel when necessary	Late arrivals, old persons
Optimize waiting filler	Whether there is any information, facilities and space for emotional comfort	Users with autism and anxiety
Annex 3: Satisfy High Frequency Behavior		
Provide necessary auxiliary facilities or tools	Whether facilities and tools are provided to assist in performing the necessary actions	Mother and infant, disabilities, wounded passengers
Provide the necessary consumables	Whether necessary health and safety consumables are provided	Mother and infant, wounded passengers
Offer more options	Whether facilities and Spaces are provided for different scales of behavior	Mother and infant

This part mainly summarizes and extracts the pain point information proposed by each subject in the experience of various facilities, as shown in the summary table of typical pain points of facilities. PPP evaluation and use universal design on the attribution of classification, then invited the provider - the airport staff to the perspective of management, operation, maintenance, facility providers - designers with product feasibility and human rationality, function realization degree for the reference, the facilities - users with their cognitive ability, behavior characteristics and emotional needs as the criterion, jointly create evaluation standard is discussed in this paper. In synergy to create a way of building for universal design.

1. Equitable use,
2. The Flexibility in the use,
3. Simple and intuitive,
4. Perceptible information,

5. How the for the error,
6. Low physical effort,
7. The Size and space for approach and use

Under the principles of seven, PPP37 evaluation items are specific to the evaluation criteria of airport public facilities. In the attribution stage of the questions raised by users, we analyzed the frequency of the questions raised by users for various PPP evaluation items, and obtained the following levels of users' universality needs by referring to the data:

Equitable use → Low physical effort → the Size and space for approach and the use

Normal obstacles the hierarchy, the deaf users for airport public facilities of the needs of the most prominent level to commonality:

Perceptible information → how the for the error → Flexibility in use

In the scene barrier level, the most prominent demand level for the universality of airport public facilities for users with babies is reflected as:

Low physical effort → Flexibility in use → Size and space for approach and use

5 Summary

According to the user definition of obstacles in airport travel scenarios based on general design principles, this study creatively proposed three user hierarchy classification methods:

1. Normal Impediment
2. Periodic Impediment
3. Scene Impediment

This paper systematically sorts out and summarizes the interactive behavior problems that occur in the whole process of airport travel for various kinds of obstacle users in *"Arriving at the airport → Entering the departure hall → Seeking information → Check-in → Security check → Waiting for boarding → Boarding the plane"*. The item attribution method of PPP evaluation of users' pain points is proposed to establish the evaluation system of airport for public facilities. It provides a systematic basis for airport to test the rationality, availability and universality of public facility contact. Based on the project members' joint attempts to construct the service construction reference guide proposed for the possible obstacles in the airport travel scenario.

The research results above, which is beneficial to the airport for usability evaluation service resources, does not affect the value of public resources to provide security, to ensure that the airport public service system more secure, efficient, flexible, predictability, and fairness are available, and continued to deepen the research and use of perfect after correction phase, form sustainable evaluation system for civil aviation service resources assessment.

References

1. General Assembly of UN: Transforming our world: the 2030 Agenda for Sustainable Development. The 70th session of the United Nations General Assembly (2015)
2. The State Council Information Office of the People's Republic of China Homepage. http://www.scio.gov.cn/ztk/xwfb/83/6/Document/1192196/1192196.htm. Accessed 10 July 2012
3. Beijing Organising Committee for the 2022 Olympic and Paralympic Winter Games, Accessibility guidelines for Beijing 2022 winter Olympics and Paralympics (2018)
4. CAAC Academy of Science and Technology: CAAC News Agency, Avic Mobile Technology co., LTD., China Civil Airport Association: 2017/2018 CAAC Passenger Satisfaction Evaluation Report (2019)
5. Future Travel Experience Website. https://www.futuretravelexperience.com/2017/10/memphis-airport-uses-smart-glasses-to-assist-blind-and-low-vision-travellers. Accessed Oct 2017
6. Evoke Website. https://evoke.ie/2018/11/23/life-style/sensory-room-shannon-airport-autism. Accessed 23 Nov 2018
7. Toronto Pearson Airport website. https://www.torontopearson.com/en/accessibility/autism-app-magnuscards
8. Baiyunport: Cordial Service, T2 edn. Guangzhou (2018)
9. AIRPORT Technology website. https://www.airport-technology.com/news/deal-news/pittsburgh-airport-cmu-develop-new-aviation-systems/. Accessed 23 Apr 2018
10. Jing Tian, F., Tingting You, S.: Airport Passenger Service, 1st edn. China Civil Aviation Press, Beijing (2015)
11. Narita Airport website. https://www.narita-airport.jp/en/bf
12. Japan Airlines website. https://www.jal.co.jp/en/jalpri/?_ga=2.20066872.1215802953.1580469431-1397460760.1580469431
13. IAUD (International Association for Universal Design) Japanese website. https://www.iaud.net/UDmatrix_userinfo
14. Li, C.: Emotion valence and emotional intelligence's effects on relations among attitudes and behaviors during the choice of trip mode. Shaanxi Normal University, Xi'an (2017)
15. Liang, L., Li, J., Jia, J.: ERP study on the effect of assessment of different properties on inhibitory function of trait anxiety. Stud. Psychol. Behav. (2008)
16. Berggren, N., Derakshan, N.: Attentional control deficits in trait anxiety: why you see them and why you don't. Biol. Psychol. **92**(3), 440–446 (2013)
17. Pessoa, L., Padmala, S., Kenzer, A., Bauer, A.: Interactions between cognition and emotion during response inhibition. Emotion **12**(1), 192–197 (2012)
18. Kumar, V.: 101 Design Methods: a Structured Approach for Driving Innovation in Your Organization. Wiley, Canada (2013)

Navigating Through Haptics and Sound: A Non-visual Navigation System to Enhance Urban Bicycling

Anette Isabella Giesa[✉]

K3 - Malmö University, 205 06 Malmö, Sweden
anette.giesa@gmail.com

Abstract. Bicyclists are increasingly shaping the picture of urban traffic. Modern navigation systems for this group of traffic participants do not offer a satisfying solution for guided navigation. On one hand, visual information is shifting the attention away from the traffic situation. On the other hand, voice instructions are perceived as distracting and the use of conventional headphones blocks the hearing of ambient sounds. Providing navigation instructions in form of vibrotactile stimuli instead of visual information and simple sounds over open-ear headphones instead of voice instructions can diminish these problems to a great extent.

This paper presents the design of a non-visual, multi-sensory navigation system for urban bicyclists. The aim is to explore how audio-tactile stimuli can replace audio-visual instructions and create a feeling of greater safety, enhancing the cycling experience.

The introduction of this paper gives information on background, relevant frameworks and theories. In Sect. 2 the methodology is presented. Section 3 describes the design process and Sect. 4 the test procedure of the final prototype as well as the test results. Section 5 and 6 cover discussion and conclusion

Keywords: Audio-tactile navigation · Non-visual interfaces · Multi-sensory · Embodied displays · Bicycle navigation · Wearables

1 Introduction

Sight is one of our most important senses that we rely on to orientate and move in space. Therefore, reacting to events that are happening around us requires a high degree of visual attention. Besides our sense of sight, the sense of hearing plays an equally important role to react to the environment. Navigating in urban space with a large number of traffic participants requires an especially high level of attention in order to react and interact with each other and to ensure a certain level of safety. This applies in particular to less-protected traffic participants such as cyclists. Besides actual safety hazards, the feeling of safety also plays an important role.

Most conventional navigation systems provide directions in form of visual information in combination with voice instructions. This additional visual information increases the risk of accidents, as the focus needs to be shifted away from the current traffic situation. Spoken turn-by-turn instructions are hardly used by cyclists because

© Springer Nature Switzerland AG 2020
A. Marcus and E. Rosenzweig (Eds.): HCII 2020, LNCS 12201, pp. 640–652, 2020.
https://doi.org/10.1007/978-3-030-49760-6_45

the information is perceived as too long and distracting. Auditive spoken information demands a greater attention span to not only be perceived but to be understood. In comparison, shorter acoustic signals require less attention and time to be recognised [1, 2]. However, they are seldom used in bicycle navigation. In addition, the use of headphones limits the ability to locate ambient sounds, resulting in a feeling of insecurity.

Providing navigation instruction should not be limited to one sense. Addressing multiple senses has been proven to optimize the riding experience and to lead to faster reaction time [3]. Besides addressing the sense of sight and hearing though, the involvement of other sensory channels is rather seldom present in navigation systems. It is assumed that the inclusion of vibrotactile stimuli for directional information is perceived faster and more intuitively [4].

Non-visual feedback is predominantly explored for guided navigation and obstacle avoidance for visually impaired people [5, 6]. In the area of pedestrian navigation, the use of non-visual interfaces has been tested in some projects. Tactile information was provided for example by a mobile phone [7, 8] or a vibrotactile belt [9–11]. The use of non-visual multi-sensory information in navigation for bicyclists however has been less thoroughly researched.

As cycling is a whole-body outdoor activity, many different factors need to be respected when designing a navigation solution. Cycling is an experience that addresses all senses. Therefore, it is important to consider which sensory channels are addressed, and in what way. Research that has been done on the usage of audio-tactile signals for navigational purpose focuses mainly on performance data. Data on perception and reaction time deliver good information on the effects on navigation tasks of the tested technology. The question of how it feels to use a certain technology solution though, is mostly not explored. From the perspective of interaction design, the emotional aspect is an equally important factor that needs to be considered.

This paper presents the design of a non-visual audio-tactile navigation system for bicyclist. Vibrotactile stimuli at the wrists in combination with shorter acoustic signals provided by open-ear headphones are used to convey navigation instructions. Such non-visual navigation interfaces have the potential to maintain attention on the traffic scene more effectively. The ability to focus more on the surroundings can thus lead to a feeling of greater safety. Furthermore, it is investigated how the exchange of visual information by tactile cues and another form of conveying acoustic signals is advantageous for the cycling experience during active navigation.

2   Methodology

This project follows the research through design (RtD) approach. RtD describes the usage of design practice to create new knowledge that can contribute to design theory [12]. Another outcome of RtD are new design artefacts "where the artifact as itself is a type of implicit, theoretical contribution." [13]. The practical explorative character of RtD has the advantage of gaining multiple perspectives on a problem by including iterative cycles, as done in this project. The development of prototypes and the implementation of experiments were performed in parallel. That gives the opportunity to use the reflection on intermediate results to redefine process steps and design prototypes that build on each other.

The design process was structured based on that designerly approach. The methods that were applied are shortly described in the next sub-sections. The reason for their selection and in what part of the process they are used is also addressed.

2.1 Videography

Audio-visual recordings allow the researcher to capture situations and activities and analyze several aspects of social interactions independently of time and place. As defined by Knoblauch, Tuma and Schnettler [14], social interactions are not only to be understood as human to human interaction, but "involve(s) any action performed by someone who is motivated by, oriented to and coordinated with others, irrespective of whether these 'others' are other participants, animals, artefacts, or whatever". [14]. The analysis of audiovisual data recorded in the field with focus on interactions in 'natural settings' is defined as videography [14]. Natural setting is to be understood as situations that are typically not created by the researcher and could happen without any intervention.

In the first phase of the design process this method was used to get a deeper understanding of the user group. In the last phase videography was used for documentation and analysis in testing.

2.2 Bodystorming

Bodystorming can be summarized as methods of brainstorming "in the wild" or as Oulasvirta, Kurvinen and Kankainen also describe it, the idea of 'being there' and living with data in embodied ways [15]. Bodystorming makes it easier and faster to understand the environment in which the explored interactions take place and to use this understanding to generate ideas. Activities like cycling are extremely complex and cannot be fully grasped by observation and collection of insights from the users. Active, bodily exploration on the other hand captures a more precise understanding of relationships and dependencies of actions [16]. Therefore, bodystorming was used in the earlier design phases to build a felt understanding of cycling and to explore the complexity and context-dependent interactions.

2.3 Unstructured and Semi-structured Interviews

Unstructured interviews were conducted in the first phase to gather insights into experiences from the user and discover problem areas and design opportunities. The conversational character and the rather loose structure give the interviewee more control, but one additional strength is that relevant aspects can be discovered that were not considered as such by the interviewer beforehand [17].

Semi-Structured interviews were used to collect data and insights during the final prototype stage and were included in the test processes. Predefined questions made it possible to collect specific information on the test experiences while leaving room for the exploration of further aspects.

2.4   Protosketching and Experience Prototyping

Sketches can take many different forms, but they always serve to explore a variety of concepts [18]. In this project sketches were mainly created in the form of protosketching. As the name indicates, protosketching means sketching by low-fi prototyping. Koskinen et al. state that, "Protosketching is particularly suitable for designing embedded systems in which one has to simultaneously define physical prototypes and dynamic interactions in response to user behaviours" [19]. Since this work aims to answer the question of how guided cycling experience can be improved by exchanging visual information through audio-tactile signals, it is necessary to include technical aspects in the exploration process, before moving on to the test stage. Koskinen et al. [19] also describe protosketching as sketching in experience prototyping.

Experience Prototyping is a prototyping method that focuses on how a situation is actually experienced. Since experiencing also depends on the actual context, experience prototyping attempts to reconstruct a tangible experience that enables the researcher to understand the interactions between users and a design artifact in a realistic way.

Looking at what "experience" means in that context, Buchenau and Suri describe experience as "a very dynamic, complex and subjective phenomenon. It depends upon the perception of multiple sensory qualities of a design, interpreted through filters relating to contextual factors" [20].

Since the research question is situated in a very specific context, it was important to go through many iterative cycles in order to be able to explore and test individual factors that are relevant to the experience of active navigation on a bicycle in urban areas. Using protosketching and experience prototyping supported prototype construction that focused on different aspects of a desired experience, while considering previous experiences and the context that surrounds it. Protosketches turned into experience prototypes, which were tested and again transformed into new protosketches. Thus, individual components could be quickly tested and revised.

3   Design Process

In the following sub-sections different process steps and their results are described. In Sect. 3.1 the collection of relevant data and their evaluation is discussed. Section 3.2 deals with technical and sensory exploration, prototyping and smaller tests. In Sect. 3.3 the development of the final prototype is described.

3.1   Research and Fieldwork

To design for urban cyclists, one first needs to understand the experience. Bicycling is an activity that is physical, sensory and social in nature [21], and, as such, it needs to be studied in the field, when and where it is happening. Methods such as desktop research and interviews are suitable to collect initial information, but they are not sufficient to capture the complexity of this activity and its dependence on contextual factors for the experience.

In order to investigate and answer the question of how a non-visual, multi-sensory navigation system for urban cyclists might be designed, a combination of videography, bodystorming and unstructured interviews was chosen to get the best possible understanding of the cycling experience. Information was collected on questions such as how people cycle, how they feel when cycling, what they perceive on a sensory level, whether they use digital devices while riding and, if so, for what purpose.

Over a timespan of 2,5 weeks videos were recorded with a GoPro action camera, mounted on a helmet while cycling. Recordings were done on a daily basis and performed in two cities. Some recordings were done to record the ride, while others also served to directly comment and document feedback on the felt experience while cycling in self-observation.

Besides self-observation, eight people in three different cities and two countries were asked to use their bicycle as often as possible for their daily routes and pay attention to how they are cycling, as well as their interactions with other traffic participants and the surroundings. They were also asked to focus on what sensations they are perceiving and how it feels in general to ride a bicycle in an urban area.

Fieldwork Results. Unstructured interviews were used to compile the results. One person additionally submitted an audio file with comments that he recorded during two rides.

The combined and compared data indicates that the bicycle infrastructure in urban areas plays an important role in the cycling experience. In the different cities in which the research, fieldwork and subsequent tests were conducted – Malmö, Berlin and Frankfurt – the cycling infrastructure is entirely different. This factor also has a higher influence on the feeling of safety when cycling than for example, time of day or traffic density. Collected information on how people ride, and experience biking shows that the safer a person feels, the better they evaluate the experience. Participants in Malmö, where the bicycle infrastructure is good developed, could give more information on how they perceived the activity on a more sensory level, while participants in Berlin and Frankfurt reported that most of their attention is required to interact with other traffic participants to stay relatively safe. Their experience of cycling is more related to stress.

When it comes to the usage of digital devices, headphones and smartphones are most frequently used. Headphones are mainly worn to listen to music, while the answers to the question of why and when a smartphone is used varied. Nevertheless, the majority indicated that they use the smartphone to check their position when having a clear destination.

From video analysis and interviews it can further be concluded that the frequency of usage is also dependent upon the feeling of safety. Participants in Malmö stated that listening to music and taking a look at the phone while riding, presented no problem, as one can feel safe on the cycle paths. In contrary, people in Berlin and Frankfurt who cycle on a daily basis mentioned that they either stopped listening to music or navigation instructions entirely or switched from headphones to a portable Bluetooth speaker that is carried around. The reasons given were that they do not feel safe enough when their hearing is blocked for the surrounding traffic noise and possible hazards. Based on these results, it became apparent that a solution is needed that allows for the simultaneous perception of acoustic instructions and environmental sounds.

3.2 Exploration and Development

To be able to test in the field, the decision was made that the whole system should consist of wearable components. Using some kind of speaker that is placed on the head to convey acoustic signals was plausible. The decision to also build the tactile component in form of a wearable was made based on interviews with other bicyclists and self-observation. Integration into the handlebars for example was not an option, since not all handlebars have the same shape, the hand positions vary while cycling and the type of road surface itself can cause strong vibrations.

In order to achieve the best solution for a directional perception of acoustic and vibrotactile stimuli, protosketches were created to investigate technical aspects and materials. The resulting experience prototypes were then tested to examine the actual experience of smaller components of the final navigation system.

The following subsections describe the exploration of the sensory stimuli separately and in combination and the development of the resulting final prototype.

Exploring Vibrotactile Stimuli. Using vibrotactile actuators to deliver navigational cues in form of a wearable, one of the first questions was, where and in which form they should be placed on the body. The option of a belt was regarded, as the body position differs depending on the type of bike. Placing actuators into gloves was also rejected as they are not worn by everybody and during all seasons. Thus, the decision was made to place them around the wrist.

Using an Arduino Uno, the number of vibration motors and their position on the wrist were tested to determine the best directional sensation (Fig. 1).

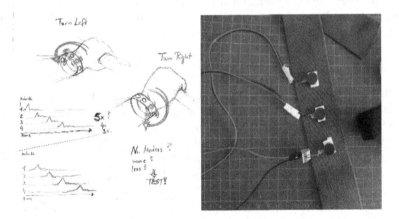

Fig. 1. Paper sketch of possible motor positioning and vibration patterns (left), a protosketch wristband to explore the perception of vibration (right).

One test was made with 4 participants using 3–5 motors and two vibration patterns. Vibration pattern describes here, a rhythmic modulation sequence of the vibration intensity. The number of only 3 motors was perceived as easiest to distinguish. Based on that result another test was conducted with 7 participants using 3 motors and 4 vibration patterns to determine patterns that result in clearer directional perception. One result was, that when using three motors at the same strength, the middle one was always perceived as "weaker". It could be observed that more irregular vibration rhythm creates a stronger feeling of being pulled into one direction. Following, a total of 12 patterns was created to be tested including further navigation instructions. The different signals should function as turn indicator, turn signal, stop or warning signal and destination reached.

Exploring Acoustic Signals. Out of interviews and desktop research it was concluded, that acoustic signals for navigation should ideally consist of simple sounds and leave out any language. As the artefact is for outdoor use, a sound that is clearly distinguishable from the surrounding sounds is necessary.

Together with a conductor, different instruments were tested to find a suitable sound. The decision was made to use a steel drum, as its sound is clearly different from traffic noise. Another reason was the deep resonance and the rich sound. From the recordings four final sounds[1] were created to be used for the instructions. To convey them a MP3 Mini Player module was used, and different acoustic actuators were tested.

Combining Haptics and Sound. The next step was to synchronize the vibration patterns with the sound files. For each navigation instruction 3 different combinations were tested. Two Lo-Fi wristbands were made of elastic fabric into which the motors were sewn. They were attached around the wrists of the participants with Velcro tape. To hear the acoustic signals, the participants had to hold the loudspeakers in their hands close to their ears.

3.3 Final Prototyping

Since the final prototypes needed to be tested in the field, i.e. while people are moving through urban space on their bicycles, the system had to be controllable wirelessly. That was realised by using an Adafruit Huzzah and the NRF Toolbox Application to send the commands to the microcontroller from a Smartphone. That also allowed changing the code "on the go" during small test sessions. The circuit was optimized and transferred to a smaller PCB (printed circuit board) (Fig. 2).

---

[1] http://giesa-a.net/navigationsounds.html (last accessed 2020/1/23).

Fig. 2. Final circuit soldered and stacked on a smaller PCB

To protect the control unit, a small box was created out of MDF. It was covered with pieces of an old bicycle tire and inner tube to make it water-resistant.

A "bend around the ear" solution was built to attach the speaker to the head. Using wire, the cables were holt in place while staying bendable. A small resonance enclosure was built on the backside of the speaker. Everything was covered with synthetic leather and foam was used to make the headphones sit comfortably.

To cover the cables and attach the control unit, wristbands and headphones to the body, a pair of suspenders, elastic bands and Velcro tape was used. Thus, the prototype cloud easily been adjusted to fit different body heights and shapes of the testers. In order to provide additional safety, reflector elements were sewn on (Fig. 3).

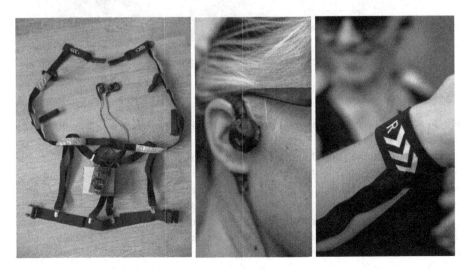

Fig. 3. Assembly of the final prototype (left), Open-ear headphone detail view (middle), wristband detail view (right).

4 Final Testing

4.1 Participants and Test Environment

In the final test round a total of 25 participants took part. 19 tests were carried out in the field, the other 6 were "dry tests", which means that the participants did not ride a bicycle during the test. These "dry tests" have been performed both indoors and outdoors, while sitting, standing or walking. 11 tests were carried out in Malmö, 8 in Frankfurt and 6 in Berlin. In addition to performing tests in cities with a different bicycle infrastructure, factors such as type of road and pavement, type of bicycle, weather condition, noise level, time of day, etc. were tried to be included where possible. The street types that could be used in the tests were, separated bike lanes, bike lanes on streets, side streets and main roads. The types of pavement were asphalt, pavers, cobblestone and gravel. Since the type of bike also influences the riding style and the vibrations that occur during the ride on the bike itself, besides "normal" road and touring bicycles three participants with a racing bike, one with a fat bike and one with a recumbent bike were tested (Fig. 4).

Fig. 4. Testers wearing the prototype.

4.2 Test Procedure

For the tests in the field, a smartphone was mounted on the handlebar of the bike from the researcher. The researcher was riding behind the participant and sent commands via the smartphone to the control unit to trigger an acoustic navigation instruction, a haptic one or a combination of both. The order in which instructions were given and over which sensory channel was randomly chosen. The participants were asked to react according to their interpretation of the information they received.

Using the think aloud method, participants were asked to verbalize their thoughts directly during the test. Based on the communicated thoughts, questions were asked from time to time and/or short conversations were held if the traffic situation allowed it.

If the participant has given their consent in advance, the entire test was recorded with a GoPro camera. After completion of the test semi-structured interviews were conducted, which were audio recorded with the smartphone. The video and audio recordings were sub sequently transcribed into notes for further evaluation.

4.3 Test Results

Although, many different factors as well as individual preferences and the perceptive ability of singular senses influenced the experience of cycling with the prototype, comprehensive results could be determined.

In comparison to conventional navigation systems, all participants mentioned that they see a non-visual solution as a better alternative. Eleven out of 19 participants that were tested in the field mentioned that they feel much safer. For a few participants it was because they perceived the system as more reliable and immediate, for some it was that they had the feeling they could concentrate more on the situation, and for others it was the fact that they did not need to use their phone to re-examine route and position. Most participants did not miss visual information, but a few would like to have a map for route planning and the possibility to look at it, if needed.

Without having experienced the instructions beforehand, not all signals could be understood clearly. Especially sound in separate was harder to understand. Based on the context though, all signals were interpreted correctly. However, if the combination of both was experienced a few times before, even instructions using only one sensory channel were understood without any further explanation. In general, it can be said that the combination of haptic with acoustic signals gives the best results. The stimuli were perceivable even in situation with a high noise level, when cycling on cobblestone and even when both occurred at the same time. All signals were interpreted and reacted to with almost no difficulties.

None of the participants had used open-ear headphones before. Most testers were surprised about how clear they could hear the sound instructions while still being able to perceive the ambient sound. The sound of the steel-drum was perceived as clearly distinguishable from the surrounding, even in loud environment. Some people suggested to use a higher pitched tone for the stop/warning signal to be more aggressive and almost force you to stop.

The noise level in certain areas had a noticeable impact on the perception of the navigation directives, in particular the sound instructions. In almost all tests that were carried out in louder environment, the results on fast perception of the instructions were poorer. This applies not only to the acoustic but also to the haptic stimuli.

The limitation to only four instructions – turn indicator, turn signal, stop/warning, destination reached – was perceived as just the right amount for bicycle navigation. This minimalist approach was particularly highlighted as positive, as the moments of possible distraction by the navigation system were reduced from the beginning.

5 Discussion

As the experience of cycling in urban space is highly influenced by context, former experiences and a variety of external factors, it is necessary to take all of them into account when designing for bicyclists. To enhance the cycling experience and improve the feeling of safety in active guided navigation, a prototype that serves as a concept for a non-visual, multi-sensory navigation system was designed. Considering the contextual dependence and influence of external factors, research and tests were done in the field in three different cities. The results of the analysis in the early phase of the design process and the results of the final tests show that factors such as road infrastructure, traffic density, noise levels, pavement and bicycle type, to name but a few, affect not only the general cycling experience but also the sense of safety in bicycle navigation.

As shown by Park, Kim and Kwon [3], addressing multiple sensory channels in navigation systems improves the riding experience and leads to faster reaction time. The results of the final tests are confirming that the perception over multiple channels is experienced as a best solution. The combination of sound and vibration could be perceived in all situations. Dependent on which sense was affected by external factors, the information communicated over the other sensory channel was considered as indispensable. Nevertheless, some testers reported that they could forgo the sound instructions if they would need to choose. The vibrotactile stimuli were experienced as much more intuitive, direct and reliable than additional information communicated through other senses. This confirms the assumption of Gustafson-Pearce, Billett and Cecelja [4], that especially vibrotactile stimuli can be perceived faster and more intuitively and are therefore effective at delivering navigation instructions. The fact that the testers reacted slower to navigation instructions in a noisy environment shows, however, that the perception of tactile stimuli is negatively affected by environmental sounds, even if these stimuli are perceived as immediate.

Based on the fact that cycling in urban areas requires a constantly high level of attention, the navigation instructions have been reduced to a minimum. It was assumed that this restriction would not only have a positive effect on the attention to the surroundings but would also be sufficient for bicycle navigation. This assumption was confirmed in the final tests and was highlighted as particularly positive.

The feedback on the sound instructions in comparison to spoken voice instructions confirms that acoustic signals are perceived as faster and easier to understand. It should be emphasised here that this is a matter of personal perception. If the actual duration of shorter spoken navigation instructions is compared with the duration of the audio files used, the audio files are often longer. As Klatzky, Marston, Giudice, Golledge and Loomis [2] conclude, this leads to the assumption that the cognitive load to understand non-verbal sound is lower than the one to understand language. In this respect however, the concept of how the designed system functions may also play an important role. Since the directional information were only provided on the respective side of the body, not only cognitive load but also body perception could play a role in perception speed. Further it was possible to show that a type of open-ear head phones enables the hearing and localisation of traffic sounds while acoustic stimuli are transmitted.

6 Conclusion

In this paper the design of a non-visual, multi-sensory navigation system for bicyclist was presented. Wristbands that convey vibrotactile stimuli in combination with acoustic signals, that are provided over open-ear headphones, are used to deliver necessary information for active bicycle navigation. It could be demonstrated that visual navigation instructions can successfully be replaced by audio-tactile stimuli. The omission of additional visual information allows cyclists to keep their attention on the main traffic scene. This results in a feeling of increased safety and contributes to a better cycling experience in urban areas. In addition, the number of instructions was reduced to a minimum, which was evaluated as significantly less distracting.

Besides conveying acoustic signals through open-ear headphones, simple sounds were used instead of spoken voice instructions. Participants experienced that as much safer compared to conventional navigation systems. The vibrotactile stimuli on the wrists were perceived as more intuitive and direct compared to other sensory stimuli.

As cycling is a bodily outdoor activity, it is highly context dependent and influenced by external factors like for example bicycle infrastructure, traffic density, noise level or pavement. It has been shown, that by involving several senses it is possible to perceive navigation directives even if one of the senses addressed is negatively influenced by these external factors. Especially the inclusion of haptic stimuli in multi-sensory systems offers a promising role for non-visual interfaces and the improvement of experiences in urban navigation. Nevertheless, the positive effects of an audio-tactile navigation system on the cycling experience cannot be generalized. The strong context dependency requires more research on the influence of various external factors on the perception of the delivered sensory stimuli. The findings presented in this paper, however, provide a basis for further research on multi-sensory embodied displays and their use in the context of navigation.

References

1. Fry, D.B.: Simple reaction-times to speech and non-speech stimuli. Cortex **11**(4), 355–360 (1975)
2. Klatzky, R.L., Marston, J.R., Giudice, N.A., Golledge, R.G., Loomis, J.M.: Cognitive load of navigating without vision when guided by virtual sound versus spatial language. J. Exp. Psychol.: Appl. **12**(4), 223 (2006)
3. Park, E., Kim, K.J., Kwon, S.J.: Evaluation of automobile navigation systems with multisensory information channels. Behav. Inf. Technol. **36**(10), 1014–1019 (2017)
4. Gustafson-Pearce, O., Billett, E., Cecelja, F.: Comparison between audio and tactile systems for delivering simple navigational information to visually impaired pedestrians. Br. J. Vis. Impair. **25**(3), 255–265 (2007)
5. Dakopoulos, D., Bourbakis, N.G.: Wearable obstacle avoidance electronic travel aids for blind: a survey. IEEE Trans. Syst. Man Cybern. Part C (Appl. Rev.) **40**(1), 25–35 (2010)
6. Jacobson, R.D.: Navigating maps with little or no sight: an audio-tactile approach. In: Content Visualization and Intermedia Representations (CVIR 1998) (1998)

7. Komninos, A., Astrantzi, M., Plessas, A., Stefanis, V., Garofalakis, J.: Non-verbal audio and tactile mobile navigation. In: 2014 IEEE 10th International Conference on Wireless and Mobile Computing, Networking and Communications (WiMob), pp. 314–321. IEEE (2014)
8. Szymczak, D., Rassmus-Gröhn, K., Magnusson, C., Hedvall, P.O.: A real-world study of an audio-tactile tourist guide. In: Proceedings of the 14th International Conference on Human-Computer Interaction with Mobile Devices and Services, pp. 335–344. ACM (2012)
9. Heuten, W., Henze, N., Boll, S., Pielot, M.: Tactile wayfinder: a non-visual support system for wayfinding. In: Proceedings of the 5th Nordic Conference on Human-Computer Interaction: Building Bridges, pp. 172–181. ACM (2008)
10. Pielot, M., Boll, S.: *Tactile Wayfinder*: comparison of tactile waypoint navigation with commercial pedestrian navigation systems. In: Floréen, P., Krüger, A., Spasojevic, M. (eds.) Pervasive 2010. LNCS, vol. 6030, pp. 76–93. Springer, Heidelberg (2010). https://doi.org/10.1007/978-3-642-12654-3_5
11. Van Erp, J.B., Van Veen, H.A., Jansen, C., Dobbins, T.: Waypoint navigation with a vibrotactile waist belt. ACM Trans. Appl. Percept. (TAP) 2(2), 106–117 (2005)
12. Zimmerman, J., Forlizzi, J., Evenson, S.: Research through design as a method for interaction design research in HCI. In: Proceedings of the SIGCHI Conference on Human Factors in Computing Systems, pp. 493–502 (2007)
13. Zimmerman, J., Stolterman, E., Forlizzi, J.: An analysis and critique of research through design: towards a formalization of a research approach. In: Proceedings of the 8th ACM Conference on Designing Interactive Systems, pp. 310–319. ACM (2010)
14. Knoblauch, H., Tuma, R., Schnettler, B.: Video analysis and videography. In: The SAGE Handbook of Qualitative Data Analysis, pp. 435–449 (2014)
15. Oulasvirta, A., Kurvinen, E., Kankainen, T.: Understanding contexts by being there: case studies in bodystorming. Pers. Ubiquit. Comput. 7(2), 125–134 (2003). https://doi.org/10.1007/s00779-003-0238-7
16. Schleicher, D., Jones, P., Kachur, O.: Bodystorming as embodied designing. Interactions 17(6), 47–51 (2010)
17. Wilson, C.: Interview Techniques for UX Practitioners, pp. 47–49. Morgan Kaufmann, Waltham (2014)
18. Buxton, B.: Sketching User Experiences: Getting the Design Right and the Right Design. Morgan Kaufmann, San Francisco (2007)
19. Koskinen, I., et al.: Protosketching: Sketching in Experience Prototyping (2009)
20. Buchenau, M., Suri, J.F.: Experience prototyping. In: Proceedings of the 3rd Conference on Designing Interactive Systems: Processes, Practices, Methods, and Techniques, pp. 424–433. ACM (2000)
21. Spinney, J.: A chance to catch a breath: using mobile video ethnography in cycling research. Mobilities 6(2), 161–182 (2011)

Understanding Engagement in the Workplace: Studying Operators in Chinese Traffic Control Rooms

Linyi Jin[(⊠)], Val Mitchell, and Andrew May

Design and Creative Arts, Loughborough University, Loughborough, UK
l.jin@lboro.ac.uk

Abstract. This paper analyses the workplace engagement of operators in traffic control rooms (OTCR) through two examples from a qualitative study of two traffic control rooms in a southwestern China province. It aims at providing an empirical basis for subsequent User Experience (UX) Design research and practice within a workplace environment. In previous research, engagement in the workplace has been well-documented to be closely related to productivity in groups and organisations. In traffic control rooms, the work performance of operators largely depends on the varying levels of their engagement with their work, which is of great importance to road safety. However, how UX design could be used to enhance the work engagement of OTCR is an area that has been largely, if not entirely, overlooked in existing literature. This paper presents the research methodology and a theoretical understanding of engagement that seeks to provide theoretically informed and empirically grounded strategies for UX based design of effective and satisfying interaction between OTCR and the technologies they use.

Keywords: Engagement · Traffic control room · Empirical study · User experience design

1 Introduction

In China, the goal of motorway management is "safety, speed, efficiency, comfort and convenience". Motorways are managed by operators working in networks of traffic control rooms (Fig. 1) located in different geographical areas [1]. The performance of operators in traffic control rooms (OTCR) and the execution of various tasks maximises motorway safety. OTCRs' tasks require active observation and the constant analysis of information regarding motorway safety, with timely evaluation of complex situations [2]. Previous research on motorway design has studied OTCR's behaviour in traffic control rooms in relation to technological improvements and human factors, whereas the user experience has been largely overlooked. This research contends that a human-centred design (HCD) approach needs to be integrated into the traditional function-orientated design approach. It is essential that some unique cognitive strengths of humans, subtle psychological demands, and knowledge about how operators feel and interact with tasks should be considered [3].

© Springer Nature Switzerland AG 2020
A. Marcus and E. Rosenzweig (Eds.): HCII 2020, LNCS 12201, pp. 653–665, 2020.
https://doi.org/10.1007/978-3-030-49760-6_46

Fig. 1. Chinese traffic control room

This research, with the case study of operators in two traffic control rooms in a southwestern China province, highlights the notion of 'engagement' as a key aspect of the OTCR's experience in the workplace. Engagement is an important determinant of performance in workplace [4], so as performance of operators in the traffic control room, that is highly relevant to road safety. Previous literature indicates that many traffic incidents are caused by inappropriate, delayed operation or omissions from operators in control rooms [5]. In addition, operators in highly automated control rooms are reported to be constantly bored [6]. This problem, from the researcher's perspective, can be partially solved by applying UX design within the workplace in order to influence OTCR's engagement. Towards this purpose, this paper sets out to firstly develop an understanding of OTCR's engagement within the workplace through empirical research, and will then attempt to operationalise this knowledge in future applied research and design.

This paper briefly reviews relevant literature and then reports on the research methodology used to understand OTCR engagement. Then, the paper illustrates findings from empirical research using three different steps. Firstly, a preliminary study was used to inform participants of the construct of engagement. In this way, participants were able to articulate their experience of engagement more accurately. Secondly, a task analysis that combined cognitive task and hierarchical task analysis was undertaken to understand task content and procedures. Thirdly, a subsequent study set out to investigate how operators perceive the construct of engagement in the real context of undertaking their work in a traffic room. Lastly, the paper discusses how these empirical findings can be operationalised within UX design in order to improve OTCR engagement, and therefore indirectly improve road safety and OTCR well-being.

2   Review of Literature

Kahn [7] introduces the concept of engagement and defines it as "the harnessing of organization members' selves to their work roles; in engagement, people employ and express themselves physically, cognitively, and emotionally during role performances". Treadgold [8] contends that engagement is closely linked with meaningful work, high level of self-integration, as well as high level of self-actualisation. Schaufeli et al. [9] provide a more comprehensive and precise description of work engagement as a ful-filling, work-related state of mind that is characterised by vigour, dedication, and absorption. That is "vigour is characterised by high levels of energy and mental resi-lience while working. Dedication refers to being strongly involved in one's work and experiencing a sense of significance, enthusiasm, and challenge. Absorption is char-acterised by being fully concentrated and happily engrossed in one's work, whereby time passes quickly and one has difficulties with detaching oneself from work".

Acknowledging Schaufeli et al.'s definition of engagement, Bakker and Demerouti [10] have created the job demands-resources (JD-R) model. According to their model, there is a positive link between job resources and work engagement, where job resources include social support from colleagues and supervisors, performance feed-back, skill variety, autonomy and learning opportunities. They illustrate job demand as including work pressure, emotional demands, mental demands, physical demands and so on. Bakker and Demerouti argue that job resources and personal resources are reciprocal, because personal resources can produce new job resources – when job demands are high the resources become especially important. Moreover, work engagement, in turn, positively impacts on job performance. And, employees who engage highly in work and perform well are able to create new resources, which then foster engagement again over time and create a positive gain spiral (Fig. 2).

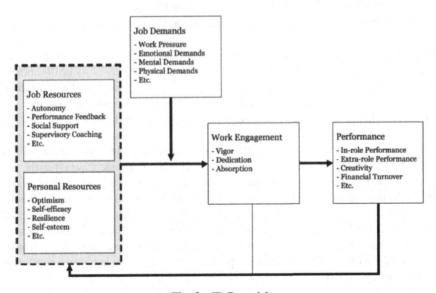

Fig. 2. JD-R model

However, the relationship between demand and engagement is still somewhat vague. Job and Personal resources are important to engagement, and are crucial when an employee is confronted with high job demand, which implies that resources and job demands can produce engagement together. For example, Bakker and Demerouti include performance feedback as one component of job resources, feedback may imply that there is still deficiency to be improved and perfected, and job demands such as work pressure, emotional demands and physical demands can allow employees to know what improvements are needed. Therefore, to some extent, job demands can enable and motivate an employee to acquire improvements. Although, employees may experience a transient positive emotion if they evade difficulty, eventually this may lead to negative emotions, and they may then fail when facing the same difficulty in the future [11]. Job demands such as work pressure, difficulties and challenge could therefore at least theoretically be designed to increase engagement.

However although the JD-R model helps define engagement, how to adjust engagement through this model is still not clear. Additionally, the phenomenon of engagement may not appear in the same way in different contexts. Therefore, in order to enhance the engagement of OTCRs, a clear understanding of engagement is necessary within the specific context of Chinese traffic control rooms. In this study, the researcher has tried to understand how job resources and demands influence engagement in the context of Chinese traffic control rooms through a three stage qualitative study in two separate Chinese traffic control rooms. The section below presents the methodology in terms of sampling strategy, data collection and preliminary analysis.

3   Methodology

Through literature review, engagement in this research is construed primarily as a psychological phenomenon which is experienced by OTCR and can be influenced by personal, social, cultural, and environmental factors. It can be studied phenomenologically by using qualitative methodologies which can help improve understanding of social phenomena as experienced by participants. This involves the systematic collection, organisation, and interpretation of data derived from interviews or observation [12]. The process of data collection and analysis can be characterised as 'iterative', meaning that each step in the methodology is interconnected and intertwined. The successful completion of each step, i.e., data collection and preliminary analysis, informs and affects the next.

To collect accurate and comprehensive qualitative data in order to understand engagement in traffic control rooms, the research consisted of three stages. Firstly, participants were informed about the construct of engagement by the researcher. This was to provide the participants with the necessary vocabulary and verbal expression for them to be able to articulate their experience of engagement, and to make sure that participants were able to identify the target experience before describing it. The three step process for transferring knowledge, developed by Ross and Munby [13] was used to inform the participants, following the sequence of 'perception, conception and abstraction'. Step one, the concepts are explained to the participants. Step two, participants interpret the concepts. Step three, participants explain the concepts to another person who is unfamiliar with them so that the researcher can check their understanding.

Secondly, based on preliminary analysis of the data collected through conversations with participants, and with the retrieval and examination of relevant control room documentation, the researcher conducted a task analysis to systematically describe the tasks confronting the research participants in their daily work. The researcher firstly identified research boundaries through analysis of relevant literature and documentation. Then, each OTCR and engineer was interviewed to establish how the target tasks should be decomposed.

With the understanding of the participants' tasks and environment of work, the research proceeded to the third stage, which was to understand engagement from the perspective of OTCRs. Many researchers probe the experience of engagement through participants' memories [14–16]. The premises of techniques for understanding engagement is that participants are able to recall these relevant memories. Because memories are unreliable, people may make many mistakes during the retrieval process [17–20]. In addition, because engagement is an immersive and unconscious psychological state, it is very hard to remember details. Therefore this research developed a systematic approach for identifying the construct of engagement in the real world context of the traffic control room. This was contained two overlapping stages. In stage one, critical incidents including engaging tasks and subtasks were identified through card sorting. The cognitive interview (CI) method was then used to understand engagement in relation to these critical incidents. CI aims to elicit credible information from witnesses by facilitating the retrieval of memories [20]. Normally, this technique is used to help police interview witnesses to help improve their recall of detail. Furthermore, an open-ended interview was used to build the image of ideal engagement and understand what characteristics can influence engagement in the control room context.

Each OTCR was asked to rank the three most engaging tasks and describe the overall experience of each task in three different sequences. Firstly, the OTCR was asked to describe in their own words the task. The researcher then divided the task into its main steps based on the task analysis and checked this with the participant. The OTCR was then asked to describe each step in detail, including their experience, thoughts, conditions and behaviours. In the third sequence, each OTCR was invited to rank the tasks and identified sub tasks based on the level of engagement and asked why they ranked the procedures in this way. At the end of the session, each OTCR was asked to explain what kind of task characteristics could increase or decrease the level of engagement of a task, and what task can create the ideal level of engagement in his or her mind.

3.1 Sampling Strategy

The sampling for this research included the selection of field sites and the selection of individual participants. Convenience sampling was used to locate control rooms that the researcher has access to and who were willing to take part in the research. The sampling of individual participants was based on a purposive sample with the target group selected using the researcher's specialist knowledge [21]. Criteria were developed through the researcher's preliminary consultation with experienced personnel in the field, including engineers and managers, and included investigation via literature review [22, 23]. The researcher developed two criteria for the selection and recruitment of OTCR in traffic control rooms, namely, 1) Experienced OTCR, 2) OTCR who are willing to take part. Software engineers were selected by two criteria, 1) working in traffic monitoring software design with rich work experience, 2) usually having contact with OTCRs. The gender of OTCR was not included into the criteria, because gender is not a criterion when hiring OTCR and engineers. A total of twenty-two participants, thirteen participants in control room A and five participants in control room B were recruited. Eighteen OTCRs attended the whole study. Four engineers in CHENGDU JINSUI AUTOMATION ENGINEERING CO., LTD. All participants were aged from 29 to 55. They had an average of three years working experience as a control room OTCR or engineer. This study was carried out in these two traffic control rooms from December 2018 to January 2019.

3.2   Analysis

This section focuses on the analysis and results of step three: understanding engagement from the perspective of the operators. Codes were assigned to major themes that emerged from the data namely:

a) the hierarchy of engaging tasks
b) the ranking of engaging parts of tasks
c) engaging tasks and their corresponding characteristics
d) engaging parts of tasks and their corresponding characteristics
e) unengaging tasks and their corresponding characteristics
f) the ideal engaging task and its characteristics
g) OTCR's perceived challenges and
h) the description of experience of engagement

Documents were imported into NVivo software for this analysis.

4   Empirical Findings

The following section describes the characteristics that influence the engagement of OTCRs in the context of Chinese traffic control rooms and how they enhance or diminish engagement and end with a construct to operationalize engagement, which provides a possible direction to enhance engagement through UX design.

4.1   Task Characteristics Influence Engagement

Unfamiliar Situations. OTCRs feel very engaged in when they need to assess, detect, scrutinize, and judge a situation. For example, OTCR A mentioned that:

"I once detected a pile-up involving 11 cars crashing into the one in front, and I had to immediately assess the situation with many road-side assistance personnel, to decide on the

type of accident and its location, (which was decided based on various clues, such as the distance markers along the road as reported by the motorway patrol), to what extent the incident had blocked the road, how the traffic police assessed the situation, and what could be learned from the CCTV. I felt nervous, stressed, challenged and inadequate, because communicating with road-side assistance personnel was very exhausting and somewhat ineffective, so I was very engaged under this kind of high pressure condition, I was afraid of making mistakes".

Additionally, challenges led to engagement but too many challenges were stressful, for example OTCR H mentioned that:

"I usually pay more attention to those challenging tasks, it is suffering, but I don't want to give in to difficulty, and I will persist in fighting with these challenges, because it felt meaningful. It can facilitate personal growth by accumulating and learning knowledge from them. When I complete it I feel a sense of achievement. However, I can not handle too many challenges at the same time, which leads me to feel strained and uncapable".

Other examples of unforeseen engaging tasks are when many emergencies happen at the same time, or coping with new tasks OTCRs had not experienced before. Such situations make OTCRs feel unable to respond to them satisfactorily. In addition, it was concluded that OTCRs feel much more engaged when they meet new unfamiliar tasks, - this happened a lot when they were new employees in the traffic control room, because there was much to learn. For example, OTCR B said that:

"The sense of engagement appeared frequently when I was a new operator here. At that time I paid attention to those unfamiliar tasks, and I used a notebook to record many new knowledges, such as road information, task procedures, operation criteria, software operation, how to cooperate with road patrol personnel and how to conduct handover with other operators"

However too much job challenge can also decrease engagement, just as OTCR E mentioned

"I feel incapable and exhausted if too many accidents happened at the same time".

A balance of workload is therefore necessary, for example OTCR A stated that:

"It is better to share workload during busy times, and taking care that the everyone feels neither too overloaded, nor too bored. For example, I had had a very enjoyable working experience: it was during a Spring Festival when I successfully responded to many emergencies because of fruitful cooperation with my colleagues".

In addition, the fear of punishment is the motivation mentioned most frequently for OTCRs to force themselves to engage with tasks. For example, OTCR C says that:

"I must be very engaged in collecting road information in an emergency, because this step is a foundation to submitting a correct report, otherwise I will be punished for an inaccurate report".

And OTCR D say that:

"I forced myself to concentrate on releasing information on information boards, and guiding motorway patrols to cope with accidents, because I had been punished for wrong execution before. The punishment is very serious, including salary deduction, blame from supervisors, and even criminal responsibility if a second serious accident is caused by an operator's mistakes".

It can be concluded that OTCRs are more engaged when they are confronted with unfamiliar and uncontrollable tasks. Also a certain amount of job demand, such as job pressure, physical and emotional demands [10] can also be positively linked with engagement if they have enough job resources, such as capability, concentration, support from colleagues and so on to cope with them. However too many job demands can decrease engagement by overwhelming them.

In addition, because the fear of punishment is a strong motivation for them to carefully conduct certain tasks, they do not enjoy the execution of such tasks, rather they feel stressed, worried and afraid.

Repetitive Tasks and Lacking Challenge. Some tasks were perceived as dull and repetitive and without challenge, making OTCRs feel very bored, for example OTCR F said.

> *"I feel meaningless and monotonous, when I was conducting transmission of repeat information, and continuing CCTV surveillance that does not reveal any incidents. After completing them I couldn't remember anything about what I had been doing".*

Eleven OTCRs mentioned that they felt extremely bored and meaningless when there are no tasks at all, and they are in a daze for a whole day. Therefore, adequate job or personal resources, but little job demands or challenges can also diminish the sense of engagement, and resources can be negatively related with engagement under this situation.

Significance of Tasks. OTCRs prefer to pay more attention to tasks which they think are important for road safety. For example, OTCR G said

> *"I pay more attention to expressing the information that should be released on information boards in different locations to guide traffic flow effectively".*

and OTCR H said

> *"I think detecting traffic jam by CCTV or on the TV wall is very engaging during festivals, I felt very engaged, because detecting accidents by checking CCTV along the roads can help solving problems. And I'm willing to invest effort in doing these tasks".*

In contract, OTCRs feel unwilling to execute tasks that they could not agree with and hence their engagement was lower. For example, OTCR F thinks

> *"It is unreasonable to submit repetitious information, and watching the CCTV for incidents on roads is very inefficient, because most incidents are not discovered by CCTV surveillance of daily".*

Therefore, in line with the definition of engagement given by Schaufeli et al. [9], people can experience a sense of significance in engagement. OCTRs prefer to pay more attention to tasks they believe can enhance road safety, even if other tasks are also very important within the job.

Management System. The degree to which the supervisor emphasizes the importance a task influences the operator's engagement in the task. For example, OTCR C said:

> *"I attached strong importance to presenting information on the information boards, because this task was given a high priority by supervisors".*

A supervisor may ask each operator to detect at least three incidents on the road using CCTV; this encourages some OTCR to intensify their surveillance with a higher degree of engagement. In addition, supervisory coaching is very crucial when OTCR meets high job demands. For example OTCR A mentioned:

"When I meet some accidents which I have no idea how to cope with, guidance and coaching from supervisors can always reassure me, making me feel confident in execution".

Feedback from managers is significant, but too much feedback can also diminish OTCR's engagement by increasing pressure and making them feel doubtful about their capabilities, for example OTCR D:

"I carefully monitored accidents on the road during emergencies, because, I have to react to the many supervisor's requests for information. And I also care about the supervisor's opinion of me, I think it's not good when they ask something from me and I can't answer. But I will feel they don't believe me if they ask me too frequently".

In short, job resources like performance feedback and supervisory coaching [10] can stimulate engagement but it is a double-edged sword - it can increase OTCR's attention on tasks, and it can also bring the sense of pressure and incapability to them.

The Sense of Responsibility and Promotion Prospects. An operator who has a higher sense of responsibility and interest in promotion is more likely to feel engagement. A very small number of OTCRs who had a very strong sense of responsibility and want to achieve success at work could even find meaning in very repetitive and boring tasks, and would force themselves to engage with them. For example, OTCR P who mentioned:

"I think it's possible to find meaning while daily CCTV detection in control room, even it's very hard I will still insist checking the CCTV, I believe it can contribute to monitoring work".

Furthermore, a few OTCR who have a comparatively strong sense of responsibility would like to pay more attention to the job, for example OTCR F said:

"I would be worry about unfinished tasks after work, and I would sacrifice my own time to finish tasks, for example once there was a continual accident which occupied roads many days and have not been solved properly, I was feel very worried and nervous about it, even I couldn't sleep well at night".

However, sixteen OTCRs say that they don't enjoy most of the tasks, and that they can't feel fully engaged in the workplace. They persist in carefully completing tasks because of their sense of duty.

A few OTCRs reported little engagement in tasks which cannot reflect their own values or give them a sense of personal development. These included tasks which don't require any assessment or judgement. OTCR F mentioned that:

"I feel very bored and lost when my task could be completed by a five year old boy".

OTCR A said that:

"I can not get any benefit from repetitious tasks, because I can not learn anything, it is very meaningless".

In short, personal resources like optimism, self-efficacy, self-esteem [10], career ambition, and responsibility can enhance engagement, while whether an operator has the required sense of responsibility and interest in promotion is decided by his or her own character traits. These are very difficult to change, and many OTCR just adopt a production line approach, working without reflection, to their work.

4.2   Ideal Tasks

Besides these characteristics which influence engagement, many OTCRs thought that to be ideal a task should be challenging while controllable. An ideal example of a very engaging task is the experience of detecting the cause of a traffic jam by using CCTV cameras along the road. In this task, OTCR can always successfully overcome difficulties. The experience of this task is very close to the full engagement: vigour, dedication and absorption, defined by Schaufeli et al. [9]. For example as described by OTCR B and F, if they can quickly discover the cause of a traffic jam, they can find a sense of significance, enthusiasm and challenge. They spontaneously concentrate on the task and time passes quickly. Even if they feel it is a difficult situation, they will try to overcome the challenges and it's hard for them detach themselves from this task. They felt capable of facing the challenge and reported that they were energetic and resilient. Sometimes work was even perceived as fun.

4.3   The Construct of Engagement

In short, engagement in the traffic control room depends on the comparison of the resources of the operator and the challenges that he or she faces (Fig. 3). The resources are defined as all that OTCRs have at their disposal to face the challenges. The resources consist of three factors: personal characteristics, the management system and the OTCR's perception about the importance of tasks. Personal characteristics, which is very similar to 'personal resources' in the JD-R model [10], include: an operator's fear of punishment, the sense of responsibility, career ambitions, and the capability (knowledge, energy and experience) to complete the task. The management system is OTCR's understanding of the emphasis managers place on a task, because an OTCR's execution of this task can influence the way a manager or supervisor views the OTCR. In addition, performance feedback and supervisory coaching can also stimulate engagement. The perception about any task is the impact an operator believes that task to have on road safety. The challenges are defined as the difficulties and obstacles that an operator faces in completing tasks, and the pressures they feel from supervisors. Ordinarily, the fear of punishment is the main motivation for an OTCR to face challenges.

Figure 3 uses the analogy of a seesaw. When the challenge is less that the resources, the seesaw tilts towards boredom, and when the challenges are more than the resources, the seesaw tilts towards anxiety. Full engagement [10] occurs when the resources match the challenges. Full engagement happens rarely in the traffic control room: only two OTCRs described such an experience when detecting a traffic jam as described above. The most common high engagement state in the traffic control room happens in response to emergencies, when an operator meets challenges that require

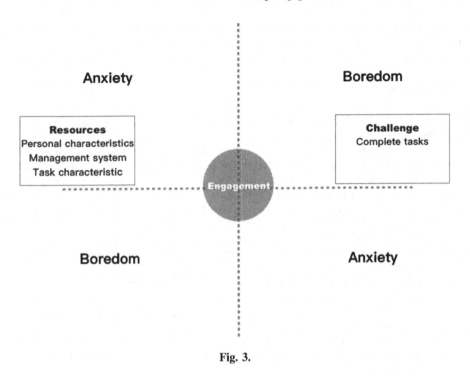

Fig. 3.

slightly more than the available resources; in this case the seesaw dips slightly towards anxiety, it is a state of partial engagement. It resembles the "full engagement experience" as described by Bakker and Demerouti [10], except that the operator feels anxious rather than happy and satisfied. Many OTCR said they couldn't stay in this state of engagement consistently because they found it very exhausting, which implies that engagement is a limited resource. The low engagement state happened the most in the control room. OTCRs meet few challenges and possess far more reources. In this state, they are bored and feel the work is very mundane and meaningless. OTCRs meet this situations a lot when they have no specific tasks at hand, when they stare at the big CCTV wall without thinking, and when they undertake surveillance of traffic flow with a low likelihood of detecting incidents.

5 Conclusion

A construct for engagement has been developed in the context of Chinese traffic control rooms, and the specific characteristics that influence engagement have been identified. Engagement in the traffic control room depends on the balance of resources (personal characteristics, management system, and OTCR's perception about tasks) and the challenges the OTCR faces. Underpinned by Bakker and Demerouti (2008)'s [10] JD-R model of engagement, this construct of engagement will be used to highlight opportunities to enhance engagement through UX design. Because full engagement impossible to maintain across all tasks, engagement should be focussed on target tasks which are crucial to safety. Future work will therefore seek to understand how to use the construct to identify the target tasks of interest.

References

1. ZhangYang, Z.J.: Expressway monitoring system theory and system application, pp. 20–23 (2000)
2. Noyes, J., Bransby, M.: People in Control Human Factors in Control Room Design, 1st edn. The Institution of Engineering and Technology, London (2001)
3. BS: Ergonomic design of control centres. Principles for the design of control centres. EN ISO 11064-1, British Standard (2001)
4. Simpson, M.R.: Engagement at work: a review of the literature. Int. J. Nurs. Stud. **46**(7), 1012–1024 (2009)
5. Ikuma, L.H., Harvey, C., Taylor, C.F., Handal, C.: A guide for assessing control room operator performance using speed and accuracy, perceived workload, situation awareness, and eye tracking. J. Loss Prev. Process Ind. **32**, 454–465 (2014)
6. Schaeffer, J., Lindell, R.: Emotions in design: considering user experience for tangible and ambient interaction in control rooms. Inf. Des. J. **22**(1), 19–31 (2016)
7. Kahn, W.A.: Psychological conditions of personal engagement and disengagement at work. Acad. Manag. J. **33**(4), 692–724 (1990)
8. Treadgold, R.J.: Engagement in meaningful work: its relationship to stress, depression, and clarity of self-concept. Dissertation abstracts international: section B. The Sciences and Engineering (1997)
9. Schaufeli, W.B., Bakker, A.B.: Bevlogenheid: Een begrip gemeten: work engagement: the measurement of a concept. Gedrag en Organ. **17**(2), 89–112 (2004)
10. Bakker, A.B., Demerouti, E.: Towards a model of work engagement. Career Dev. Int. **13**(3), 209–223 (2008)
11. Parker, P.D., Martin, A.J.: Coping and buoyancy in the workplace: understanding their effects on teachers' work-related well-being and engagement. Teach. Teach. Educ. **25**(1), 68–75 (2009)
12. Malterud, K.: Qualitative research: standards, challenges, and guidelines. The Lancet **358**(2), 483–488 (2001)
13. Ross, B., Munby, H.: Concept mapping and misconceptions: a study of high-school students' understandings of acids and bases. Int. J. Sci. Educ. **13**(1), 11–23 (1991)
14. Bakker, A.B., Demerouti, E., Verbeke, W.: Using the job demands-resources model to predict burnout and performance. Hum. Resour. Manag. **43**(1), 83–104 (2004)
15. Schaufeli, W.B., Bakker, A.B., Salanova, M.: The measurement of work engagement with a short questionnaire: a cross-national study. Educ. Psychol. Measur. **66**(4), 701–716 (2006)
16. Saks, A.M.: Antecedents and consequences of employee engagement revisited. J. Organ. Eff. **6**(1), 19–38 (2019)
17. Köhnken, G., Milne, R., Memon, A., Bull, R.: The cognitive interview: a meta-analysis. Psychol. Crime Law **5**(1–2), 3–27 (1999)
18. Conway, A.R.A., Skitka, L.J., Hemmerich, J.A., Kershaw, T.C.: Flashbubl memory for 11 September 2011. Appl. Cogn. Psychol. **716**, 698–716 (2008)
19. Fober, D.: Eyewitness memory enhancement in the police interview: cognitive retrieval mnemonics versus hypnosis. J. Appl. Psychol. **70**(2), 401–412 (1985)
20. Memon, A., Bull, R.: The cognitive interview: its origins, empirical support, evaluation and practical implications. J. Community Appl. Soc. Psychol. **1**(4), 291–307 (1991)

21. Tongco, M.D.C.: Purposive sampling as a tool for informant selection. Ethnobotany Res. Appl. **5**, 147–158 (2007)
22. Kirwan, B., Ainsworth, L.: A Guide To Task Analysis. CRC Press, Boca Raton (1992)
23. Militello, L.G., Hutton, R.J.B.: Applied cognitive task analysis (ACTA): a practitioner's toolkit for understanding cognitive task demands. Ergonomics **41**(11), 1618–1641 (1998)

Interactive Behavior Model for Physically Disabled People Based on Airport Travel Scene

Yi Liu[1], Jiang Chen[1], Wa An[2], and Tao Wang[2(✉)]

[1] Guangzhou Academy of Fine Arts, No. 257 Changgang Road,
Guangzhou, China
[2] Province Key Lab of Innovation and Applied Research on Industry Design,
No. 257 Changgang Road, Guangzhou, China
64947357@qq.com

Abstract. With the rise of Chinese civic consciousness, social equity has become an important yardstick for measuring the degree of civilization in a society. As an important part of social public services, the respect and attention given to vulnerable groups by airports has become a symbol of the social civilization of the city where the airport is located. In this context, this article takes the disabled groups that are commonly seen in the airport travel as the research object, carries out in-depth analysis of the behavior mechanism of the disabled groups by studying the behavior characteristics of the disabled groups in the airport travel, and summarizes the core factors that have affect the airport travel experience of the disabled groups. Furthermore, provides feasible theoretical basis for improving airport construction and services, so as to improve the quality of airport services and improve the airport travel experience for disabled people. This research aims at the behavior characteristics of disabled people, adopts field survey methods, selects Guangzhou Baiyun International Airport Terminal 2 as the observation site, and carries out on-site observation and actual measurement of the physically disabled people and healthy people in airport travel. Through a comparative analysis of the behaviors of different groups, we learned the behavior characteristics of disabled people during airport travel. By summarizing the airport travel satisfaction and behavior characteristics of disabled people, clarifies the key issues that disabled people are facing in airport travel, and abstracts the disabled passenger behavior model into a mathematical model combing with the airport service process through the data model.

Keywords: Passenger travel behavior model · Behavioral obstacles · Behavior characteristics · Service design

1 Introduction

Airport is the core elements and travel link for citizens of a city. The research on the travel behavior modeling of people in the airport is not mentioned in the related research and literature. However, there have been many achievements in data modeling for the entire transportation travel behavior based on traffic scenes and taking passengers as objects.

A. Marcus and E. Rosenzweig (Eds.): HCII 2020, LNCS 12201, pp. 666–682, 2020.
https://doi.org/10.1007/978-3-030-49760-6_47

The establishment of a travel behavior model consists in the regularity of the abstract behavior itself and methodologically establishing a structured description method of the interrelationships between the travel behavior itself, and travel services, travel-related scenarios. As for the travel behavior modeling methods, various scholars have widely used the knowledge and concepts in the fields of operations research, computer science, and transportation science. The key scenarios and links represented by nodes are abstracted, and the behaviors and interaction modes in each node are linked according to the travel behavior patterns in different scenarios. Define the scenes in the travel behavior in an abstract way, and screen out the typical scenes. At the same time, dynamically evaluate the behavior of users between two key scene nodes, and this behavior is defined as the link between the two nodes. This is a general method for abstract model building for travel behavior. This method is widely used in the study of path planning in traffic problems, and it is used as the basis for the most reasonable solving algorithm for travel plans. Classic travel scheme algorithm research appeared in the 1950s and 1960s, such as Dijkstra [1], Bellman-Ford [2], and D'Esopo-Pape [2] algorithm and so on. In recent years, with the development of the domestic high-speed rail network, domestic scholars have begun to study more about passenger travel mode, and research on rationalization solutions for travel plans for passengers' travel needs. The research in this field mainly focuses on three aspects: the construction of the transportation network for passenger departure, transfer, and arrival [3], the establishment of travel behavior models [4], and the solution of travel plans [5].

Modeling of passenger travel behavior is the basis of research on travel planning issues. Different levels of travel needs and behavior patterns can be constructed based on different information sources. Based on railway travel services, Shi Feng has constructed different levels of passenger rail travel behavior and transfer behavior patterns based on information of the railway network, train travel plans, and train operating time, combined with data on passenger transfers and exits in travel behaviors. Cui Bingmou has taken the minimum of the sum of the travel target value and the transfer target value as the objective function value, established the mathematical model for selection of passengers' transferring plan, considering the constraint conditions of passengers departing from the starting station, eventually arriving at the terminal station, and entering and leaving the transit station. Jiangnan has determined the constraints of the passengers' transportation scheme, and established the optimization model for the minimum number of transfers through analyzing the constraints for selection of the passengers' transportation scheme [6]. As for existing researches based on transportation problems, researchers are mostly focused on three aspects: travel efficiency, convenience and travel cost. Relevant research on the reliability and satisfaction of travel services is rare. With the popularization of high-speed rail around the world, the frequency of people travelling gradually increases. The convenience and punctuality of high-speed rail has brought significant challenges to the traditional aviation market. Comparing to high-speed rail travel, the punctuality of aircraft travel is often delayed as impact of many uncertain factors due to air routes, weather and other reasons, resulting in a decline in user experience. Furthermore, the overall service of domestic high-speed rail was initially established based on airport services as a model. Therefore, currently high-speed rail travel can get more positive feedback on the user experience, when the punctuality rate is higher than that of air flight. For this reason, the aviation industry has begun to adopt scientific methods to study how to improve the service level and overall service quality of the airport under the pressure of high-speed rail competition.

2 Research Results and Development of Travel Behavior Models

The service evaluation research of the transportation industry started in the 1980s, which evaluates the reliability of the transportation industry itself. The reliability discussed in this type of research is carried out from two dimensions of "connectivity reliability" and "capacity reliability" in transportation hubs. Connectivity reliability is the evaluation of physical connectivity of transportation hubs from the spatial dimension. It was first proposed by Mine Kawai from Japan in 1982, and respectful Handa and others made further research. It reflects the probability that any two nodes in a transportation hub remain connected. In the whole travel service link, every two adjacent pairs of contacting points can be regarded as a pair of Origin & Destination (OD). Mine's research aims to provide an evaluation system to evaluate the smoothness between two nodes. He believes that smoothness between nodes is the key to the entire transportation hub system. From the perspective of evaluating products, these two dimensions are only limited to evaluating the "availability" of travel service products. He has not carried out a higher-level study facing of the travel efficiency and emotion of users from the "experience" level. On the basis of travel reliability, Anthony Chen et al. Proposed the concept of capacity reliability in 2002. Unlike Mine, Anthony has looked at the reliability of travel from the perspective of a traveler. It is defined as the probability that a transportation hub can meet a certain level of travel demand at a certain service level. He analyzed the capacity constraints of different transportation hub scenarios, considered the travelers' movement route selection behavior, and made up some shortcomings of connectivity reliability. The proposal of capacity reliability can be seen as the entry point for researchers who are engaged in travel service to start using a user-oriented perspective for research.

In addition to the dimensions of travel capacity reliability and connectivity reliability, Asakura and Kashiwadani initially proposed the time dimension of travel service evaluation in 1991. It is an index system that evaluates the stability of travel behavior on the basis of satisfying space accessibility. It has complemented the one-sidedness and shortcomings of the initial capacity reliability and connectivity reliability that carry out research on travel scenarios from a one-dimensional perspective. It furthermore has built a reliability system for travel scenario services that is more comprehensive from the two dimensions of time and space. Domestic scholar Xiong Zhihua has established an evaluation index system for travel time reliability in transportation service hubs from the three levels of the target level, the criterion level, and the index level based on the theory of time reliability [7].

As for the research on travel service, scholars at home and abroad have experienced the development process from one-dimensional to multi-dimensional, from single factor to multiple factors, from the physical level to the service level, from the service provider-oriented to the travel user-oriented. And related research on the service evaluation has also developed from the evaluation basis of one-dimensional spatial connectivity evaluation and two-dimensional space-time to the establishment of various-dimensional evaluation methods from service reliability and service experience interface friendliness to the acceptance of users upon service experience centering on users' experience. In terms of service-focused research, earlier research focused on the reliability of transportation stations and system services from the perspective of passengers. Sterman has firstly proposed the concept of public transport service reliability, and qualitatively analyzed the factors affecting reliability. Chapman has defined the reliability of public transportation services [8]. The definition of public transportation reliability has been proposed by Polus as "the ability to provide stable services over a period of time" [9]. The essence of the research on the reliability of public transport services is the differences between the service content, methods and time proposed by the service provider and the actual service provided[], and the user's tolerance for deviations in service quality, as well as the range and probability of the deviation.

Domestic research on service reliability in the field of public transportation is still at the stage of studying network reliability (operation). Most scholars who conduct service research in the field of transportation are still more concerned about the capacity, speed, capacity, and reliability of related transportation network. For example, Mao Linfan has used the bi-level programming method to study the reliability of the public transportation network, Liu Rui, Dai Shuai, Gao Guifeng have defined and analyzed the reliability of the public transportation network [10]. Wei Hua, Zhao Hang, and Heng Yuming have conducted research on the reliability of public transportation services. Such kind of researches still start from aspects of the punctual rate of services provided by the public transportation system to users and the probability of completing transportation tasks. If we take the public transport system as a "product" of a large city service, such kind of research is still based on the basic "availability" of the product, which does not penetrate into the research of deep user experience such as user emotion and user perception. However, previous research scholars in the field of transportation's abstraction of traffic problems, as well as the refinement and summary of user behaviors, service processes, the flow of travellers, and various key factors in the traffic scene, have all become the solid foundation for my research on travel services for disabled passengers.

3 Core Elements of Travel Behavior Experience

Experience is an important part of the behavioral model. Human behaviors are generated based on scenes. In specific scenes, people's perceptions, emotions, and cognitions of things have a fundamental impact on behaviors. And the perception of experience in the scene itself has a decisive effect on behavior. For example, people will consciously whisper in church, or avoid talking to keep the environment solemn and dignity. People sing freely instead in the entertainment scene. Therefore, we must conduct in-depth research on human experience and perception in specific scenarios when study human behavior patterns. And define the decisive factors that have a core influence on the experience in this scene. Research and summary of factors based on travel behavior experience are relatively rare in China. Runyan et al. [11] have used students as the research object, and studied people's experience and perception of social life based on social behavior and multicultural background. Tikhomirova [12] and others have studied the experience of young groups in social consumption behavior from the perspective of biological awareness research. Foreign scholars 'research on experience design is mostly focused on the research of users' market consumption behavior and Internet-related product behavior experience. This type of research, on the one hand, starts with sociology to make a deeper analysis of the changes and impacts of human behavior in the new digital society. On the other hand, further digs and summarizes of changes in the living forms brought about by the application of Internet technology in current society from the business point of view. It is hoped that such type of research will provide a basis for product and service innovation, social and public policy formulation. Professor He Renke of Hunan University in China proposed the "conversion process" generated from user behavior and experience in service scenarios for user-based behavior experience. And proposed four semantic forms experienced by the user for reproduction of behavior experience in the service scenario: perception semantics, feature semantics, demand semantics, and state semantics. In different service processes and links, the interaction between user behavior, service processes, and contact points have formed the interactive narrative context in the service scenario [12]. In this study, we also consider the behavior of passengers in travel scenarios as a scene of daily behavior of passengers. Therefore, we borrowed the perspectives and angle of user experience based on service research in our research.

Combining the previous results of research on travel issues, we can divide passenger airport travel issues into six indicators: intensity, distance, time-consuming, travel mode, time distribution (peak, flat peak), and travel space. Meanwhile, the experience of travel behavior is divided into four dimensions: perceived performance, passenger expectations, user complaints, and brand loyalty. The service process is a coherent chain of behavior, and the service process itself does not directly output the user experience to passengers. The user experience of airport travel comes from the behavior process of interacting with the service process. Therefore, we need to analyze the four dimensions of perceived performance, passenger expectations, user complaints, and brand reputation to dissect the emotional experience and cognitive experience of passengers in the course of airport travel. And then explain why users develop specific perceptions during airport travel.

3.1 Passenger Expectations

Starting from the characteristics of passenger airport travel behaviors, we can make a reasonable assessment of the expectations of passengers on the travel experience in the airport scene. In different scenarios from check-in, security check-in to boarding, the expectations of passengers are all "psychological expectations" thresholds that can be perceived. For example, regular passengers usually arrive at the airport two hours before the flight. Therefore, starting from the arrival at the airport, from the check-in behavior in the airport departure hall scene to the security check-in, the time value expected by the users will be controlled at about one hour. According to previous research, the passenger will be upset if the time exceeds the users' expectation under the circumstances of the large passenger flow during the peak period, the long walking distance, and the change of terminal due to incomplete terminal information, which exceed the users' expectation. The quality of the passenger travel experience depends on their perception of travel expectations. Therefore, it is an effective way to achieve better user expectations by interference of the passenger expectations in the early stage.

However, the travel problems of disabled people are far more complex than those of normal people. In the airport scenario, disabled people often need to check in wheelchairs, check prosthetics, and submit suitable flight certifications, which usually make the airport travel process uncontrollable. Therefore, it is difficult for disabled people to define a more reasonable "expected value" for their own airport travel that covers aspects of time, intensity, and distance. In previous research, we found that disabled passengers would normally arrive at the airport six to eight hours earlier for relevant procedures. This time span is unimaginable for normal healthy people. Therefore, improving the transparency of the airport travel process for disabled people and making airport travel costs to be controllable and predictable for disabled people are the primary conditions for improving the user experience of the group.

3.2 Perceived Performance

A good service system is not just about being able to provide efficient services for users to achieve their intended goals. Moreover, it should be able to make users feel the care and warmth of the service provider through the service provided. The service system is not a cold and dead mechanical system. It is an organic system composed of personnel, equipment and other factors in the service scenario through certain process bonds. Each interface in the service system that is in contact with the user should be temperature-sensitive. Especially in the current context of the internet, cold service machines are more criticized by users, let alone providing users with a good experience. The airport is a social public service window; thereby the service of the airport should make every traveler feel warm and caring. In recent years, guided by the government's advocacy of service awareness, the service awareness of airport has been greatly strengthened. Many improvements have been made in service efficiency, quality of service personnel and service response. However, as we have learned from the interviews with airport travelers in the previous research, many efforts and attempts made by passengers on the airport service provider side cannot be perceived. On the contrary, passengers often have conflicts with airport service providers due to force majeure, such as weather and flow control, resulting in complaints.

From a service design aspect of view, service perceived performance is an important indicator of whether a service system can communicate and interact well with users. A good service system shall be able to fully make users feel the emotion and warmth of the service side to users, and make the service popular with many details. Even if the force majeure of the service system occurs, it could still allow users to better understand the difficulty of the service side through empathy. Thereby provides a more relaxed and harmonious environment for the development of services. Airport is such a typical scenario that needs to improve service perceived performance. Passengers' perception of service is weak in the current airport service. On the one hand, the airport service side bears passenger complaints caused by force majeure factors, and on the other hand, passengers experience the cold and non-opaque service mode in the airport service. Therefore, strengthening the construction of empathy on the service side of the airport and "delivering" the service to passengers through the interface of each users' touchpoint is an important means of solving the airport service experience at present.

Service perception improvement is more important in the service of disabled people. Behavioral disabilities include people with both congenital and acquired disabilities. Through previous in-depth interviews and research on disabled people, we can know that people with behavioral disorders are more vulnerable on a psychological basis than healthy people. One is that the physical disorder itself makes them feel different from the normal people in society. There is a certain gap between them and the mainstream groups in their psychological identity; The second is that for people who have acquired disabilities after having complete psychological consciousness, their psychological trauma is huge. Therefore, they will be particularly sensitive in social interactions with people. How to provide service to the behaviorally disabled groups so that they can feel the respect from the airport service, this is an important aspect that needs attention in the design of airport service systems. The construction of user perceived performance shall be comprehensive, not only include service processes, but also include more detailed service links such as body language, speech, etc. of servicing personnel.

3.3   Users' Complaint

The user's judgment of the service experience comes from the gap between the user's expectations of the service and the actual service experience. In the case of equal service perception performance, if the user expects a higher service, but the actual service quality perceived in reality is lower than expectation, the user's experience of service quality must be poor. Conversely, if the actual quality of service experience is better than expectation, the user's experience of service quality would be positive. Therefore, users' grumbles and complaints in the actual service process will be important core elements in service quality.

User grumbles and complaints are generally divided into two approaches in service research. One is the collection of data on service complaints. This can be used to record complaints from users in the daily service process through the service complaint hotline and service record book. This type of data can be summarized and sorted through data sorting and analysis. This type of information is mostly generated by users' complaints actively. Companies often make structured complaints in response during the handling and recording of such complaints, allowing users to express and record their opinions in a systematic way. Therefore, such type of information is better processed and summarized. However, it requires active user intervention since the acquisition of such information is passive on the service provider side. The willingness and cost of the users will be relatively high. If not left with no choice, users are often reluctant to invest time to complete complex complaint procedures. To this end, in the service process, the service quality assessment actively invited by the service provider is added, and the active acquisition of user complaints and opinions on service quality through questionnaires and interviews is the core element of service experience quality evaluation.

3.4   Brand Reputation

Modern society is a highly commercial society. Brand is an important basis and symbol for people to recognize and judge things in modern business society. The role of brands has become more obvious in the commercial space. Users choose goods and services based on personal perception upon the brand in a market environment. Meanwhile, many cultural factors have been added to the current brand building. Brand has become a spokesperson for a certain "value" in society. French scholar Baudrillard proposed in the "Consuming Society" that brand as a "symbol", people's consumption of "symbol" is not a demise of the value of the product itself and the value of use, but pursue of the meaning behind the product. For example, MUJI has become synonymous with quality life, low-key luxury, restrained lifestyle and value orientation. Apple brand has become synonymous with fashion and digital survival for the younger generation in urban life. The value system referred to by the brand allows different groups in the society to naturally cluster people according to their preferences and value identity.

In the highly Internet-based business market, people naturally form different groups according to their attributes and labels—fan groups. The construction of the brand has been separated from the traditional visual design field and expanded to a broader level of content construction. The current Internet brands are more adhesive and guiding to users due to the expansion of the content level and the impact on user values. They can lead the users' life form from the perspective of values.

Social and Cultural Factors of Brands. Brands have become important creators of social culture. The current social culture is formed by the joint action and influence of many brands. With the rapid development of the internet, all aspects of people's social life have been 'internet oriented'. Brands in the internet market have transformed from symbols of original goods to symbols of cultural communication. Nike represents the attitude and values of healthy life, for which Nike constantly outputs tweets and content in social media that are consistent with its brand identity. And it affects a wider group of people through the promotion of specific new media. Furthermore, the 'fan oriented' user group will become a new boost for the brand. Brands no longer belong to companies; they are generalized as gathering place for specific fan groups instead. The relationship between the company and the client has also changed from the former "publisher"-"recipient" relationship to "recipient-reviewer-producer-communicator". In the process of interacting with the brand, users become brand promoters, content producers, and become a part of the brand also.

The Formation of Fan Culture. Fan culture represents the state of the diversified pattern represented by internet media as the new media is becoming more and more deeply involved in social life, in the spiritual field during the social transition period. In this era, the values and ideologies of people are also diversified. The formation of fan culture represents the trend of social equality. The internet soil is good in China. With the promotion of huge internet fans, the collective power of fans has been valued to a certain extent and even in many occasions. It has been greatly respected especially in business. The balance of business interests is gradually tilted towards the fans (users). Fans not only have the right to choose their preferences, they are not limited by commercial factors and interests. Meanwhile, with the further development of the fan culture, it is pushing the mainstream consciousness of the society back and gradually let the will of the group speak in the mainstream public opinion. As a result, the initially commercialized narrative gradually turned into a popular will.

Brand is an Important Means of Managing Emotional Capital. In the era of experience economy, the essence of experience is feeling and emotion. Therefore, emotion itself has been given new meaning in the era of experience economy, and it has become a new kind of capital that enterprises have in the market-emotional capital. In the social environment of the internet, pan-socialized applications allow the output of products and services to expand from a simple function and application level to a deeper level of cultural and content output. A variety of communication tools such as Tiktok and WeChat public accounts provide users with various product-related experience cognitions. These experiences are prior to the user's true perception, and are put into the user's cognitive system before the user actually interacts with the product. Therefore, the current Internet experience economy is an era of "verification" experience and perception. It is different from the commodity economy era in which one first obtains goods and services, then gaining experience perception during the usage. The current internet experience economy is "transcendental" in nature. This "transcendental" is not the same to what Kant said: "All those that are not related to the object, but related to the way we know the object, are known as 'transcendental' as long as they are innately possible. 'Transcendental' does not mean something that transcends experience (that will be 'transcendent'), but something that has not been further specified other than making the experience possible, although it precedes experience ('innate'). "This transcendental comes from the perception and experience implanted by the internet. It is also an important part of the work that designers undertake in the era of the internet experience economy. It not only caters to consumers, but also participates in shaping consumers' values, which in turn shapes consumers' dreams, illusions, emotions, desires and "needs." Luo Yonghao's hammer mobile phone is an example of gaining sales by invoking fans' feelings about "craftsmen", mobilizing the fans' emotion and investment, and providing the fans with the unique experience and perception gained through the product. Airport services must also follow the objective law of the internet society. Through the dissemination of internet content, airport brands and passengers have formed a specific perception of the airport. So as to better grasp and guide the passenger experience and passenger emotional management.

4   The Travel Process Characteristics of People with Behavioral Disorders

The airport travel service design is to study the out-of-control sequential organization of various services, processes, and behaviors during the travel of passengers at the airport. In terms of conventional airport, station, and other travel service design, the "path" is mostly designed from the space or time, the service considered is limited to the "traffic behavior" in passenger travel. From the service process, how to divert and guide rapidly from the perspective of transportation, and how to make passengers smoothly board the corresponding flight or train should be considered more. In the past, the "experience" of passengers has not been considered as an important factor in the service design of public transportation. In previous studies, the evaluation and research of passenger behaviors focused more on the effectiveness evaluation of "travel behaviors". In other words, the behavior research of passengers in the airport and other scenarios related to the process and steps of baggage check-in, check-in and boarding, and walking transportation. However, the actual process of passenger travel is a combination of multiple travel behaviors. The latitudes considered by the existing studies are not comprehensive enough to fully meet the diverse needs of passenger travel experiences. It is also not possible to put travel behavior into the scene, and analyze the purpose and meaning behind the behavior phenomenon of passengers in the scene. Therefore, it is necessary to analyze and abstract the characteristics of service design in travel scenarios and conduct theoretical research. A general model for passenger travel service design will be built in this chapter, to analyze its relationship with related issues in existing research. And to provide general solution method of passenger travel service design as the basis for subsequent research.

The result of the airport travel service design is to design a service scheme that covers the entire journey of the passenger's airport travel. But for different travelers, their preferences are different. For example, some people are more sensitive to time and want to reduce the time length of stay at the airport; some are sensitive to the price and would prefer to spend more time to save their travel costs; others are more interested in service quality and want to reduce the journey and physical strength consumed, also hoping that the process from waiting to departure can be more comfortable. Therefore, for different people and needs, we need to screen common needs and individual needs. In public service scenarios, service resources are limited. Although public scenarios such as airports also have commercial properties, their public attributes are stronger than commercial attributes. Therefore, the service resource allocation in public scenarios should be fair and reasonable. The investment and configuration of individual needs can only be considered after the common needs of the vast majority of passengers are addressed. Furthermore, some individual needs that require significant service resources investment should not be considered or included in the goal of service design optimization. Meanwhile, an evaluation system should be established through research methods such as questionnaires and experience evaluation for personalization and commonality issues in travel scenarios. The individual and common preferences of different passenger groups for service needs shall be annotated and studied. This chapter will discuss the travel service experience at different levels, analyze and summarize the characteristics, commonalities and differences of various types of travel service experience problems, and propose an airport travel behavior model.

4.1 Airport Travel Process Analysis for Disabled People

The passenger airport travel service design is the optimization and decision-making of designing the connection schemes of various behaviors in the travel process according to passenger travel needs. This section carries out analysis upon the actual physical process of passenger travel to abstract the general characteristics of airport travel service design issues.

The whole process of a disabled passenger traveling in an airport scene is a sequence of a series of actions between the start (arriving at the airport) and the end (boarding the plane). These behaviors occupy a certain time interval and space interval, and there are different manifestations, such as check-in, inquiries, walking, security, riding (ferry), waiting, boarding, etc. The following figure describes the behavior of a typical passenger airport. Total 10 intermediate locations are passed through from the start to the end, which are walking, inquiries, check-in, baggage check-in, security, boarding, inspection, ferry, and boarding. The whole process of airport travel for disabled passengers is an orderly connection of these behaviors (see Fig. 1).

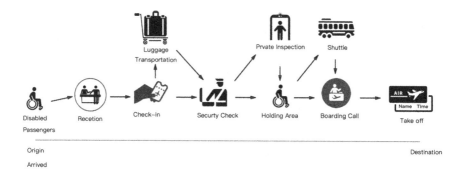

Fig. 1. The process of disabled passenger carrying out in the airport.

It can be seen from the figure that the basic elements of the physical process of a disabled passenger's airport travel are walking, check-in, and security check. The spatial or temporal transitions between the key elements are indicated by dashed lines. This article refers to the autonomous behavior of disabled passengers as "travel behaviors". They share common characteristics: 1) they all occupy a certain space interval; 2) they all occupy a certain time interval; 3) they all have a certain form of expression or a certain added value. For example, the space occupied by walking behavior is the spatial connection of various contacts from the arrival at the airport, from the drop-off point to the inquiry and check-in. It takes a certain period of time to complete this behavior, and its manifestations are walking, transportation by shuttle bus, etc. For another example, the place where the waiting process takes place is the same space "point", which can be regarded as a space "line segment" with the same starting and ending points, and the occurrence time is a time segment. Its value is that it has realized the relax needs of travelling passengers. For another example, a certain period of time is required for transfer and connection behaviors. The spatial scope can be a "point" of space (connected in the same place) or a spatial segment (connected in different places), and its expression can be It is the same mode of transportation or different modes of transportation. Take the travel for disabled people at Baiyun Airport as example, the wheelchairs for the disabled people are not allowed on board. Therefore, people with disabilities need to check in their wheelchairs when they arrive at the airport, and use the airport's substitute wheelchairs. Thereby even if it is the same mode of transportation, due to the problems related to shipping, replacement, etc., people with disabilities still need to involve linking and connection in this contact. The value of this behavior is to achieve the connection between the previous two travel behaviors of the disabled traveler. And the connection point in the service process is often the crux of the problem.

Since travel behaviors occupy a certain area of time and space, the start and end of travel behaviors have corresponding starting and ending points in both time and space dimensions. In addition, travel behaviors have certain forms of expressions and added value. Even for behaviors at the same time and space, their expressions of behaviors are not the same. For example, the behavior of taking the plane from the subway to Guangzhou Baiyun Airport, due to different flight schedules, different times, and different arrival and departure times, the resulting behaviors of people must be different. Therefore, an arbitrary travel behavior can be uniquely represented by a combination of its initial state, process state, and final state. In this article, the initial state, process state, and final state of travel behavior are collectively referred to as the travel state, and each travel state includes attribute values such as time, space, and added value. The change of the state of every two adjacent trips is realized through the promotion of travel behavior in the service process. The state of the passenger at the starting point of the trip is called the starting state, and the state of the ending point is called the target state. Therefore, the change process from the initial state to the target state is realized through a series of travel behaviors. These travel behaviors shall meet the cohesive constraints of time and space. In other words, these travel behaviors can be connected sequentially in the time and space dimensions. Therefore, in summary, the airport travel behavior of disabled passengers is the process of changing the travel status of passengers by implementing several travel behaviors from an abstract level.

5   General Characteristics of Travel Service Design for Disabled Passengers

In the discussion in the previous section, we analyzed the actual physical process of travel for disabled passengers. And from the perspective of demand, the whole process of a passenger's travel is described as: a process of continuous changes in a number of travel behaviors performed by a passenger. These travel behaviors need to be provided with corresponding travel services in order to be realized. Then, from the perspective of providing, the entire process of passenger travel can be described as: the process of changing the travel status through providing travel services.

From the perspective of the provider of the travel service and the airport, the entire journey of a passenger is a chain of travel behaviors composed of different travel services. Each travel behavior corresponds to a specific travel service and scenario. Then, the entire process of a passenger's travel can be abstracted into a travel plan that is made up of several travel services connected over time and space. Therefore, the entire process described in the above passenger travel flowchart can be abstracted into the logical process shown in the figure below (See Fig. 2). Among them, the travel service provides physical support for the travel behavior so that the travel behavior can be realized from the perspective of the provider. The service on the provider side in each scenario corresponds to the travel behavior of the passenger. Each travel behavior is associated with the start and end, and is connected one and another. Therefore, they can be expressed logically as a combination of initial and final states. Each set of travel behaviors has attributes such as time, space, and added value.

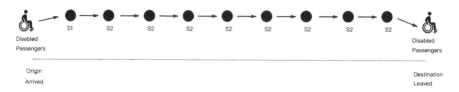

Fig. 2. The abstract of logical process of the airport service.

As mentioned earlier, the essence of airport travel services is to select a number of travel services from a specific service system under the conditions of knowing the starting and target states, and allocate them in space and time to meet the changes in travel status demand. The whole process of the chain of travel behaviors of passengers at the airport is formed eventually. The general structure of a travel service design is shown below. The essence of the travel is a series of processes that match the travel services with the demand for travel. According to their own needs and expectations, passengers in the service resource pool select the most suitable resources and combine them to create a personalized solution. The degree of matching of service resources and passenger service requirements determines the efficiency and experience of airport travel services. The richness of service resources and the efficiency of service response are the key factors for disabled passengers to obtain a quality travel experience.

In a realistic airport scenario, the airport is a giant space system with multiple functional spaces. Meanwhile, passenger capacity, transit efficiency, and time are all factors that need to be considered in this system. It is not only the relationship about the presence or absence of service resources, but also the proportional relationship of the allocation of service resources. The ratio of resources during peak and flat peak periods is critical. Therefore, the rationality of the allocation of service resources and ensuring a consistent experience for 24 h passenger travel is an important challenge for airport services.

6   General Model of Airport Travel Services for Disabled Passengers

In service engineering, service is defined as an action taken by a service provider (servicer side) to meet the requirements of the beneficiary (recipient side) and cause some or all of the status changes of the service recipient. The service system is a combination of multiple services, and the recipient can accept all or part of the services in the service system. We traditionally refer to each service point in the service system as a service contact point.

If the service system of the airport departure hall is taken as the research object, according to the characteristics analysis of the entire process of the passenger experience service system, the service process manifests itself as the passenger starts at the entrance of the departure hall, passes through various service contact points, and finally boards. That is, the behavior of the service system to provide services can be described as the sequential combination of the recipient receiving the services of a series of contact points from the start point to the end point. According to this, the service quality evaluation of the service system can be described as a weighted average value of the evaluation values of each service contact point in the service system. Its mathematical expression is:

$$W_{i=1}^{n} = \sum ki \cdot wi_{i=1}^{n} \left(\sum ki = 1 \right) \tag{1.1}$$

In which, W is the quality evaluation value of the service system, n is the total number of service contact points in the service system, ki is the weighted value of the quality evaluation of the entire service system by each service contact point, and wi is the quality evaluation value of each service contact point. It can be seen that the way the evaluation value of service contact points are mathematically described is very important. It can be concluded from the above definition of service that the state of the service recipient refers to the physical state of the recipient, such as location, feeling, emotion, etc., and the psychological factors that perceive the service, such as passenger expectations, perceived performance, user complaints, the overall feeling of service brand reputation. Services associate and interact with passengers through various service contacts, and "service" and "deliver" service experiences to service recipient through service content and service channels in each service contact. The content of the service (such as materials, energy, and information) directly changes the status of the recipient. Business is the blueprint of travel. The airport travel business method finally lands in the airport scene and "interpreted" into on-site service processes, such as check-in, security, waiting and boarding. Passengers can finally achieve the purpose of travel and fulfill their travel needs. The business method is to indirectly affect the status change of the service recipient by transmitting, amplifying and controlling the business content. This definition assumes that both the provision of a service and the changes caused by a service can be represented by a combination of multiple service composition parameters.

These parameters can be divided into the following two categories: parameters that indicate the status of the recipient and parameters that directly or indirectly affect the status of the recipient. The parameter that represents the status of the recipient is called the "recipient status parameter" (RSP). Recipient satisfaction is indicated by changes in RSP. The latter consists of two types: parameters directly related to recipient state changes are called "content parameters" (CoPs); parameters that indirectly affect RSP changes through content parameter intermediaries are called "channel parameters" (ChPs).

According to this analysis, the service quality evaluation value of the service contact point can be described as: the starting state and target state of the channel network, the recipient, and the channel scheme (that is, the service completion method). The absolute value of the difference between the end state and the target state after the start state changes and the smaller the value, the more the program can achieve the intended service purpose.

Before establishing a mathematical model, define and explain the relevant variables.

G: The channel network G is an n-dimensional Euclidean space, which is composed of a node set P and an arc set S, and $G = (P, S)$. Now suppose that the channel network G described below has three latitudes of psychological state, service content, and space, and the attributes of these three latitudes are represented by E, C, and V respectively.

p: Recipient status. p $(\forall p \in P)$ is a node in the channel network, which represents the state of the recipient in the channel network, and is denoted as $p = (E, C, V)$. Among them, E, C, V represent the mental state, service content and service interface of p, respectively.

$p0$:   The initial state of the recipient, recorded as $p0 = (E0, C0, V0)$

pn: the end state of the recipient, denoted as $pn = (En, Cn, Vn)$

pn':   the target state of the recipient, denoted as $p\ p\ n' = (E\ n', C\ n', V\ n')$

s: channel. s $(\forall s \in S)$ is an arc in the channel network, which indicates the process of changing the recipient's state through a certain behavior. It can be uniquely represented by the order pair $<$initial state, final state$>$ of its initial and final states, denoted as $s = <pi, pj>$ $(pi, pj \in P)$.

Plan: Channel (service execution) plan. The channel plan plan is a sequence composed of a limited number of channels in the channel network G, and is denoted as $plan = \{s1, s2, ..., sn\}$. Where $s1 = < p0, p1, s2 = <p1, p2>$, ..., $sn = <pi, pj>$ can be sequentially connected to the recipient states $p0$, $p1, p2, ... ,pn$, constituting from the initial state $p0$ to channel chain of target state pn.

Set $\lambda(s)$:   The set of channels available to the current recipient. That is, the channel set that can provide service content to the recipient and change the status of the recipient.

$Wi(plan)$:   The target attribute value of the channel plan.

Based on the above definitions, the service quality evaluation value model of the service contact point can be established as follows (Table 1):

Table 1. Table evaluation value model of the service contact point.

$wi(plan) = \mid pn' - pn \mid$	(1.2)
s.t.	
$G = (P, S)$	(1.3)
$plan = \{s1, s2, ..., sn\}\, s1, s2, ..., sn \in \lambda(s)$	(1.4)
$sk = <pi, pj> \forall Sk \in \lambda(s), pi, pj \in P, k = 1, 2, ..., n$	(1.5)
$p0, pn, pn' \in P$	(1.6)
$s1 = <p0, p' > p' \in P$	(1.7)
$sn = <p', pn > p' \in P$	(1.8)

Equation (1.2) is the objective function of the model, which represents the difference between the recipient state and the ideal state upon completion of the service. Equation (1.3) is the value constraint of the travel network G. All channels and recipient states are in this network.

Equations (1.4) to (1.8) are the constraints of the model. The detailed meaning of each constraint is as follows:

Equation (1.4) is the relationship between the channel plan and the channel set, that is, the value constraint of the channel plan, that is, all channels in the channel plan must belong to the available channel set.

Equation (1.5) is the relationship between the channel set and the recipient state, that is, the value constraint of the travel service.

Equation (1.6) is the value constraint of the starting state, ending state, and target state.

Equation (1.7) is the relationship between the channel scheme and the starting state, that is, the channel scheme should start with the starting state p0.

Equation (1.8) is the relationship between the channel scheme and the end state, that is, the channel scheme should end with the end state pn.

7 Summaries

After discussion about the nature of travel problems, travel influencing factors and airport scene interactions for disabled people are discussed in the previous chapters, integrate the previous research data and perspectives and summarize into several core dimensions as user psychological factors, service content, and spatial scenarios etc., and the psychological factors from the service provider side and service recipient side of the image of disabled group are divided into three key factors: passenger expectations, perceived performance, user complaints, brand reputation. Therefore, a multi-dimensional method and a three-dimensional model are used to construct an airport travel behavior model for disabled people. This chapter mainly completed the following aspects through constructing of airport travel behavior model for disabled people:

1. Defined the core elements of travel behavior experience for disabled people. And analyzed the weights of core elements by using data from passenger satisfaction surveys on airports;
2. Summarized the basic characteristics of each contact point and behavior process based on the analysis of the satisfaction of the disabled people during the entire travel behavior process;
3. Discussed the problem of airport travel for disabled people, and analyzed the performance and causes behind for disabled people in service scenarios combining airport service processes and characteristics;
4. Constructed airport travel behavior models for disabled people through establishment of multi-dimensional methods and three-dimensional models; and provided

more verifiable service design research methods for subsequent design research by constructing airport travel behavior models for disabled people. To provide methodological support for improving airport service quality.

References

1. Deng, Y., Chen, Y., Zhang, Y., Mahadevan, S.: Fuzzy Dijkstra algorithm for shortest path problem under uncertain environment. Appl. Soft Comput. **12**(3), 1231–1237 (2012)
2. Cheng, C., Riley, R., Kumar, S.P., Garcia-Luna-Aceves, J.J.: A loop-free extended Bellman-Ford routing protocol without bouncing effect. ACM SIGCOMM Comput. Commun. Rev. **19**(4), 224–236 (1989)
3. He, X., Zheng, H., Peeta, S.: Model and a solution algorithm for the dynamic resource allocation problem for large-scale transportation network evacuation. Transp. Res. Part C Emerg. Technol. **59**, 233–247 (2015)
4. Handy, S.: Methodologies for exploring the link between urban form and travel behavior. Transp. Res. Part D Transport Environ. **1**(2), 151–165 (1996)
5. Enoch, M.: Sustainable Transport. Mobility Management and Travel Plans. Routledge, London (2016)
6. Li, Q.Y., Li, Z.P.: A network optimal model for railway passager transfer. J. Lanzhou Jiaotong Univ. **3** (2012)
7. Xiong, Z.H., Shao, C.F.: Review on the reliability of transportation network with prospect. Commun. Transp. Syst. Eng. Inf. **2** (2003)
8. Andreassen, T.W.: (Dis) satisfaction with public services: the case of public transportation. J. Serv. Mark. (1995)
9. Polus, A., Schofer, J.L., Ushpiz, A.: Pedestrian flow and level of service. J. Transp. Eng. **109**(1), 46–56 (1983)
10. Liu, Z.Q., Song, R.: Reliability analysis of Guangzhou rail transit with complex network theory. J. Transp. Syst. Eng. Inf. Technol. **10**(5), 194–197 (2010)
11. Runyan, J.D., Fry, B.N., Steenbergh, T.A., Arbuckle, N.L., Dunbar, K., Devers, E.E.: Using experience sampling to examine links between compassion, eudaimonia, and pro-social behavior. J. Pers. **87**, 690–701 (2019)
12. Tikhomirova, A.M., Zhuravleva, L.A., Kruzhkova, T.I.: Ecological consciousness as a factor in consumer behavior of young people in the context of new industrialization: sociological research experience. In: Proceedings of the 2nd International Scientific Conference on New Industrialization: Global, National, Regional Dimension (SICNI 2018) (2019)

Research on the Influence of Emotional Valence and Road Environment Monotony on Driving Behavior

Siyao Lu, Xin Xin$^{(\boxtimes)}$, Nan Liu, Yiji Wang, and Yanrui Qu

Beijing Normal University, 19 Xinjiekouwai Street, Beijing, China
xin.xin@bnu.edu.cn

Abstract. In order to optimize road environment construction, vehicle interior function design and safety improvement, this paper systematically sorts out the existing driving behavior research. Based on the literature research, it is necessary to deeply explore the effects of emotional valence and environmental monotony on driving behavior. The research has determined methods, and will convey the further research next step. This study hopes to provide effective suggestions for future car and road design from the perspective of cognitive behavioral characteristics and driver emotions.

Keywords: Driving behavior · Environmental monotony · Emotional valence · Driving load · Situational awareness

1 Introduction

According to statistics released by the World Health Organization, in 2004, 1.2 million people worldwide died in traffic accidents and 35 million were injured. According to statistics from China, there were more than 510,000 road traffic accidents in 2004, with 107,077 deaths and an average of 293 people per day. Almost every minute, people were disabled or even buried in traffic accidents [1]. In fact, what is more serious than the accident is the damage it causes. Therefore, reducing traffic accidents has always been a research topic that people have been paying attention to for a long time. The traditional method is to improve the safety of roads and vehicles by improving the traffic safety legal system, clarifying traffic safety responsibilities, strengthening government management functions, and promoting and using new technologies and methods [2]. However, with the continuous development and continuous maturity of technical means, these technologies that have greatly improved the traffic safety situation have been improved day by day. The space where traditional means can play a role is getting smaller and smaller, which is not enough to further effectively solve the problem of traffic accidents.

The study found that drivers who are prone to accidents often have potential, specific psychological characteristics, namely 'accidentality', making them more prone to accidents than the average driver [3]. Some psychological states can easily leads to traffic accidents, 1) blind self-confidence, ideological paralysis, unexpected surprise when there is an abnormality, panic, and helpless; 2) lucky, psychological,

A. Marcus and E. Rosenzweig (Eds.): HCII 2020, LNCS 12201, pp. 683–693, 2020.
https://doi.org/10.1007/978-3-030-49760-6_48

troublesome; 3) attention shift leads to decision-making rush, busy error; 4) proud arrogance, overestimate yourself, do not care about the abnormal situation, not easy to detect the danger; 5) tired of work, lack of concentration, slow response, low activity; 6) bad mood, abnormal mood swing, Will go to extremes and weaken control [4]. When the driver is under the anger, sorrow, and fear temperament, the individual's sensibility and rationality are reduced, and the level of ability to observe and think is degraded. Eventually, under these bad emotions, driving is more likely to cause traffic accidents.

For example, many people in daily driving drive 'Fighting car' mostly come from some bad emotions. Under these emotional states, people's analytical ability is restrained, their ability to control themselves is weakened, and they become unable to restrain their behavior, cannot correctly evaluate the meaning and consequences of his actions, and ultimately lead to accidents. Therefore, the study of driver's emotional valence, driving analysis and decision-making ability from the perspective of psychology is a research hotspot, scholars should pay close attention to.

As drivers who play an important role in traffic accidents, their behavior will directly and indirectly cause traffic accidents. Therefore, research on driving behavior has been concerned since the 1930s. However, most of the early models only focused on low-level Behavioral control, such as process changes such as lane changes and vehicle turns [5]. As a comprehensive and high-level driving behavior research, driving cognitive behavior research has been gradually introduced since 1964, but because human understanding of itself is also in the simultaneous exploration, it is not profound, especially in depicting itself. Cognitive behavior was also limited by the research techniques of the time, so the research on driver cognitive behavior did not make an achievement in more than 50 years of work. Recent research has shown that psychotherapy can play a role in reducing traffic accidents, which in turn brings new opportunities for traffic safety research.

Based on the above research, the traffic problems around the world are getting worse and worse. The number of road traffic deaths in China is still rising, and the traffic safety situation is very serious. At the same time, with the continuous advancement of technology, new theories, research methods and technical means are constantly emerging. The research on driving behavior, especially the combination of computer science technology and life science research methods has become a new research hotspot. At present, research in the field of traditional driving behavior has made significant progress, and many research results have been widely adopted by the automotive industry. However, the research on cognition, emotion and behavior in the driving field has just begun. The research on cognitive behavior involves more subject areas. There are many research work worthy of development, and it has broad application prospects.

Therefore, this study will analyze the driving behavior, driver's mood and road environment. It is hoped that the return to the driver-oriented, from the new perspective of the road environment and driver emotions, the driver's cognitive behavior research, Provide a theoretical reference for road setting and driver mood adjustment for the future driving field.

2 Driving Behavior

2.1 Factors Affecting Driving Behavior

Driving behavior studies, including the characteristics of driving ability, the psychological and physiological capabilities related to driving tasks, and the number of road traffic accidents caused by drivers. The earliest research on driver behavioral models was the field-analysis theory of vehicles proposed by Gibson and Crooks in 1938. The overall situation of driving behavior research is: the research on the external performance of driving behavior has made great progress in these years, many driving behavior theories have been proposed, and many achievements have been widely used in the automotive industry; while the research on the internal mechanism of driving behavior is It has been valued by researchers, but its research results cannot be applied substantively, and there are still many work worth exploring.

In 2001, Vaa analyzed the theory and models of past driving behaviors and pointed out that cognition and emotion are good tools for predicting, evading and evaluating dangerous situations in driving missions [6]. Both Salvucci and Olivier have made progress in the study of driver behavior in cognitive architecture [7, 8]. The University of South Dakota's Driving Research Laboratory's main work is the study of quantitative assessment techniques for the psychological load of driving and driving-related activities, including driving simulation environments and real environments. Dr. James, a professor of psychology at the University of Hawaii, studies driver emotions, cognition, and perception movements from the field of social psychology. His research team observes his driving behavior and the perception of other drivers. When they perform daily driving tasks, they use the tape drive to record three aspects of their driving behavior, including emotions (feelings and motivations)., cognition (understanding and decision making), and perceptual movement (feeling, perception, and verbal performance) [9]. The results of the previous studies can be found that the driver's psychological state is an important factor in driving behavior, including emotional uneasiness, cognitive bias, perceived movement incoordination, and emotional impulses.

2.2 Research Progress on Driving Cognitive Behavior

Traditional driving behavior research objects include steering behavior, driver workload research, safety behavior, and longitudinal behavior. When investigators conduct driving behavior studies, the types of vehicles used in the experiments will basically involve vehicle types such as cars, minivans, buses, trailers, and construction vehicles. There are researchers based on the definition of the driving environment analysis of the current environment, the goal is to develop driving ecological information (data collected in the real driving environment) analysis and processing of the models, methods and cognitive engineering tools, in order to develop driving awake The psychological model of perception uses the "inference-based experiment" method in the field of artificial intelligence to deal with the relationship between experimental data and psychological theory, and proposes a research program based on software simulation [8].

Based on the above literature, although the research on driving behavior and related theories are very rich, the research on driving cognitive behavior has just started, and it is still in the laboratory or research stage, such as Salvucci's research on the influence of mobile phone on driving behavior in the car [10], and the aforementioned mention of Olivier Georgeon et al. Driving behavior modeling and evaluation of driving situational awareness tools.

3 Environmental Monotony

3.1 Relevant Theory of Environmental Monotony

The road landscape can be divided into an internal landscape (within the land area) and an external landscape (outside the land area). The internal landscape can be divided into an attraction-like landscape (a pedestrian's viewpoint) and a series of landscapes (driver's viewpoint) depending on the viewpoint. The landscape of the monotonic study of the scene can be considered as a series of landscapes, that is, the continuously changing landscape perceived by the driver during driving [11]. Monotony is related to the visual stimuli that appear in a specific environment. At present, scholars have not reached a consensus on the monotony of the environment, and different scholars have different definitions. As early as 1970, McBain proposed monotonicity when the stimulus did not change or changed within a predictable range. Oran-Gilad believes that monotony is a state that occurs when visual stimuli are a constant or highly repetitive [12]. Some scholars have also suggested that lack of alertness is monotonous, and less stimulation or stimulating changes lead to lower arousal [13].

With regard to environmental monotony, there are currently mainly Resource Theories and Dynamic Models of Stress and Sustained Performance. Resource theory believes that people can provide a certain capacity-restricted resource to handle the attention process. When there are not enough resources available to match the resources required by the task, the operational efficiency is reduced. Configuring resources at different stages of the task is the root cause of the decline in functionality. For example, when an overloaded driver maintains vehicle control, it may reduce the level of attention to the traffic environment [14]. Dynamic model refers to the concept of adaptability based on task requirements. When the load changes, the driver can maintain a certain level of operation, but at low load or high load, the adaptability is very poor [15]. The possible hazard of fatigue is that the energy required for the task may be compromised because fatigue reduces the scope and efficiency of the conditioning strategy. Adjustments to mission requirements are ubiquitous because driving involves rapid changes in driving load. Hancock and Weaver's research found that, under normal circumstances, the demand for driving is lower than the driver's best attention, but in an emergency, the driver reacts to an emergency by focusing all the attention on the emergency. In the case, this is the so-called "narrowing of attention" phenomenon [16].

3.2 The Influence of Environmental Monotony on Driving Behavior

In addition to Resource Theories and Dynamic Models of Stress and Sustained Performance, scholars have carried out a series of relationship studies, hope to explore some effective countermeasures to solve driving fatigue and stabilize driving performance. As the study by Oron-Gilad et al. suggests, driving operations are a function of driver status and environmental demand. The driver's state is expressed by Fitness to Drive, which is a series of continuous streams of information or uncertainties that the driver must handle [17]. When the demand for the environment is high (for example, in a complex traffic environment), when the driver is not suitable for driving (for example, the driver is a beginner or the driving ability is reduced), the driver is in an overload state; when the demand is low (for example, In a monotonous scene), the driver is very suitable for driving (for example, the driver is experienced) and the driver is under load. Between these two extremes is the optimal operating area. In view of the monotonic nature of the road environment, it is currently mainly through the installation of anti-glare facilities on long-distance road sections. Wang Jianjun and others proposed that in the monotonous landscape, the length of a single landscape is recommended to be about 5 km, which can give the driver appropriate stimulation.

At present, China has no clear norms for the construction of the road environment, and the United States has clearly defined the location of traffic signs, the choice of information, the lane markings, and the use of various logo colors in the Handbook of Unified Traffic Control Facilities. In the manual, there are also chapters specially established for the specification of overpasses, which require planners to consider the information of the travellers in order to meet more complicated traffic data information and avoid overload and discontinuity of traffic sign information [18]. In 2010, Bendak S conducted a simulated driving test on 12 volunteers and conducted a questionnaire survey of 160 drivers to study the psychological impact of the driver's driving process due to roadside billboards. The results show that roads with roadside advertisements are more likely to cause driver distraction and the risk of deviating from the lane [19]. In 2013, Liu and others conducted a pilot logo visibility study under real road conditions. The experiment selected a number of people to drive the experimental vehicle equipped with the eye tracker Smart Eye Pro4.0 and GPS to conduct experiments in the actual traffic environment, and then analyzed the different drivers (professional, non-professional) in different lighting and vehicle speed. Recognition characteristics [20]. In 2014, Costa et al. studied the visual response and characteristics of the driver's opposite sign through a real vehicle experiment conducted by 22 volunteers wearing eye point tracking devices [21].

China's urban roads and highways are committed to healthy and rapid development, which puts new demands on road safety facilities, especially the reasonable setting of highway safety facilities, and how to improve road traffic capacity, avoid traffic accidents, and prevent illegal driving. The requirements, the unreasonable design of the signs on both sides of the road will inevitably increase the probability of accidents and affect road traffic safety.

The monotony of "overcoming" road scenes is undoubtedly beneficial, and many studies have shown that road traffic accidents are more likely to occur on environmentally monotonous roads. At the same time, for the current trend of vehicle design intelligence, the study of the monotonicity of the road environment will also be of great benefit to the exploration of integrated multi-element driving fatigue detection system. In a monotonous environment, the driver lacks stimulating attention, the perceptual sensitivity to the surrounding things is reduced, and the thoughts are loosened or transferred to things that are unrelated to the road traffic and attractive to the driver, causing the driver to become overly tired and enter the fainting state. The state of sleepiness, so many scholars have studied monotony. It can be shown from the above literature that the definition of monotonicity is very long, but the research in this area is still very slow so far. The main reason is the lack of indicators to measure monotonicity, both in field experiments and simulated cabin simulation driving experiments. Much of the research remains in qualitative analysis, and there is a lack of methods and models for evaluating road landscapes from the driver's perspective.

4 Driver Emotion

4.1 Driving Emotion Research

Emotion is the attitude experience of a person's attitude towards whether an objective thing meets his or her needs. Everything that meets or meets people's needs will lead to positive affirmation, such as happiness and affection. Anything that fails to satisfy the cravings of human beings or that contradicts the will of the human will cause negative negative emotions such as disgust, pain, fear, anxiety, pessimism, and tension.

A person's emotions have an important influence on his understanding, will and behavior. For the driver, this kind of influence needs to be paid more attention. The driver is the receiver and processor of the information in the road traffic system. On the one hand, the driver's emotional valence will directly affect the safety of driving, on the other hand, the superposition of individual behavioral states. It also affected the entire traffic situation. If the driver drives the vehicle under certain adverse emotions, it will directly interfere with the driving behavior and pose a threat to their driving safety. A large number of traffic accident cases also show that traffic accidents caused by drivers driving with negative emotions account for a considerable proportion of the total number of accidents.

4.2 Driver Emotions and Driving Behavior

In recent years, research on emotions and driving behavior has rapidly warmed up. Researchers focus on the effects of individual emotional changes on their driving behavior during driving. These analyses are important for a deeper study of the quantitative relationship between driver psychological characteristics and lane change behavior. In foreign research circles, many scholars began to explore from their respective perspectives. In general, they can be divided into two types, one for extreme driving situations and the other for general driving situations. The extreme case study is to focus on some extreme situations that are likely to cause traffic accidents or some of the more threatening driving behaviors. In contrast, it is more inclined to target specific dangerous situations, in addition to its own scientific theory. In addition to the meaning, it also reveals the threat of extreme emotions and dangerous driving, and also has a warning effect to the public.

For example, some scholars have studied the behavioral characteristics of drivers under anger, and found that individuals with anger are prone to aggressive and adventurous driving behavior. Drivers with low public self-awareness are more prone to aggressive driving behavior when driving anger [22]. Stephens and Groeger began with the anger of prolonged anger and the anger caused by emergencies, and studied the effects of anger on the driving process. The results show that the emotional valence of anger is indeed It will make drivers tend to be more dangerous driving behavior [23]. But it's worth noting that the study also found that anger also increases the driver's ability to handle emergencies.

Listening to music is one of the favorite activities of most drivers during their driving. Music is an important medium for their emotions. Pecher, Lemercier and Cellier use music to induce participants' emotions. In the experiment, various price-effective music and no music are played alternately to participants, and then the influence of emotion on driving behavior is analyzed. The results show that happy music is the easiest to distract drivers, making their average speed drop unexpectedly, lateral control weakening, and sad music slowing down, but with smaller amplitude and better lateral retention [24]. In the study of the effects of emotional and emotional adjustment techniques on driving behavior issues, scholars explore the effects of changes and adjustments in mood on drivers. It has been found that although the happy mood will increase the speed of the car, the driving performance and the ability to deal with the problem will be greatly improved. The unpleasant emotion will make the lateral control weaken and the driving performance will be reduced. At the same time, the driver The emotional appeal for positive valence is significantly higher than negative and neutral [25].

Through literature review, it is found that personality, emotion, attention, self-protection awareness and other aspects are the main psychological factors affecting driver safety. The bad mood often causes the driver to illegally change lanes, overtake, car, speeding, etc., and even cause the driver to distract and increase the error rate, which has buried a huge hidden danger to road traffic safety. Therefore, studying the driver's emotional factors and emotional behavioral characteristics will help to explore psychological countermeasures to effectively prevent traffic accidents.

5   Research Methods

With the development of economy and technology, the number of vehicles is increasing, and the road traffic situation is becoming more and more serious. Traffic safety is the direct cause of exploring driving behavior. Much research shows that driving behavior research can play a positive role in improving road traffic safety. The driver is the recipient and processor of the information in the road traffic system, as shown in Fig. 1. The behavioral characteristics of the driver with bad emotions will also have an impact on traffic safety. Accurate and efficient identification of the driver's emotions, timely intervention and adjustment, can reduce unnecessary driving mistakes, reduce or avoid the cause Road traffic accidents caused by anger. The monotony of the road environment affects the driver's cognitive load. In the case of too high or too low load, the driver's adaptability to emergency situations is very poor, and it is impossible to maintain a stable level of operation. The study of the monotonicity of the

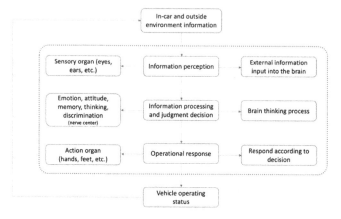

Fig. 1. Driver's driving behavior mechanism.

environment contributes to the improvement of the road environment and the supporting construction of the interior functions of the vehicle, and jointly achieves the improvement of safety.

Through a large number of predecessors' research, this study proposes that it is necessary to further explore the impact of the road environment on driver behavior, and whether the emotional valence plays a role in regulating the two, hoping to solve the driver-oriented emotional factors in driving behavior. And several problems of road environment cognition factors provide certain technical support for road traffic safety management, thereby reducing the occurrence of traffic accidents and increasing the safety of people's travel safety.

At present, this research has developed research procedures and experimental methods, the experimental method and questionnaire method were used to conduct quantitative research on the driver's behavior characteristics, and combined the interview method to conduct qualitative investigation on the special behavior and emotional feelings in the car. The driving simulation experiment was conducted in the Car-Human-Computer-Interaction Laboratory (Car-HMI Lab) of Beijing Normal University. The study selected 60 drivers who were driving for more than one year, and the research was mainly divided into three stages, as follows:

1. **Pre-experiment: material selection for different monotonous road environments**

   The purpose of the pre-experiment is to screen out the driving scene that can be effectively perceived by the subject in the monotonous dimension of the environment. Based on the number of lanes, straight/curved sections, and the length of each section of the road, the simulated driving scenarios were set to three types of road environment monotony (High, medium, and low), see Fig. 2. Using the Swedish Occupational Fatigue Inventory Questionnaire (SOFI-C) to measure the subjective fatigue state of the driver before and after driving.

Fig. 2. Schematic diagram of scene setting.

2. **Experiment 1: The impact of environmental monotony on driving behavior**
   Based on the pre-experimental results, three environmental monotonous scenarios (high, medium, and low) will be set in the experiment 1, and 10 subjects will perform simulated driving in the laboratory. The research records the driving operation performance (speed, steering wheel control, brake depth, number of collisions), eye movement data during driving (average gaze duration and number of saccades), and interview data. Through the driving performance, eye movement data and post-driving interview results, the influence of different monotonous road environment on driving behavior was explored.

3. **Experiment 2: Under the different levels of monotonous environment, the influence and mode of emotional valence on individual driving behavior**
   In the second experiment, 40 participants will participate in the experiment, they were randomly divided into positive emotion group and negative emotion group, using Mozart's G Major String Serenade and Mahler's Fifth Symphony as emotion-inducing materials [26]. The PANAS Emotional Self-Assessment Scale (Chinese version) was used to test the emotion-induced effectiveness. Through the data of driving operation performance, it is analyzed whether there is a significant difference in driving behavior characteristics between different groups of subjects (positive/negative emotion).

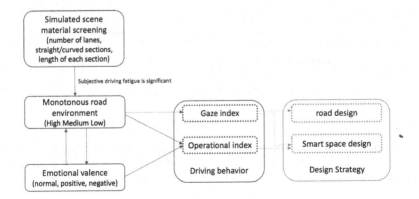

Fig. 3. Variable relationship diagram.

Finally, the study will analyze the relationship between driving performance and the road environment monotony by data fitting, combined with the interview material to explore the behavior characteristics associated with the scene characteristics, explore whether the emotional factors can temporarily adjust the driving performance of the subjects, as shown in Fig. 3.

6   Conclusion

The driving behavior problem is researched by the driver as the object. Due to the diversity of human characteristics, differences and influencing factors, the complexity of the research on driving behavior is determined. By combing the research of predecessors, this study proposes a new perspective in the field of traffic safety. By understanding the driving cognitive behaviors in different monotonous environments and the adjustment of behavioral characteristics of emotional valence, the driving behavior is studied at the cognitive level. At the same time, it also proposes a specific research process, paying attention to the psychological changes of driving behavior at the level of road cognition. Through the driving laboratory simulation, eye movement equipment and subjective interviews, the data is collected uniformly to realize the road environment change and the driver's subjective feelings. Unified analysis.

In the next step, a series of experiments will be carried out. It is hoped that through the phenomena found in the research, it is possible to propose feasible suggestions for improving the driving performance of individuals in a monotonous environment, and to propose a design strategy for road construction and vehicle design centered on the driver.

References

1. Wang, S.: New concepts and control strategies for road traffic injury. Prev. Med. Forum **02**, 253–256 (2005)
2. Bo, D., Wang, Y., Wang, J., Wang, J.: Analysis of the current situation of public security traffic safety management and countermeasure research. J. Chin. People's Public Secur. Univ. (Nat. Sci. Ed.) **01**, 82–85 (2008)
3. Shen, S., Zhang, W., Kang, Y., Jiang, Y.: Research status of psychological characteristics of accident drivers. Chin. J. Trauma **28**(1), 37–39 (2012)
4. Yue, H.: Research on the psychological types that affect drivers' safe driving. Business **20**, 169 (2012)
5. Liu, Y., Wu, Z.: Modeling of driving ACT-R cognitive behavior. J. Zhejiang Univ. (Eng. Ed.) **10**, 1657–1662 (2006)
6. Vaa, T.: Cognition and emotion in driver behaviour model-some critieal view points. In: 14th ICTCT Workshop (2001)
7. Salvucci, D.D., Lee, E.J.: Simple cognitive modeling in a complex cognitive architecture. In: Human Factors in Computing Systems: CHI 2003 Conference Proceedings, pp. 265–272. ACM Press (2003)

8. Olivier, G., et al.: Driver behaviour modelling and cognitive tools development in order to assess driver situation awareness. In: Workshop on Modelling Driver Behaviour in Automotive Environments (2005)

9. James, L.: Data on the private world of the driver: affective, cognitive and senorimotor (1984)

10. Salvucci, D.D.: Predicting the effects of in-car interfaces on driver behavior using a cognitive architecture. In: Human Factors in Computing Systems: CHI 2001 Conference Proceedings, pp. 120–127 (2001)

11. Zhao, X., Fang, R., Rong, J., et al.: Experimental study on comprehensive evaluation method of driving fatigue based on physiological signals. J. Beijing Univ. Technol. 37(10), 1511–1516 (2011)

12. Oran-Gilad, T., Hancock, P.A.: Road environment and driver fatigue. In: Proceeding of the Third International Driving Symposium on Human Factors in Driver Assessment, Training and Vehicle Design, pp. 318–324 (2005)

13. Thiffault, P., Bergeron, J.: Monotony of road environment and driver fatigue: a simulator study. Accid. Anal. Prev. 35, 381–391 (2003)

14. Xia, A., Wang, B., Song, B., Zhang, W., Qian, J.: How and when workplace ostracism influences task performance: through the lens of conservation of resource theory. Hum. Resour. Manag. J. 29(3), 353–370 (2019)

15. Hancock, P.A., Warm, J.S.: A dynamic model of stress and sustained attention. Hum. Perform. Extreme Environ. 7(1) (2003)

16. Hancock, P.A., Weaver, J.L.: Temporal distortions under extreme stress. Theor. Issues Ergon. Sci. 6(2), 193–211 (2005)

17. Oron-Gilad, T., Ronen, A., Shinar, D.: Alertness maintaining tasks (AMTs) while driving. Accid. Anal. Prev. 40, 851–860 (2008)

18. Manual on uniform traffic control devices for streets and highways. FHWA, U.S. Department of Transportation (2009)

19. Bendak, S., Al-Saleh, K.: The role of roadside advertising signs in distracting drivers. Int. J. Ind. Ergon. 40(3), 233–236 (2010)

20. Liu, X., Lu, J.: The technology of road guide signs setting in large interchanges. Procedia-Soc. Behav. Sci. 96, 538–547 (2013)

21. Costa, M., Simone, A., Vignali, V., et al.: Looking behavior for vertical road signs. Transp. Res. Part F Traffic Psychol. Behav. 23(23), 147–155 (2014)

22. Millar, M.: The influence of Public self-consciousness and anger on aggressive driving. Pers. Individual Differ. 43(8), 2116–2126 (2007)

23. Stephen, A.N., Groeger, J.A.: Anger-congruent behaviour transfers across driving situations. Cogn. Emot. 25(8), 1423–1438 (2011)

24. Pecher, C., Lemercier, C., Cellier, J.M.: Emotions drive attention: effects on driver's behavior. Safety Sci. 47, 1254–1259 (2009)

25. Gwyther, H., Holland, C.: The effect of age, gender and attitudes on self-regulation in driving. Accid. Anal. Prev. 45, 19–28 (2012). http://www.soc.hawaii.edu/leonj/leonj/leonpsy/instructor/driving1.html

26. Storbeck, J., Clore, G.L.: With sadness comes accuracy; with happiness, false memory: mood and the false memory effect. Psychol. Sci. J. Am. Psychol. Soc. 16(10), 785–791 (2005)

Research on the Interactive Relations of People with Mobility Difficulties in the Airport Service-Scape

Weifeng Xue, Yi Liu, Miao Cui, and Jiang Chen[✉]

Guangzhou Academy of Fine Arts, No. 257 Changgang Road,
Guangzhou, China
826153519@qq.com

Abstract. With the rapid development of the national economy and great improvement of people's living standards, air travel embraces increasing popularity. Meanwhile, as the most efficient choice for traveling around the world, the airport has functioned as a national portal and city symbol. The majority of airports aspires to transform themselves to multi-functional space to satisfy the needs of various traveling scenarios. However, in the process of designing this public space, necessary considerations for the people with mobility difficulties are always neglected.

To meet the interaction relationship of people with daily travel difficulties and provide a constructive reference for improving spatial interaction, the paper starts researches from perspectives of service and space. As for the research methods, the paper adopts a literature study, field measurement, interviews, document analysis, and induction. Based on the analysis of the airport's main service procedures and layout of the airport's spatial architecture, the paper summarizes the key factors affecting the interactive experience of public service space following a comparative analysis of touchpoints between passengers with and without mobility difficulties in the airport service-scape, as well as the study on spatial ergonomics.

The paper sorts out and summarizes relations between service and space, coming to the conclusion that only through complete information exchange and match between service and space, can the airport better meet passenger's needs. At the same time, the paper provides a reasonable reference and evaluation standard of interactive relations for providing ultimate and premium services for people with mobility difficulties.

Keywords: Airport · Public space · Service-scape · People with mobility difficulties · Interactive relation

1 Introduction

In recent years, the civil aviation industry has maintained stable and rapid development in the world. In 2017, more than 4 billion passengers chose air travel, of which China's transportation volume ranked second, with the highest growth rate of 14% among the top ten countries or groups. In order to meet the increasing transportation demand,

A. Marcus and E. Rosenzweig (Eds.): HCII 2020, LNCS 12201, pp. 694–715, 2020.
https://doi.org/10.1007/978-3-030-49760-6_49

China is building or renovating a large number of airport terminals [1]. In the context of the rapid development of the aviation industry, the analysis and research on the interaction between passengers in airport service scenarios have become particularly important and critical. In this paper, the behavior barrier population is the main research object. Its specific definition refers to people with a physical disability and sporadic behavior disorder. Through the study of their interaction in the airport service scene, we can find their pain points and needs in the airport, and provide help for their smooth and convenient travel. At the same time, we can provide reference suggestions and suggestions for improving the service quality and space construction of the airport. The evaluation criteria also contribute to the excavation of new directions and requirements of airport construction.

1.1 Research Background

According to the information provided by the 13th five-year plan for the development of civil aviation in China issued by the Civil Aviation Administration of China, the national development and Reform Commission and the Ministry of transport, in 2017, there are 229 urban airports in mainland China. It is estimated that by the end of 2035, the number of airports will increase to more than 400 [2]. At present, China's civil aviation industry is growing at an amazing speed, and the development of the civil aviation industry is not only reflected in the number of airports but also reflected in the service quality of airports.

With the rapid development of civil aviation in China, people have a new angle and standard to judge the service quality level. In the 2030 agenda of sustainable development, the United Nations has also proposed to strengthen the power of vulnerable groups and provide further support for removing obstacles and restrictions. Its specific provisions are: by 2030, all people, especially children, women, the elderly and the disabled, will be provided with inclusive, safe, accessible and green public space. With the continuous improvement of social civilization, people's cognition and attitude towards people with behavioral disorders have changed a lot, and more and more attention has been paid to the provision of barrier-free facilities and the construction of humanistic services. In the service industry, the improvement of standards is not only reflected in the improvement of service quality requirements but also requires the integration of humanistic spirit and human warmth into the service.

For service design, Sharon Prindiville and Nancy bocken mentioned in "sustainable business models through service design" that the early description of service design focuses on providing creative and functional services, including planning and shaping the available and shaped elements of service experience, and designers transform intangible experience into tangible, such as personas, user journey maps Service blueprint, scene, experience prototype, story version, etc. Through service, innovation to improve customer satisfaction, improve the efficiency and competitiveness of the company. At the same time, there is another view that service design is a human-centered design thinking method, which is a human-centered service system that pays more attention to stakeholders. Optimize and improve the service system (personnel, technology, resources) through service design, so as to create value for the enterprise [3]. In Luo Shijian, Zou Wenyin's "research status and progress of service design" also mentioned that the essence of service design is to design effective models, which can be used to organize and plan various components of people, infrastructure, communication and tangible materials in the service system, so as to improve the quality of an entity product or intangible service [4]. In today's service economy era, service design plays a more and more important role in society, and also creates great value for the development of the social economy.

Service design started in China not long ago, but it has a huge market demand in China. The popularity of a people-oriented concept also indicates the great potential of the service design industry. In the transportation industry, service design is more and more widely used. In the research on service design of urban public transport system – a case study of Chengdu written by Xu Bochu and Wei Feng, this paper analyzes the composition of service design in public transport system from the perspective of "user experience", explores the relationship between the planning and construction of public transport system and the needs of user groups, and puts forward four service design modes for use function, emotion, path and interaction The paper takes Chengdu public transport as an example to analyze and study and discusses and verifies the applicability and application value of service design theory in public transport system [5]. This paper takes the airport as a case study. There are many similarities between the planning and construction of the airport and the planning of the public transport system. Through the service design, it can provide the construction of the airport with more programs and suggestions that meet the needs of the public, are more humanized and experience better.

The service system of the airport consists of several service contacts, and the connection between these contacts is an important part of the service system of the airport. From entering the airport to completing different tasks to achieve different purposes, users need to have corresponding interaction behavior to connect. Through the study of the interaction relationship between different contacts of users, it is easier to find the problems and solutions in the service system chain.

This paper hopes to provide reference suggestions and evaluation criteria for the development and construction of the airport through the research on the interaction of the behavior barrier population in the airport service scene, and also trigger other public service spaces in the society to think and improve actions, so as to provide better services and experience for the travel of the behavior barrier population.

1.2 Purpose and Significance of the Study

(1) Theoretical significance: At present, with the continuous improvement of social civilization, people's cognition and attitude towards people with behavioral disorders have changed dramatically. Urban environmental construction and facilities have gradually included the use of people with behavioral disorders into the scope that must be considered. Although great progress has been made, the matching of barrier-free facilities are not applicable in many scenarios, and the corresponding services can not really capture their needs. Before the planning and construction of services or facilities and equipment space scale, there needs to be corresponding research and analysis to support the rear practice.

The airport is a public service space, serving all people. To meet the needs of so many users, it is necessary to classify users and conduct specific in-depth research and analysis, which is conducive to meet more users' needs and provide more reasonable solutions. At the same time, the classification research of users can find the differences and advantages and disadvantages of the services received by different users and corresponding service contacts in the airport service scenario, which can more pertinently fill in the loopholes and omissions in the service system, so that different users can enjoy the ideal service experience that meets their own requirements.

In addition, in the process of studying the interaction relationship of behavior barrier people in the airport scene, we can explore, refine and accumulate relevant research methodology, and use specific service design methods in the analysis of passengers and space construction research in the airport scene, so as to provide evaluation reference standards for the spatial interaction construction of behavior barrier people in the airport travel.

(2) Practical significance

With the rapid development of China's aviation industry and the continuous implementation of the airport construction plan, the service interaction design can play a huge role in the optimization and upgrading of the airport and improving the service experience of users in the airport. If the professional theoretical guidance of service design can be included in the planning before the airport construction, the landing implementation of the specific space facilities of the airport will be in the use sustainability of users Satisfaction can get higher evaluation.

In addition, the standards and suggestions for the spatial functional spatial layout of the specific spatial scale provided by the Research Institute of the interaction relationship of the behavior barrier population in the airport service scene can be used as guidance suggestions in the practical landing process. It can help the airport and society to embody the spirit and culture of humanistic care, provide good example materials for the construction of airport brand image and social city image, integrate the service concept of people-oriented into the service planning and design of the airport, trigger the thinking of the industry and strive to integrate the service design thinking into the construction of the airport.

1.3 Research Methods

The objects of research methods are mainly divided into two categories: the first is about service research, and the second is about space research. The main methods of service research include literature research, questionnaire survey, interview, data analysis and induction, qualitative research, etc. The main methods of space research include field surveys, literature research, data analysis, and induction.

The below figure is the research framework of this paper, which studies the public service space for travel demand from two perspectives of the service system and space conditions. In the service research, through the collection and analysis of service-related data, the behavior and travel process of passengers as the service receiving side, as well as the different service related systems provided by the airport as the service supply side for health and behavior impaired passengers are summarized. In the space research, the specific spatial function, scale, and layout are analyzed, and the differences between the contact points of the behavior disorder population and the healthy passengers in the airport scene are compared (see Fig. 1). Combined with the research on the human factors of the space environment, the key factors affecting the interaction experience of public service space and the human-computer interaction scale in the contact interaction of the airport service process are summarized Use.

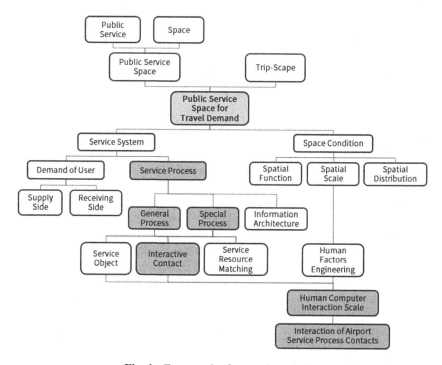

Fig. 1. Framework of research methods.

2 Public Service Space for Travel Scenarios

Public service space serves the public and is a part of social life. In Xu Haosheng's "Research on the design strategy of public service space in small and medium-sized museums from the perspective of New Museology", it is mentioned that public service space can be divided into traffic service space, information service space, cultural education service space, social entertainment space, etc., which is a multi-functional space. The public service space mentioned in this paper is a multi-functional application space, emphasizing the functionality of the public service space. It is true that the construction of public service space is to provide people with places and ways to deal with social relations and participate in social services. It is a relatively common functional space scene in people's lives [6].

With the rapid development of China's economy, the gradual enrichment of material products and the improvement of people's living standards, the national demand for public services is gradually becoming diversified, and higher requirements are put forward for the original public services. Therefore, the public service supply functions of local governments and other public spaces are in urgent need of improvement, optimization, and upgrading [7].

With the advent of the era of the experience economy, the society has higher requirements for public service space, not only to meet the functional needs of the people but also to bring different psychological satisfaction to the people. It also needs to carry the historical culture of the society, the humanistic characteristics and unique charm of the city, so that the people can more comfortably and smoothly complete the functional objectives and feel the high-quality service experience. The open public space of a city is not only a single functional place, but also a place for cultural communication. Every public space is the epitome of a city. We should strive to become a representative of the city, including more services for social and cultural life [8].

Public service spaces for travel scenarios include airports, bus stations, subway stations, ship terminals and so on. Such public service spaces are closely related to people's lives, and they almost touch these scenes and spaces every day. The number of public service space is so huge, so whether it is to study a kind of public service space or single public service space, to find out the commonness between them and to explore their own unique places is the key to study public service space.

There are many commonalities in public service space. In terms of service objects, these public service spaces serve all kinds of people every day, whether they are stations, subway stations, docks or airports. They are part of society and the city. Secondly, in terms of functions, they not only complete the tasks of transportation hubs but also carry the functions of promoting economic development, satisfying people's social interaction, satisfying people's entertainment, etc., which are well interpreted In terms of social effect, these public service spaces are the epitome of the city where they are located. They spread the cultural spirit of the city and reflect the spirit of a city.

In front of these commonalities, the individuality of each public service space is also obvious. The airport is a huge public service space, which has the commonness of other public service spaces, but its individuality is very prominent, which is attributed to the fact that although the airport is also a passenger's travel space scene, it is not the ground transportation mode. The differences between the airport and the ground travel space can be classified as: (1) safety differences: in addition to explosion-proof detection, the airport also has special luggage security and personal security inspection areas, with higher requirements for safety. (2) process differences: from entering the airport to boarding, the operation process of the passenger airport is more complicated than other public service spaces. The relatively complex process setting before waiting is also due to the huge airport system, the high safety factor, and the restrictions and requirements of flight tools. This ensures the orderly and smooth operation of Airport Flights, as well as the interests and safety of every passenger. (3) Time difference: compared with other public travel service spaces such as high-speed railway station, station, subway, etc., the airport is different in terms of time arrangement. Most domestic flights require to check-in at the airport 90 min in advance; most international flights require to check-in at the airport 120 min in advance. The time of passengers at the airport is relatively long, so it also requires a large area of the airport itself, which can add diversified services to help passengers spend their time at the airport. (4) Image difference: the airport is connected with the world. It is often the first space for international friends to contact when they arrive and the last space scene when they leave. It has a representative significance for the spread of national and urban culture and spirit.

No matter the airport or other public service spaces, how to keep pace with the times and how to meet the increasing requirements of the public society today? This requires a comprehensive analysis of the service system and space conditions under specific scenarios and a high degree of exchange and matching of the information between the two.

2.1 Relationship Between the Overall Service Process of the Airport and Each Service Space Function

According to the classification system of government functions of the United Nations, government public services include general public services and public security, social services, economic services, expenditures not classified by categories, etc., which shows that public services are services provided by the public sector represented by the government to meet public needs. The important characteristic of public service is "public attribute". In addition to the main characteristics of non-competitiveness and non-exclusiveness, public participation, simultaneity, perishability, un-certainty, and heterogeneity are also the more significant characteristics of public service.

This paper takes the airport as the research object. The airport is a public service space under the travel scenario. The public service areas of airport passenger activities include departure hall, security inspection area, waiting area and arrival area. Based on the research of airport service systems around the world, the whole service system of the airport includes two parts: passenger departure and passenger arrival. In the service system of passenger departure, the services provided by the airport mainly include check-in, security check, waiting and boarding, while in the service system of passenger arrival, the services provided by the airport only include baggage collection, ticket purchase, waiting, etc. These functions have changed greatly in the internet background. In Wang Xueyun's "Research on the supply of civil aviation airport passenger services under the background of the Internet", we can clearly see that with the support of "Internet plus" and big data technology, the self-service equipment is becoming more and more perfect, and the reconstruction of service process has become the inevitable development direction of public service [9]. Great changes have taken place between the two, and the service system has become more huge and complex. In the past, the solidification of airport service mode can be realized only when the specific functions are in a specific area. For example, to handle check-in, you need to use a manual channel or self-service check-in terminal in the check-in area, to handle catering and entertainment, you need to go to the waiting area or the catering area, etc. The specific functions cannot be realized through online or other channels in the huge space of the airport, and the passengers need to go through no The movement of the same contact point meets the demands of different services; now the flexible and personalized service mode breaks the previous fixed mode, such as online ticket check-in, electronic check-in, online airport delivery, etc., and integrates the Internet into the service construction of the airport (see Fig. 2).

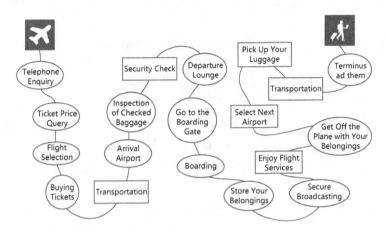

Fig. 2. Research on the supply of civil aviation airport passenger service under the internet + background.

When we study the public service space of airport travel scenarios, we can divide the problem into two parts: the service system research in the scenario and the space system research in the scenario. On this basis, we can carry out the comparative analysis of information exchange. Taking Guangzhou Baiyun International Airport as the research object, based on a large number of studies on the contact sequence of passengers in the airport travel scenario and field observation and follow-up of different passengers, the service process architecture provided by the airport for departing and arriving passengers can be analyzed.

Taking the arrival of passengers at the airport as the starting point and the boarding of passengers as the endpoint, the overall service process provided by the airport during the departure process can be shown as follows: arrival at the airport → entering the departure hall → seeking advice → going to check-in & consignment → going to security check-in → security check-in → going to the gate → waiting → boarding (see Fig. 3).

Taking the arrival of passengers at the destination airport as the starting point and the departure of passengers from the airport as the terminal, the overall service process provided by the airport during the airport arrival process can be presented as follows: arrival at the airport → going to the baggage claim hall → finding the corresponding conveyor belt → baggage claim → leaving the isolation area → finding the airport pick-up person/parking lot/ticket sales office/subway entrance → leaving the airport (see Fig. 4).

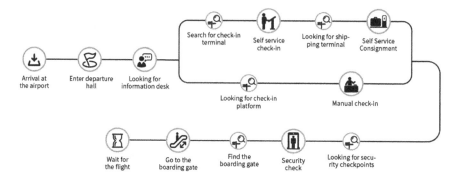

Fig. 3. Overall service flow of airport departure.

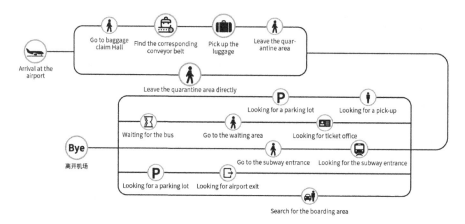

Fig. 4. Overall service flow of airport arrival.

Although there are many catering, entertainment, fitness, and recreation services in the public service space facing the travel scenario, the airport is still a functional public service space based on travel. Passengers can experience different services in different airports, but the main contacts in the airport scenario are still similar, and the overall main service process of the Airport is roughly the same.

After sorting out the travel contacts of airport passengers, we can clearly see the sequence relationship between each contact and contact. In order to meet the needs of different passengers in each contact of the airport, the airport has considered the function, scale, and layout of each service function space in the construction planning, and then carried out the micro information structure after planning the macro spatial information structure Planning of spatial function, scale, and layout. Among them, the relationship between the function, scale, and layout of space is interrelated. The function of space affects the scale and layout of space. On the contrary, the scale of space also affects the function and layout of space. The layout of space affects the function and scale of space. The research of these three should start from the spatial function. Because space itself has no function, in order to make the space without function become a public service space with social value and service value, space must meet the requirements of public service space and meet the basic functions as a public service space.

As the service supply side, there is no doubt that the airport has planned the main behavior content process of passengers in the airport in advance, and through the way of spatial information guidance and staff guidance, the passengers can comply with the process and actively meet their other needs. The functional types of airport service space are based on the contacts and user behavior in the overall service process of the airport. According to the behavior and demand of different contacts of passengers in the airport service process, based on this information about the over-all service process, the functions of each service space of the airport need to be optimized and iterated on the original basic functions and diversified and rich upgrading. For example: in the overall service process of the airport, consultation and check-in are the first, and check-in, security check-in, waiting and boarding are the second. These processes have been set up before the space construction planning. On this basis, the airport only considers the service content in each link, which determines the space function. All in all, the overall service process of the airport determines the function of each service space. The function endowing and iterative upgrading of the space is to better serve passengers to realize the function of the space itself in the process and maintain the normal operation of the process.

2.2   Relationship Between the Overall Service Process of the Airport and the Layout of Each Service Space

The relationship between the layout of each service space and the overall service flow of the airport is relatively simple and direct compared with the spatial function and spatial scale. In the limited site space, the location of the layout function partition from macro to micro adjusts the spatial scale. The main characteristic of the spatial layout is the reliability of spatial connectivity. Its connection with the overall service process of the airport is more reflected in the user's behavior dynamic line in the airport scene. Considering the uncertainty of user's behavior, the planning of each service space layout of the airport needs to be based on the overall service process of the airport, and guide the passengers to complete the travel purpose step by step and experience the natural and comfortable service (see Fig. 5).

Taking the spatial layout of the third floor of Guangzhou Baiyun International Airport as an example, after passengers enter the airport from gate 44 or enter the departure hall from the subway, parking lot, etc., their behavior moving line will be basically considered in the macro layout of the airport. After checking in the departure hall for check-in, they can have dinner and farewell with friends in the catering rest area, and then enter the waiting area through the security inspection area to find the registration area Waiting or shopping in the waiting area.

In terms of the macro spatial layout, the macro layout of the airport corresponds to the overall service process of the airport one by one and maintains a clear and high matching relationship. From the micro perspective, the airport spatial layout is based on

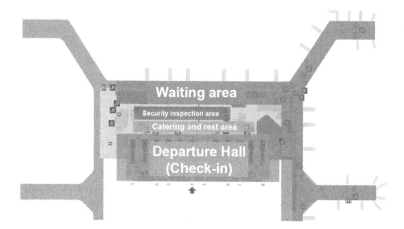

Fig. 5. Airport macro layout division.

the macro spatial scale and layout. The relationship between the micro spatial layout and the overall service process of the airport is more in-depth and detailed, which is the deepening and focus of the macro layout.

3   Comparison Between the Travel Process and the General Process for People with a Behavior Disorder

The content of this chapter is mainly to study the travel process of the disabled people in the airport scene, the service system set for them by the airport and the setting of the service interaction contact point of the disabled people in the airport. On the basis of this research, the paper compares with the general travel process and service system of healthy regular passengers and obtains the difference of demand as service receiving side and the difference of service received at the supply side of the airport, as well as the pain point and demand of interaction contact setting and service resources in the airport scene of behavioral barrier passengers The purpose of this paper is to provide evaluation reference and examples for the service system of the airport construction behavior barrier population.

3.1   Travel Process of Behavior Impaired People in the Airport Scene

As the object of this study, the definition of behavior disorder population in this paper is people with a high degree of behavior disorder. It is quite common to distinguish users by the degree of behavioral barriers in service design. All people have certain barriers to their behaviors. Through the degree of behavioral barriers, people or their needs in specific scenarios can be classified, and corresponding services and solutions can be provided. For example, pregnant women, the elderly, in a specific scenario are classified into the group with behavioral disorders because their physiological and psychological barriers in a specific scenario are much larger than those of normal people. Older people are physically vulnerable to leg and foot inconvenience, slow response and poor understanding, which leads to greater obstacles when they use the facilities and equipment designed for healthy people, such as taking the escalator in public places, or using some terminals for printing bills or handling business in public places such as banks and stations. They often need someone to guide them Guide or help. The reasons why pregnant women are listed as the group with behavior disorder are: in physiology, their waist and legs bear greater pressure and bondage, they are not convenient for walking for a long-distance, they are not convenient for bending and squatting, and their body response speed is also greatly reduced; in psychology, pregnant women are often in high tension and small in their daily life because they are worried about the collision injury of the fetus The state of mind, therefore, long-term mental tension and concentration will lead to pregnant women prone to fatigue and anxiety.

In the airport travel scenario, the research on the travel process of the behavior barrier population is similar to the research on the travel process of healthy passengers. Taking Baiyun International Airport as a case study, the first step: We analyzed and arranged the service interaction contacts of the disabled people at the airport. The second step is to investigate the behavior, moving line, pain point and satisfaction of the behavior barrier population in the terminal area. First-hand data and information about airport travel of behavior impaired people are obtained through follow-up and block visits on site. Step 3: sort out and analyze the collected data, and output our summary and summary of the travel process of the behavior barrier people in the airport scene and the corresponding views.

First of all (see Fig. 6), the interaction contacts of the behavior impaired people are different from those of healthy passengers, and the interaction contacts of different behavior impaired passengers will also be different. First of all, people with behavioral disorders need to arrive at the airport in the same way. Due to the inconvenience of their actions, most of them are mainly friends and relatives or colleagues. After arriving at the airport, they entered the departure hall differently. Taking wheelchair passengers as an example, when wheelchair passengers arrive at the airport and enter the departure hall, due to the large volume of wheelchair and the limitations of the movement mode, wheelchair passengers can not take the walking elevator to the departure hall on the third floor, only the straight elevator can meet their functional requirements, so the straight elevator is the key contact point for the disabled people to arrive at the airport.

Link	Arrival at the airport	Check-in	Security check	Wait for the flight	Boarding
Interactive contact for people with behavioral disorders	Parking lot, airport entrance, subway station, sign board, gate, escalator, vertical ladder, staff Special passenger parking space	Information desk, self-check-in terminal, self-check-in terminal, manual counter, special counter, special passenger counter	Security check counter, security check door, security check box, staff, special passenger security check channel, private check room	Seats, signs, shopping malls, food stores, special functional areas, trolleys, battery cars, special passenger rest areas	Staff, inspection gate, ferry car, disabled boarding car

Fig. 6. Interactive contacts of people with behavioral disorders.

Due to the height limitation of the wheelchair, the operating range of the arm of wheelchair passengers is relatively low for normal passengers when they check-in. When they use the self-service check-in terminal and self-service check-in terminal, they still have the problems of unclear perspective and difficult to click the interface at the top of the screen. Therefore, they generally prefer to choose the manual channel check-in and check-in together. Baiyun, Guangzhou The departure hall of the International Airport is also equipped with corresponding manual check-in channels for special passengers. In addition, when the inspection technology of the self-service terminal and artificial channel fails to meet the requirements, the wheelchair can only be checked in the special luggage consignment area. The long-distance and long-term movement is more physical consumption for wheelchair passengers. If wheelchair passengers travel alone, the help of the staff is particularly important. The airport has the service of providing assistance for people with behavioral disorders, which also increases the normal use and important interactive contacts different from the normal passengers, namely, online reservation service and airport service application counter.

In order to ensure the safety of the security check, some people with behavior disorders need to use a private examination room in the process of security checks because they use their own wheelchair or wear artificial limbs. In the private examination room, they need to dismantle and check the metal equipment on their body or provide a more comfortable and easy environment for them to leave the wheelchair and wait for the security check personnel to carry out security scans on the wheelchair.

After arriving at the isolation area through security checks, wheelchair passengers can choose to repair in the rest area of special passengers. The relatively isolated space can isolate external interference. For disabled passengers with psychological barriers or who do not want external interference, this is a good relaxing environment. When the flight departure time is close, or the flight information is adjusted, the airport staff will also give tips and help.

Finally, when they board the plane, some behavior disabled people need to use the disabled boarding car, which can help the disabled directly arrive at the cabin entrance of the plane and avoid the process of walking stairs. All of the above are multiple service interaction contacts different from those of healthy regular passengers that will be used by people with behavioral disorders in airport travel scenarios. Connect the service interaction contacts of the disabled people in the airport in chronological order. We can see the travel process of the disabled people in the airport scene.

As shown in the figure, the travel process of wheelchair passengers in the airport scene is shown (see Fig. 7). The interactive contacts of their travel in the airport are arranged and sorted according to the time sequence. The airport travel process of the disabled is more complex than that of the healthy passengers. Whether it is physical space and hardware facilities contacts or communication and interaction with the staff, it shows more contacts and higher contact frequency. Some constraints of its own conditions lead to its relatively narrow choice of the travel process, but also make it more difficult to simply and directly realize the most convenient travel process in the airport scenario. Looking for and waiting for the vertical ladder, looking for and waiting for the manual check-in channel and special passenger check-in channel, checking in the wheelchair for special luggage, leaving the wheelchair for security inspection, waiting for the wheelchair to be picked up, etc. The travel process of them

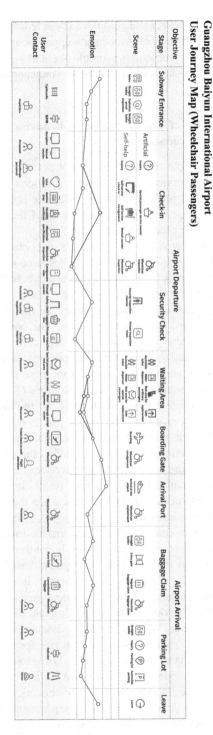

Fig. 7. Guangzhou Baiyun international airport user journey map (wheelchair passengers).

in the airport scene is more tortuous and complex. These tedious operation steps add a lot of burden to the travel of the behavior handicapped people both physically and psychologically. They are the problems we should see and pay attention to when we understand the airport travel process of the behavior handicapped people and optimize their travel process.

3.2   Comparative Analysis of Travel Process of Behavior Barrier Group and General Travel Process in Airport

The needs of the disabled people in the airport are not exactly the same as those of the healthy passengers, and the service-related systems provided by the airport are also different. In their airport travel process, the main difference between the travel process of the disabled people and the general travel process is the difference in the number and function of the contacts in the process (see Fig. 8).

In the same service process stage, the difference of contact function and contact number can be attributed to the difference of service resource allocation, that is to say, we can make a comparative analysis on the service of the behavior barrier population and healthy population from the perspective of service resource allocation.

In the process of airport travel, service resources are mainly divided into human resources, equipment resources, and space resources. The configuration of the three service resources constitutes the realization of the service contact function. Taking Guangzhou Baiyun International Airport as an example, this paper analyzes the airport travel process of the disabled and healthy people from these three aspects.

In the aspect of human resources, the human resources of the related services for the behavior handicapped people intersect with those for the healthy regular passengers. The allocation of resources in the intersecting part is relatively rich and appropriate, but the unique human resources in the related services for the behavior handicapped people are still in a state of shortage. Taking the special check-in counter as an example, it is defined as the counter providing services for special passengers, but usually, it is not only for special passengers, which results in that special passengers can not enjoy the services of special counters in time when they arrive at the check-in Island, and the main lack of human resources is to open a separate manual check-in channel. If the special check-in channel fails to perform its original functions, it is the lack of human resource allocation of service contact. In contrast, the general process of healthy regular passengers, no matter where they go, is basically guided or implemented by relevant staff. With sufficient human resources, healthy regular passengers can quickly experience services and achieve operational goals.

In terms of equipment and resources, the application and use of airport wheelchairs often need a long scheduling time. When wheelchair passengers arrive at the airport site to apply for replacement of airport wheelchair or apply for assistance services, the insufficient number of wheelchairs and the slow speed of resource allocation make the service system unable to provide the right to use airport wheelchair on the site immediately while ensuring the smooth completion of network application services It is the problem of insufficient equipment resources and equipment resource allocation. In addition, some equipment resources, such as self-service check-in terminal, battery car and so on, do not well consider the use scenarios of some people with behavioral

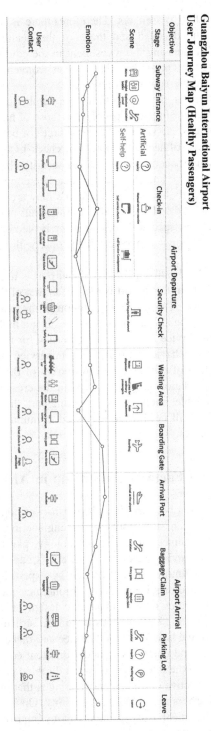

Fig. 8. Guangzhou Baiyun international airport user journey map (healthy passengers).

disorders, such as wheelchair passengers. Therefore, there is a big gap between the equipment resources of the disabled and those of the healthy people in terms of "quantity" and "quality". Increasing the investment in the equipment resources of the disabled and developing the products and services convenient for their use are important ways to improve the equipment resources.

In terms of space resources, there are also a large number of intersections between the space resources of behavior impaired people and those of healthy people. Different from the equipment resources, the service space resources of behavior impaired people are more abundant than those of healthy people. The check-in area is equipped with an independent special passenger check-in channel, the security check-in area is equipped with a private inspection room, and the waiting area is equipped with a special passenger rest area, a mother and child area, a children's play area, etc. These spaces are designed for their special needs. However, due to the small number of users and the consideration of privacy, these special spaces are often isolated from the outside world and the number is small. It is not convenient for people with behavioral disorders to find and go to these spaces.

The travel process of the disabled people in the airport is relatively more complex, and their number of contacts in the airport is more than that of the healthy people, but they are not dense in space. That is to say, although the number of their service interaction contacts is large, the allocation of resources is not high, which can meet the corresponding function of service contacts, but it is easy for the lack of resources to affect the experience of the behavior barrier people in service contacts.

In general, the allocation of related service resources of the behavior barrier population and the healthy population has some cross. In the cross part, the allocation of resources is rich and reasonable, but in the non-crossing part, the related services of the behavior barrier population still need to be improved in human resources, equipment resources, and space resources.

4   Analysis of Human Factor Relationship in Airport Space

The research on the interaction between the behavior barrier population and the scene in the public service space can start from human engineering. Human factor engineering involves many disciplines, including physiology, psychology, management, engineering, safety science, environmental science, etc. it has a wide range of applications, but its name and definition are not unified by experts from all countries. In China, the definition of ergonomics in the Book Ergonomics edited by Professor Zhu Zuxiang is a science that studies how to make the design of human-machine environment system conform to the characteristics of human structure and physiological psychology, so as to realize the best match of the three and make people work and live effectively, safely, healthily and comfortably under different conditions.

The reason why we study the interaction between disabled people in different parts of the airport from the perspective of human engineering is that disabled people have a higher level of behavior barriers and weaker adaptability. Optimizing their interaction with equipment and environment is very important to improve their airport travel experience, which involves the research scope of human engineering. The airport belongs to a large public service space, and its service scope and depth are at a higher level than other public service spaces. Through the research on the interaction relationship of the behavior disabled people in the airport service scene from the perspective of human engineering, we can provide reference cases and standards for the interaction relationship of the behavior disabled people in most public service spaces, and specific to human-machine Environment is of great significance to the practice of theory.

4.1 Human-Machine Scale Analysis of Service-Related Contact Points for People with Behavioral Disorders in Airport

We have measured and analyzed a large number of service space contacts and equipment and facilities in the process of investigation of Guangzhou Baiyun International Airport. Through a follow-up survey, we also conducted a lot of relevant scale experiments and discussions with wheelchair passengers.

When we study the relationship between space and human, we can't avoid the problem of man-machine scale. There are a large number of service-related contacts between behavioral disorder people and airport space, and the human-computer scale relationship between them and these service contacts is more complex than that of healthy people. In this paper, wheelchair passengers are taken as the research object. From the perspective of ergonomics, the scale problems existing in the three main travel processes of airport check-in, security check-in, and waiting are analyzed.

(1) Check-in: after the passenger arrives at the airport, the first step is usually to choose consultation or check indirectly. With the rapid development of the Internet, Guangzhou Baiyun International Airport has also set up self-service check-in terminals in front of each check-in island. The appearance of the terminal is mainly vertical base plus an inclined operation panel, which is convenient and quick for normal passengers to operate, but for wheelchair passengers, the terminal does not meet the basic man-machine scale. First of all, from the perspective of the analysis of the hand touch range, the bottom of the self-service check-in terminal is a vertical shape. Wheelchair passengers can't operate the operation panel in the front like normal passengers. They need to side to be closer to the terminal to achieve the operation. Second, in the analysis of hand touch height, the height of the terminal is high, and wheelchair passengers with short arms cannot touch the buttons on the top of the panel, which is easy to cause danger. Third, from the perspective of visual field height analysis, the terminal has no adjustable height and no movable panel. The lowest part of the operation panel is 1.08M away from the ground, and the area of the operation panel is almost above the head position of wheelchair passengers. Wheelchair passengers need to keep their heads up to obtain the information of the operation panel. Finally, from the angle of view range analysis, the operation panel of self-service check-in terminal is designed to be close to 60° to the ground for the convenience of normal passengers, but for wheelchair passengers, such angle of tilt panel will cause reflection, from their view angle, it is almost impossible to obtain the information of reflection area (see Fig. 9).

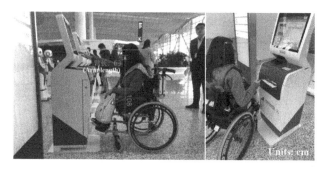

Fig. 9. Wheelchair passenger is using self-check-in terminals.

(2) Security inspection link: in the security inspection link, wheelchair passengers first contact the identity verification counter, and then contact the security door and the security personnel detection or private inspection room. In this link, there are two extremely troubling contact human-computer scale problems. First, the width of the security door can only meet the needs of wheelchair passing. If wheelchair passengers push the wheelchair forward by themselves, their arms will be blocked by both sides of the security door, resulting in their inability to move forward. Second, the wheelchair detection of wheelchair passengers still needs to be manually checked by the staff using a metal detector. In this process, wheelchair passengers with lower extremity obstacles need to stand temporarily or move to another platform to wait for the inspection of the staff. In the process of transferring the body and cooperating with the examination, they need three kinds of help: fixing the wheelchair, providing the supporting point of the hand and providing a suitable transfer position. However, in reality, this process only satisfies the first one. These three are the important interactive contacts to ensure the safety of wheelchair passengers from secondary injury in the process of security check. We should provide guarantee and support for their safety and comfort from the perspective of the human-computer scale, and use the human-computer scale data in the configuration and construction of facilities, equipment, and space (see Fig. 10).

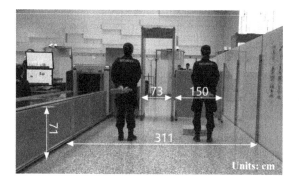

Fig. 10. Field investigation of security inspection channel.

(3) Waiting link: during the waiting process, wheelchair passengers can choose to enter the rest area for special passengers. The rest area for special passengers can provide rest places, boarding tips, and other services for special passengers and their peers, but the facilities and equipment are still lack of human-machine consideration for wheelchair passengers and other special passengers. As for the seats in this area, if the comfort of the seats in the rest area is low and the risk coefficient of the transfer process is high, the wheelchair passengers can not get the physical and mental comfort and relaxation, which can not reflect the particularity of the rest area and the care for the special passengers, and its function and name can not match.

From the perspective of the human-computer scale, human-computer interaction problems in service space can be analyzed from the physical scale of space equipment contacts to find the hardware problems that affect the experience of passenger service interaction. Adding human-computer scale system analysis to the hardware configuration and setting can solve the problems from the source and obtain long-term results. It will be an inevitable trend for the construction of public service space in the future to strictly follow the rules of the human-computer scale and create relevant service contacts suitable for most people with behavioral disorders based on this standard.

4.2   Analysis of Contact Interaction In-Service Process

In physiology, we have established an ergonomic environment space through a scientific human-computer interaction scale, but it is not in accordance with the design of a human-computer scale that can make passengers feel comfortable, which involves the psychological level. When we meet their physiological needs, we tend to ignore the psychological feelings of passengers, while the psychological feelings seem to be nihilistic but play a huge role. Psychological research often can guide the design of man-machine scale in some fields. For example, in the design of the seats in the waiting area, the requirements for comfort are not high, too comfortable seats will make the passengers sleepy and forget the boarding time; however, in some special cases, when the passengers are very tired and need a good rest, the requirements for the comfort of the seats will be greatly increased, at this time, they will choose comfortable massage chairs to wait, in order to prevent missing the boarding time, press The motorcycle chair should be equipped with boarding prompt function. Therefore, different types of passengers will have different physiological and psychological needs on the contact point of the waiting seat, and the interaction analysis should have higher judgment and analysis standards of universality and effectiveness.

When analyzing the interaction in-service process contact, it is more rigorous and humanized to analyze the interaction between humans and contact from the perspective of human-environment emotion. The relationship between humans and the environment belongs to the physical level, while the relationship between the environment and emotion belongs to the spiritual level. Different feelings of passengers in different scenarios can reflect whether the interaction between different service contacts and passengers is good (see Fig. 11).

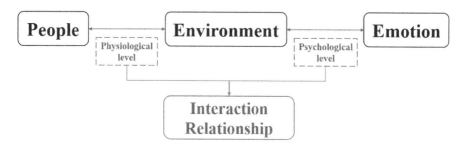

Fig. 11. Research framework of airport contact interaction.

Taking the private inspection room of Guangzhou Baiyun International Airport as a case study, when we analyze the interaction between them, we will not only capture and cut the internal scenes and analyze the human-computer relationship, but also analyze the emotional changes of passengers in each scene. When the special passenger enters the private inspection room, the space scale, hardware material, hardware modeling, floor material, main color of the environment, light brightness, light color temperature, air temperature, air humidity, etc. this interaction has occurred before the physical contact between the passenger and the space, it will directly affect the first feeling of the passenger for the space contact, and the first feeling is lower than It is expected that passengers will have resistance and affect their perception of service space contact.

5 Summaries

China's civil aviation industry is growing at an amazing speed, and social civilization is also constantly improving. As the most timely travel space connecting the city to the world, airport service quality needs to be systematically improved from multiple perspectives. As a public service space, to meet the basic travel needs of more people, providing better travel services and travel space is its basic responsibility. In the past, the airport travel process and contact points of the behavior disabled people have not been considered as a single group in the airport construction, resulting in the existing airport service-related system is not perfect, and the travel of the behavior disabled people is more inconvenient than that of the healthy people.

By comparing the airport travel process and service-related systems of the disabled with those of the healthy people, it can be seen that there is a huge difference between the processes they need to operate and the related systems they need to serve from the moment when the disabled decide to travel. When they come to the airport to enjoy the service, the airport prepares for them The allocation of service-related resources and the resources of healthy people have a large number of cross, while the noncrossing resources are relatively limited, and the allocation of human resources, equipment resources, and space resources still need to be adjusted.

All kinds of service resources are provided by the airport as the supply side, and the main feelings of the passengers with behavioral disorders as the receiving side are divided into physiological and psychological aspects. The interaction between them and the airport service contact point still needs to be improved and considered on the human-computer scale from the perspective of physiological Ergonomics, while from the perspective of psychological analysis, the passengers with behavioral disorders and the airport service In order to establish a good interaction relationship between contacts, we need to dig into their psychological emotions in each service scene lens and optimize them through relative service specifications and contact environment atmosphere.

The airport is the epitome of urban culture and civilization. It is important to work and responsibility of the airport as a public service space to provide convenient travel and high-quality services for all people, including healthy people and people with behavioral disorders. It will be a new policy for the airport service industry to convey warmth and care, and to tell the world the service concept of people-oriented.

References

1. Air transport statistical results (2017). https://www.icao.int/annual-report-2017/Pages/the-world-of-air-transport-in-2017-statistical-results.aspx. Accessed 30 Jan 2020
2. The 13th five-year plan for the development of civil aviation in China (2016). http://www.caac.gov.cn/XXGK/XXGK/ZCFBJD/201702/t20170215_42525.html. Accessed 30 Jan 2020
3. Prendeville, S., Bocken, N.: Sustainable business models through service design. Procedia Manuf. **8**, 292–299 (2017)
4. Shijian, L., Wenyin, Z.: Research status and development of service design. Packag. Eng. **39** (24), 43–53 (2018)
5. Bochu, X., Feng, W.: Research on service design of urban public transport system – taking chengdu as an example. Decorate (2), 126–127 (2016)
6. Haosheng, X.: Research on the design strategy of public service space of small and medium-sized museums from the perspective of new museology. South China University of Technology (2017)
7. Lan, H.: A study on the dilemma and strategy of government purchasing public service – taking district w as an example. Innovation **13**(01), 73–80 (2019)
8. Yiqi, G.: The introduction of public space culture to serve the city's tourism image – a case study of Taoyuan airport in Taiwan. Beauty Times (City Ed.) (8), 91–92 (2015)
9. Xueyun, W.: Research on the supply of civil aviation airport passenger service under the internet + background. Hefei University of Technology (2017)

User Research on Digital Consumption Behavior and Design Guidelines in Connecting Vehicle Context

Di Zhu, Wei Liu$^{(\boxtimes)}$, and Yanrui Qu

Beijing Normal University, Beijing 100875, China
{di.zhu,wei.liu,yanrui.qu}@bnu.edu.cn

Abstract. Connecting Vehicle's design of driving has increased rapidly in functionality, but the service design has evolved less. This study reports on a quantitative user research study (N = 314) and qualitative study (N = 30) that uses an online questionnaire and semi-structured in-depth interviews to get insights into digital consumption behavior and design guidelines in the Chinese context. The results show that people are interested in the wellbeing field, they like seeing records of not only their performance but also of the reactions and highlights experienced by their family members. And analysis reservation behavior and their attitude toward virtue cost. This paper also concludes seven design guidelines to instruct future relating research and give a vision of how third-level autonomous vehicles work for users who get used to digital consumption.

Keywords: User research · Connecting vehicles · Digital consumption · User interview · Design guidelines

1 Introduction

Mobile Internet is evolving towards the Internet of Things through enabling technologies [1]. The high-quality internet allows vehicles to share Internet access with other devices both inside as well as outside of vehicles. Many automobile companies noticed a growing trend and significant business opportunities for connecting their vehicles. Moreover, China is globally pioneering a new wave of digital lifestyles through its hyper-connectivity, rapid smartphone adoption, centralized service ecosystems by Internet companies. Furthermore, Chinese's openness to adopt new technologies and social behaviors and, as such, using the context of China today to explore user behavior and needs can give researchers insights into what the rest of the world might require in the future.

There are two types of digital consumption [2], the one is as a kind of currency, for instance, you can buy a book online, and use WeChat Pay to pay the money, that is called digital consumption. The other one is non-currency consumption that users read the text, listen to audio, or watch videos through digital platforms, such as mobile phones, laptops. Connecting Vehicles field focuses more on technology research, but not on user research. Because this field is pretty novel in a user study, in other words,

© Springer Nature Switzerland AG 2020
A. Marcus and E. Rosenzweig (Eds.): HCII 2020, LNCS 12201, pp. 716–729, 2020.
https://doi.org/10.1007/978-3-030-49760-6_50

no user experienced it before. However, based on user research methods, we can explore users' behavior and create design guidelines for future HMI design. This paper concentrates on non-currency consumption in connecting vehicle context. Customized digital consumption services provide more possibilities for automobile companies, which can collect users' information through digital platforms to estimate users' preferences to advertise and enhance users' loyalty accurately [3]. With the development of technologies, more and more activities users can do on vehicles [4]. It will be more kinds of services and stakeholders involved in the service system.

This paper did research based on Level 3 conditional autonomy. According to the National Highway Traffic Safety Administration (NHTSA) defines five degrees of car autonomy which varies in the penetration of cars with Advanced Driver Assistance Systems (ADAS). This paper concentrates on Level 3 conditional autonomy, which system capability is in specific traffic or environmental conditions. The vehicle can manage most aspects of driving, including monitoring the environment [5]. The system prompts the driver to intervene when it encounters a scenario it cannot navigate. The driver will be available for occasional control, but with sufficiently comfortable transition time [6]. In other words, drivers can do some digital consumption activities in conditional autonomous vehicles; for instance, they can watch movies, buy clothes, and browse news.

2   Quantitative Research on Digital Consumption Behavior

In order to dig out valuable user research insights, the researcher conducted an online questionnaire and in-depth interviews to combine quantitative research and qualitative research within these points to clarify the target user group's behavior, attitude, and perspectives. Quantitative research methods can help researchers to narrow down study directions because of great certainty features and investigate a big scale of users [7]. Based on desk research of digital consumption, the online questionnaire consisted of three sectors, necessary information, commute preference, and consumption value emphasized on digital consumption.

2.1   Questions Setting

On necessary information, this questionnaire included gender, age, career, accommodation, and salary. Of commuting preferences (as Table 1 shown) including how they commute, they have experience in the driving or not, and they know how to do an emergency rescue or not. On consumption value (as Table 2 shown), we asked the most two kinds of products they bought online, paying tools they like to use, they spend money on buy souvenirs, membership, and copyright or not, what kind of attitude towards these consumptions.

Based on the two social platforms of WeChat and QQ, the survey was developed and hosted on survey platform 'Tencent Questionnaire', to post the online survey to WeChat friends circle, WeChat group, QQ group, etc. This study used SPSS software to analyze the data.

Table 1. Commute relevant questions.

Question	Type
What is the commute method you use most often?	Single choice
Who are you with when you go out to play?	Single choice
When I go out to play, will I go?	Multiple choice
Which of the following do you want to do most in travel?	Single choice
What do you do often when using mobile devices (mobile phones, tablets, car systems) in your car?	Multiple choice
When you are in trouble during driving, what do you do?	Single choice
When other people's vehicles are in an emergency, do you tend to?	Single choice
Do you know about the car emergency rescue knowledge?	Single choice
When using the car center console, do you prefer to use it?	Multiple choice
What kind of mitigation will you take when faced with stress?	Multiple choice

Table 2. Consumption value questions.

Question	Type
Under what circumstances will you bring a gift to your family and colleagues when you are traveling or on a business trip?	Single choice
Which two types do you spend the most on the Internet?	Multiple choice
What reason do you usually make an appointment before?	Single choice
Which type of card are you most commonly used in cards bundled with third-party payment platforms?	Single choice
Which of the following members have you applied for?	Multiple choice
Why are you handling this membership?	Single choice
What is your current attitude towards paying for copyright or knowledge?	Single choice

2.2   Participants

Three hundred and forty-one participants varied in gender, work domain, and job title answered the online survey. It consists of 42% of males and 58% females. One-third of them are students, while others are officials, managers, contractors, etc. They lived in different provinces of China, covering the whole country except for three provinces. They belonged to different generations, but they all use smartphones and connected to the Internet. The birth year is between 1965 to 2010, with an average age of twenty-four years old. Every participant has an individual WeChat or QQ account.

2.3   Procedure

The online questionnaire has twenty-two questions after screened from more than thirty questions. This study planned a pilot of the questionnaire in order to address any usability and design issues. It targeted large online social networks due to users' superior using bases. Online surveys consist of an introduction page, single-choices, and multiple-choices questions, and a thank-you page is displaying after submission [8]. Finally, we analyzed data and defined user behavior. The online survey process included several steps, as showed in Fig. 1.

- Start with questions of online questionnaire brainstorming, brainstorm as more as possible. Use affinity diagrams to cut down the question number.
- Set the sequence of questions. The start of the online survey should be an interesting topic that talks about their daily digital life. Moreover, put questions of the same topic together to create a context for participants.
- Answer an online survey with a pilot. Recruit several target users to answer and ask their feedback. Compare outcome and questionable purpose, then redesign questions and screen some questions.

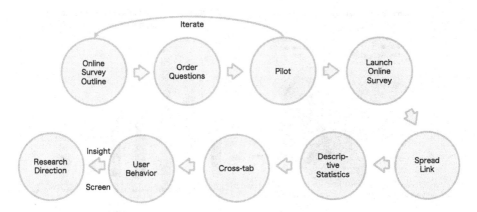

Fig. 1. Online survey analysis steps.

- Based on feedback, iterate outline, question, and sequence. We moved demographic questions to the end of an online survey to decrease the probability of loss of participants who think these questions are too tedious to answer.
- Launch an online questionnaire and share the link to WeChat friends circle, WeChat group, QQ group, etc.
- Use descriptive statistics method to analyze the data to cluster user behavior and attitude.
- Use the crosstab of SPSS to analyze the potential connection within data.
- Find consumption, driving, socializing behavior, and screen research directions.

These steps help the researcher to ensure the quality of online survey research to discover users' preferences and behavior.

2.4   Online Questionnaire Analysis Result

By integrating the results of descriptive statistics and crosstab, the research found that the current acceptance of digital consumption is high in a wide age range. 94.3% of them trust third-party payment platforms such as WeChat Pay and Alipay. 80.3% of the participants had at least one online member of application or virtual services. The research will focus on the three topics, make appointments daily, pay attention to health issues, and high dependence on music and video-related services, which will be further discussed in the next step.

As showed in Fig. 2, only 12.4% of the participants reported that they never make an appointment. The most significant proportion is a user who feels safe when they have made a reservation. Therefore, in the interview phase, we will study what kind of services users prefer to make an appointment, what kind of information users will search or need when they decide to book it or not, how can a service provide safe feeling to users.

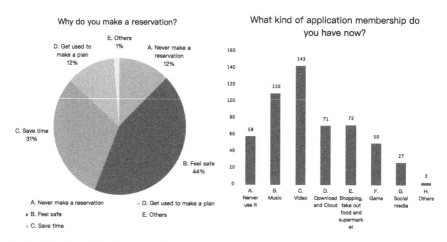

Fig. 2. Pie chart of why you make a reservation question (left), bar chart of what kind of application membership do you have now question (right).

At present, users pay more considerable attention to health, and we can take advantage of health concerns to better improve users' loyalty. Cross-analysis found that the higher the annual income, the more likes to do sports together when they feel high stressful. The higher the annual income, the higher the proportion of choosing "sports", indicating that with the increase in income, the health awareness will be stronger. Moreover, government officials are more inclined to do sports together. Therefore, in the interview phase, we will concentrate on how users will judge their health state and detect their health problems. We will also discover how users care about the health of their families.

With the transition from TVs and radios to smartphones and tablets, users' needs for multimedia services such as video and music are becoming more and more personalized. Not only will they consume free streaming media, but they will also choose to pay for a membership to improve quality of service, for instance, enjoying exclusive copyright steaming media, high-speed downloading, more considerable cloud shortage, high-quality of streaming media.

As Fig. 2 shown, video membership (143 participants) and music membership (110 participants) are the most popular. According to the analysis of the membership and jobs relevant crosstab, this study found that participants who work as a teacher, lawyer, or doctor are more inclined to apply for video members. Most of the participants have a positive attitude towards paying for copyright. They thought that copyright would be more and more critical, and the company will spend more resources on protecting them. As Fig. 4 shows, 31% of participants buy membership of an application because they attracted by a feature of an application, 26% of participants since they can save more money by using the membership. Therefore, in the interview, we should consider the potential impact of occupation on the choice of multimedia service types. In the following interviews, it is necessary to focus on the target users' multimedia consumption types and their consumption levels.

In conclusion, this study concentrated more on users' specific behaviors in a specific context that can help us to understand the motivation behind these behaviors and get more insights into the next research phase.

3 Qualitative Research on Digital Consumption Behavior

According to probability theory and mathematical statistics, analysis results showed user commonality in the same context and users' preference. Then the paper chooses a semi-structured interview to understand participants' perspectives on their lives, experience, or situations as expressed in their own words. And the outline of interview divided into three topics: before digital consumption, during digital consumption, and after consumption.

3.1 Participants

Thirty participants varied in gender, work domain, and job title were selected. They were students, engineers, designers, freelancers, and other office workers. They lived in different cities of China, varying from the first-tier city such as Beijing, Shanghai to the fifth-tier city such as Chifeng, Liaoyang. They belonged to different generations, but they all use smart phones and connected to the Internet. The age range of participants is between ten and fifty-three years old, with an average age of twenty-five years old. In the driving situation, eleven participants had no driving experience, sixteen participants have little driving experience, and the rest of them have a rich driving experience. Nine of the participants lived with their parents, eight were living independently, seven were living in a school or a corporate quarter, and six were living with a partner.

3.2 Procedure

Each interview started with demographic information [9]. The participants described their digital consumption activities, including subscript information, make an appointment, help others to buy products online, buy a digital product, focus on the health problem, and pay a bill. Participants especially recall their experience in interacting with IT tools and were encouraged to refer their experience of the information [10]. The actual interview analysis included several steps, as showed in Fig. 3.

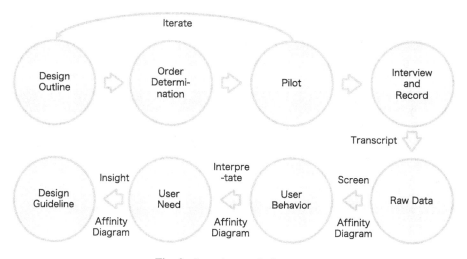

Fig. 3. Interview analysis steps.

- Start with a draft outline.
- Decide the sequence of questions. The start of the interview should be an easy topic that talks about their daily digital life. Moreover, combine tedious topics and interesting topics with helping participants maintain a level of arousal.
- Interview with a pilot. Recruit several target users to interview and ask their feedback. Compare outcome and question purpose, then redesign questions.
- Based on feedback, iterate outline, question, and sequence.
- Conduct interviews and record every word that a participant says. Take note to capture informal conversations and observations.

- Make a transcript of every sentence into documents, including interjection. Furthermore, use a single side to print it.
- Screen sentences which closely related to behavior and attitude.
- Use the affinity diagram to cluster user behavior and attitude.
- Reformulate transcripts to nail down a specific user's need and to build a shared understanding among the researchers.
- Get insights into user needs, probe design guidelines of digital consumption.

These steps help the researcher to use a whole procedure of an in-depth interview to explore digital consumption behavior and user need.

3.3 Results

All thirty participants were very open and cooperative in describing their daily activities and tools involved and explaining their ways of making digital consumption decisions. We found that most of the users will pay close attention to health issues to keep subhealth away. They will contact the family regularly but do not understand how to communicate with their family members, especially the elder members. They will make a reservation to take control of the pace of life and save time. Most of them will listen to music but do not spend much money on it.

How Users Check Physical and Mental Status? Keeping good health has good awareness over target user groups. Participants all have their way to check physical states such as apply for a membership card in a fitness gym, set a daily goal of walking steps, go jogging once or twice a week, do physical examination regularly, or weigh themselves. As for mental status, some of them will consider stress levels recently. They would like to adjust themselves to a better mood in a short time, for instance, females like shopping in a big mall and chatting with a close friend, males like doing some sports to fresh up. Many participants said WeChat sport encourages them to walk more because they do not want to be the last one of walk rank. Moreover, when they have the most steps, they will be very proud of themselves. They prefer a visualized approach to present their achievements and get professional instruction so that they can encourage them to keep a good habit.

Participants care about not only their health but also family members' health. They will judge physical status by looking at the face, listening voice, or even asking them face to face or on the phone. Most of them will call their family regularly, especially the special festival evening. It is a good time calling family after daily work because users and family members will be available. Asking health status is a Chinese customer to concern about their parents and find a good chatting topic. It will be a warm way to take care of people around users. Most of them have an idea to care about family. However, some of them cannot figure out their way to show their feeling and caring.

Through the collation of the affinity graph method, the analysis results out four types of core services in the service system. As found in the 1-to-1 interview process, most users not only pay attention to their health but also set the number of steps and apply for fitness cards, weighing themselves, conduct physical examination regularly, and other means of concern. At the same time, they are also very concerned about family health. They will talk to his family regularly, giving priority to his or her health level, and focusing on recent health issues. Therefore, the concern about these conclusions and the advantages of driving vehicles [11]. It divided into health care services and family communication services.

When Users Make a Reservation? Most users make a reservation because they want to secure their appointments in the case of spending more time on unnecessary accident. It will ensure a perfect date. During the reservation service, they want a complete service, including a detailed information and comments system. However, they only use the comments system to critic terrible experiences. In China, it is widespread to make an order online while waiting for a delivery man to ship it. Moreover, most white collars in first-tier cities do not have enough time to go to a market or cook. So, they will choose to make an order online in advance. Arriving time is a crucial factor; it can help the user to save time or waste time. Delivery ship too early, the home will be empty, and no one can answer the door. On the contrary, users may wait for an extended period. They prefer to pick up delivery or take away food by themselves to save money and make sure that delivery will arrive on time. Moreover, some of the users want to book popular shows or tickets in advance. They will also book a parking lot in that place. However, reservations cannot secure the delivery ship on time because of several uncontrollable factors. Vehicles as a moveable container, many reservations will be made on vehicles.

What is Attitude Towards Cost Virtue Media? Every participant has media consumption, not only listens to music, watches movies to browse media, but also buys a virtue membership to update their experience. It is trendy to buy a virtue membership to listen to an album, watch a movie, or get an advanced version. Most of the young generation have an open mind to buy a virtue product, while elder generation thinks that "it is not worth, why should I buy a virtue one, I would rather not buy it." and people who spend money on it, they will buy a good deal of membership and compare the same type of membership and make a final decision. They would like they charge them a fee by month and show detailed information that includes cost and services. Most users think that media charging is a trend, but they will consider the amount of money and resource they can provide. Users are affected by bundled sales promotions, and as long as one of the bundled products is needed. The users are more likely to purchase. For instance, a participant said he likes playing Fate Go mobile game, and he usually spends some money on it. Furthermore, he uses Bilibili to watch the animation. When he saw a promotion that the same amount of money, he can change the game account and watch the animation in advance, he decided to buy membership in Bilibili. Membership is small amount of money in everyday life. However, users will consider does it worthy or not. Consideration of the third level of autonomous vehicles [12], music service will be more suitable for connecting vehicles' digital consumption service systems.

In conclusion, the service system can divide into four services health care service, family communication service, reservation service, and music service.

3.4 Design Guidelines

This study translated these results into a set of design guidelines, which will subsequently apply to cater to user needs in a future connecting vehicle services context.

Avoid Meaningless Activities to Save Energy. Participants would like to mail gifts they bought on a business trip because they will not spend too much energy to carry a gift, and they want to lower their luggage and ensure gifts are fresh and local. They want their low-cost members with high-frequency use can automatically renew without multiple interactions. They want to select food that they will eat and the time which expects to deliver. So, they can save time on waiting for the food. They dislike learning how to use complicated software or application, and if they have a problem. They prefer to find a reliable expert, especially a family member, to help them remotely. They cannot remember all procedures because they rarely meet the same difficulty in a short duration.

Effective and Traceable. Some of the participants will go shopping rather than have a holiday to take a quick break from a busy and stressful environment. When they saw what they have bought, they will feel fresh to face more challenges. They think that the goal is to have a rest so that they will choose an effective way to achieve it. Some of them have select confidants to address different kinds of problems. Special confidants should be reliable and available, and confidants will leave essential information to help them in the future. When participants are chatting with family, they want to know their previous health status. It can help them effectively prioritize different chatting topic. Most of the participants want to collect physical souvenirs instead of the digital version, such as books, hand drawing maps.

Maintain Social Network. Connecting vehicles system not only connecting vehicles and infrastructures but also connecting human beings. Based on the connection, users can build their social network. Users spend much time maintaining these connections, especially to family members, no matter users are enjoying chatting with the family or not, because Chinese culture emphasizes family bonding. As a result, they want to find or create more chatting topics, and they want to find a more comfortable way to understand their friends' or families' life more. Furthermore, every user tries his or her best to catch up with the latest fashion that they thought.

More Professional and Comprehensive Information. Users never lack information as a result of the Internet, but they value professional and comprehensive information. Participants mentioned they are not experts, so they need very kinds of professional information to help them make decisions. They will be confused when they only see the results. Reasons and background information can allow users to build trust between machines and humans. However, users have the authority to choose to see this information or avoid it. Moreover, information can combine online recourse and data collected from users. It will be more reliable and have more orientation. The way to present information is represented proficiency of the information. So, users like a visualized way to show the results, because they can understand the meaning of it in short period of time, and it can last longer in users' memory.

Rational Consumption Attitude. Participants hold a rational consumption attitude; for instance, they bought a monthly music membership to download music that collected over a half year. It is unnecessary to purchase for non-sustainable needs. When they see a promotion, they will predict their need to save money, but they are usually overestimating it. As a result, they will buy many unnecessary items that meet their preference. Users will make a quick comparison between the previous consumers' behavior, according to the user research clusters, it has four criteria: low-cost advantages, including the final purchase an equal number of products at lower prices, they can buy more products at the same price. The advantage of saving money is that the membership fee is less than the price that they can save, such as membership discount products, membership coupon, and membership free trails. The purchased product meets the compelling needs of users and is eager to have music or video copyright. Get priority rights, including the ability to see the show as soon as possible, see the unabridged version, get better quality of service, and prioritize delivery. In conclusion, participants use these criteria to judge whether they should purchase or not, and most of them have rational consumption behavior and attitude, but they sometimes overestimate their needs.

Guarantee Success Rate in Advance. All of the participants mentioned that they like good results. So, they will use more positive approaches to ensure they can succeed. Some of the participants prefer to make reservations in advance to reserve a table, a parking lot, seats, etc. When it comes to the digital payment method, they mentioned that they like to choose the most common platform to pay. It all depends on what is the most common way among their neighborhood. Some of the participants said they would do a physical examination regularly to check hidden danger in advance to avoid having a more severe disease without feeling it. Many participants use digital devices such as smartphone, i-Watch, Mi band to check their physical status. The elder focuses more on walking steps, and the younger prefer to run.

Implement Healthy Habits. Every participant wants to keep a healthy habit, but consideration of realistic challenges in daily life, it is challenging to implement the habit. Some of the participants will choose the best combination of their life and healthy habit. For instance, a participant mentioned that she spends much time to find a good recipe and cook food, so she designs a healthy food menu that contains nitration, vitamin, and good taste. It will be more achievable when it combines with an existing habit, not create a new one. Moreover, use statistics to quantity indicators, the number will set a clear goal for users so that they can follow every small step to approach the final objectives. Participants need real actions to help them to keep healthy.

The design guidelines above are for digital consumption behavior, attitude in connecting vehicles to context. Furthermore, design guidelines will be used to design future digital consumption services system in the connecting vehicle context.

3.5 Vision of Future Services of Digital Consumption in Connecting Vehicle Context

In the context of connecting vehicles, it will have various limitations [13]. Vehicles, as the third room of users, provide a temporary room to users. It is a private space, and users can be themselves, such as singing in the vehicle, scheduling user's workday, calling their family members. There are fewer distractions than outside of vehicles. Vehicles are also mobile transportation, not only can move people from a location to destination but also can move products, boxes, food, deliveries, for instance. A visionary services system was created to illustrate how the design guidelines could have implications for designing future digital consumption services. Below is the visionary system map of digital consumption services in connecting the context of the vehicle (see Fig. 4): The center of this service system is a vehicle that has connected to the Internet for vehicles. It connects four services, music service, family communication service, reservation service, and health care service.

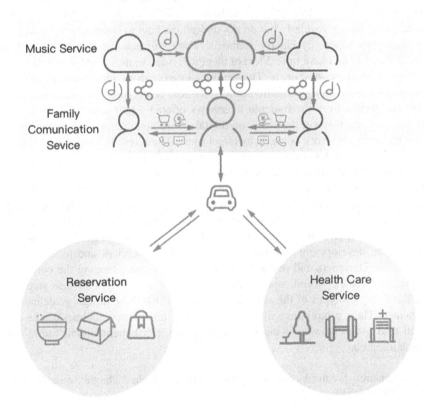

Fig. 4. The visionary system map of digital consumption services in connecting vehicles context.

In the core of the service is communication of friends. And the psychological connection is strengthened through the sharing of information. More in-formation exchanges will build more connections. Technically, sharing geographic locations based on data interoperability, so the location can be shared with different services. Music service and family communication service rely on cloud service technology.

The reservation service and health care service involve the service stakeholders, aiming at providing more customized services and making the user more viscous.

4   Conclusion

A series of interviews has been described involving thirty participants from different work domains and backgrounds, focusing on how they interact with digital devices and make a purchase decision to conduct digital consumption activities. From learning and comparing this user behavior and attitude, we found that digital consumption services have a lot of potential opportunities in connecting the context of the vehicle. We found that most users will pay close attention to health issues to keep subhealth away. They will contact the family regularly but do not understand how to communicate with their family members, especially elderly members. They will make a reservation to take control of their life and save time. Most of them will listen to music or browse news but do not spend much money on it. The service system can divide into four services: health care service, family communication service, reservation service, and music service. The results from the in-depth interviews offered a rich source of experience, anecdotes, and routines on the ways of digital consumption interacting and mental mode in the home and work contexts by target users. These results were then translated into a set of design guidelines, which will be subsequently used to cater to user needs in future connecting vehicle services systems.

These findings have implications for the development of future connecting vehicle services that should utilize the power and advantages of user research. This study resulted in a set of design guidelines for supporting digital consumption activities, specifically focused on behavior and attitude. Many of these design guidelines can also be used in the development of other connecting vehicle services and tools for conceptualization. Designers and researchers who focus on understanding the context of the connecting vehicle would benefit from the result of our study. Our next step is to design detailed prototypes of the services system in which these design guidelines are implemented. These prototypes will demonstrate how the design guidelines can be used and will also assess how well the design guidelines can benefit digital future consumption research.

Acknowledgments. We thank our teaching team, students, and the Fulbright Research Scholar Grant (ID: PS00284539).

References

1. Vermesan, O., Blystad, L.C., Hank, P., Bahr, R., John, R., Moscatelli, A.: Smart, connected and mobile: architecting future electric mobility ecosystems. In: Design, Automation & Test in Europe Conference & Exhibition, pp. 1740–1744. IEEE (2013)
2. Zhang, Z.: Digital Consumption Behavior and Trend Analysis in Chinese Context. Doctoral dissertation (2017)

3. Xu, J.: The development of the digital economy in China, new trends, new models and new path. Chinese economic and trade (THEORY EDITION) (2017)

4. Romano, B.: Managing the Internet of Things. In: ACM SIGCSE Technical Symposium, pp. 777–778. ACM (2017)

5. Rödel, C., Stadler, S., Meschtscherjakov, A., Tscheligi, M.: Towards autonomous cars: the effect of autonomy levels on acceptance and user experience. In: International Conference on Automotive User Interfaces & Interactive Vehicular Applications. ACM (2014)

6. Pettersson, I., Ju, W.: Design techniques for exploring automotive interaction in the drive towards automation. In: Proceedings of the 2017 Conference on Designing Interactive Systems, pp. 147–160. ACM, June 2017

7. Merolli, M., Sanchez, F.J., Gary, K.: Social media and online survey: tools for knowledge management in health research. In: Australasian Workshop on Health Informatics & Knowledge Management. Australian Computer Society, Inc. (2014)

8. Harms, J., Wimmer, C., Kappel, K., Grechenig, T.: Gamification of online surveys: conceptual foundations and a design process based on the MDA framework. In: Nordic Conference on Human-Computer Interaction (2014)

9. Kuniavsky, M.: Observing the User Experience: A Practitioner's Guide to User Research. Elsevier (2003)

10. Schoor, R.V.D., Zijlstra, J., Daalhuizen, J., et al.: Delft design guide. Faculteit Industieel Ontwerpen, Delft, Netherlands (2010)

11. Cycil, C., Perry, M., Laurier, E.: Designing for Frustration and Disputes in the Family Car. IGI Global (2014)

12. Kanchanasut, K., Boonsiripant, S., Tunpan, A., Kim, H.K., Ekpanyapong, M.: Internet of cars through commodity V2V and V2X mobile routers: applications for developing countries. KSCE J. Civ. Eng. 19(6), 1897–1904 (2015)

13. Polaine, A., Løvlie, L., Reason, B.: Service Design: From Insight to Inspiration. Rosenfeld Media (2013)

Author Index